Following 9/11

Following 9/11

Religion Coverage in the *New York Times*

Christopher Vecsey

SYRACUSE UNIVERSITY PRESS

Copyright © 2011 by Syracuse University Press
Syracuse, New York 13244-5290

All Rights Reserved

First Edition 2011
11 12 13 14 15 16   6 5 4 3 2 1

∞ The paper used in this publication meets the minimum requirements of the American National Standard for Information Sciences—Permanence of Paper for Printed Library Materials, ANSI Z39.48-1992.

For a listing of books published and distributed by Syracuse University Press, visit our Web site at SyracuseUniversityPress.syr.edu.

ISBN: 978-0-8156-0986-5

Library of Congress Cataloging-in-Publication Data

Vecsey, Christopher.
  Following 9/11 : religion coverage in the New York times / Christopher Vecsey. — 1st ed.
    p. cm.
  Includes bibliographical references and index.
  ISBN 978-0-8156-0986-5 (cloth : alk. paper) 1. New York times.   2. Religion and the press—United States—History—21st century.   3. Journalism, Religious—United States—History—21st century.   4. Journalism—Objectivity—United States.   5. Islamic fundamentalism—Press coverage—United States.   6. Muslims—Press coverage—United States.   7. September 11 Terrorist Attacks, 2001—Religious aspects.   I. Title. II. Title: Following September eleven.
  PN4899.N42N38 2011
  070.4'492—dc23   2011020044

Manufactured in the United States of America

Hailing from a family of journalists, **Christopher Vecsey** is Harry Emerson Fosdick Professor of the Humanities, Native American Studies, and Religion at Colgate University. *Religion & Ethics Newsweekly* of WNET (PBS) has featured his classroom design in "Using the News to Teach Religion." Vecsey has also authored and edited a dozen books about American Indians. Since 2001, he has served Syracuse University Press as editor for the series "The Iroquois and Their Neighbors."

Contents

Acknowledgments

Consider this book an act of filial piety.

Both of my parents were journalists. George S. Vecsey spent almost his entire adult working life in news media, especially sports, at the *Long Island Press,* the Associated Press, and the *New York Daily News* (with a short-lived stint at an experiment called the *Huntington Bulletin*). May Spencer Vecsey was society writer and editor at the *Long Island Press* until she began her career in maternity.

They cared about the newspaper business. In our New York City home—graced over time by past, present, and future newsmen and newswomen (my parents, my siblings, and now the third generation in my nieces and a nephew)—we received more than a half-dozen papers every day, and we *read* them. Our fingers were often black from handling the newsprint. My father died just after his seventy-fifth birthday in 1984, having just perused several newspapers before falling to sleep.

I remember conversations in the living room among my parents' friends: *Who* (which paper, which writer) handled such and such story the best? *What* effect would a labor strike have on press jobs and salaries? *When* did newspapers develop their codes of professional ethics? *How* was layout and writing style changing at the various dailies? *To what degree* was advertising influencing news coverage? *Why* all the typos these days? To this day, newsroom lingo still conjures up vivid images for me. When someone refers to "spiking a story," I can't help but picture the bandages on my father's hand after he impaled himself spiking some wire service copy.

The bookshelves held—amidst the literature, the history, the philosophy, and the religion—a variety of titles, old and more recent, regarding journalism: Oliver Gramling's *AP: The Story of News* (1940); Leo E. McGivena's *The News: the First Fifty Years of New York's Picture Newspaper* (McGivena et al. 1969); Gay

Talese's "new journalism" treatment of the *New York Times, The Kingdom and the Power* (1970); Phillip Knightley's *The First Casualty* (1975), in which he decried the co-optation of the press in modern wartime propaganda; Tom Wicker's *On Press* (1978), regarding his years at the *Times* and his meditation on the vocation and vicissitudes of journalism; Richard H. Meeker's study of S. I. Newhouse—*Newspaperman* (1983)—who treated his papers (including the *Long Island Press,* where both my parents were expelled in the 1930s for their American Newspaper Guild activities) as a for-profit business; Ari L. Goldman's *The Search for God at Harvard* (1991), telling how a young Orthodox Jewish man (Goldman) became religion correspondent for the *Times* and then took a course of study at divinity school. All of these tomes bore the marks—including marginal notes—of having been studied.

My mother, whose funeral fell on my birthday in 2002, used to stuff the books in our house with newspaper articles. She clipped pieces she thought relevant—to something or other—and inserted them into what she considered the appropriate books. I have most of these volumes now in my office, rather like a parental shrine, and I am edified regularly by what I can find between the pages about Anne Morrow Lindbergh, Vladimir Nabokov, Chaim Potok, P. G. Wodehouse, and many others.

Her devoted son number three did her one better. He professionalized her obsession. Over the past four decades, first while earning a Ph.D. in the history and literature of religion and then while teaching history and religion at several colleges, my daily routine has included research (more than just casual reading) in the *New York Times* for all manner of religion coverage. Although my scholarly focus has been on Native American studies in general and on American Indian religions in particular, I have never lost sight of contemporary religious developments worldwide. I now have in my office almost twelve file drawers, three complete file cabinets, filled with *New York Times* clippings about religion and related matters dating to the early 1970s. That doesn't count the several other cabinets filled with American Indian materials. (Yes, I know: it's all on the Web now.)

I come from a family of journalists; I chose a life as an academic. Having produced, as writer and editor, a dozen books about Indians, and having spent many years teaching students about religions in America and around the globe, I now turn my scrutiny and my piety to a career path not taken. In 1971, my father introduced me to George Cornell of the Associated Press, perhaps the first

American journalist to identify religion as his specialization. I had just completed my master's degree in religious studies. Cornell encouraged me toward religion reporting, but I had other obligations at the time, including several years of alternative service to the military draft as a conscientious objector.

Several years later, on the verge of returning to graduate school, I spent a day with Edward B. (Ted) Fiske at the *New York Times,* where he was the religion writer, observing him on the job and discussing his trade. It wasn't for me: too many desks, too many typewriters, too many *people* in one room, too much noise, too many assignments, too many deadlines, not enough time and freedom, and, on my part, perhaps not enough gumption. It was back to the historical archives for me.

Not long afterward, a most forceful argument appeared in the *Times* itself for "freedom *from* the press: An Essay on the daily addiction of news and why, if the reader were to take the author's argument to heart, this would be . . . the last article" (Harris 1974) he or she would ever read in the newspaper. Mark Harris, novelist and erstwhile reporter, now deceased, let journalism have it: for its superficiality, its secondhandedness, its inaccuracy, its endless repetition of stereotypical trivialities, or, as Henry David Thoreau called them, "myriad instances and applications" of the same old thing. "To a philosopher," Harris quoted Thoreau, "all news, as it is called, is gossip."

Harris wrote that George Bernard Shaw had once called the newspaper "the poor man's university. . . . Unfortunately, nowadays the media appear also to be the university man's university, his own having failed to impress upon him the possibilities of his own mind." Harris called upon us all—I felt him calling upon me—to trust our own intelligence, our powers of observation, our circle of friends, the books we read, the arts we encounter, our intuitions, our imaginations, to know what is important, now and for the future. "The media are the opiate of the people," he chided. He confessed how, as a journalist, he had been required to use the word *today* in the first sentence of every article in order to impress upon the readers the urgency of learning what is happening right now, to be "'up on current events.'" And he winced to think that school children now have a "*duty* to read the newspaper and watch the news on television." Harris's advice? Make his the last newspaper article you read. "You, whoever you are, if you *must* buy a newspaper, don't read it. Save it. Read it in 10 years. You'll see how much you could have skipped."

I was moved—almost—to follow his directive. But the addiction was too strong in me. Not only did I read on, but I persisted in clipping. I placed Harris's article in its proper clip file. And here I am, not ten, but almost forty years later, reviewing it and everything else I've saved to see whether it was worth the reading and the reflecting.

When I landed my first teaching post in 1976, my oldest brother, George—now a longtime *Times* sports columnist, but then already a seasoned *Times* correspondent, weighing between sports and other forms of news coverage—took a multiyear assignment covering religion for the *Times*. His position intensified my interest in religion journalism, but only from the vantage of my office in the halls of academe. As the decades have passed, I have collected, examined, and cataloged *Times* clippings about religion, sharing them from time to time with my classes, waiting for the appropriate moment to analyze them in full.

In the fall semester of 2001, I taught a seminar at Colgate University designed for first-year students who had just arrived on campus. "American Religion in These Times" aimed to assess the depth, scope, and slant of religion coverage in the *New York Times*. I planned to have the students investigate religious developments in contemporary America in a global context by reading the *Times* every day to learn what is new and newsworthy: in Christianity, Judaism, Islam, and the many other religious traditions (in their diversity) that coexist in the United States; in the interplay between church and state within that realm sometimes referred to as "civil religion"; in emerging forms of spirituality, community, and ethical discourse; and in the relationships between religiousness, on the one hand, and the arts, sports, ethnicity, politics, sexuality, and secularism, on the other. I assigned several scholarly books about Americans' religious experiences and institutions (Albanese 1999; Benowitz 1998; J. Lewis 1998; Lippy and Williams 1988; Queen, Prothero, and Shattuck 1996; Roof 2000; Schultz, West, and MacLean 1999; Wuthnow 1998) and about religious journalism (Proctor 2000; Silk 1998); however, I determined that most of the course topics would arise directly from the pages of the *Times*.

My students and I were fortunate to be linked to Colgate's scholar of politics, Timothy A. Byrnes, who taught us all in his course "America as a Democracy." Byrnes is the author (Byrnes 1991, 2001) and editor (Byrnes and Katzenstein 2006; Byrnes and Segers 1992; Segers and Byrnes 1995) of several books regarding religion and politics in the United States and in Europe, and he enhanced our understanding of contemporary religious developments by educating us to the constant interplay between the religious and the political dimensions of human life.

As if we needed reminding. Two weeks into the semester, the attacks of September 11 took place. We found ourselves on September 12—Byrnes, myself, and our nineteen students—sitting around our seminar table, poring over the catastrophic aspect of the *New York Times*. In grim words and images, the newspaper chronicled the events of the previous day. From that juncture through the end of the semester in December, the paper explicated the complex set of phenomena that we all came quickly to call "9/11." Within that story and perhaps at its core, the *Times* focused on the complicated character of religion. Rarely did a day pass in which the *Times* neglected to run an article about the varieties of religious causes of and responses to 9/11 in the United States (particularly in New York City) and in the world among the adherents of all the major (and many of the more local) religions.

The semester ended, but the *Times*' coverage of 9/11's religion angles has not ceased. Nor has my interest in the *Times*' treatment of religious phenomena. In the fall of 2003, Byrnes and I once again linked our classes—his first-year seminar "Politics and World Religions" and my introductory course "Religion and the Quest for Meaning." And among the assigned books and scholarly articles, we once again examined the *Times* as a text, asking ourselves not only what is happening religiously in our day, but also how the *Times* is defining religion—especially in its relationship to politics (see "Using the News to Teach Religion" 2004). Then in the fall of 2005, Byrnes and I taught a seminar together, "Religion and Politics in These *Times*" (2004), in which we made *Times* religion coverage the primary subject matter in a seminar setting. I taught a similar course in spring 2008.

This book is the result of collaboration, growing out of my work at Colgate University with Professor Byrnes and our students, who have shared in our spirit of learning: Courtney Collins, Kristen Forry, Todd Garvey, Ebony Geiger, Christine Hart, Catherine Hartman, Gabriel Herman, Sergio Jackson, Laura Kenny, Cory Kilpatrick, Whitney Lang, Caroline Langdale, Kate Levine, Nicholas MacDermott, Kevin Meehan, Brian Spence, Alissa Valiante, Margaret West, Adam Wolk, Michael Barnes, Amar Bhakta, Samuel Bruce, Jacqueline Couture, Natalie Dean, Tina DiMonda, Allison Frumin, David Gelman, Laurabeth Harvey, James Hlavacek, Thomas Leonard, Abhinav Maheshwari, Natalie Mendoza, Bernadette

Sarlo, Alex Weinberg, Brandon Weiss, Evan Winter, Hyun Eric Yoon, Mary Acoymo, Cole Banning, Ashley Becker, Claire Beste, William Birnie, Jonathan Calfee, Rachelle Dennis, Robert Fenity, Anne Gruppo, Matthew Grygiel, Jennifer Jackson, David Kaplan, Andrew Lane, Colleen McCue, Naseema Noor, Darcy Richardson, Jarman Russell, Rebecca Sadowsky, Erin Silver, Megan Sobel, Christine Swanson, Jeff Turney, Michael Ventura, Saul Waller, Dolan Wallis, Caitlin Whiteaker, Katelyn Wilson, Benjamin Camper, Casey Dalcher, Daniel Fichtler, Matthew Fortin, Sarah Greenswag, David Hussey, Adam Iwamoto, Sarah Kruse, Katherine Lamb, Stephanie Macomber, Melissa Madaio, Jessica Mawhirt, Claire McConnaughey, Lyle Morgan, Scott Nicholson, Dylan O'Hearn, Marla Pfenninger, Samantha Plummer, Sara Radin, Lisa Robison, and Erin Senker. I offer my sincere thanks to all of them.

I also appreciate the time and direction given to me by *Times* writers past and present: Joseph Berger, Kenneth A. Briggs, David W. Dunlap, Erik Eckholm, Steven Erlanger, Alan Finder, John W. Fountain, Clyde Haberman, Ari L. Goldman, Laurie Goodstein, Chris Hedges, Corey Kilgannon, Neil A. Lewis, Andy Newman, Gustav Niebuhr, Alan Riding, Serge Schmemann, Peter Steinfels, John Tagliabue, George Vecsey (my brother), Daniel J. Wakin, Edward Wong, and religion journalism maven Mark Silk.

I dedicate this book to Tim Byrnes and our Colgate colleagues and students in religious and political studies.

Prologue

This book examines the *New York Times* coverage of religion after September 11, 2001 (9/11). The *Times* followed the religion stories represented by the events of 9/11 and its aftershocks as they developed over time. I determined to wait five years after 9/11 before organizing this study in order to see how the stories played out, and it has taken almost a full decade for the work to see print. I found that 9/11 of course makes good copy, but it also provides what I consider an unveiling of persistent themes in the *Times* treatment of religion. At the moment of 9/11 crisis, the *Times* turned to its standards of journalistic comprehension, its institutional memory regarding religious phenomena, grasping the new with customary tools of cognizance. Whether these conventions proved appropriate or adequate is a question to be asked along the way.

The events of 9/11 were political as well as religious, and we shall see—by pondering *Times* coverage—how religion and politics have defined one another in our times. I draw attention especially to the volatile public phrases *culture wars* and *clash of civilizations* to perceive the ways in which 9/11 crystallized and recast those concepts, so important in understanding the political dimension of religion over the past decades.

Day in, day out, the *New York Times* is arguably the most important source of information about the contemporary world. Having perused almost every *Times* article about religion from 1970 to the present (about fifteen thousand of them from 1970 to 2001, available to readers on my Colgate Web site [see Vecsey 2009], and tens of thousands since then), and having come to judgments about the *Times'* definitions of religion's dimensions over that period of time, I now seek to investigate "religion" reported in the *Times* in the crux of 9/11, perhaps the most galvanizing event concerning religion in our lifetime.

Through the pages of the world's preeminent journalistic institution, one can compile an encyclopedic analysis of religion in our times. Here is my claim: you can get an education in religious studies by reading the *Times*. A study of *Times* religion coverage, focusing on 9/11 and its upshots, shows not only how the *Times* reported on the events of the subsequent years, but also how the paper presented its conventional themes—diversity, tolerance, institutional organization, interfaith cooperation, ethical judgment, social amelioration, sectarian strife, scandal, political entanglement, church–state relations, sexuality, gender, artistic expression, ritual activity, community celebration, local identity, supernatural power, and so on—regarding the shapes of religious traditions on the crucible of crisis.

It is said that the *Times* from its earliest incarnation in 1850 "has always displayed a sensitivity to the role of religion in society" (Petit 1986:184). Furthermore, "*the Times* from Adolph Ochs' day was hypersensitive in its coverage of religion, ever fearful of offending one group or another" (Talese 1970:125). From the 1850s to the 1920s, both before and after Ochs's purchase in 1896, the *Times* revealed the religious fault lines in American society. The paper's foundations were Christian: uttering Christian sentiments and arguments; proffering support for Christian endeavors; reporting regularly on churchly activities. Its allegiances were Protestant, yet it reported fairly on the animus between Protestants and Catholics. Its allegiances were with the Union, yet it allowed that both sides in the Civil War believed God to favor their cause. Its allegiances were with public schools and their evangelical piety, yet its coverage demonstrated the competition between public and parochial schools. The *Times* informed its readers about the conflicts in American culture: between mainstream Protestants and their competitors; between patriotism and sectarianism; between civil religion and the separation of church and state; between evangelical fervor and secular pursuits; between pious homiletics and clerical scandal; between social reform and conservatism; between scientific rationalism and faith; between supernaturalism and materialism; and between religion and journalism as competing frameworks for societal interpretation.

In 1925, the *Times* carried these concerns into its reporting about the controversy between modernism and fundamentalism, focusing on the teaching of Darwinian evolution in public schools. The paper seemed to regard the changing place of religion in American life, in light of scientific progress, to be a crucial issue in defining the culture of those times. The paper quoted and described not only the proponents of evolutionary theory, but also the various theological camps regarding the infallibility of the Bible, the divinity of Jesus Christ, and the doctrine of the Virgin Birth. Fundamentalists against modernism proclaimed Jesus's miracles, resurrection, ascension, and Second Coming on the pages of the *Times*. Sermons cited in the paper asked, "Is Christianity dying?" "Is education taking the place of religion?" "Is the Bible being discredited?" (quoted in Petit 1986:219). These topics were newsworthy issues of the day.

By the 1930s, the *Times* had begun to depend for its local religion coverage on the reporting of a single, specialized writer. Rachel K. McDowell became the religion news editor of the *Times* in 1929, "the first and only religious news editor *The New York Times* had had in its first 100 years" (Dugan, Nannes, and Stross 1979:4). She was also one of the only four women reporters who worked in the *Times* city room in the four decades of Adolph Ochs's ownership. Born into a Presbyterian family, "she enjoyed nothing so much as a hellfire-and-brimstone sermon." She was a "tiger of a reporter" (Robertson 1992:49) who had covered church news for the *New York Herald* since 1908 but switched to the *Times* in 1920, where, according to the *Times'* Meyer Berger, she "haunted churches and cathedrals, presbytery meetings and Bible conferences" until her retirement in 1948 (quoted in Dugan, Nannes, and Stross 1979:4). She was said to be a "puritanical" woman, was known in the ranks as "'Lady Bishop'" (Talese 1970:75) of "the religious department"(E. James 1945:11), and under the city editor was "the only woman reporter in the city room" (Robertson 1992:51). She founded the "Pure Language League" and made a point to "pin back the ears of anyone . . . who swore in her presence." She seemed like "a freak and a figure of fun to the men on the staff, but she was formidable on her own turf" (Robertson 1992:51).

She was succeeded by George Dugan, who had worked for Religious News Service before joining the *Times*. Over the decades, the *Times* hired an impressive string of religion editors and writers, including John Cogley, John Leo, Edward B. Fiske, Kenneth A. Briggs, George Vecsey, Eleanor Blau, Ari L. Goldman, Joseph Berger, Peter Steinfels, Gustav Niebuhr, Laurie Goodstein, Daniel J. Wakin, Andy Newman, Michael Luo, Neela Bannerjee, Samuel G. Freedman, Paul Vitello, and Mark Oppenheimer—most working out of the *Times'* New York offices, for both the national and metropolitan desks.

During the 1940s, the *Times* paid close attention to the tensions of pluralism within the United States. America had often been declared a Christian—indeed, a Protestant—nation. During World War II, however, the United States needed to emphasize its multicultural, multireligious unity, and it was challenged to do so by the events of the day. Most churches backed the war effort as just, but pacifist denominations such as Jehovah's Witnesses were considered unpatriotic and were prosecuted (some would say persecuted) when they refused to recite the Pledge of Allegiance. Some Jehovah's Witnesses sought conscientious objector status in the military draft. The *Times* drew attention to these tensions in American civil life with sober care and with little editorializing. America was coming to grips with its multiple religious identities and the need to incorporate them all into a single civic unit. The courts would prove to be the mechanism for this assimilation, and the *Times* would cover these trials throughout the rest of the twentieth century.

From the end of World War II into the 1960s, *Times* coverage of religion emphasized the affiliation of God and state during what was perceived as a "'religious revival'" (Petit 1986:238). Christian and Jewish leaders called for greater religiousness in America to cure its moral ills and ambiguities. "If religion was an essential component of Americanism, then the Cold War was also a spiritual conflict" (Petit 1986:240). The Christian message, said a Baptist minister, was America's greatest weapon against godless communism. In this regard, the *Times* reported on the addition of "under God" to the Pledge of Allegiance on Flag Day in 1954.

The religion stories of the 1960s began with the election of John F. Kennedy as the first Catholic American president, followed over the next several years by Roman Catholicism's Second Vatican Council. John Cogley initiated the salad days of religion writing at the *Times* in the early 1960s. A liberal Catholic recently of *Commonweal*, he covered the Second Vatican Council with élan and depth. Here was a world-class story of great change covered by a world-class reporter. He "tackled the big issues, especially those roiling his faith" (Phelps 2009:201). The story of the civil rights movement, begun in the 1950s with black Christian ministers such as Martin Luther King Jr. and their congregations in the forefront but supported in the 1960s by white clerics, nuns, rabbis, and priests—a story of religious social engagement and societal change—filled the pages of the *Times* for more than a decade. The spread of the Nation of Islam was an important related story, especially concerning Elijah Mohammed, Malcolm X, and Mohammed Ali. The Vietnam War had a religious angle as religious groups protested the military engagement. The *Times* also reported on youths finding their churches hypocritical and insufficiently involved in social issues. Religion was significant in several prominent Supreme Court cases concerning the separation of church and state at school, at work, and in the post office.

When James Reston came to New York as executive editor of the *Times* in 1968, he began to initiate a change he had been mulling over for some time. He had once said in a speech about journalists: "We are not covering the news of the mind as we should; we minimize the conflict of ideas and emphasize the conflict in the streets" (quoted in Talese 1970:619). Now he introduced in the *Times* more coverage of legal thought, artistic creativity, humor, economic theory, and what he called "the news of the mind." Religion coverage would be upgraded, too, but it would take time.

Robert B. Petit (1986)—whose work I have relied on in reviewing the history of *Times* religion coverage—states that from the 1850s to the 1970s one can find "accumulating evidence for the secularization thesis" through the pages of the *New York Times*. What he found was that the *Times* over a century and more carried fewer stories and fewer headlines regarding religion as well as less news space and less prominence for religion on the front page (249–51). Religion references in advertising also declined and almost disappeared by the second half of the twentieth century. Even the religious revival of the 1950s did not necessarily make religion more salient in the news because religion was considered a private affair rather than a matter of public concern. If one compares mid-1900s reporting conventions to those in the 1850s *Times,* there is a world of difference, a dramatic shift from committed Christian to decidedly secular reportage.

Petit is not arguing that the *Times* ceased to cover religion by the 1970s, but rather that religion had been eclipsed as a major news item by matters considered more worldly, more weighty; and religious exponents—preachers, rabbis, priests, and pious-minded reporters—were far less likely to find their faith expressed directly on the pages of America's leading newspaper. Although the *Times* paid attention to movements questioning religion's hegemony, it also took part in that overall movement of secularizing American society.

Debra L. Mason (1995) says of the *Times* at the end of the twentieth century that it paid more attention to religious "beliefs/practices"—a type of phenomenology of religion in our times, including thoughtful essays—than most other American newspapers. Its other interests are religion's relations to "foreign government" and "social action." It is less likely to report on religious "announcements" and "routine business" than most other major papers in the United States, she comments (179).

It wasn't always this way. In midcentury, a generation of *Times* reporters learned about journalism by recounting sermons in New York churches and synagogues. It was a minor beat for neophytes, but it had the potential to open their ears to different ways of speaking. Peter Steinfels (2005b) says that for many reporters, it was the "first time they had gone to a religious service other than their own church," which made them careful listeners.

While at City College before World War II, Abraham M. Rosenthal served as a campus correspondent for the *Times,* and, like other such stringers, he wrote brief accounts of sermons for the Monday edition. The religion news editor watched out for "any signs of irreverence" in his reports (Talese 1970:331). He was paid three dollars a story—twenty-five cents of which he was to deposit in the collection basket. It was felt at the paper that if you could not cover a sermon and write a reliable report about it, you probably were incapable of covering anything. It was foundational coverage of phenomena considered rudimentary: spell the preacher's name right; quote correctly; interpret the message accurately. Rosenthal penned summaries of "dozens of impeccable sermons" (Talese 1970:332) and thereby proved his mettle. Before long, he had dropped out of college and was covering the United Nations on page one of the *Times*. He had moved on from the insignificant to the monumental, from local religion to world politics. That is how he saw it, and that is how the *Times* saw it, although it is said that Rosenthal "maintained a deep interest in religion" to the end of his career (Phelps 2009:201).

By the 1960s, the *Times* no longer reported on routine sermons about town, in part because such pieties were no longer considered newsworthy and in part because the paper was no longer willing to kowtow to religious institutions. When Rosenthal became metropolitan editor in 1963, he discontinued the coverage of Sunday sermons. "I realized every Monday, we were giving a page of coverage to handouts, and they were boring as hell and had nothing to do with religion," he said. Instead, he suggested that reporters cover the "experiences of believers in their neighborhoods" (quoted in Goldberg 1996:302)—observing the people, not the official church viewpoints. The overall effect, however, was that by the mid-1970s religion was a diminished *Times* topic.

That is not to say that the *Times* neglected religion or that its editors aimed to misrepresent it. In the 1976 *Manual of Style and Usage* (Jordan 1976), care was taken to honor the doctrines, terminology, and titles of religious organizations: for example, "Ascension. Capitalize when the reference is to Jesus" (17); "Resurrection. Capitalize when the reference is to Jesus, or to the rising of the dead at the Last Judgment" (177); "Capitalize *He, Him* and *His* when the reference is to Jesus, God or the Holy Ghost (or Holy Spirit)" (105, italics in original); "*Christ* is also proper" (105, italics in original) in reference to Jesus in articles concerning the Christian religion. Reporters and editors were instructed to refer properly to religious officers such as bishop, archbishop, cardinal, and chief rabbi and to denominations such as the Church of Jesus Christ of Latter Day Saints. In Christian Science—that is, the Church of Christ, Scientist—"there are no clergymen in the church; thus *the Rev.* should never be used" (39, italics in original).

There was also an attempt not to offend religious readers: "Devout. Use with care, to avoid cliché writing. Applied unthinkingly, as in the overworked phrase *devout Catholic,* the label may offend some readers by implying that there is something extraordinary about strong religious convictions" (61, italics in original); and "Evangelical. A term for conservative Protestants that is preferred to *fundamentalist,* which sometimes has pejorative connotations" (72, italics in original).

Furthermore, there was an attempt not to identify people by religion so as to avoid bias: "Religion of a person in the news. Religion should be specified in a news story only when it is clearly pertinent. The same stricture applies to ethnic and racial identifications" (175–76).

One gets the impression from such a style book that *Times* journalists were secular people trying to explain religious people to secular readers in terms that would not be offensive to the religious. One would not find in the *Times* a jaded religion reporter who would refer in print to "Jesus, the alleged son of God," as in a Calvin Trillin novel (quoted in Steinfels 2005b). The *Times* was determined not to appear antireligious; indeed, it aimed and still aims to respect the theological beliefs of whatever religious group is being featured, without judging the validity of truth claims. At the same time, however, one might ask if most of its reporters and editors lacked and still lack personal experience in religion. Have *Times* journalists been nonreligious?

Surely not all. Kenneth A. Briggs, *Times* religion editor in the 1970s and 1980s (now adjunct professor of English at Lafayette College), was an ordained

Methodist clergyman; however, he makes it clear (Briggs 2007) that he was not hired from his earlier job at *Newsday* in order to provide a Protestant presence at the *Times*. Nor did he function as a "minister" there. Always eager to keep "advocacy" and "reportage" separate, Briggs "made it a point not to cover things I thought were too close to me," including religious groups associated with his denomination. He had been in the newspaper business since the age of fifteen, and his "vocation" rested in his "ability to tell the truth" about religion—a serious topic—without "stereotypes" or "false fronts."

Senior *Times* editor Serge Schmemann (2007) says of himself, "I belong to the Orthodox Church," with a knowledge of its beliefs, traditions, and contentions. In his experience, *Times* staff members are not keen on revealing their religious faith. "In the newsroom," he says, "you will never guess who is devout," and you are surprised when a colleague says grace before meals. "Believing in God is not fashionable"; indeed, it is considered "retrogradish" in the social milieu in which the *Times* exists, Schmemann states. "Doctrine" is "something you laugh at at your editorial meetings," while placing politics on the front page. No wonder, then, that "a major gap" exists in the depth of *Times* religion coverage, he states.

Of New York, Irish, Catholic birthright, Corey Kilgannon (2007), a former "jock" and Columbia University alum, is less sure that religiosity is a virtue in a reporter like himself. "I'm not religious," he avers, but that does not prevent him from highlighting the lives of people who are. For example, he has penned many pieces about Jews—"I'm fascinated by people I didn't even know existed, growing up"—much to their appreciation. "I'm the Shabbos goy of the newsroom," he exclaims. The *Times* is said to be "a godless place" filled with "cynical" types— "not the most spiritual" people around—and yet religion gets a good press at the paper in Kilgannon's view.

At the same time, Kilgannon recalls John McCandlish Phillips of the city desk, an evangelical, Bible-reading street preacher, who is famous in *Times* lore. In 1965, Phillips covered the story of Daniel Burros, a New York City Klansman and American Nazi Party member who, it turned out, was born a Jew. After Phillips finally interviewed Burros, and Burros had threatened the reporter's life if he revealed the bigot's Jewish identity, Phillips tried to convert him with spiritual exhortation: "What you have to do to break the grip fascism has on you is to call upon the name of Jesus Christ" (quoted in Talese 1970:446). When the story broke and Burros's Jewish identity was revealed, he shot himself dead. Some accused the

Times of invading Burros's privacy; others defended the accuracy of the reporting. What did Phillips think of the affair? That this was "the God of Israel acting in judgment" (quoted in Talese 1970:448), but he did not say so on the pages of the *New York Times*. Such a statement would have been permissible in the 1850s, even conventional, but not in the secularized setting of the 1960s or 1970s.

How much could *Times* reporters express of their religious views in print? Would they be stigmatized if they did? Might they get scolded, as Linda Greenhouse did for taking part in a pro-choice demonstration? The *Times* did not want its Supreme Court reporter publicly identified with a cause or a position. Indeed, the *Times* advised its reporters not to take part in demonstrations. Its attitude was: be objective; look objective. Religious reporters were not supposed to demonstrate their faith in their writing or in public displays (Schmalzbauer 2002:169–70).

How many demonstrably religious reporters worked for the paper in the 1970s? Phillips (2005) claims that "when the *Times* put me on its reporting staff, I was the only evangelical Christian among some 275 news and editorial employees, and certainly the only one who kept a leather-bound Bible on his desk." Through his tenure on the metro desk, he was always a "spiritual outsider." A man who had chosen his job by consulting God on his knees in prayer had little in common with the gambling and cursing of the newsroom. The cofounder (in 1963) of a church called the New Testament Missionary Fellowship—offering respite to believers from a world of pornography, drugs, fornication, and abortion—was accustomed to convening with his prayer group each morning, after which he "entered the secular world at the *Times*" (Auletta 1997). Although Phillips did nothing to "impose his values on others" in the newsroom, "he was widely said to be a religious fanatic of some sort," according to a former colleague (quoted in Auletta 1997). He was writing books on the supernatural and the spirit world. No matter that "he kept his religion strictly segregated from his work" or at least tried to, he was regarded with some suspicion, even as his "Jewish editors"—as he called them (Phillips 2001:19), referring to Arthur Gelb and Abraham M. Rosenthal—praised his professionalism and compositional prowess.

For his own part, Phillips (2001) had become disgruntled with his working conditions at the *Times,* where he found himself at *"war,"* especially in the newsroom, which he called "spiritually . . . a swamp for me just about all the time" (8, 13, italics in original). According to Terry Mattingly (2000), he was living in "two radically different worlds. Few journalists appreciate what goes on in churches, he said, and few church people understand what goes on in newsrooms." He came to believe that this disparity "warps the news." He found it galling that his editors could not recognize the power of religion in people's lives, its soteriological effects on the addictions of contemporary existence. They did not take religion seriously; they did not regard it as newsworthy, at least not as he did. As a result, he quit his job at the *Times* for a life as a "Pentecostal preacher with a small urban flock" (Mattingly 2000).

Phillips was one of a kind at the *Times;* however, others corroborated his experience with editors tone-deaf to religion. When George Vecsey was named a religion reporter on the city desk in the late 1970s, he was working under A. M. Rosenthal, but his immediate boss, the city desk editor, said Vecsey was too good a reporter to be covering an unimportant topic such as religion. He told Vecsey that he wanted to move him to another aspect of city life. Vecsey mentioned this comment to a rabbi he had come to know on the job. (Vecsey felt that he was becoming popular with the rabbis because he covered their stories, quoted them as they might have wished, and represented them well.) The rabbi was upset that the *Times* was possibly going to cut back on its religion (and Jewish) coverage. By the time Vecsey got back to his office, the city desk editor told him to forget the change; he was going to stay on religion. It was clear to Vecsey that the rabbi had gotten one of the *Times'* brass on the telephone and persuaded him to call off the editor (G. Vecsey 2002).

Vecsey (2010) says that in the late 1970s, when the paper had a very large staff and only rudimentary computer facilities, there basically was no cohesive structure for the *Times* editors to plan coverage of religion. He adds: "It's a great newspaper, and it knows how to cover major stories." He recalls Joe Lelyveld, then an editor in foreign news, organizing a major symposium on Shiite Islam after the taking of hostages in Iran and himself covering a papal conclave and the trips of Pope John Paul II to Mexico and the United States, the Lubavitchers and other Hasidic sects, as well as the growing tension between mainline and evangelical Protestantism. Vecsey considers several personal interviews during the Dalai Lama's first visit to the United States to be a highlight of his fifty-year career in journalism.

Kenneth A. Briggs, the religion editor, could write what he wanted now and then; it didn't matter. No one was in place to guide Vecsey or encourage him in any thematic way regarding religion coverage. Religion was something local—say, a church burning down—but religion as a dimension of human life seemed to fall through the cracks (G. Vecsey 2002).

Vecsey tells how Rosenthal called him over one day. "What's the attraction of these Eastern religions?" Rosenthal asked. He wanted Vecsey to write a *Times Magazine* piece on Asian religious influence in the United States. Rosenthal seemed bemused by these religions. Someone speculated to Vecsey that a Rosenthal family member might be involved with meditation or something—thus Rosenthal's sudden interest in the topic. So Vecsey did some interviews and wrote a piece on Buddhist growth in the United States, but the magazine editors were uninterested in it. A month later Rosenthal asked Vecsey, "I thought you were a good reporter; what happened to the Eastern religion story?" Vecsey told him that he had filed it long since. Next thing Vecsey knew, Rosenthal had called the magazine chief on the carpet, and the story ran shortly thereafter (G. Vecsey 2002).

This story is an example of the haphazard, personalized manner in which religion stories were generated in the late 1970s. "Lapsed Catholic editors would order up stories on lapsed Catholics; Jewish editors would suddenly get curious about Passover about 2:00 PM before a seder; and so on," says Vecsey (2005). He hastens to add that one executive, Seymour Topping, had a feel for religion coverage, "particularly Tibetan Buddhism," whereas others—such as Rosenthal, Lelyveld, Mike Levitas, and David R. Jones—had active journalistic curiosity.

In January 1980, Vecsey was working up a story about an up-and-coming Protestant preacher named Jerry Falwell who had founded an organization called Moral Majority the previous year. Falwell and other "so-called conservatives" among evangelical Christians were intent on changing America's culture by influencing its politics. "You couldn't miss that these guys were flexing their muscles, and people were listening. Huge attendance at conventions, clearly a national happening[.] Much kow-towing at religious broadcasters' conventions, etc.," Vecsey (2007) recalls. So, as a religion writer, Vecsey wanted to follow "something important," and he arranged to spend several days with Falwell, whom he already knew and liked, "but it got caught in a jurisdictional dispute" at the *Times*. As a metro writer, he was not supposed to travel. "Isn't there religion right here in New York?" his metro editor asked, making Vecsey think of church fires. Vecsey and other reporters interested in religion coverage "had to sell our stories to one desk or another—usually National, sometimes Metro, sometimes Foreign, sometimes Week in Review, once in a while Magazine. There was no one person to bounce ideas off," and even the religion editor, Briggs, "didn't have much power." Vecsey recognized what he felt was a "bad situation" as a "Lone Ranger" on religion coverage and "got out," back to his first beat, sports, which had vast budget, staff, and space, but he is still "disappointed about being called off" (Vecsey 2007) the "planned trip to Falwell's world in Virginia" (Vecsey 2005). As for the position of religion reporter at the *Times,* "it got much better afterward, I think," Vecsey (2005) muses. "I'm hoping it is easier to find an editor with curiosity and power and access to space in the paper than it was in the bad old days of the late '70s" (Vecsey 2007). However, Alan Finder (2007), who has worked in sports and education, suggests that little has changed at the *Times* regarding the allocation of resources and space; sports still rates over religion.

Ari L. Goldman (1991), now dean of students at Columbia University's Graduate School of Journalism, adds to Vecsey's impression that religion "had a bad name at the paper" in the 1970s, left over from its dull repetition of Sunday sermons in the "'Church News'" days of the 1930s and 1940s (197). Perhaps in order to compensate for an earlier heritage of platitudinous religion coverage, "one of Ari Goldman's *New York Times* editors told him that he wanted more conflict and controversy in religion stories" (Hubbard 1990:13). Goldman was perplexed how he could report responsibly about religious events if his newspaper was insisting on sensational elements.

George Dugan, one of the pioneers of religion coverage, once brooded a whole day in his hotel room because the *Times* had "spiked" a story he had written on a religious convention (Cornell 1990:25). He cared about religion coverage much more than his editors did. Briggs (2007) is still bemused over the choices *Times* editors made during his tenure to plug or impede the publication of certain viewpoints. An article questioning the wisdom of a Manhattan church construction project was "spiked"—in his view—because it countered the agenda of "a lobby" popular with *Times* management. When Liberation Theology was making the news in Latin America during the 1970s, an article by Michael Novak appeared in the Sunday magazine, "knocking the legs out of its legitimacy. . . . Novak had a pipeline to Abe Rosenthal," Briggs remarks, so the piece was printed. Did Rosenthal and Novak plan this together? Briggs says, "I can't prove it, but I think so."

In Briggs's (2007) view, serious religion coverage was always threatened by the "cocktail party influence," the "hanging around effect." *Times* editors would come back to the office from a "hotsy-totsy" weekend in the Hamptons, filled with ideas gathered in conversations with "important" people. The word then would go down to the staff that there were "stories we ought to look after."

Back then, the *Times* was not an ideal place to cover religion. Now it's different, Vecsey (2002) says. Religion coverage suffuses the paper locally, nationally, thematically, internationally, and there are layers of management that suggest stories, send reporters out, check facts, call in the usual suspects to write expert reports and op-eds. There has been substantive change in *New York Times* religion coverage from the late 1970s to the twenty-first century (see also comments by Briggs in Hoover, Handley, and Radelfinger 1989:103).

In the post-9/11 world, religion is constantly in the news. For an obsessive paper clipper of *Times* religion stories (such as myself), the rising tide of coverage seems like a tsunami set off by a volcanic eruption. I used to clip an article now and then, perhaps one each day. Now it's religion all the time in almost every section. In the decade after 9/11, the volume of religion reportage in the *Times* has become overwhelming. On some days, several front-page articles are focused on religion, and several full pages inside the daily *Times* are replete with religion articles. Martin E. Marty (2005) observes about religion headlines in American newspapers, including the *Times*, "Never, never let go unchallenged the observations that our nation and its world used to be more religious, that citizens used to pay more attention to religion, that the media used to do more with religion than they do today."

The "religion coverage industry," says Briggs (2007)—such as the Religion Newswriters Association and other aspects of the "establishment" funded by Lilly grants—still claims that "religious coverage never matches religion's importance" and that "religion is always misunderstood." In fact, religion is an ever-present and highly respected subject in the American press today. Indeed, if anything, he comments, there is perhaps "too much deference" given to religion, "a reluctance to look at the downside of American religion, except in extreme cases."

What happened from the 1970s to the early twenty-first century to create this tidal wave of religion in the news? I can offer a few explanations. First, a paper such as the *Times*—management and staffers alike—has come to recognize the importance of religion in contemporary society. Second, the *Times* has come to realize, as have other journalistic institutions, that there is a sizable audience for religion news and that it is prudent to give readers what they want. Third, religion has become a powerful force in public, political life at home and abroad, and both consumers and producers of the news are now cognizant of this fact. Whether one points to Jimmy Carter's successful presidential campaign in 1976 or to the ascension of Pope John Paul II in 1978 or to the Islamic Revolution in Iran in 1979 or to the creation of the Moral Majority in that same year, it is clear that since the late 1970s religion has become deprivatized. Secularization, an earlier trend perceived as inevitable, has been overturned over the past several decades; the *Times* has documented the revival of public religiousness as it has swept across the globe. And finally, of course, there is 9/11.

In paying greater attention to religious trends and events, the paper developed conventions of religion coverage. Did the *Times* rest upon its conventions, its institutional memory, to understand the religious dimensions of 9/11, and if so, were these conventions sufficient for the task at hand? Or did the *Times* refashion them or rise above them? In the foreword to a book about media coverage of the 9/11 story, Victor Navasky (2002) ponders what we have learned about journalism during this time. He suggests that most news media fell back on their conventional views of the world and their accustomed modes of reportage and commentary and that those modes proved insufficient.

What of the *Times*? The following pages show that the paper employed its conventions, its institutional memory, its portrayals of religion's defining dimensions. It carried out its traditions of moderatism (representing US centrist values in a manner aiming toward detachment, fairness, balance, even objectivity) and modernism (sympathizing with contemporary, Western standards, practices, ideas, and characteristics in light of, for example, scientific perspectives), well used to grappling with an ascendant, related paradigm, the "clash of civilizations," in its understanding of the "culture wars."

On the first anniversary of the 2001 attack, Martin E. Marty (2002) depicted America's crisis of faith as it lost its sense of security and its confidence in its way of life as the best or only reasonable culture in the world. Marty also spoke of the sense of trust that Americans evoked and maybe even embraced in the days following 9/11. These feelings are aspects, he said, of the religion of the hearth, the deep, experiential faith more profound than rituals, institutions, statistics.

How well, one might wonder, did the *New York Times* capture that loss of faith and that sense of trust? Did the *Times* capture the projects that America engaged in to get right again, to cope, to define aspiration, heroism, and values? Did the *Times* capture the paradoxes of American religious life—the fundamentalism and the liberalism, the hospitality and the hatred? Did the *Times* capture the sacred silences in grief, in remembrance, in the shrines and the prayer services? These aspects of American life, according to Marty (2002), constituted "the sensitive crown of the human heart" in the days, weeks, and months following 9/11. Is it too much to judge a newspaper by its ability to locate and reveal these profound aspects? This we ask of the *Times.*

In this first-anniversary lecture at Colgate University, Marty spoke of Lincoln's Second Inaugural Address, which used a biblically grounded, ironically informed message, transcendent of conventional prejudices, reaching across boundaries. Who, in the days following 9/11, was able to reach beyond convention to express the signs of the times? And did the *Times* recognize such a voice or voices? More important, did the *Times* serve as a vehicle for such transcendence?

Newspapers are supposedly about the new, the absolutely contemporary, refreshed each day. But much in the headlines, the leads, the captions, the closing, climactic kickers are repetitions of "evergreens"—that is, the same old stories rewritten. Did post-9/11 religion coverage in the *Times* have that quality of repetition and conventionality? September 11, 2001, was an axial moment for many Americans, maybe for many people in the world. Was it an axial moment for *New York Times* coverage? It definitely inspired an overwhelming amount of coverage in the several months that followed 9/11 and even for several years. But to what degree did the *Times* fall back on its conventional coverage of religion in order to understand 9/11, and to what degree did 9/11 inspire new ways of understanding religion? Was the *Times* able to transcend or employ those conventions in its coverage of a shatteringly new "news" event?

My rather old-fashioned conclusion is that the *Times* made use of its institutional memory, its accustomed coverage of religion, religions, and religiousness, in order to ask probing questions about religion news in light of 9/11. Its tradition of religion coverage proved more than adequate to the task. The paper was able to inform its readers about a monumental, breaking story of religious import. In short, the *Times* possessed the capacity to provide insight to religious phenomena in its complex coverage of 9/11. I might not go as far as Hal Espen (2006), who wrote in the *Times Book Review* a few years ago that the paper's 9/11 coverage was "one of the transcendent achievements in the history of journalism," but I would say that the coverage was impressive. And it demonstrated a thoroughgoing journalistic discipline regarding religion, worthy of emulation.

Many *Times* reporters who brought these religion angles stemming from 9/11 to the public are ironically not even aware of the religious import in their stories. Neil A. Lewis, who wrote about legal issues facing Muslims in American institutions; Sarah Lyall, who depicted British Muslims; David Rohde, who risked his life covering Islam in Pakistan and elsewhere; Katharine Q. Seelye, who told of reputed insults to the Koran; Jodi Wilgoren (now Rudoren), who portrayed American Muslims; and Edward Wong, who corresponded extensively from Iraq—all demurred when asked in interviews in 2007 about their religion coverage. They have "no memory of . . . having written especially on this topic" (N. Lewis 2007a; see also N. Lewis 2007b), "except in the most peripheral of ways, usually when it comes up in the context of another story" (Lyall 2007), but "never . . . as a beat" (Rohde 2007), neither "directly [n]or indirectly" (Seelye 2007), not "very much" (Rudoren 2007) or as a "sole or primary focus" (Wong 2007a).

Metro writer Corey Kilgannon (2007) denies any special place for religion in his coverage since 2001. "Being religious is just another attribute," he says, like being "homeless" or "a blind guy who plays the violin behind his back." If there is "news value" or "human interest" to what the subject is doing, then it is worth the ink. In the "curiosity shop" of "P. T. Barnum" stories favored by Kilgannon—of miraculous talking fish (Kilgannon 2003b) and weight-lifting gurus (Kilgannon 2004d)—there is little "navel gazing" or "tedious discussions of scripture." Religion catches his eye when it is "new to me," the "believe-it-or-not" kind of event. It has been no different since 9/11 than it was before.

Nevertheless, religion infused much of the 9/11 news in the *Times*. "I cannot pretend to have added to understanding of religion as such," writes cultural correspondent Alan Riding (2007), "but I may have helped to spotlight the political and cultural repercussions of religious beliefs since 9/11." Edward Wong (2007b) writes, "I absolutely agree with you that religion is an integral part of Iraqi politics and the Iraq war, as well as [of] daily life in that country." Yet "I don't consider myself to be an expert on religion, and . . . religion in Iraq or the Islamic world hasn't been my 'beat' per se, but rather I have covered it as part of the larger canvas of the social and political upheavals in Iraq."

But we are getting ahead of ourselves. What were the 9/11 news stories? How important were their religious dimensions? The immediate event was absolute news. All you had to do was tell the story or show the images (Chermak, Bailey, and Brown 2003a:9). The attacks of September 11 embodied the excruciatingly apt aspects of the Now, the newsworthy event par excellence. Its enormity, its shock: the United States is actually under attack! Here we are, protected geographically by broad oceans and cordial ally-neighbor-nations, and yet an enemy has somehow invaded our sacred space. And this enemy is not even a nation, but rather a pack of fanatic outlaws. One did not need to employ sensationalism to cover this occurrence (see Schmemann 2001b). Instead, the *Times* employed saturation news techniques. The immediate 9/11 stories included pieces on terrorism and terrorists, Osama bin Laden, his database (called Al Qaeda), the impact on New York City, the failed World Trade Center architecture, airport security, US intelligence, President George W. Bush's proclamation of war on terrorism, the competing values of national security versus civil liberty in America, the trauma in civil society, and so on—all at the local, state, national, and global levels (Navasky 2002:xiii).

Navasky (2002) speaks of the "signal journalistic achievements of the *New York Times* and others in crisis mode" in covering 9/11 (xiii); however, he seems to contrast that achievement with most mainstream media behavior, which—in his view—was jingoistic regarding the United States, including what he sees as the "demonization of the Muslim world." The impression one gets is that the *Times* stood out in its thorough and perceptive coverage of 9/11 and its aftermath. As another media analyst writes, "The work of the *New York Times* staff was little short of miraculous in covering the terrorist attacks and their aftermath intensely, humanely, and in large measure fairly" (Schedson 2002:37).

It is suggested that "journalism is a curriculum . . . , with breaking news only the intro course. After that comes the human interest side-bar, the biographical sketch of the person in the news, news analysis, the lengthy magazine piece, later the book" (Schedson 2002:38). The *Times* created an extensive 9/11 curriculum right from the start. It did so through news coverage; through features, which are necessary to provide a sense of what is happening on a personal level in the culture; in the "Week in Review" summaries, which put things into contexts that make sense to the *Times;* in the "essays beyond the news," the op-eds, the magazine articles, which allowed for a great deal of opinion; and of course in the reviews of books, which provided the accumulating 9/11 bibliography. The *Times* moved beyond political coverage to the social, the cultural, the artistic, the intellectual, and the religious. Above all, however, the paper showed how politics and religion can be mutually defining dimensions of human life.

PART I | A Newspaper Challenged

There is no question about it: 9/11 was a religion story, an event that revealed just how important a force religion could be in modern times. As former religion writer George Vecsey (2007) says, "My frequent role while covering religion . . . was to assure editors, no, seriously, some people actually believe this stuff—and act on it. Jonestown just being one example. Then Jonestown arrived downtown." The religion angles were interpretations of causation: What motivations brought about 9/11, and how did people respond to it? What meanings did people construct about 9/11, and how did they behave as a result? The religious foci were religion in America, Islam at home and abroad, and the wars kindled around the world by the 9/11 attacks. In addressing these topics on the pages of the paper and beyond, *Times* personnel pondered the significance of these galvanizing events.

Pre-9/11

Conventions of Religion Coverage, Institutional Memory

Professor Timothy A. Byrnes and I began teaching our linked Colgate courses—his "America as a Democracy" and my "American Religion in These Times"—in the last week of August 2001, using the *New York Times* as our daily touchstone. Our first day of *Times* reading was August 27, and the first religion story that caught our attention came out of Kabul, Afghanistan's capital, where twenty-four employees of a German organization, Shelter Now (sixteen Afghans and eight foreigners, including two American women), had been arrested for the alleged crime of preaching Christianity under Taliban rule (Bearak 2001m).

During that year, beginning in February, the *Times* had carried Agence France-Presse and Associated Press (AP) reports about the Taliban, as Afghan officials ruled for the demolition of two prominent and ancient Buddhist sculptures in Bamiyan, northwest of Kabul, and of other Buddhist relics in the capital and elsewhere. Representatives of the art world pleaded with the Taliban to forego this "'global cultural catastrophe'" ("Taliban Decree" 2001). "They are destroying statues that the entire world considers to be masterpieces," decried the head of the United Nations Educational, Scientific, and Cultural Organization (UNESCO). "And this is being done in the name of an interpretation of the Muslim faith that is not recognized anywhere else" (quoted in "Pre-Islam Idols" 2001). Nonetheless, "the Taliban's supreme leader, Mullah Muhammad Omar, issued an edict . . . ordering the destruction of all statues, declaring, 'These idols have been gods of the infidels'" ("U.N. Pleads" 2001).

Times art critic Holland Cotter (2001c) wrote a short piece about the massive Buddhas of Bamiyan, offering the hope that the artifacts of age-old Buddhist tradition would survive the Taliban threat, perhaps for the reasoning of Islamic scripture. "'I do not serve what you worship; nor do you serve what I worship. You have your own religion, and I have mine.' This terse statement of live-and-let-live religious tolerance is from the Koran," Cotter concluded. Karen Armstrong (2001), author of a book about Islam, wrote an op-ed cautioning the Taliban against "vandalizing the priceless statues of Buddha," not because the artworks were "'idols'" representing a deity—such was not the case in the Buddhist tradition—but because of the tradition of "tolerance" practiced by the sixteenth-century Mogul emperor Akbar, whose successors' "intolerance helped hasten the decline of Muslim India. The Taliban would do well to contemplate this example," she warned.

By the middle of March, however, the destruction of the Bamiyan Buddhas was complete, as reported from New Delhi by the *Times* bureau cochief there, Barry Bearak (2001c, 2001k). In New York City, *Times* correspondent Barbara Crossette interviewed a Taliban envoy, who explained the demolition as an indignant protest to world powers such as UNESCO who—he implied—cared more about artworks than about Afghans starving as a result of United States economic sanctions against their country. "In our religion," the envoy argued, "if anything is harmless, we just leave it. If money is going to statues while children are dying of malnutrition next door, then that makes it harmful, and we destroy it" (quoted in Crossette 2001d). Several of the Taliban articles made references to the fact that Osama bin Laden was ensconced in Afghanistan and that the United States had conducted bombing raids against him in the wake of violence to Americans abroad in 1998, for which he was the suspected mastermind.

In covering this story, the *Times* made it clear that issues of religious freedom and diversity were important, newsworthy matters. The Taliban, the Afghan ruling party since 1996, had received *Times* attention since then; however, its explicitly religious aspects had been somewhat muted in *Times* coverage until the articles by Barry Bearak and were now coming to the fore, and its members were presented as religious bigots. (The *Times* gave far less coverage, just a photograph and two sentences, when French authorities destroyed a one-hundred-foot statue of the "Cosmopla[n]etary Messiah," the founder of a "cult" called "Mandarom." No protests were reported. See "Cult Statue Destroyed" 2001.)

In May, Bearak (2001o) issued a dispatch from Kandahar with the following lead: "The Taliban rulers, worldwide pariahs for their harsh treatment of Afghan women and Buddhist statues, face further scorn with a proposal that would force Hindus to wear an identity label on their clothing to distinguish them from Muslims." He referred to the "notorious" Taliban Ministry for the Promotion of Virtue and the Prevention of Vice and quoted a US State Department official who spoke of bringing the Taliban "into compliance with international norms of behavior on all human rights issues."

In a later communiqué with a Kandahar dateline, Bearak told of a mock-heroic television repairman and movie smuggler in subversive skirmishes with the "austere edicts" of the Taliban against the representation of the human form in moving or still images. "This dictum" against television and movies, especially those containing sexuality, "is enforced," Bearak (2001j) wrote, "by religious policemen from the Ministry for the Promotion of Virtue and the Prevention of Vice. They ride around in pickup trucks with scowls on their faces and automatic weapons at their sides."

In early August, this Taliban ministry closed Shelter Now's office under the accusation of Christian proselytizing, a punishable crime according to Taliban "edict." The Christian organization "denied" the charges, and the AP brief gave some credence to the denial by characterizing the Taliban as "members of a religious militia that espouses a harsh brand of fundamentalist Islam" ("Afghanistan Closes a Christian Relief Office" 2001; see also "Afghans to Keep 24 Christian Aid Workers in Jail" 2001 and "Taliban Suspect Christian Plot" 2001).

Although maintaining a critical stance regarding the Taliban, Barry Bearak presented the Taliban evidence against the Christian aid workers, including the two Americans, Dayna Lesli Curry and Heather Mercer, both of whom were caught, in a Taliban official's words, "as you say, red-handed, in an Afghan's house, where they know they were not to go. They were trying to show a video about Jesus, from his birth to his, what is the word, I think it is crucifixion." An anonymous American upbraided the women for having broken a well-known law and for having "dragged their Afghan workers into this." The Taliban suggested that the women could be put to death for their crime; however, Bearak (2001n) offered his own view about the appropriate punishment: "If the reclusive, one-eyed Mullah Muhammad Omar is indeed the last word, he might consult his own Edict No. 14, a July 31 decree concerning the behavior of foreign nationals. It regards 'inviting Afghans to any religion apart from Islam' as a less serious offense than 'taking photographs of living creatures' or 'eating the meat of the pig.' Punishment is 3 to 10 days in prison and then expulsion." A subsequent article (Bearak 2001m) expressed Bearak's skepticism about the gravity of the jailed Christians' offenses—"This may not exactly sound like the centerpiece of some grand collusion, . . . the tentacles of a far-reaching Christian plot," he said—but the evidence was sufficient regarding Christian evangelizing among the Shelter Now workers: "'Bibles, Bibles, Bibles'" as well as a CD, music, and instructional booklets about Jesus and Christianity. By August 27, the two Americans admitted "showing a video CD about Jesus. But 'we did not think it would cause so much trouble,' because Jesus is also regarded as a prophet by Muslims, reads a statement by both Ms. Curry and Ms. Mercer. 'We again are very sorry.'"

In the weeks to come, the *Times* played out the drama of the imprisoned aid workers in Kabul as lawyers, parents, judges, mullahs, diplomats, and foreign ministers jockeyed for the women's lives because they were condemned to die for attempting to convert Muslims to Christianity, an evangelical faith suspect among Afghan Muslims, despite their great respect for Jesus as a prophet and healer (Bearak 2001a, 2001b, 2001d, 2001e, 2001g, 2001p).

On August 29, the *Times* carried the op-ed commentary "Teaching the Taliban about Human Rights" by Karl F. Inderfurth (2001), who had been assistant secretary of state for South Asian affairs in the Clinton administration and was in 2001 a senior associate at the Institute for Global Engagement, a faith-based think tank concerned with religious freedom worldwide. The op-ed recounted Taliban abuses: periodic massacres of Shiites, ordinances forcing Hindus to wear identification badges, the campaign against the Buddhist statues in Bamiyan, and so on. He called on Muslim governments worldwide (the fifty-five nations that make up the Organization of the Islamic Conference and in particular the three—Pakistan, Saudi Arabia, and the United Arab Emirates—that recognized the Taliban government as legitimate) to "persuade the Taliban to pursue a path of greater tolerance." He also suggested that the United States, with $124 million in aid to Afghanistan in 2001, flex its economic muscle to influence Taliban policies. The *Times* also ran an editorial on August 30 titled "Pakistan's Cruel Blasphemy Law" (2001), commenting on a law that condemned a man to death for teaching the obvious: "that before receiving God's words at the age of 40, Muhammed and his family were not Muslims and did not follow Muslim practices" (see also Bearak 2001h; Kristof 2002f).

Our Colgate students commented that the *Times* as an institution seemed to perceive a public duty to report on issues of religious pluralism, with praise for diversity, ecumenism, and interfaith cooperation, but with scorn for individual and governmental intolerance. The Taliban served in the summer of 2001 as fundamentalist bogeymen in the worldview of American media such as the *Times,* primarily because the Afghan Muslims made a sharp contrast to religious, freedom-loving America (and perhaps in part because the Taliban could be seen as an extreme example of religious fundamentalism, an oblique warning about any state, including the United States, that might wish to establish church organizations with governmental sanctions).

The paper was rewarded for this coverage. Barry Bearak (who, with his wife, Celia Dugger, reported on eight countries in South Asia, one-fifth of the human race, Bearak [2003] said) received the 2002 Pulitzer Prize and the George Polk Award in international reporting for his illumination of Afghanistan in 2001. Remarking that the Taliban expelled Bearak from their country while he was covering the trial of the Christian workers, a proud *Times* colleague, Roger Cohen (2002), praised the reporter, stating that he is "guided by a moral compass that sets him apart among correspondents." Furthermore, Cohen said, "he is disinclined to write about anything he has not himself seen, and he is deeply suspicious of all conventional wisdom."

And yet it is a *Times* convention to praise religious diversity and religious tolerance as positive values and to condemn religious intolerance both at home and abroad. Bearak and his *Times* colleagues carried out that convention in their treatment of the Taliban. The *Times* showed the potential political ramifications of hidebound religious attitudes in foreign and international contexts.

Another article in the *Times* on August 27, 2001, enhanced this convention on the domestic front. Page A4 carried an article about the Taliban, but on page A10 there was a piece on the mass murder of six Ukrainian immigrants in California by one of their relatives focused on a congregation, the Bethany Slavic Missionary Church, whose members had come to the United States seeking religious freedom, but who did not mix well with other Ukrainians in the area. "Residents who fled persecution feel fear in their new home," read a caption, suggesting that their in-bred clannishness had somehow led to the killing. "They don't mix too well with us," said the president of the Ukrainian Heritage Club of Northern California. "They are from a very strict fundamentalist background that doesn't allow social dancing. Our club promotes folk dancing and social dancing as part of Ukrainian culture. They feel we're nonbelievers and sinners" (Navarro 2001). Our Colgate students felt that the implication in the *Times* report was that "fundamentalist" religionists were antisocial and intolerant of their fellows and that their attitudes could lead to friction and even violence.

The August 27, 2001, issue was rich in religion news. On A12, as a sidebar to an article on stem cell research debate, Gustav Niebuhr (2001s) cataloged the ways in which religious leaders in the United States "ponder the stem cell issue." Niebuhr quoted opinions from Roman Catholic, Unitarian-Universalist, Episcopal, United Methodist, Mormon, Presbyterian, and United Church of Christ leaders, as well as from Reform and Conservative Jews, Muslims, Hindus, and Buddhists, noting that "many major religious groups have yet to be heard from." The overall effect was to show that America is a land of many religions with many "nuanced" opinions on knotty ethical questions such as abortion and stem cell research.

On the stem cell debate, the *Times* followed the convention of quoting a variety of ethical opinions from leading religionists regarding crucial contemporary issues. Over the next two weeks, the *Times* carried several stories about abortion and stem cell research, indicating the role of religious activists and leaders in making their viewpoints public (Fountain 2001d; Goodstein 2001a; Sack and Niebuhr 2001) and addressing ethical concern about unbridled scientific experimentation on human embryos (Steinfels 2001a). In effect, the *Times* provided a forum for religious commentary. There were no surveys or polls yet, suggesting national opinion regarding stem cells, but the paper was laying out a spectrum of religious opinion on the subject. Our students remarked that the diversity of religious perspectives tended both to highlight the importance of the ethical issues and to relativize the views of any one religious group.

On August 27, 2001, the paper's regional coverage in the "Metro" section contained a short item from Waterbury, Connecticut, "An Afternoon of Prayer in a Wounded City" (Herszenhorn 2001a), in which a priest, a rabbi, and a Protestant minister led prayers, hymns, and readings on the village green to comfort a community shaken by the arrest of its mayor on charges of "luring a child for sex" (a trial that concluded with a conviction in March 2003). "The crowd was a reflection of the city," the reporter declared, "Christian, Muslim and Jewish, Hispanic, white and black, retirees and young couples with children"—that is, the American ideal *(e pluribus unum)* of a unified community composed of the diverse many, coming together for prayer, spiritual healing, and forgiveness in a common crisis.

The *Times'* interest in interreligious activity as a means toward social unity between Christians and Jews was marked at the deaths of Robert McAfee Brown, a renowned "champion of ecumenism" and "a theologian who fought for causes like civil rights and liberation theology" (Martin 2001), and "David Hunter, 90, pioneer in interfaith ties" ("David Hunter" 2001). In the Saturday "Religion Journal," Gustav Niebuhr (2001o) reviewed favorably a film and book devoted to the notion of common faith between Christians and Jews, offspring of "'Our Father Abraham.'" It was clear to our students that, according to the conventions of *Times* coverage, interfaith solidarity can serve a healing role in times of crisis and that America's pluralistic society is well served by emphasizing common religious roots and values.

The *Times* played other conventional stories in the waning days of the 2001 summer. The paper reported on tensions within religious traditions (Pace 2001) and on the regular appointments of church personnel, especially within Roman Catholicism in and around New York City (Kershaw 2001b). In so doing, the *Times* reminded its readers of the institutional structures of churches, with their hierarchies and internal politics, as was its wont. For the *Times,* particular denominations constituted the building blocks of religious organizations—the named, cumulative, religious traditions.

At the same time, the paper highlighted several religious actors deemed newsworthy:

• A feature on a black Baptist minister defying drug dealers, despite the threat on his life (Bragg 2001a)

• An analysis of a "faith-based effort to save ailing marriages" (Niebuhr 2001f)

• A brief report on a religious "drive against gossip" (Schemo 2001a)

All of these stories conveyed the impression that religious organizations exert influence for the good of society and its foundational relationships—hence, the shock that Benedictine sisters in Rwanda would have collaborated with Hutu militiamen in the massacre of thousands of Tutsis in 1994. Religion was normally a force for societal good, according to this convention of *Times* coverage. "What mixture of terror and hatred," the *Times* writer asked, "led these nuns to betray the promise of their faith?" (Ignatieff 2001).

The *Times* also paid attention to hatreds either fostered or exacerbated by religious strife:

• "New Accusations of a Vatican Role in Anti-Semitism" (E. Eakin 2001a) examined the papal campaign against Jews in the decades preceding the Holocaust; and a second article raised questions about the papacy's insufficient resistance to Nazi annihilation of Jews (Henneberger 2001d). The *Times* also ran several articles about the Holocaust and its remembrance (Bohlen 2001b; Erlanger 2001b; P. Green 2001), reminders of how much hatred and violence can be directed against a religious minority, the Jews, under particular historical circumstances.

• Protestant attacks on Catholic schoolgirls in Northern Ireland were highlighted in an incident that elicited "revulsion" and "disgust," even from "hardline Protestant politicians" and "Protestant paramilitary groups" (Lavery 2001). A follow-up headline called Catholic–Protestant strife in Northern Ireland "a cycle of hatred" (Cowell 2001a).

• Religious violence between Muslims and Christians in Nigeria "left smoke rising in the sky and charred bodies in the streets" when a Christian woman in the city of Jos tried to cross a street where Muslim men were gathered for Friday prayer ("Religious Strife in Nigeria" 2001; "Religious and Ethnic Clashes in Nigeria" 2001).

• A short piece served as a reminder of the 1994 Brooklyn Bridge killing of an Hasidic yeshiva student and the wounding of two of his peers by a Lebanese immigrant gunman "in retaliation for the massacre of Muslim worshipers in Hebron, in the West Bank, by a Jewish settler from Brooklyn" (Fried 2001).

It was plain to our students that, according to the *Times*, religion can foster hatred and violence, especially when mixed with political and ethnic conflict.

On less sanguinary notes but with substantial gravity, the *Times* reported on scandalous behavior by the personnel of religious organizations: cases of sexual abuse alleged against a United Church of Christ Sunday school teacher (Goodstein 2001c) and a Mormon church member ("not a member of the clergy" [Niebuhr 2001i]).

With a tinge of titillation, the *Times* Vatican correspondent told about a Zambian Catholic archbishop who married a follower of Reverend Sun Myung Moon in a Unification Church multiple wedding, but who recanted his marriage vows under hierarchical peer pressure (Henneberger 2001n). An article quoted the prelate: "'My commitment to the life of the church including celibacy, does not allow me to be married,' wrote the archbishop, who is 71. 'The calling of the church is my primary pledge and the right one." His rejected spouse said "her immediate plans were uncertain but spoke of meeting her husband again in the hereafter" (Henneberger 2001a).

Our students suggested that in this coverage the *Times* was acknowledging that representatives of religious traditions sometimes engage in scandalous behavior, often of a sexual nature, that belie their ideals and vows of faith. According to the journalistic convention, religious bodies are peopled by fallible members and are enmeshed in the secular institutions of the world.

Churches also own properties and sometimes considerable wealth, and their members can be political agents. Hence, the *Times* reported on real estate owned by the Episcopal Church (Garbarine 2001), a mayoral endorsement by an Hasidic rabbi (Sengupta 2001a)—both in New York City—and the death of the US congressional chaplain ("Rev. James Ford" 2001). A large feature focused on a Midwest Catholic abbey that was supporting its "'contemplative life'" financially through the manufacture and sale of coffins. "It is all fine and good to rise at 3:15 in the morning to pray," the reporter opined, "but prayers do not pay the bills" (Barry 2001a).

More significant, according to the paper, the institutions of religion and government can enter into relations, which are especially newsworthy when the interaction arouses concern. The *Times* ran several articles about church–state relations, including a leading editorial against President George W. Bush's "faith-based initiative" ("Church, State, and Joe Lieberman" 2001). Other church–state articles dealt with Alabama Supreme Court chief justice Roy Moore's installation of a monumental sculpture of the Ten Commandments "in a prominent place [in his courthouse] to acknowledge the supremacy of God as the basis of the law" ("Alabama Court" 2001) and the contested observance of religious holidays by New York City public-school teachers (Wyatt 2001b). In the *Times* of late summer 2001—as in the preceding decades—church and state relations were matters of public importance and controversy.

The *Times* conventions of religion coverage include observation of the tensions not only between religions and within religions, but also between religious and nonreligious values. Religious convictions can sometimes be at odds with the secular mores of society at large, as epitomized in the notion of the "culture wars" in the United States. In the past generation, both in the United States and abroad, journalists have commented on the ways religions have been embroiled in the issues of the day and in many cases have constituted the issues themselves as societies have struggled to define their orienting values and consequent policies. In the United States, this struggle has been termed the "culture wars" (J. Green et al. 1996).

The term *culture wars* approximates the nineteenth-century German word *Kulturkampf,* meaning the public argument in the German states concerning "the moral character of the nation" forged by Otto von Bismarck (Hunter 1991:xii). The "culture wars" in the United States have their surface issues—prayer in public schools, abortion, gay rights, arts funding, women's rights, child-care policy, church–state relations, multiculturalism, and other issues regarding family, education, popular media, law, electoral politics, sexuality in general, and so on—but in aggregate they reveal a cultural "struggle" (might we call it a *kampf* or a jihad?) about how to "define America" (Hunter 1991).

American newspapers such as the *Times* exist in order to participate in the "struggle to define America." Their task is to report on and to teach about current controversies that define the nation. Sociologist James Davison Hunter (1991) acknowledged that the news media treat these issues of "deep concern for the character of life" held by those committed to the struggle (33, 32). He adds, *"At stake is how we as Americans will order our lives together"* (34, italics in original).

In early September 2001, there was a feature in the "National" section of the *Times* about evangelical Christians who were opting out of the sexuality of dating in favor of celibate courtships under the guidance of home-schooling conferences and parental oversight. This American movement was described in the paper as the "counterculture of Christian home schoolers who are accustomed to seeing themselves as mavericks cutting fresh paths in an ungodly society" (Goodstein 2001l). The *Times* has covered the "culture wars" in the United States since the 1980s, and this piece can be seen as an aerial view of one particular battleground.

Religion reporter Laurie Goodstein wrote this article in a sensitive manner, without critical comment about its protagonists. This is the type of story Goodstein (2004b) says she likes to emphasize in her reporting—"religion in the living room." One might call it an optional story, run by the *Times* without the need for a breaking-news peg, in order to define religious developments as its editors and reporters see them. Goodstein notes, however, that the story is about an important religious "trend," so even though it is a "feature," it is truly newsworthy and not really optional. She remarks that Joshua Harris's book *I Kissed Dating Goodbye* (1997)—mentioned in Goodstein's (2001l) article as an influential text—had sold close to a million copies by 2001, and so something was really going on in America, something worth covering. Why did the *Times* put the dating story on the front page of the Sunday paper? She says that it was a "slow news day," but she also states that there was real human interest in the story, and she hopes that one might say it was well written.

American evangelical Protestants sometimes say that the *Times* is hostile to them, and yet Goodstein's story was not hostile. She calls it a "sympathetic" story. Her editors questioned her skeptically about the people in her piece, arranging marriages for their teenage children. "What year are we living in?" they asked. For the editors, for many *Times* readers, and for our students—who, I attest, found the evangelicals in the article off-putting to their own liberal, northeastern sensibilities—the story had a certain kind of "shock value." Goodstein (2004b) emphasizes that the people in her story were "smart people" who had reasons for doing what they were doing, and she feels that her job was to "translate" their reasons to her readers.

Much *Times* religion coverage contains affecting portraits of its subjects, even though they might elicit ambivalent reactions from readers, such as our students. In September 2001, the *Times Magazine* contained a touching portrait (many pages of words and photographs) of a Lubavitcher rabbi's wife in Brooklyn and her fourteen children, emphasizing her devotion to the late leader of the movement, Menachem Mendel Schneerson. The headline pointed to the "paradox" in Doba Levin's life, which is contained in the author's statement: "Levin devotes her life to serving a system that excludes her and her 10 daughters from formal positions of authority or leadership. . . . It is also, perhaps unexpectedly, a movement with a fairly extensive infrastructure for women, including national conferences and Torah study groups and a line of rhetoric about women's power" (Mark and Shapiro 2001).

Our students commented on the feminist angle that the *Times* carried in many of its religion articles. In recent decades, the paper has made it a convention to interpret contemporary religion through women's eyes and interests, remarking that women's goals are often at odds with religious institutions' ends. The article on Levin was a feminist take on Jewish orthodoxy, but it was placed, perhaps ironically, our students said, amidst the fashion ads and articles. My eye was caught by the page following the feature, which carried the heading "Beheld" under the rubric "Beauty." Concerning the "alternate reality of the prettiest girl," we learned about Sara Ziff, the blonde in the hip-huggers and tank top who received an ogling from a construction worker in SoHo. "She is as aware of her effect on strangers as they are," the caption said (Greenfield and Spindler 2001). Our students suggested that the *Times* caters as much to fashion and pretty girls on its pages as it does to feminism or to religion.

One aspect of *Times* religion coverage that often goes overlooked—indeed, Professor Byrnes and I had to coax our students to read or even acknowledge the arts articles—is the interplay between art and religion. Just as a university has its departments and therefore tends to see the universe in terms of its named disciplines so that it might offer psychological, philosophical, historical, art-historical, literary, sociological, anthropological, and perhaps even economic, educational, political, and geographical perspectives on religion in its curriculum (not to mention its interdisciplinary angles: women and religion, Native American religion, environment and religion, and so forth), the *New York Times* categorizes the world through its sections: "International," "National," "Metro," but also "Arts," "Fashions," "Sports," "Business," "Science," "Travel," "Book Reviews," and so on. The arts are very important to the *Times,* meriting their own section every day, like business and sports do; but more than the latter two, the arts are frequently linked with religious themes. Indeed, art is a means by which religions are humanized in the paper, showing them in their most beautiful, personally expressive aspects.

On September 7, 2001, the *Times* ran a review of the exhibition Meeting God: Elements of Hindu Devotion, which had opened at the American Museum of Natural History. The exhibition "is tailored to its moment," said the reviewer. "It comes at a time when Asian Indians form one of the fastest growing immigrant groups in the New York metropolitan region" (R. Smith 2001). So not only did the art "display . . . Hindu ritual with reverence and graciousness," but it also served the museum's (and the newspaper's) multiethnic constituency. The review praised the exhibition for displaying *puja* (daily worship), *darshan* (seeing and being seen by God), and various shrines of the gods Krishna, Ganesha, and so on, thus demonstrating how a people worship. Hence, the *Times* employed a display of spirituality to show the importance of religious ritual in human culture.

In another corner of town on September 10, the Jewish Cultural Fund for the Performing Arts organized "'holy partying'" at a cruise marking *selihot,* "observed shortly before Rosh Hashana, the Jewish New Year, which begins at sundown next Monday." Here were "revelers enjoying the salt air, summer breezes and skyscraper silhouettes" (Kilgannon 2001), showing *Times* readers how rituals invigorate religious sensibilities and how—in one specific instance of Judaism—religious liturgies comprise the seasons of the year. This celebration was not your typical ritual; indeed, it was the "unlikelihood" (Kilgannon 2007) of the gathering—in a boat with "offbeat characters" circling Manhattan rather than in a staid temple—that appealed to the reporter. Nevertheless, it lent light to contemporary Jews' ceremonial lives.

On the same day, the *Times* ran the pictorial spread "At Historic Temple, a Joyous Revival" (Wadler 2001), regarding Central Synagogue on Fifty-fifth and Lexington (one of my favorite spaces in New York City, built in 1872 and modeled after a Budapest synagogue), which had been torched accidentally in 1998 but was now restored and ready for reopening. A beautiful color photo showed young men and women carrying Torahs, "where trumpeting shofars heralded" the temple's rededication. Although at the moment the *Times* did not have a single reporter who covered religion in the metropolitan area (it later hired Daniel J. Wakin for this beat), the paper did illustrate religious life in communities around the boroughs, celebrating diversity on the local level, which made sense in a city in which more languages are spoken than in any other municipality in the world. The *Times* has made it a habit—like any other newspaper—to celebrate local religious communities. In this case, the celebration was on the streets of Manhattan.

Finally, still looking through the pages of the August 27 *Times,* we examined page A4 once again in order to observe another convention in *New York Times* religion coverage. Here was a report from Indonesia, "An Outpatient Exorcism (It Was Only a Crab)" (Mydans 2001c), in which a reporter mocked a "faith healer" who, "mixing mysticism with chicanery," treated a patient by removing a crab from his belly. According to the feature, the healer "pokes . . . slaps . . . scribbles . . . listens . . . prods," while his trained parrot cries out "Allah!" In the end, the healer tells the patient to say a prayer and "return the crab gently to a pond."

From time to time, the *Times* makes skeptical fun of magical supernaturalism—the belief in the human ability to harness the powers of the spiritual world—usually by focusing on religionists from the Third World: Africa, South

Sea Islands, and so on (see, e.g., Lacey 2001 regarding "traditional spirits" in Uganda). But even American magical supernaturalism has received its share of *Times* skepticism. On August 28, 2001, the *Times* ran an AP story about the accreditation of the Astrological Institute in Scottsdale, Arizona, where "courses include a 'master class on the asteroid goddesses.'" The article closed with the following: "Astrology contends that a person's character and fate are directed at birth by the position of the sun, the moon and the planets. This is charted in a horoscope, which is often done these days with computer software. Scientists scoff at the pursuit" ("First School of Astrology Is Accredited" 2001).

Some of our students thought that the *Times* was expressing an overall distaste for religion in its stories about exorcism and astrology. Others argued that the paper seemed to distinguish between religious people's individual faith experiences, which might be presented sympathetically, and claims of spiritually enhanced prowess in matters such as healing the sick and divining the future.

In any event, Professor Byrnes, our students, and I encountered about a dozen salient conventions of *Times* religion coverage during the first two weeks of our term in 2001. These conventions coincided with but differed somewhat from the categories of coverage in religion journalism that several scholars had cataloged (Hoover, Handley, and Radelfinger 1989:72; cf. Steinfels 1993a:4):

individual faith experiences
local church news and announcements
other local religious issues
national denominations
ecumenical, cooperative, interfaith movements
beliefs of various religions besides your own
major American religious movements (e.g., evangelicalism)
alternate, new movements
national religious scandals and controversies
religion and American politics
religion in foreign and international politics
ethical and social issues
social and ethical positions by major faith groups
opinion and commentary by religious leaders
humor or cartoons regarding religion
surveys and polls on religious topics

The conventions we encountered during a two-week period in late summer 2001 represented only a sliver of *Times* religion coverage. Nevertheless, they point out the *Times'* usual interests in religion stories. They show that conventionality does not mean single-mindedness, as if there were THE *New York Times* coverage of religion. Instead, there seemed to be many complementary conventions at work, with many reporters acting according to their own biases, sensitivities, and agendas. In addition, conventionality did not mean dull reportage. The *Times* of August and September 2001 showed that the paper had come a long way from being the "good gray lady" of its past. Its coverage was lively and colorful, with literary and photographic flair.

In observing these conventions of religion coverage, one has to ask: What did the *New York Times* delineate as "religion" in its coverage? From the examples, one might be able to tell that the *Times* employed in those two weeks a considerable degree of semantic range when treating what we might call a "religion" story. And that range coincides with the *Times'* definitions of religion over the previous three decades.

In the *Times,* a "religion" story is any coverage of the cumulative, institutional traditions—Christianity, Islam, Judaism, and so on—that are conventionally regarded as the identifiable religions of the world. These collectivities, with their hierarchies, authority, history, and internal diversity, are treated as the major agencies for organizing people's religious lives: fostering piety, transmitting meaningful worldviews, encoding ethics, validating and criticizing cultures, passing down wisdom, providing the means of facing ultimate concerns, arranging the means of attaining links with the divine or the transcendent, and redeeming humans in their most profound predicaments. By and large, religious people around the world identify themselves as members of these traditions. These traditions' edicts, their personnel, their ministries, their real estate, their congregations, their calendars, their rituals, their ponderings, their internal and interfaith relations—all are potentially suitable as "religion" news.

But it is also clear that the *Times* portrays certain dimensions of religious life, and by focusing on those aspects, the *Times* serves to define "religiousness" in several ways.

• In the *Times'* view, religions are newsworthy when their representatives attempt to define or reassess their teachings about the transcendent, spiritual world and its relationship to the material universe and people's lives within it.

These teachings—sometimes called "beliefs" or "doctrines"—constitute a religious worldview, defining what religious communities believe about the cosmos and expressing shared symbols, concerns, questions and answers, values, even conflicts, made sensible within an overall structure of the universe common across a religion's culture. Worldviews are correlative, positing ultimate interrelatedness of all beings in a single web of connection. Religion is informed by worldview and the motivating attitudes dependent on it.

• People behave religiously when they conceive of a supernatural, spiritual realm whose powers are felt to sustain or endanger human existence. These beliefs—dearly held concepts—often seem unconvincing and even irrational to nonbelievers, but to believers they are true beyond doubt. The *Times* does not answer the question of God's existence but rather treats religious people's utterances about the divine as sincerely formative in their motives and behaviors. When held in common by members of a religious tradition, these beliefs can bind diverse persons into a community of shared faith and practice. Religion is belief in invisible, transcendent, powerful, divine, eternal realities and communication with them.

• People behave religiously when faced with life crises (disease, death, disillusion, scandal) or at times of great joy (birth, rebuilding, the seasonal celebrations of renewal and forgiveness)—in short, when facing critical, imminent concerns. As a dimension of human life, religion exposes and addresses crucial, ultimate human questions, to which humans express their deepest feelings, their beloved ideals, their emotions, their spirituality with serious intent, with a sense of awe and reverence, with commitment, and with faith. Religion is a faithful grappling with ultimate matters, for individuals and especially for communities.

• People behave religiously when they take defined moral positions, espousing principles that entail doing good and avoiding evil, grounded in their religious traditions of piety and reverence or in individually conceived, spiritual philosophies of life, and when, molded by ethics and in light of ultimate concerns, they act upon their moral convictions for the good or ill of their community (conceived locally, nationally, internationally, and even cosmically). Religion is a code of ethics, a set of values, with concrete ramifications in daily life and in public policies.

• People behave religiously when they act in concerted, repetitive, obsessively proper, stylized ways. These ways are ritualized means by which religions inculcate value and provide emotional release or practical training. Rituals sometimes attempt to control situations through magical incantations, hoping to harness the invisible powers of the universe through ritual compulsion in order to further one's health, wealth, and happiness; at other times, they cede power to the supernatural realm. Religion is a ritualized set of behaviors, grounded in shared beliefs and a common way of life.

• Finally (although the definitions might go on), certain people behave religiously when they celebrate their ethnic identity as something greater than their individual selves *and* when they set themselves off against other peoples, absorbing themselves in their community and setting themselves against those outside it, whom they may sometimes come to perceive as enemies. Religion has the function of fostering community consciousness, providing principles of organization, and informing legal and political structures. A shared way of life, a shared set of ultimate concerns, shared ethics, a shared belief in God, and shared ritual activities—over time and space—are the real stuff of religion because they are shared. Religions are thus foundational in the creation of culture: the shared way of life with its common symbols and meanings. Religion is a means of forming social solidarity. Indeed, it might be argued that whatever serves to bind humans together is religious, including social and political systems. The *Times* is especially interested in religion's place in these systems, both at home and abroad.

In sum, what does religion in the national society called the United States of America look like on the pages of the *Times?* The *Times* has shown interest in religion's roles in the national cultures of the world, beyond the borders of the United States. How has the *Times* informed Americans (its main readership) about worldwide religious phenomena, placing US patterns in global contexts? What are the moral conundrums that vex other national cultures? How do other nations deal with church–state questions? The stories have flowed in from Asia, Africa, the Middle East, Latin America, Europe, and elsewhere throughout the globe, depicting national identities either formed or fractured by religious loyalties.

Each country, each nationalism, has its own religious patterns, complexities, church–state relations, tensions, even hatreds and "culture wars." In the United States, Jews, blacks, American Indians, and other ethnic minorities have been studied in the *Times* for their special religious dimensions within mainstream America for better or worse and for how those dimensions have held communities together or split them apart. Religious identity can sometimes foster enmity toward those outside the pale or the veil. The *Times* has not forgotten historical American Protestant intolerance for Catholics, nor has it neglected racism, imperialism, or anti-Semitism as faith-based, societal forces.

Indeed, if one of the defining characteristics or dimensions of religion is its community formation—its nationalism, as it were—there is also the political aspect of religion: What roles does religion play in holding these communities-nations together, and what roles does it play in setting interest groups against one another? Religion not only plays a role in politics—we know that—but also is one of the ways in which groups identify themselves within the body politic. It is one of the ways in which groups identify their goals, their "goods," and how they locate them against others' interests. The "culture wars" in any society are religious matters because religion is how a people think about and communicate their concerns and interests and how they organize to promote their plans. Politics thus takes place both within each religious group—as its members argue over their ultimate and immediate concerns—and within larger countrywide polities; religions (churches) thus function as interest groups that press their ideals on the culture as a whole.

If these definitions of religions are inherent in the *Times*' treatment of religion, the paper, as noted, seems to care little about defining religion, fathoming its essence, or tracing its human history. The paper's interests—like that of all mainstream American journalism—are persons, institutions, ideas of current importance, not "religion" per se. The *Times* is interested these days in the religious dimensions of contemporary life, but it is not a religion textbook.

Nonetheless, *Times* coverage defines religion according to the conventions of its institutional memory. The question facing us is how the *Times* defined and redefined religion in light of the events of September 11, 2001.

Civil Religion in America

Newspapers have the duty to cover the public displays of national consensus and conflict. One might even say that in the context of American civil religion journalists are the scribes, both priestly and prophetic, recounting celebrations and tragedies, rites of communion and rites of crisis, and holding up the sacred canopy of civic life for admiration and scrutiny. The events of September 11, 2001, gave rise immediately to a matrix of national ceremonies, not explicitly religious in a denominational sense, but part of US public-square solidarity, incorporating the churches but focusing on the nation. How did the *Times* depict the national spirit in this time of challenge? How did religion serve to hold the country together and express consensus values? To what degree did religion play a divisive role? And what role did the *Times* play as a participant-observer in American civil religion after 9/11?

Times religion writer Laurie Goodstein (2004b) says that Executive Editor Howell Raines—on the job only one week when the attacks occurred—had already put in place a technique of *Times* news coverage that subsequently served the immensity of 9/11 issues admirably. Its operative directives, she explains, were to "flood the zone" and "beat the competition." *Times* editors sent reporters out to cast light on every angle of 9/11 they could imagine, even if the overall effect was redundancy. In 2002, the *Times* used the same saturating method to cover the Catholic sexual abuse scandal. In the latter case, the saturation seemed to many readers like too much, but for 9/11 it seemed appropriate. Raines (2004) himself—after having been fired from the *Times* in 2003—declared that his staff's dedication in covering 9/11 for the first six months was "the most inspirational performance I've ever seen" in four decades of his journalistic experience.

The immediate vehicle for the *Times'* saturating coverage of 9/11 was a section unto itself called "A Nation Challenged." It won a Pulitzer Prize in Public

Service, one of seven awarded to the paper in 2002. Howell Raines (2002b) says in the introduction to the book *A Nation Challenged: A Visual History of 9/11 and Its Aftermath* (*New York Times* 2002) that the special section "gave editors the freedom to show readers the breadth and depth of the unfolding story . . . with unsparing intellectual balance" (9).

When one reads *A Nation Challenged* under a single cover, one can see how the *Times* perceived the 9/11 story line: the attack itself; the collapse of the World Trade Center; the ruins at Ground Zero; local and national leadership; the mourning—around the city and around the world; the thanks to the firefighters, including the icon Father Mychal Judge (41); the "misplaced anger" (86) directed at US Muslims; the recovery at Ground Zero, with the cruciform girders positioned upright in the rubble (123); the anthrax panic; the campaign against Osama bin Laden and the Taliban in Afghanistan; the "holy war against America" (142); "Islam ablaze" (145); Osama bin Laden himself; the "creed of the Wahhabis" (148). There is little explicitly about religion on its own, but it is also ever present. "Unlikely Foes" (184) pictures Muslim convert John Walker Lindh and American soldier John Michael Spann. "Behind the Burka" (212) shows the effects of the Taliban, now apparently defeated. The book ends with an upbeat photo from Afghanistan, "The Doves Are Back" (232).

Victor Navasky (2002) states that the *Times* displayed an "ideology of the center" (xv) in its immediate 9/11 coverage, a position of moderatism that looked hard at all manner of extremists—around the world and in the United States. One would agree by looking at *A Nation Challenged*. In book form, the *Times* 9/11 narrative is closer in content to the patriotic story told by other news outlets and criticized in the books about 9/11 coverage. *A Nation Challenged* cleaves to the center, castigating fundamentalists on all sides and espousing societal acceptance of US Muslims. Yet the book lacks the idiosyncratic voices on all sides that appeared in the pages of the real *Times* and comes to a conclusion perhaps too facile: that victory was securely at hand in Afghanistan and relative peace of mind in America. In this way, the *Times* inscribed an American cultural narrative in response to 9/11.

Mark Silk (2001a) says that 9/11 opened a "new chapter" of civil religion in America, and the newspapers covered it. When President George W. Bush offered his thoughts at a prayer service for the victims of the September 11 attack, it was an act of civil religion, as defined most famously by Robert N. Bellah (1967). Silk writes, "If civil religion is about anything, it's about war and those who die in it." What makes this angle so intriguing—as Americans tried to define that national, public, inclusive religiousness—is "whether such inclusive religiosity can persuasively be marshaled against an enemy that thinks of itself as supremely godly" (1).

So there were two primary themes to be covered at home: (1) the varieties of American civil religious response to 9/11 and (2) the varieties of Islamic response. Of course, the Islamic responses came from abroad as well as from home, and that was the crux of the conflict: How does global Islam fit into the fabric of American life? I address this question more fully later, but first I look at the varieties of American civil religious responses. The American nation was being challenged and potentially redefined.

Dan Barry has worked at the *Times* since 1995, covering New York City, its environs, and now the whole of America. He has written a column, "About New York," and he has published a memoir, *Pull Me Up* (2004), which depicts the romance of his Irish American upbringing. At St. Bonaventure University, he discovered his vocation as a writer, received a B.A. in journalism, then went on for a journalism master's at New York University. According to the book's reviewer, he employs the language of his Catholic upbringing in his memoir: "'Baptize me in ink,' he says, and seeks a sanctuary in the newsroom, 'as though journalism was a kind of priesthood.' Some of the book's most lyrical passages capture the routines and rituals of newspaper life, with a wry understanding of its endless repetitions: 'The contents of these filing cabinets sang of life's inevitabilities, the distressing and the reassuring'" (Lopate 2004). In a feature about Barry on the St. Bonaventure School of Journalism Web site, Barry says that for New Yorkers, life is divided into two epochs: before 9/11 and after. He is no different: "'I wrote hundreds of stories for the New York Times but all of them seem like they were 20 years ago after 9/11,' he said" ("Dan Barry" 2003).

It fell to Barry (2001c) to write a summary, profusely illustrated with color photographs, of the vigils around the world that meditated soulfully on the 9/11 attacks. At the Washington National Cathedral in a national service of prayer and remembrance, President Bush addressed his fellow mourners not only in the cathedral, but around the country: "'We are here in the middle hour of our grief,' he said. 'So many have suffered so great a loss, and today we express our nation's sorrow. We come before God to pray for the missing and the dead, and for those who loved them.'" He also "vowed to fulfill what he said was the nation's responsibility to 'rid the world of evil'—to respond to attacks that appear to have killed thousands of people. 'God bless America,' the president said, before heading north to Manhattan for a tour of a fresh crater in American soil."

What effects would the 9/11 attacks have on the practice and depth of American religion? At Rosh Hashanah services at Temple Emanu-El in Manhattan, "a new song was added to the traditional liturgy: 'God Bless America.'" At many Jewish temples, attendance was unusually heavy. "There are no atheists in foxholes," one Jewish official commented, "and we're all in one big foxhole right now" (A. Newman 2001; see also Nathan 2001).

Within two weeks of the Washington ceremony of mourning, the *Times* was suggesting a shift in religiosity in the headline "Terror Attacks Could Change Paths of Faith" (Wakin 2001h). American clergy—evangelicals, Jews, Muslims, Catholics, and others—were reporting that they perceived among the American populace a turning in religious institutions of all sorts. Attendance at church services was way up. People were willing to listen to Jehovah's Witnesses at the door. There was an outpouring of "charity and noble behavior" at Ground Zero and around the country. Almost suddenly now people were willing to believe in evil and in the need to counteract it with active good. "A brief turn to religion in itself is not surprising after a disaster, and the mood could soon evaporate," Daniel J. Wakin stated in the article. "But many religion experts and clerics suggest that the terror attacks could herald a deeper change in religious patterns because of the enormity of the tragedy and because many feel the nation is in for a long struggle with the forces of terrorism."

Wakin (2007) is now skeptical of these claims that 9/11 deepened American religiosity. "I would hesitate to link cause and effect," he demurs, despite suggestive anecdotes and surveys. It would be "virtually impossible," he says, to link any long-term changes in the practice of religion in the United States with the events of 9/11, although in the weeks immediately following 9/11 it was reasonable to suggest such a connection.

As Americans in the post-9/11 era were said to be taking the reality of evil more seriously, Peter Steinfels (2001c) reported on a book that took account of God's existence "in a world of so much evil." The author (Adams 1999) challenged contemporary thinkers to "seek an explanation of how God might 'make good' on evil—that is, not only balancing each individual's suffering with some greater good for that person, as in heavenly reward, for example, but also integrating the experience of evil into each person's relation to God in some way that makes sense."

If Steinfels hoped to engage Americans theologically with the related questions of divinity and evil, educational institutions seemed keen on inculcating in their students the rituals of patriotic participation, including pledges and prayers. The *Times* reported that "the New York City Board of Education unanimously adopted a resolution last night to require all public schools to lead students in the Pledge of Allegiance at the beginning of every school day and at all schoolwide assemblies and events." The resolution also stated that "students and staff members will neither be compelled to participate nor disciplined if they choose not to recite the pledge" (Wyatt 2001a). At the same time, school prayer was revived as a response to 9/11, particularly in the American South, but also in Illinois among Prayer Warriors for Christ (Fountain 2001c), despite a recent Supreme Court ruling that banned prayer over public-address systems at schools. The president of the Ethics and Religious Liberty Commission, which supports school prayers, said that religious expression in public places had "taken a quantum leap in the public consciousness. . . . Post-Sept. 11, the secularists are going to have a harder time making their case" (quoted in Schemo 2001b).

Under attack, Americans were reinforcing or redefining their national values and loyalties. Some school officials saw a mandated—but not individually required in order to protect personal scruples—Pledge of Allegiance as a means of expressing national solidarity against an enemy perceived as religiously compelled. Other educators saw a confrontation between Christian America, on the one hand, and another religion as well as secular Americans, on the other. In short, one's place in the already existing "culture wars" influenced one's definition of America and defined the threats it faced.

The *Times* tried to keep pace with expressions of national unity, but it also kept an eye on religious diversity in the United States, including a brief piece on atheists. As "America's culture of civil religion" took to singing "God Bless America" and printing "In God We Trust" on billboards, atheists were wondering how they could be part of the national consensus of mourning. Atheists lacked any comfort in believing in an afterlife, and they were also eschewed by the religious mainstream as the 9/11 rituals of mourning took place. Thomas W. Flynn, editor of *Free Inquiry,* the quarterly published by the Council for Secular Humanism, said, "I'm an American, too. Don't shut me out" (quoted in Niebuhr 2001p).

In the first month after 9/11, the *Times* continued to cover some of the institutional religious stories in Christian America: "Episcopal Diocese Welcomes Its
15th Bishop" (Peterson 2001); "Archbishop Is Installed for the Newark Diocese"
(Hanley 2001); "Black Order of Nuns in Harlem Celebrates 85 Years" (Day 2001).
However, in each case the terrorist attacks loomed over individuals' religious
lives. As the *Times* examined the Trappist monks of the Abbey of Our Lady of
Gethsemani in Kentucky, "theoretically removed from the distractions of the
everyday world," they were confronted with the horrific impact of modernity,
and so they watched their television on 9/11 and were now reflecting on violence and love, with mixed feelings about flag waving and talk about national
revenge. Said one monk: "Violence rests on the assumption that the enemy and
I are entirely different: the enemy is evil and I am good. The enemy must be
destroyed and I must be saved. But love sees things differently. It sees that even
the enemy suffers from the same sorrows and limitations that I do" (Rimer 2001).
In Harlem, the black nuns said that they were praying for the foreign terrorists as
well as for the mourners of America (Day 2001).

In November 2001, the nation's Catholic bishops wrote "the pastoral message on the aftermath of Sept. 11." "'Without in any way excusing indefensible
terrorist acts, we still need to address those conditions of poverty and injustice
which are exploited by terrorists.' . . . 'We cannot say religion is the problem, as
some would say,' wrote Cardinal Bernard Law of Boston, the committee's chairman. 'We cannot say Islam is the problem, as some would say.' Indeed, the document calls for Catholics to step up efforts at religious dialogue with Muslims"
(Niebuhr 2001a).

The *Times* offered no critique of Christian Americans who responded to the
attacks of 9/11 in a spirit of forgiveness (see Goode 2001); however, in one article
(Sack 2001) it took a more skeptical tone toward Christians who saw 9/11 as an
omen of millennial combat: "the Sept. 11 attacks have invigorated the apocalyptic brand of theology embraced by many Christian evangelicals and fundamentalists, who view the collapse of the World Trade Center towers as the latest
harbinger of the end times. . . . That, of course, is not necessarily the view within
the mainstream of Christianity," which, according to the *Times* reporter, considered apocalypticism an "aberrant Christian theology." In the article's kicker, a
professor of American religion criticized the prophetic trend: "Rather than looking to improve or reform the world, they simply are opting out and predicting

judgment. They talk about individual regeneration rather than social amelioration, and to emphasize one at the price of the other is a distortion of the gospel."
One can see in this article the combatants of the "culture wars" fighting over how
to interpret an impending "clash of civilizations." It seems easy at first to tell on
which side of the cultural divide the *Times* stood and how the paper defined the
moderate middle of American religion.

President Bush's (2001) Thanksgiving Proclamation stated the central tenets
of American civil religion: "Thanks to God for the many blessings we enjoy as a
free, faithful and fair-minded land"; "thanks for the millions of people of faith
who have opened their hearts to those in need with love and prayer, bringing us
a deeper unity and stronger resolve"; and the "hope" that "Almighty God, who is
our refuge and our strength in this time of trouble, [will] watch over our homeland, protect us and grant us patience, resolve and wisdom in all that is to come."

How long did it take for the religious surge of the 9/11 aftermath to ebb?
On November 26, Laurie Goodstein (2001b) wrote a piece entitled "As Attacks'
Impact Recedes, a Return to Religion as Usual." As she saw it, church attendance
was back to normal, and so was spiritual fervor. Whereas Franklin Graham hailed
the religious surge "as an enduring turn toward God," and Pat Robertson said
that "the terrorist attack was 'bringing about one of the greatest spiritual revivals
in the history of America,'" the evidence seemed to contradict their hopes and
claims. Indeed, a Gallup poll editor stated that "it looks like people were treating
this like a bereavement, a shorter-term funeral kind of thing, where they went
to church or synagogue to grieve. But once past that, their normal churchgoing
behavior passed back to where it was." Sociologist Robert Wuthnow said that the
waxing and waning of intense religiosity showed Americans' reservoir of spirituality, but also their habits as "consumers." As things returned to normal, he
observed, "as long as we can kind of paste together a sense of control through
our ordinary work and our ordinary purchases, we're pretty happy to do that.'"

Indeed, American leaders were already trying to gauge how to channel the
new religious mood of sobriety. In the "Business Day" section of the *Times,* mer-
chandisers were wondering how to market the cultural holiday of Christmas in
2001 in light of 9/11. "Santa is going to look a lot like Uncle Sam this year," suggested the operator of a dozen malls. The problem with such a strategy was that,
"for many people, shopping and celebrating seem inappropriate at a time when
families are grieving and flags only recently stopped flying at half-staff." There

seemed to be a consensual sense of "'survivor guilt'" throughout the land. As a result, the article stated, "Americans are being encouraged to shop, both as an act of patriotism and to help them get on with their lives after the attacks" (Kaufman and Hays 2001). To aid the "personal shopper," the *Times* displayed several "modern" menorahs, with prices ranging from $98 to $495 (Rohrlich 2001).

Times coverage of the short spike of American religiosity, from September 11 to November 11, was "typical," according to Andrew Walsh (2002), writing in the journal *Religion in the News*. There was a boom followed by a predictable recession. Psychologists, seeing religion as a "coping mechanism" (26), were not surprised. Neither were Catholic priests, Jewish rabbis, and Islamic clerics, professional religionists who understood that people respond to crisis with intensified devotion, then return to a steady state of religious feeling. But evangelical Christians were disappointed. They wanted "signs of God's forceful action to change human hearts," Walsh stated (27). Evangelical Americans once again had acted on their long tradition of preaching "'jeremiad,'" the "proclaiming revival"; "once again, America has failed to be converted" (28), at least for an appreciable period of time.

As books began to sound the tone of American civil religion after 9/11, the *Times* listened in. Michael Lind's (2002) essay "Their Country 'Tis of Them," a review of three books about America under siege, discerned two different messages. One of the books, *Why We Fight: Moral Clarity and the War on Terrorism* by William J. Bennett (2002), tolled bellicose righteousness, equating the chosen nation of America with the chosen nation of Israel. In *What's So Great about America*, Dinesh D'Souza (2002) extolled the America of trade, commerce, tolerance, and the separation of church and state. The reviewer concluded: "One need not agree with D'Souza about everything to hope that his optimistic, secular understanding of America's role in the world prevails over Bennett's religious triumphalism."

The *Times* was interested in the phenomenon of American solidarity, the civil religion resulting from the 9/11 attacks; however, its writers reserved their highest praise for the moderating, quotidian forces of local and national unity. Robert Stone's (2003) review of *After: How American Confronted the September 12 Era* by Steven Brill (2003) concluded, "The primary lesson of 'After' is Brill's insight into the way various special interests, the eternal antagonists of the American arena, came together in extreme circumstances to repair the damage.

His book gives a sophisticated demonstration of the strengths and weaknesses of 21st-century commercial democracy under pressure." Indeed, Brill (2003) cited the *New York Times* Neediest Cases Fund, which raised special money for victims of the 9/11 assaults, as an example of American charitable enterprise–civil religion in action, through the agency of a supposedly secular newspaper, one might add (161). Before a month passed, $25.9 million had come in to the fund, compared to the $8.3 million raised by the fund in the year 2000.

Interfaith Relations

Just before 9/11, religion scholar Diana Eck had published *A New Religious America* (2001), in which she praised the religious multiculturalism that made the United States "the world's most religiously diverse nation." The 1965 Immigration and Naturalization Act had brought millions of people from Asia, the Middle East, Latin America, and elsewhere to the United States—thirty million immigrants, a million a year—and she found that fact wonderful in that most of them were practicing religions different from the ones that helped establish America as a "'Christian Country.'" Pluralism was for her an accomplishment for which America could be proud. The events of 9/11 raised questions about how wonderful religious pluralism really is, considering it as a problem to be solved as well as an ideal to be achieved.

In the journal *Religion in the News,* Andrew Walsh (2001) told us after 9/11 that media coverage emphasized the single-mindedness of the American response to 9/11. Stories emphasized American unity and played down (or ignored) aspects of American identity that might be seen as divisive. At the same time, "American religious diversity received a new, and perhaps decisive, level of recognition" (3). Interfaith Protestantism set the tone at the National Service of Prayer and Remembrance on September 14 at the National Cathedral in Washington—respecting all traditions, the prayers proclaimed. "Henceforth," Walsh predicted, "when religion is presented to the American public, the picture will include Hindus, Muslims, Buddhists, and Sikhs, as well as Protestants, Catholics, and Jews." In the media, there was an emphasis already on the "'ecumenical,'" the "'interfaith'" picture (3). The *Times* built on this convention to help make sense of the religious picture of post-9/11 America.

The pages of the *Times* sometimes looked like advertisements for interfaith wish fulfillment. Indeed, the Ad Council published (September 19, 2003) a staged snapshot of "a priest, a rabbi and an imam . . . walking down the street" engaged in discussion. The text lauded America's culture of religious freedom and coexistence and called on Americans—including Buddhists and Hindus—to consult "the spiritual leader of your choice." But this was an ad, not news reporting or commentary.

Laurie Goodstein (2004b) describes the 9/11 *Times* coverage as taking place in "chaos." She does not think highly of the first story she wrote after 9/11 (Goodstein 2001n), about the relations between Muslims and Jews in the United States. To her eye, it was obviously hurried, put together out of pieces, wherever she could grab them, trying to chronicle how beleaguered religionists were respondents to the momentous horror. Nevertheless, one can also look at that article and see how Goodstein knew almost instinctively what the proper angles were and what they would be for months to come: (1) There is already a worldwide rift between Muslims and Jews. (2) Do not assume that Muslims did this terrible deed; remember Oklahoma City before rushing to conclusions about the perpetrators. (3) Quote and report on the tensions between Jews and Muslims, with Israeli and Palestinian sympathies. (4) But also show that Muslims are part of the US community. The kicker—quoting a Muslim academic—emphasized the basic decency, even patriotism, of American Muslims, who faced "a tragic situation that has to be condemned by everyone who has an iota of decency."

The *Times* examined the shared, communal responses—emotive and moral—of diverse American religionists, showing how they pulled together as one for mutual support in a time of tragedy. Gustav Niebuhr's (2001n) "Religion Journal" column "Clergy of Many Faiths Answer Tragedy's Call" stated that "ministers, priests, rabbis and imams have led prayer services." He thus laid out the four main religious groups in America—Protestant, Catholic, Jew, and Muslim—and stressed their common functions within their congregations: comforting, reassuring, explicating God's will in overwhelming circumstances. One Protestant minister said, "God wills the death of no one and invites people into abundant life," a theme echoed by his cohorts from other religious traditions. Not only did the religious leaders have similar roles and messages, but they also reached out for one another. A Catholic archbishop stated, "It's important that we pray with our Muslim brothers. . . . I think it's important that we put our arms around our Muslim brothers and sisters right now, and they know we love them, and they know we care."

The *Times* "Religion Journal" served as an interfaith site on occasion (e.g., "Religion Journal: Abhorring Terror at an Ohio Mosque" 2001), recording the religious perspectives of Muslims, Jews, Buddhists, and Christians on the evils unleashed in our days, applying their core messages to help resolve moral conflicts and to understand the human condition in crisis.

At Yankee Stadium, twenty thousand persons attended an interfaith service, a "Prayer for America." Celebrities such as James Earl Jones, Bette Midler, and Oprah Winfrey; politicians such as Mayor Rudolph Giuliani and Governor George Pataki; religious leaders including Cardinal Edward M. Egan of the Roman Catholic Diocese of New York and Imam Izak-el Mu-eed Pasha of the Malcolm Shabazz Mosque in Harlem; as well as Muslim, Jewish, Sikh, and Hindu mourners shared a common space and common sentiment of spiritual patriotism (McFadden 2001), finding "emotional catharsis" in a public arena.

Throughout the fall of 2001, the *Times* emphasized that the response to 9/11 in America transcended any denominational identity or concern. Whether people of different traditions joined together in rituals, their prayer was at heart interfaith: a common upswelling of spiritual need in a time of trouble. On October 6, an article on Kennedy Airport's interdenominational prayer rooms featured large photographs of Muslim and Catholic worshippers, separate in prayer but joined in a hope to "soothe souls" (Kershaw 2001c).

If rituals could be shared across religious lines, and if prayers possessed deep elements of commonality, then members of different faiths could engage in meaningful dialogue. At the Cathedral of St. John the Divine in New York, the Iranian president, Mohammed Khatami, spoke at an event called "The Role of Religion in the Dialogue among Civilizations." Mr. Khatami showed not only his Islamic learning and his knowledge of Western philosophy—Kant, Hegel, Nietzsche, Freud, Marx—but also his commitment to pluralism and a condemnation of terrorism and nihilism. He impressed the recently ordained Episcopal bishop of New York, Mark Sisk, and a representative of the World Conference on Religion and Peace praised Khatami for "proposing an alliance of thoughtful, religiously rooted moderates, from across faith lines, who could offer a vision for society that used neither materialistic secularism nor religious fundamentalism as its starting point" (Niebuhr 2001q).

Commentators noted a conscious effort among Americans to recognize Islam as part of the fabric of religious life in the United States. In an America in which

Attorney General John Ashcroft had said a mere year earlier, "We have no king but Jesus," we now had President Bush "holding an iftar dinner at the White House, breaking fast during the holy month of Ramadan with 50 ambassadors from Muslim countries. . . . The terrorists want to define their war with us as a religious conflict. Our response has shown that the freedom to practice our religions as we see fit is one of the qualities that defines us as Americans" (Smaby 2001).

In early December, a *Times* essay described a conference in North Carolina, planned more than a year earlier, espousing cooperation between Muslims and Christians. In light of 9/11, there was still a sense among the ninety-three religious leaders in attendance that "'there are a lot of things they can do, not internationally but at home. . . . Reconciliation itself can be as intimate as within a family or a community. It has to start there'" ("Religion Journal: Christianity and Islam" 2001).

Not content to rest with post-9/11 sentiments of "goodwill" and intents toward "toleration" and "pluralism," the president of Union Theological Seminary, Joseph C. Hough Jr., replied to questions posed to him by Gustav Niebuhr (2002) in an article titled "Acknowledging That God Is Not Limited to Christians." "Since the Sept. 11 tragedy," Niebuhr began, "Americans of different faiths have joined together in public prayer services to show national unity. Have you found something essential missing in those gatherings?" Hough hoped that American Christians could recognize that "religion is something that we human beings put together in an effort to give some cultural form to our faith. Our faith is a response to the experience of the presence of God." After gaining "a greater understanding of religious traditions other than our own," Christians must acknowledge they have helped foment religious conflict "because we have made our claim to God's revelation exclusively ours." "Are you saying that all religions are equal?" Niebuhr asked. Hough replied, "No, all religions are not equal for me. For my faith, Jesus Christ is decisive." At the same time, he affirmed God's hand in all religions: "Wherever there is peace and movement toward peace, where there is justice and movement toward justice, God is present and working."

In 2002, the *Times* followed the ironic outcome of the interfaith service "A Prayer for America" held at Yankee Stadium the previous September. As Daniel J. Wakin (2002i) described this outcome, the Reverend David Benke, a Lutheran leader, was condemned of "heresy and idolatry" for "sharing the stage with a Muslim imam, a rabbi, Cardinal Edward M. Egan, and Sikh and Hindu holy men. (Not to mention Oprah Winfrey, Bette Midler and a flock of elected leaders.)" Seventeen of Rev. Benke's fellow pastors in the Lutheran Church Missouri Synod accused him of "tolerating syncretism, the combining of Christian and non-Christian views. Their charges," Wakin reported, "could lead to his dismissal as a clergyman." *Times* photographs of the Yankee Stadium event emphasized the patriotic solidarity it engendered: people holding hands, police and firefighters in uniform, the ethnic diversity of New York City, etc. One photograph by Ozier Muhammad (Wakin 2002g) shows Benke just behind Mayor Rudolph Giuliani, who is waving an American flag.

The overall effect of the photos and Wakin's text was to make the Lutheran Synod seem out of touch with the ecumenical American spirit of the day and of the time. Wakin (2007) hopes that he did not portray Benke as a martyr and his denomination as a flock of bigots. Indeed, the reporter aimed, he says, to strike a balance between the minister's outreach and his church's need to "avoid dilution." Even "mainstream" Christian bodies, such as the Lutheran Church, "have the characteristic of drawing the line." In a multicultural city such as New York, sensitive to sectarian slights, religious organizations may feel the need to display the "rectitude" or "standing up for principles," even though "it might sound like intolerance to some." Wakin thinks that the Lutheran authorities had the right to defend their sense of propriety, and he hopes that his articles represented their position fairly.

Although Benke was found guilty of syncretism and "unionism"—joining different Christian groups in the same ritual or doctrine—and although, according to his accusers, he broke the first and second commandments by placing God amidst other gods and therefore was suspended from his post as president of the Atlantic District of the Lutheran Church–Missouri Synod, he refused "to apologize, as demanded in exchange for lifting the suspension, and has appealed the ruling. . . . He says he is waging war against religious intolerance." In the end, in 2003 the synod "cleared" Benke of all charges and "restored the pastor's church membership to 'good standing,' finding that his prayer was Christian" ("Lutheran Panel Reinstates Pastor" 2003).

In the months following 9/11, the *Times* emphasized the convergence of religious faith(s) in America. As tensions and violence increased in Israel, the paper returned to the particular locus of Jewish–Muslim relations in the United States, contrasting hatreds abroad to commonalities at home, especially in and around New York City. According to one report (Saulny 2002), New York Arabs and Jews, in a demonstration of the American melting-pot ideal, were able to talk to one another about conflict between Jews and Palestinians overseas without hating one another.

The view from the *Times,* however, was not always so irenic. In a 2003 "NYC" column, Clyde Haberman (2003a) reported on "rational talk by 2 faiths across divide." "Jew met Muslim" was the lead. Haberman told how Seyyed Hossein Nasr, an Iranian-born Islamic scholar, spoke for an hour about his faith at the Jewish Theological Seminary. There were four hundred in attendance, almost all Jews. Nasr was introduced by the seminary's chancellor, who said that at this time of mutual suspicion, "we make a small contribution to the perpetuation of reason in an irrational world." The fact that Purim—founded in the book of Esther and set in Persia—was about to begin made it fitting that we should have a real Persian in our midst, according to the chancellor. "It may be worth noting, though," commented Haberman, "that Esther is one of the Bible's bloodier books, a reminder that hatred and violence have walked arm in arm for thousands of years. The story is that of a foiled pogrom, with Persia's Jews being saved and then allowed to strike back at their enemies. The death toll, as described in Esther 9:16, is astounding: 75,000."

Nasr spoke of Muslim protection of Jews in the Middle Ages. He also acknowledged that today there is an Islamic trend toward "extremism," but he said that the extremists' numbers are small. He received warm applause, and then there were skeptical questions: Why are Muslim moderates not speaking out against the extremists? Why do madrassas teach radicalism? Does the Koran teach Muslims "'to kill nonbelievers'"? Why is Osama bin Laden so popular? If Haberman's column represented the state of American interfaith dialogue by 2003, the early emotional goodwill was now tempered by serious concerns— Nasr's questioners raised many issues prominent on the pages of the *Times* since 9/11—and by a sense of history's repetitive experience of the tragic. (For continuing Jewish–Muslim discord, see Ramirez 2004.)

In the early days after 9/11, most prominent, centrist Americans in public places and certainly on the pages of the *Times* were encouraging a calm assessment of the forces behind the attack. Whereas it became clear to most that Muslims were responsible for the violence, President Bush and others distinguished between Islam's ideals and the perpetrators' motives and stated that Islam was not America's enemy. Civic leaders called for a spirit of respect and unity within the American populace, emphasizing tolerance and eschewing any blame mon-gering that would poison the commonweal with division.

A discordant note was struck, then, when in a televised conversation with Reverend Pat Robertson "the Rev. Jerry Falwell said . . . that the American Civil Liberties Union [ACLU], with abortion providers, gay rights proponents and fed-eral courts that had banned school prayer and legalized abortion had so weak-ened the United States spiritually that the nation was left exposed to Tuesday's terrorist attacks." "The A.C.L.U.'s got to take a lot of the blame for this," he is reported to have said, according to a transcript of *The 700 Club* program. Falwell later explained that he wasn't blaming God or shifting blame from the terrorists. "He said he did not believe God 'had anything to do with the tragedy,' but that God had permitted it. 'He lifted the curtain of protection,' Mr. Falwell said, 'and I believe that if America does not repent and return to a genuine faith and depen-dence on him, we may expect more tragedies, unfortunately'" (Niebuhr 2001g).

The *Times* did not make much of the story, providing only nine para-graphs. The following day in another short report, the paper noted the presi-dent's response: "Falwell's Finger-Pointing Inappropriate, Bush Says" (Goodstein 2001f). At the same time, the article noted that the initial remarks were "based in theology familiar to and accepted by many conservative evangelical Christians, who believe the Bible teaches that God withdraws protection from nations that violate God's will."

Falwell issued a quick public apology "that during a week when everyone appropriately dropped all labels and no one was seen as liberal or conservative, Democrat or Republican, religious or secular, I singled out for blame certain groups of Americans." According to a follow-up article, he also acknowledged that his statement "ran counter to his lifelong theological conviction that it was impossible to know whether an event reflected God's judgment" (Niebuhr 2001l, another brief piece; none of this was front-page stuff).

Michael E. Naparstek (2001) observes in *Religion in the News* that both Jerry Falwell and Pat Robertson used 9/11 to rail against their enemies—"the pagans and the abortionists and the feminists and the gays and the lesbians," in Falwell's words—and to blame them for "God lifting his protection over this nation," as Robertson had it. The media treated these comments as unforgivable breaches in the American code of civic unity. Walter Cronkite in the *New York Times* called Falwell's comments "the most abominable thing I've ever heard"

(5). Why this response, Naparstek asks, when it has been common in American religious history for leaders to deliver jeremiads, blaming immoral behavior for God's wrath. Abraham Lincoln, in his Second Inaugural, treated slavery as the sin that brought down the Civil War. So why could these ministers not employ a traditional preaching device? Robertson refused to apologize, saying that it was his duty to "bring God back into the national consciousness" (27).

In the "Metro Matters" column a few days after 9/11, the *Times* noted that it was "the racial, religious, political" diversity of "Sin City"—"our daily tribute to differences"—that Falwell and other outsiders (such as the overwrought Atlanta baseball player John Rocker) hated so much (Purnick 2001). New York City's hometown newspaper was defending the practical American ideal of oneness out of multiplicity *(e pluribus unum)*, so often experienced in the urban streetscape, against parochial bigots of all stripes.

Religion professor and leftist critic Bruce Lincoln (2003) has compared the transcript of Pat Robertson's interview with Jerry Falwell on *The 700 Club,* September 13, 2001, to Osama bin Laden's videotaped address of October 7, 2001, finding in both an expression of "maximalist" religiosity, a signpost of fundamentalism. He declares the "televangelists' religious ideal" to be an "equally maximalist, if Christian rather than Muslim" message parallel to bin Laden's (50). The *Times* did not make such an explicit comparison; indeed, its treatment of the evangelists in fall 2001 was understated, demonstrating the spirit of national decorum rather than engaging in cultural combat. As participant-observer in the "culture wars," the *Times* seemed to know when to moderate its reportage on the Religious Right.

No more was heard in the *Times* of the ACLU as the moral scapegoat for the 9/11 assault. Two months later, however, Reverend Franklin Graham, Billy Graham's son and president of Samaritan's Purse, a Christian relief organization, stated that "Islam had attacked the United States on Sept. 11. He said that Muslims worshiped a different God than Christians and that he believed Islam to be 'a very evil and wicked religion.'" Muslim leaders wished to discuss his remarks with him, at a time "when many public figures have emphasized inter-religious understanding, not least Mr. Bush, who has asked Americans not to blame the faith for the acts of Sept. 11" (Niebuhr 2001d). Graham declined their offer. Several weeks later he was still "responding to criticism of his comments about Islam." He now averred that "he did not believe Muslims were 'evil people' but lamented evil done in the religion's name" ("Graham Modifies Comments" 2001, a one-paragraph story).

In the meantime, the *Times* carried a small AP item, "Baptist Head Urges Prayers for Muslim Conversion" (2001), which stated: "Calling Christianity 'the only true religion,' Mr. [James G.] Merritt said that 'every other religion gives a false hope of having a relationship with God. . . . That's not what I say,' he added. 'That's what Jesus says,'" as he called on Southern Baptists to fast and pray for the conversion of Muslims. The article also contained a paragraph-long reply by an American Muslim, which stated, among other things: "It's a free country. . . . If he wants to have Christians fast and pray, we're hardly in a position to tell people not to."

In 2002, another Southern Baptist, Reverend Jerry Vines, a past president of the Southern Baptist Convention, "illustrated how hate speech against Muslims had become a staple of conservative Christian political discourse." He called the Prophet Muhammad a "'demon-possessed pedophile' and declared that Muslims worshiped a different God than Christians." The *Times* reporter opined that "open scorn for Islam as a religion has become a staple ingredient in the speeches of conservative Christian leaders in the months since the Sept. 11 terrorist attacks." According to the reporter, these Christians were uncomfortable with President Bush's efforts to "emphasize that the United States does not consider Islam an enemy." A subhead emphasized that "Jewish and Muslim groups join in protest" of the comments (Sachs 2002b).

The evangelical critique of Islam continued through 2002 and 2003. Some of the attention rested on Franklin Graham—whose father had recently apologized for anti-Jewish comments he had made in President Richard M. Nixon's tape-recorded confidence thirty years earlier (Firestone 2002b; "Graham's Son Defends Him" 2002). As presented in the *Times,* the story was that "nine months after calling Islam 'a very evil and wicked religion,' the evangelist Franklin Graham said yesterday that Muslims had not sufficiently apologized for the Sept. 11 terrorist attacks and that they should help compensate victims' families." Graham added that "terrorism is part of 'mainstream' Islam and that the Koran 'preaches violence.'" In this instance, "Muslim groups dismissed Mr. Graham's statements" as inaccurate (Wilson 2002a).

Then Jerry Falwell weighed in about Islam on the CBS program *Sixty Minutes.* The AP announced: "Falwell Calls Muhammad a Terrorist" (2002). Pat

Robertson—with financial and legal problems of his own, according to the *Times* (Ayres 2001; Blank 2001; Finley 2002; Winter 2001b, 2002)—held forth on an ABC news program with the charge that Islam was "violent at its core." Even as President Bush spoke publicly of Muslims' "'spirit of tolerance,' distancing himself from an increasingly assertive campaign by some American conservatives to cast Islam as hostile to the United States and a breeding ground for terrorism," Robertson characterized the president's remarks as "political. . . . ' The president does not want to be fighting all of Islam and he didn't want to set this thing up as a holy war and he was very wise,' Mr. Robertson said. Still, he said, Mr. Bush's decision not to speak negatively about Islam has 'caused a great deal of consternation, especially among his base, who know better'" (Stevenson 2002).

A *Times* headline, "G.O.P. Web Site Apologizes for Anti-Islam Link" (2002), indicated how far an anti-Islamic Web site had infiltrated mainstream political domains; however, IslamExposed.com, which referred to Islam as "the greatest evil on our planet," a "false religion . . . nothing more than a barbaric occult [*sic*] invented by savages for savages," turned out to be the work of an atheist, author of a similarly defamatory site, ChristianityExposed.com. In this obscure locale, Muslims and evangelical Christians had a common enemy.

On *The 700 Club*, however, in the revving up period before America's invasion of Iraq, Islam was being touted as the major threat to America and to Christianity. In an AP article, "The Religious Right: Islam Is Violent in Nature, Pat Robertson Says" (2003), the show's host was quoted as saying about Muslims: "They want to coexist until they can control, dominate and then, if need be, destroy." An Arab American spokesman called Robertson's accusations akin to anti-Semitism.

American Muslim leaders were equally dismayed when in the midst of the Iraq War Franklin Graham was chosen to lead Good Friday services at the Pentagon. They accused him of carrying "a message that is divisive and bigoted, and they urged the Pentagon to cancel his invitation" rather than convey the impression of a "'government endorsement'" of his anti-Muslim views (Marquis 2003). A professor of theology at Dallas Theological Seminary came to Graham's defense, asking in an op-ed for *Times* readers to give Graham a chance to prove his Christian compassion through his relief agency in Iraq (Pyne 2003).

In an article in the journal *Religion in the News,* Andrew Walsh (2003) focuses on Franklin Graham from his earliest public response to 9/11: "We're not attacking Islam," Graham stated, "but Islam has attacked us. . . . The God of Islam is not the same God. . . . It's a different God, and I believe it is a very evil and wicked religion" (7). Graham did not back down from this statement. Over the next year and more, he pushed for missionary efforts to convert Muslims, as he had for more than a decade—for example, during the Gulf War, when he wanted US troops to distribute Arabic-language New Testaments in Saudi Arabia, Iraq, and Kuwait—much to General Norman Schwarzkopf's anger.

Walsh (2003) is far more critical than the *Times* was of the evangelical critics of Islam and of the missionary efforts. He concludes, "Like it or not, American evangelicals of the 21st century must recognize that their religion is perceived as political, at home and abroad" (27). The *Times* was not so pointed in its articles or in its editorials or op-eds.

Trauma Around New York City

The *New York Times* covered the grisly events of 9/11 in vivid detail. As befitting a national newspaper, it assayed their impact on the consciousness of Americans, with datelines representing diverse regions of the country. At the same time, the *Times* functioned as a hometown New York press, depicting the reactions around the city and especially at the site of the fallen World Trade Center, which came quickly to be known as Ground Zero. In these articles, religious dimensions often prevailed.

On the day after 9/11, two metro reporters described "the reaction" with the headline "A Tough City Is Swept by Anger, Despair, and Helplessness" (Dwyer and Sachs 2001). A large photograph by James Estrin took visual command of the page. It pictured New Rochelle's Iona Grammar School eighth graders in prayer, hands clasped in gestures of Catholic piety, a crucifix on the wall. The last two columns of the lengthy story described ways in which "many sought solace in prayers, either alone or in the great holy spaces of the city." Street preachers suddenly had respectful audiences. Cardinal Edward M. Egan offered mass and last rites. "Places of worship" opened their doors to the stunned people of New York City.

The September 13 *Times* featured the story "A Place of Solace in a Time of Grief" (Raver 2001), containing photos by Meg Henson of the biblical garden at the Cathedral Church of St. John the Divine, which—the author said—offered a space for "solace" and "soul-searching," where New Yorkers could "contemplate" the city's damaged state. The garden's designer recommended the "secluded" place for its "peaceful, tranquil . . . luminosity." The cathedral's canon for liturgy and the arts remarked, however, that "the garden is a respite, but it is not removed from the world." The horrors of 9/11 were not to be erased, even as a church's green yard could offer momentary succor. Three years later a *Times* reporter noted "a chilling augury of September 11 in the Portal of Paradise [at the Cathedral Church of St. John the Divine], carved from 1988 to 1997" (Dunlap 2004c:217, illus.): a statuary pedestal showing the World Trade Center toppling under a cloud of smoke; however, no mention was made of this ominous presence in 2001.

In the weeks to come immediately after 9/11, the *Times* returned repeatedly to churches around the city—especially St. Patrick's Cathedral (see Archibold 2001)—to record the processes of mourning and condolence taking place. The *Times* "Weekend" section advised New Yorkers where they could find "an oasis of peace and contemplation" for a "weekend excursion" in the ambience of eighteenth-century architecture built by German quietistic communities around Ephrata, Pennsylvania (Ruda 2001). For those in need of soothing, the "Sunday Styles" section offered "spiritual balm, at only $23.95" (Kuczynski 2001). The "Travel" section recommended "centers of solace for the self"—Catholic, Quaker, Jewish, Hindu, Buddhist, and nondenominational holistic establishments in quiet locales—noting that "spiritual retreats of various faiths hold particular appeal these days" (Benzel 2001).

On the streets of the city, New Yorkers constructed "spontaneous shrines" as "personal displays of grief." In a contemporary America, without an established religious tradition of public mourning, individuals invented their own rituals. At the same time, however, the patterns of grieving were "influenced by confessional talk shows and New Age therapies" as well as by a record of televised funerals—from John F. Kennedy's to Princess Diana's. Technologies allowed for private but consensual mourning in the home: "virtual sympathy cards on message boards" and the "'televigil'" on cable channels (Kakutani 2001).

The *Times* reported on the demonstrations of mourning but also participated in the display. Witness a September 19 photograph by Ruth Fremson (2001b) of a yoga teacher in lotus position at Union Square in front of a flag-bedecked memorial to the World Trade Center victims one week after the attack. Or, on the same day, under no headline, Chester Higgins Jr. (2001) snapped "a makeshift shrine at the statue of Washington in Union Square Park" (Higgins 2001), with the message "love" lettered repeatedly on the statue's base. By carrying the photographs, the *Times* was in effect printing its own shrine for its audience. Showing the Hindu devotee emphasized the multireligious, patriotic response to the attacks. The message "love" bridged the realms of politics and religion.

In order to analyze New Yorkers' behavior in the immediate aftermath to 9/11—fabricating shrines to the dead and missing, marking off Ground Zero as a kind of holy field, ritualizing public mourning—Gustav Niebuhr (2001r) interviewed the cultural anthropologist who had curated the exhibition Meeting God: Elements of Hindu Devotion at the Museum of Natural History not long before the attacks occurred. It was not a big story; however, it provided insight. The scholar found New Yorkers to be acting like the Hindu devotees he had studied in India: creating "sacred spaces" where something had been "sanctified"—by good or by evil—and thus was to be "set apart" as a "shrine . . . to honor the sacred."

The next day *Times* feature writer Marshall Sella (2001) published "Missing: How a Grief Ritual Is Born" in the *Times Magazine,* examining the posters and shrines that sprang up all over New York City. Sella observed that the first human response to the 9/11 disaster was denial—people assuming that their beloveds were missing rather than dead—and humanization—mourners displaying the faces of the missing publicly through photographic portraits. Then the posters became shrines, ways of communicating with the dead and with one another in the symbolic presence of the dead. The stages of grieving were acted out—improvised but also copied—in an urban American milieu without a unified denominational tradition. Chalk writing on the streets, the placement of flowers, teddy bears, and other objects at the shrines, as well as other behaviors were imitated by firsthand observation from site to site, but also paradigms were found on television and the Internet.

Some theorists are interested in the question of how the press treated a traumatized public in 9/11 coverage (Zelizer and Allan 2002a:1–5). Did the trauma knock journalism loose from its moorings, without a script to follow? Did journalists circle the wagons and rest on conventions? Did they aim to soothe their readers? It would seem that many media turned to the patterns of religiopatriotism to interpret 9/11. Patriotism spurted forth from the traumatic wound in a surge of civil piety, hoping to heal the hurts. According to this notion, papers not only reported on religious responses to 9/11 but also served themselves as media of functional religious consensus.

The *Times,* for example, "ran more pictures and in more prominent places" (Zelizer and Allan 2002a:7) as a response to trauma, as a way to depict it, to express it, to treat it. Barbie Zelizer (2002) contends that there is a "template" (53) for recording horrific events like the Holocaust that employs the photograph for "bearing witness" (54). The *Times* used this template in featuring twice as many photos after 9/11 than before in order to bear witness to trauma, helping to shape people's grieving and to focus it and "moving people through the grieving process" (57). The most horrific images in the *Times* were those on September 12 of people falling to their deaths or clinging to upper-story windows of the World Trade Center. The *Times* editors debated the propriety of their use and struck a balance between grisly reality and anonymous distance. There was little human gore. Rather, the *Times* showed "witness" photographs, which exhibited devastated buildings, people in shock at the site of the violence, and then the shrines, where grieving New Yorkers stared at photos of the missing and the dead.

On September 15, 2001, the *Times* ran a two-page spread of photos, "After the Attacks: A Day of Prayer," showing Americans across the country in poses of prayer in a time of grief. A photo showed Muslim women at prayer in Los Angeles. There were also photos from around the world: Taiwan, Kenya, India, Palestine. "Hundreds of Palestinians rallied to support the United States," said the caption of a photo taken in Hebron. On this same day, the *Times* began what would soon be called its "Portraits of Grief," eulogies of the World Trade Center victims: a snapshot along with a paragraph of text. Each was a "photograph of witness." More like a vignette than an obit, each was about two hundred words. Touching word paintings, democratic in scope, these portraits were real innovations in journalism that helped the public express and contain trauma and grief.

Howell Raines (2002b) says that the "Portraits of Grief" were "independently conceived and executed by our Metro Desk" (9). The "Portraits of Grief" were the result of Christine Kay's concept, Wendell Jamieson's management, and metro editor Jon Landman's leadership. They comprised 2,310 stories, and 155 reporters took part in the project. Writers included religion reporters Gustav Niebuhr and Daniel J. Wakin, former religion writer Ari L. Goldman, as well as Iver Peterson, Jere Longman, David Chen, Adam Clymer, Abby Goodnough, and many others. It is said that reporters wept in this "heartbreaking" but also "uplifting" work (J. Scott 2003:ix–x) as they interviewed mourners—combining professionalism and empathy in recording this so human, momentous catastrophe.

Gustav Niebuhr (2001h, 2001t) has spoken at length about the care he took in writing his "Portraits." He was getting information from devastated people, so he wished to be considerate, yet he wanted to get the best portraits he could. He invariably called the mourners back, reading them what he wrote, to make sure that he got their portrayals right. The portraits had to ring true, as if they were coming right out of the mourners' grieving memory. He brought to this task what it takes to write good religion journalism: sensitivity to emotional expressions of existential profundity, a caring ear to utterances of faith.

Daniel J. Wakin joined the project, following the lead of Christine Kay—a colleague with a keen sense of religion's importance—whose desk was within his view. "You have sightlines to a body" in the newsroom, he remarks (2007), and that influences assignments. However, he says he is not sure why he was among the many asked to contribute. Producing the "Portraits" was an "emotional" experience, "of course," but also "very liberating" to a journalist: a chance to write in a "unique genre, . . . a cross between an obit and a tribute," a piece "with poignancy," in which he had the freedom to "pick the thing" upon which to focus.

Raines (2003) remarks that "nothing published in the *New York Times* during my twenty-four years on the newspaper has elicited a reader response like the one we've gotten on 'Portraits of Grief.'" He suggests that their journalistic power comes from "the democracy of death" (vii), to which they bear poignant witness. The book-length collection *Portraits: 9/11/01* (2003) contains 663 pages of texts, from Gordon M. Aamoth to Igor Zukelman. The "Portraits of Grief" did not include Pentagon victims (679–80) or those who died on United Airlines Flight 93 (681). For those who say that Jews knew about the attack in advance and stayed away from the World Trade Center, one might check out the Cohens, Jacobs, Goldsteins, and other members of the tribe who apparently failed to get the word.

Peter Steinfels (2005a, 2005b) says that the "Portraits" broke new ground in the *Times* treatment of religion, emphasizing as they did the importance of faith, spirituality, ethics, and denominational affiliation in the personal lives of common Americans. Although the *Times* was offering emotional release and comfort to its readership through its "Portraits" (consolation usually provided by religious bodies), it was also highlighting the role of religions in providing meaning and community in a time of national grief.

The *Times* writers were well aware that they were playing a religious role in publishing the "Portraits of Grief." Janny Scott (2001), a metro desk reporter who composed some of the first portraits, said that, "for many people, reading the profiles became a daily ritual—observed at breakfast tables, on the subway, before computer screens late at night." Scott wrote that hundreds of email messages and letters to the *Times* professed strong emotional attachment to the daily reading; it "was a way of paying homage. Others said it was a means of connecting, a source of consolation. . . . One reader, a lawyer in Manhattan, called reading the profiles 'my act of Kaddish.' Some said they found the stories uplifting, a guide to how to live a better life." The *Times* "Portraits of Grief" became a "sort of national shrine," as Howell Raines claims (quoted in Zelizer and Allan 2002a:8).

The "Portraits of Grief" were, in the words of a media investigator, "a form of journalism as tribute, journalism as homage, journalism as witness, journalism as solace, and journalism aspiring to art." "In moments of tragedy," he states, "journalists assume a pastoral role" (Schedson 2002:39, 41). The "Portraits of Grief" had the capacity for that function.

In assessing the ways in which various American institutions had helped America cope with the trauma of 9/11, one book reviewer said: "The *New York Times* managed an extraordinary feat of journalism with its pages of short, lively obituaries of the victims of the September 2001 terror bombing. With a picture and a few paragraphs, each stranger's severed life was considered and honored most movingly. They were sentimental and ritualized, but in running them, *The Times* did about as much for the memory of its subjects as a hometown newspaper can do" (Stone 2003).

The *Times* closed its official coverage of 9/11, "A Nation Challenged," on December 31, as the war on Afghanistan seemed to be winding down (but the two main quarries were still at large). The continuous "Portraits of Grief" feature ended on that day, although the portraits were to endure during the year to come as family members of the victims agreed to speak with reporters.

The last day, December 31, 2001, began with the firefighters' chaplain, Mychal Judge, and ended with midwesterner Andrea Haberman, who had never been to New York City before September 10, 2001. "But when her company asked her to go there for a day of meetings, she steeled herself. She arrived late Monday night, Sept. 10. She had a 9 a.m. meeting in the north tower on Tuesday. She was there 20 minutes early" ("Andrea Haberman" 2001). In effect, the portrait intimated, her death resulted from her sense of duty.

According to one critic, the *Times* "Portraits of Grief" were part of the media treatment of US "trauma," based on the assumption that "memorializing is a form of healing" (Briethaupt 2003:73). But Fritz Breithaupt does not believe in such a simple formula. The "Portraits," he says, were verbal monuments, akin to the ones in the street and the images on television. These shrines, he avows, "are not a means of therapy. Rather, they are institutions that master and rule over memories in such a way that the institution echoes the violence that accompanied the initial shock." His view is that the media "become 'traumatic,' produce 'trauma,' and then pose as the cure" (73). "The media's employment of 'trauma' only formally mimics therapy to set up a ritual instead." And by this he means what Durkheim meant by ritual: "that which unites a people by bringing about the consciousness of society as such." This is the "means by which one can achieve the union with this higher being: America" (77). In this sense, the *Times* played a priestly role in highlighting trauma for its constituency, the congregation called the American nation.

Daniel J. Wakin (2007) is unconvinced by this line of analysis. He does not think that the "Portraits" made the *Times* into New York City's pastor or America's church. To call such reporting "pastoral" or "healing"—to think of the *Times'* role as "religious"—strikes him as a semantic stretch. If publishing the "Portraits of Grief" is "religious, then anything could be called religious," he replies. He acknowledges that certain readers may have responded to "Portraits" as one might to eulogies in a house of worship; however, in writing them, Wakin did not feel "religious." Rather, his task was "journalistic" in the midst of catastrophic, breaking news.

Consolers, Heroes, Survivors

The *Times* was not the only New York institution dealing with trauma. The city's vast machinery began the enormous and sensitive task of restoring the World Trade Center site and its neighborhood to at least a semblance of normality. Religious groups from near and far responded to the shock and the restorative undertaking. One feature focused on a minister of the Church of Scientology, whose corps of volunteers tried to offer psychological therapy for workers and residents about Ground Zero. "'They bring people back, so to speak, so they are in control of their mind and environment,' said John Carmichael, the president of the Church of Scientology of New York. 'You want to help get rid of the fatigue and the fuzziness.'" The story did not criticize the Scientologists for what might have appeared to some as a brazen attempt to capitalize on others' pain; indeed, the paper quoted Scientology spokesmen uncritically—for example, when they testified to the aid they were bringing, alongside the Red Cross and the Salvation Army, to people at the World Trade Center remains. "When he drove down to the site on Tuesday, Mr. Carmichael said, a police officer waved him through. 'You're a Scientologist,' he recalled the officer saying. 'You're good.'" "'It's not proselytizing,' Mr. Carmichael said. 'It's us trying to help'" (Waldman 2001a).

Roman Catholics were prominent in the 9/11 religion angles around New York. At Ground Zero, a Franciscan priest "blessed" with "holy water" a "piece of debris" made of two smashed World Trade Center girders in the shape of a "symmetrical cross," an inspirational symbol to many and termed "miraculous" by a fireman (Steinhauer 2001, photo by Ruby Washington). A mixture of denominational and civil religiousness filled the air at Ground Zero. People played "Amazing Grace" on the bagpipes and sang "God Bless America," and the crowd cheered, "USA! USA!"

Roman Catholicism prevailed in media coverage of post-9/11 New York City, especially given the heroic role of the largely Catholic fire and police departments in the events of 9/11. As a media commentator said, "Workers at Ground Zero treated the site as a holy place in a specifically Catholic way, asking priests to bless the area and creating crosses made from steel girders" (Walsh 2001:4). The paper featured New York City's most prominent Catholic prelate, "Edward Cardinal Egan, who presided when the attack of September 11, 2001, turned St. Patrick's [Cathedral] into a focal point of the city's mourning and its quest for some kind of spiritual response to the horror" (Dunlap 2004c:237).

"Most powerful of all was the crystallization of an intense and now global devotion to Father Mychal Judge, the Franciscan priest and fire chaplain who died at Ground Zero" (Walsh 2001:4). The *Times* took note of the man with a short piece on September 13, 2001: "Mychal Judge, 68, Chaplain for Fire Dept." On November 11, 2001, an uncaptioned photo by Agence France-Presse pictured Pope John Paul II in St. Peter's Basilica in the Vatican blessing Father Judge's helmet, held by a New York City firefighter. A feature on the priest who replaced Judge as chaplain to the firefighters proclaimed the late Franciscan a "charismatic" figure (Collins 2001). The last day of the "Portraits of Grief" said the following of him: "He had no use—none—for physical things, said Steven McDonald, the police officer paralyzed by a gunshot who accompanied Father Judge on peace trips to Belfast. Give the father a cashmere sweater, he said, and it would wind up on the back of a homeless person. Go to him with a troubled soul and he would listen intently for as long as it took. He went where he was needed. On Sept. 11, he faced the inferno with the firefighters" ("Mychal Judge: Where He Was Needed" 2001).

All of which presented Judge in heroic light—if not much illumination—during a time in which media convergence on heroism served civic needs. An op-ed stated that in recent decades Americans had avoided heroes for being too simple-minded, too fascistic, too male. We looked instead, the commentator said, for "winners and celebrities"—athletes, movie stars, and billionaires. But our firemen, he said, have always been heroes, such as Big Mose, a nineteenth-century New York metropolitan folk hero, based on a real fireman (Dubner 2001).

Media analysts remark that "the celebration of the many heroes of September 11 helped people process the loss, restored faith and confidence in society, connected people together in unexpected ways, and provided justification for a significant response" (Chermak, Bailey, and Brown 2003a:1–2). It was time for Americans to praise and emulate heroic, moral exemplars, and Father Judge seemed to be a perfect paradigm.

Perfect, that is, "except the fact that Judge was a relatively high profile gay man" (Walsh 2001:5)—a fact that all the major papers except for the *Village Voice* ignored. Why did the press, including the *Times,* more or less exclude that aspect of Judge's life? Mainstream journalists acknowledged the homosexuality of Mark Bingham, who was among the resisting passengers on United Airlines Flight 93. So why was Judge's sexuality hardly mentioned in the *Times* for more than a year after his death? Was his identity as a gay Catholic priest considered too scandalous, too divisive, at a time when Americans (and American media) were focusing on traits of national consensus? *Times* columnist Frank Rich (2002) raised the issue as a kicker to a piece on the ways in which "politicians hijack religion," when he spoke of the "heroism" and "self-sacrifice" evidenced in Judge, "a Catholic priest, who, not that it should matter, happened to be gay."

On September 27, 2002, Daniel J. Wakin (2002e) published an extensive retrospective on Judge, "the sandal-shod fire chaplain" who had "become the center of a fervent following," but also of some contention. By that time, there was already a Web site promoting his canonization, a movement decried by his fellow Franciscans. A legend had developed among his fellow priests—who wished to think of him performing his priestly functions at his death—claiming that he died giving last rites, even though evidence showed otherwise. A photo by Shannon Stapleton of Reuters showed his body being carried from the World Trade Center; it was called "a modern Pietà." Wakin treated Judge's status as "larger than life" and tiptoed carefully around his putative homosexuality. His article stated that "gay rights advocates . . . have spoken openly about what they say was his homosexual orientation." But, Wakin reported for balance, others charged that gays were using him "to further their agenda." (For more about Mychal Judge's Catholicism and homosexuality, see A. Newman 2005a.)

In retrospect, Wakin (2007) thinks that he located the right perspective to his 2002 piece about Father Judge. When he "stumbled" onto Web sites devoted to making the priest "a saint," when he accompanied devotees to Judge's burial ground, he found it "very moving," more than worthy of *Times* attention. "The gay thing didn't interest me as much," Wakin acknowledges, although he paid it heed—not enough, according to gay critics. Wakin thought it proper to balance the gay community's association with Judge against those firemen who could not imagine Judge as a gay man. Indeed, Wakin suggests that the priest's sexual orientation was perhaps irrelevant. Judge's Catholic colleagues said that the man was celibate, so maybe it did not matter if he was gay or not. Wakin states that the church supposedly respects all people regardless of sexual orientation—as long as they do not act on their sexuality outside marriage. What difference, then, did it matter in theory how Judge's sexuality was to be characterized? In his death, the priest made a deep impression on many people, straight and gay, not for his imagined sexuality, but for his heroic deeds.

Time outlasted the initial acts of consolation and heroism. In the months following 9/11, New Yorkers were in shock, according to one woman, "still struggling to figure out what it all means" (quoted in Jacobs 2001). Street preachers from across America converged on New York City to disseminate their tracts at Ground Zero. They "bellowed about sin and redemption," one of them saying of New York City that "the only difference between hell and New York is one of them is surrounded by water." On one occasion, a Muslim preacher told a mostly Christian crowd, "Allah loves you," which prompted an evangelical Protestant to retort, "You can believe in Muhammad all you want, but you're still going to hell" (all quoted in Jacobs 2001). At Union Square, Tibetan Buddhists—who "had sometimes felt neglected when it came to official memorials"—held a service, with several hundred in attendance, for the World Trade Center victims (Wakin 2001c). In honor of Trade Center dead whose bodies were unrecovered, Jewish women performed "the most selfless of Jewish commandments: to keep watch over the dead, who must not be left alone from the moment of passing until burial "(Gross 2001a). This Orthodox ritual, known as "sitting *shmira*," took place "round the clock" at the morgue in New York City for eight weeks after 9/11, led by a student at Stern College for Women, a division of Yeshiva University.

Various Christians, Muslims, Hindus, Buddhists, and Jews were depicted on the pages of the *Times* in sincere postures of pious bereavement. Articles demonstrated the ways in which religious people's faith was tested. At Manhattan's Xavier High School, whose Catholic students and staff grieved for alumni and relatives, sixty all told, spiritual and visceral concerns conjoined. A reporter noted that "in religion classes, instead of murky abstractions, questions of the deepest and most painful kind are asked and, at least sometimes, answered." An assistant headmaster commented, "Of course it tests your faith. But faith is a choice and this is an environment that nurtures it" (Gross 2001b). A Presbyterian church in Ridgewood, New Jersey, lost a dozen congregants to the 9/11 attack. The minister reflected publicly on the deaths (as well as on an electrical fire that gutted the church): "I don't know why this happened to us. . . . But I do know for certain that God did not cause this to happen. I don't believe we live in a if-you-are-good-God-will-reward-you-and-if-you-are-bad-God-will-punish-you kind of world. . . . I don't know why it is raining on us right now, . . . but I don't think we've done anything to deserve this" (quoted in G. James 2002).

The *Times* paid mind to the effects of 9/11 on religious institutions and the role of churches in responding to the needs of communities and individuals. It ran ads from Jewish and Christian institutions offering condolences to those in grief. A two-page spread of sermons from across the nation (Niebuhr 2001e) featured Cardinal Egan saying mass in New York City (Barron 2001), but it also included messages from Protestant, Catholic, Jewish, Hindu, and Muslim spokespeople, all asking how to respond to evil, exhorting mourners to put faith in God and love, and encouraging their congregations to comfort the bereaved. Many rabbis deemed a traditional Jewish New Year's prayer reflecting on "who shall live and who shall die; who shall see ripe old age and who shall not; who shall perish by fire and who by water" to be too unfeeling to utter at a time when so many so greatly needed condolence. The *Times* page headings showed how such an issue was nestled within the greater 9/11 story. The section "A Nation Challenged" considered Americans "turning to faith," including Jews: "Rosh Hashana: Rabbis Revise Sermons to Soften a Stark Prayer" (Waldman 2001f).

Clergy as well as laypersons were in need of condolence and guidance in a time of crisis (Niebuhr 2001c). Michael Winerip (2001a) composed a poignant portrait of a Catholic priest on Long Island who sagged physically and emotionally under the pressure of conducting funerals for the 9/11 dead and the added pressure of adjudicating among distraught, feuding family members of the deceased. At night, he sat with his aged parents, confiding in them "the horrors of the day."

Throughout the fall of 2001 and for years to come, the *Times* memorialized Trinity Church's Episcopal contributions: the food, the counselors, the volunteers, the emotional support, all available as a facet of Christian ministry for the denizens and work crews at and around Ground Zero (Genzlinger 2001). *Times* reporter David W. Dunlap (2004c) writes that Trinity Church "played a vital role on September 11, 2001, and in the months that followed. Indeed, it offered what may have been the very first institutional response to the attack, just after the second jetliner hit the World Trade Center: an impromptu service for those who streamed into the church for shelter and solace. In the midst of a hymn—'O God, our help in ages past'—there came the thunderous collapse of the south tower, casting the church into Stygian pitch and ash. Both Trinity and its chapel, St. Paul's survived the attack and ministered to the needy. Having survived wars, rebellion, riots, and plagues, it was a role for which this parish was well suited" (276–77).

The good deeds of one church found their generous echo in the gesture of another. Our Lady of the Rosary Catholic Church is a shrine of St. Elizabeth Ann Seton, the first native-born American to be canonized and a convert from her Trinity Church Episcopal faith. Dunlap (2004c) recalls that "after Trinity was shut down on September 11, 2001, the Rev. Peter K. Meehan offered Our Lady of the Rosary as a place of worship for the Episcopal parish, reuniting Seton and Trinity, at least temporarily. In the first service on September 16, the Rev. Samuel Johnson Howard, vicar of Trinity, allowed himself the gentle humor of noting, 'She was *our* daughter before she was *their* mother.' Worshipers laughed, some perhaps for the first time since the attack" (167, italics in original).

Help came to the city from across the country. A thousand Southern Baptists, known as the "God squad," many of whom had aided disaster victims in other countries, traveled to New York City to help out, cleaning many apartments around the fallen trade center. A *Times* reporter attested to these religious volunteers' altruism, stating that they "do not take money for their work" and that "the group has not sought publicity" (Cowan 2001). Nor did they seek converts.

Christian and Jewish philanthropies were portrayed as financial benefactors, helping businesses and individuals hurt by the 9/11 attacks. "We just wanted to spend God's love," said an evangelical pastor from Kentucky as he wrote out a check to the owner of a toy store near Ground Zero. "Thank you, I'll do good things," the shopkeeper replied, "her eyes tearing. They hugged" (Wakin 2001a). The Salvation Army raised more than sixty million dollars to help victims of the September 11 attacks and were "overwhelmed" in the task of distributing the proceeds of "this generous gesture" (Henriques 2002). New York City's Buddhists continued to offer their neighbors "messages of peace and compassion"; however, they found their "nonviolence out of fashion after Sept. 11" (Crossette 2002).

Ritual condolences continued to come in, even from afar. A front-page article, "Where 9/11 News Is Late, but Aid Is Swift" (Lacey 2002b), with a dateline from Kenya, contained a color photograph with the following caption: "In a remote Kenyan village, William Oltetia presented 14 cows to aid victims of the attacks of Sept. 11." In the picture by Mariella Furrer/Corbis Saba, the "chief of the young warriors" poses beside the cows; he carries an American flag erect. His hair is orange, and he is wearing a pink, flowery wrapper and beads over his undershirt. Behind him is a thatched building and many red-cloaked villagers, some shielding themselves from the sun with umbrellas. These are Masai people, for whom "skyscrapers are a foreign concept." A local man had recently returned from studying in the United States and had told about the 9/11 attacks. His village "wanted to do something." So they held a "solemn ceremony, . . . blessing 14 cows being given to the people of the United States." These animals are "held sacred by the Masai," and after the blessing, they were given to an official of the US embassy in Nairobi. In the article, the Masai spoke of the cows' sacrality— "far more than a source of meat and milk"—and of the need for revenge against a man such as Osama bin Laden. The *Times* seemed to be validating the mythic tale at home—of victims and villains and power of faith-based consolation for the bereaved—by virtue of a distant, naive people's authentically sincere and romantic expressions. It is almost as if the Masai expressions of sacrality and justice—a multicultural affirmation by a simple, faithful folk—had universal application (see Gettleman 2006 for the follow-up).

Not long after 9/11, its survivors were having their say, holding forth about their personal, salvific, spiritual experiences in the wreckage. Sujo John, a native of Calcutta, worked on the eighty-first floor of the north tower of the World Trade Center. He made it as far as the mezzanine when the building collapsed around him, amidst a dozen people or so. Facing death, "he prompted them to shout out the name of Jesus—just before everyone but him was crushed to death." This was the story that he told in "fundamentalist" churches across America, according to the *Times* reporter. "'My heart was sad,' he said on Sunday, 'but I rejoiced.' . . . Many hear his story, weep, and praise God," the *Times* stated with only the slightest hint of apprehension. According to the report, he received "no money for this new-found ministry, other than donations to cover his modest expenses. . . . With thousands of people dead, he is loath to be seen as promoting himself. All he knows, he said, is that he was spared to prepare others for their own deaths." That was his message: you all must prepare for your death. Thus, he shouted, "There is no name that can save you other than the name of Jesus" (Barry 2001b).

A New York City Transit worker, John B. McMahon, spoke to a *Times* reporter about a miraculous something that saved his life on 9/11. McMahon rushed to the World Trade Center that morning to help anyone who might be caught in the subway below. When he got there, the south tower collapsed around him, and he escaped by holding someone's hand and following two lights. When he emerged from the debris, "he realized that he was not holding anyone's hand. He was alone. . . . He still has no idea what the lights were, and no idea how he found his way out of the debris. 'I'm a Catholic,' Mr. McMahon said. . . . 'But I only go [to mass] about once every five years. I don't know what that was that day. I don't know how to explain it. Somebody got me out,' he said" (R. Kennedy 2001).

The *Times* treated the testimonies of Suro and McMahon with serious attention. A "Styles" section article took a different edge. As we have seen, the *Times* runs stories from time to time on clairvoyance and parapsychology—usually with a mocking tone. These phenomena represent the superstitious, magical end of the religious spectrum (like shamans pulling crabs out of people's bellies). Thus, the paper reported with some wariness that "since Sept. 11, grieving family members of the victims have sought comfort from the clergy, psychotherapists, groups of neighbors and their fellow bereaved. And some have turned to mediums who say they can reach the spirit of loved ones." As mourners struggled and sought comfort after 9/11, a "British-born best-selling author who maintains that she speaks with the dead, was conducting a free private session for the grief-stricken." There she was, describing for women whose loved ones had died in the World Trade Center the details of their final moments on Earth and their spiritual condition in the hereafter. Some of these depictions rang true to the grievers. "If she wasn't so right on the money," one woman said, "I wouldn't have believed it." The *Times* author stated that some of the deceased "have been the subject of newspaper obituary articles, and they are listed on the Internet," thus suggesting the preparatory research that a medium could perform before the session. For context, the *Times* referred to "a national fad for communicating with the dead." But "the notion of spirit mediums elicits the deepest skepticism of many people, and when the spirits supposedly being contacted are connected to Sept. 11, questions of insensitivity come into play, along with the possibility of exploitation. . . . Beyond questions of appropriateness (including why a reporter would be invited to observe the . . . event . . . for any reason other than publicity), there is the more basic question of whether victims' relatives, raw with emotion after such sudden deaths and desperate to 'talk' to their loved ones, are being taken advantage of." The article continued with references to James Randi, "a well-known debunker of the occult," with whom the diviner "faced off" on *Larry King Live* last year. Then the author showed the medium's technique—for example, fishing for answers, as in "Which of your husbands was the football player?" or using descriptions of 9/11 that were familiar to television news, then switching to comforting vignettes of "light coming through windows at the moment of 'passing,'" encounters with angels, and "reassurances that the victims acted courageously and didn't suffer long." The author did not neglect to say that the medium "worked the room in an elegant tweed blazer, with gold necklace and diamond bracelet glimmering," details that suggested the proceeds of a successful charlatanry. And the author showed how the diviner got details wrong. Even so, one mourner exclaimed in the kicker, "I know it shouldn't really help, but it does" (Morris 2001).

Place and Time

Sacred and Secular

Before the end of 2001, the site of the fallen towers was becoming a destination for pilgrims seeking an experience of the terrible, violent power unleashed there. The *Times* documented the fascination Ground Zero held for innumerable seekers. The place where the World Trade Center lay ravaged soon became a ritual center space in the American civic religion, as "fabricated" by the media (Breithaupt 2003:78), including the *Times*.

Over the years, the *Times* had covered many a fire in the city's houses of worship—some by ill-intentioned vandals—and the paper had tracked the ways in which congregations had rebuilt their wrecked edifices. Now the same would be done for the leveled trade center.

Nearby churches were part of the picture. A photo of Ground Zero taken by James Estrin (2001) focused on the spot where St. Nicholas Greek Orthodox Church stood before it was destroyed by the toppled towers on 9/11. A service was held "to honor the church and members of the faith killed on Sept. 11." The devastation was almost total. A *Times* reporter remarked, "Two suitcases hold all the remains" of the church: a paper icon, an ornamental cloth bible cover, an oil-burning lamp, a bell clapper. The Greek Orthodox archbishop, Demetrios, faced the "shocking destruction" of his church. However, "within a month of the September 11 attack, Demetrios pledged that the church would 'rise in glory once more in the same sacred spot as a symbol of a determined faith'" (Dunlap 2004c:103, 233). In the new year, students at New York City Technical College in Brooklyn were already designing a model for a rebuilt version of St. Nicholas (Arenson 2002a).

Early in 2002, New Yorkers were beginning to have mixed and competing feelings about how to treat the sacred site. As visitors wrought with emotion and curiosity arrived at Ground Zero, mourners, survivors, and neighborhood denizens began to object to the attention, calling a viewing platform "ghoulish." "'It is like a freak show,' one grieving mother complains" (Murphy 2002).

For January 25, 2002, John Tierney's "The Big City" column was entitled, "Downtown, a Necropolis Is Rising." He wrote of Lycia in Turkey, which is famous for its "'distinctive type of funerary architecture.'" He wondered if downtown Manhattan, like Lycia, was in danger of becoming "'the land of tombs.'" "While their Greek neighbors were creating art and literature," Tierney said, "the Lycians were building memorials to the dead," and he worried that we might be devoting too much time and space to the 9/11 victims. Downtown Manhattan already had memorials to fallen police officers, victims of the Holocaust, and the Irish potato famine. Now Rudolph Giuliani and some relatives of the September 11 dead were proposing to turn "the entire 16-acre site of the World Trade Center into a memorial." This was too much for Tierney. The World Trade Center had been a commercial place, and it deserved to become so again, he thought, even though commercialism might be seen as a "desecration of hallowed ground. . . . Some of the victims' families will never be reconciled to seeing new commerce on the site, but there are some who see no sacrilege in it." Tierney suggested maintaining the twin towers' footprint and a memorial "showing firefighters going into the towers, or helping people escape . . . ," something heroic like that. But he wanted Ground Zero to become a site of vibrant commerce once again.

In the years before 9/11, the *Times* (Goldberger 1996) had represented the World Trade Center as an architectural symbol of New York City's commercial eclipse of religion. Ironically, the World Trade Center buildings were attacked because they *were* commercial centers, the symbolic core of secular American culture. Now the victims' mourners were finding a revival of that commercial spirit sacrilegious.

Six months after 9/11, the atmosphere around Ground Zero was shifting noticeably. St. Paul's Episcopal Chapel on Broadway and Fulton Street had served as a sanctuary to recovery workers at Ground Zero. But in March 2002 it was due to close for cleaning. It was a sign that, as one construction worker said in the kicker of a *Times* article, "everything has got to stop. . . . It goes back to normal" (Kelley 2002). The crisis period of mourning downtown was phasing out, and there was a question of how long public mourning should persist.

According to Dunlap (2004c), St. Paul's Chapel's

> noblest and most tireless role came after September 11, 2001, when it sheltered and comforted the police officers, firefighters, rescue workers, and laborers engaged in the heroic effort of combing through and carting off the ruins of the World Trade Center, directly across Church Street. Washington's pew became the podiatrist station. St. Paul's offered its great iron fence as the setting of a magnificently impromptu people's memorial. For months, it was covered with missing-person posters, family snapshots, baseball caps, T-shirts, teddy bears, origami cranes, candles, and poems—inspiring a reverential hush from almost everyone who approached. (280)

For more than a year, St. Paul's Chapel of Trinity Church displayed on its perimeter along Vesey Street a collection of 9/11 memorabilia, a shrine of left objects, in what became "the world's guest book" at Ground Zero. Finally, the question loomed for the chapel's keepers: "how to say 'enough,' gracefully." An accompanying *Times* photo of the memorial by Don Hogan Charles manifested the chaos of the place. "New York is thick in Sept. 11 imagery," the reporter said, but St. Paul's had become an eyesore. Visitors who first arrived there thought the shrine wonderful but the neighborhood seems to have had enough. The chapel's vicar declared, "It is an impediment to our continued recovery" (Wilson 2002b).

The church's authorities determined to clear the area of the "unsightly collection . . . and sidewalk vendors hawking 9/11 memorabilia," as a neighbor put it (Wilson 2002c). One day a week workers removed the materials, "one flag, one shirt, one doll at a time," and stored it all for possible display in the future. The chapel, which had been called "'heaven's outpost' for its ground zero relief operation," serving as "a refuge of sanity for rescuers and workers at the World Trade Center site" (Wakin 2002b), aimed to redefine its mission beyond its legendary status as "a national shrine" to 9/11.

By June 2002, it was time "to mark the passing of ground zero from recovery site to construction zone" (Kershaw 2002). Only portions of about a thousand of the 2,800 victims' bodies had been recovered and identified; nevertheless, it was time to move on. There was an "interfaith service" and a last Catholic mass beneath "a cross of steel beams," beginning with "Amazing Grace" and ending with "Taps."

Ground Zero still remained an attraction to visitors to the city, and 9/11 persisted as a momentous event to be memorialized. The Reverend Bill Minson could not turn away from the "huge tomb" of Ground Zero. In the "Public Lives" column, Chris Hedges (2002b) wrote, "For a year, Mr. Minson, 52, a stocky minister who wears a clerical collar but who never went to a seminary and who was ordained in an independent church set up to provide spiritual direction, including astrology and numerology readings, to musicians and entertainers, has haunted the site." This mildly mocking piece spoke of the minister's "unwavering self-confidence and charisma that entices listeners" and that left the impression of a self-promoter, drawn to what he called "a different kind of light, a different type of excitement."

Dan Barry (2003b) chronicled the mission of another man compelled to "[preach] the gospel of ground zero" from morning to night at the edge of the sixteen-acre "gouge in Lower Manhattan," telling visitors what happened on 9/11 to "his beloved twin towers." The man wanted everyone to remember everything about the buildings and how they were destroyed. Why was he doing this? About a year earlier, he had heard someone tell his son that the towers' collapse was the result of "an accident, that a jet had made a wrong turn." He could not bear to have the truth undone, and so he was "preaching the gospel of Sept. 11 to visitors." Some listeners tied 9/11 to the war with Iraq; others said they are completely unconnected. The man said nothing on that issue. Someone called him a "warmonger. No, he answered. This is only history." His mission was never to forget.

In the lead of his column "Looking for God in the Details at Ground Zero," Dunlap (2003b) asked: "Does God have a place at ground zero? This is not a metaphysical inquiry but a planning question, although the quick rejoinder might be: which god? Or, whose god? Or, *what* god?" Dunlap reported that the architects who made their plans for a reconstructed Ground Zero treated churches—St. Paul's Chapel, St. Nicholas Church—mostly with attitudes ranging from "diffidence to indifference, though some attributed an innate overall spirituality to their projects."

Dunlap was one of the *Times* reporters who covered the religious implications at Ground Zero and around New York City. The paper's senior real estate writer, Dunlap has published widely about architecture, design, landmarks, and urban history for the *Times* and elsewhere. He has produced two books about Manhattan's sacred structures and spaces (Dunlap 2004c; Dunlap and Vecchione

2001), and his expertise regarding church architecture was on display at the New-York Historical Society in the exhibition From Abyssinian to Zion: Photographs of Manhattan's Houses of Worship during the summer of 2004.

With his sensibilities and expertise regarding New York's churches, synagogues, and mosques, Dunlap has reflected in his writings—in the *Times* and beyond—on 9/11's impact on the city's diverse religious communities and their roles in ministering to the city's stunned populace.

Given Dunlap's knowledge about the religious dimensions of church architecture, it made sense to ask him, "To what degree, in your view, has ground zero functioned as an evolving 'sacred space' (however that might be defined) or even as a 'place of worship' since 9/11?" (Vecsey 2004). His reply: "I'm afraid I haven't given your excellent question enough thought to offer a useful answer" (Dunlap 2004b). Perhaps he had not put this development of Ground Zero as sacred space into conceptual form; however, the *Times* coverage of Ground Zero and its environs taught its readers plenty about the ways in which powerful events and meaningful human responses create sacrality in a particular locale.

Through 2003, 2004, and beyond, Dunlap (2004e) and other *Times* reporters conveyed in articles and longer works the news of architectural plans for rebuilding Ground Zero. Whatever spirituality may have existed in architects and city planners' minds, it did not manifest itself in the models or the mission statements for the future. The former World Trade Center site did not cease to carry enormous emotional freight, especially for survivors and the relatives of victims who died there on 9/11, nor did the planning discussions lack gravitas. Nonetheless, Ground Zero seemed to evolve from a short-lived sacred space to something with more secular import.

New Yorkers behaved religiously in mourning: they constructed shrines, delivered sermons, said prayers; they respected their dead, turning them into heroes, saints, martyrs, paradigms (our incipient ancestor worship). Their prayers referred to "God," seeking comfort and meaning in supernatural contexts. At the same time, New Yorkers eventually returned to their normal lives and were encouraged by religious and political leaders to do so. Don't overmourn, embrace life, they along with other Americans were told.

In the year following 9/11, through the liturgical cycle that marks sacred time—Christmas, Good Friday, Easter, Passover, Yom Kippur, Ramadan, and the new holy day in the American spiritual calendar, September 11—the *Times* took stock of the changing shape of 9/11's implications at Ground Zero, around New York, in America, and around the world.

On Christmas Day 2001, the *Times* carried articles on the monsignor in charge of ceremonies at St. Patrick's Cathedral, where "the symbol of red, white and blue stands for something that can never be destroyed, even by the most evil act we can imagine," according to the monsignor (quoted in Wakin 2001f), and on the remains of St. Nicholas Greek Orthodox Church, which was crushed by the World Trade Center on 9/11, losing a safe containing, among other things, a relic of "St. Nicholas himself, from whom Santa Claus evolved" (Dunlap 2001a; see also Dunlap 2001b). At the north end of Manhattan, worshippers regarded the survival of St. John the Divine from a five-alarm fire as a "miracle" (Christian 2001).

On Christmas "in the heartland," the *Times* reported from Indiana that "red, white and blue join the icons of the season" (Kilborn 2001) as patriotism and cultural Christianity coalesced. In Bethlehem, West Bank, Palestinians claimed a parallel to the life "'Jesus lived—the poverty, the misunderstanding, all these things'" (Bennet 2001).

But the most dramatic Christmas story appeared on December 26, and it focused on Ground Zero: "Christmas Mass Beneath a Cross of Fallen Steel" (Murphy 2001). A photo by Dean E. Murphy revealed a Catholic priest saying mass at Ground Zero for fifty or so firefighters, police officers, construction workers, and volunteers under a split beam "in the perfect shape of a cross" that fell into the rubble of the World Trade Center and that "immediately became an inspiration for many Christians and others working at ground zero. On Christmas Eve, two Muslims were among the people who attended midnight Mass there." "It is hallowed ground, all of it," a firefighter said of Ground Zero.

Months later "Good Friday Ritual Is Cast with the Backdrop of 9/11" read the headline to a story (A. Newman 2002a), featuring a Nancy Siesel photo of Catholics bearing a cross over the Brooklyn Bridge. The lead: "The last time so many people crossed the Brooklyn Bridge on foot, a little more than six months ago, it was on a panicked exodus. But yesterday, following a man carrying a simple wooden cross, more than 2,000 people walked across the bridge toward ground zero. They walked in the hope that grafting Jesus' journey onto the geography of contemporary tragedy, they could find some comfort and meaning from the tenets of their faith: his death and resurrection." It would be hard to find an article more sensitive than Andy Newman's to the sacramental power of ritual in the face of calamity. In a newspaper that had long observed religious rituals as means of consolation and solidarity, this piece had especial fidelity to such an insight.

Newman published a dozen *Times* articles about 9/11 with religious dimensions (see, e.g., A. Newman 2002d), including several he composed as religion writer for the "Metro" section (A. Newman 2005a, 2005b, 2005c). He found the Good Friday piece a "moving" experience (A. Newman 2007). Assigned by an editor, he considered the big crowd a worthy topic as the congregation began its pilgrimage from church to Ground Zero, and he was determined to capture the expression of post-9/11 Christianity. The son of "vehemently atheistic Jews," Newman had become "more spiritual than they are" and fascinated by "big squishy things" such as "faith" and the "infinite." "Knowing nothing about Christianity" but attracted by the pilgrims' fervor, Newman set out to illustrate their soulfulness.

His boss congratulated him on the story; several years later he was asked if he wanted to replace Daniel J. Wakin as the metro religion reporter. Newman's parents—and some of his colleagues—"questioned my sanity" when he took up his new beat, he recalls (2007). He lasted only a matter of months—replaced by Michael Luo. "I wasn't tremendously productive," he acknowledges, in part because he resisted the stories about religious institutions and in part because "it was harder than I thought to see into people's souls". For one moment in 2002, however, his intuition was perspicacious.

The evergreens of Passover and Easter took a solemn hue in spring 2002. In New York, the disaster of 9/11 continued to be felt even as Jews considered "next year in Jerusalem" (quoted in Chen 2002) and Christians donned their Easter hats. "Heads Turn and Eggs Roll, but Perilous Times Darken Easter" was one headline's description (McFadden 2002b). It was a "furtive Easter Sunday for foreigners" in Pakistan: "Bomb Attack Chills Churchgoers in Islamabad," read another headline (Mydans 2002e). And another told readers, "Hopes for Easter Release of Missionary Couple Held in Philippine Jungle Prove Unfounded" (Perlez 2002a).

The anniversary of 9/11 in 2002 became a holy day of remembrance in American civic life and a time for searching concerns. In his "Beliefs" column, Peter Steinfels (2002c) queried, "Where was God on Sept. 11?" A PBS documentary and several books asked this same question, and it was a conundrum on the minds of many. Steinfels suggested that "not a few voices have answered that God was right in the midst of the horror, especially in the heroism and self-sacrifice."

In Steinfels's essays and elsewhere in the *Times* (e.g., Wakin 2002c), one could find searching, theological, existential questions, answers, and more questions. The *Times* epitomized religion as quest(ion), seriousness, ultimacy, faith. Amidst the frivolousness of fashion, there was commitment to the search for meaning. Was the *Times* secular in its engagement with 9/11 as the first anniversary approached? Of course. It was also religious—not just conventionally religious, but responsively, responsibly, seriously religious.

Daniel J. Wakin (2002c) reported on "clerics' daunting task" in "forming 9/11 sermons." New York's mayor Michael R. Bloomberg decided that there should be no original oratory on September 11, 2002, during the city's official commemorations. Instead, New Yorkers were to hear "the nation's secular scriptures: the Gettysburg Address, part of the Declaration of Independence and the Four Freedoms." This left the task of original sermons to the preachers. "It is the moment for the sermon of a lifetime," said the lead to Wakin's article, for "the city's priests and rabbis, imams and ministers, to give spiritual comfort and moral compass." There was "a need to crystallize in words the meaning of the disaster." These sermons would refer to the tragedy itself, to biblical stories, to the "selflessness of the rescuers." They would try to avoid using clichés, claiming to know God's will, or presuming that good has come from the disaster. Their aim was to give people a chance to think and pray. To be a comfort. There needed to be an emphasis on interfaith communities coming together. "The heroism and post-attack togetherness show humankind's true face." This was the advice Wakin heard from the clergy preparing their sermons. His kicker: "On the other hand, some New Yorkers may agree with Ralph Waldo Emerson, who wrote in the essay 'Self-Reliance': 'I like the silent church before the service begins, better than any preaching.'" Perhaps silence would be more eloquent than words as a response to such moral and emotional enormity.

The *Times* provided its own civic sermons around 9/11's first anniversary. Its Sunday op-ed page was entitled "Reflections on an America Transformed" (Carter et al. 2002), with short essays by Stephen L. Carter ("what America most needs today may be prayer: prayer that God may yet help us, before it is too late"); Cynthia Ozick, Tom Daschle, Muhammad Ali ("Islam is a religion of peace and tolerance—not one of hate and revenge. Killing all of those innocent people will count against the terrorists on their judgment day. Those wishing evil on the world cannot call themselves Muslims, for they are hijacking an honorable faith"), Newt Gingrich ("Reactionary Islam, as distinct from modern Islam, will always oppose us because our very existence threatens its values. . . . [O]ur national security policy must be to pre-empt and defeat our enemies. That is the lesson of Sept. 11"), Martha Nussbaum, William J. Bennett, and others. To match the words, photographs in the *Times* pictured "ceremonies of healing, old and new" ("Ceremonies" 2002): a Coptic sanctification of Ground Zero by Ruth Fremson; a Lummi Indian totem pole dedicated in Monroe, New York, by Susan Stava; a Harlem water ballet in honor of the dead by Ozier Muhammad.

For New York Muslims, September 11, 2002, was an "uneasy anniversary" (Wakin 2002d), an impending date with a special burden, reminding them of their many brothers and sisters in faith who died in the World Trade Center, yet they, as Muslims, felt blamed for the 9/11 deaths. Muslims helped at Ground Zero, trying to prove that there are "good" Muslims in America, but they were still mistrusted by their fellow citizens.

Mona Eltahawy (2002), an Egyptian-born, New York–based freelance writer and managing editor of *Arabic Women's News,* wrote in the op-ed "Keeping Faith with Islam in a New World," "I am dreading the anniversary of Sept. 11. . . . I brace myself for a renewal of blame." How many times, she asked, must she and other Muslim Americans apologize and explain and "reclaim the stage from the maniacs who want to take over the mosques? All Muslims cannot be held accountable for the murderous actions of 19 men." She did not feel a burden to apologize; however, she concluded, "We must question, criticize and speak out. Only by reclaiming our own voice can we silence the zealots." On September 11, 2002, many American Muslims were still feeling distrusted, alienated, and threatened, even as they continued to grieve a year after 9/11 (Wilgoren 2002b).

On the first anniversary, Gary Laderman (2002) reported in *Religion in the News* on the commemorations of the dead, "communal rituals to create social solidarity" (2). The United States is sometimes called a death-denying or defying culture, he said, but in this case the dead were to be honored. The World Trade Center location became a sacred site visited by pilgrims. But, more significant, many people across America gathered "the residue of decimated buildings and annihilated bodies mixed together and thus transformed it into sacred ruins" and "Ground Zero dust" (2). The *New York Post* reported on this activity on September 12, 2002. Why this phenomenon? Laderman theorized that it was because so few bodies were recovered from the debris. Another aspect was "the rhetorical effort to transform innocent, unsuspecting civilians into national heroes who sacrificed their lives—implicitly comparing them with American soldiers who died fighting for the country in wars past" (3).

On February 27, 2003, the *Times* took a moment on the tenth anniversary of the 1993 World Trade Center terrorist attack to recall the six people who died there. A memorial mass at St. Peter's Roman Catholic Church provided the opportunity for several relatives of the victims, "whose loss has often been obscured by the enormity of Sept. 11, 2001," to state that "their wounds were still fresh" (Cardwell 2003b).

Meanwhile, tourists and peddlers trafficked Ground Zero, and, according to some city officials and relatives of the World Trade Center 9/11 deceased, the "'sanctity of the site'" was being marred by "a certain tackiness" of "knick-knacks" and "knockoff watches," "hot dogs" and "NYC sweatshirts" (Haberman 2003b). Although sympathizing with a desire for "dignity" and the impulse to banish the moneychangers from the temple of doom, Clyde Haberman noted that at "sacred" sites around the world—the Vatican, the Western Wall, Lourdes, Buddhist temples in Japan, and so on—"commercialism" is "inseparable" from "hallowed ground." Also to be remembered is the fact that the World Trade Center was itself a "temple of commerce."

At the second anniversary of 9/11, the *Times* observed New York City's memorials of remembrance:

• A vial of a dead firefighter's blood was "laid to rest" after a ceremony in a Roman Catholic church (von Zielbauer 2003).

• A troupe of actors read from the "Portraits of Grief" in "a chorus of grief at ground zero," captured in a photograph by Stephen Crowley (Crowley 2003).

• Parents on Staten Island continued to tend a memorial to their lost son. Fred R. Conrad's photograph displayed the angels, the cross, the flowers, the American flag, the son's picture, and the inscription "WTC 9/11/011." Said the father of the house about the shrine, "I see it as always being there" (Barry 2003a).

On the morning of September 11, 2003, "people who lost family members in the attack on the World Trade Center placed flowers and other tokens at two reflecting pools where the twin towers once stood" ("Two Years Later" 2003). A *Times* photo by James Estrin recorded the service. In the stories of the second anniversary, there was some mention of implicit religiosity; however, the religious symbolism was mostly muted, and pictures of witness in general took the place of verbal description or interpretation. St. Paul's Chapel seemed to be the repository of "'sacramental expression'" around Ground Zero, not only for its exhibitions Out of the Dust: A Year of Ministry at Ground Zero and Unwavering Spirit: Hope and Healing at Ground Zero, but for itself as a surviving aspect of spirituality at the site. Said St. Paul's rector, "St. Paul's has become a symbol, whether we wanted it to be or not. There's nothing symbolic you can identify with across the street except a big iron fence" (Dunlap 2003a; see also Dunlap 2004d).

Hundreds of "relics"—huge hunks of scrap metal—lay in hangar storage at Kennedy International Airport (Lipton 2003). Even the steel girder cross from the ruins of the World Trade Center was uptown in Inwood at the Roman Catholic Church of the Good Shepherd (Dunlap 2003c, photograph by Barton Silverman), far from Ground Zero. In his book *From Abyssinian to Zion,* Dunlap (2004c) notes that Good Shepherd was once known as "'the unofficial capital of the Irish diaspora.'" Thus, "when a large number of Irish-Americans were killed in the attack of September 11, 2001, Good Shepherd felt the impact terribly" (86), and it seemed appropriate to place the trade center relic in its churchyard. Dunlap wrote in 2004, the "dented steel cruciform salvaged from the site of the World Trade Center—'Ground Zero,' the sign says—stands in the churchyard" (86). It was later returned to the World Trade Center site, where it became a bone of contention as well as a "potent religious symbol" (Dunlap 2006a).

Even as the "NYC" column (Haberman 2004b) quoted from poignant 9/11 memorials inscribed on the benches of Central Park, and Hoboken, New Jersey, continued to mourn its fifty-three residents who died in the World Trade Center (Applebome 2004), the Sunday *Times* announced closure of 9/11 on the third anniversary, not once but several times. In the *Times Magazine,* Walter Kirn asked on September 12, 2004: Was it not time to "forget it? If 9/11 is going to exist mostly so politicians can manipulate our souls and psyches, maybe it's time to move on." As exhilarating as it had been to experience "the sense of pure victimization," and as strong as the "nostalgia for the lost unity" is, "when everyone was crying together and when the rest of the world was crying for us," and even though the "healing process . . . felt sinful," it was clear for some Americans that 9/11 had moved "from tragedy to policy. How sad," Kirn said, but "the passage of time" transforms things.

On the same day in the *New York Times Book Review,* Pete Hamill (2004) said the same thing in regard to Ground Zero: "Three years are gone, and the shock of the great wound has faded from New York. Sorrow and rage have ebbed. The void of ground zero is another construction site." In "those emotional early months . . . New Yorkers expressed their own visions. The most extreme ranged from wanting nothing at all to be built on 'sacred ground' to demanding duplication of the twin towers." As *Times* articles have shown over the past few years, anything associated with sacrality has been missing from the stories about rebuilding. Architects vie for contracts. Investors press for advantage. "When the symbolic cornerstone of the Freedom Tower was laid on July 4, 2004," Hamill reported, "the city yawned."

Over time, some New Yorkers may have lost interest in Ground Zero, but the most noticeable yawning was the chasm left by the World Trade Center despoliation. And the *Times* did not avert its gaze from the emptiness of the ruins. Dunlap (2004a) rued the "commercialism" impinging on the place where Americans had "mournfully contemplated" the thousands who had "perished" there on 9/11.

Ground Zero might have become a battleground between forces of commerce and commemoration, but its artifacts inspired gravity far and wide. At St. John's University in Queens, a small cross "of rusty World Trade Center steel" proclaimed the "gospel of tragedy and redemption" in a newly dedicated church, featuring a shrine to the victims of the 9/11 attack. The president of the Catholic university called the cross "a reminder of God's presence" (Kilgannon 2004c).

More than three years later, most people in the world were thinking of things more immediate, more mundane than of that ravaged day on September 11, 2001. Yet on two days in December 2004, the *Times* reminded its readers of 9/11's horror and the ways in which New Yorkers have recovered and helped others toward recovery from the trauma. Reading like a postscript to the "Portraits of Grief," a "Sunday Styles" feature under "Weddings/Celebrations," with a gorgeous photograph by Cary Conover, recounted the story of a woman whose fiancé died in the 9/11 assault and whose "grieving process" fell apart two years later in a "'massive breakdown,' she said. 'I couldn't get through the day.' She added: 'I felt like everyone else had forgotten about it. I was resentful. Lonely.'" She "sought therapy." Enter a man she had known from schooldays, a man who had interviewed at Cantor Fitzgerald on the morning of 9/11 and had left the World Trade Center just before the first plane hit. "Everyone I just interviewed with was dead," he recalled. After a courtship, they married in an "interfaith ceremony," with a Christian minister and a Jewish rabbi cocelebrating. "In lieu of bouquets, bridesmaids carried candles, placing them on pedestals, creating an inner circle under the huppah." Without forgetting the deceased—not only the bride but also the maid of honor lost a boyfriend in 9/11, and the latter also lost her brother— the wedding ritual celebrated love's healing balm in a world of mortality. The maid of honor spoke of the bride's bravery and vulnerability: "It gives the world, and me, so much hope." "It's great to have a person in your life now, to go through the joys and sorrows together," the bride commented. "Everyone assumes you're going to live till 90 years old; it's not necessarily true." At the ceremony's conclusion, a quartet played "Ode to Joy" "as the bride raised her bouquet in jubilation" (Quealy 2004).

In this story, the *Times* found restoration from the trauma of 9/11 in a marriage. The next day, in the "Metro" section, another young woman made her rounds in Lower Manhattan with the terrorist attack of 9/11 very much on her mind. Set to be married on that day in 2001, she and her fiancé "struggled with the wrenching decision of whether to proceed with the wedding. After consulting with a rabbi, they went ahead." She recalled, "The rabbi said, 'Look at it as Osama bin Laden did something evil, and you are doing something small but good.'" Then she and her spouse decided to move to the area around Ground Zero. "It was churning inside us that it was providential that we got married on a day of an evil plan. We wanted to spread goodness and do kindness." So they began an organization, World Tikkun Center, "that memorializes those killed on Sept. 11 and fosters a Jewish cultural life in Lower Manhattan." Her hope is to start a synagogue in the area. In the meantime, her "mission" is to provide "a taste of Jewish life" downtown by baking about a dozen loaves of challah every week and delivering them to neighbors, including New York's mayor, Michael Bloomberg (Steinhauer 2004, photographs by Nicole Bengiveno).

In the "Public Lives" column on December 24, 2004, Chris Burke recounted his continuing grief: "He sleeps fitfully, the haunting faces of his brother and scores of friends," lost in the World Trade Center on 9/11, "crowding out dreams. He began seeing a therapist because he felt that he was about to fall apart. 'I was hiding from 9/11 in 9/11,' he says." To channel his horrors, he founded Tuesday's Children, a "nonprofit organization that tries to boost the spirits of children who lost a parent in the Sept. 11 attacks." Even so, he is still "fumbling toward the light" as "he still counts off the dead. 'It's starting to be a manageable reality, where they are guests in my house and they are intent on staying. I talk to them now. I'll say to them at 3 a.m.: "Go away. I love you, but please go away""" (Richardson 2004). (For Burke's feet of clay, see Barron 2006.)

None of these stories was "news," but all provided crucial details to the still unfolding 9/11 narrative. They revealed spiritual dimensions to the drama of trauma, grief, consolation, and recovery: earthy dimensions embodied in weddings and foods, in memory, in commitment, and in giving.

Religious Functions
of Media Coverage

Beginning on September 12, 2001, the *Times* responded to the most traumatic single event in modern American history, an attack instigated in the dark spirit of a religious zealotry and responded to not only by military force, but also by faith. If we follow *Times* coverage over time, we see the unfolding of an American paradigm, the range of inflections of an American language and worldview. The *Times* not only reported and commented on Americans' expressions of their civil religion but also was a vehicle of that religion in reportage and commentary. In its posting of prayers and sermons, in its depictions of ritualized exhortations to togetherness, in its praise of interfaith solidarity and its disapproval of sectarian divisiveness, the *Times* touted a consensual American faith in a time of crisis. In its photographs of witness and in its "Portraits of Grief," the paper became a shrine to the dead and a comfort to the bereaved. In its delineation of mourners, victims, survivors, consolers, and heroes, it charted a compass of character, local and national, idealized and humanized. In its focus on Ground Zero and its environs, including its churches, it surveyed a geography of sacred spaces and places. And as the months became years, the *Times* let go of the anguished moment and allowed its readers to recover from their dolors.

The *Times* has demonstrated over time that religions are means by which peoples establish consensual identity, in part by defining their lineage, character, and institutions and in part by distinguishing them from their neighbors and enemies. Religions serve the function of creating, maintaining, blurring, and calibrating the dichotomy between "us" and "them." National newspapers such as the *Times* serve the same function, which is to say that they are religious or quasi-religious (maybe pseudo-religious) entities. In covering the religious dimensions of 9/11 (including public "us/them" dichotomizing and blurring [see Sreberny 2002]), the *Times* also dichotomized and blurred—that is, participated in—the national religious response to 9/11.

Newspapers try to appeal to a readership's sense of itself and its values in the news; reporting reflects the character of a paper's presumed community. In its religion coverage since the late 1970s, the *Times* came to reflect America's growing interest in its own religiousness. It is more secular than mainstream America, but only somewhat so. Over the last generation, the *Times* tried to keep more in step with American religious mores. At 9/11, it came very close to the American gestalt, although critical of supernaturalist religiosity. Did the *Times* reflect the American character? It tried to do so in enumerating American virtues.

Academic and former journalist Jack Lule (2002) argues that *Times* editorials responded to 9/11 through the structures of myth: lamenting the loss of US innocence, extolling the victims, calling for vengeance, celebrating heroes, mobilizing for war. In looking at eighty-four editorials, from September 12 to October 12, 2001, produced under the guidance of Gail Collins, who had just taken over as editorial page editor in August 2001, Lule says that "*Times* editorials . . . strained to understand a struggle between good and evil. They tried to make sense of almost senseless events. In doing so, they took up the role of myth" (276). Drawing upon the themes of world mythology, they constituted "a formidable array of strategies for dealing with the enormity of September 11" (286). Both a national and metropolitan medium, the *Times* "offered myths for a nation—but *especially a city*—in crisis" (287, italics in original).

Lule says in explanation: "Myth, of course, has long played a crucial role in society. Myth explains origins and history. Myth affirms values and beliefs. In this view, the central role of myth is to proclaim and promote social order. Mythic stories help shape and maintain the structures and forces that keep a society together: its laws and codes, its government and economic system, its assumptions and beliefs" (287). In effect, myths—in this case pronounced on a newspaper's editorial page—are means by which a culture defines ultimate questions and proposes ethics of good and evil for a populace.

Lule says further, "The myth-making of the *Times* did offer one surprise. The myth of the Enemy was missing from the editorial pages. The absence is notable. The *Times* [editorial page] rarely mentioned bin Laden. It avoided bellicose and belligerent talk of vengeance. It did not draw upon structures and stories of the Enemy myth" (286).

This may have been true of *Times* editorials; however, in its news reportage and commentary, on the pages of its magazine and the "Week in Review," in its op-eds and features, the *Times* surely defined America's apparent enemies and in the process served to define Americans in their unity and diversity.

PART II | Islam Observed

While portraying victims, mourners, survivors, consolers, and heroes, the *Times* also endeavored to identify the villains: not only the nineteen men who were profiled as the agents of destruction on 9/11, but what they stood for and against.

In so doing, the *Times* came to face the human contours of global Islam: a billion and more Muslims, including millions in the United States. It was the paper's daunting task to distinguish between, on the one hand, American Muslims, who were part of the story of American religion and who by and large were as innocent of causing the 9/11 destruction as any other Americans, and, on the other, an Islamic challenge and threat to America and its civic culture. The *Times* expressed consistent themes of interfaith dialogue and cultural tolerance regarding Muslims in the United States, especially in the first few months after 9/11; however, by the second week of October the *Times* made room for a more bellicose trope regarding Islam, employing "clash of civilizations" rhetoric through columnists, pundits, and reporters. It engaged in the ambiguity of defining American religion, with its Muslims more or less included, while contrasting the faith, the values, the sacralized institutions of the American way of life to those of an enemy identified with the Islamic religion.

Islam in the Eyes of the *Times*

Laurie Goodstein (2004b) says that in the aftermath of 9/11 there was a "bottomless appetite" in America and especially in the *New York Times* for stories on Islam. The events of September 11, 2001, produced an avalanche of press about Islam, but this religion was hardly new to the *New York Times*.

Over the previous three decades, the *Times* had produced articles and reviewed books about Islam and about Muslims in the United States. It had covered the persistence of Islam in the former Soviet Union and offered many stories about the tug between modernization and traditionalism in Islam worldwide, including Africa. In 1974, Edward B. Fiske wrote four extensive pieces in the series "Islam Today" (Fiske 1974b, 1974c, 1974d, 1974e; see also Fiske 1974a, 1974f). Other pieces dwelt on converts to Islam, pilgrimages to Mecca, and Libyan attempts to spread Islam around the world. In 1978, the *Times* noted that a "religious revival is sweeping across the world of Islam" (Kandall 1978), with a dateline from Tehran. In the same year, the "Week in Review" reported, "the Moslem world rekindles its militancy" (Wren 1978). When the Iranian Revolution took hold in 1979, Flora Lewis wrote her famous (or infamous) three-part piece "Upsurge in Islam" (F. Lewis 1979a, 1979b, 1979c).

The *Times* covered Islam in many countries during the 1980s—Nigeria, China, Saudi Arabia, Egypt, the USSR, the Philippines, Malaysia, Pakistan, and so on, with an emphasis on its growth, and contained in those stories were the motifs "Moslem world is unsettled by surge in fundamentalism" (Miller 1983) and at home "Moslem students in U.S. rediscovering Islam" (Colin Campbell 1984). There were occasional book reviews regarding Islam and politics in Iran as well as stories about the internecine rivalry between Sunni and Shiite Muslims. At the same time, the newspaper started to write the first evergreens about

Ramadan in New York and across America, especially as work began on the mosque and cultural center on East Ninety-Sixth Street.

In the 1990s, the *Times* followed Islam in the news in Bosnia and Central Asia, and the terms *fundamentalists* and *fundamentalism* appeared fairly regularly in describing Islamic movements. Headlines spoke of "an Islamic identity crisis" (Zonis 1994) and "militant Islam" (Ajami 1995). In 1993, there was a review (Mitgang 1993) of a book (Juergensmeyer 1993) that asked in its title, "The New Cold War?" and defined that new war as one in which "religious nationalism confronts the secular state." Similar books, warning of the threat of politicized Islam in the modern day, found review through the 1990s. The continuing saga of Salman Rushdie and the infamous fatwa issued against him by Ayatollah Ruhollah Khomeini of Iran occupied the *Times* for many years and made readers wonder about Islamic values and policies in the modern world.

In 1993, Richard Bernstein (1993), Ari L. Goldman (1993), Peter Steinfels (1993b), and others wrote the expansive series "Muslims in America," followed by diverse articles on Muslim life in the United States: mortgages, hate crimes, foods, fasts, architecture, Muslims on campus, and Muslim schools. As Muslims spread through Europe, stories started to appear on the phenomenon and on the nascent discussions among Muslims, Christians, and Jews. The *Times* started to examine sharia (Islamic law), and of course there were stories on Islamic women, often focusing on the veil, but surprisingly often focusing on Islamic women's sense of freedom and autonomy beneath the veil. In the heyday of women's liberation, the *Times* investigated Muslim women as objects of commiseration for their apparent second-sex status in Muslim cultures.

Above all, the image of Islam was clouded by a political agenda, which came to be known as "Islamism." Militant, extremist, fundamentalist, this movement defied the values of modernism and moderatism espoused by the *Times* and seemed to pose a threat to peace and security in many locales. In 2001, Karen Armstrong (2001)—a scholar sympathetic to Islam—bemoaned in an op-ed that in the present day "a history of Muslim tolerance is overturned."

One might say that the *Times* view of Islam was conventional for news media in the West. In 1981, Edward Said (who died in 2003) published his influential book *Covering Islam,* building on his analysis of Orientalism, in which he argued that "the media and the experts determine how we see the rest of the world" and in effect "cover up" more than "cover" Islam (163). Said acknowledged that there was a very real "resurgence of radical nationalism in the Islamic world"; however, he objected to US media coverage of Islam as "traumatic news" (x). He charged that "inaccuracy," "ethnocentrism," "cultural and even racial hatred," and "free-floating hostility" (xi) filled the Western news about Islam. This pattern, he said, grew out of a millennium and more of hostility on the part of Christendom toward the "demonic religion" (5) of the "false prophet" (5) Mohammad. Now colored by oil economics, the hostility was more textured and no less pervasive. Islam was seen as a long-violent threat to Western interests. According to the media, Islam resists "modernization" according to Westerners' rules and thus seems to the West to be marked by "its fundamental intransigence" (29).

Israel's existence was an important factor, Said stated, in forming American views of Islam. Israel's *religious* nature is downplayed in the news because it serves as a "foil for Islam"—presented always as the Middle East's "'only democracy'" and "'our staunch ally,'" "a bastion of Western civilization" (31).

We all arise out of "communities of interpretation" (41), Said argued, and the media play a large role in forming that cultural worldview. Given the fact that most Americans don't know much firsthand about Islam, they tend to swallow whole the relatively uninformed reports on Islam by reporters such as Flora Lewis, who wrote about "the oddities of its beliefs, and [the] illiberal totalitarianism of its domination over its faithful" (39). For Said, the media *create* the news as much as they *report* on it, and they do so with such supposed authority and objectivity that we must worry about how powerful their effect is—even though there is no single propaganda machine in America or in any one newspaper, not even such a powerful corporation as the *New York Times*. It isn't a plot; it is a matter of "culture" or "consensus" (49).

One of Said's most sustained critiques was of Flora Lewis's 1979 series "Upsurge of Islam." There are some "excellent things" (85) in her articles, he wrote—such as "complexity and diversity" (85)—but it was clear that she did not know much about Arabic language, poetry, theology, or philosophy. She relied on experts such as Bernard Lewis and admitted in an *Esquire* (May 1980) interview that she overreached her knowledge to serve her desperate *Times* editors. In the end, commented Said, her piece was "merely a collection of attitudes displayed for the benefit of suspicious and frightened readers" (88) in the midst of the Iranian

Revolution. The *Times* did better in the months and years to come; the Iranian crisis made the paper *think* about Islam. Nonetheless, Said concluded, "today Islam is defined negatively as that with which the West is radically at odds, and this tension establishes a framework radically limiting knowledge of Islam" (155).

Despite all of this critique and with all his emphasis on the diversity of the Islamic world, Said still wrote: "Nevertheless, the conflict between 'Islam' and 'the West' is very real" (61), and each camp solidifies its identity by reflecting upon the other.

Said's critique of the *Times* held, though. The paper is apt to refer to the "'Shi'a penchant for martyrdom'" (xi) rather than really understanding Iran's resistance of Iraq's invasion. The *Times* (e.g., Kifner 1980) shows Islam to be "simple, mono-lithic, totalitarian," argued Said (11). We are apt to see the *Times* reporters, like orientalist scholars, try to "deny" and "cover" "their deep-seated feelings about Islam with a language of authority whose purpose is to certify their 'objectivity' and 'scientific impartiality'" (23). In its ideology of modernism, the *Times,* like orientalists, tends to see Muslim societies as "an archaic set of superstitions, pre-vented by its strange priests and scribes from moving out of the Middle Ages into the modern world" (28). Whereas the liberal press makes heroes of some intense religionists—Pope John Paul II and Alexander Solzhenitsyn, for example—it never does so of Islamic religionists (30). American reporters *do* play a role in representing and supporting their country, and most are quite aware of doing so (47). They also represent their corporate culture, especially at the *Times* (48). Beginning in 1979, the *Times* employed its "maximum authority" (82), its "catho-licity" (83), to view Islam "from the viewpoint of national security" (83)—for example, in the two-page symposium "The Explosion in the Moslem World: A Roundtable on Islam" (December 11, 1979), where Muslim countries were dis-cussed in terms of how friendly they were to the United States. The *Times* did good political reporting on Iran in 1980; the crisis made the *Times* think about Iran and even about Islam in more complex terms. Reportage had improved from those days (116–17, 124), Said wrote, but it still fell far short of accuracy, espe-cially insofar as the paper tended not to allow Muslims to speak for themselves, to define themselves or their religion.

Considering that journalistic discipline is based on getting subjects to speak directly through reportage—quoting sources accurately and giving those sources voice—how well in 9/11 coverage did the *Times* let Muslims speak for themselves, and to what degree did the *Times* cover up those voices with conventions and clichés?

One might compare the *Times'* ability in this regard with the techniques of a religious studies academic such as Mark Juergensmeyer. In his 1993 book, Juergensmeyer employed the tropes of the "culture wars" when he identified himself in clear opposition to religious nationalists—in Iran, Egypt, Israel, India, and even the United States—who "threaten a confrontation with secular government" (xiii). His loyalties were firmly with "our own ideology and politics," by which he meant "secular Western democracy" (xiv). For Juergensmeyer, the most pressing threat was Islamic nationalism, at least since the Iranian Revolution in 1978 and the taking of American hostages in 1979, for "what appeared to be an anomaly when the Islamic revolution in Iran challenged the supremacy of Western culture and its secular politics in 1979 has become a major theme in international politics in the 1990s" (1).

For the most part (but not always; see Juergensmeyer 2003:202–10), Juergensmeyer demonstrated the enviable skill of a phenomenologist interviewer. He did not agree with the views of the religious terrorists he engaged, but he quoted them, often without editorial comment. A reader could reject the terrorists' claims or feel how twisted their rhetoric may be, how self-deluding, but Juergensmeyer mostly left that to the reader, as a journalist would wish to do.

Has the *Times* done as well in its coverage of the same topic? Has it followed the story of Islam's political surge from 1979 to 2001 with a wise eye on the religious aspect of religious nationalism? And when the story exploded in 2001, did the paper try to understand the varied experiences and reactions of Muslims at home and abroad as well as the motives of the Muslim perpetrators?

When Juergensmeyer (2003) asked Mahmud Abouhalina, a 1993 World Trade Center bombing participant, what he considered the West's greatest harm to Islam, the terrorist replied, "Media misrepresentation. He told me that secularism held a virtual lock on media control and that Islam did not have news sources to present its side of contemporary history" (142). In particular, Abouhalina found the *New York Times* "scurrilous" in its disregard of Muslim viewpoints.

Abouhalina does not get the privilege of speaking for all of Islam, but, like other committed religionists—Catholics, evangelicals, and so on—he offered the opinion that media such as the *Times* are secular and therefore incapable of doing their religion justice. Let us test that thesis.

In his essay "Islam Is Everywhere" (originally delivered as a lecture at Colgate University on November 16, 2001 [Silk 2001c]), Mark Silk (2001d) says that "the dominant impulse of the U.S. news media at the moment of 9/11 was to show American Muslims as loyal, law-abiding people who should not be blamed for terrorist acts apparently committed by a few of their co-religionists." It was necessary, therefore, "to show that Islam was a religion that did not condone such attacks—that it in fact opposed suicide and the killing of innocents" (6). Silk recalls that the *New York Times* on October 8 began a story with the following: "Leading American scholars and practitioners of Islam said yesterday that Osama bin Laden had twisted and debased Muslim theology in a video-taped statement in which he called on 'every Muslim' to 'rush to make his religion victorious' by emulating those who attacked the United States on Sept. 11" (quoted on 6). Since the 1980s, Silk says, newspapers had covered events in the Islamic liturgical calendar, such as Ramadan, and had quoted local imams condemning acts of violence by Muslims in other countries. Now the papers sought to quote Muslim leaders and agencies regarding the attack, and American Islamic leaders obliged on their own Web sites. "After September 11, the Islamic Circle of America posted on its web site a 'sample letter to Media' stressing the anguish and sorrow of American Muslims, their fear of backlash, and the un-Islamic nature of the attacks" (6–7). Islam was not the enemy, many people (including George W. Bush) avowed, and the newspapers quoted them at length.

Silk adds, however, that "it was open to question how long this period of good feelings would last" (7). A month later it still held, at least for American Muslims. He refers to the *New York Times* of October 18, 2001, which featured patriotic Muslim families in Laramie, Wyoming (the locus of antigay violence in recent American past). At the same time, however, by mid-October the *Times* was printing stories about the Islamic schools (madrassas) in Saudi Arabia, Pakistan, and elsewhere that had spread the Wahhabist gospel of xenophobia and fundamentalism. The *Times* continued with this type of coverage, "the comfortable contrast between the good patriotic Muslims at home and the bad ones over there," states Silk (2001d:8)—Africa, the Middle East, South Asia, and so on. But even this dichotomy broke down, with stories about the ambivalence American Muslims had toward American society. Yes, "America was 'an example of freedom and democracy we can learn from,'" but it was also "'an immoral, corrupt society,'" according to the survey *The Mosque in America* (quoted in Silk 2001d:8). Silk comments, "Ambivalence was one thing. Speaking out of both sides of your mouth was another" (8). News reports found American Muslims who were moderates, some who were extremists, and some who pretended to be one or the other, depending on context. *Times* articles featured all types and took a range of viewpoints on Islam, from sanguine to paranoid (see Andrew Sullivan's "This *Is* a Religion War" [2001] and Salman Rushdie's "Yes, This Is about Islam" [2001]). Daniel Pipes had employed the term *Islamism* to contrast with the more benign, spiritual aspects of Islam. He wrote in the *New York Post* that "many American Muslims are Islamists who would like to turn the United States into an Islamic state" (quoted in Silk 2001d:28). Silk concludes, "After September 11, making America safe for Islam was one side of the coin. Making Islam safe for America was the other" (28). Silk might have said that making America safe *from* Islam was a third.

Karim H. Karim (2002) writes that journalistic coverage of Islam after 9/11 already had a pattern on which to rely. The pattern of coverage regarding "violence, terrorism, and Islam" (102) was already in place on 9/11, and the media continued its pattern. For three decades, US media had already decided that terrorism was used only by those who oppose the United States or its allies, such as Israel. When the United States trained repressive regimes or bombed other nations, that was not to be called terrorism. Nuclear weapons were not terrorism. As Max Weber had declared, only the state has the authorization to use violence. To use violence against the state is terrorism.

The story line, then, in the US television media was clear and monolithic on 9/11: Islamic terrorists attacked the United States; therefore, the United States must defend itself and destroy them. The media followed the president in this regard. Countervailing voices were brushed aside as "interviewers sought confirmation for their perceptions about an endemically violent Islam" (Karim 2002:105).

Karim acknowledges that part of the problem in American mass-media mystification of Muslim societies was that Muslims have not made their ethical, humanistic aspects known in the West—or, as he calls it, "the North." Muslim societies have not developed their democratic potential, and they have allowed political extremists to serve as Islam's spokesmen. Nor have Muslims seemed

to understand liberalism, secularism, materialism, multiculturalism—the kalei-
doscope of Western ideologies (106–7). In addition, Muslims have allowed their
resentment of Israel to turn to anti-Jewish sentiments, thus the Western view of
"Islam as being anti-Judaic" (107).

Yet Western media often seem disingenuous in their treatment of Muslim
topics. They claim to want to liberate Muslim women from Islam, but the constant gaze makes Muslims defend female honor all the more. Western media
regard the *hijab* and communal Muslim prayer as signs of fundamentalism or
fanaticism, whereas Western religious symbols and gestures are considered normal. Western media do not see the diversity of Muslim cultures, and they pigeon-
hole Muslim political criminals as exponents of Islam. If white supremacists use
Christian symbols, that usage is not really Christianity, but if Al Qaeda uses
Islamic symbols, that is considered real Islam.

More deeply, Karim argues, we have one thousand years of Western images
of Muslim violence and treachery. For example, the assassins of the eleventh-
century Mideast are seen as the forebears of today's "'Islamic terrorists'" (110).
Even the *Times* mentioned the assassins in an article on Muslim science, he
points out (111).

Karim concludes that because there is "the lack of knowledge and unease
among many Northern journalists about religion in general" (112), spiritual
motivations and symbolic meanings are underplayed in favor of the "rational-
istic" (113), the political, the socioeconomic. Religious discourse—Islamic religious discourse above all—is considered bizarre and fanatical.

In the new, post-9/11 edition of his book *Islamic Peril: Media and Global Violence* (2003), Karim writes: "'The world has changed forever,' we were told repeatedly. But despite the radically unusual events, the responses of the authorities and
the media have been largely predictable" (vii). He says that media coverage of 9/11
drew upon "primary stereotypes of Muslims that have been [in] existence [for]
hundreds of years. . . . The term 'Islamic' was used indiscriminately to describe
acts of murder and destruction" (ix).

Did the *Times* do better in its post-9/11 reporting on Islam than Karim suggests? Another media critic, Aslam Abdallah (2005), asserts that post-9/11 news
reports and opinion columns in the *Times* contributed in "creating a public perception of Islam that is directly contradicted by Muslim denunciations of terrorism, and the reality prevalent in the Muslim world" (125–26). Even though the

Times tried to improve its coverage of Islam after 9/11, Abdallah writes, using Muslim experts to explain Islam, allowing Muslims to hold forth on its op-ed page, and hiring Muslim writers, the paper—like other mainstream American news media—has nevertheless projected Islam "as a faith"—a religion prone to "terrorists" and "violence"—"that needs to be changed if it is to exist in the modern world" (125–26). Let us see.

US Muslims

In her book *A New Religious America* (2001), published on the eve of 9/11, Diana Eck observes that there are now more Muslims in the United States (six million) than Episcopalians, and an equal number of Muslims to Jews (2), including a million Muslims in New York City alone (65). The first Muslim prayer offered in the US House of Representatives was in 1991 (25). Eck recounts the centuries of Islamic presence in the United States (223–86), including among African Americans, and in a subhead she proclaims, "America Is Part of the Muslim World" (260). And yet in 1997—or maybe for that reason—one could encounter a South Carolina education official saying in support of the Ten Commandments being posted in public schools: "Screw the Buddhists and kill the Muslims" (quoted on 7) if they had any objections.

In 2001, Muslims were claiming both a long history and large numbers in the United States; however, mainstream American popular opinion still perceived Muslims as outsiders to its culture. At the same time, it was said that American society, with its aims at "global consumerism" (Palmer and Gallab 2001:112) was a threat to global Islam. The media offended Muslims by demonizing them as terrorists, and the mass culture's emphasis on alcohol, gambling, and permissive sexuality was also offensive to Islamic ethics. Could Muslims ever become absorbed fully into American life?

The very notion of the cultural melting pot—the assimilation of foreigners into the American mainstream—was first popularized as an image in a 1908 play (discussed in the *Times* that year) that envisioned the melting away of the religious "'feuds and vendettas'" (Eck 2001:54) inherited from the Old World. The melting pot became the most famous of American ideologies in which all ethnicities would dissolve and a standardized American would emerge.

But what would happen to the sustaining religious bonds of the many ethnic groups? *Cultural pluralism* was the term—first used in the *Times* in 1924—that characterized an ideology less ruinous than *melting pot* to ethnoreligious particularities. According to the ideal of pluralism, America should be a symphony of many instruments, all of them beautiful.

In the decades before 9/11, the *Times* proclaimed the ideal of pluralism in regard to religions—the interfaith services and dialogues, the public codes of ethics among the Abrahamic faiths to "love" (quoted in Eck 2001:69) one another, and so on. But the paper also pondered the problematic of pluralism, mutual suspicions and tensions among groups of religionists, including mainstream stereotypes of Muslims as unmeltable ethnics in America, even though many American Muslims thought that Islam and American society were perfectly suited for each other in that both recognize freedom and diversity and the dignity of the individual (Eck 2001:222–23). If one held a sanguine view of pluralism in the United States in 2001, 9/11 was to offer a challenge with respect to Muslims' place in American life.

The post-9/11 *Times* aimed for a complex treatment of Muslims in the United States and around the world. Even if one might argue that individual articles presented stereotypes—the moderate, the militant, and so on—the overall effect was to see Muslims in a great variety of snapshots, as individuals as well as in groups, at the dinner table as well as at the mosque, as sexual as well as political beings, as students as well as mullahs. There was a humanizing effect even as there was a problematizing of the American Muslim's dual identity within the problematic of pluralism.

When it became immediately clear that Muslim individuals were suspects in the 9/11 hijackings, threats and recriminations were directed to Islamic individuals, communities, and organizations, including mosques. The *Times* followed this story from the very beginning, noting that mosques were taking extra security against potential violence directed at them. In New York City, police sentries guarded many mosques. The *Times* made a point of saying that "American Muslim groups, vastly more integrated into American society today than they were at the time of the 1993 World Trade Center bombing, were swift to denounce the terrorist acts" and that Muslims around the city were eager to donate blood and volunteer for other types of community service in the 9/11 aftermath (Sengupta 2001d).

During the first days after 9/11, the *Times* reported that ".the incidents [against Muslims] are increasing despite numerous interfaith prayer services and calls from President Bush and other officials for the public not to target anyone because of religion, race or ethnic origin" (Goodstein and Niebuhr 2001). Harassment in the form of telephone, Internet, drive-by, and face-to-face aggression—"taunts, physical attacks and arson" (Goodstein and Niebuhr 2001)—were directed at Arabs and other Middle Eastern Americans, whether Muslim or not. Muslims around the city feared for their safety and for their children as "targets of bigotry" (Hartocollis and LeDuff 2001). Some hid at home or withdrew their children from school, at least during September 2001. Horrified by the 9/11 assaults, many Muslim Americans were faced with a "confounding choice. In discussions about the loss of innocent life, do they talk about Muslim life, or do they stay silent for now?" (Sengupta 2001c). Some Muslims were mortified in the presence of non-Muslims by the hijackers' behavior; they were also suspicious of their fellows in faith, for there decidedly were pro–bin Laden and pro-Taliban contingents in their own mosques (Filkins 2001).

In New York City, a blade of mistrust cut into relations between Muslims and their neighbors and officials. Police tried to reassure Muslims in Queens that they were not targets of investigations: "We are after evil. We are not after your religion. We don't want revenge; we want justice," they said (Zhao 2001).

For all the tension in New York City, violence did not turn deadly there. In Texas, however, a Pakistani Muslim was shot to death, and in Arizona a Sikh was murdered by a man who mistook him for a Muslim. "I stand for America all the way," the killer shouted as the police handcuffed him (Lewin 2001). Mosques in several states were subjected to assault, perhaps encouraged by a "grass-roots backlash" on the Internet, which called for Americans to "'kill all of those who worship Allah'" (Lohr 2001). Christian Arabs, too, found themselves "harassed" (Niebuhr 2001b) in the unsteady weeks following 9/11.

"Perhaps even more than Muslims," reporters noted, "Sikhs in the United States have been singled out for harassment since the terrorist attacks, perhaps because the long beards and turbans prescribed by their Indian religion give them a visual resemblance to the terrorist Osama bin laden and the Taliban" (Lewin and Niebuhr 2001). The *Times* quickly printed a front-page story about the half-million Sikhs in the United States, identifying them as members of a monotheistic religious community begun in India by Hindu-born Guru Nanak in the fifteenth century, with more than eighteen million members, the world's fifth-largest religious group and completely distinct from Islam. With Sikhs under attack or at the least on the receiving end of baleful stares from mainstream Americans and the "focus of profiling at airports" (Goodstein 2001d; see also Goodstein and Lewin 2001), one young Sikh man in New Jersey cut his beard and hair in order to look "like an All-American guy," thereby provoking his family and relatives' faith-inspired rage. In post-9/11 America, the young man exclaimed, "I have to, if I can live in this country." His uncle insisted that the young man's parents should "kick him out of the house!" (Winerip 2001b; see also Lueck 2004; on Sikhs in Canada, see Krauss 2002). It was ironic and newsworthy several years later to see the prominent role of an American Sikh group, Sikh Dharma of New Mexico, in the Department of Homeland Security (Wayne 2004).

The tenor of the *Times* coverage was clear in expressing a desire for religious and cultural tolerance. Its reports about ethnic or religious bigotry carried implicit and explicit disapproval. Its stories regarding the backlash against Arabs, Muslims, and any swarthy people with beards, veils, and turbans tended to humanize those people under threat of attack. The paper emphasized the patriotism and goodwill of America's diverse citizens under suspicion simply by visual association. Recognizing the power of images to trigger aggression against Muslims, the *Times Magazine* printed "The Looks They Get" (Saint Louis and Serrano 2001): five photographs of New York City Muslims who felt very much under siege for their appearance as well as for their religion. The photo captions gave them an opportunity to express patriotic American sentiments, including the desire for revenge on the perpetrators of the 9/11 attacks.

Into early October 2001, the *Times* continued to emphasize Muslim American communities' plight under post-9/11 siege. Pakistani Americans in small-town Illinois were shown to be middle-class, patriotic, antiterrorist, anti-Taliban Muslims worried about their future and feeling the need to educate Americans about Islam (Wilgoren 2001c). The *Times* told its readers that African Americans make up 25 to 40 percent of the American Muslim population. The Muslim American Society of W. Deen Muhammad (Sunni) has 2.5 million members; the Nation of Islam has perhaps 100,000, the *Times* reported, and they, including the Nation of Islam leader Louis Farrakhan, have roundly condemned the attacks. The black American Muslims stated their love for America, but right now, they said, in the atmosphere of post-9/11 suspicion, "it's sort of like being black twice"

(Fountain 2001a; see also "2 Gatherings Reflect U.S. Muslims' Divide" 2003; "Muslim Leader among Blacks Resigns Post" 2003).

Over the weekend of October 6–8, however, the *Times* began to get more critical of Islam and even of religion more generally as its stories started to face up to some edgy tensions between Muslim and American loyalties. It would appear as if *Times* editors urged their writers to move beyond the treatment of American Muslims as innocent victims of bigotry and to ask more conflictual questions about American Islam. The pivot of coverage seemed to coincide with the beginning of American military action against Afghanistan, a new phase of the 9/11 story. When asked about the notion of this coordinated pivot of post-9/11 coverage, *Times* religion writer Laurie Goodstein (2004b) said that the reportage was "more organic" and less directed from editors than an outsider might suspect. Individual writers were trying in their own ways to examine every angle they possibly could about the topic of Islam in America and to express what had not yet been said, so the attitude merely unfolded and evolved over the weeks and months after 9/11.

Daniel J. Wakin (2007) concurs that it would be folly to define or decipher a *Times* strategy in religion coverage, even in response to 9/11. There is "ebb and flow" to topical angles, a "subjective" current that depends on reporters' impulses and editors' receptivity. Despite appearances, published attitudes should not be thought of as "systematic." Nonetheless, *Times* coverage turned a corner around October 6–8.

On October 6, Gustav Niebuhr (2001j) wrote an article about "strong and neighborly . . . ties between a mosque and Fort Bragg" in North Carolina, suggesting that black American and other Muslims were serving in the American military without apparent contradiction of loyalties. The next day, however, Laurie Goodstein (2001i) wrote a more complicated story of Muslim military clerics. There were fourteen Muslim chaplains in US service; the first, Captain Abdul-Rasheed Muhammad, was appointed in 1993. In a follow-up article written a few days later, Goodstein (2001h) wrote that although Chaplain Muhammad perceived "no conflict between being a loyal soldier and a loyal Muslim," others among the four to eight thousand Muslims in the US soldiery worried about the "'awkward situation'" of having to fight a Muslim nation were they to be sent into action in Afghanistan. When Chaplain Muhammad "sought guidance for Muslim military personnel uneasy about being deployed in the operation against

Afghanistan, . . . a panel of prominent Muslim scholars in the Middle East . . . issued a fatwa, or religious opinion, denouncing the terrorist attacks on the United States and saying it is the 'duty' of Muslims to participate in the mission to apprehend the terrorists." This unbinding edict pleased some American Muslims but "outraged" others, who saw it as a "political statement" of arguable merit according to Islamic jurisprudence. According to William Glaberson (2001), the difficulty in interpreting Islamic law in America was due not only to the "decentralized" nature of Islam, "without an institution like the Supreme Court to resolve the countless questions," but also to the "disorganized" state of Muslim communities in the United States, lacking any recognition for their legal concepts in a secular society. US Muslims were caught between their American habits and their Muslim scruples.

Mixed loyalties were made more explicit in interviews with Muslim American teenagers at the Al Noor School in Brooklyn, a private Muslim school where parents send their children to avoid secular American schooling. These teens were critical of the United States (it bullies Muslim nations, they charged) and of US anti-Muslim bias ("America is intrinsically anti-Muslim," one opined). Some doubted that Muslims actually carried out the 9/11 attack and held the United States to "blame for the ills of the Muslim world through its support of more secular Muslim rulers." The students preferred a national system based on the "perfect blueprint" of the Koran to the "separation between religion and state," and they said that they would go to jail rather than fight for the United States against a Muslim people. "In the meantime, they said, they want to become doctors and lawyers and teachers in the United States . . . , the one place where Muslims are free to be themselves." In the kicker, the school principal wondered if his students were not "too paranoid" about their position in the United States, noting that Al Noor had received nothing but "goodwill" from its neighbors since 9/11 (Sachs 2001a).

The *Times* began to record a variety of Muslim viewpoints about 9/11 and the Muslim condition in America. "Caught in the middle," American Muslims expressed "disdain for bin Laden and criticism for the U.S." (Belluck 2001). Some continued to doubt bin Laden's complicity in the 9/11 crime. "Farrakhan Wants Evidence Released in Terrorist Attacks" (2001), read a headline on October 18 concerning the Nation of Islam leader, who called on President Bush to make public any evidence he had that Osama bin Laden was responsible for the 9/11 assaults. Farrakhan had earlier "condemned the 'wild beasts' who carried out the terrorist attacks," but he nevertheless did not trust the US government's credibility. In like manner, Imam Omar Saleem Abu-Namous, leader of the Islamic Cultural Center of New York, condemned the 9/11 strike but did not accept proof yet that Muslims were responsible for the violence.

Other Muslims remarked that their fellow religionists "were living in denial, unwilling to accept that Muslims could do something so horrible" (Wakin 2001b). Some American Muslims blamed Israel for the hijackings; others suggested that "white supremacists" or "fanatical Christians" were possible perpetrators, hoping to "start the battle of Armageddon and hasten the return of Jesus," according to a Muslim professor of Islamic studies and comparative religion (Goodstein 2001j). Among the many emails Thomas L. Friedman received immediately after 9/11 from Muslim friends around the world, one asked if it was true that four thousand Jews had stayed home from the World Trade Center on 9/11 because they knew what was to come, having been tipped off by Israeli intelligence. Friedman (2003a) wrote later of "an epidemic of denial that spread throughout the Arab-Muslim world, which refused to really face how this outrage could have come from its bosom" (327). Only when a tape of Osama bin Laden demonstrated his advance knowledge of the attacks did American Muslim opinion leaders finally overcome their inherent distrust of American media and accept the United States government's version of events.

Muslim Americans had proclaimed their patriotism and muted their criticism of the United States in order to appear 100 percent loyal. They had suffered from abuse on the streets and in the supermarkets. In places such as Laramie, Wyoming—a land of bigotry, from the gay community's perspective, because of the killing of Matthew Shepard there in 1998, but also of civic responsibility because of the subsequent community condemnation of homophobic violence—the few Muslim families, there for a generation, responded to anti-Muslim bias with prayers at interfaith services, invoking the name of Mr. Shepard (Egan 2001). American Muslim leaders asked their fellows to tone down whatever criticisms they had of American policies at home or abroad (Goodstein 2001g). Then, "in a shift, Muslim groups cast themselves as loyal critics." One Muslim man who lectured on college campuses and at Christian churches noted, "After the attack . . . there was a need for differentiating between Islam as a religion and the terrorist attacks. Now that we've done that, we need to look at how our foreign policy, intentionally or not, breeds frustration among many people" (Winter 2001c).

At the same time, however, a feature on a New York Muslim woman, Aasma A. Khan, presented her as "a daughter of Islam, and an enemy of terror." Khan was "co-creator of Muslims Against Terrorism, a month-old coalition of urban professionals dedicated to educating fellow New Yorkers—and beyond—that Islam neither endorses nor tutors terrorists." She was described as a "citified, New Age Muslim who shopped at Ikea, skated in Central Park and made profitable use of her law degree." Once she had spoken out against Al Qaeda and Osama bin Laden, she was more worried about being attacked by Muslim terrorists than by mainstream Americans in a backlash against Islam. "'It's like our religion was hijacked,'" she declaimed, quoting a California imam, Hamza Yusuf (Finn 2001).

Muslim Americans had been proclaiming their numerical growth in the United States for many years, making a point of their presence and strength in the body politic. Some claimed Muslim population figures in the country were as high as 6 or even 7 million. Yet several surveys of religious affiliation in 2001 suggested much lower figures: between 1.1 and 2.8 million (Niebuhr 2001u). These divergent numbers were significant in gauging the potential impact of Islam in American life. They also made apparent how little was known for certain about Muslim Americans. The *Times* was making the point, however, that among the millions of Muslims in the United States, there were differences of opinion about America, about politics and terrorism, and about Islam. Some Muslims were very much at odds with one another; at the same time, most Muslims were stretched between their religious and national identities, "struggling to be both Arab and American" (Wilgoren 2001d).

The *Times* began to suggest that some American Muslims were a danger to the country. Law enforcement officials said that Dearborn, Michigan, with the oldest and most established Muslim community in the United States, was "crawling with 'sleeper cells'" (Wilgoren 2001d; cf. Harden 2001b). A report on Sheik Muhammed Hisham Kabbani accented that a "Muslim leader who was once labeled an alarmist is suddenly a sage" (Goodstein 2001e). Kabbani had been warning Americans for several years that 80 percent of American mosques were infiltrated by extreme and dangerous forms of Islam. He charged that plans for large-scale attacks on American soil, including nuclear weapons, had been afoot for some time. His message to Americans was "to beware the Muslims in their midst." This article treated his warnings seriously but warily, reflecting the mainstream and official responses to him in post-9/11 America.

An American convert to Islam expressed her concern not only about the threat of Islamic terrorism, but also about the "tyrannical" mood of Islamic religious expression in general. American Muslims, she cautioned, "need to realize there are really extremist elements that need to be countered openly" (quoted in Wakin 2001d). In recent years, she recounted, her mosque leadership in Oregon had taken to ordering her to stay at home rather than work, to cover her head, and so forth. She refused, determining to practice her faith in private. Her experience was said to be typical of many Muslim "moderates" in the United States.

But also representative was the sentiment of Muslims eager to differentiate themselves from mainstream America in liberal settings such as college campuses: wearing head scarves, eating specially prepared foods, and associating separately with fellow Muslims. "I am Muslim first, not even American Muslim," said one co-ed from Queens. "Because so much of the American culture is directly in conflict with my values as a Muslim, I can't identify solely as an American, or even as an American Muslim" (quoted in Goodstein 2001k). A feature in the *Times* special supplement *Education Life* returned to Al Noor school in Brooklyn, one of about 375 such Muslim schools in the United States, to explain how Muslims in America aimed to retain their religious heritage and to establish boundaries with the American way of life. The principal told how he tried to have his students take a critical look at their own community, learning to distinguish between the religion of Islam and various cultural traditions. An English teacher explained how he encouraged students to see Jewish points of view by reading *Exodus*. Nevertheless, the school's emphasis was on "lessons from the Islamic point of view . . . in a strict and sheltering atmosphere" discrete from the melting pot (Bahrampour 2001).

As the holy month of Ramadan neared in 2001, the *Times* carried on November 16—under the section heading "A Nation Challenged"—a romantic photo by Bob Rives (2001) of four Muslim women in North Carolina lighting lanterns, which illuminated their charming faces. Inside the section, illustrated by another appealing Rives photo, Laurie Goodstein (2001m) reported that American Muslims were finding themselves scrutinized but also accepted by their non-Muslim neighbors. "This Ramadan," she wrote, "mosques are opening their doors. Mosques around the country report that church and school groups have been inundating them with requests for tours, and many are planning to hold open houses for the holiday. Meanwhile, churches are inviting mosque members to get acquainted." The image conveyed by the photos and the article was that of a peaceable people—all women, their visages in full view—taking part in the pluralistic spirit of America, aiding in the progress of interfaith understanding.

The *Times* seemed to be a partner in that undertaking during Ramadan. Drawing on the habit of "mandatory Sunday parish stories" (Schmemann 2007) with "pretty pictures" of the faithful at church, the paper now turned its lens toward Muslims, presenting them in its best light. With words and pictures, the paper displayed Islamic "faith and tradition" (Wakin 2001g), both of which nurtured communities of Muslim immigrants—for instance, West Africans newly settled in the Bronx.

A photo by Steve Hart (2001) in the November 18 *Times* showed Muslim men saying their Friday prayers outside a mosque in Brooklyn. According to the caption, "Some Muslims said they feel like targets in a larger society where 'Muslim' is often equated with 'terrorist.'" The picture seemed determined to dispel that biased formula. So did the recognition of the first Muslim-designed American stamp, issued by the US Postal Service ten days before the 9/11 attack. After a five-year campaign by Muslims to have it adopted, the stamp—commemorating "the two most important Muslim holidays: Eid al-Fitr, the end of Ramadan fasting and Eid al-Adha, at the end of the pilgrimage to Mecca"—made Muslims such as the executive director of the American Muslim Council feel "as if their country has recognized them." The stamp's designer remarked that he knew Christians and Jews who planned to use it for their holiday cards. "People want to make a statement," he concluded (Goodstein 2001q).

Since Ramadan coincided with Thanksgiving in 2001, the *Times* examined the competing or complementary requirements of the two seasonal rituals for American Muslims. "Thanksgiving in a Time of Fasting: In Brooklyn, Healing Rhythms of Ramadan" (Wakin 2001i) showed an Arab American family, with a son in the National Guard, fasting and feasting for Ramadan but not celebrating Thanksgiving. For them, Ramadan took precedence. "It is a time of listening to Koranic verses in the mosque while going without Britney Spears at home," according to the reporter. Even in years when the feast day of American civil religion stands alone, the family does not celebrate Thanksgiving. "I try to teach my kids that we should be thankful all the time," said the man of the house.

In Illinois, a black American family made up of Muslims, Jews, and Christians celebrated Thanksgiving during Ramadan. "The spirit of Thanksgiving is probably the one celebration in the American calendar that really goes to the heart of Islam," said one Muslim man, "that is to always and continually be thankful to God" (quoted in Fountain 2001; cf. Herszenhorn 2001b and Severson 2001).

In the 1990s, the *Times* seemed to regard the shift from the Nation of Islam to orthodox Islam with some relief, regarding black Muslims as a threat to American society but Islam as a reputable, great religion of the world. Participation in Islam might pacify these American militants, make them less racially hostile to whites. Ironically, after 9/11 black American Muslims were treated somewhat like the "safe Muslims," uninvolved in international terrorism. Now Islam was the danger, not these homegrown black Americans, most of whom had Christian relatives and were once Christians themselves.

The *Times* coverage of African American Muslims was deepened by the reporting of John W. Fountain, who was then a national correspondent based in Chicago, his hometown. Now a professor of journalism at his alma mater, the University of Illinois at Urbana-Champaign, he was already in 2001 a "licensed minister with Pentecostal roots" (Fountain n.d.), having served as a youth minister in his grandfather's church. In his memoir *True Vine* (2003), this black man tells of his religious calling from poverty to "real faith, . . . from hard times to *The New York Times*" (n.p.). He has also written about the God who became his real father when his alcoholic father had abandoned his family (Fountain 2005a). Although not writing about his Christian roots in the *Times,* Fountain was able to capture the familial spirituality and vulnerability of Muslims in the months following 9/11.

In order to "find a fresh news angle" in the "over-saturation" of Muslim coverage—"reading the same stories over and over again"—Fountain (2005b) hoped to interview members of Chicago's Nation of Islam about the post-9/11 American "backlash" against Islam. He was told, however, that Minister Louis Farrakhan had forbidden his followers to speak with the mainstream media. "We can't talk," Fountain was told repeatedly by black Muslims, and so "the story went dry." Instead, Fountain made contact with African American Muslims beyond the nation—in restaurants, in mosques, by telephone—and "they were much more willing" to give the *Times* their story for what Fountain called a "think piece, a mood piece," which appeared on October 5, 2001 (Fountain 2001a).

His editor assigned him the story about Ramadan's overlap with Thanksgiving described earlier, and Fountain was fortunate to find a family who allowed him into their home. The man of the house even gave the reporter a Koran as a parting gift when the story was filed. Fountain (2005b) recalls that although he knew that "Jesus Christ is my Lord Savior" and that Christianity and Islam "differ strongly," as a reporter of faith he brought "a kind of reverence, a kind of respect," to people of other faiths, especially when he saw the "commonality" of Muslim "faithfulness" with his own.

Fountain's African American identity gave him both the "sensitivity" and the "entree" to these stories, to African American Muslims who had been targeted by racism. So, too, his Christianity was a point of contact with the subjects of his reporting. His religious experience provided "insight" rather than "bias" in writing his stories—about Muslims, Catholics, evangelicals, missionaries, exorcism and evolution, and prayers in time of war. "I'm secure in my Christianity," he says (2005b). His faith is "not intolerant," he remarks, and it is "not my job to convert everybody I come into contact with." At the same time, he is already familiar with faith experience: "I don't have to learn about the joy. I already know it." For these reasons, he considers himself a good reporter of things religious. He was pleased in the fall of 2001 to slake the "great thirst" at the *Times* and in America "to understand Islam." He and his journalistic colleagues were "forced to do a better job" of reporting on Islam in America. "We still have a long way to go," he concludes.

As Christmas approached in 2001, the *Times* ran an article on the "silent, secular majority of American Muslims" in the United States—the investment bankers and other professionals who go to mosque once or twice a year; who aren't "into rituals," as one man said, who practice "moderation" in their religion, and who claim that the Koran sanctions such moderation. "Sometimes called Id (pronounced eed) Muslims, because they take part in the major Islamic festivals of Id twice a year, cultural Muslims are akin to the so-called cafeteria Catholics, as Roman Catholics who pick and choose the customs they observe are popularly designated." They feel pressure from other Muslims to be devout or at least to feign devotion, but they are not that way. "I had the privilege of being exposed to other religions from the very beginning, so I wasn't so fixed on the idea that Islam is the only way to live," commented a banker, pictured with his wife before a Christmas tree in their Los Angeles living room (Goodstein 2001p).

When asked about this article and especially the revealing photograph by Misha Erwitt, Laurie Goodstein (2004b) remarked that photographers are journalists in their own right and that they convey news stories and features in cogent ways. In this case, Goodstein interviewed the couple on the telephone (there was no dateline on the article). She had wanted to write a story on secular Muslims because she was frequently encountering them in her research for other post-9/11 stories. She thought that cultural but somewhat unobservant Muslims deserved a hearing in the press. After speaking with them and writing her piece, she did not know what this couple looked like until she saw the photograph. She was impressed—as anyone would be—with the picture's effectiveness in expressing the subjects' character. There are "so many decisions" that go into the total story, she explained, with text editors and photo editors working together to create a meaningful narrative out of independent parts. The result in this case was a commentary on the variety of Muslims in post-9/11 America, the persistent secularism in American private life, and the many ways in which Americans observe Christmas—themes that have interested the *Times* for years.

Before 2001 came to a close, a distinguished professor of international relations and a specialist on conflict and security in the Third World at Michigan State University, Mohammed Ayoob (2001), reflected in an op-ed on his fellow Muslims' position in American society. Why were they subject to suspicion and tainted with terrorism in the aftermath of 9/11? Many of them, he argued, "fail to recognize that the link between Islam and terrorism is also the result of extremist groups' appropriation of the Islamic idiom to legitimize their actions. Worse, such appropriations were rarely, if ever, denounced by mainstream American Muslim organizations before 9/11. Had responsible Muslim leaders in America been vigilant and forceful in condemning such extremism," he proposed, "the connection between terrorism and Islam would not have been so readily fixed in the public's mind. The Muslim community is now paying dearly for this failure." What was his suggestion for a "Muslim American agenda"? He wrote, "Muslims, especially first-generation immigrants, need to define themselves as Muslim Americans—with a focus on issues in this country," including those important to native-born, African American Muslims. In effect, they should immerse themselves in the melting pot, not only culturally but also politically.

In 2002 and beyond, the *Times* continued to report with frequency about Muslims in America. They were said to be under siege in the United States, suspect for their religious beliefs and associations, including their charitable organizations (see, e.g., Firestone 2001a). While reporting on the many charges made against American Muslims, the *Times* quoted them liberally in their own defense, often citing their professed ideals. The *Times* emphasized the ways in which Muslim Americans were similar to other religious Americans in their spiritual practice, in their need for professional guidance, and in their tensions with a society perceived as secular. Muslims were often torn between their religious duties and cultural influences as well as between their Muslim and American loyalties.

In the year following 9/11, US Muslims found themselves persistently designated as potential enemies in their country. According to Mark Silk (2002) in *Religion and the News,* "President Bush largely ceased his public outreach to America's Islamic community. Politicians down the food chain seemed to follow suit" (1). The condition of Muslim Americans was not anywhere nearly as bad as that of the Japanese after Pearl Harbor, but it was knotty enough to be reported on by newspapers such as the *Times* on the first anniversary of 9/11 (Egan 2002).

In 2002, vandals in the American heartlands continued to strike occasionally at mosques. Even when non-Muslims offered all manner of support to those under attack, American Muslims felt the threat daily ("American Muslims" 2002). Federal prosecutors brought charges of terrorism against African American Muslims living in a handful of "isolated Islamic settlements established across the country by followers of the Muslims of the Americas, a group that promotes advanced studies in Islam and encourages its members to live in small villages, 'free from the decadence of a godless society'" (Thomas and Blumenthal 2002). In the "Book Reviews" section, under the heading "Suspect Thy Neighbor," *Times* editorial page editor Ethan Bronner (2002), reviewing Steven Emerson's *American Jihad: The Terrorists Living among Us* (2002), reported on the argument that "there are secret terrorist cells" conducted by Muslims "in cities all across America." Emerson's book was built on cautionary arguments he had made in an earlier book on the destruction of Pan Am Flight 103 and in the pages of the *Times* and elsewhere since the World Trade Center bombing in 1993. Bronner concluded that Emerson may have gone too far in his accusations, "but he is an investigator who has performed a genuine service by focusing on radical Islamic groups in this country. His information should be taken seriously—just not at face value."

In the climate of distrust, officials at Muslim schools such as Al Noor were intent on "steering clear of politics" (Zhao 2002b). As related in the *Times,* a *Washington Post* article located "anti-Semitic and anti-Christian views" in the classroom of an Islamic academy in Virginia. Al Noor teachers were directed to focus on "'academics,'" and not to "'fire up the kids'" with any expressions—in speech, in assigned books, on the blackboards—that would reflect badly on the school, or on Islam, in the American media (Zhao 2002b).

For whatever public attention was directed to wholesome or quotidian activities by American Muslims—their search for spiritual guidance while at college (Goldscheider 2002); their keeping to the dietary rules of "halal, which are similar to those that govern kosher" restrictions among the Jews (Donovan 2002); their attempt to function according to the antiusury moral code of sharia in attaining home mortgages (McDowell 2003); their "embracing the American prom culture of high heels, mascara and adrenaline while being true to a Muslim identity" (P. Brown 2003); their responses to a New York voter-registration campaign (Healy 2003; see also Hauser 2004); their participation in the eighteenth annual Muslim Day Parade down Madison Avenue (see Ozier Muhammad's photograph of Muslim police officers at prayer, "A Day to Honor Their Faith," September 29, 2003)—they still lived their lives under a cloud of distrust.

Muslims near Washington, DC, accused the Bush administration of "racial and religious harassment, citing the Justice Department's request that 3,000 Muslims living in the United States submit to voluntary interviews, as well as a series of federal raids . . . on homes, businesses and charities in Northern Virginia" (Kahn 2002). A Zogby International poll found that, based on their experiences in the workplace and in public after 9/11, "57 percent of American Muslims believed Americans held unfavorable opinions of Muslims and Arabs" (Sachs 2002c; see also "Bias Incidents Against Muslims" 2002). It was even a matter of doubt that a Muslim accused of terrorism could receive a fair trial in the United States (Lubet 2002). Some Muslims found it necessary to surround themselves with American flags—as illustrated by a Joyce Dopkeen photograph on April 25 (Sachs 2002c)—and with other symbols of American patriotism. Others were discouraged regarding their prospects in America and thought either to submerge their Muslim identity in order to assimilate or to leave the country.

An op-ed headline exclaimed: "Moderate Muslims under Siege" (Abou El Fadl 2002). Khaled Abou El Fadl, a professor of Islamic law at the University of

California–Los Angeles (UCLA) and author of several recent books about Islamic law, authority, aesthetics, tolerance, rebellion, violence, and women, wrote that "Muslims like me are grieving and in utter misery." Since 9/11, he explained, American Muslims had to counter "proponents of a clash of civilizations," maligners of Islam and Muhammad, Israeli propagandists, and "fellow Muslims," who denied any Muslim role in 9/11—blaming it all on the U.S. Central Intelligence Agency (CIA) and Mossad (Israel's equivalent of the CIA). And not least of it, he wrote, "in this country, moderate Muslims have had to deal with a presidential administration that is systematically undermining their civil liberties."

Abou El Fadl (2003) expanded on this plaint in a longer essay to make his point even more clear: that there was a culture war among the many exponents of Islam, even in America (see also Jackson 2003). Amidst the intrafaith contention over modernity, authority, colonialism, and authenticity, American Muslims were in a conflicted position. In his "Beliefs" column on December 7, 2002, Peter Steinfels (2002d) remarked that "Abou El Fadl's defense of Islam's classic legal tradition against what he terms modern 'Muslim puritanism' made him persona non grata in some Muslim circles even before 9/11 and an object of death threats afterward."

The PBS documentary *Caught in the Crossfire* highlighted the current tensions of being a Muslim American. A *Times* review of this program written by Samuel G. Freedman (2002), a professor of journalism at Columbia University, complained that PBS, "so concerned with promoting tolerance," failed to probe potentially unpleasant questions about the "possibility of divided loyalties" among Muslim Americans in the United States. Freedman sought more than an image of a Muslim "victim" at the first anniversary of 9/11. However, his critique presented such a victim in a sympathetic light. The *Times* photo by Harvey Wang, taken from the documentary, showed Ahmed Nasser, a New York City police officer, prostrating on his prayer rug, a public servant in a pious pose and a difficult position. Freedman's review noted the Arab American policeman's condemnation of the 9/11 attacks; the streetside taunts hurled at his wife and children for being Muslim; his son's artistic obsession with the image of a plane hitting a tower. The whole family seemed still to be "caught in the crossfire" of events beyond their comprehension or control.

American propaganda to Muslim people around the world (a form of communication that the United States termed "public diplomacy" and that a *Times* headline writer called "Muslim-as-apple-pie videos" [Perlez 2002e]), trying to show how happily assimilated American Muslims were, failed to allay Muslims' "skepticism." With "hate crimes up against Muslims" in the United States ("Hate Crimes" 2002); with the Federal Bureau of Investigation (FBI) ordering field supervisors to "count local Muslims and mosques," which "Arab groups and others see as a new form of racial profiling" (Lichtblau 2003a); with American Muslims "resentful of treatment" but still attempting to "work with authorities" in law enforcement (Goodstein 2003b); with Muslims protesting uncharged detentions of their fellows and subversions of the Bill of Rights by Homeland Security and the war on terrorism (Swarns 2003); with threats of deportation against Muslim immigrants already swimming the American mainstream (Kilgannon 2003a), evidence accumulated of a troubled relation between American Muslims and their chosen land. Justice Department officials called a "great success" a program that checked up on well more than a hundred thousand Muslim "male immigrants and visitors, predominantly Muslims," and that targeted more than thirteen thousand for deportation. Whereas many Muslims understood the US government's needs, many were "fearful, angry or confused" (Swarns and Drew 2003; see also Swarns 2003a and Cardwell 2003a).

Times reporter Corey Kilgannon (2007), who wrote sympathetically about one Pakistani American teen threatened with deportation, says that Muslims were "demonized" in the years following 9/11. Kilgannon wanted this story (Kilgannon 2003a; see also the photographs by Marilynn K. Yee) to show the young man's humanity and the impropriety of expelling an assimilated immigrant from the country he loved. Indeed, at the youth's hearing before an immigration judge (see Kilgannon 2003c), Kilgannon's article served as evidence of the fellow's adjustment to American life. "It was the best thing I ever did," Kilgannon (2007) avows. The *Times* article "kept [the teen] from being deported." It "shamed the bureaucrats," and "the kid hugged me" after the decision was rendered.

Not all stories turned out so well. Some Muslims in Brooklyn perceived a collapse of their community as a result of post-9/11 hostility toward them (Elliott 2003). With a poll showing that many Americans thought of Islam as "more likely than other religions to encourage violence among its adherents" (Steinfels 2003e), the *Times* perhaps needed to make a point of calling "an accident" a fire at a mosque in Elizabeth, New Jersey, so as to dissipate suspicions of anti-Muslim arson (M. Newman 2003). As the second anniversary of 9/11 approached, a

Muslim fellow at the Brookings Institution, Muqtedar Khan (2003), found that many American Muslims—chafing under a "civil rights environment" that had "declined drastically with the passage of the USA Patriot Act and other anti-terrorism measures"—were feeling their "American citizenship" to be "fragile." Even the former executive director of the American Muslim Council and president of the American Muslim Foundation, Abdurahman Alamoudi, who had met with President Bush, was arrested on charges of terrorism in regard to his advice to Muslim chaplains in Guantánamo Bay, Cuba ("U.S. Charges Islamic Leader" 2003). Other Muslims claimed bias at their jobs (Saulny 2003).

Some New York Muslims—African Americans and African immigrants— were willing and eager to serve the FBI as informers in a "'citizen academy'" against "suspicious visitors" who might foster terrorism. An Ivory Coast immigrant who became an imam in Harlem and who lost a cousin in the World Trade Center attack exclaimed, "'We came here for the American dream ourselves,' . . . adding that terrorists 'don't like us'" (Moss and Nordberg 2003).

Many Muslim soldiers took part in the US invasion of Iraq in 2003. Nevertheless, Muslim Americans encountered suspicion and hostility from their non-Muslim counterparts. "'Just Shoot Me'" (Clemetson 2003), read the headline of a short piece on Petty Officer Naveed Muhammad, one of two Muslims on the carrier *Abraham Lincoln*. Muhammad, who had immigrated to Dearborn, Michigan, at age nine, was confronted by several sailors, one of whom asked "when he was going to become a terrorist." His reply: "I told him if I was such a danger and he was such a patriot, why didn't he just shoot me now and save everyone the trouble later." When interviewed, he was meditating on his prayer rug in the chapel aboard ship.

The very pillars of Islam were under federal investigation. Almsgiving *(zakat),* one of the primary religious duties of faithful Muslims, was institutionalized in various charitable organizations. In an attempt to freeze assets that might support terrorism, the US government seized funds of Muslim charities such as Holy Land Foundation for Relief and Development, especially if they supported Hamas and other "militant" Palestinian groups. American Muslims seethed: "'Palestine is occupied! The Israelis are the occupiers!' they shouted at first, and later: 'Holy Land is helping the persecuted! The widows! The orphans!'" They accused the Bush administration of "merely trying to appease the Israeli government. 'This is politics, pure politics. . . . This is trespass from the war on terrorism to an attack on Muslims.'" Holy Land chairman Ghassan Elashi decried the charges: "The government is using Israeli information to take away the civil rights and due process of American Muslims. . . . It is the same thing as McCarthyism, and we are going to request a meeting with President Bush" (Milloy 2001a).

The *Times* continued to cover the story of Muslim charities: their possible connection to the "financial web" of terrorism (Eichenwald 2001a); the seizing of assets (Shenon 2001); accusations of money laundering in order to funnel many millions of dollars to Al Qaeda (Lichtblau and Glaberson 2003; Newman and Khan 2003); testimonies of innocence by the heads of "'faith-based humanitarian'" agencies engaged in "'charitable work around the world'" (N. Lewis 2002); judicial judgments against charitable groups (Firestone 2002c); an occasional guilty plea ("The Money Trail" 2001). In some cases, American Muslims grew wary of donating funds to Muslim charities because they feared being fingered as a terrorist fellow traveler (Goodstein 2003j). Given the federal investigation of the local Al Farooq Mosque for alleged Al Qaeda fund-raising, the article "Brooklyn Muslims, Disputing Any Ties to Terror" (A. Newman 2003) closed with an expression of anguish by a Muslim from Uzbekistan, now of Bay Ridge: "Every place they collect money, but nobody knows where it's going." In an op-ed, the director of the Muslim Public Affairs Council, Salam Al-Marayati (2002), argued that the United States should "indict individuals, not charities" if the charge of abetting terrorism were found to be true. He stressed, "American Muslims take seriously their duty to help other Muslims around the world. We also take seriously our duty as American citizens. There is no reason these two values cannot coexist." Nevertheless, the government investigation of Muslim charities continued in 2004 and beyond (Lichtblau 2004; Ruethling 2004; Shenon 2004; Strom 2004), including an investigation into the peculiar activities of a government witness, Mohamed Alanssi (Files 2004; Glaberson 2004).

Over the several years after 9/11, the *Times* continued to peruse the lives of American Muslims in a manner both sympathetic and investigatory (e.g., Baker 2004; Berger 2004b, 2004c; Bernstein 2004; J. Brown 2004; Capuzzo 2004; Dao 2004a, 2004b; Elliott 2004b; Goodstein 2004a, 2004d; Hedges 2004b; Herszenhorn 2004; Kilgannon 2004a, 2004b; Leland 2004; Lipton 2004; Luo 2004; A. Newman 2004; Preston 2004; "Repeated Vandalism" 2004; Safire 2004a; Wakin 2004a, 2004b; Zezima 2004).

Part of the sympathy arose from the realization that Muslims faced similar strictures to Jewish and Christian religionists in the secular city. For instance, Joseph Berger—who had covered religion for *Newsday* and the *Times* in the 1980s—was focused on a project concerning urban change and immigration. In 2003, his father died. "I needed places to say kaddish for him," Berger (2007) writes. "I was stunned at how many choices I had in midtown—a reflection of the growing clout of the Orthodox in the Jewish life of the city." As a result of this "personal experience," Berger came to pen a piece on Muslim "prayer amid the office machines" of Manhattan (Berger 2004c). Later in 2004, an illustrated feature on family foods at Ramadan (Nathan 2004) was surely a sign of the *Times'* acceptance of Muslims.

Official American suspicion regarding foreign Muslims—the scholar Tariq Ramadan, the singer Yusuf Islam (formerly known as Cat Stevens), and others—seeking to enter the United States three years after 9/11 was a newsworthy matter (Fouquet 2004; Kinzer 2004; Ramadan 2004; Sontag 2004a; Tyler 2004b). On occasion, the *Times* also described post-9/11 Muslim lives in Canada (Krauss 2004a, 2004b). The Muslim American story clearly had legs.

It may have seemed ironic in a post-9/11 climate of American distrust toward Muslims, but Islam continued to be "the nation's fastest-growing religion." By the thousands, largely among the black population, Americans were converting to Islam, and "many say the events of Sept. 11 only confirmed their commitment" (Wilgoren 2001a). A *Times* article by Jodi Wilgoren (2001a) featured white converts, some of whom had to cut their familial ties when they became Muslims. An accompanying photograph by Tim Parker showed a St. Louis lawyer who had studied to be a Jesuit priest before converting to Islam, on his prayer rug in a meditative posture.

An article surveying the twenty-five thousand or so Hispanic Muslims in the United States—especially women—noted that whereas some converted in order to marry a Muslim, others had grown tired of Catholic hierarchy or dogma and wanted a change (Nieves 2001a). Some sought a religious tradition that resisted modernity better than Catholicism. A follow-up article focused on Alianza Islamica, one of the oldest organized Latino Muslim groups in the United States, founded in 1975. One of its leaders, a Puerto Rican in the Bronx, spoke of Islam's appeal to a social critic in the 1970s: "The culture was becoming more commercial. We didn't want to give up the struggle, so we looked in different places. Islam represented a place for us to be part of a larger community. When we realized that within Islam there was every spectrum of people, regardless of class, regardless of race, we were attracted to that universal principle of human interaction and communion with the divine" (Wakin 2002h).

In contradistinction to these several sanguine reports on Muslim converts' piety and community, the *Times Magazine* conducted a page-long interview with V. S. Naipaul, the new Nobel laureate for literature, who had been prominent for years for his criticism of Islam. He was especially worried, he said, about the converts to Islam because they feel they must prove themselves to their newfound cause. Their strong sense of piety, their engagement in Islamic "brotherhood," their desire for paradise will goad them toward extreme manifestations of religious zeal, he claimed regarding "the neurosis of the convert" (Shatz 2001).

As if on cue, in the midst of the war in Afghanistan a sensational American Muslim convert materialized. Enter John Walker Lindh, an ambitious news editor's dream. Whereas there had been a few stories about homegrown Americans— blacks and whites and Latinos—who had converted to Islam and even about some Muslim Americans who felt the tug between their religious and national loyalties, here was a story about a convert who fought for Islam against the United States. "A U.S. Convert's Path from Suburbia to a Gory Jail for Taliban" (Nieves 2001) introduced Lindh, whose parents—the lead said—"knew he was a different sort of boy." No football, no fast cars, but rather "holed up in his room studying thick treatises on world religions, Buddhism, Native American religions, Hinduism. Raised a Catholic but encouraged by his parents to choose his own spiritual path, Lindh studied them all. That is, until Islam captured his heart and soul and propelled him on a journey that ended over the weekend when he was captured as a fighter for the Taliban in northern Afghanistan." This story read as a scary advisement against comparative religion, a case study of a spiritual seeker leaving behind his native religion, experimenting freely with various forms of faith. Converted to Islam at sixteen, Lindh "left Marin County, known for its progressive politics and millionaires, because he found it too difficult to be a Muslim there." He traveled to Yemen, and before long he was a soldier in the ranks of the Taliban.

The *Times* carried many articles on the legal aspects of this convert's capture and trial (e.g., N. Lewis 2001). More interesting for the study of religion was a dichotomous article, "One for His Country, and One Against It" (Harden and Sack 2001), contrasting the lives of John Walker Lindh (referred to here as

"Walker") and an American soldier, Johnny Michael Spann, who was killed in battle in Afghanistan and whose death, some say, was Lindh's fault. Spann grew up "foursquare" in Alabama; he wanted to be a CIA officer. He felt at home in American society. Lindh was a "walker," seeking a path beyond the American garden of possibilities. "Every place has its culture, but I like the Muslim culture the most," he was heard to say.

To many Americans, Lindh was a traitor to the American way of life, its civic culture, and potentially a criminal to be convicted and punished in a "conspiracy to kill Americans." As the case developed against him, the *Times* reported: "A cousin, also a convert to Islam, calls Lindh a 'true hero' and says he is innocent" (Nieves 2002). Lindh's relative compared him to the boxer Muhammad Ali, who converted to Islam and saw the side of a people under attack by American might in the Vietnam era. The *Times* reporter quoted these claims but remained neutral regarding their validity. A *Times Magazine* interview with another white American convert to Islam—a "holy warrior" who had fought against the Russians in Afghanistan and had written a book about it—raised concern about his passion for fighting, while printing his judgment that "ultimately Islam is peace" (Barrett 2002).

The paradox of Muslim converts' embrace of peace and violence, repentance and criminality, was the subject of a *Times* "Religion Journal" feature about prison inmates searching for the "true nature of Islam" (M. Fuchs 2002). In the past generation, Islam had become the most prominent religion in many prisons and even more prevalent since 9/11. Most prison converts to Islam were African Americans seeking not only sources of comfort and strength, but also channels for their anger. Some greeted the World Trade Center destruction in vengeful celebration; others aimed to locate what they could call "'the true Islam'" (M. Fuchs 2002). When H. Rap Brown, now a Muslim convert named Jamil Abdullah al-Amin, went on trial for a killing in Atlanta, the *Times* (Firestone 2002a) made no overt reference to 9/11, leaving it to readers to imagine any connection to radical Islam. When John Allen Muhammad and his youthful partner were captured after their murderous rampage around the suburbs of Washington, DC, the *Times* examined Muhammad's 1985 conversion to Islam and the religion's help to him in finding "his identity as a black man." But there was also a hint that this unbalanced man was unhinged by hidden religious extremism, leading him to proclaim, "I am God" (Harden 2002).

Converts to Islam could be heroes or victims or villains. Along with other Americans and many Saudis, Sergeant Obadiah Y. Abdullah—"who loved Islam and basketball and ancient history"—was killed by "Islamic terrorists" in a bombing in Riyadh. His wife, "who did not convert to Islam herself, attested that "her husband was not dogmatic, and never insisted that she follow his path" (Schemo 2003). Nevertheless, converts in the military were under suspicion, especially when one—Sergeant Hasan K. Akbar—was accused of attempting to kill several comrades because of having overheard jokes about "'raping and plundering' Iraqis" (Gettleman 2003). Another convert-soldier, Ryan G. Anderson, faced charges in 2004 for allegedly trying to help Al Qaeda (Janofsky 2004; Kershaw 2004).

An extensive treatment (Sachs 2003f) of a Muslim missionary group, Tablighi Jamaat (a name translated as "'group that propagates the faith'"), threw light on one means by which Americans were converted to Islam and possibly to Muslim militance. Founded in India in the first half of the twentieth century as a response to Hindu proselytizing, the group had become an attractive spiritual organization in South Asia, with a network ranging into Britain, Canada, and the United States, its main American headquarters in Queens. Describing itself as "nonpolitical" and "nonviolent," interested in "nothing more than proselytizing and bringing wayward Muslims back to Islam," Tablighi Jamaat was suspect after 9/11 as a recruiting aid to Al Qaeda. The FBI suggested that "extremists" plucked converts from the group, using their initial enthusiasm "as an assessment tool to evaluate individuals with particular zealousness and interest in going beyond what's offered." This was said to be the case with John Walker Lindh's "path to militancy." Having worked as a proselytizer for Tablighi Jamaat (a Reuters photograph showed what he looked like in those days), he found the group's apolitical spirituality insufficient for his desire to link the political and the spiritual; therefore, he moved on in "his odyssey toward Afghanistan." In a similar way, six Yemeni American men from a Buffalo suburb—not converts to Islam, but rather Muslims whose faith had been quickened by Tablighi Jamaat efforts—got involved in military training in Pakistan and ended up pleading guilty to providing support to Al Qaeda (see the "Lackawanna Terror Case" coverage [e.g., Purdy and Bergman 2003]).

Susan Sachs's (2003f) article about Tablighi Jamaat exhibited the *Times* technique in reporting a 9/11 religion story. The front-page headline attracted readers with its notice that "a Muslim missionary group" was "draw[ing] scrutiny" in the United States. Sachs's lead told how Al Qaeda operatives used Tablighi Jamaat's name to "disguise their intentions" in obtaining airline tickets. She told of the group's spiritual origins in India, its international growth, and its religious dimensions. A photograph by G. Paul Burnett gave an impression of Muslim missionaries with their travel bags on the move in Queens. But the news story was about Tablighi Jamaat's political implication, the 9/11 angle, presented through accusations quoted from US officials. Sachs gave the group's American leadership an opportunity (but not on page one) to reply to the charges: "It's a very great accusation, a total lie. . . . Anybody who has been active in our work, who spends at least three days, will have an understanding of our peaceful nature." For a fourth perspective (after the historical provided by the author, the accusatory, and the denial), Sachs called on the scholarly: Khaled Abou El Fadl, professor of Islamic law at UCLA, who had been a member of Tablighi Jamaat twenty years earlier in Cairo: "I don't believe there's a sinister plot where they're in bed in Osama bin Laden but are hiding it," he said. "But I think that militants exploit the alienated and withdrawn social attitude created by the Tablighis by fishing in the Tablighi pond." Keeping these perspectives in mind, Sachs concluded her account with a firsthand description of "Tabligh acolytes" having coffee in Queens. As one man tried to interest the waitress in Islam, a recent convert, "sprouting a small reddish beard and dressed in a long tunic and loose trousers," spoke excitedly of his newfound faith. When asked, "Was he also interested in political causes like Chechnya, Kashmir or the Palestinian–Israeli conflict?" he "blurted," "'Man, I know I'd kill anybody who killed another Muslim.'" Sachs noted that "his two companions glared at him. One kicked him sharply under the table. 'We respect all people,'" said the man who had been engaging the waitress. "'Tablighi Jamaat taught me that you don't need to protest, that we respect the prophets of the Christians and Jews.'" That was the kicker, leaving the reader with an uneasy sense about the spiritual sincerity of this Muslim missionary enterprise active in the heart of New York City.

In the stories about Captain James Yee, American convert to Islam and chaplain to Muslim prisoners at Guantánamo Bay prison whom the US military accused of spying, the *Times* examined the contours of his conversion to Islam and his enthusiasm for his Muslim faith (Kershaw 2001a). According to David W. Machacek (2003) in *Religion in the News,* many in the news media followed the US military's lead in concluding that Yee was a "religious turncoat" like John Walker Lindh (7). Why did Yee convert? Islam seemed to fulfill Christianity, Yee said, but the media questioned his values and loyalties after his conversion in the 1990s. When charges against him proved unsupportable and were downgraded, and new charges (adultery, pornography) brought against him, most coverage failed to express indignation at the shoddy treatment Yee received from his military and his government.

The *Times* did far better in its coverage than the media treatment characterized by Machacek. Its reporters provided opportunities for avowing Yee's innocence as well as for cataloging the charges laid against him ("Army Rebukes Muslim Chaplain" 2004; "Convictions Dropped" 2004; Goodstein 2003k; "Groups Lose Sole Authority" 2003; Kershaw 2003; N. Lewis 2003a, 2003b, 2003c, 2004; Lewis and Shankar 2004; Schmitt 2003, 2003; "Washington: Army Chaplain Quits" 2004). Moreover, its commentators and editorial writers offered sympathy for him and criticism of the government case against him ("Captain Yee's Ordeal" 2003; Conover 2003), which in the end proved groundless (Golden 2004).

The US military seized the other prominent American convert to Islam, Jose Padilla, in June 2002 and kept him in confinement for years under an accusation of plotting a "dirty bomb" attack in the United States (Sontag 2004b). In an exceptionally long feature, the *Times* traced Padilla's "journey from Pentecostal child preacher to Muslim convert to suspected terrorist, from a Taco Bell in Davie, Fla., to a pilgrimage site in Mecca, to the Charleston, S.C., brig."

With Lindh, Yee, Padilla, and others, the impression in *Times* coverage of Muslim converts was that they were "unconventional" Americans (Broder 2004), with potential proclivities toward militance, yet deserving of fair legal play.

The Islamic Threat

The *Times* examined Muslims' place within America's religious and ethnic pluralism, which was under serious stress after 9/11. By and large, the paper defended innocent American Muslims from unwarranted abuses, either from emotional outbursts of bigotry or overzealous official accusations. As a longtime exponent of America's trust in interfaith understanding and cooperation, the *Times* displayed a liberal attitude toward individual Muslims, assuming their goodwill and national loyalty. In keeping with its essentially friendly view of religion's societal role, the paper perceived Islam as an ethical, community-minded force in American life.

At the same time, the *Times* recognized in Islam worldwide a mighty movement of militance—an antiworld to the paper's code of moderatism—epitomized in its extreme by Osama bin Laden and Al Qaeda, but characterized more generally by a radical austerity and intolerance. Insofar as this movement represented a substantial aspect of contemporary Islam—throughout the world, including the United States—and insofar as the movement prompted terrorism, the *Times* considered it a significant threat to America, especially to its security and that of its allies, but also to its cultural and political foundations (cf. P. Marshall 2009).

Osama bin Laden, of course, was the posterized figure of Islamic militance. Judith Miller (2001b), who had written much for the *Times* about the upsurge of militant Islam, characterized bin Laden as a "child of privilege who champions holy war," a man with a "self-proclaimed jihad, or Islamic holy war, against the United States and its allies," a foe who had declared that "it was 'the duty' of Muslims everywhere to kill Americans."

Bin Laden's was not a solitary Muslim voice. Even though the *Times* located expressions of "moderation" among Muslims everywhere, it was clear that "more extremists" were finding a "basis for rebellion in Islam" (Jehl 2001e)—rebellion against American hegemony, but also against the rulers in many Muslim lands. John L. Esposito, an oft-quoted academic expert on Islam, said, "You're talking about a small but very deadly minority" espousing the cause of violent jihad. In Saudi Arabia, bin Laden was often called "'the conscience of Islam,'" according to a *Times* report. The rich and powerful did not like him, but the "puritanical Wahhabi sect" revered him, and he was seen on the street as a "champion of Islam" (MacFarquhar 2001d).

The *Times* began to examine Osama bin Laden, Al Qaeda and its operatives, the Taliban, and militant Islam more generally, trying to understand—but not excuse—Muslim terrorism and its underlying motives, including religious ones. When the will of the alleged leader of the 9/11 hijackers, Mohamed Atta, was discovered, the *Times* emphasized its manifest devotion to Allah and Islam (Shenon and Johnston 2001). The *Times Magazine* carried a feature on Atta's conversion from the "easy secularism" of Egypt to the "anxious, belligerent piety" of Islamic religious cells. "A cultural war" broke out in Egypt, and Atta joined a cell in Germany, a "country of unbelief," as a "consolation," a "way of doing penance for the liberties" of the West (Ajami 2001a). There was considerable psychologizing in this piece. During the week that followed, a long biography of Atta rationalized his religious zeal as a function of his familial upbringing: how he was babied by his mother and treated like a girl (Yardley 2001b). The story did not take seriously his religious motivations as such but rather explained them away as a case study in arrested psychological development.

It was one thing to treat Mohamed Atta or even Osama bin Laden as deviant personalities, but what of the broader spectrum of Islamic militance? Stories began to edge toward the idea that Islamic terrorism was less marginal to Islam than some might wish to believe. Reports from Indonesia and Pakistan emphasized angry demonstrations of would-be jihad soldiers. "Go to hell America," shouted one Indonesian man, who ironically had an American girlfriend and was fond of many aspects of American popular culture. So were other Indonesians (Michael Jordan was a sports hero to many). Nonetheless, their loyalty was to Islam, and, as Muslims, they wished to sweep Indonesia clear of Americans (Mydans 2001e). Thousands in Pakistan rallied for the Taliban and bin Laden and against the United States and Israel, both of whom were denounced as indifferent to Muslim lives. A mullah blamed the Jews for the 9/11 terrorism; everyone in the audience agreed. "Osama talks to Allah," said another orator to exclamations of affirmation (Bragg

2001). In a *Times Magazine* portrait, an Islamic militant in Pakistan readied himself for "battle. Somewhere. . . . 'I like jihad the most, when it's at its peak,'" he confided to the interviewer, and he looked forward to the unification of the Muslim world, which would be expedited by an American assault on Afghanistan (Maass 2001a). In full-voiced public, Pakistani Islamists rallied their followers against the United States (Frantz 2001), including its journalists, such as *Wall Street Journal* reporter Daniel Pearl, who was brutally murdered in early 2002.

As the United States began bombing Afghanistan in its campaign against Al Qaeda and the Taliban, the *Times* reported on bin Laden's videotaped "taunts" and praise for "'Almighty God'" and for the "'vanguard Muslims'" who had attacked America. "May God bless them and allot them a supreme place in heaven," he said in his statement ("Bin Laden's Statement" 2001; Burns 2001b). In mosques throughout the world—India, Egypt, England, Pakistan, and Kenya, for example (Dugger et al. 2001), Muslims "gathered for Friday Prayers, and in many instances the preaching was political and sharply anti-American." "We feel that the United States is the terrorist," said a sheik in Nairobi. "Every single Muslim is being targeted by the United States. Every Muslim is Osama bin Laden" (quoted in Dugger et al. 2001). It became difficult in reading the *Times* to ignore the widespread Muslim sentiment that "it is the duty of every Muslim to stand up with the Afghan people and fight against America"(quoted in Jehl 2001b).

In order to understand the hijackers' motives, the *Times* published a "terrorist manual" supposedly used by bin Laden's Al Qaeda network, which stated its objectives up front: "The confrontation that we are calling for with the apostate regimes does not know Socratic debates . . . Platonic ideals . . . nor Aristotelian diplomacy. But it knows the dialogue of bullets, the ideals of assassination, bombing and destruction, and the diplomacy of the cannon and machine gun." In its code of ethics, it advised that "religious scholars" (Weiser 2001) permit the killing of hostages. One of bin Laden's closest associates, Ayman al-Zawahiri, published an autobiography in the fall of 2001 in "'an attempt to revive the consciousness of the Islamic nation, to tell them about their duties and how important these duties are,' he wrote. Muslims need to know 'how the new crusaders hate Muslims and the importance of understanding the difference between our enemies and our friends'" (MacFarquhar 2001c).

For all their identification with bin Laden against America, many Muslims continued to deny his complicity in the 9/11 attacks, even as his taped speeches from Afghanistan professed unending "'hostility between us and the infidels'" (MacFarquhar 2001f), at least until a videotape recorded his gleeful reaction to the 9/11 news. The lead article on the front page of the *Times* announced: "Bin Laden, on Tape, Boasts of Trade Center Attacks" (Bumiller 2001). Other articles quoted ("Scenes of Rejoicing" 2001) and analyzed his candid comments, with his "guard down" (Miller 2001a). Bin Laden followed with a videotape filled with kudos for "these blessed and successful strikes," which battered America's "arrogant power" ("Bin Laden's Words" 2001).

Bin Laden was surely responsible for 9/11. Americans might regard him thus as an international criminal; however, many Muslims in many lands applauded his actions and were inspired by his continuing call for battle against Islam's putative enemies. In "Bin Laden Stirs Struggle on Meaning of Jihad" (Burns 2002a), with a dateline from Pakistan, a bearded young man proclaimed that "jihad will continue until doomsday, or until America is defeated, either way."

Throughout 2002, the *Times* reflected on the nature of Islamic militancy, particularly in book reviews. Robin Wright (2002), author of *Sacred Rage: The Crusade of Militant Islam* (1985, with a new edition under a slightly different title issued in 2001), reviewed a book by a French academic who argued that the militant Islamic theocracy movement had "run its course." *Jihad: The Trail of Political Islam* by Gilles Kepel (2002) was published in France in 2000, tracing militant Islam from the 1960s to the new millennium, and Wright cautioned that the book may have seemed more convincing in its sanguine forecast before 9/11. In her own book, Wright, a journalist with ties to *Times* writers such as Thomas L. Friedman and John Kifner and three decades of experience in the Middle East and beyond, had predicted that "the growth of fanaticism, accompanied by anti-Western attitudes, is likely to mean more attacks, particularly against the U.S.— and particularly in light of the potential staying power of the crusade and the Iranian revolution" (1985:262). Even with her criticism of Kepel's book, she was not persuaded regarding the existence of America's putative "'clash of civilizations' with Islam." Instead, she asserted that a distinction needed to be made "between Muslim militancy and Islamist activism. One is malignant; the other can be benign—potentially even positive" (2001:288).

Daniel Pipes, whose earliest book was a published version of his 1978 Harvard dissertation on Muslim military systems and who had written several other books in the 1980s and 1990s on the Islamic threat to the West, produced *Militant*

Islam Reaches America (2002b), a collection of alarmed essays. "Does Islam threaten the West?" he asked. "No, it does not. But militant Islam does threaten it in many and profound ways. There is, indeed, no comparable danger in the world today" (3). With Islam, he said, there was a battle raging between secularists (e.g., Turkey's government) and Islamists. Moderate Muslims existed, but there were no moderate Islamists. The latter were antidemocratic, anti-Semitic, antimoderate, and anti-Western. Their goal was to "'conquer America'" (111) through conversion, infiltration, and terrorism.

Historian David Schoenbaum (2002) penned a review of Pipes's book, "Opening Western Eyes to a View of Islam," noting Pipes's claim that "Islamism" is an ideology of perhaps 70,000 of the 1.3 billion Muslims in the world—a "global menace," to be sure, but more comparable to "the great totalitarian heresies, fascism and Communism," than to old-time Islam. A second assessment of Pipes's book, by Judith Miller (2002), said the following: "The administration has resisted defining militant Islam as the enemy, particularly at home. Bush has been vague about the identity of America's enemies. They were not militant Muslims, nor Islamists who espoused violence, but generic 'evildoers,' 'parasites,' those 'motivated by hate.'" Pipes was not reticent to name America's foes. He said bluntly and polemically that Islamism was the enemy, and wherever it had triumphed (Iran, Sudan, Afghanistan), its record was horrendous. Pipes distinguished between Islam and Islamism, but he also asserted that moderate Muslims had been "complicit" in Islamism's rise. Miller called Pipes "intemperate" but said that he could be "forgiven" because he had been warning the United States of Islamism for a decade, and almost nobody took him seriously—until 9/11.

Indeed, in his book Pipes (2002) wrote that political correctness had kept Americans from recognizing hard truths about Islamists. He said that we must "demand objectivity from the media, which has shamefully covered up what might be criticized about Islam and Muslims" (143). "The message of September 11 was clear," he said, "allowing for no ambiguity about who is the enemy: it is militant Islam" (245), spreading its message—as the *Times* had demonstrated—through madrassas and other means. However, he concluded that "Americans are *not* involved in a battle royal between Islam and the West, or what has been called a 'clash of civilizations'" (248, italics in original); indeed, Muslims were eager to be rid of their militant rulers, as shown by *Times* reports from Afghanistan.

In the first days after 9/11, while the *Times* was reporting on America's religious response to 9/11, with US spokespersons proclaiming the innocence and spirituality of the American character, the paper was also disclosing the militant Muslim world's perception of America, a view of it quite at odds with America's self-image. "International Memo: America Inspires Both Longing and Loathing in Arab World," announced a headline (Burns 2001d). The story beneath the headline demonstrated America's enormous global impact on the economies, cultures, and imaginations of Muslims. It was America's "freewheeling, secularist ways" that both attracted and repelled the Muslim world. With transparent reference to Islam's five pillars and the etymological essence of Islam, John F. Burns wrote, "Freedom itself can be considered deeply disturbing in many of the world's poorer societies that are anchored to the old pillars of faith, tradition, and submission." Burns continued: "When the Taliban began their rule in Afghanistan in 1996 by hanging television sets from trees, banning radios and tape recorders, and outlawing music and films, they were at the extreme edge of an uneasiness that is widespread in traditional societies that have begun to feel inundated by Western, and particularly American, culture." In effect, the article seemed to say, Islamic militance was in part a reaction to America's way of life and its hegemony. Furthermore, Burns concluded, "the United States and its allies, in their military actions against Iraq, and Israel, in its violent confrontations with Palestinians, exercised within the laws of democratic nations, have endowed their actions with presumptions of moral rectitude that are widely disputed among the disempowered peoples."

If Burns represented Islamic militance as a response to American cultural and political power, Lamin Sanneh (2001), professor of religion and history at Yale University, stated that many Muslims perceived some of America's most valued traditions and institutions as odious. In an op-ed titled "Faith and the Secular State," Sanneh asked, "Why America?" Why would Al Qaeda wish to destroy the United States? Did not the United States confront the Soviet Union in Afghanistan and Chechnya, and did not the United States protect Muslims in Bosnia and Kosovo? At home, the United States offered a friendly haven to millions of Muslims. Perhaps America's support for Israel or its infidel presence on the "holy soil of Saudi Arabia" angered many Muslims. But, he argued, "what most inflames anti-American passion among fundamentalist Muslims may be the American government's *lack* of religious zeal. By separating church and state, the West—and America in particular—has effectively privatized belief, making religion a matter of individual faith. This is an affront to the certainty of fundamentalist Muslims." What was Sanneh's message? That "Muslim leaders need to embark on programs of democratic renewal—with the support of the West, if necessary. The West needs to overcome its insistence that the nation-state must be secular to be legitimate." Indeed, as Douglas Jehl (2001d) noted, "the traditions of Islam emphasize submission to religious law, leading many scholars to question whether Islam is even compatible with democracy." In this context, "moderate Muslims" in the Middle East and elsewhere worried that their voices were unheard beneath the cry, "'Jihad is the solution!'"

Even in Muslim nations such as Kuwait, once "saved" (Smith 2002a) and still defended by the United States, there was resentment toward US power, ambivalence toward its culture, and attraction to the martyrdom claimed by the 9/11 terrorists. A common theme in *Times* interviews with young Muslim men was their moral conflict between wanting to be part of the Western economy and wanting to make war on it. As depicted in the *Times Magazine,* a young Jordanian was not sure "what his life's mission should be: computer programming or jihad." The headline read, "Loves Microsoft, Hates America" (Davidson 2003).

The *Times* did more than define militant Islam as a reaction to American culture. It tried to make historical sense of the religious upsurge of Muslims worldwide and in so doing focused on a particular strain of Islam called Wahhabism. The *Times* described Wahhabism as "an austere, stringent form of Islam," the sectarian ideology of bin Laden and his followers. This -*ism,* founded in the eighteenth century, was characterized by its opposition to "modernization" in all forms (telephones, etc.); its thrust was toward adherence to the "fundamental teachings of the Koran." The Wahhabist movement—one amidst the "diversity, and complexity, of the Muslim world," as shown on a *Times* map—helped create Saudi Arabia with its military "ferocity." But Wahhabists, in their "ascetic" and proselytizing zeal (Neil MacFarquhar—who went to school in Libya, was *Times* bureau chief in Cairo, and is fluent in Arabic—compared them to Christian "Puritans"), had become dead set against the present Saudi government and its supporters, including the United States (MacFarquhar 2001e).

A subsequent article sought to explicate what it called "the deep intellectual roots of Islamic terror"—a medieval tradition called "Salafiyya," of which the later Wahhabism was an offshoot, "a minority Islamic tradition with a wide following and a deep history." In the eyes of the *Times,* present-day Wahhabists were "radicals" and "Islamists" who declared Muslim governments infidels and Westerners barbarians and who struggled violently and valiantly against authorities in Egypt and elsewhere before turning their attention to the United States on 9/11 (Worth 2001).

Then, the *Times* divulged that Saudi Wahhabists had sought for decades to recruit US Muslims to their sect, although trying not to mention Wahhabism per se when spreading the faith in America. The Saudi government had even supported this activity, with the result that as many as 25 percent of the two million Muslims in the United States who attended mosques regularly adhered to the "structures" of Wahhabism. In Russia's eastern republics, too, Wahhabism was growing and was regarded by authorities as a form of political-religious extremism. "At Friday Prayers," the *Times* reported, "the mosques are packed with young people who say that feeling persecuted by their own government only drives them deeper" (Harden 2001a; see also Waldman 2001g).

Among the most influential engines for the spread of Wahhabism and militant Islam, according to the *Times,* were the seminaries called "madrassas, that have become incubators in Pakistan for the holy warriors who say they will die to defend Islam and their hero, Osama bin Laden, from the infidels." Seventy-five hundred of these madrassas in Pakistan alone were shaping as many as a million students to "learn to recite and obey Islamic law, and to distrust and even hate the United States." These schools constituted "an assembly line for the jihad," a place where people blamed the Jews for the 9/11 attack even as students celebrated it, running through one of the madrassas, "stabbing the fingers on one hand into the palm of the other, to simulate a plane stabbing into a building" (Bragg 2001d; see also Ziad 2004). Many of these madrassas were funded by Saudi Arabia, whose schools at home were said to recruit future jihadists. According to a *Times* headline, "Anti-Western and Extremist Views Pervade Saudi Schools," and a religion lesson warned of the "dangers of having Christian and Jewish friends." As one informant said, "It is compulsory for the Muslims to be loyal to each other and to consider the infidels their enemy" (MacFarquhar 2001a).

Several articles in the *Times* reiterated the message that madrassas were training youths in Pakistan, Indonesia, and elsewhere to "'make jihad'" (Eckholm 2002) against Israel, the United States, and the West more generally, urging a "'personal jihad' in the steps of bin Laden" (Perlez 2002b). A photo by James

Nachtwey showed an Indonesian student wearing an "Osama bin Laden T-shirt under the blazer of an Islamic school said to have recruited for Al Qaeda." The clear impression from Pakistan was that madrassa clerics and students would resist any attempt by the government to curtail their functioning. Said one madrassa director, "Madras[s]as are the foundation of Pakistan" (quoted in Eckholm 2002). "'This is the lesson of the madras[s]as,' said one student . . . 'that Western Civilization is not good for Muslims'" (Fisher 2002c).

Times reporter Erik Eckholm (2007a)—Beijing bureau chief in the years around 9/11 and an experienced editor of religion coverage—recalls his brief experience in Pakistan in 2002: "I tried to let madras[s]a leaders tell what they were about in their own words; if readers got the impression that this element of Pakistan society saw the U.S. as an enemy and even refused to believe Osama was responsible for 9/11, that was an accurate perception at the time." He adds, "Of course this is in the context of the *NY Times*'s extensive efforts to fairly portray other sides of Islam: as far back as 1993, when I was a special projects editor/ writer, I edited a big (and I'd say sympathetic) series about the rising presence of Islam in America." One could be sympathetic to American Muslims; it was more difficult to appreciate "Islamic extremism" (Eckholm 2007b) in Pakistan's madrassas.

Mohamed Charfi (2002)—Algerian minister of justice and former president of the Tunisian Human Rights League—composed an op-ed that suggested how madrassas might be "modernized," as Tunisia had done when he was minister of education there. Charfi confirmed the *Times*' concern regarding the "educational systems prevalent today in Muslim countries and their role in promoting hostility toward the West." Despite the "rebirth and modernization" of Muslim countries in the previous century, schools continued to teach what Charfi called "the ancient ideology of a triumphant Muslim empire, an ideology that held all non-Muslims to be in error and saw its mission as bringing Islam's light to the world. . . . Osama bin Laden, like the 15 Saudis who participated in the criminal operations of Sept. 11, seems to have been the pure product of his schooling. While Saudi Arabia is officially a moderate state allied with America, it has also been one of the main supporters of Islamic fundamentalism because of its financing of schools following the intransigent Wahhabi doctrine."

The *Times* pointed to Saudi Arabia as the primary exporter of Wahhabism, yet 9/11 caused some Saudis to question their own Wahhabist attitudes, including their "intolerance" toward other religions. This self-scrutiny—a small stirring amidst a "facade of disavowal" regarding Saudis' role in the 9/11 hijackings—was a "significant shift in a society whose Wahhabi branch of Islam tends to make such questioning taboo." *Times* reporter Neil MacFarquhar found himself confronted with the face of Saudi Wahhabism in a conversation with a professor of Islamic law in Riyadh: "Well," said the professor, "of course I hate you because you are Christian, but that doesn't mean I want to kill you'" (MacFarquhar 2002c).

Richard Bernstein's (2002) review of Stephen Schwartz's *The Two Faces of Islam: The House of Saud from Tradition to Terror* (2002) manifested a thoroughgoing suspicion of Saudi Wahhabism and its politics. Under the headline "The Saudis' Brand of Islam and Its Place in History," Bernstein led with this statement: "In April 2002, eight months after the attacks of Sept. 11, a Saudi cleric named Sheik Saad al-Buraik, preaching in a mosque in the Saudi capital of Riyadh, called for the enslavement of Jewish women by Muslim men. 'Do not have mercy or compassion toward the Jews,' Mr. al[-]Buraik said. 'Their women are yours to take, legitimately. God made them yours.' Mr. al-Buraik, it is important to note, was a member of the official Saudi delegation that accompanied Crown Prince Abdullah during his visit to President Bush in Crawford, Tex., at the end of April 2002." Bernstein then reported on Schwartz's book, a condemnation of the "deep hypocrisy and corruption of politics in Saudi Arabia, a country that promotes and fosters an extreme, intolerant, terroristic Islamic cult even as it presents itself, in Crawford and other places, as pro-Western and moderate." The "cult" was Wahhabism, which, Bernstein said, had "waged a bitter struggle against all other variants of Islam, most particularly the tolerant, peaceful, poetically mystical schools of thought that, in Mr. Schwartz's view, are the true and admirable historic Islam." Schwartz's message, according to Bernstein, was that in our day "'the war against Wahhabism is therefore a war to the death, as the Second World War was a war to the death against fascism.'" When Bernstein wrote that Schwartz "minces no words," he meant it as a compliment, and his review was overall very positive. Indeed, in his book *Out of the Blue: A Narrative of September 11, 2001* (Bernstein and the staff of the *New York Times* 2002), Bernstein expressed similar views of Saudi Wahhabism.

Stephen Schwartz was an editorial writer for Voice of America, Washington bureau chief for the *Jewish Forward,* and interfaith activist in the Balkans. He wrote about communism in the Soviet Union, the Spanish Civil War, California radical culture, and the background to the war in Kosovo. For all the hard-headed thoroughness with which Schwartz exposes the threat of Saudi Wahhabists in *The Two Faces of Islam* (2002)—not only in Saudi Arabia's leadership and mainstream, but also as far afield (or close to home!) as the United States—the book seems equally intent on revealing the humanity of Muslims worldwide. Schwartz urges especially that "the United States should begin by reaching out to the Muslims of Bosnia-Herzegovina, Kosovo, and the other Balkan Muslim societies, which represent an authentically indigenous European Islam that is fully Westernized in its social norms while often permeated with a profound Islamic spirituality" (282). In his conclusion, Schwartz says that people in the United States had seen images only of "the evil face of Islam" (286): Wahhabism, the nineteen hijackers, the Arab street glee at the World Trade Center destruction, bin Laden and his henchmen, and John Walker Lindh's "evil glare" (287); "rich Saudis, as so often before, smiled lovingly at Americans while measuring our heads for the cut of the terrorist's blade" (287).

> But the other face of Islam waited patiently, seemingly hidden, but no less present: the face of pluralism and coexistence, of Sufis preaching love and healing, of scholars seeking new routes for the Islamic imagination, and of millions upon millions of ordinary Muslims around the world looking confidently toward a world of prosperity and stability. In tearing the benign mask away from Wahhabi–Saudi hypocrisy, paradoxically, the democratic powers and traditional Muslims had the opportunity to reveal anew at the same time the inspiring and inviting face of an Islamic civilization that could offer fresh and valuable contributions to humanity. For Westerners to miss such an opportunity would be worse than folly; it would be suicide. In defeating terror, let us therefore clasp the hands of traditional Muslims, and recognize in them our cousins, or sisters, our brothers. (287)

Reading Bernstein's review, one would not come quite to Schwartz's interfaith exhortation. And yet Schwartz's book expresses the *Times'* balance between encouraging understanding between mainstream Americans (read Christians and Jews) and Muslims of goodwill, on the one hand, and warning against the threat of Muslim extremists to America and Americans, on the other. In reviewing books such as *The Two Faces of Islam,* the *Times* pointed its readers to a larger world of ideas and opinions beyond the pages of the paper. A book such as

Schwartz's epitomized the inclusive moderatism of the *Times* as well as its sense of modernism's struggle with cultic religiosity—reading like an extension of the paper's corporate worldview.

Since the late 1970s, the *Times* had been investigating the roots of Islamic militance, while informing its readers of an Islamic revival, which it characterized as fundamentalist, extremist, and politically militant. The events of September 11, 2001, forced the *Times* to delve more fully into the religious underpinnings of Muslim terrorism, and Wahhabism was a fitting ideological catchall to explicate the jihadist movement that, like a tracer, led to the World Trade Center.

"The Philosopher of Islamic Terror" (Berman 2003b), the cover story in the *Times Magazine* for March 23, 2003, provided a name, a face, a person, and a set of clearly articulated ideas to stand for Islamic militance. An excerpt from Paul Berman's book *Terror and Liberalism* (2003c), the article was a thorough analysis of the philosophical groundwork for contemporary Islamic militance contained in the life and writings of Sayyid Qutb, a twentieth-century Egyptian theorist and activist who had studied briefly in the United States. "Qutb is not shallow. Qutb is deep," Berman said in his analysis of the ideas in Qutb's multivolume work *In the Shade of the Qur'an*. "Some of those ideas may be pathological . . . ; yet even so, the ideas are powerful" (all quotes from the excerpt, Berman 2003b).

Berman wrote that Qutb's ideas were "'Islamist.' He wanted to turn Islam into a political movement to create a new society, to be based on ancient Koranic principles. . . . Qutb wrote that, all over the world, humans had reached a moment of unbearable crisis. The human race had lost touch with human nature. Man's inspiration, intelligence and morality were degenerating." The fault lay in ancient Jerusalem, with Judaism, which, Qutb's book said, had made "'a system of rigid and lifeless ritual.'" Christianity had completely garbled the ideas of Jesus, creating an asceticism that "lost touch with the physical world," which, as Qutb characterized it, was a "'hideous schizophrenia.'" Islam possessed the right balance, the divine message, but Christian Crusaders and secularists over time had undermined Islam.

In recent centuries, the West had created a system that Qutb regarded as its most "truly dangerous element": "America's separation of church and state." According to Berman, Qutb "opposed the United States because it was a liberal society, not because the United States failed to be a liberal society." Qutb felt that there was in his day an "effort by Crusaders and world Zionism to annihilate

Islam . . . in order to rescue their own doctrines from extinction." And to make matters worse, Islamic states were coming to accept the secular ideas of the West. Qutb regarded modernity as an epoch of "jahiliyya," the dark period corresponding to the days before Muhammad's reception of the Koran, an era of "spiritual malaise" marked by political systems that placed "man above God"—including "representative democracy as well as Communism—and all culture inconsistent with Islamic law" (Shulevitz 2001). Qutb said that sharia was the answer to the threat of cancerous secularism. "Shariah, in a word," commented Berman (2003b), "was utopia for Sayyid Qutb. It was perfection. It was the natural order in the universal. It was freedom, justice, humanity and divinity in a single system." It would take a "'jihad,'" Qutb wrote, an intense, prolonged struggle, to establish sharia. Some Muslims would have to accept a "martyr's death" for the sake of giving sharia its rightful place in the world.

Berman, who had written about several aspects of American ideological life—the 1968 generation, political correctness on college campuses, charter schools, the relations between blacks and Jews—asked in his essay if the West had a contemporary philosophy to counter Qutb's, a galvanizing, motivating set of ideas worth living by and dying for. No wonder, then, that a reader said of Berman and his *Times Magazine* editors, "You are the best history teachers" (Cox 2003). According to Edward Rothstein's (2003c) review of Berman's *Terror and Liberalism* (2003c), Berman's "most important argument" was that "the war on terror doesn't just *resemble* the war on totalitarianism, it is *literally* a continuation of it. The intellectual and political roots of Islamic terror, [Berman] suggests, lie in the West" (italics in original). Berman, Rothstein said, treated Islamism not only as a homegrown Muslim movement but also as totalitarianism akin to communism and Nazism, with "intellectual and political roots . . . in the West." Qutb, Ayatollah Ruhollah Khomeini, and Osama bin Laden were as much exponents of Western fascism as they were of the Koran. In totalitarianism's assault on liberalism, the latter had—Berman argued, according to Rothstein—"too-readily succumbed, seeking to treat even its enemies as reasonable when they were not." In Berman and in Rothstein, there was a call to know not only who America's enemies were, but also what they believed. But to understand the Islamic militants' worldview was not enough. Berman—and the *Times*' Rothstein—saw the necessity to counter those beliefs with an aggressively effective liberalism. Indeed, Berman said that America needed to face this totalitarianism—which was not Islam, but only an aspect of the larger whole of the tradition—and do so in the spirit of liberalism, promoting democratic forms and attitudes. Beware of totalitarian responses to terrorism, he wrote.

Gary Rosen (2004) noted a similar caution in his review of *Occidentalism: The West in the Eyes of Its Enemies* (2004) by Ian Buruma and Avishai Margalit, which, according to Rosen, interpreted Qutb's writings as typical of a "deeply anti-liberal theme" found among Maoists, Nazis, and other demonizers of the West, including jihadists. In a second *Times* review of Berman's *Terror and Liberalism*, Rosen (2003), managing editor of *Commentary*, drove that point home. Rosen termed Berman "a banner waving liberal interventionist," steering a middle course between "right-wing 'realists,' with their cold calculations of national interest, and left-wing 'anti-imperialists,' who recoil at their country's every international move." With the war in Iraq under way, a "raging debate over what to do about Islamism and Iraq," according to Edward Rothstein (2004), was occurring on the pages of the *Times* as well as in Berman's book, leading many to define Islam's contours as counterposed to those of the West but also having some roots among Western, antimodernist intellectuals.

Who Is Truly Muslim?

From the first days after 9/11, Muslims themselves—confronted by the horror of the assault and the "foreboding" (Crossette 2001a) of accusations against the perpetrators—struggled to define their own faith. Could Muslims have carried out this massive immorality, and if so, what kinds of Muslims could they be? "Islam doesn't accept killing innocent people," said a Canadian Muslim. "If somebody is doing this, it is not Islamic." Faced with these questions, the *Times* directed its reporting toward the angle of Islam's essence, asking who is truly Islamic and who and what is not. Even on the sports pages, the question resounded. Boxer Muhammad Ali, pictured in his fighting days, a "Fruit of Islam" fez on his head, was quoted: "I am a Muslim. . . . I am an American. If the culprits are Muslim, they have twisted the teachings of Islam. Whoever performed, or is behind, the terrorist attacks in the United States of America does not represent Islam. God is not behind assassins" (Berkow 2001).

What beliefs were emblematic of Islam? And what behaviors? Many Muslims in the United States, including scholars, stated "unequivocally that nothing in Islam countenances the Sept. 11 actions," wrote Laurie Goodstein (2001o). They explained that "certain scriptural passages are distorted by Islamic extremists like Osama bin Laden." When may Muslims fight, and in what manner? Muslim scholars said that "the terrorist acts clearly violated the ethics of battle spelled out by Muhammad," both in the Koran and the hadith. America had not forced Muslims from their religion or from their homes. The victims in the World Trade Center were noncombatants. Moreover, suicide was a punishable offense to God. "Even the term Jihad, which means struggle and is associated in the West with radical Islam, means something different to most Muslims," explained Goodstein. "To them, it can refer to an individual's internal spiritual struggle, for example, and opposition to bad morals in a culture, as well as to armed conflict.

But jihad is not among the five pillars required of Muslims." As a result, the scholars said, no good Muslim could have carried out the attacks. Indeed, some Muslims distrusted the US government's report of finding the terrorists' writings with references to "'eternal paradise'" as their hoped-for reward for their martyrdom. Were the letters fake? Was Islam being framed? they wondered. Goodstein's article showed perplexed Muslims trying to come to grips with aspects and exponents of their tradition, just as Christians and Jews might have to explain the violence in their scriptures and their history.

As Goodstein pointed out, a term such as *jihad,* used in the *Times* and other news media in most stories about Islamic militance as a synonym for the phrase *holy war,* possessed a semantic range within Islamic circles, even as it was voiced as a military epithet on the streets of the Muslim world. An op-ed by Harvard professor of Islamic studies Roy Parviz Mottahedeh (2001) on Islam's tradition regarding war emphasized that "a majority of learned Muslim thinkers, drawing on impeccable scholarship, insist that jihad must be understood as a struggle without arms." To Mottahedeh, the term *jihad* did not equal *holy war* in most Muslims' minds. Furthermore, lawful war meant no harm to civilians. Terrorists are a minority in Islam, he argued, just as terrorists are a minority in Northern Ireland, and they do not represent the essence or the totality of the Islamic tradition.

The *Times* printed two views of the term *jihad* that had appeared in *Dawn,* the largest English-language newspaper in Pakistan (Husain and Haykel 2001). The first, written by a Pakistani, tied concepts of jihad to those of *qital,* or combat, justifying them when they oppose "oppression," which is "worse than killing." The second, written by a professor of Islamic law at New York University, stated "unequivocally that the war bin Laden has engaged us in cannot be labeled a jihad" because "he has acted contrary to the tenets of Islam and can be ostracized from the community of believing Muslims. Moderate Muslims will agree with me," said the professor.

An examination of the etymology and ambiguity of the term *jihad* in Islam— its spiritual meaning in personal redemption, its social application in building a just society, its present political uses in the varieties of Islam—was informed by various *Times* articles, showing how thoroughly the *Times* addressed the subject after 9/11 as a means to assess Islam's ethics (see Church 2002).

In 2002, when a Harvard student was chastised for delivering a commencement speech entitled, in part, "My American Jihad," the *Times* covered the story (Zernike 2002b) and gave op-ed space to a columnist for the *Harvard Crimson* (N. Hasan 2002) to explicate the term *jihad*. Some people at Harvard are upset at the word, Nader R. Hasan said, but uttering it is a means of "reclaiming what is ours." "Jihad," he explained, refers to the internal struggle of a Muslim of faith, and the word has been stolen by violent Muslims, creating suspicion of American Muslims. We must "show our fellow citizens that America has nothing to fear from Islam."

If one followed Daniel Pipes's (2002b) view in "Harvard Loves Jihad," published in the *New York Post, jihad* had only one meaning: "military action with the object of the expansion of Islam." But if one read Chris Hedges's (2004) portrait of an Indian-born, English-raised Muslim actor living in New York, one could observe, as the actor did, "I never heard the word jihad until it came out of the mouth of an American television reporter, . . . and I was raised Muslim." The *Times* tried to understand the violent and the peaceful aspects of the term, an indication of the *Times'* "openness," according to one scholar (Strawson 2003:20), to plumb the rich and shifting vocabulary of a religious tradition. Defining *jihad* in various ways helped to perceive the many representations of Islam from its proponents.

It also provided an opportunity for commonality between Islamic and American interests, centered in each of their senses of moderatism. Noah Feldman's book *After Jihad: America and the Struggle for Islamic Democracy* (2003a), reviewed in the *Times* (Tepperman 2003), distinguishes between the two types of jihad and argues that the time has come, already in the Islamic world, for the deeper, introspective sort: "Jihad as a struggle waged to make sense of one's own values might not be the worst way of thinking about future American efforts to encourage Islamic democracy" (234). In Feldman's view, the United States should eschew the temptation toward a military jihad of its own and should instead join forces with "Muslim democrats" to foster Islamic democracy through the principles of jihad. "After jihad," he writes, "comes a turn within, to self and to community. It is a turn away from opposition and toward combination. The mobile ideas of Islam and democracy have the flexibility, universality, and simplicity to make their encounter into a struggle for synthesis rather than supremacy" (234).

One can see if one looks at the paper over the space of even only a day or two shortly after 9/11 that *Times* personnel were trying to locate the spiritual center of Islam and at the same time to depict the widespread aberration of Islamic terrorism. While Muslim scholars debated meanings of the term *jihad* and interpretations of lawful warfare in Islamic tradition (Goodstein 2001o; Mottahedeh 2001), and Indonesian "radicals" issued "threats of holy war" (Mydans 2001e), there was a sympathetic treatment of Pakistani Muslims' faithful reverence toward the Koran (Frantz 2001e). The devoted Muslims presented in Douglas Frantz's feature tended their underground repository for thousands of their holy books, playing the role of the good Muslims, the nonpolitical Muslims, ostensibly the real Muslims for readers of the *Times*. A month later another feature from Pakistan (with photographs by Robert Nickelsberg) portrayed a local Muslim shrine where almsgivers prayed for "miracles" to sate their most pressing needs. Said the *Times* reporter, "This is Islam, but it is not the kind practiced by hard-line, politically minded Muslims of the Taliban. . . . Inside this courtyard, Islam is rich and wild and loud and imperfect, a religion in which people pray not for victory over the infidels but for a new baby, for blood to flow through a withered leg, for hands locked by arthritis pain to open like flowers" (Bragg 2001c).

Where was a *Times* reader to locate Islam? In spiritual beliefs, in ethical judgments, in ritualism, or in the politics of identity? Turn to the headline "Bin Laden's Journey from Rich, Pious Lad to the Mask of Evil " (McFadden 2001a). The title told the whole story of this biographical sketch. While explaining the development of bin Laden's hatred for the West and his motives for organizing Al Qaeda—especially his reactions to the Soviet invasion of Afghanistan, the US presence in Saudi Arabia, and Israel's treatment of Palestinians—the article pictured him as an unsophisticated thinker, not truly or deeply Muslim, but rather an extreme aberration from authentic Islam.

In a September 30, 2001, *Times Magazine* interview (P. Scott 2001), Martin E. Marty, coeditor of the Fundamentalism Project, emphasized that Muslim fundamentalists do not represent Islam. Fundamentalism *is* religious, fanatically so, he said (imagine the years of flight school, all aimed at suicide); however, "this is not Islam," he opined. "This takes Islamic texts . . . and skews them." Islamic fundamentalism, according to Marty, pretends a single reading of texts, a political, hateful, reactionary reading, and says you must act on it. In the same issue of the magazine, a portrait of "the zealot," a Muslim in Pakistan ready to fight for the Taliban, served as a proof text for Marty's characterization of fundamentalist mentality. The man spouted his hatreds and his denials. "Israel did the attack" on 9/11 to "defame" Muslims, he said. The *Times* writer did not need to comment on that notion for the readership to find the idea preposterous (Maass 2001b). Which Pakistani Muslim better represented his faith? The pious keeper of Korans, the supplicant in search of miracles, or the zealot primed for jihad?

The same question reverberated across the Islamic world; however, the *Times* seemed more intent on answering the question than many public Muslim representatives. In "Guardians of the Faith: Speaking in the Name of Islam" in the "Week in Review" section, Douglas Jehl (2001c) analyzed "the relative timidity of mainstream Islamic authorities in the face even of mass murder. . . . In fact," he stated, "Islam teaches that violence is not only justified, but obligatory, in the defense of the faith. Muslim clerics, who see themselves as the protectors of the umma, or Islamic community, have often looked tolerantly on those who claim to be using violence against Islam's foes, or to keep society on the right spiritual path." In a search for the authentic Islam, Jehl noted that, "beyond a handful of on-air and newspaper commentaries, there has been no sustained and comprehensive rebuttal of the radical theology put forth by Mr. bin Laden." Why was that? Jehl explained that Islam lacks central authority; however, the reasons also have a political dimension: Muslims are afraid of the terrorists and do not want to offend them. Muslims want to uphold a common front. Muslim leaders do not want to threaten their own power. No Muslims want to be seen as "lackeys of the West." And so, Jehl concluded, there was moral failure among Muslims worldwide to proclaim the true faith, and so the militants got to claim that true faith as their own.

Since the late 1970s, the *Times* had been covering the "culture wars" between "fundamentalists" and "secularists" in America. Over the decades, it had pointed up the distinctions among the competing parties, serving to define the issues that separated and enjoined many Americans. When 9/11 came around, the paper found another "culture war" in the world, a Muslim version of the American story, in which parties vied for the heart of their tradition.

As Ramadan came to an end in 2001, the annual fashion show by the Pakistan Student Association at the University of Houston was "a showcase of modesty. . . . But the show was not modest enough for a small group of young men from the more conservative Muslim Students Association who protested outside.

'Itaqallah,' they told the arriving guests, meaning, 'Fear God.'" The *Times* found in this vignette a struggle between "secular norms" and "a fundamentalist view that regards alcohol, the mingling of the sexes and other commonplaces of college life as sinful." The university Muslims agreed in their condemnation of the 9/11 attacks, but in regard to their personal lives one could perceive "Wahhabi interpretations of Islam from Saudi Arabia" in critique of "a fraternity in which Muslims join Hindus and Christians" (Yardley 2001a).

The *Times* made it clear that even an "orthodox Islamic school of thought" need not approve of the "virulent expression" of its own principles, as found in the Taliban's code. "A peaceful form of Islam," Deobandism, arose in a section of India "where Hindus and Muslims peacefully coexist to the eternal rhythms of sowing and harvesting." The movement "was altered as it spread" to Afghanistan, and Deoband adherents in India wished to distinguish their spirituality from the divergent "fundamentalist" politics of the Taliban (Dugger 2002f). "From bin Laden's native land," Saudi Arabia, the *Times* located "a voice to calm the angry American" and to represent the more irenic side of Islam. Khaled Al-Maeena, the editor in chief of the English-language Saudi newspaper *Arab News,* was depicted as "an unabashed America-lover" who composed comforting, embracing missives—for example, "Let's all pray for a peaceful and tolerant world"—to Americans who were outraged by the 9/11 attacks (Sciolino 2002f). Might he represent the soul of Islamic faith?

James Carroll (2002), a scholar of Catholicism, remarked that when after 9/11 President Bush distinguished between "true" Islam and the "perversions" of it by the terrorists, he received public praise, and many Americans followed his lead. "But," Carroll wrote in this review of Seyyed Hossein Nasr's *The Heart of Islam* (2002), "this radical distinction between the nefarious deeds of the terrorists and a blameless religion of Islam results in a shallow reiteration of the discredited idea that religion as such is an essentially virtuous phenomenon. The evidence suggests that religion is ambiguous, a source of consolation, hope and compassion but also of intolerance, contempt and even violence." Christians and Jews have had to face the question of evil growing directly from their religion, Carroll wrote. After 9/11, a similar question became the property of every Muslim. "That is a question Seyyed Hossein Nasr works very hard not to address in this book."

Nasr's book arose from his distinguished career as a scholar of Islam: its spirituality, science, philosophy, and art. In 1984, he left his native Iran for George Washington University, and he was the president of the Foundation for Traditional Studies. *The Heart of Islam* (2002) was a direct response to "the tragic events" of 9/11 (xi). Believing Islam's message—of God and revelation—to be crucial to the modern world, Nasr wished to disabuse the West of its "misinformation" (xi) about Islam, which had proliferated for more than a thousand years and which had reached by 2001 "cacophonies" (xiii) of rejection, despite its theological closeness to Judaism and Christianity.

"The prevalent image in the West," Nasr wrote, "that all Muslims are united as the faithful against the infidels—even if some well-known Christian preachers repeat to their flocks this assertion made by some extremists within the Islamic world—is simply not true" (45). "As a matter of fact," he said, "secularism is the common enemy of all the Abrahamic traditions, and the erosion of moral authority in secular societies that we observe today poses as many problems for Jews and Christians as it does for Muslims" (45–46).

Whereas some evangelical Christians marshaled battle lines against two sets of enemies after 9/11, American secularists and Islamic adherents, and whereas many writers for the *Times* saw fault lines between liberal, democratic traditions (including the secular separation between church and state) and the fundamentalist tendencies of Christianity, Islam, and other belief systems, Nasr perceived secularism as the common enemy of faithful Muslims, Christians, and Jews. Indeed, he wrote of secularism as a contributing factor in the disaster of modernity in the West. Tens of millions of deaths occurred in twentieth-century Europe, he said, due to "modern means of warfare, combined with the loss of the meaning of life, the secularization of the world, the dehumanization of humanity, the breakup of the social fabric, the unprecedented destruction of nature" (310), and so on. "Are all these criticisms to be forgotten and modern civilization made the norm that is right and in comparison to which everything else is considered wrong?" Nasr's answer—which was, in fact, a retort to "the recent condescending question about Islam, 'What went wrong?'" (Carroll 2002), and a rebuttal to the "clash of civilizations" thesis—was clearly "no," as he called on moderns—Muslims, Christians, and Jews in particular—to immerse themselves in traditional religious values.

Although Nasr was intent in his book to criticize the secular West, the *Times* reviewer (Carroll 2002) wished for a more thoroughgoing critique of Islam, one that would not hide behind pieties about the basic goodness of authentic Islam (and religion in general) and deny the dysfunctions inherent to the Abrahamic faiths.

After 9/11, the *Times* surveyed Islam, perceiving a large majority of Americanized Muslims as moderates who practiced their religion—more or less—and who posed no threat to America or its hallowed institutions. As for Islam, the global faith with its diverse sects, it was characterized as essentially spiritual but rife with a militant zeal that threatened civilized order both in Muslim nations and in the West as well as within Islam itself.

In a study of American journalism in the nineteenth and twentieth centuries, Kenneth Dayton Nordin (1975) shows how newspapers initially regarded Jewish and Catholic immigrants as a threat to the United States, but over time they came to be treated as an audience as well as a subject of inquiry (73–74). In the process of change, news media performed acts of surveillance on the suspect populations, not only to acquaint the mainstream readers with the newcomers, but also to pressure the immigrants into assimilating American behaviors and attitudes. It can be said that the *Times* was engaged in a similar process regarding Islam after 9/11. Perhaps the *Times* was presenting portraits of assimilated Muslims to allay non-Muslims' fears *and also* to establish a model for other Muslims who had become *Times* readers. In particular, the paper posited a divide between moderates and zealots within Islam and exhorted the moderates to criticize their zealous siblings in the faith—in effect, to engage in an intramural Muslim "culture war."

Muslim moderates' reticence to criticize Islam's reputed excesses wore on the patience of some *Times* writers, including even Muslim authors of op-eds (e.g., Nomani 2004). Those who already harbored suspicions about Islam—and one should not necessarily think of *Times* employees as Muslim friendly—found their antipathy intensified, to say the least, after 9/11 as they waited for Muslims, at least those in America, to condemn Islamic terrorism in an unqualified manner. One could even hear rumblings from one *Times* writer off the record that American Muslims should be "rounded up and deported." So much for the basic goodness of the Islamic religion in the eyes of the *Times*. When the *Times* published post-9/11 articles about suicide bombers, jihadists, and the like, its editors seemed startled when readers replied by saying that "nothing is off limits in fighting terrorism—not racial profiling, not restricting civil liberties" ("Jihad's Women" 2001, letters to the editor). This unliberal response should not have been startling, considering the "scary reality" portrayed in *Times* articles that "these people simply want to obliterate us." As one letter to the editor said, "Islam does not teach this," despite "one or two unfortunate references in the Koran to the destruction of infidels," and yet the *Times* depiction of radicalized Islam was "frightening—and frustrating."

More than three years after 9/11, when the Progressive Muslim Union of North America launched itself "as a counterweight to the 'oppressive or dysfunctional practices' that have come to define Islam for many people, both inside and outside the religion," Clyde Haberman's (2004a) "NYC" column bore the headline "A Little Late, but a Stand Against Hate." Haberman characterized the organization as "a small band of American and Canadian academics, writers and community activists. Not a head scarf or beard was in sight." After quoting the union's executive director, Ahmed Nassef—"We will not be intimidated into silence as narrow and authoritarian interpretations of our faith are presented"— and its spokeswoman, Sarah Eltantawi, to the effect that the union "would not tolerate . . . intolerance, whether by Muslims or toward Muslims," Haberman commented, "Brave words, deserving to be heard." But then: "It was impossible, too, not to notice a conspicuous absence in the discussion yesterday. Is it possible to talk about Islam in the post-9/11 world without a single reference to the dread T-word? Nowhere in the group's mission statement or in the members' remarks was terrorism mentioned. Why is that?" The members made it clear that although they were "unequivocal about condemning terror," they were "not going to equate Islam with terrorism."

Fanaticism and Islam Worldwide

Some *Times* articles expressed an appreciation for Islam's religious core; others took a more skeptical stance. The same could be said for religion in general, and the word that smeared religion's good name was *fanaticism.*

It did not take long after the events of September 11 for the first 9/11 op-ed response to appear. On September 14, Israel's Amoz Oz (2001) wrote ominously of "a tide of religious and nationalistic fanaticism" on the rise in Islam, but also in Christianity and Judaism, inciting religionists toward hatred. Oz called the link between fanaticism and hatred "'The Great Satan'" and warned: "Let us be very careful not to be infected." Writing from Lebanon, Saad Mehio (2001) gave a similar warning against the "immoral, unscrupulous and irreligious exploitation of Islam as a political weapon—by everyone. The West, the United States, Arab and other Muslim tyrannies have all used the weapon of Islam. And all are paying their different prices for it."

Nikki R. Keddie (2001), an historian who had written about Iran's revolutionary response to the modern world, wrote an op-ed about "divine inspiration" pegged to the mention of predictive dreams and visions in Osama bin Laden's taped conversations. This notion of direct communication from the holy, fueling messianic hopes, is typical of Islam and Christianity, she said. In a secular critique of religious motives and assumptions, she concluded: "Many combatants throughout history—including Americans—have believed that God is on their side, though there can never be empirical evidence of this. In this conflict, as in others, dreams and visions will have little to do with the outcome."

In like manner, a report on a new book, *The Quest for Paradise: Visions of Heaven and Eternity in the World's Myths and Religions* (Ashton and Whyte 2001), commented on Muslim terrorist-martyrs seeking their virgins and other rewards in paradise. In many religious traditions of the world, including Christianity, there have been "many heavens, many ways to get there," the article reported, displaying "images of eternity, from endless war to excellent sex" (Kimmelman 2002). The overall impression presented by this article in the "Arts & Ideas" section of the Saturday *Times* was of overwrought religious imaginations engaged in obsessive wish-fulfillment.

Times columnist Maureen Dowd (2002b) joined the chorus of religion's critics in "Sacred Cruelties." She wrote that "not long after Sept. 11, somebody scribbled these chillingly profound words on a wall in Washington: 'Dear God, save us from the people who believe in you.'" Surveying the waywardness in Christianity, Islam, and Judaism—the three Abrahamic faiths "roiling" with each other in the world—she asserted that "at precisely the moment when religion should have a calming influence, it has a dispiriting influence. Just when people need religion to bring them peace, it brings them war or crisis or abuse or just plain pain."

Dowd was referring in part to the sexual abuse crisis in the Catholic Church and not just to aspects of fanaticism. On January 9, 2002, the *Times* had begun its coverage of pedophilia among Roman Catholic priests (Henneberger 2002b), a topic that the paper treated with its famed saturation reportage. Throughout 2002 and 2003, the 9/11 offshoot stories constituted perhaps less than half of *Times* religion coverage, as other stories such as the scandal in Catholicism came to the fore. Some *Times* commentators tried to relate the crisis brought about by the sexual scandal to the devastation of 9/11, most prominently Laurie Goodstein (2002c) in "O Ye of Much Faith! A Triple Dose of Trouble" in the "Week in Review." She tried to pull together the crises for Muslims, Jews, and Christians (especially Catholics with the sexual abuse scandal), and although avoiding any blanket condemnation of religion per se, she let it be known just how far from "above criticism" religions were. The article ended with a quote from Martin E. Marty: "'We're seeing now that religion is not an innocent force in the world,' he said, 'but it shares the same problems as the rest of the world.'"

More than at any time in previous decades, the *Times* was carrying pieces critical of religion per se for its tendency toward extremism—both in its supernaturalism and in its clannishness. The criticism was aimed at the Abrahamic faiths, but also others. Throughout 2002 and beyond, the *Times* observed the flames of violence fanned by religious antipathies in many parts of the world, but particularly in India, where Hinduism's "political resurgence" was coming to be seen as "the other South Asian fundamentalism," potentially dangerous (Mishra

2002). (Pankaj Mishra [2003a] also saw Islam as a "time bomb" in India.) When "Muslims set fire to a train carrying Hindus planning to build a temple on the site of a mosque in Ayodhya that Hindus razed a decade ago," the "touchstone of Hindu-Muslim tension" set off "three days of the worst Hindu–Muslim violence in nearly a decade" (Dugger 2002g; see also Dugger 2002c, 2002e), leaving hundreds dead in western India. A Hindu "fundamentalist" justified the killing of "innocent Muslims" as a means of teaching them a "lesson," which was, as the fundamentalist put it, "the end of toleration" (Dugger 2002d). As the Indian Supreme Court tried to prevent the "fundamentalists" from performing a ceremonial "provocation" at the site of the destroyed mosque and proposed temple (Dugger 2002a), the residents of Ayodhya "braced" for a "Hindu mob" bent on worshipping their god Ram in a display of Hindu nationalism (Sengupta 2002b; see also Sengupta 2002e). Thousands of soldiers prevented the demonstration in a test of "India's integrity as a secular democracy." Nevertheless, many Muslims were said to "fear for their future" after the "wave of rioting across India by fervent Hindu mobs" (Sengupta 2002a). Both "friendships and faiths" (Sengupta 2002f) were shaken by the violence, even though some Hindus and Muslims were able to maintain their fidelity to one another in the midst of the "mythic hatreds" (Nair 2002) between their peoples. "Hindu mobs" continued to kill Muslims in Gujarat State, causing as many as one hundred thousand people to flee to relief camps. "Leaders of the Hindu nationalist-led government . . . warned Western nations . . . to stop lecturing India about the official failure" to prevent the killings. "But the issue refuses to die," said Celia W. Dugger (2002b), the *Times* co–bureau chief in New Delhi. The "Hindu Right" (Sengupta 2002d) especially pushed its views, including in schools, to "build a Hindu nation" in the secular state of India—in effect, "hijacking India's history" (Friese 2002) by rewriting national textbooks.

Sure enough, a *Times* headlines proclaimed: "Deadly Violence Erupts Again in India's Hindu–Muslim Conflict" (2002). In another article, Celia W. Dugger (2002h) wrote with irony and indignation about "religious violence," the Hindus' "unspeakable savagery against Muslims" in Ahmedabad, "the adopted hometown of Mohandas K. Gandhi, the great apostle of nonviolence." Before too long, Muslim assailants had left their own trail of human carnage at a Hindu temple in Gujarat (Waldman 2002b), "a grim omen for all India" (Waldman 2002e), whose secular status seemed in jeopardy (Waldman 2002g), with "Hindu nationalists" winning a "landslide" victory in the state of Gujarat (Waldman 2002c), where the

Hindu–Muslim riots had occurred. When it came time to put some of the Hindu rioters to trial, many Muslim witnesses recanted their testimony for the prosecution, leading to acquittals (Rohde 2003e). Before long, though, the headlines read once again: "Hindu Temple Plan in India Stokes Tensions" (2003; cf. Rohde 2003b) and "Anxiety Rises in a Muslim Enclave near Bombay" (Waldman 2003b; see also Waldman 2004b, 2004c; however, cf. Waldman 2003c regarding shared Hindu-Muslim devotions in India).

The *Times* reports about India in 2002 and especially those by Celia Dugger elicited charges of an "anti-Hindu spin" (Rao 2002) and "anti-Hindu . . . bias" (Talwalkar 2002). The *Times,* it was said, blamed Hindus for all the religious conflict in India and pandered to Muslims, just as Indian "secularists, . . . academics, editorialists, and . . . politicians" did. "Lest we forget, India has the second largest Muslim population of any country in the world, and one of Osama bin Laden's primary target [*sic*] of hate is India" (Rao 2002).

Pankaj Mishra (2003b), the Indian essayist, novelist, and travel writer who had warned *Times* readers about the dangers of fervent Hinduism, looked back with horror at a year of Hindu–Muslim violence in his native land, noting that "while the West worries over Islamic fundamentalism, India's Hindu nationalists thrive by stirring up a murderous anti-Muslim frenzy." His article in the *Times Magazine* was entitled "The Other Face of Fanaticism."

Before 9/11, the *Times* had already weighed in on religion as a political force worldwide. In its coverage of conflicts in Indonesia, Burundi, eastern Europe, Northern Ireland, and elsewhere, the paper had to decide how important religion was as a factor in societal violence. Was religion the cause, or was ethnicity or economics or a combination of many aspects of society? In *Religion in the News,* Mark Silk (2000) had examined this issue and the contrasting positions taken by different writers such as Seth Mydans and Chris Hedges in the *Times* and had stated that we must look at each conflict "case by case" (3) to determine religion's relative role in fomenting political conflict. It was clear, however, that whatever role religion played in causing the ferocity of 9/11 and whatever role, exacerbating or ameliorating, it might play in its aftermath, at least some authors in the *Times* feared the fanatical aspect of religions, including Islam, and conveyed that fear in their writings.

Whatever concerns the *Times* may have had about religious "fundamentalism" or "fanaticism" at home and around the world, its primary concern was

Islam. Religion writer Laurie Goodstein (2004b) regrets that since the first anniversary of 9/11 the *Times* has lessened its commitment to Islam within the borders of the United States as a story. Whereas the deluge of articles on American Islam slowed to a mere rivulet, another steady stream of stories about Islam around the world continued to flow through the presses. The paper ran dozens of stories about global Islam—in Nigeria, Indonesia, Malaysia, Singapore, Thailand, the Philippines, China, Pakistan, Bangladesh, Iran, Turkey, India's Kashmir, Egypt, Saudi Arabia, Tanzania, Senegal, Russia, Kenya, and so on—and about Islam more specifically in western European countries—especially France, England, Italy, and Germany—in order to gauge the impact of this transnational religion on various national cultures and politics. Many of these articles were of considerable length, and together they constituted a series called "The Force of Islam." The unmistakable impression gained from these articles—with notable exceptions that served to prove the rule—was of a growing and glowering religious potency, verging on violence to its neighbors and threatening to secular states.

"Religious and Ethnic Clashes in Nigeria Spread, Killing at Least 165" (2001), read one headline, continuing a story of Muslim–Christian violence that had begun in Jos, Nigeria, before 9/11 and had spread to Kano ("13 Nigerians Die" 2001) and possibly serving as a proof text of the "clash of civilizations" in an African context. An expansive story analyzed the ways in which "rising Muslim power in Africa causes unrest in Nigeria and elsewhere" (Onishi 2001b). It quoted an Anglican bishop in Nigeria who said of the contest between Islam and Christianity, "The Muslims are winning—they have won. . . . Islam is growing very fast. For many Africans, it makes more sense to reject America and Europe's secular values, a culture of selfishness and half-naked women, by embracing Islam." Maps showed which African nations, mostly in the north, had majorities of Muslims and which Nigerian states had instituted official sharia functions for its populace. Nigeria was split in two between Muslim and Christian majorities. A photograph by Norimitsu Onishi captured the image of Osama bin Laden on a newspaper on display in Kano, Nigeria's largest Muslim city.

A year later "sectarian violence" brought about by a planned Miss World beauty competition led to more than a hundred deaths as Christians and Muslims fought one another in the city of Kaduna. Muslims had complained about the pageant for "promoting promiscuity and offending female modesty and sexual morality" (Cowell 2002). A newspaper article ignited a firestorm by asking,

"'What would Muhammad think? In all honesty, he would probably have chosen a wife from among them.'" "Nigerian State Government Urges Muslims to Kill Fashion Writer" (2002), read a headline regarding Zamfara State, where the authorities evoked sharia and issued a "'fatwa.'" Nigeria's "secular government . . . dismissed the decree as 'null and void' and unconstitutional and said it would not be enforced." President Olusegun Obasanjo and other Nigerians recognized that their country's problem was not the matter of a beauty contest, but rather of deep-seated religious hatred between Christians and Muslims brought to a head by sharia laws being enacted in the North's Muslim-majority states. "Religious riots" were a tradition among a population that "has shown itself to be devoutly religious but also quick to kill" (Lacey 2002a). A "Week in Review" analysis of Nigeria's "radical" form of Islam emphasized the relatively recent history of sharia enforcement under British rule: "by the mid-20th century, northern Nigeria was the only region outside the Arabian peninsula where Islamic criminal law was fully enforced." And although independence in 1960 had introduced a "secular constitution," in the past decade one-third of Nigeria's thirty-six states had reinstituted Muslim rules (Steinglass 2002). A follow-up article to the Kaduna riots tried to see past Muslims and Christians' competing piety to ways in which local Nigerian politicians scored points by "playing the religion card" in assigning jobs and police protection and in electing individuals to office (Sengupta 2003c; see also "Muslim Mobs" 2004).

Elsewhere in Africa the picture was mixed. The paper found a "war being waged" on Tanzania's island of Zanzibar, "more of a clash of cultures than an international battle over terrorism," as its "dual role as both an Islamic society and a tourist spot" pitted religious and economic interests. News service photos contrasted a white woman in a bikini on a beach with a "local woman" in "head-to-toe covering," a recurring type of image in the post-9/11 *Times* (Lacey 2002c).

Sufi Muslims called "Mourides"—entrepreneurs who sell watches and other wares on the streets of New York and other Western cities—financed an autonomous, "Vatican-like" enclave and pilgrimage site in Senegal called Touba, where they demonstrated a "moderate, essentially African vision of Islam" (Onishi 2002a). This report served as a contrast to most stories about international Islam. "In few places in West Africa is Islam so well organized and politically powerful as in Senegal," the author wrote, "a country at the same time considered the region's most open and Western-oriented." A related story featured the leader of the Mourides, Sheik Mourtada Mbaké, among some of his far-flung follow-ers, striving toward the "twin virtues of hard work and prayer" at the House of Islam in Harlem (Sachs 2003e). Senegal seemed an anomaly (Pareles 2004) in an African continent where Muslims often seemed embattled with Christians and traditional religionists, as well as often among themselves, as in Sudan (Lacey 2004; cf. Zanganeh 2004 regarding Mali's cosmopolitan intellectualism in the distant past).

The bombing of a Jewish resort in Mombasa, Kenya, in late November 2002 stirred the local Muslim minority's feelings of being "victims of discrimination at home." According to a *Times* article, "While none of the city's Islamic lead-ers publicly praised the attacks on an Israeli-owned hotel and an Israeli airliner, many blamed both Israel and the United States as making such acts inevitable" by their frequent flexing of military muscle (Filkins 2002a).

"Militant Islam" was described as an unsettling force of rebellion and social tension in Southeast Asia, including Indonesia, Malaysia, Singapore, and the Philippines (Mydans 2001d). The latter was especially volatile as a former gover-nor of the Autonomous Region of Muslim Mindanao staged a revolt (Kirk 2001a), and guerrillas continued to hold several Christian missionaries captive, having already beheaded several others (Kirk 2001b). As US troops planned a foray on the Abu Sayyaf rebels holding the hostages, the *Times* reviewed the history of American military power in the Philippines and its effects on Christian–Muslim tensions, which were ongoing (Brooke 2002; see also Conde 2003).

Indonesia and Malaysia were of especial interest because they had long developed traditions of a "tolerant Islam" (Mydans 2001b; cf. Mydans 2001a), which had recently turned "rigid" under the influence of Middle Eastern Mus-lims—especially Saudis—who had impressed their "austere" notions of Islamic authenticity on the region (Crossette 2001b; see also Perlez 2003c). The *Times* "Week in Review" carried an essay arguing that the West must make and main-tain substantial business connections in Muslim countries such as Malaysia to counteract the influences of "fundamentalists" (Kahn 2001).

At the same time, Indonesian Muslims and Christians on the island of Sulawesi—"once friendly neighbors who shared their religious holidays—have been massacring, torturing and beheading one another in the most recent and worrying of Indonesia's communal conflicts" (Mydans 2002d). "Jihad Seethes, and Grows" proclaimed the headline, and Osama bin Laden's visage decorated a poster in one of Seth Mydans's photographs from the region. With the Indonesian government struggling "to hold the amorphous center together," a Muslim party sought "nothing less than to impose the traditional Shariah, or Koranic law, on this secular nation" (Perlez 2002i). As the United States attempted a "propaganda war" to win back "a 'lost generation' of young, radicalized Indonesian Muslims" brought up on an "anti-American creed," Muslim politicians continued to "ramp up their appeal to voters on a religious basis" (Perlez 2002h). Indonesian voters rebuffed the Islamic parties, continuing a long tradition of "resisting Shariah as the law of the land" (Perlez 2002c), and the "profoundly moderate kind of Islam, . . . a practical Islam, . . . Islam Lite" (Perlez 2002c), once again seemed to prevail, at least for the moment. The *Times* even found reason to celebrate a "reverence for tolerance" between Christians and Muslims who averted violence when "a mob came close to attacking a mosque" (Perlez 2003b).

When the United States invaded Iraq, reporter Seth Mydans (2003c) found in Southeast Asia—the Philippines, Malaysia, and Indonesia—an attitude critical of America, "but hardly pro-jihad." And when Indonesian prosecutors charged Abu Bakar Bashir in the bombings of several churches in Indonesia in December 2000 and a plot to blow up the American embassy in Singapore, his indictment was said to indicate a "shift" in Southeast Asia from ignoring the growth of Islamist "terror" to doing something about it (Bonner 2003a). Nevertheless, the killing of more than two hundred people by terrorist bombings at two nightclubs in Bali "shocked Indonesia" (Mydans 2003a), and the trial challenged the country's will to enforce its antiterrorism laws. But when Abu Bakar Bashir was acquitted of the charges that he ordered terrorist attacks in Indonesia—although he was found guilty of aiding and abetting treason by trying to set up an Islamic state (Bonner 2003b)—the *Times* found "Islam Lite" "looking more scary" (Perlez 2003a) and the United States more "unloved" (Perlez 2003d), even among relatively secular Indonesian Muslims (Liddle and Mujani 2003).

In Singapore, authorities risked alienating Muslims by enforcing a ban on head scarves and other "religious symbols" in public schools (Mydans 2002b). Thailand experienced tensions between Buddhists and Muslims in 2004 (Mydans 2004b; Perlez 2004; "Threats Close Thai Schools in Muslim Area" 2004).

China "intensified a crackdown" (C. Smith 2001b) on the nine million Turkic-speaking Muslim Uighurs in its western regions, calling the people a threat to national unity and claiming evidence of ties between Uighur "separatists"

(Eckholm 2001a) and terrorist groups abroad. The *Times* placed the "repression and the drumbeat of executions" in historical context, presenting Uighur claims to autonomy, and cited "mainstream" Uighur fears that China's actions might "turn a small ethnic-based movement into a more volatile religious one" (C. Smith 2001a). China's government "asserted that Mr. bin Laden himself had met with radical Chinese Muslims" and had "allocated 'a fabulous sum of money for the training'" of Uighur "'terrorists'" (Rosenthal 2002).

Among the many stories about Islam in Pakistan was a prominent report on the death of sixteen Christians, murdered in church by Muslim gunmen (Burns 2001c). A color Reuters photograph of the dead made the front page of the *Times* beneath the fold. A full-page follow-up, with a handful of photographs, appeared several days later, emphasizing the Christians' sustaining prayers after the "massacre" (Burns 2001e; see Bragg and Fremson 2001). Another Muslim attack on a Christian church left two Americans dead in Islamabad (Bonner 2002). In Karachi, a bomb killed a dozen Muslims at a mosque, presumably an incident in "a long-running feud between Sunni and Shiite Muslim sects that has taken more than 2,000 lives over the past decade" (Mydans 2002a). Nonetheless, the continuing story for the *Times* was Muslim violence against Christians. When Muslim gunmen murdered six guards at a Christian school for foreigners, Pakistan authorities called the assault "terrorism" (Rohde 2002e), and when an additional bomb attack on a Christian hospital killed several nurses, "officials voiced concerns that Islamic militant groups might be mounting a new challenge to one of the United States' most important allies in the war on terrorism, President Pervez Musharraf" (Rohde 2002g). Yet another raid—the execution of seven workers at a Christian charity in Karachi—brought more horror to the pages of the *Times* (Rohde 2002f), and yet again: "Raid on Church: Grenade Attack in Pakistani Village Kills 3 at Christmas Service" (2002), the story of an incident that the *Times* called an "atrocity." The paper warned that even members of Pakistan's "elite" were beginning to "gravitate toward Islamic religious parties," but certainly not toward terrorism, in an anti-American upsurge brought about by the US invasion of Afghanistan and its sword rattling in the direction of Iraq (Rohde 2002h). As the United States took control of Afghanistan, Taliban operatives found refuge in Pakistan's borderlands, creating a "resurgence" of Taliban strength there (Gall 2003a; see also Rohde 2003i). After a 2002 lull in sectarian fighting between Shiites and Sunnis in Pakistan, Sunni "militants" killed several dozen Shiite worshipers and wounded many others in Quetta ("Pakistan Holds 19 Suspects in Mosque Raid" 2003; Rohde 2003a, 2003h). Religious violence persisted in Pakistan in subsequent years (Masood 2004a, 2004b, 2004c, 2004d, 2004e), and, beyond the scope of this survey, Pakistan became a primary concern for successive American administrations as the Taliban solidified its military and religious presence there.

Agence France-Presse reported that a Bangladeshi court had acted "to protect Hindus" from "'terrorist attacks'" by Muslims in the "Muslim-dominated country," where Hindus composed about 10 percent of the population and where "Muslim fundamentalism" was on the rise ("Bangladeshi Court" 2001). "With India and Pakistan facing the prospect of a fourth war," the *Times* reported on "fear and flight in deadly Kashmir: Islamic militants brutalize Hindus, dramatizing a land's divisions" (Sengupta 2002c; see also Burns 2001f). When Hindu devotees made their annual pilgrimage to the Amarnath Cave and its shrine to Shiva in the Kashmiri Valley (Rohde 2002d), Muslim militants killed nine of them, who were among the thirty-five thousand people who had lost their lives in the thirteen-year "separatist insurgency in Kashmir, India's only majority-Muslim state" (Rohde 2002a). Ten others were murdered in a Hindu temple several months later (Waldman 2002a). In 2003, the FBI accused Muslims of "conspiring to wage 'jihad' against India in support of a terrorist group in Kashmir" (Lichtblau 2003b; see also Waldman 2004d).

In reporting from the Middle East that "Iran Shiites celebrate and mourn a martyr"—Imam Ali, the Prophet Muhammad's son-in-law, who was killed in 661—the *Times* presented a celebrative aspect of Islam, calling Ali a "hero, a saint and a philosopher" (Waldman 2001c). This story had no ostensible link to 9/11, but the fact that Imam Ali was regarded as a "martyr" served to remind readers of the "martyr complex" in present-day, militant Islam, in which "war is always religious" (Naby and Frye 2003). In the Islamic Republic of Iran there were signs of liberalization, a possible retreat from the Islamic Revolution of 1979. Over the opposition of Muslim "hard-liners," legislators gave equality to women in divorce proceedings (Fathi 2002c). Iran's president, Mohammad Khatami, proposed legislation to weaken the power of "hard-line clerics," especially the "religious panel called the Guardian Council, which has turned back reforms before" (Fathi 2002e). While President Khatami pressed for "reforms," the *Times* announced, "Iran Pardons Cleric Who Was Jailed for Insulting Islam" (2002);

however, two days later Iran's "hard-line judiciary" sentenced another "reformist to death for insult to Prophet Muhammad," although it appeared that Professor Hashem Aghajari's association with Khatami and his "criticisms of the system made him a target of hard-liners" (Fathi 2002d). Thousands of university students protested the death sentence in Tehran (Fathi 2002a; Fathi 2002f); however, Aghajari refused to challenge his death sentence for "apostasy" (Fathi 2002b). *Times* columnist Thomas L. Friedman (2002c) called Aghajari's plight and the student protest against "hard-liners" the "battle for the soul of Iran." He stressed the political aspect of the struggle, noting that the professor was arrested "after giving a speech on the need to rejuvenate Islam with an 'Islamic Protestant-ism.'" Friedman also looked to the "student-led democracy movement" for its "deepening understanding . . . that to thrive in the modern era they, and other Muslims, need an Islam different from the lifeless, anti-modern, anti-Western fundamentalism being imposed in Iran and propagated by the Saudi Wahhabi clerics. This understanding is the necessary condition for preventing the brewing crisis between Islam and the West—which was triggered by 9/11—from turning into a war of civilizations."

The *Times* found a reason more potent than the student demonstrations to think that change was coming to Iran: "The Shiite clergy who a generation ago called for the establishment of a fundamentalist, religious government are having second thoughts. Religion, many are now saying, belongs in the mosque" (Fathi 2003c). When Iran freed Grand Ayatollah Hossein Ali Montazeri—who had been under house arrest since 1997 and who once was in line to succeed Ayatollah Khomeini until breaking with him over the fatwa against Salman Rushdie and other issues—the *Times* listened for his "'reformist'" message against the "conservative clerical establishment" (Sciolino 2003c; see also Sciolino 2003g). The paper also covered Iranian student demonstrations against their religious leaders, even as Ayatollah Ali Khamenei blamed the United States for fostering disorder in his country (Fathi 2003d; MacFarquhar 2003q, 2003u). And the *Times* celebrated Shirin Ebadi, Iranian lawyer and human rights activist, who became the first Muslim woman to be awarded the Nobel Peace Prize (Alvarez 2003b). (For Iran's continuing religious developments, see Farzami 2004; Fathi 2004a, 2004b, 2004d, 2004e; Kristof 2004c; "Tehran's Well Veiled" 2004.)

"The Force of Islam" series presented the story "Turkey, Well along Road to Secularism, Fears Detour to Islamism" (Frantz 2002), featuring a photograph by

Staton R. Winter of veiled Turkish women in front of a sexy billboard at Istanbul's airport. The caption read: "Veils vs. Thongs. Turkey seeks to balance its Muslim customs, reflected by these women, and Western mores." The story examined the potential of a political victory for a national candidate, Recep Tayyip Erdogan, "trying to shed his fundamentalist background and wrap himself in a cloak of moderation." On November 4, 2002, the front page of the *Times* announced the democratic elevation of Erdogan's Justice and Development Party, which, having received one-third of the votes, vowed to uphold Turkey's "'secularism'" as "'the protector of all beliefs and religions'" (Fisher 2002e). A Turkish professor of politics said in an op-ed that "in the post-Sept. 11 environment, when the compatibility of Islam and democracy has been questioned, the current Turkish experiment is of utmost importance. If successful, Turkey will have shown that secularism can indeed be liberal and tolerant—and that democracy can function properly in a Muslim environment." The future, he said, depended in part on the European Union's acceptance of Turkey as a member, "reducing the so-called civilizational barriers between Muslim countries and the West. Here is a challenge for us all" (Ozel 2002). Nevertheless, many in Turkey wondered about the "public mythology" of Erdogan's shift from Islamism to a "new moderation." Was it a matter of campaign rhetoric, and was there, indeed, a "'secret Islamic agenda'" (Fisher 2002d)? The election of Abdullah Gul, a "moderate" within the "Islamic party," to the position of Turkish premier soothed some concerns in the West (Filkins 2002c). "The symbolism was striking," observed a reporter in an article in the "Week in Review" (Filkins 2002b). "The first thing its soon-to-be prime minister did was swear to defend Turkey's secular state. The next thing he did was declare his group an example for the entire Islamic world. . . . 'We want to prove that a Muslim identity can be democratic, can be transparent and can be compatible with the modern world.'" The *Times* analyst noted that in Turkey there were Muslims who consider the Koran "'inadequate as a basis for legislation'" and others who think that "modernity is a trap, . . . and [that] the Islamic world is best served by returning to the religion's purist roots. Bring back the veil. Smash the television. . . . Across the Islamic world, the clash of the two has produced one upheaval after another: civil war in Algeria, an authoritarian government under constant pressure from Islamist terror in Egypt, theocracy in Saudi Arabia. Iran's 20-year-old theocracy is divided between a reformist, elected president and his authoritarian, doctrinaire rivals." Turkey's future might be a beacon of hope in such "tumult." As if for illustration, the *Times* featured a book dually authored in Turkey by an "Islamist" and an "atheist," with "a joint plea for tolerance" (Fisher 2002b). A *Times Magazine* article offered the hope but also pointed to the "pretty big problems" ahead for "the Erdogan experiment," a "devout Muslim in a secular country and a pro-Western pragmatist in a nation inflamed by anti-American passions" (Sontag 2003). In 2004, Thomas L. Friedman (2004a) saw Erdogan's Turkey as a bridge between the Muslim Mideast and Judeo-Christian Europe, and he encouraged the European Union to grant Turkey admittance. Erdogan needed to convince "secular Europeans," however, that Turks would "practice their religion with the same moderation as European Catholics" (C. Smith 2004q).

An electoral victory for Muslim "traditionalists" in Kuwait (Kifner 2003a) made it clear to *Times* readers that public will—at least among the men eligible to vote—was turning against "liberals" in several Muslim lands, including Lebanon and Bahrain (MacFarquhar 2004b). In Algeria, however, Islam and democracy were holding hands publicly after a "decade-long civil war with radical Islamists that left as many as 150,000 dead" (C. Smith 2004l)—a sign of hope to a *Times* correspondent in North Africa.

Despite the popularity in Egypt of a "Muslim televangelist" who preached a message that was "neither dangerously political nor terribly strict" (Sachs 2001b), and despite the longtime presence of Coptic Christians throughout the land (Sachs 2001c), the Muslim Brotherhood, with members of Parliament "elected as independents to get around the formal ban on their movement," pursued its goal of establishing an "Islamic state." Some regarded the brotherhood as a moderating means to "rid the world of Osama bin Laden and his ilk." Others feared that the "slogan, 'Islam Is the Solution,' masks a link to the dark side of Islamic politics" (MacFarquhar 2002b). An article from Cairo regarding "one of the Islamic world's leading Web sites, Islam-Online.net," examined what the *Times* reporter called "a leading example of efforts by moderate Muslims to push for the Islamization of societies by nonviolent means" (Wakin 2002f). In general, the Muslim Brotherhood and its Islamist goals had become acceptable in Egyptian polity ("Egyptians Mourn an Islamic 'Guide'" 2004). Through 2004 and beyond, the *Times* noted the success of the Muslim Brotherhood within the religious and political culture of Egypt (MacFarquhar 2004a).

Saudi Arabia was portrayed as a land where "Bin Laden's wildfire threatens [the] might of Saudi rulers" (MacFarquhar 2001b) and where "religious freedom is lacking" for all non-Muslims, including American servicemen and women, and thus "discretion is the key" to their worship on military bases. "For years, the Saudi-born terrorist Osama bin laden has vowed to purge the kingdom of the "infidel' American military presence from the country of the two holy shrines. Those threats have made American military commanders particularly uneasy about discussing religious services for their troops. "But not the soldiers themselves. 'I have three bibles,' said one young M.P. at an American military installation, who said he was able to attend Protestant services. 'Just let someone try to take them away'" (Sciolino 2002a). Another article quoted a pious architect about "religious extremism" and "religious fanatics" in his homeland (Sciolino 2002b). It was hard to tell how large the "ultraconservative" Islamic movement was in Saudi Arabia, but clearly it was substantial. Its members were said to resent deeply the US presence in their holy land and were sure that "'the United States is against Islam'" (C. Smith 2002c). They thus blamed America for their own militancy, according to one *Times* article. But an op-ed by a Saudi journalist facing "the whip" for advocating freedom of speech and for criticizing Wahhabism argued that his country was "bogged down" by religious "extremism." Its schools and mosques, he said, were "breeding grounds for terrorists" (Al-Nogaidan 2003). In 2004, when Riyadh was rocked by jihadist bombs, the *Times* found it ironic that Saudis were outraged by such violence at home even though some of their countrymen supported "a jihad in Iraq" (MacFarquhar 2004e). Indeed, the *Times* found much about Saudi attitudes toward religious violence to be troubling (see MacFarquhar 2004d).

Also troubling was the news from Russia, the link between Asia, the Middle East, and Europe. After the disastrous assault in late October 2002 by Russian security forces at a Moscow theater where Chechen rebels held 700 hostages (disastrous because 120 hostages and all 40 of the rebels died), Russian president Vladimir V. Putin "accused rebels in the breakaway province of Chechnya of being international terrorists who believe that all non-Muslims deserve to die." The *Times* quoted President Putin at length about his "Chechen opponents. 'If you are Christian, your life is threatened. If you reject your religion and become an atheist you are also in danger. If you will decide to become Muslim, even this will not save you because traditional Islam is from their perspective hostile to their purposes and goals." Putin, the *Times* stated, continued to "taunt" the "Islamic radicals" with "vitriol and insults," exclaiming, "If you want to become a complete Islamic radical . . . and are ready to undergo circumcision, then I invite you to Moscow. We're a multidenominational country. We have specialists in this question as well. I will recommend that he carry out the operation in such a way that after it nothing else will grow." He also claimed—even as he himself was called a "terrorist" by protesters—that "it is also becoming increasingly clear that there are international terrorist elements involved in the insurrection in Chechnya" (Sciolino 2002d).

Those elements were displayed in "one of the most horrific terrorist acts in recent times," the "massacre of hundreds of children, parents and teachers" by Chechnyan separatists in a North Ossetia schoolhouse near Chechnya (Mydans 2004a; see also Chivers 2004 and "Prayers for the Youngest Survivors" 2004). Even in Moscow, Russians feared for the future as rumors filled the air regarding planned terrorist acts against churches and other cultural centers. A Russian Orthodox priest gathered with his faithful in a memorial service for the dead, proclaiming in anguish, "World War III has begun." The Muslim press of the Middle East decried the massacre, calling on Muslims everywhere to scrutinize their deeds. One Muslim publisher declared, "It is a certain fact that not all Muslims are terrorists, but it is equally certain and exceptionally painful, that almost all terrorists are Muslims" (Kifner 2004). A subhead excoriated Chechnyan "'butchers in the name of Allah,'" quoting a Saudi news source.

For all of its failures in Chechnya, Russia seems to have been more successful in allowing the growth of a homegrown Islamic revival in Tatarstan, "an easygoing, secular, peaceable, multicultural society that is, in a small way, a model for its neighbors." In Tatarstan, several varieties of Muslim piety prevailed, and the Russian state "decided to create a space for Islam to flourish—within limits" (Keller 2003b).

We can see that in the years following 9/11 the *Times* provided its readers with a collection of stories about Islamic trends around the globe. Although not constituting a unilineal development, these narratives served to warn *Times* readers—in particular those in the United States, perhaps—about a rising swell of religious fanaticism. The events of September 11, 2001, were the most momentous eruption of this surge and warranted daily attention.

Western Europe's Muslims

In the months following 9/11, *Times* readers learned about the force of Islam in regions of the world conventionally associated with large Muslim populations, either as majorities or as significant minorities. For several decades, the paper had been mapping the Muslim areas of the world—Africa, South and Southeast Asia, the Middle East, eastern Europe—with frequent dispatches from these zones. Simultaneously, the *Times* had attended to the growing Muslim populations of western Europe. The attacks of September 11 made it necessary to revisit the European theater not only because some of the 9/11 hijackers, such as Mohamed Atta, had lived in Europe, where they engaged in Al Qaeda cells, but because nations such as France, Germany, Britain, Italy, and Spain (C. Smith 2003d) were now populated by sizable Muslim minorities who were affecting the cultural mosaic of those lands.

The first post-9/11 *Times* dispatch on western Europe's Muslims came from a Parisian suburb where French-born Muslims of Algerian and Moroccan descent chanted bin Laden's name during the French national anthem at a France–Algeria soccer game; where a Moroccan immigrant told the reporter, "We want more Americans to die so they can begin to see what it feels like"; and where "Death to the Jews" was scrawled on the wall of an apartment building. The chilling "echoes of jihad" emanating from the "suburban squalor" were explained in socioeconomic terms. "'There is little in their lives that validates them,' said a French Ministry of Interior official. 'They find in radical Islam a cause'" (Hedges 2001b).

No wonder, then, that Europe's majorities were "wary of wider doors for immigrants" from Muslim lands. Even though Muslims in Britain, France, Germany, and the Netherlands accounted for probably no more than 5 percent of their populations (Austria and Yugoslavia had Muslim minorities approaching

20 percent)—many of whom had immigrated for employment possibilities over the decades since World War II—the numbers were worrying politicians and others. "I am not saying that immigration equals terrorism," said the mayor of a Paris suburb. "But people come here and we don't know much about them and we don't know when they actually leave. And, in fact, many do not leave" (Daley 2001). Reuters reported that "Rightists" were "protest[ing] in Milan, seeking curbs on Muslims in Italy" ("Rightists Protest" 2001), where Muslims composed but one percent of the population. Italians suddenly seemed intent on protecting the practice of displaying crucifixes in the public schools: "'Muslims . . . should know when they come here that this is a Catholic state'" (Henneberger 2001m; see also Henneberger 2001k). Greek Muslims—perhaps one percent of the population—were merely looking for places where they could worship (Bruni 2003). In Britain, a "tug of faith" (Cowell 2001b) unsettled Muslim loyalty to their adopted land and thus roiled British attitudes toward the Muslims in their midst, especially after an English Muslim was arrested after reportedly attempting to blow up an airplane with a shoe bomb (Hoge 2001).

Muslims numbered fifteen million in Europe, including the Balkans but not Russia, as illustrated on a *Times* map (Fisher 2001). September 11 had brought home the reality of a "clash of cultures" not only between Muslims and non-Muslims, but also between "moderation" and "extremism" within the diverse Muslim culture. In some cases, there were "two visions of Islam, . . . wrestling" with one another over the visceral politics of identity. In concluding about "the force of Islam" in Europe, *Times* reporter Ian Fisher (2001) said: "Most, for now, seem to think they can be good Muslims in the West without compromising their faith any more than Christians or Jews do. But, with so much hostility against Muslims after the terror attacks, experts say Europe itself is also facing a test: accepting that whatever terrible acts may be done in the name of Islam, Muslims are now an inseparable part of the continent."

Inseparable perhaps, but not necessarily at ease. The *Times* showed England's concern about young Muslim men who turned to the structures of their religion to overcome their anomie, only to be drawn further to "jihad" (Waldman 2002d). Some of them went so far as to join the Taliban in Afghanistan and were soon US captives in Guantánamo Bay, Cuba. British authorities investigated the Muslim leadership and infrastructure, and the Charity Commission banned a London imam, Abu Hamza al-Masri, from preaching, not only because he praised the nineteen 9/11 hijackers as "martyrs" and because "he declared that the crew of the demolished *Columbia* space shuttle—five Americans, an Indian-born Hindu and an Israeli—represented a 'trinity of evil' punished with death by God," but, more important, because he purportedly recruited "violent Islamic militants" for terrorist activities (Van Natta 2003b). Not all Britains agreed with the ban on the imam (witness the photograph by Chris Steele-Perkins of a young white English-man holding a placard that said "Respect Muslims" in protest of the Charity Commission ban [Taylor 2003]). Nonetheless, Britain moved to deport the imam (Hoge 2003), and it continued to puzzle over its Muslim citizens' motives in becoming anti-Western bombers (Lyall 2003).

Europe had become a haven for diverse Muslim sectarians and latter-day prophets ("Correction: Hadhrat Mirza Tahir Ahmad" 2003; P. Lewis 2003). Germany, too, worried about an imam known only as "al-Fazazi" who preached "hate-filled," anti-Western sermons heard by Mohamed Atta and other 9/11 hijackers (Frantz and Butler 2002), perhaps providing a religious basis for the 9/11 attacks.

In France, the concern initially was not with causative links to 9/11 or with recruitment for jihad (there were arrests), but rather with Muslims' place in French society. Especially after 9/11 and the kind of Muslim responses reported by Chris Hedges (2001b), France had outspoken critics of Islam, even one who called it "the most stupid religion," thus risking charges of "inciting racial hatred" (Riding 2002b), although he was acquitted. Brigitte Bardot, "the pouting 1950's sex symbol turned sexagenarian scold," aroused official complaint for declaring in her book *A Scream in the Silence,* "I am against the Islamisation of France. For centuries, our forefathers . . . gave their lives to chase all successive invaders from France," with the implication that she hoped her contemporaries would do the same (quoted in "Footnotes: Brigitte Bardot" 2003).

French officials worked to produce a nationally elected council for its five million Muslims, similar to such councils for Catholics, Jews, and Protestants. The *Times* called it "a government effort to mainstream France's Muslims" (Sciolino 2003f), some of whom had long been "integrated into middle-class life," but others who had "a feeling of alienation from French society" (Sciolino 2003i). When French Muslims, with their "maze of identities," voted for their delegates in "'an official Islam of France,'" about 20 percent of the Muslim communities, "including some of the country's most conservative Muslim groups," boycotted the election (Sciolino 2003d). The majority of Muslim voters supported candidates whom a "moderate" French Muslim called "hotheads," promoting a "militant fundamentalist Islam" that would "try to build a model of Islam that endangers the French model of integration particularly among young people" (quoted in Sciolino 2003j). Other French Muslims called these fears "unfounded."

Despite these efforts, France—perhaps the most avowedly secular state in Europe—had an ongoing problem with its Muslim populace. In the minds of French officials were images of "model Muslims": integrated into French culture, tolerant of all other religious groups and of secularists, showing few outward signs of their Islamic faith. "Model Muslim women would not try to wear head scarves in the workplace; model Muslim girls would not try to wear head scarves to school. Most important, model Muslims would call themselves French first and Muslim second" (Sciolino 2003h).

At the second anniversary of 9/11, France was still pondering Muslims' place in the country's public life and especially the public education. The first French Muslim high school opened in September 2003, giving Muslims "an alternative to public school education, like those that French Catholics, Protestants and Jews have long enjoyed." Yet "the challenge for France is to preserve the country's secular identity as codified under a century-old law on the separation of church and state, meet the demands of its second-largest religious community and discourage religious and ethnic separatism all at the same time" (Sciolino 2003k; see also C. Smith 2003g). *Times* reports from France and Germany in the fall of 2003 and into 2004 had much to say about the conundrum of religious displays by Muslims in schools and other public settings, where secularism was supposed to hold sway (see Coq 2004; "Critics Say Draft of Head Scarf Ban" 2004; "German Cause Célèbre" 2003; Sciolino 2004a, 2004c, 2004e, 2004h, 2004j, 2004k, 2004m). The most knotty symbols were Muslim women's (and girls') head scarves and veils, which set them off from men and from non-Muslim women. The secular French state—unhampered by a bill of rights as in the United States, which a *Times* editorial, "Muslims in European Schools" (2003), put forth as a paradigm—held firm in "'banning the ostentatious wearing of all religious symbols'" (Sciolino 2003e), even under extreme pressure from Iraqis holding French hostages (Sciolino 2004i, 2004n, 2004p, 2004q). Germany's courts were more liberal (Landler 2003).

European Muslims continued to make news in 2004 and beyond: in France ("Chirac Condemns Attacks" 2004; Sciolino 2004b, 2004d; C. Smith 2004h, 2004o), Spain (D. Fuchs 2004; McLean 2004b, 2004c; Simons 2004d), Germany (R. Bernstein 2004c, 2004d, 2004e), and England (Tyler 2004a). It became a matter of concern on the *Times* front page that "militants in Europe" were calling openly for "jihad and the rule of Islam" (Tyler and Van Natta 2004), especially in England (Alvarez 2004; Cowell 2004), but elsewhere, too (C. Smith 2004f, 2004g), incited in part by the conflict in Iraq (Smith and Van Natta 2004) and in part by alienation from European institutions (C. Smith 2004k). The terrorist attack on trains in Madrid on March 11, 2004, especially unnerved Europe that year. European leaders worried over Muslims' lack of assimilation into the cultural mainstream, while hoping to "train [a] new breed of Muslim clerics" more adaptable to European mores (Sciolino 2004g). It was also possible that Islam might become—like Marxism before it—an "ideology of the repressed" in Europe (C. Smith 2004i), beckoning to the rejected Muslim masses.

The unsettling Muslim presence in the Netherlands became front-page news when Theo van Gogh—filmmaker, writer, and "scathing critic of Islamic militants and clergy" in his homeland—was murdered in Amsterdam ("Dutch Filmmaker Critical of Islam" 2004). His book *Allah Knows Better* might have been reason enough for an outraged Muslim to have sought van Gogh's death; however, the immediate impetus for the assassination was the short TV film *Submission, Part 1,* created with Ayaan Hirsi Ali, which depicted the "sexual and physical abuse" of Islamic women (Simons 2004b). The killing led to arrests of suspected "Islamic militants" (Simons 2004c) and shocked the Dutch to question the place of Muslim immigrants in their country. A five-page letter pinned to van Gogh's body declaimed against Ali, Jews, and the United States, all of which, it vowed, "Islam will conquer with the blood of the martyrs" (C. Smith 2004b). Dutch authorities investigated links between the accused killer, the "Dutch-Moroccan" Muhammad Bouyeri, and "a possible militant network in Europe and North Africa" (C. Smith 2004c). In the meantime, Dutch arsonists set fire to several mosques, and a Dutch Muslim school was bombed, likely in retaliation for van Gogh's murder ("Arson Suspected at Dutch Mosque" 2004; C. Smith 2004d). The Dutch were suddenly faced with the limits on their highly prized "tradition of tolerance." "Now, it's war," said one man. Another declared, "Islam is the most hated word in the country at this point" (C. Smith 2004j). The nation seemed to undergo a crisis of democratic faith, with questions about the future of Europe as a whole. Said one Dutch commentator, "Words such as diversity, respect and dialogue fade against the dark context of this ritual assassination" (Bawer 2004; see also C. Smith 2004e). Thus, in post-9/11 Europe as well as in Africa, Asia, and the Middle East, Islam displayed a fanatical face in the eyes of the *Times*.

Sharia and Gender

Much of the story of Islam around the world was about competing rules of law: those of the secular nation-states versus sharia. Whose laws would prevail? In particular, the place of women under sharia intrigued the *Times* in the post-9/11 world. The *Times* combined the women's angle—long an interest at the paper—with the sharia angle, not a difficult thing to do because the most newsworthy cases of sharia's application seemed to regard sexual life and women's lives themselves as matters of religious oversight. Hence, the paper observed Muslim women living in countries such as Nigeria, where sharia rules in some areas.

"This Woman Has Been Sentenced to Death by Stoning" (Dowden 2002), shouted the headline in the *Times Magazine* on January 27, 2002. "In northern Nigeria, as in Afghanistan under the Taliban, adultery now warrants the ultimate punishment—for half the couple, anyway." A photograph by Stephan Faris showed the woman sentenced, nursing her baby. A sharia court in Sokoto State found the divorced woman guilty of having sex out of wedlock—her baby served as proof; she said the man forced himself on her after trying in vain to use "fetish charms" to woo her—and the Sokoto attorney general vowed to see her die and would be happy to "cast the first stone." In its coverage of this story and of several others in northern Africa as well as in its commentary, the *Times* was clear in its condemnation of the sentences, the courts that determined them, the sharia system, and the worldview that underlay it all. In his column "Stoning and Scripture," Nicholas D. Kristof (2002e) wrote that Muslim laws condemning women to death for sexual infractions were at odds with "modern times." Islam must "adapt," as Judaism and Christianity have to some degree, he argued, especially in its treatment of women. A second Nigerian sentence of stoning for adultery ("Court Upholds Stoning for Nigerian Mother" 2002)—the first had been overturned on an appeal—rekindled *Times* interest in the subject of sharia corporal punishments, even as the Nigerian government declared them unconstitutional. Nigerians claimed that the sharia courts were as corrupt as the secular ones, favoring the rich over the poor (Onishi 2002b). "Nigeria Stands Trial" (Sengupta 2003a), read a headline over an AP picture of the accused madonna and her child with regard to the faith-based system of (in)justice found in its Muslim-dominated states. Concerned citizens in the West, spurred by Amnesty International, signed an email petition in protest of what they thought was the imminent execution of one of the accused Nigerian women, Amina Lawal, an act that threatened her life even as it was meant to defend her (Sengupta 2003d; see also Habila 2003). She was eventually acquitted by the Islamic court (Sengupta 2003b), as announced on the front page of the *Times* with a Reuters color photo of Lawal, her daughter, and her Nigerian female lawyer wearing a black robe and blond court wig ("Nigerian Woman Cleared" 2003; see also "Nigerian Woman Condemned to Death by Stoning Is Acquitted" 2003) and as cheered by a *Times* editorial ("Saved from Stoning" 2003).

Similar stories came out of Pakistan, where "rape victims are the 'criminals'" under Koranic jurisprudence (Mydans 2002c). "Public outrage" (Mydans 2002f) forced a Pakistani court to free one such victim. Nonetheless, the *Times* painted a portrait of a "brutal society" in Pakistan where Muslim-grounded values assigned "low status" to women (Fisher 2002a). From neighboring Afghanistan, photographs by AP's Suzanne Plunkett showed intrepid women imprisoned by sharia courts for refusing to marry against their will (Waldman 2003a).

During the course of the war in Afghanistan, the *Times* carried many stories about Muslim women there. Newspapers and other media emphasized the women's angle, presenting the intensified Muslim society as degrading to women and suggesting that American troops came as their liberators. The *Times* played this refrain, as did the rest of the country (Eckholm 2001b). The American public seemed excited by the issue of female subjugation under the Taliban, so much so that the Bush administration—including Laura Bush and Vice President Dick Cheney (Stout 2001)—spoke out in favor of justice for Afghan women. Maureen Dowd (2001) found this sudden political interest in Muslim women's rights a bit tendentious. Why not a word from the president's circle, she asked, about "oil-rich" nations such as Saudi Arabia, where women are under similar strictures? (See also McMorris 2002.)

The *Times* recognized that many Muslim women were willing and eager participants in their intensified cultures, even in their militance. The *Times Magazine* carried a photographic essay called "Jihad's Women" (Addario 2001), featuring girls and women at a madrassa in Pakistan. "In some of the larger cities in Pakistan," the text read, "many women work, go to the movies, eat at McDonald's, wear pants and otherwise live a modern, Western-influenced life." But in certain areas, women regard themselves as followers of Osama bin Laden. They name their boys after him, and they raise them for war against the United States. In a photo, a woman kissed her son. The text beneath said that she would gladly sacrifice him and her other five sons as martyrs in the jihad against the United States. "If they get killed it is nothing," the woman exclaimed, and she herself was prepared to be a martyr for the cause of jihad: "If America attacks, we will put our hands on the throats of Americans and kill them." Other stories found Palestinian women uttering the same determination of religious sacrifice and triumph.

Nevertheless, the prevailing lens focused on strictures placed on women in Islam, symbolized by various head coverings. Ruth Fremson's (2001a) full-page photographic essay "Allure Must Be Covered: Individuality Peeks Through" showed Afghan women wearing burkas and other cloth veils as they observed "purdah or hijab (Urdu and Farsi words, respectively, that mean 'covering')." The *Times* made the point in another essay (Crossette 2001c) in the "Week in Review" that "Islamic extremism" over the past two decades had pushed women from their public roles of authority, creating what looked like "a world without women." "It's a Man's, Man's, Man's Man's World," read the jump-page headline (a punning reference to the 1963 film *It's a Mad, Mad, Mad, Mad World,* making not so subtle ridicule of contemporary Islamic social roles). An accompanying photograph by Vincent Laforet displayed the fierce visage of a bearded man wearing an Arabian-style kaffiyeh at a pro-Taliban rally in Pakistan.

The *Times* tried to make scriptural and cultural sense of Islam's taboos regarding women's hair and men's beards in "Hair as a Battlefield for the Soul" (Sciolino 2001) in the "Week in Review." The author cited Koranic words governing the concealment of women's hair: "Say to the believing women that they should lower their gaze and guard their modesty. . . . They should draw their veils over their bosoms and not display their ornaments." "Ornaments" came to mean "hair" in Muslim tradition. And why should men wear beards? Not because of any Koranic sanction, but rather because Muhammad did, because the prophets (such as Moses and Jesus) did, because beards came to symbolize wisdom and spirituality. With these symbols firmly in place, the strictures adopted against them during Turkey's secularization in the 1930s made the veiling and the display of hair contentious issues thereafter.

A study of gender roles in Islam required an examination of clothing's relationship to sexuality. Gelareh Asayesh, Iranian-born journalist based in Florida and the author of a memoir (Asayesh 1999) of her journey between America and her native land, wrote in the *Times Magazine* about wearing the veil. "Shrouded in Contradiction" (Asayesh 2001) made dichotomies between the "miniskirt" and the "veil," the "sundress" and the "women swathed in black." In Iran—which she described with nostalgia in her memoir as a land of prayer and strict religious and civil rules—she would like just to wear clothes, but whatever she wore marked her for or against official Islam. "To wear *hijab*—Islamic covering—is to invite contradiction. Sometimes I hate it. Sometimes I value it," she said. The veil is meant to cover up sexuality, but, she stated, "moments of passionate abandon, within the circle of invisibility created by the veil, offer an emotional catharsis every bit as potent as any sexual release."

Recognizing that in Muslim societies "the ideological war over modernism has focused on the emancipated Muslim woman as the symbol of Westernization and as a threat to the integrity of the authentic and Islamic way of life," Rina Amiri (2001) of the Women Waging Peace Initiative at Harvard cautioned against the "premise that Islam is anti-woman." Not all Muslim countries are the same regarding women, she said, and in some places women have held powerful political roles, even where they wear veils. In the United States, one Columbia University Muslim co-ed attested, "Wearing a scarf just makes me feel more liberated" (Goodstein 2001k), serving to set her apart from her non-Muslim peers.

The *Times* took account of the restrictions placed on Muslim women, but also of the power women wield. In the series "The Force of Islam," the paper examined "a woman's place" under the title "Where Muslim Traditions Meet Modernity" (Sachs 2001e). This article began: "Islam preaches equality, yet in most Muslim countries a woman's place is determined by a man's will. It's the law." A paragraph later: "But the days when Muslim women could be kept housebound, cosseted and remote from society are long gone in most parts of the Muslim world." With the help of the Internet, modern legal consciousness, and a desire to be part of modernity, Muslim women were demanding their rights, according to the *Times*. "Their challenges to Islamic orthodoxy have placed these women at the heart of the main political battle in the Muslim world."

In defining gender roles—both male and female—as a site of contention within the Islamic cultural struggle and within what the *Times* defined as modernity, the paper took note of gay Muslims, "reviled even by mainstream Muslims because of their sexual orientation." "In most Islamic societies, homosexual behavior is a crime, punishable in some cases by death," reporter Robert Worth (2002) commented. "Even in the United States, many Muslims say they cannot be openly gay for fear that they would be rejected by other Muslims or attacked by extremists." The only Muslim gay and lesbian society in the United States was said to be Al-Fatiha, a New York City organization. "We're challenging 1,400 years of dogma," its founder stated. "There's bound to be a battle" (see also Hays 2004).

In the articles about gay Muslims as well as in the many stories about Muslim women, the *Times*—for all its attempts not to demonize Islam—represented Muslim society, if not the spiritual core of Islam, as basically repressive to any personal expression that might deviate from the norms. In Saudi Arabia, for example, even American servicewomen needed special dispensation from their commanders so they did not have to wear the requisite head scarves and robes when away from their military bases (Sciolino 2002). When Rina Amiri (2002) came into contact with Afghan women after the American military action there, she found "fear beneath the burka," preventing them from removing their veils after what they called the "dark period of the Taliban." The *Times Magazine* article "The Sullen Majority" (Judah 2002) looked at disaffected Iranians who yearned for Western fashions and had to contend with puritanical rulers. A photograph by Seamus Murphy showed two "fashion-conscious" women veiling their facial identity with their scarves. These young women said their prescribed clothes were "torture."

The premise of these and other stories was that a male-dominated society made rules of behavior and dress for its women, who suffered under the limitations and yet found personal space for individual expression. In his column "Saudis in Bikinis," Nicholas D. Kristof (2002d) asked whether Saudi women "choose to be repressed?" The lead: "On my first evening in Riyadh, I spotted a surreal scene: three giggly black ghosts, possibly young women enveloped in black cloaks called abayas, clustered around a display in a shopping mall, enthusiastically fingering a blouse so sheer and low-cut that my wife would never be caught dead in it. Afterward, I delicately asked a Saudi woman to explicate the scene. 'What do you think the 'black ghosts' wear underneath their abayas?' she replied archly." In a veritable follow-up (C. Smith 2002b), a Robert McKim photograph of a marketing director in a lingerie store in Jeddah found her holding up some flimsy item among "tropical-colored thongs and teddies and tango-cut panties and bras." The kicker: "'Arab women spend much more money on lingerie than American women do,' she says, adding that despite their black wrapper, Saudi women are very colorful a few layers down. 'Because they live in such a closed society, many Saudi women enjoy themselves by wearing fancy lingerie all the time.'"

The repression of Muslim women carried into the immigrant communities in the West and at least in the headlines was still symbolized by the veil. "Behind the Veil: A Muslim Woman Speaks Out" (Simons 2002b) comprised a heroic profile of Ayaan Hirsi Ali, also known as "the Dutch Salman Rushdie." A refugee from Somalia, she spoke out for Muslim assimilation into Dutch culture and against the mistreatment of women in Islam (including genital cutting). Her stouthearted oratory made her the target of Muslim death threats, "calling her a traitor to Islam and a slut." She left the Netherlands temporarily, but then she was elected to the Dutch Parliament and continued to live in the Netherlands under constant guard. In 2004, she wrote the script for the short political film *Submission, Part 1,* discussed earlier, which dramatized the subservient place of women in Muslim society. The film so "shocked" Dutch viewers, Muslim and non-Muslim, with its "graphic" imagery of Muslim brides tattooed with hegemonic Koranic verses that Ali and the film's director, Theo van Gogh, were accused of "blasphemy" and their lives were in jeopardy (Simons 2004a). Ali's bodyguards kept her secure, but van Gogh was indeed assassinated, and Ali further menaced (see "Letter on Filmmaker's Body" 2004).

Ayaan Hirsi Ali became a bona fide symbol of courage to those in the West who regarded Islam as inimical to women's individual rights (see Alvarez 2003a). Others tried to ride to fame on her stalwart shoulders. Norma Khouri escaped from Jordan to Australia after having written *Honor Lost* (2003), a book about her childhood friend who was "stabbed to death by her own father because she had been seen in public walking with a man" (Mydans 2003). Khouri's family outlawed her for writing the book—or so she claimed. So, too, Kola Boof claimed a life of female heroism against Islamic odds, although it was not clear from a *Times* feature whether the Sudan-born author of *Long Train to the Redeeming Sin* (2001) was "fatwa victim or a fraud" in her claims about the mistreatment of Muslim women in North Africa or about her having been Osama bin Laden's mistress (Salamon 2002a). In 2004, it was revealed that Khouri's tale was what an Australian humanist in a *Times* op-ed called a "fabrication" (McCalman 2004), and her book was withdrawn from sale. Boof disappeared from the headlines; however, the op-ed author rued the West's predilection to have its "prejudices" confirmed about "any enormity of Muslim males," including Khouri's charges, in the anxious and xenophobic post-9/11 era.

Times photos of Ali, Khouri, and Boof showed them returning the gaze of the camera in frontal displays of face and hair, unflinching poses of liberated female status. In addition, *Times* readers could witness the face of Irshad Manji, "Osama bin Laden's worst nightmare, . . . a lesbian intellectual with spiky hair and a sharp tongue, . . . calling for radical change" in Islam from her body-guarded refuge in Canada (Krauss 2003, photo by Christine Muschi; see also Glassie 2003 and Sullivan 2004). In a *Times* op-ed written after Theo van Gogh's murder in the Netherlands, Manji (2004) affirmed her "modern" religiousness as a challenge to European "secular humanism" as well as to Islamic "terrorism," thus making herself a "blasphemer" to "rationalists" as well as to "countless Muslims."

The post-9/11 interest in the condition of Muslim women, their position beneath the law as well as behind their veils, took a twist in the story of one Sultaana Freeman, an American convert to Islam who moved to Florida in early 2001 and applied for a driver's license. The issue was with the picture taken for a license application, which showed her wearing her *niqab,* a veil with a piece of cloth that covers the lower part of the face—just like her previous license in Illinois. In December 2001 and thus after 9/11, Florida said that for security reasons it would not grant Freeman the license bearing her veiled photo. The ACLU supported her case, saying it was a fundamental tenet of her religion not to show her face to male strangers. Three times in three different states since 1978, state supreme courts had ruled for exemptions regarding Pentecostal Christians who regard it as religiously impermissible to be photographed for drivers' licenses. But in June 2003 the Florida Circuit judge ruled against Freeman, saying that the law did not "constitute a 'substantial burden'" on her exercise of religion (A. Rothstein 2003:9).

How did the news media cover this story? They seemed uniformly against her, according to *Religion in the News* author Adam Rothstein (2003), which he said was atypical for journalists regarding cases of security versus individual rights. One newspaper compared her to a Ku Klux Klan member wearing a hood. Others said, "Driving is a privilege, not a right" (10). Do Muslims not have the same rights as Jews and Christians? Rothstein asked. Apparently not after 9/11, he asserted. But the *Times* treatment was more interesting than Rothstein's critique would have it. First, the paper's initial story (Canedy 2002) presented the argument given by Freeman's lawyers in some detail: that Florida's "demand is subjective, unreasonable and violates her religious freedom as well as her right to privacy and due process"; that "at least a dozen states permit people to obtain driver licenses without photographs for religious reasons"; that Florida "was in violation of its own Religious Freedom Restoration Act. The act says that laws that substantially burden the exercise of religion must have a compelling government purpose and must be the least restrictive as possible"; and so on. In quoting the state attorney general's office, the *Times* put into scare quotes the notion that Ms. Freeman was "'hypersensitive'" and that "'the reasonable person in Florida is not offended by having to sit for a driver license photo.'"

A later summary in the *Times* "Week in Review" (Pristin 2002) suggested a less compelling case for the plaintiff because of the precedent of the 1990 Supreme Court decision in *Employment Division v. Smith,* which held that "there was no constitutional requirement to grant exemptions to laws that applied to everyone else. Like antidrug laws, driver's license requirements are likely to be viewed as broadly applicable." The *Times* covered the trial and the judge's ruling against Ms. Freeman because of the state's "'compelling interest' in identifying its drivers" ("Muslim-Americans: Florida License Trial" 2003). Edward Rothstein (2003a) went further, however, by reporting what information was not permitted in court: that Freeman had been convicted of beating her children, and when child welfare workers sought to see the three-year-old twins, she "invoked religious modesty to hinder investigators from looking under the children's Muslim garb, where one daughter had a broken arm, and both were covered with bruises. The mother's mug shot was taken without a veil."

Rothstein added, "At any rate, even religious pilgrims to Mecca have to have uncovered faces in their passport photographs." Drawing on the ideas of "liberal dissident" Khaled Abou El Fadl, Rothstein chided American Muslims for supporting Freeman's case—not because of the incriminating tale of her ill repute as child beater and cover-up artist, but because they seem not to have made "a serious commitment to American democracy."

The *Times* seemed fascinated to the point of obsession about veils, hair, and female fashion during the American occupation of Afghanistan in 2001–2002. Through 2003, the paper was still following the same trail in its coverage of Iranian women. Elaine Sciolino (2003a) headlined the notion that "in Iran's hair salons, the rebels wield scissors," concluding that, regarding women, "the hair issue . . . remains a political pillar of the Islamic structure." Sciolino (2003b), who documented the politics of schoolgirl veils in France in 2003–2004, penned a piece about Iranian Muslim women forced to wear the veil; only this time it was about the granddaughter of Ayatollah Ruhollah Khomeini, Zahra Eshraghi, whose husband was a leading Iranian politician. Khomeini had called the veil "the flag of the revolution," and because of that statement the veil was politicized. Eshraghi hated to wear it. She said, "People have lost their respect for it. I only wear it because of my family status." In Italy, however, a Muslim woman was fined one hundred dollars for wearing a veil in public—in response to which fashion icon Giorgio Armani argued that "a woman should wear what she likes, even if what she likes is a veil that hides her face completely" (Fisher 2004b).

The *Times* seemed to find no post-9/11 irony in Western talent scouts' scouring the Kenyan countryside for the next "new African supermodel," peering from their cars, past the head scarves of "predominantly Muslim" tribeswomen, where "virtually everybody scurries for cover." But it found a heroine in an English convert to Islam, Donya al-Nahi, who currently devoted herself to retrieving the children of Western women married to Muslims, who took the youngsters away to Islamic countries. "'I believe you've only got one mother and I don't believe anyone has a right to take you away from your mum,' Mrs. al-Nahi said in an interview" (Lacey 2003b).

Michiko Kakutani's (2003) review of *Reading Lolita in Tehran: A Memoir in Books* (2003) by Azar Nafisi went well beyond veils in showing how university women in Iran read Western books as acts of intellectual freedom and "insubordination." Nafisi, who was part of the 1979 Iranian student movement but who found its success more despotic than the Pahlavi dynasty, left Iran in 1997 and came to the United States to teach at Johns Hopkins University. Her book validated for *Times* readers the idea that the ayatollahs of Islam—in Tehran but also potentially anywhere—were freedom-crushing despots anchored and pulled down by the past. They were rapists of the spirit of Muslim intellectuals, women especially. Nafisi (2003) compared herself and her circle of students to the title character of the Nabokov novel: "like Lolita we tried to escape and to create our own little pockets of freedom. And like Lolita, we took every opportunity to flaunt our insubordination" (25). Nafisi dramatized the control Iran's Muslim leader exerted over everyone's thought: "We had become the figment of someone else's dreams. A stern ayatollah, a self-proclaimed philosopher-king, had come to rule our land. He had come in the name of the past, a past that, he claimed, had been stolen from him. And he now wanted to re-create us in the image of that illusory past" (28). She paralleled *Lolita*'s undergirding plot with the plight of Iranian intellectuals under the ayatollah: "The desperate truth of *Lolita*'s story is *not* the rape of a twelve-year-old by a dirty old man but *the confiscation of one individual's life by another*" (33, italics in original).

(For the continuing *Times* interest in "female repression," creativity, and rebellion in the 9/12 Islamic world, see "Backer of Wife-Beating" 2004; Bannerjee 2004b; R. Bernstein 2004f; Filkins 2004a; Goodstein 2004c, 2004e; Lévy 2004; Schillinger 2004; A. Scott 2004; Waldman 2004a; Zinser 2004.)

The Arts in Portraying a Religion

Nafisi's book, which became a *New York Times* best seller, illustrated one possible point of intersection between religion and the arts, in this case a liberated, Western-friendly, critical account of Islam's repressive culture. In the period following 9/11, the *Times* delved several times into Muslims' artistic creativity—in the visual arts, on the stage, in music, in the literature of the Koran. These articles constituted one means of assaying Islam from the humanistic angle of religious studies, an angle that in years past had tended to portray Islam in its most favorable light.

The lead article in the "Arts & Leisure" section on October 7, 2001, was Holland Cotter's (2001b) "Beauty in the Shadow of Violence," a review of Islamic art in the Metropolitan Museum of Art in New York City. As Cotter had done before, he focused on Islam's calligraphy, grounded in the Koran, which was to Muslims a "visual icon" as well as "*the* book, the last word." According to Cotter, the aesthetic and the spiritual are combined in Islam—in its intricate ornament, its holistic pattern "that sees the faithful as all part of a single unity."

The author was not content to savor Islam's visual beauty. In the article's concluding paragraph, Cotter wrote: "If you look, you can find the seeds of zealotry in Islamic art just as surely as you can in Christian art: in exclusionary emblems, in flashes of messianic fervor, in an insistent control of objects and images that can be used in many ways. What you will also find, though, are the tools of transformation: generosity, patience, intellectual alertness, a thirst for balance and a trust in the fragile beneficence of beauty that is both actively utopian and utterly reality-based, as the experience of art should be." (See also Cotter 2001d, 2001e, 2001f, 2003a, 2003b, 2003c, 2004). As always, Cotter's analysis of religious art—for example, African works from Mali—saw its potential for "kicking up a storm," but also its power "to keep chaos and evil at bay" (Cotter 2001a).

Having examined the traditional connections between Islamic spirituality and aesthetics, the "Arts & Leisure" section featured a contemporary artistic
interpretation of Islam with a feminist vision. Muslim American artist Ghada
Amer (her parents were Egyptian; she was raised partly in France) commented
through her art on the ways in which Islam in her day attempts to repress sexuality. Her *Encyclopedia of Pleasure* installation in SoHo was named after an
eleventh-century book written by a Muslim man who cataloged "all aspects of
sexual pleasure for both men and women." The installation consisted of fifty-
seven boxes covered with printed erotic passages from pornographic magazines.
A photograph by James Estrin showed the artist kneeling in their midst. "What I
find so fantastic about this book," she said of the *Encyclopedia of Pleasure,* "is that
it's profoundly religious." Furthermore, she asserted, Islam serves to hide its own
tradition by denying sexual expression to its women today (Sheets 2001).

A Muslim from Pakistan and a Hindu from India, both women, exhibited
their work at the Asia Society in New York, "joining . . . icons" from their two
traditions "in a testament to the bonds and fractures" between their two homelands. Their "iconoclastic approach" was attractive to the *Times* reporter (Sengupta 2001b).

A year after 9/11, the Grey Art Gallery of New York University exhibited modern Iranian visual art, showing the ways in which the world's cultures, including
Muslim ones, have borrowed from each other. "Modernism Gets a Revolutionary
Makeover in Iran," read the headline to Holland Cotter's (2002) review of the
exhibition, where some work referred to the Shiite martyrs who died in 680 and
some referred to the militant Islam of the 1979 Iranian Revolution. The forms of
Western abstraction mixed with the pictorial and the calligraphic, and passages
from the Koran possessed "the visual weight of an icon." The overall effect was a
modern Islamic visual worldview.

The *Times* twice reviewed *The Ta'ziyeh,* a Shiite musical drama in several
versions based on legends of the Battle of Karbala in AD 680 in which Imam
Hussein and his followers were killed. The Lincoln Center productions were
called "moving yet mysterious" (Weber 2002a), even "bewildering" for their
expressive religious motives and archaic references; however, "by the end, you've
been immersed in a whole other cultural vocabulary. And you understand what
it's like to go to the theater to pray" (Weber 2002b).

The *Times* was intrigued by artistic and theatrical expressions of Islamic religiosity; it was also interested in newer concoctions of Muslim creativity. Always attracted to entertainment's many forms, the paper presented several pieces about humor as a response to 9/11. The *Times* treated staged comedy as one means of identifying the fault lines revealed by 9/11—between Islam and the West as well as between pious and more secular Muslims—and of dealing with them through the rituals of laughter. One article with a Toronto dateline, "The Mideast Optimist Jewish Muslim Comedy Night" (Clark 2001), told about the show put on by six comics—both Jews and Muslims—as an attempt "'to restore a bit of balance'" and to "'release some of the anger'" in a time of tension. These comics were "'bacon'" Jews and Muslims, part of Toronto's multiethnic mix (200,000 Muslims, 175,000 Jews). "Nobody here is fanatically religious," the comics said, and of course they were Canadians, removed somewhat from the turmoil in the States.

Almost a year after 9/11, a Muslim American comic was finally able to "turn fear into funny" in a US comedy club. The club owner commented on the unfolding of mainstream American sensitivities over time: "'Now it seems like people are feeling it's finally O.K. to laugh' about the war on terror" (Wilgoren 2002a). It was not so clear that European Muslims were ready to be amused by jokes about their faith. A feature about Shazia Mirza, a British-born daughter of Pakistani immigrants, described her comedy routine in London, dealing with "a single, complicated issue: living the dual life of a religious Muslim as well as an engaged citizen of secular Western culture" (Fisher 2001). She risked getting her neck wrung by fellow Muslims who did not find it funny or acceptable to laugh at their religion. Yet after 9/11 she "became famous by telling a single (some think abominable) joke . . . : 'My name is Shazia Mirza,' she said. 'At least that's what it says on my pilot's license.'" Some did not find Mirza's humor illuminating or charming. She commented: "If the comedy doesn't work out, . . . I'm going to become a suicide bomber. I went to see my job counselor, and he said, 'Previous experience not required.'" The reporter responded, "And on this night, in this club, the moans are drowned out by laughter" (Sella 2003; see also C. Smith 2003j, 2004m).

On the one hand, theatrical humor might serve as a means of alleviating the tensions of a post-9/11 world. On the other hand, it might just as easily exacerbate hurt feelings and mutual animosities. The play *Paradise* by Glyn O'Malley, about a young, female, Palestinian suicide bomber, was "fatwa'ed in Cincinnati" when

O'Malley gave an unrehearsed reading, and Muslims in the audience found the production incendiary and unfit to tour local high schools. One Muslim man objected to the bomber's donning of a head covering as she went out to her suicide mission. Did this act give the impression that anyone who puts on a hijab is dangerous? The man's daughters wore head coverings to high school, and he worried about how they would be perceived: "What is the message?" he asked. "To promote hatred? Are we trying to scare people in this country? We need to promote peace and not to promote war." The play's Muslim critics said that there were too many stereotypes of the Palestinians, and there was insufficient analysis of "crimes against Palestinians carried out by the Israeli government during the last 54 years of brutal occupation." Even though the Muslims reportedly called *Paradise* "a Zionist piece of propaganda," they were not objecting to its enactment in a theater: "It's a free country. The problem I have is to take it to schools. I'm not censoring anything. If I'm defending the rights of my children, is that extremist?" Nevertheless, the playwright felt threatened. "The fact that I was called anti-Islam is very dangerous. People get killed for that," O'Malley contended (Gussow 2003).

In discussing Islam's relation to the arts (see Riding 2004), the *Times* tried to balance its concerns for multicultural religious appreciation, on the one hand, and individual creative expression, on the other. The paper's personnel did not wish to offend Islam, nor did it wish to minimize the jeopardy posed by Islam to the freedom of artists and intellectuals pursuing their investigative, creative goals. A feature on the "silenced music" of Iran (Toumani 2003) repeated the motifs of Afghan Taliban coverage, pitting artistic creativity—including Rumi's lyric poetry—against repressive Muslim religiosity. A similar review of a television documentary, *The Rock Star and the Mullahs,* acknowledged the "confrontations" between "positive-thinking" rock music and "restrictive Islam" (Pareles 2003).

Alan Riding (2007)—veteran *Times* cultural correspondent in Latin America, Europe, and elsewhere—describes how "culture . . . has been affected by the rising tension over religion, notably Islam, since 9/11." His approach as a reporter has been "to see *(a)* how the arts can serve as a bridge between the West and the Islamic world; *(b)* how religious intolerance encourages censorship or self-censorship in the arts; and *(c)* how the arts can throw light on the Islamic world's resentment towards the West." Like other *Times* correspondents, he has "written extensively about the West's reawakened interest in Islamic art—new departments and galleries in major museums as well as prominent temporary exhibitions—in the belief that growing awareness of the roots and quality of this art can help Westerners distinguish between religion and culture on the one hand and terrorism on the other." He is also aware that an "emphasis on Islamic art"—in museums and presumably in the *Times*—"can also make locally born or immigrant Muslims feel their culture enjoys greater respect in the West." At the same time, he is cognizant of the tensions between "Muslim pressure (actually threats)" and Western cultural freedom; witness Rushdie or, worse, Theo van Gogh.

It was significant, therefore, that in an article about recent scholarship regarding the Koran, the paper stated that to interpret the Koran critically (historically, contextually, and linguistically)—as the Bible has been analyzed for a century and more—is to risk fatwa, violence, and even death at the hands of Muslim dogmatists (Stille 2002). "Even many broad-minded liberal Muslims become upset when the historical veracity and authenticity of the Koran is questioned," the author wrote, and the effect is to stifle any thoroughgoing Muslim enterprise in Koranic study that would match the critical treatment received by the Bible. At the same time, "a handful" of Islamic scholars are trying to engage in textual criticism, using similar techniques that historicized and secularized the Bible in the nineteenth and twentieth centuries. Indeed, some of these scholars intend for secularization to take place among Muslims as a result, just as higher criticism began to shake doctrinaire Christianity and Judaism a century or so ago. The *Times* reported that a return to the oldest sources of the Koran suggests that contemporary readings of the Holy Book are sometimes incorrect. For instance, the virgins in paradise, which the 9/11 hijackers and other jihad martyrs hoped for as reward, were in the earliest texts actually "'white raisins' of crystal clarity" (Stille 2002), a phrase mistranslated in transcriptions at a later date (see Kristof 2004b).

Some scholars of Islam wished for Muslims to think more critically about the Koran, especially in light of 9/11. In the United States, academics thought that it was high time for Americans to learn something about the Koran and about Islam. At the University of North Carolina–Chapel Hill, the administration assigned its 3,500 incoming students the summer reading of translated excerpts from the Koran in Michael A. Sells's *Approaching the Qur'án: The Early Revelations* (2001), with the expectation that they would discuss the book when they arrived on campus. A conservative Christian group tried in vain to get a court to stop the assignment, calling it "forced Islamic indoctrination." The students at Chapel Hill did not agree with this characterization, according to a *Times* report (Zernike 2002a). They saw the book as part of their education, introducing them—almost all Christians and Jews—to things they knew little or nothing about, and 9/11 made Islam an especially important subject for investigation. One student said, "I don't believe that intolerance of other religions is the guide that Christ set before us to follow. . . . He wanted us to show that he was the way and the truth, but not through ignorance and intolerance. I think reading books like this is a good way to make people more open-minded."

The *Times* reported on the book and the controversy, and at least one columnist found the attempt at censorship "embarrassing" for America (Friedman 2002a). But the paper did not review Sells's book and did not evaluate it as an introduction to Islam. The book was meant to provide a sympathetic beginning to understanding Islam among American college students, focusing on the earliest, most spiritual, and least political writings from the Koran. A letter to the *Times* editor from a Jewish studies scholar said that "the real issue . . . is that students are being asked to read selections from the Koran that do not include the controversial and important writings that speak about jihad, war and how infidels should be treated. How will that foster honest inquiry?" (Michael Dobkowski in "Does the Koran Belong in Class?" 2002).

In fact, however, Sells's translation of the Koran does include some passages condemning unbelievers and the unrighteous, so students reading it could have gained an introduction to Islam's dogmatic qualities as well as to its spirituality. Neither the university nor the newspaper intended Islamic studies to begin and end with a single book. In the period following 9/11, Americans were turning to many sectors of the marketplace to learn about Islam and more generally about religion. Americans were buying up books about Islam, but also about putative Western prophets such as Nostradamus for what might be construed as his prescient take on the terrorist attacks (E. Eakin 2001b).

On television, Oprah Winfrey offered "Islam 101" to show her audience the human—especially the female and modern—faces of Muslims. The *Times* praised her efforts at introducing her viewers to aspects of Islam (C. James 2001). PBS produced "television's crash course in Islam," a two-hour special that had been in the works since 1999, but whose completion was made timely by the immediacy of 9/11. The *Times* reviewer, Julie Salamon (2002b), wrote that "in its determination to be fair, to present an open-minded view of Muslims and how they've dealt with expanding Western influence, the producers seem"—despite their testimony to the contrary—"to have shied away from the most inflammatory and powerful imams and mullahs and their destructive exhortations against the United States and Israel." The reviewer found two themes noteworthy in the PBS documentary: (1) that Muslim women are agents of Islamic reform and (2) that Muslims are engaged in "balancing tradition and modern life." Alessandra Stanley's (2002b) review of the PBS documentary *Muhammad: Legacy of a Prophet* termed it "the first serious attempt to tell the story of Muhammad on television and also as a testimony to the hypersensitivity of our times." She found in it a "cozy, comforting portrait of Muslim communities in America," featuring "heartwarming depictions" of a New York City fireman who was on duty at Ground Zero. In effect, the documentary was, to her, a "lengthy infomercial for Islam," brought to viewers by Muslim American sponsors "eager to have the story told in the most favorable light possible." Instead of investigating potential controversies in Muhammad's life, there were rationalizations for his behavior. For instance, regarding his polygamy, the program stated: "It was an act of faith, not an act of lust." And regarding Muhammad's execution of a Jewish tribe in Medina that had supported his enemies: "The filmmakers quickly refute any argument that this incident is part of a larger historical animosity between Muslims and Jews," wrote Stanley. As the film stated, "'Muhammad had nothing against the Jewish people per se, or the Jewish religion. The Koran continues to tell Muslims to honor the People of the Book.'" (See also Elliott 2004a and Stevens 2004 for reviews of an animated film about Muhammad.)

Americans and others wanted to know about Islam, and various academic experts were suddenly in demand for their knowledge (see Lee 2004). The members of the Study of Islam section of the American Academy of Religion—"the chief academic association for professors of religion—immediately set about creating a Web site on Islam after the Sept. 11 attacks" (Stille 2001), and within two months the site had already "several thousand visits," according to Professor Omid Safi (2001–2004), then of Colgate University, "and they are coming from all over the world, including places I didn't know had Internet access." American Muslim media—such as Amana Publications—tried to fill in the gap of knowledge about Islam with their English-language Korans and other works (Niebuhr 2001m).

As American undergraduates sought to learn about the "volatile world now facing them" after 9/11, professors debated over the ways Islam might be portrayed in the classroom. Some felt that the reality of Islam included its militance, which must be analyzed—despite Edward Said's cautions against reinforcing "negative Western stereotypes" of Muslim violence. Martin S. Kramer hoped, for example, "that the attacks of Sept. 11 will shake up academics who have played down the threat of Islamic fundamentalism." Others, such as John Voll, taught their courses about Islam with exactly the opposite goal in mind: "I would hate to see the reaction be, 'Oh, my god, we have to learn more about Islam because it threatens us,'" he commented. "That would just create a new structure of polarities: the West versus Islam, the Huntingtonian 'clash of civilizations,' which is one of the worst ways to reorganize the curriculum" (Press 2001).

Arabic language was suddenly a hot academic topic in addition to the study of Muslim religion (Dillon 2003b). Unfortunately for American scholars of Islam, anti-American sentiment in the Islamic world—especially after the American invasion of Iraq—made firsthand fieldwork nigh impossible (Dillon 2003a). In *Times* coverage, scholarly representations of Islam were no more sacrosanct than televised fare. Any attempt to portray the spirituality of Islam without taking account of its politics was regarded as a potential whitewash. When the death of Annemarie Schimmel—"one of the 20th century's most influential scholars of Islam"—was reported, it was noted that her fellow German intellectuals roundly criticized her being "'a welcome guest in totalitarian Islamic states like Iran, but in her entire work there is not a single reference to human rights violations in those countries'" (Kinzer 2003).

Of course, as we have seen, the *Times* itself served as a public repository of knowledge about Islam in the post-9/11 period. The paper did not reproduce the kind of extended primer on Islam like the one published thirty years earlier (see Fiske 1974a, 1974b, 1974c, 1974d, 1974e, 1974f) but rather addressed questions regarding Islam, which seemed apt in light of 9/11. Unless readers could turn back the pages to the earlier series, they would be forced to seek other sources beyond the *Times* to learn the basic history and theology of Islam. In *Times* coverage from 2001 through 2004, 9/11 was the starting point for inquiry about Islam. Rather than trying to explain the deep structure of the religious tradition, the paper began with a crucial event and filled in enough background about Islam to make sense of the religious motives for the hijacking. As always, news stories were more about issues than about structures, at least when it came to fathoming religion. It took Peter Steinfels (2002d) the effort of surveying several books, excerpts from *Beliefnet,* a symposium on tolerance in Islam, and a PBS special on Muhammad in order to summarize what we had learned about Islam since 9/11. He concluded that Muslims as well as non-Muslims were still learning about Islam: "With more than a year gone by, American Muslims debate Islam, intolerance, terrorism and the significance of Sept. 11."

Significantly, it seemed impossible to discuss Islam without its political embroilments. As the *Times* looked at Ramadan a year after 9/11, there was less an attempt to explain Ramadan's spiritual significance than there was a critique of Islamic culture. Maureen Dowd (2002c) wrote of "a gnashing negotiation between ancient and modern—to see pilgrims in white robes carrying black laptops" on a Saudi Arabian Airlines flight from Riyadh to Jidda. She said that, "after 9/11, wised-up Americans started trying to figure out what toxic desert flowers were growing behind the kingdom's walls." Right above Dowd's column was an op-ed by Asma Gull Hasan (2002), who reminisced about the Ramadans of her schoolgirl past; however, "this year, I don't have much enthusiasm for telling people I'm fasting." With various Protestant reverends denouncing Islam, and with all the suspicion of Muslim charities and mosques, she wrote, "I can't help but feel that anything that sounds Islamic will be perceived as anti-American." Hasan was the author of *American Muslims: The New Generation* (2000), and she has since written a personal account of her Islamic faith in an American context, *Why I Am a Muslim: An American Odyssey* (2004). In 2002, however, this American-born attorney and self-proclaimed "Muslim feminist cowgirl" could not find the wherewithal to proclaim her Muslim identity or to explain her religion, so strongly did she feel American prejudices against her.

In like manner, the *Times* coverage of the 2002 pilgrimage to Mecca emphasized the "cautious" politicized "chill" created by 9/11 (Sciolino 2002c). Even as pilgrims returned to America, their "joy" was tempered by "concern" about "the growing gap between the Muslim world and the American world" (Hedges 2002a). In 2003, an Agence France-Presse photograph, "Annual Pilgrimage to Mecca nears Culmination" (2003), showed hundreds of thousands of hajjis (pilgrims); however, a Reuters dispatch regarding the mandatory hajj, "retracing the footsteps of the Prophet Muhammad 14 centuries ago," stated that "this year's pilgrimage has been overshadowed by a buildup of American troops in the Persian Gulf region for a possible attack on Iraq" ("14 Killed in Ritual" 2003). As American Muslims returned from Mecca, they expressed fear that they would be held up in airport security as potential terrorists, with their newly shaved heads and growing beards—both received in the hajj—especially as a war seemed imminent in Iraq. An American Muslim noted that "we've been connected to terrorism and it's not fair" (Sachs 2003a). The *Times* quoted his words, and yet to some degree the paper was doing precisely that—linking Islam to terrorism—by emphasizing a political angle to the sacred pilgrimage to Mecca. With an opportunity to expand the public's knowledge of Islam's spiritual aspects, the *Times* treated both Ramadan and the hajj as occasions to portray a religion colored by the concerns of 9/11, showing the intricate connections between religion's ritual and its political dimensions.

In the years to come, the *Times* continued to cover the hajj ("244 Die" 2004; "Pilgrims near End of Hajj" 2004). *Times* photos portrayed Muslims worldwide at festival times, such as Id al-Adha and Ramadan ("Cleansing before the Fasting" 2004; "A Festive Time for Muslims" 2004; "Holy Month Comes to End in Kashmir" 2004; "Milk and Dates at Sunset" 2004; "Visiting the Shiite Ancestors" 2004). Meanwhile, an op-ed by a Columbia University journalism student suggested that public discourse about Islam should stop treating Islam as a religion both foreign and at odds with the West. He recommended, for starters, that newspapers should refer to the God of the Muslims as "God" rather than "Allah" so that Christians and Jews could say to their Abrahamic brethren, "My God Is Your God" (Kearney 2004). No one at the *Times* seemed to take up his recommendation.

PART III | Religious Worlds at War

For several decades, the *Times* had run articles about the upsurge of Islam: the upsurge of fundamentalism, the upsurge of politicized religiosity, the upsurge of violence, and the links to terrorism. After 9/11, these themes became preeminent, yet the paper's personnel did not wish to portray the basic religion and culture of Islam as inherently flawed, as some American evangelicals did. The question, then—as essays in the *Times* framed it—was what had "gone wrong" with Islam over the centuries and in recent decades. In a newspaper with an abiding reverence for empirical science as an identifying mark of modernity, an answer quickly arose: that Muslims had come to hobble scientific investigation—hence, the religion's degeneration. The "Science Times" section on October 30, 2001, carried the story "How Islam Won, and Lost, the Lead in Science" by Dennis Overbye. The article reported on the "Golden Age of research and discovery," from the ninth century to the thirteenth century, but then "decline" set in, with humiliating result: "the notion that modern Islamic science is now considered 'abysmal,' as Abdus Salam, the first Muslim to win a Nobel Prize in Physics, once put it, haunts Eastern scholars." Today's Muslims might look back on Avicenna, the eleventh-century philosopher and physician, and to many other Muslim scientists of the past centuries, but "fundamentalists" turned Islamic practice to "rote learning" and eschewed rational inquiry. The spirit of scientific method has been dulled in Islamic cultures, the article stated.

By reading between the lines and recalling the *Times'* history of covering conflicts between scientific and religious cultures, one might infer a warning against religious fundamentalism in the West and its potentially dire effect on the rational culture of modernity. Progress versus degeneration; science versus supernaturalism; tolerance versus fanaticism: these dichotomies applied to *us* (Americans, mostly non-Muslims) as well as to *them* (Muslims, worldwide, including in America). Each time the *Times* pointed to the "culture wars" in Islam, its vectors reflected on American "culture wars."

As Americans reflected on the 9/11 attacks and the ensuing battles between America and Muslim nations—Afghanistan and then Iraq—the interpretive impetus was to blame the conflict on Islam's sorry state. Bernard Lewis produced two books—*What Went Wrong?* (2002) and *The Crisis of Islam* (2003)—that found disastrous fault in degenerative Islam. A review of the latter book by Kenneth M. Pollack (2003), senior fellow in foreign-policy studies at the Brookings Institution and the author of *The Threatening Storm: The Case for Invading Iraq* (2002), led with the following: "Even now, with American troops in Iraq, the wound of 9/11 has begun to heal, salved by the balm of victory over the Taliban, the destruction of Al Qaeda's Afghan sanctuary and the seeming success (perhaps illusory) of our new defensive measures for homeland security. With this distance must also come greater reflection and deeper inquiry." Bernard Lewis did very well with *What Went Wrong?* Pollack wrote. In *The Crisis of Islam*, Pollack stated, Lewis "argues that the failure to modernize is what has turned so many Middle Eastern radicals to Islamic fundamentalism; modernization and reform can't work, their alternative is to return to traditional Islamic ways. But he fails to go beyond this 'what' to address the 'why,' and it is the 'why' that we most need to understand now." Lewis should be telling us *why* Islam is so frustrated with itself and *why* it produces terrorism. Pollack was disappointed: "[Lewis] still has not offered his explanation for why the Islamic Middle East stagnated, why its efforts at reform failed, why it is notably failing to become integrated into the global economy in a meaningful way and why these failures have produced not a renewed determination to succeed . . . but an anger and frustration with the West so pervasive and vitriolic that it has bred murderous, suicidal terrorism despite all of the Islamic prohibitions against such action."

The reasons were more pervasive than a turning away from scientific discipline. An AP photo illustrated Pollack's review. It pictured "Jordanians packing a mosque in downtown Amman on the last Friday of Ramadan." Thousands of Muslims filled the street for prayer under the thrusting minaret. The caption continued: "Bernard Lewis writes that some aspects of Islamic doctrine can encourage terrorism, but that killing innocents and suicide attacks have no basis in Scripture or tradition." One might ask what the relation was between the photo and the caption or between the photographic ensemble and the review. What was the illustration meant to illustrate? The implication was that "faith and terrorism in the Muslim world"—as indicated in the review's title—were mutually generating forces in contemporary, unmodern Islam.

Afghanistan and the Taliban

Exhibit A in the *Times'* treatment of Islam "gone wrong" was the Taliban's religious rule in Afghanistan and its relation to Osama bin Laden. The paper began its post-9/11 coverage of the Taliban on September 13, 2001. Barry Bearak (2001f), who had written on the topic throughout 2001, had this to say: "Women have been forced into head-to-toe gowns known as burqas and evicted from schools and the workplace. Men are obligated to wear long beards or face jail. Banned are musical instruments, chessboards, playing cards, nail polish and neckties. Cheers at soccer matches are restricted to 'Allah-u-akbar,' or God is great. Freedom of speech has bowed to religious totalitarianism." This paragraph's portrayal was typical of the coverage to come as American troops prepared to attack the Taliban and their Al Qaeda allies. Bearak (2001l) followed with a brief history of "the [Taliban] purists," "from vigilantes to strict rulers," telling how the Taliban grew out of the outrage against the Soviet invasion and subsequent lawlessness. The abduction of two young girls in 1994 led to the formation of an armed militia from cadres of religious students *(taliban)* bent on restoring order to their country. By 1996, the Taliban, under the leadership of Mullah Muhammad Omar, had entered Kabul and taken over Afghanistan, placing the Koran as the law of the land. The *Times* described how Mullah Omar and Osama bin Laden "spent many hours in deep discussion of the intricacies of Islam" and thus "forged jihad ties," especially when bin Laden declared the mullah a "caliph, a title reserved through the 1,400-year history of Islam for the leader of the faithful" (Frantz and Rohde 2001). A feature described Mullah Omar's rise to prominence and especially how in 1996 he "literally cloaked himself in the trappings of the Prophet Muhammad." He unsealed a shrine in Kandahar and took out a cloak supposedly belonging to the Prophet Muhammad—it had not been touched since the 1930s—and in a public display placed it on his own shoulders and thus "declared himself the commander of the faithful, the leader of all Islam. No one had claimed that title since the Fourth Caliph, more than 1,000 years ago" (Weiner 2001; see also Onishi 2001c).

In the fall of 2001, the Taliban constituted a worthy subject for study (see Sifton 2001). For all their political intrigue, noble ideals and ritual brandishments, however, the Taliban served primarily as puritanical bogeymen in the *Times*, especially as US troops overran Afghanistan in search for bin Laden and Mullah Omar. The article "No TV, No Chess, No Kites: Taliban's Code, from A to Z" (Waldman 2001d) told of Taliban officials enforcing the minutiae of sharia edicts. In the "Week in Review" in early December 2001, Amy Waldman (2001h) produced a mocking tableau of Taliban codes promulgated by the Ministry for the Promotion of Virtue and the Prevention of Vice. The article's title said it all for the *Times* attitude: "Word for Word / Taboo Heaven: More No-Nos Than You Can Shake a Stick At. (Hey, No Stick-Shaking)." The Sunday "Week in Review" carried this sort of sarcastic essay that one would rarely find during the week, except perhaps on the op-ed page, and yet the viewpoint was consistent with a general *Times* scorn for the Afghan religious rulers: "The Taliban will go down in history for many reasons, but their determination to encode in law their unique vision of an Islamic society will certainly be one." Kite flying, music playing, shaving, photograph displaying, gambling, money changing, cockfights—all banned; avoidance between women and men, covering of women's faces—strictly enforced; banned from import: satellite dishes, movies, musical instruments, "'all instruments that produce music, cassette tapes, computers, VCR's, television and anything that provokes sex or nudity, . . . sewing catalogs with pictures,' neckties, and necktie pins." All these rules demonstrated how far the Taliban was willing to go in ruling over a somewhat reluctant population of fellow Muslims. In an act of cultural revenge, one Taliban official "was chased down and shot to death by a group of youths" (Waldman 2001d), as the US-supported forces defeated the Taliban.

By early December, US troops seemed victorious, and the *Times* seemed to share the spirit of triumph over the Taliban. Bearak (2001i) described how "Kabul retraces steps to life before [the] Taliban." Robert Nickelsberg's photographs expressed the article's tone toward Afghans' liberated "joy": the accoutrements of a beauty shop window, an accordion fingered by a musician, an unfurled oil painting, all retrieved from their hiding places; men and women speaking "freely" with one another once again. In Kabul, an "Afghan artist [erased] layers of repression imposed by the Taliban." The intrepid Afghan physician and artist "saved his oil paintings from the Taliban's wrath by covering them with watercolor, which he later removed," once safe from Taliban control (Landler 2002a).

Two photographs by Andrew Testa (2001) of Sufis banned by the Taliban bore the caption: "In a Kabul mosque, there is new vigor among dervishes [as] the Nakshbandi dervishes in Kabul prayed openly" once their Taliban masters were removed from power. Other photographs illustrating Afghan "hunger" for "a new, better, life" (Waldman 2001b) showed the glee of girls on a carnival ride in Kandahar (Ruth Fremson's) and the devotion of worshippers at the Shrine of Ali Mosque in Mazar-i-Sharif (Chang W. Lee's), both presumably enhanced by the Taliban's fall. Jews (Landler 2002b) as well as Sikhs and Hindus (Waldman 2002f) who had survived the restrictions and threats of Taliban rule were eager to restore their worship and their rivalries. The Agence France-Presse photo "Hoping to Give Buddha Back to Afghanistan" (2002) showed the cliffs in Bamiyan where the Taliban had destroyed one of the giant statues of the Buddha a year earlier. The interim Afghan government commissioned a native sculptor to organize the reconstruction of at least one of the Buddhas if the government was able to raise funds. Religious diversity and tolerance seemed to be on the rise where the Taliban once enforced uniformity. A year later, however, UNESCO officials had persuaded the Afghan government not to rebuild a Buddha—despite an offer from the Japanese—on aesthetic and political grounds (Gall 2003b).

With the Taliban officially undone, the *Times* made much of 9/11's first anniversary by proclaiming the freedoms that Afghanistan's women had gained by the American takeover. In keeping with the paper's fascination with fashion, two prominent articles emphasized the beauty shop angle. "After the Veil, a Makeover Rush" (Halbfinger 2002), read the headline of a Sunday "Styles" feature with four color photos by Natalie Behring-Chisholm showing how "American companies provide Afghan women with cosmetics and ideas" and how "Afghan women who left return to teach a new generation basic haircuts and manicures." The difficulty was in "trying to overcome a shortage of beauticians, combs, gels, rinses and powders" in order to accomplish the apparently heroic tasks of teaching "how to apply . . . makeup" and providing "a lesson in cutting and layering." Sadly, "Kabul salons have lacked even the basics like mirrors" under repressive Taliban rule. Afghan women were said to be "relishing beautiful new freedoms in

Kabul," especially when on Fridays—"Afghanistan's wedding day—beauty salons in Kabul fill up with brides." Amidst photos by Tyler Hicks of beauty products, the *Times* reporter commented: "In the Taliban's scheme of things, the only true beauty lay in the contemplation of God. So, no question, the Taliban mullahs with their hairshirt version of Islam, chased from power 10 months ago by American bombing, would take a wretched view of what has been happening lately on Fridays in Kabul and many other Afghan cities and towns" (Burns 2002c). With the help of military firepower, the hairdressers and cosmeticians had triumphed over the puritans, much to the glee of the *Times*.

For that victory to occur, however, the United States needed to commit its troops to fight. Here the *Times* examined the motives and justifications for military action in Afghanistan, reporting on American and international religious leaders' qualms and weighing the arguments for and against the war and the particulars of its conduct. As the United States geared up for its attack on Afghanistan, the Taliban mullahs asked bin Laden to leave their country and asked America for mercy against their poor people. At the same time, they were furious at President Bush's use of the word *crusade* to describe the US response to terrorism (Burns 2001a); even the code name for the military operation against terrorism, "Infinite Justice," was considered offensive to Muslims ("Choice of Words" 2001).

At home on September 21, 2001, various religious groups—Catholics, Protestants, Jews, and Muslims, according to the *Times*' ecumenical tally—expressed "nuanced" support for what they termed America's "right of self-defense," but they also called for adherence to international law and respect for all domestic religious groups (Niebuhr 2001v). Thus, the paper carried out its accustomed survey of religious perspectives on the ethical issues of the moment. The next day the *Times* reviewed St. Augustine's and St. Thomas Aquinas's classic formulations of the Christian notion of "just" warfare. The article featured two contemporary scholars—Michael Walzer and Reverend J. Bryan Hehir, S.J.—who expounded on "just-war" theory, especially the intent to prevent injustice, to establish a just peace, and to limit violence to minimize deadly dangers to noncombatants. At the same time, Stanley Hauerwas, a pacifist, was "'absolutely dumbfounded' at the ease and haste with which Christian leaders in the United States adopted a belligerent stance that in his view is at odds with the teachings of their religion" (Bohlen 2001a).

Journeying in Kazakhstan, "a model of religious tolerance" (Pala 2003), Pope John Paul II urged "restraint" (Henneberger 2001h; see also Henneberger 2001i, 2001o) in response to the 9/11 attacks. The pontiff "obliquely spoke against war," cautioning against "any overzealous military response by the U.S" (Henneberger 2001e)—a message delivered by Vatican officials to the new American ambassador to the Holy See a few days after 9/11 (Henneberger 2001j). The pope also "drew a sharp distinction between "'authentic Islam' and the extremism that led to the recent terrorist attacks in the United States" (Henneberger 2001g). Then Vatican spokesmen "worried that the pope had come off as too pacifistic, or even anti-American," and so "the Vatican foreign policy team went to work, stressing that he had never precluded the use of force," a qualification that served as a "reminder that the church was not only a spiritual body but a geopolitical one, with an agenda and internal struggles of its own" (Henneberger 2001f). (See the pope's careful way of deploring the 1915 Armenian "'genocide'" without condemning the Turks [Henneberger 2001] and his expressions of generalized concern for peace [Henneberger 2001b; "Pope Urges World" 2001].)

Different national units of Catholic bishops issued their own statements of understanding regarding political leaders' responsibilities in crises. Italian bishops, for example, said that it was "a duty, to neutralize international terrorism," within "just war" constraints, of course: the war must be a response to evil; it must have the purpose to protect lives; the good must outweigh the evil; there must be an attempt at civilian immunity; there must be no more force than necessary; there must be a chance of success. Vatican officials tried to balance the need to combat terrorism with the need to provide "social justice" around the world (Henneberger 2001l).

Simply to report on the attitudes of "the world's intellectuals and politicians" was to place the American moral position in waging a war against terrorism into a shadow of perspectivism. Not much more than a month after 9/11, the *Times* reported, "More and more, the war is being seen abroad as 'America against Osama,' not, as the Bush administration would prefer, 'All of us against terrorism.' The intense Sept. 12 rush of 'We are all Americans' seems to have faded in the breasts of all but Tony Blair" (McNeil 2001).

Three years later a Pentagon study found the United States failing to explain its policies regarding terrorism to the Muslim world. "Muslims do not 'hate our freedom,'" the report stated, "but rather they hate our policies." Moreover, the report said, "when American public diplomacy talks about bringing democracy to Islamic societies, this is seen as no more than self-serving hypocrisy" (quoted in Shanker 2004). Furthermore, the *Times* claimed, "The United States has a strategic problem: its war on terror, unlike its long fight against Communism, is not universally seen as the pivotal global struggle of the age. Rather, it is often portrayed abroad as a distraction from more critical issues—as an American attempt to impose a bellicose culture, driven by the cultivation of fear, on a world still taken with the notion that the cold war's end and technology's advance have opened unprecedented possibilities for dialogue and peace" (R. Cohen 2004).

In the United States, strains of opposition arose to the gathering military response to 9/11. The new Episcopal bishop of New York City, Mark S. Sisk, called for reconciliation, not hatred (Peterson 2001). Peace marches in Washington, DC, included Quakers bearing witness against what they called a "war of revenge" (Becker 2001). A sketch of an American Catholic priest "devoted to nonviolence" cited his belief in "the God of Peace" and his devotion to antiwar "icons" such as Mahatma Gandhi, Martin Luther King Jr., Dorothy Day, Philip Berrigan, and Oscar Romero (Kifner 2001). The American Friends Service Committee, Pax Christi USA, War Resisters League, and other groups planned "vigils and rallies to urge alternatives to war" (Niebuhr 2001k), stressing that the proper response to the 9/11 attacks should aim for justice and international tribunals rather than for war. A black American imam in Brooklyn allowed that "President Bush 'should use any legitimate means to go after the perpetrators'" of the 9/11 attacks, "but he cautioned that the quest for justice could cause the United States to itself be unjust. 'If we kill innocents, we create the conditions for another Osama bin Laden. Don't seek vengeance; seek justice'" (Waldman 2001e).

The *Times* gave attention to antiwar religious viewpoints before the fighting began, raising the question of what a "just" military reply to 9/11 might be. One could see by reading the *Times* that there was not a monolithic religious viewpoint on the ethics of warfare; even within particular denominations there was a range of moral judgments. Both the tension and the congruence between churchly and patriotic loyalties were visible in the reportage. Once the fighting was taking place, the *Times* made note of questions being raised about its conduct. If by and large "violence begets violence" (Steinfels 2001d), was it possible that violence might produce "justice" in some situations? Should the United States cease its military action during Ramadan? Daniel J. Wakin (2001e) wrote that such cessation rarely happened within Muslim cultures; indeed, "Muhammad himself led his followers in battle during Ramadan in 624." In his "Beliefs" column, Peter Steinfels (2001b) noted the diversity of Christian American opinions about the American retaliation in Afghanistan and about war in general, saying, "Most U.S. church leaders back the war, with a 'but.'"

The *Times*—and especially Steinfels—had long been concerned about the ethics of warfare. Over the next few years, Steinfels devoted at least ten of his "Beliefs" columns to an evaluation of warfare's ethical dimensions and especially of America's war-making activities. When asked if he feels particularly committed to this issue, Steinfels (2005a) replied that the ethics of war is "a great, long-standing interest of mine." The antiwar *Catholic Worker* was regular reading in his childhood home. One of his brothers was a conscientious objector; another was critical of the war in Vietnam even when serving in the armed forces. Steinfels' Ph.D. dissertation concerned the Left in Europe, and he respects citizens' duty to criticize their government as well as their church. In short, he believes in "moral constraints" concerning the "paramount military power in the world," and he wrote his columns accordingly.

At the same time, the *Times* ran many prominent 9/11 commentaries that justified the American military action against Osama bin Laden, Al Qaeda, and the Taliban as a matter of prudent, patriotic defense. Whereas *Times* editorials were far from bellicose in tone, there was clear support for President Bush's decision to invade Afghanistan. *Times* coverage of the war described American soldiers in sympathetic terms—for example, a December 3, 2001, article on marines in Afghanistan that included a paragraph on a Roman Catholic intelligence officer who led a lay service and that compared Advent's preparation for Christ with the soldiers' preparation for the culminating battles to come (Myers 2001). Here was a poignant instance of religiosity's inspiration in warfare; the article more generally served to support the American effort in the war by presenting American soldiers in appealing terms.

On the same day, the *Times* ran a critical story in the "Business Day" section about Fox network's coverage of the war: "Fox Portrays a War of Good and Evil, and Many Applaud" (Rutenberg 2001). According to Fox, Osama bin Laden was "'a dirtbag,' 'a monster' overseeing a 'web of hate.' His followers in Al Qaeda are 'terror goons.'" This commentary constituted, according to the *Times* reporter, "unabashed and vehement support of a war effort, carried in tough-guy declarations often expressing thirst for revenge." The *Times* explained: "The [Fox] network's motto is 'fair and balanced,' a catch phrase drafted to imply that it is objective while its competitors carry a liberal bias. But in this conflict, Fox executives say, to be unequivocally fair and balanced is to participate in the worst kind of cultural relativism. Giving both sides equal credence is to lose touch with right and wrong, they contend. . . . 'What we say is terrorists, terrorism, is evil, and America doesn't engage in it, and these guys do,' said Roger Ailes, the *Fox News* chairman." As a result, Fox "avoided giving too much weight to reports about civilian casualties in Afghanistan. . . . ' In the final analysis, Mr. Ailes said, 'I don't believe that democracy and terrorism are relative things you can talk about, and I don't think there's any moral equivalence in those two positions.' He added: 'If that makes me a bad guy, tough luck. I'm still getting the ratings.'"

Writing in the *Times* about the Muslim world's own news coverage of the war in Afghanistan, Fouad Ajami (2001b) observed Arabic television network Al Jazeera's take on Osama bin Laden and George W. Bush and found that it was not "objective." Ajami wrote that Al Jazeera's "Hollywoodization of news is indulged in with an abandon that would make Fox News Channel blush." But James J. Napoli (2002) remarked that, truly, nothing could make Fox blush. Not "professional egoist Geraldo Rivera," whom Fox hired to cover the war in Afghanistan; not the American flags on the sets; not the use of the "patriotic 'we.'" Fox as well as CNN and MSNBC "were, in short, Al Jazeera's secret sharers, mirroring it with reverse images" (20). When we look at Islamic journalism, Napoli argued—for example, in Egypt—we should not be surprised to find chauvinism, bias, blaming of the West, and antisecularism; each culture's media reflect its cultural biases and concerns.

National culture is the context from which news perspectives are drawn, especially in times of conflict. Nonetheless, the *Times* drew on its critical capacities and on the judgments of religionists from home and abroad in assessing US war making after 9/11. The *Times* carried reports of religious exponents critical of the American military campaign in Afghanistan and took seriously religion's ethical commentary on the conduct of war. At an ecumenical gathering—including Muslims, Jews, Buddhists, Hindus, Zoroastrians, and Christians—the pope denounced "violence in religion's name" (Tagliabue 2002a). Speaking in Azerbaijan, the pope once again enunciated "his message of peace" (Stanley 2002a). As the US war in Afghanistan continued, Steinfels (2002b) composed a "Beliefs" column on "keeping civilians immune from direct attack." He feared that "the moral line against directly attacking civilians" was "going to be crossed once again to fit the circumstances. . . . Does the end justify the means? Who remembers?" he asked. Daniel J. Wakin (2003b) memorialized "Christian charity to help a mosque." According to the article, "Criticism [arose] as [an] Episcopal church [rebuilt] an Afghan house of worship" that American bombing had destroyed during the war. The kicker was a quotation from the chairwoman of the New York City Episcopal–Muslim Relations Committee, which organized the effort. "Christianity teaches unconditional love," she said in an expression of values contrasting the spirit of warfare, "and what love could be more unconditional than to build a house of worship for a community other than your own?"

In reporting on religious organizations' concerns about the war, the *Times* contrasted to the jingoistic coverage of media such as Fox. Nonetheless, the *Times,* like most American newspapers, included vast coverage that tilted toward American interests, values, and institutions, including democracy, Christianity, and Judaism. In so doing, the paper reflected its primary constituency's viewpoints. When President Bush tried to turn the memorial of 9/11 into a crusade of good against evil, most American newspapers let him get away with it. Even as September 11 Families for Peaceful Tomorrows launched a countercampaign with the slogan "Our Grief Is Not a Declaration of War" (Napoli 2002:22), the majority of Americans resonated to Bush's war cry. When he claimed that a war against Iraq was part of a larger war against terrorism, a continuation of the 9/11 story and its religious angles, the American news media did not contradict him frontally—not even the *Times* and its primary reporter, Judith Miller, to its eventual chagrin.

Regarding this absence of critique of the administration's claims, John Tagliabue (2007a) recalls how one of his articles "faced resistance from editors" at the *Times.* He wrote a piece from Prague quoting Czech intelligence officials to the effect that there had been no meeting in Prague between Mohamed Atta and an Iraqi diplomat. "At that time," Tagliabue remembers, "the Bush administration was pushing the view that such a meeting took place, and used it as grounds for going to war in Iraq." Rather than confront the Bush justification, the *Times* "hesitated for several days before running my story," Tagliabue reports, "and then in shortened form and deep inside the paper."

Critics writing before the US invasion of Iraq charged that "September 11 has been narrativized by way of the media into a primary, recognizable discourse, one with a distinct logic—a clear beginning (September 11, 2001), forceful middle (war), and moral end (democratic victory)" (Chermak, Bailey, and Brown 2003a:5). Surely the *Times* provided news of critical commentary on such a myth during the war in Afghanistan; however, the paper also articulated and even espoused the myth. The *Times* and Fox might have seemed worlds apart in their coverage, but seen from the perspective of, say, Al Jazeera, the differences between the two Western news outlets appeared less definitive.

In the course of the Afghan War, a flurry of attention centered on the American workers and their cohorts accused by the Taliban of Christian proselytizing and imprisoned since the eve of 9/11. Even before the American invasion, the parents of the two American women, Heather Mercer and Dayna Curry, feared for their daughters' safety and denied that they had broken Taliban law by trying to convert Afghan Muslims (Frantz 2001a). While promising the accused a "'fair trial'" (Burns 2001g), the Taliban seemed to threaten their lives if the United States carried out its invasion.

The incursion took place, and before too long the *Times* reported the rescue of eight imprisoned workers, including the two American women, with a front-page headline on November 15, 2001 (Schmemann 2001a; see also Burns 2001h). After their "ordeal" and their dramatic release, the two American women told how they had engaged in religious dialogue with their Taliban captors. "They explained their faith and they asked us what we believe," the women said as they and their fellows proclaimed their Christian faith and their forgiveness (Onishi 2001a). In Waco, Texas, the women's sponsors and friends were "jubilant," calling the deliverance a "godsend" (Milloy 2001b). On November 17, the two American women acknowledged that some of the Taliban charges against them— perhaps 20 percent—were true. Indeed, they had shared their Christian books and a film about Jesus with their Afghan associates, and these offenses were punishable under the law at the time. The Taliban were respectful toward the women in prison, they attested, allowing them to pray. But the two saw Afghan women beaten by the Taliban for running away from their abusive husbands, so the Americans experienced "fear" as well as "faith" during their imprisonment (Frantz 2001b). President Bush shortly thereafter praised them for their courage under duress.

In the journal *Religion in the News*, Dennis R. Hoover (2002b) analyzed the media's coverage of the two women accused of "Christian proselytizing" (16).

Hoover claimed that the press either hid or did not discover that the charges against the women were surely true. Their employer was Antioch Community Church in Waco, Texas, a missionizing organization that set them up as volunteers with Shelter Now Afghanistan. The Taliban did not allow visas to "'missionaries,'" so the women called themselves "'aid workers'" (16), a phrase that the press picked up uncritically. Hoover found the "religion reporting" on this incident "anemic" (16), including in the *Times,* either because the media did not want to endanger the women while in Taliban prison or because they were lazy in tracking the facts. The women were, indeed, using a famous missionizing film about Jesus and a Bible translated into Dari for the purposes of evangelizing. Whatever they might have said to their captors about having merely "'natural conversations'" with their Afghan associates, the women were missionaries, as they acknowledged after their release (16).

Was the *Times* coverage of the two women's story as anemic as Hoover asserted? Barry Bearak (2001n) hinted at the facts, but Douglas Frantz (2001a, 2001b) seemed to have missed the truth about Antioch Community Church's proselytizing agency. There certainly was no criticism of the women or any implication that their activities were a matter of ethical, legal, or political concern.

In subsequent years, however, when the *Times* followed the issue of Christian missionary activity among Muslim populations, it raised a question about the prudence of such evangelism in the milieu of an aroused Islam. There was no issue raised in an article about "campus evangelists" (Zhao 2002a) seeking out foreign students at US universities for possible conversion; indeed, their targets seemed primarily to be non-Muslim Chinese. Abroad, however, the political ramifications were serious and even violent. And Hindu as well as Muslim self-assertion might lead to missionary deaths ("Claim in Killing of Christian Family in India" 2002).

In the Philippines, Islamic revolutionaries killed a Christian missionary and injured his wife when Filipino troops trained by the United States confronted the guerrillas, who had held the couple captive for more than a year (Fountain 2002b; Perlez 2002f). The *Times*—which had presented a feature on the faith of the missionaries' children, who wondered about God's plan for their parents but "begged God to stop their suffering" (Wilgoren 2001b; see also "Muslim Rebels in Philippines" 2001)—attested to the steadfastness of the missionaries' evangelical community back in the United States.

When a US medical missionary was murdered in Lebanon, the paper reported on the "resolve" of students at the Moody Bible Institute in Chicago, which had trained the young woman for her Christian enterprise abroad (Fountain 2002a). The *Times* also noted, however, that Lebanese Muslims had "denounced" aggressive proselytizing in previous months, and attempts by native Christians and Muslims to limit the evangelicals' activities, for their own good, had been "rebuffed." It appeared that "derogatory remarks about Islam and Muhammad made by leading evangelists like the Rev. Jerry Falwell and the Rev. Pat Robertson had added to the ill feeling toward Christian evangelists" in the area (MacFarquhar 2002d). The *Times* took the sole killing and the death by bombing of a Lebanese convert (Wakin 2003e) as symbolic of the "enmity" between evangelists and Muslims in Lebanon, and not all Christians found the missionaries blameless. "I think she was killed because she was preaching Christianity to Muslims," said a local Catholic archbishop "who has criticized the evangelist movement's assertive efforts at conversion. 'She was in the habit of gathering the Muslim children of the quarter and preaching Christianity to them while dispensing food and toys and social assistance,' he said, and her actions upset the city's Muslim hierarchy. 'In these times, there are people in the Muslim community who don't even want to hear the word 'conversion'" (MacFarquhar 2002d).

In December 2002, when three American Southern Baptist missionaries were slain in Yemen, a "Religion" sidebar announced, "With Missionaries Spreading, Muslims' Anger Is Following." American Christian missionaries have become a "lightning rod" in Yemen, the reporter said. "More recently the number of volunteer missionaries has exploded," leading to hundreds of thousands of Muslim conversions to Christianity. "Under Muslim law," however, "conversion from Islam is punishable by death." The evangelicals could think of those who died as "martyrs." They could perceive in the violence "a conflict between God and Satan, between good and evil," as they put it (MacFarquhar 2002a; see also Fisher 2003e). Nonetheless, Christian proselytizing enraged Yemeni Muslims, and at least some felt justified in preserving the status quo through violence, even when the evangelists felt "affection" for the Yemeni people they knew (McFadden 2002a).

With the war in Iraq under way in spring 2003, Deborah Caldwell (2003), senior producer of the online magazine *Beliefnet*, wrote an essay in the *Times* "Week in Review": "Should Christian Missionaries Heed the Call in Iraq?" The photo by Mark Mainz was of the singer Bono and Reverend Franklin Graham, the latter of Samaritan's Purse. "Evangelical groups want to help. They also want to spread the Gospel," said the raised caption. The article quoted Graham: "We're in an Arab country and we just can't go out and preach." But, he said, "God will always give us opportunities to tell others about his son. We are there to reach out to love them and to save them." Some, including conservative evangelists, were worried that the Muslim world would perceive this effort as a crusade, part of the American national agenda, especially given Graham's closeness to George W. Bush. Since 1990, Caldwell wrote, the number of Christian missionaries in Islamic countries had quadrupled, led by Southern Baptists. There was even a special master's degree program at Southwestern Baptist Theological Seminary in Texas for missionaries ministering to Muslims. A major tool in this missionary effort was the *Jesus Film,* created by the founder of Campus Crusade for Christ in 1979 and translated into 811 languages. It was this film that helped get the American missionaries in Afghanistan arrested in 2001. Evangelical Christians did not understand why they should be criticized for carrying out Jesus's command to spread the faith, but others—especially but not exclusively Muslims—found the Christian outreach offensive and unwise in a time of war between America and a Muslim nation.

At the least, some evangelical leaders wished to offer what they called a "loving rebuke" to Reverends Graham, Falwell, and Vines, who had made public "anti-Islam remarks," not only because such comments "tarnished American Christians," but also because they "jeopardized the safety of missionaries and indigenous Christians in predominantly Muslim countries." At the same time, they "accused mainline Protestants and groups like the World Council of Churches of holding 'naive' dialogue sessions with Muslims that minimized theological and political differences." Falwell replied, "In this media-sensitive world, we must be cautious that we walk a tightrope that does not allow offending others while at the same time never compromising what we believe. . . . At the same time we cannot expect hundreds of thousands of evangelical church leaders to go silent when somebody asks what they think about any religion, just because those religions might kill their missionaries'" (Goodstein 2003n).

If anything, many evangelicals stiffened their determination to criticize Islam and to bring "'the love of Christ'" to Muslims everywhere (Goodstein 2003m). Laurie Goodstein recorded the words of "evangelical Christians from several states gathered for an all-day seminar on how to woo Muslims away from Islam." She heard them say, in their comments and in their writings, that "the Koran's good verses are like the food an assassin adds to poison to disguise a deadly taste. . . . Better to find the same food, sans poison, in the Bible." Representing the thousands of American Christian missionaries trained to proselytize in Muslim lands, "they assert that while the vast majority of Muslims are not evil, they have been deceived by a diabolical religion based on a flawed scripture that can never bring them salvation." Even when their critics charged that "'evangelicals have substituted Islam for the Soviet Union . . . [and that] [t]he Muslims have become the modern-day equivalent of the Evil Empire,'" and historians noted that "'Islam is the only religious tradition that has ever threatened the existence of Christianity,'" and even when President Bush depicted Islam as a "peaceful religion that has been 'hijacked' by extremists," the missionaries and their supporters held steadfast to their evangelical beliefs and strategies. (See also Onishi 2004 regarding Korean Christian missionaries to Muslim populations.)

The Jewish Angle

When on 9/11 the hijacked planes smashed into icons of the American land-scape—its financial, military, and political symbols (the fourth flight was to be diverted to destroy the US Capitol)—the Muslim radicals' target seemed to be America itself. Over the months that followed, the *Times* pieced together the motives for Al Qaeda's assault on the United States: its imperial breadth, its mili-tary presence in the holy land of Saudi Arabia, its satanic obsession with unholy matters such as sexuality, and its unwavering support for Israel.

Israelis and Americans sympathetic to Israel's cause commented immedi-ately that "when the unimaginable happens and it's right outside your window," Americans must be asked: "Do you get it[?]" "It was simply a question for those who, at a safe remove from the terrorism that Israelis face every day, have damned Israel for taking admittedly harsh measures to keep its citizens alive." The *Times* "NYC" columnist, who had reported on Israel in the early 1990s, suggested in his column that "Jerusalem offers a glimpse of what New York may become" (Haber-man 2001a). The Israel-friendly Committee for Accuracy in Middle East Report-ing in America (CAMERA) gave a "thumbs up to Clyde Haberman" ("Thumbs Up" 2001) for this column and for his reports (e.g., Haberman 2001b) on the fears that Israelis live with daily under Palestinian threat. Americans needed to see the Muslim world as did Israelis, according to CAMERA, because now both America and Israel were targets of Muslim terrorists. CAMERA found Haber-man's column "candid" and "truly refreshing," especially "in a newspaper which continues to designate those killers who target American civilians 'terrorists,' and those killers who target Israeli civilians 'militants.'"

Ari L. Goldman, a former (and still occasional) *Times* writer, wrote an essay in the *Jerusalem Post* for September 14, 2001, in which he asked if he and his family would "avoid Israel so we can be safe and sound in New York?" "All New

Yorkers became Israelis this week," he said. "After the last few days in New York, we are not just New Yorkers. We are Israelis. We belong there. We're going." Goldman, like Haberman, brought his associations with Israel in his immediate reaction to 9/11 and not least of all because of his Jewishness. In the aftermath of 9/11, Jews in America, in Israel, and in other places on the globe—as reflected on the pages of the *New York Times*—felt the attacks to be part of a more general assault on Jews.

A third anecdote: *Times* foreign-affairs columnist Thomas L. Friedman was in Israel on 9/11. He told how an Israeli secretary reacted in Jerusalem to the news of the assault on the World Trade Center and the Pentagon: "'Now the world will finally understand what we've been facing,' she declared. Then, with barely a pause, she added: 'Oh my God, they're going to blame us.'" Friedman commented, "She was right on both counts" (from Friedman 2003a:322).

The *Times,* always keen to the question of anti-Semitism, continued in post-9/11 coverage to address the catastrophic outpouring of anti-Jewish thought in the Holocaust—including the putative role of the Vatican in fomenting such hatred (R. Bernstein 2001a; Wills 2001). However, Jonathan Rosen (2001), former editor of the Jewish weekly newspaper *The Forward,* brought the Holocaust up to date in the *Times Magazine* by addressing "the uncomfortable question of anti-Semitism." Rosen related how he had thought he was living in a post-Holocaust world, but now he wondered after 9/11, if perhaps it was "a pre-Holocaust world as well." Would Jews be blamed as the fundamental cause of the 9/11 attacks, especially if the Muslim motive turned out to be revenge for Israel's treatment of the Palestinians? But there was a deeper way, he said, in which Jews *are* the essence of difference between "the terrorists and their fundamentalist defenders," on the one hand, and "Americans and Jews," on the other. Jews, he contended, are basically religious relativists. For centuries, "Jews believed that adherents of other faiths could find their own path to God. Christianity and Islam, which cast unbelievers as infidels, did not share this essential religious relativism." The United States, Rosen said, came to that laissez-faire conclusion in creating its pluralist nation-state. And so Jews and Americans *are* the enemy to the Islamists, who are religious absolutists at heart. This realization, he concluded, "redoubles my patriotism and steels me for the struggle ahead."

Letter writers found Rosen's article "chilling and moving," a "disturbing glimpse at what the future might bring" ("The Uncomfortable Question" 2001).

For many, anti-Semitism was entangled inseparably with Israel, although opinions varied regarding the ways of interpreting the connection. To one, the issue was "'kosher' anti-Semitism that under the guise of sympathy for the Palestinian cause attempts to isolate Israel and undermine its legitimacy—even as it once again demonizes Jews" (Goldsmith 2001). Another reader distinguished between the inclination to "think critically about Middle Eastern politics," on the one hand, and "unfair" charges of anti-Semitism, on the other. "My American Jewish friends," the letter writer said, "whisper to me that even they cannot question Zionism to other Jews without being labeled anti-Semitic" (Amy Logan in "The Uncomfortable Question" 2001). This difference of perspective played out in the *Times* over the years to come.

More immediately, the *Times* commented repeatedly on the "nonsensical" view held by many Muslims and others that "only 'international Zionism possessed the means and will'" (Gerges 2001) to carry out the 9/11 assaults in order to set off armed conflict between the United States and Muslim nations in the Mideast. There clearly were many who held Israel—and Jews in other lands—responsible for a variety of unnamed world problems. Through 2002 and 2003, the *Times* recounted dozens of anti-Jewish attacks, including violent crimes, in the United States and around the world. American Jews, "long known for their outspoken defense of civil liberties," were especially sensitive to the threat of Muslim terrorism and were "silent on or even supportive of the Bush administration's counterterrorism legislation, breaking with their allies in the civil liberties movement who have criticized the new measures as potentially repressive" (Goodstein 2002b). In Brooklyn, the Jewish Defense Group planned armed patrols in the likelihood of Muslim attacks, although police prohibitions against such vigilantism halted the plan ("Jewish Group" 2002; A. Newman 2002b, 2002c).

An Anti-Defamation League poll found that 17 percent of Americans held "'hard-core' anti-Semitic views, as measured by reactions to an array of time-tested stereotypes about Jews: they have too much power, they're not honest in business, their first loyalties lie with Israel, and so on. Pre-9/11, a similar poll pegged that hard core at only 12 percent," said "NYC" columnist Clyde Haberman (2002). Haberman correlated the statistical rise with the Israeli–Palestinian violence, although he asked, "Can't one find fault with Israel, not to mention with the iron-fisted policies of Prime Minister Ariel Sharon, without being labeled an anti-Semite?" Not all the news was bad, he said; "it seems too early to reach for panic buttons. . . . Yet an 'end is at hand' fear has spread among American Jews. . . . Some even see a 'second Holocaust' on the way."

Hence, Jewish houses of worship throughout New York City constructed protective barriers, as discussed in the article "Messages in Concrete: The Aesthetics of Safety" (Dunlap 2002). The captioned *Times* photograph by Don Hogan Charles told it all: "The concrete barriers at the Central Synagogue at 55th Street and Lexington Avenue were installed after a warning from the F.B.I." Central Synagogue had completed its restoration two days before 9/11 "to the flourish of trumpeting shofars," wrote David Dunlap (2004c) a few years later. Now, "like so many synagogues," including Congregation Shaaray Tefila, also Reform, "it was ringed with concrete barriers after the attack on New York in 2001" (40, 259). But there were no barriers to protect two dozen cars in a Jewish neighborhood in Brooklyn from the spray painting of swastikas, one of which was displayed in a photograph by William C. Lopez (see "Two Dozen Cars Vandalized" 2003; cf. Fried 2003).

In two cases, American Jews were accused of plotting preemptive attacks on Muslim institutions. Jewish Defense League leader Irving D. Rubin and a confederate were said to have plotted an attack on a mosque in Los Angeles and at the office of a Congressman of Middle Eastern descent (Winter 2001a). A sidebar explained the history of Meir David Kahane's Jewish Defense League, founded in 1968, and its Los Angeles offshoot, known for its "militancy" (Lueck 2001). The league's Web site offered the following exhortation: "We pray to G-d Almighty to help us avenge the deaths of every single victim of Arab/Islamic terror" (quoted in Winter 2001d). A Jewish man in Florida was also charged with plotting to blow up an Islamic education center and dozens of mosques ("Doctor Is Charged in Plot" 2002; "Police Say Man Accused in Plot Had Explosives" 2002). As for Rubin, he was murdered in prison while awaiting trial ("California: Jewish Radical Is Dead" 2002; "Jewish Defense League Leader Is Declared Dead" 2002; LeDuff 2002), a fatality in the struggle between extremists among American Jews and their imagined—but not imaginary—enemies.

In France, a wave of anti-Jewish threats and crimes crested after 9/11, reflecting tensions between Muslim and Jewish communities and their strong differences in loyalty regarding Israel and its policies toward Palestinians, which reached a point of crisis in 2002 (Daley 2002b). Hundreds of incidents, including arson and shootings, worried Jews throughout Europe, caused governments in France and Belgium to declare emergency protective measures ("Defending France's Jews" 2003; McNeil 2002a; "Shooting in France" 2002), and was reason enough for Germany to raise the legal status of Jews in the country (Butler 2002). Nonetheless, firebombing and other assaults persisted (Tagliabue 2002c), especially during the siege of the Church of the Nativity in Bethlehem in April 2002, a symbol of an exacerbated Israeli–Palestinian conflict. In close to a dozen French cities, "synagogues, classrooms, school buses, a clubhouse" were "targets . . . of home-made bombs," and when fifty thousand people marched in Paris to "protest anti-Jewish attacks and to support Israel," fights broke out with pro-Palestinian counterdemonstrators (Simons 2002a). In Germany, anti-Semitism reared its head in a political campaign (Erlanger 2002c) and in literary circles (Erlanger 2002a); in Russia, "Death to Yids" was the "ugly message" on a sign rigged to a bomb, which wounded a woman who tried to tear it down (Tavernise 2002); in Italy, Jewish graves were "desecrated" (Bruni 2002), although a follow-up headline retorted, "Vandals' Motive Wasn't Anti-Semitism" (2002).

"Europe Knows Who's to Blame in the Middle East," stated a "Week in Review" headline (Erlanger 2002b), and by and large those to blame were not the Palestinians. A member of Germany's Parliament noted that "the general attitude has change in Europe and it is a very dangerous moment. . . . It could open anti-Semitic doors, and we must do important work in the next days and weeks to forestall that." Americans, too, worried about the European shift against Israel, especially considering Europe's Holocaust past. The *Times* stated succinctly that "since Sept. 11, there has been considerable empathy among Americans for the threat faced by Israel. Moreover, Washington, now publicly committed to opposing all terrorism, is more understanding of Israel's need to defend itself as it sees fit. The Europeans, in contrast, generally don't consider the Middle East a security threat, except insofar as their own Muslim populations become violent in support of Palestinians or Afghans."

Steven Erlanger (2007b), who wrote several pieces in the *Times* about the post-9/11 images of Jews—especially in Europe, where he became Berlin correspondent—is not content to assign the label of "anti-Semitism" to European "disquiet" over Israel and the Palestinians. In his analysis, an "unthought-through European leftish sympathy for the underdog" attached itself to the Palestinians," along with "a sense of schadenfreude, almost that the victims have become the victimizers, that the Jews, too, have been somehow corrupted by power and the use of force." Europeans' attitudes toward multiethnic Israel have been complicated by "their own colonial sins that produced such large and growing Muslim populations in essentially mono-ethnic and mono-cultural" European enclaves and by the "sense of glee some felt" that Israel's ally, the United States, "got its nose punched by someone, that Americans finally understood for a time that foreign policy has consequences." These views, Erlanger thinks, are not about "'Islam' or 'Judaism' per se," and anti-Semitism is but a sidebar to a more complex set of issues.

Nonetheless, the *Times* kept a focus on anti-Semitism. On April 13, 2002, cultural essayist Edward Rothstein (2002a) explained contemporary "anti-Semitism as fear of too-rapid change," stating that

> the hatred of Islamic radicals for the United States is also inspired by fear that their own traditions and order are being undone by alien ideas. It is no accident that anti-Semitism has also been dragged into the ideological mix. Even before recent events in the Middle East, the idea of the Jew as a power-hungry, manipulative destroyer of traditions and culture was not unfamiliar. But during the current crisis, in which a Jewish state is involved and the nature of a modern Middle East is at stake, that Nazi-like caricature has been resurrected with a vengeance—and not just in many state-run newspapers in the Arab world that have given voice to virulent forms of anti-Semitism.

On the same day in an op-ed on Holocaust Remembrance Day, Israeli educator Daniel Gordis (2002) reflected on the deaths of fourteen members of the Israeli Defense Force. "Needing Israel" was the piece's title, and the point was that Israel was necessary for the safety of Jews in a world in which the memory of the Holocaust still burned as a daily lesson. "One thing important to Jews is remembering," Gordis wrote. "We won't forget the 20th century and the world's complicity" or its present "double standard" in blaming Israelis for protecting their national security. He was not going to let Jews become scapegoats for 9/11.

Nonetheless, violence struck a synagogue in Tunisia (McNeil 2002b, 2002c) and a Jewish soccer team in Paris (Daley 2002a). The latter could be rationalized as the work of "petty delinquents rather than [as] an organized campaign" ("Jews Discuss Attacks" 2002); however, the Tunisian explosion was decidedly the result of determined jihadists, part of a campaign against what they called "all the godless pigs of the world" (Andrews 2002; see also Hedges 2002d). In either event, the *Times* saw evidence of "a new and threatening wave of anti-Semitism" in the Old World (C. Smith 2003c).

The *Times* tried to explain why "anti-Semitism is deepening among Muslims" and how "hateful images of Jews are embedded in Islamic popular culture" (Sachs 2002). The *Protocols of the Elders of Zion* was readily available in Arab hotels; the Israeli flag had a swastika superimposed on it in Islamic newspapers. How did Muslims come to embrace the virulent stereotypes long associated with Nazism? In an op-ed, anthropologist David I. Kertzer (2002)—author of a book about the Vatican's role in the rise of modern anti-Semitism—called the "demonization" a "singularly unoriginal human impulse" based on the "historical role of Christianity in promulgating such hatred."

The *Times* was particularly interested in the uses of the *Protocols,* "which purports to depict Jewish leaders plotting world dominion" and which "has long been recognized as a fabrication by the czarist secret police. It was used in early 20th-century Russia and in Nazi Germany as a pretext for persecution of Jews," and yet Egyptian television employed its ideas for part of a "blockbuster Ramadan series, . . . 'Horse Without a Horseman,'" about Middle East history. Egyptian officials were unapologetic when questioned by a *Times* religion reporter (Wakin 2002a). Closer to home in New York, "the leader of New Jersey's branch of the Anti-Defamation League demanded an apology . . . from the publishers of a local Arab-American newspaper that printed excerpts from a century-old anti-Semitic tract . . . 'The Protocols of the Elders of Zion.'" *The Arab Voice* editor "defended the decision to publish the tracts, saying that he thought it could be an educational tool for his readers." He also said that he printed a disclaimer that the tracts were not true—small consolation according to his accuser (Jones 2002).

Several conferences sponsored by Jewish organizations in the United States and Europe analyzed "hatred of Jews," "the old virus freshly seeping through Western culture, taking new pathways, seeking new hosts and posing new threats," particularly susceptible in a time of global "political crises" (E. Rothstein 2003b). But when asked to head the US delegation to a security-oriented conference on "combating anti-Semitism" (R. Bernstein 2003a), former mayor of New York City Rudolph W. Giuliani went beyond analyzing the causes of ethnic and religious hatred and offered comprehensive policing tips for European countries to "stop the hate." Giuliani (2003) presented his hometown—"where every conceivable ethnicity can be experienced within a few square miles"—as a model not only of multiethnic cooperation, but also of hard-nosed refusal to condone hate crimes. He wrote: "Europe must address the climate that has allowed anti-Semitism to return with such force. Hate flourishes when excuses for the conduct are accepted, or justified by vague connections to international politics. If a synagogue is torched, the response must not be, 'The act is wrong, but we can understand the reasons the arsonist feels he must resort to such extreme measures.' The perpetrators must not be allowed to advance their so-called cause through violence." Giuliani praised—and quoted—himself for his mayoral response to the 9/11 attacks: "I made it clear that the city would not tolerate the blaming of groups for the terrorists' actions: 'Nobody should attack anybody else. That's what we're dealing with right now. We are dealing with insanity, with sick hatred.'" Those "principles," he wrote, were the "true bulwarks of our security and safety." And because of them, "all faiths suffered on Sept. 11, but they also all were strengthened."

Anti-Semitism stayed in the news in the years to come (Berger 2004a; R. Bernstein 2004; Dillon 2004; Eberstadt 2004; "France Scolds Sharon" 2004; "France: Students to Protest Anti-Semitism" 2004; Nunberg 2004; Sciolino 2004f, 2004o; C. Smith 2004a, 2004n, 2004p), including "a flurry of stories . . . about anti-Semitism in France" linked "tangentially" to 9/11 (Berger 2007).

Did the *Times* overemphasize Islamist hatred for Jews as a contributing factor in the events of the era? If anything, one might argue the opposite. When Islamists associated with Al Qaeda assassinated an American businessman named Nicholas Berg in Iraq in 2004, supposedly in revenge for "American mistreatment of Iraqi prisoners at Abu Ghraib prison," it made front-page news. The fifth paragraph described the murder, including the Islamist shouts, "God is Great!" Only on the jump page did the *Times* relate this "particularly gruesome" attack to the slaying in 2002 of Daniel Pearl, the *Wall Street Journal* reporter beheaded by "Muslim militants" in Pakistan. The *Times* stated flatly, "Both Mr. Berg and Mr. Pearl were Jewish" (Filkins 2004c).

If one returns to the initial *Times* coverage of Pearl's death (e.g., among more than a hundred stories, Barringer and Eckholm 2002; Cooper 2002; Kristof 2002c), it is striking to see how little was made of his Jewishness. His murder was interpreted as an assault against hated Americans, and he was hailed for his intrepid journalistic spirit. ("There but for the grace of God go I," said Pearl's friend, *Times* correspondent Barry Bearak, considering the risks he himself had taken while covering Afghanistan and Pakistan in the summer of 2001 [quoted in Aronson 2003].) Even when Pearl's father, Judea Pearl (2002), an Israeli citizen living in the United States, wrote of his son's life and death, he emphasized Daniel's American identity, his "humanity," and only in passing did he mention his son's concern for "anti-Semitism." It took letters to the editor to make the blanket charge: "His murder was the result of a vicious hate crime because he was a Jew" (Spiegel 2002; see also Dowd-Timonen 2003). During the trial of his murderer, the Pakistani court revealed a videotape of Pearl's beheading, an excerpt of which had Pearl telling the camera, "My father's Jewish, my mother's Jewish, I'm Jewish" (French 2002). Nevertheless, *Times* coverage downplayed the Jewish angle in Pearl's death, although others, such as the Frenchman Bernard-Henri Lévy (Riding 2003), thought Pearl's Jewish identity was the key to understanding the murderous Islamist hatred directed to him.

Israel

The events of September 11, 2001, caught Jews and Muslims in the midst of already heightened tensions caused by Israel's very existence; indeed, the attacks seemed to some like "echoes of [the] rift of Muslims and Jews" (Goodstein 2001n). Some Jews said immediately after the attack that now the United States would know what terrorism Israel lived with every day, and televised footage of Palestinians, jubilant at 9/11's devastation, did nothing to diminish the sense of Muslims at war with Jews and their Christian allies. Among the casualties of 9/11 were some longstanding relationships between Jews and Muslims. Some Jews walked out of interfaith dialogues because Muslims refused to condemn what the Jews called terrorist bombings in Israel. Muslims claimed that Jews were taking 9/11 out on Palestinians, ending the possibility of peace in the Mideast (Firestone 2001b). So the 9/11 story included, by extension, all the future Israeli–Palestinian stories and all the debates about that issue throughout the world. The *Times* (e.g., Myre 2003a) covered the Israel–Palestinian story over the next several years, through its cascades of recrimination and violence, and after 9/11 that story's dimensions seemed inseparable from a consideration of 9/11's religion angles.

In the weeks after 9/11, Christians and Muslims in the course of dialogue in Rome exchanged "harsh words" (Henneberger 2001c)—mostly regarding Zionism and Israel. The *Times* described a "split" in opinion among US Jews regarding the idea promulgated by the United States that there should be a Palestinian state. Would the United States attempt to appease the Muslim world by selling out Israel to Palestinian interests? Or would America join with Israel in combating "'violent extremism'" in a common effort "'to conquer global terror'" (Eichenwald 2001b)? American Jews worried for Israel's future, and the *Times* carried news of that worry.

No story carried more punch than Joseph Lelyveld's (2001) piece in the Sunday magazine, "All Suicide Bombers Are Not Alike." The former executive editor of the *Times* composed a lengthy and significant analysis of the connection between 9/11 and the Palestinians, based on his firsthand reporting, with stops in Egypt and Germany. He examined in particular the "latter-day cult of martyrdom," denied by some Muslims but expounded upon by others he met. A prominent photo by Agostino Pacciani displayed a Gaza suicide bomber's family holding pictures of their martyred loved one. "'I hope,' said his mother, 'my other children do the same.'" In Cairo, the Muslims Lelyveld interviewed claimed either that 9/11 was "a Zionist plot" or that "if the attackers were Muslims, 'they were misguided people who did evil.'" In either case, the bulk of the blame was assigned to the United States "for not having resolved the Palestinian question." Finally, in Germany Lelyveld encountered what he considered the most frightening Muslims—personally threatening to him and potentially emblematic of uprooted Muslims throughout the West, in contrast to the Palestinians and Egyptians, who were polite and culturally grounded. Lelyveld's conclusion? "War on America, as far as I could tell, made perfect sense" to the Muslims he met in Germany, including a Libyan who gushed, "Sept. 11 was the happiest day of my life."

One imam in Germany said of Lelyveld's *New York Times:* "I know it is controlled by Jews,'" clearly implying that the paper and he, Lelyveld, were incapable of fairness in treating questions concerning Jewish–Muslim relations, especially the relations between Israel and the Palestinians. The *Times,* in the midst of celebrating its 150th anniversary, ironically took itself to task for "turning away from the Holocaust" in an attempt during World War II to prove to itself and its readers worldwide that it was not a "parochial" Jewish-run newspaper. Its pro-assimilationist editorial policies in the 1940s led to charges that the *Times* managers had been "'self-hating Jews' and 'anti-Zionists'" (Frankel 2001). It would seem that the paper's bosses tried to make amends for downplaying Hitler's extermination of Jews by supporting Israel's existence—if not its every policy—from 1948 or some time thereafter. The *Times'* commitment to the memory of the Holocaust and to the recording of its legacy, at least from the 1970s into the new millennium, was part of the paper's unstated but apparent commitment to the survival of the Jewish people. In light of 9/11, the *Times'* dedication to treating Muslims fairly and adequately in its news coverage and editorials was severely questioned in theory by Lelyveld's Muslim interlocutor and was seriously challenged in practice.

In analyzing the *Times'* 9/11 coverage, one must raise the question of the paper's relationship to Jewish identity and to Israel's national interest. Did the *Times* connect 9/11 to the question of Israel's relations with Palestinians (and the Muslim world) because of the paper's longstanding concern for Israel, or was the paper expressing an obvious reality, which is that the 9/11 attacks were largely about US support for Israel? And in its coverage, did the *Times* balance properly its concern for Israel with its concern for the Palestinians?

Neil MacFarquhar (2002f), who wrote many articles about the Middle East and other dimensions of the 9/11 story for the *Times,* took heed of Arab complaints about US policies toward Israel, Palestinians, and the Muslim world in general. "Across the Middle East," he said, "the region that spawned the terrorists of Sept. 11, the Afghan conflict and American support for Israel in the intensifying Arab–Israeli crisis have clearly left a sour aftertaste. . . . Educated people confess to unease that despite all denials, the United States appears to be making Islam its enemy." One wonders if the same "educated" Arabs would say the same about the *Times.* Would they notice Chris Hedges's (2002c) profile of Henry Seligman, American Jew and senior fellow at the Council on Foreign Relations, who worried over an American Jewish "swing to the right" due in part to the conflict between Israelis and Palestinians? "And as the conflict intensifies, the voices of opposition to Israeli policy among American Jews have withered away," commented Hedges. "The support for Israel fills a spiritual vacuum," Seligman stated. "If you do not support the government of Israel then your Jewishness, not your political judgment, is in question." Or would they see a feature on an Israeli "crusader against state-subsidized Judaism," hoping to "separate religion and state" (Bennet 2003c)?

A *Times* op-ed about suicide bombers found not only an "ever-rising support for 'martyrs'" among Muslim populations worldwide and a grounding of that support in "faith" and "religion," but also a strong respect among the same populations for

America's forms of government, personal liberty and education. . . . It is our actions that they don't like. . . . Shows of military strength don't seem to dissuade terrorists: witness the failure of Israel's coercive efforts to end the string of Palestinian suicide bombings. Rather, we need to show the Muslim world the side of our culture that they most respect. Our engagement needs to involve inter-faith initiatives, not ethnic profiling. America must address grievances, such as the conflict in the Palestinian territories, whose daily images of violence engender global Muslim resentment. (Atran 2003)

The *Times* also produced a quotation-rich profile, "Defining Hamas: Roots in Charity and Branches of Violence" (Fisher 2003a), that presented a range of Palestinian views of the organization. "Hamas is not some dark, shadowy organization in a corner," said a scholar; "they are part of Palestinian society." An op-ed made the case that groups such as Hamas have rational aims and that "what nearly all suicide terrorist campaigns have in common is a specific secular and strategic goal: to compel liberal democracies to withdraw military forces from territory that the terrorists consider to be their homeland. Religion is rarely the root cause, although it is often used as a tool by terrorist organizations in recruiting and in other efforts in service of the broader strategic objective" (Paper 2003). The *Times* offered several profiles, both critical and sympathetic, of Palestinian suicide bombers in 2003 and 2004.

Despite this kind of reporting and op-ed punditry, it is doubtful that Palestinian champions would be satisfied with *Times* Mideast coverage, nor would most Arab nationalists. A perceptive article by Ervand Abrahamian (2003) in *Third World Quarterly* posited that the *Times* and most other "mainstream quality media" (529) in the United States failed to connect 9/11 causally to the Palestinian cause, preferring religiocultural angles to political analysis. In the months following 9/11, he wrote, the *Times* "buried political news in reams of articles on theology," thereby obscuring valid complaint against Israeli policies in the Mideast (535). When Saudi journalist Mansour al-Nogaidan published a *Times* op-ed claiming that his country was "the real culprit" in spreading Muslim terrorism, he was arrested. At his trial, the Saudi judge shouted at him, "How did you dare to write in the enemy's newspaper?" (E. Rubin 2004). The *Times* does not have to be "controlled by Jews" to be insufficiently hospitable to Muslim ideas, especially Arab Muslim ideas about the Mideast. As much as the *Times* might want to please its Muslim readership and represent its worldview on occasion in print, those tasks are not the primary goals of the paper's editorial leadership, at least not at this time. Of course Mideast Muslims were going to find the *Times* biased (toward Israel and toward Jewish viewpoints) in its treatment of their interests (see, e.g., Gross 2002).

Even a Jewish American critic of Israeli policies such as journalist Richard Ben Cramer, "arguing that Israel should return land and apologize" to the Palestinians, called the *Times* "'the former house organ of American Zionism'" (Jonathan Rosen 2004). However, many others found the *Times* insufficiently supportive of Israel and insufficiently critical of Muslim agendas. CAMERA, Israel's advocate, had long censured the *Times*, including its correspondents in Jerusalem. Serge Schmemann, for instance, was said to play a role in the "herd impulse among members of the media, the aversion to deviating from views of other journalists," for finding fault in the "tiny Jewish state" (Levin 1997). The events of September 11, 2001, did not reduce the tensions over Israel in the news (see, e.g., "Action Alert: Whose Human Rights Matter?" 2007).

Daniel Okrent (2005b), the first *Times* public editor, has called the paper's coverage of Israel and Palestine "the hottest button," with passions flaring on both sides. Pro-Palestinians have "expressed the belief that unless the paper assigned equal numbers of Muslim and Jewish reporters to cover the conflict, Jewish reporters should be kept off the beat," a position Okrent found "profoundly offensive, but not nearly as repellent as a calumny that has popped up in my e-mails with lamentable frequency—the charge that *The Times* is anti-Semitic." Okrent commented, "This is an astonishing debasement. If reporting what is sympathetic to Palestinians, or antipathetic to Israelis, is anti-Semitism, what is *real* anti-Semitism? What word do you have left for conscious discrimination, or open hatred, or acts of intentional, ethnically motivated violence? *The Times* may be—is—imperfect. It is not anti-Semitic. Calling it that defames the accuser far more than it does the accused," he concluded (italics in original).

Martin S. Kramer's book *Ivory Towers on Sand* (2001) blamed scholars of Islam and the Middle East for not facing the reality (as he saw it) of militant Islam's rise. According to Richard Bernstein (2001), these scholars, Kramer said, were "afflicted with so much political bias and wishful thinking that most [of them] have missed 'the major evolutions of Middle Eastern politics and society over the past two decades.'" In reviewing the arguments in Kramer's book and those of the scholars Kramer criticized, such as John L. Esposito, Bernstein stated that "the disagreements have a good deal to do with Middle East politics themselves, with Mr. Kramer and his scholarly allies tending to be more pro-Israeli and more critical of the Arabs than his scholarly adversaries." The *Times*, as always, took note of the controversy and paid attention to the positions on either side, trying to station itself in the moderate middle. And assaying the full 9/11 religion story meant an assessment of the relations between Muslims and Jews in Israel in the context of Middle Eastern, Israeli–Arab politics.

"Ramadan Begins, Outside the Walls," a photograph by Rina Castelnuovo (2001), showed Palestinians praying in Jerusalem, Israeli soldiers in the background. The caption said that Israeli guards prevented Muslim worshippers—the young men in particular—from passing into the Old City for their Friday prayers. In a city fraught with sacred sites and competing sensibilities, the practice of religion was perforce gripped by politics. In reviewing a novel about the Dome of the Rock in Jerusalem (Makiya 2001), Chris Hedges (2001a) remarked, "The rock is the heart of Jerusalem. It was the spot where Adam is said to have landed on his fall from Paradise. Abraham attempted to sacrifice Isaac here. This is where Solomon's Temple stood and where Jesus preached. It is, as well, the place from where the prophet Muhammad is believed to have ascended to heaven." The dome was "the first great architectural and artistic work of Islam . . . built to rival the synagogues and churches in Jerusalem, especially the Church of the Holy Sepulcher." It has been "a point of contention" ever since the seventh century, when it was built (see Schmemann 2002c).

In Nazareth, too, the construction of a mosque by the city's Arab majority was considered a symbol of "assertiveness" (Greenberg 2002b) by Muslim "militants" (Schmemann 2002b) because of its proximity to a Christian shrine devoted to Mary. Under "stiff pressure" from Christian authorities to halt the "'fanatic people'" (Schmemann 2002b) from challenging Christian hegemony, Israeli officials blocked the mosque's completion several years after it was begun. On Easter 1999, violence had occurred between Christians and Muslims at the site. Now Israel was firmly siding with the Christians and in 2003 dispatched bulldozers and jackhammers to tear down the mosque's foundation (Myre 2003b).

Such solidarity did not prevent the Vatican from taking a neutral stance in calling for an end to Mideast violence (Tagliabue 2002) or from criticizing what it called Israeli "reprisal and retaliation" against Palestinians, and for "imposing 'unjust and humiliating conditions'" upon them (Riding 2002a). While condemning "all acts of terrorism in the Middle East" (Riding 2002a), the Vatican urged Israel to engage in peace talks with Palestinians when hundreds of the latter took over the Church of the Nativity in Bethlehem as a form of protest and as a sanctuary under siege by Israeli troops (see "Holy Places" 2002; Henneberger

2002a). During the month-long standoff at the "holy site" (Brinkley 2002; see also Cowell and Greenberg 2002; Greenberg 2002a; Rohde 2002b, 2002c), the *Times* examined various "religious sites in Jerusalem and the West Bank" that had "repeatedly become flashpoints in the struggle between Jews and Arabs" over the years ("Holy Sites, Bitter Passions" 2002), including Joseph's Tomb in Nablus, the Cave of the Patriarchs in Hebron, the Dome of the Rock (the "Temple Mount" to Jews or the "Noble Sanctuary" to Muslims [Bennet 2003d]), the Western Wall, and the Mount of Olives in Jerusalem, and the besieged Church of the Nativity in Bethlehem. Upon closer scrutiny, warfare in the "Holy Land" was not about sacred sites per se—many of which archaeologists have shown not to carry the historical import reputed by Jews, Christians, and Muslims' "faith." "The Middle East conflict is in part about conflicting narratives" grounded in communal identities and loyalties, according to Stephen Kinzer (2002). "These arguments over protecting sites are used as excuses," a biblical archaeologist told Kinzer. "They're symptoms of much deeper problems. But the religious overlay does point up an inherent contradiction that's obvious and very disturbing. You have war raging in the places where Jesus and other great religious figures preached their message of peace. You can hardly imagine a greater contradiction than that."

Thus, an academic, as a kicker in a *Times* essay, scolded the Abrahamic religious traditions about falling short of their lofty ideals. The ideals of academia were soon roiled by "strife" (Schemo 2002) echoing that of the Mideast. In Europe, scholars signed petitions calling for a boycott and denial of grants to Israeli institutions. Longtime colleagues broke their associations with one another not only over Israel's policies—called by some a "Holocaust" for Palestinians, which to Israeli loyalists was an "obscene" comment—but over Israel's very right to exist. One might perceive the brouhaha as a European phenomenon; however, the question soon came to the United States, where the president of Harvard University decried what he called "growing anti-Semitism" on campus, symbolized by demands that Harvard "remove all Israeli investments from its endowment" (Arenson 2002b). Middle East Forum's director Daniel Pipes created a Web site, Campus Watch, in order to keep "dossiers" on academics who were, in his view, not sufficiently worried about "the dangers of political Islam" and who were overly concerned about Palestinian rights. He claimed that such scholars were guilty of "anti-Semitism" (Lewin 2002). In reply, Rabbi Michael Lerner, editor of *Tikkun* ("the liberal Jewish magazine of politics and culture"

[Lee 2002]) and organizer of the Tikkun Campus Network, said, "There is real anti-Semitism. . . . But right now, we have Jewish political correctness run wild. The new McCarthyism in American society is that anyone who criticizes Israel is an anti-Semite." Lerner's group was designed to emphasize "respect and tolerance" and "a common humanity" among "pro-Palestine and pro-Israel" factions engaged in "standoffs" and "turmoil" on dozens of American academic campuses (Lee 2002). The *Times*' Edward Rothstein (2002b) assayed the distinction in "Hateful Name-Calling vs. Calling for Hateful Action," a column about anti-Israeli views expressed by invited speakers at Harvard. "Not all criticism of Israel is anti-Semitic," Rothstein concluded, "but not all criticism of Israel is *not* anti-Semitic," and some of it—for example, saying that "'Brooklyn born' Jewish settlers on the West Bank . . . 'should be shot dead'"—can have "hateful consequences" (italics in original).

The *Times* observed the ripples of anti-Semitism in international arts. Thus, the article "Jewish Groups Want a Teenager's Novel Withdrawn in France" (2002) told of a book, *Dream of Palestine,* that presented a Palestinian viewpoint against Israel. Was the article anti-Semitic? And was the opera *The Death of Klinghoffer* (Rockwell 2003)—based on the death of Leon Klinghoffer during the hijacking of the Italian cruise liner *Achille Lauro* in 1985—anti-Semitic or merely "prohuman"? It treated the Palestinian plight with care, but the hijackers themselves were presented as villains.

Video games are no works of art, but they also reflect the cultural milieu in which they are created. *Special Force,* the "hottest video game for the teenagers of Beirut's southern Shiite neighborhoods," constituted a simulated war against Israel. "'Victory comes from no one but Allah,' exhorts the screen before the mission begins." The *Times* took this game as an example of virulent anti-Jewish "propaganda" (Wakin 2003a).

On the political scene, anti-Semitism among the world's Islamic leaders continued to concern the *Times* through 2003 and 2004 (R. Bernstein 2004b; "Islamic Anti-Semitism" 2003). Especially prominent was Malaysian prime minister Mahathir Mohamad, who at a conference distributed copies of Henry Ford's anti-Semitic tract *The International Jew,* which includes the infamous *Protocols of the Elders of Zion* ("Anti-Semitic Book Distributed" 2003).

As the effects of 9/11 took deadly hold in the Israeli–Palestinian conflict, and as various religionists and academics (as well as journalists) took sides, the

Times announced in a June 9, 2002, headline: "Evangelical Christians and Jews Unite for Israel" (Firestone 2002d). Ralph Reed, former executive director of the Christian Coalition, and Rabbi Yechiel Z. Eckstein, president of the International Fellowship of Christians and Jews, helped create a new group, Stand for Israel, aimed to "draw on the fervent support for Israel among conservative Christians who wish to have a voice in the country's Middle East policy." Maureen Dowd (2002a) derided the "Rapture"—referring not only to the "alliance that began in the Reagan era between conservative Jews and evangelical Christians," but also to the "biblical vision of a terrible final war in Jerusalem between the forces of light and darkness and the consequent ascension of 'saved' Christians, snatched up to Heaven from their cars, computer terminals and food courts." Listening to Reverend Jerry Falwell, she realized how little the Jews would get once the final "Rapture" took place, but in the short run the political "rapture" would surely benefit the Bush push toward 2004.

The events of September 11, 2001, had become a dimension of Middle East politics and its religious loyalties. In *Religion in the News,* Dennis R. Hoover (2002a) reported on the process of "choosing up sides in the Middle East," as reported in the news media. Samuel P. Huntington, he noted, had defined the "Clash of Civilizations" (8) about ten years earlier as a looming conflict between Judeo-Christianity and Islam. The events and aftermath of 9/11 suggested that Huntington's prediction had some truth to it. In the debate over the thesis of a religiously grounded "Clash of Civilizations," the "domestic 'culture war' divisions—liberals vs. conservatives *within* the Judeo-Christian traditions" (8, italics in original)—took their sides. Conservative Protestants and many Jews were in favor of war against Palestinians—and, in turn, against Iraq—whereas liberal Christians were against these wars. Israel under Ariel Sharon portrayed its battle against the Palestinians as part of President Bush's war against terrorism and Al Qaeda. Reverends Franklin Graham, Jerry Falwell, and Pat Robertson railed against Islam, calling Muhammad a terrorist. Some evangelicals and Jews joined forces, at least temporarily, in 2002. And as the United States and Israel continued to regard each other as allies, at least until the "Rapture," some termed their common interest "'not just an alliance between nations but between religions'" (21).

That alliance was unsettling to one *Times* commentator, who perceived the "vision long cherished by Israel's religious and secular hawks . . . that the new

Palestinian state must be Jordan." With the "strengthening alliance between those Jews who favor a Greater Israel and conservative Christians in the United States who are moved by the same ancient dream, based on what evangelicals call the 'Abrahamic covenant,'" there was a possible confirmation of what was being called "the real subtext of the war on terrorism: that it is a battle between Judeo-Christian and Islamic values, beliefs and territorial ambitions" (Bennet 2003a). (For a study of the argument that "the United States was singled out by Al Qaeda in large part because of American support for Israel's occupation of the West Bank and Gaza and that a significant motivation for the invasion of Iraq was to improve Israel's security," as sponsored by "a Jewish lobby," see Finder 2006.)

War in Iraq

In the fall of 2002, as the United States made its preparations for an invasion of Iraq, an action depicted by administration officials as a campaign in the global war against terrorism, Iraq began to loom as a religion angle to the 9/11 narrative in the news media. Whether Iraq's policymakers, especially Saddam Hussein, had anything to do with the 9/11 attacks or not, the American president (and thus the United States) acted as if they did, and media such as the *New York Times* began to examine diverse religious implications of the military expedition there. Articles in the *Times* surveyed the varieties of Islam in Iraq, raised questions of the war's justification, followed the gathering of jihadists to counter the US presence there, and paid close heed to the interplay between religion and politics in the country. By the time the 9/11 religion story got to Iraq, one could hardly separate religion from politics from culture from ethnicity. It seemed almost boneheaded to ask of a story, Where is the religion here? Or where *isn't* it? Defining religion seemed at this point to be an exercise in artificiality because virtually every story was about people who identified themselves largely through denominational, sectarian loyalty. Reading the *Times* about Iraq became a saturated case study in the embedded role of religion in the lives of millions of people. Whereas the domestic American angles to the 9/11 religion narrative became more and more muted in 2003 and beyond—for example, Ground Zero became less and less a religion story—the war in Iraq became the stuff of civilizational conflict, not because Iraq was implicated in 9/11, but because the Bush administration made it so rhetorically, and the media followed his lead. What began with 9/11 was playing out in US bellicosity toward a nation largely of Muslims, in a president's evangelical faith, in soldiers and civilians' behavior in the crises of wartime.

Iraq had played little part in the *Times'* survey of global Islam in the year following 9/11. But as President Bush's intentions toward Iraq became apparent, it emerged in a series of religion-related stories. An op-ed cautioned the US foreign-policy makers to work with "Iraq's forgotten majority," the Shiites, who made up two-thirds of the population but who had been kept from power, along with the Sunni Kurds (20 percent), by the Sunni Arab minority (16 percent). "Shiite Muslims would be the largest voting bloc in any democratic Iraq," the author wrote, and so far the United States had ignored them for fear that they would be too closely tied to Iran, "where the Shiite faith predominates" (Smyth 2002). An analysis by the *Times*' Neil MacFarquhar (2003n) underlined the importance of the Shiites—here estimated at 55 percent of the Iraqi population—as "'the most dangerous threat to the regime'" of Saddam Hussein, considering its attempt to unseat him in 1991 and his murderous retaliation. "The Shiites want more power, want their religious authorities to be autonomous," said a Western diplomat.

As the Bush administration made its case for a preemptive attack on Iraq, American "churches and ethicists" opposed the war, calling it "unjust and immoral" (Steinfels 2002a). Peter Steinfels (2002a) wondered why, "for all its reputed piety, the White House shows no sign of concern about the moral objections swelling up from an imposing portion of American church leadership. How many divisions does the Pope have, Stalin is supposed to have sneered. Karl Rove can much more reasonably ask, how many voters [does mainline Christianity influence]?" Although those in the pews seemed not to follow their leaders' lead, "in religious circles," stated Laurie Goodstein (2002d), "the antiwar voices are vastly outnumbering those in favor of a war." According to Goodstein's article, "to counteract the chorus of negativity," a Southern Baptist, Dr. Richard D. Land, issued a statement that "using military force against Iraq would fit the theological definition of a 'just war,' because it would amount to a defensive action against a biological or nuclear strike from Mr. Hussein." Several "prominent evangelicals" signed the statement, including Bill Bright of the Campus Crusade for Christ and Charles W. Colson of Prison Fellowship Ministries. In a *Times* op-ed, Wheaton College graduate, Heritage Foundation fellow, and National Public Radio commentator Joseph Loconte (2003) added his voice against the "religious liberals" by reminding them that "Jesus talked a great deal about punishment, and the moral obligation to oppose evil with a strong and swift hand. Human evil must be confronted," he said, and "'the Prince of Peace'" was also known in the Bible as "'the Lion of the tribe of Judah,' the one 'who judges and wages war.'" Loconte did not determine that Jesus's words were "an argument for a pre-emptive strike on Baghdad. But it's a good reason for a little more humility among the apostles of diplomacy," who were "oversimplifying the Bible."

American Catholic bishops said that they could not "find a moral justification for a pre-emptive war against Iraq because there is no adequate evidence that Iraq is about to attack" (Goodstein 2002e; see also Goodstein 2002a). Pope John Paul II made clear the Vatican's "stepped-up opposition to any war with Iraq" with an appeal for peace in the Middle East ("Pope Makes Plea" 2003), followed by an even stronger rebuke, calling the American plan a "defeat for humanity" (quoted in Bruni 2003f). Although reprimanding the United States for its war plans, the pope sent an envoy to Baghdad to "try to persuade Iraq to cooperate fully with weapons inspections and to prevent an American-led military strike" (Bruni 2003e). Iraq responded by sending Tariq Aziz—vice president, deputy prime minister, and an Assyrian Christian—to meet with the pope, warning European countries, with their sizable Muslim minorities, against joining the pending US assault, "saying that it would be seen as a crusade against Muslims and have bitter consequences." At the least, it "would poison Christian–Muslim relations" (Bruni 2003b). In the "public relations battle between Baghdad and Washington," Aziz journeyed to Assisi, following "the footsteps of St. Francis, the patron of peace and protector of the weak," and prayed publicly for peace (Bruni 2003d). Various world leaders made a path to the pope's door seeking his counsel and support in the debate over the looming war. Although continuing to reject "'the underlying rationale for war as preventive'" (Bruni 2003g), the pope maintained political neutrality, hence serving "'on behalf of humanity'" in general (Schmitt and Bruni 2004; see also Stevenson 2004).

As Peter Steinfels did for the American war in Afghanistan, he examined the US rationale for war in light of the "just-war tradition," finding that "however straightforward and sensible the notion of going to war only as a last resort may sound in principle, the world is demonstrating how difficult it is to apply in practice" (Steinfels 2003d; see also Steinfels 2004c). Steinfels (2003f) recalled the moral power of Pope John XXIII's encyclical "Pacem in Terris" (Peace on Earth) as a guide to national policy, keeping the "gestalt" of "peacemaking" in mind: "a total configuration of endeavors that encompassed disarmament, human rights, economic development, sensitivity to the dignity of weaker nations," and so on. He also (2003c) assessed the effectiveness—and lack thereof—of papal pronouncements and diplomacy in opposition to the war in Iraq and other conflagrations.

On the verge of the US-led war, Laurie Goodstein (2003a; see also Goodstein 2003f and 2003l) stated that in the United States "most Christian denominations have taken a stand against going to war"; however, American Jews were experiencing a "'profound ambivalence,'" wishing to support President Bush "because he has been a reliable ally of the Israeli government," but also "fearful of a backlash if the war goes badly." Hence, according to Goodstein, most Jewish organizations "remained silent" on the issue, even when, as David Firestone (2003) reported, Representative James P. Moran, Virginia Democrat, blamed Jews "for the buildup toward war with Iraq." "Under pressure from Jewish groups," Firestone stated, Democratic congressional leadership rebuked Moran for what they said were "insensitive remarks."

On the eve of war, "mainline" religious leaders were "frustrated that they have not been able to see Mr. Bush to express their anxieties" (Bumiller 2003) about the impending invasion. Elisabeth Bumiller commented: "George W. Bush is turning out to be one of the most openly religious presidents in American history. He prays daily. He delivers speeches and national radio broadcasts that sound like sermons. He oversees a White House full of Bible study groups. Most important, he favors lowering the barriers between church and state by giving government money to religious charities." It was ironic, then, that the president would not meet with the many religious leaders opposed to his policy regarding Iraq. An op-ed by an historian of American culture took the president to task for his "slide into self-righteousness," greased by his belief not only in "Providence," but in God's plan for himself, his presidency, his country, and its wars (Lears 2003; cf. "When Faith Guides a President" 2003). As per the op-ed's title, this was "how a war became a crusade." It was not that President Bush was the first American to be taken by a "providentialist spirit." Indeed, many American leaders—political and religious—had spoken of God's support in time of war (Wills 2003; see, for example, the exhortatory sermons by a Presbyterian minister in Manhattan in 1776 [Wakin 2003g]). For Lears and other critics, it was the president's inability to hear other voices of American religious faith that worried them so.

The *Times* paid mind to those voices; however, the paper also made room for *their* critics—for example, in a review by Paul Berman (2003a) of Jean Bethke Elshtain's book *Just War Against Terror* (2003) and of Richard Falk's *The Great War Terror* (2003b). In February 2002, the Institute for American Values released a statement, "What We're Fighting For," signed by Elshtain; Laura Spelman Rockefeller, professor of social and political ethics at the University of Chicago Divinity School; and other intellectuals such as Samuel G. Freedman, Francis Fukuyama, Claire Gaudiani, James Davison Hunter, Samuel P. Huntington, Daniel Patrick Moynihan, Michael Novak, Michael Walzer, and others. The document (republished in Elshtain 2003:182–207) justified American military response to the 9/11 attacks on moral and religious grounds, and Elshtain's book was an extension of the argument, thoughtfully made and well documented.

In short, Elshtain drew on the Christian realism theology of Reinhold Niebuhr and Paul Tillich to say that one must recognize the evils in this world and respond to them morally and forcefully when necessary. There are just wars, she argued, and the war against terrorism is one such enterprise. Osama bin Laden and his followers, she said, are not reasonable men; they call America a land of infidels, and they mean to destroy us. Hence, we must defend our people, our values, our democracy, and our freedom of religion.

As for American Christians opposed to American military fronts, Berman (2003a) explained that Elshtain considered their arguments "simplistic, senti- mental, utopian and unrealistic," holding a nation to a "form of Protestant per- fectionism—an attitude of moral purity that cannot begin to cope with the awful consequences of even the most justified of wars." Elshtain contrasted bin Laden's "demonizing" of America to US officials' warning against "any such tendency" in reciprocation and thus found in America a willingness to respond appropriately to evil without the collateral damage of religious hatred. Berman found her case compelling, even though it led in the direction of "a new kind of American 'impe- rialism' devoted to nation-building, which seems to be the Bush administration's current position too." Berman did not comment on it, but it was instructive that to build a case for American warfare against terrorists far and wide, Elshtain (2003:179–80) drew on two aspects of the *Times* 9/11 narrative—the picture of individual innocents found in the "Portraits of Grief," who must be protected by government, and the depiction (e.g., Frantz 2001c) of Muslim would-be jihadists who would live in America if only they could.

Berman's review gave less space to international-relations professor Richard Falk, who "regards the United States mostly as an imperialist bully." Falk's book *The Great Terror War* (2003b) says that the most dangerous agents of destruction are the "dogmas of reassurance that commend the established order, whether emanating from religious or secular sources, asserting unconditional claims that a truth is being served and any resistance to what the power-wielders propose is evil. Such a mentality makes killing and dying fully justified, even an occasion of glory. In the end only a rejection of all fundamentalisms will enable humanity to grope toward a safer, fairer, and more sustainable and hopeful future than now seems in the offing" (190).

Falk (2003a) got to express some of these ideas in a *New York Times* review of Jonathan Schell's *The Unconquerable World* (2003), in which Schell describes the ways in which 9/11 had awakened US militarism. Schell wrote: "The United States, facing the threat of further attack from a global, stateless terrorist network, launched its war on terrorism. Then it embarked on a full-scale revolution in its foreign policy that, while taking September 11 as its touchstone, adopted goals and means that extended far beyond the war on terror. The policy's foundation was an assertion of absolute, enduring American military supremacy over all other countries in the world, and its announced methods were the overthrow of governments ('regime change') in preemptive, or preventive attacks" (6). Falk found himself in agreement with Schell's critique.

In Kuwait, American servicemen and women prayed as they waited for the "battle ahead" (Weinraub 2003). Once war began, Americans at home prayed "for the safe return of one of their own" (Fountain 2003b) and thanked God for the soldiers' homecoming (Halbfinger 2003). American Indian tribes such as the Hopis and Navajos—often at odds with one another—found a common-faith, intertribal unity in praying for a Hopi soldier, Lori Piestewa, who was killed in the first military engagements (Janofsky 2003a). Prominent clerical critics who had accused the president of "'hubris'" suddenly fell silent, feeling it inappropriate to "'go on a crusade while the war is going on'" (Wakin 2003c). Yet Steinfels (2003b) stated that "the United States has probably never gone to war with less backing from the nation's religious leaders." The Southern Baptist Convention, the Lutheran Church–Missouri Synod, and the Union of Orthodox Jewish Congregations endorsed the administration's actions; however, most other national denominational leaders found America's justifications wanting. "So much for the leaders," Steinfels wrote. In a poll cited in Steinfels's article, 60 percent of Americans seemed to favor American military action in Iraq, and a plurality of Americans (more than 40 percent) leaned most heavily on "what they had seen or read in the media" in forming their opinions. Only 10 percent mentioned "religious beliefs" as the primary influence on their thinking about the war. Steinfels was struck by the disparity of opinion between the views coming from national religious leadership or local clergy and the judgments coming from most Americans on such an important moral issue. He was also impressed by the seeming power of the press—which was perhaps ironic, given Frank Rich's (2003) take on the media in the *Times* "Arts & Leisure" section. In "They Both Reached for the Gun," Rich fashioned an analogy between the plot of the movie *Chicago* and the story line justifying the invasion of Iraq. In both, the press played the role of gullibles, believing any justification the authorities came up with. Regarding Iraq, reporters dutifully asked President Bush about his "faith," and he gave them a "faith" reply, but no one, commented Rich, asked him why it was that "virtually every religious denomination in the country, including Mr. Bush's own, opposes his war."

In this light, Peter Steinfels's (2003a) report on the book *Warrior Politics: Why Leadership Demands a Pagan Ethos* (2002) by Robert D. Kaplan suggested that "history's pagans might have approved of President Bush's Iraq policy." A pagan ethos, Steinfels said, derives from (or is similar to) "the harsh world of the Peloponnesian Wars between Sparta and Athens as recounted by Thucydides, the Punic Wars between Rome and Carthage as recounted by Livy, and the era of the Warring States in China in Sun Tzu's 'The Art of War.'" In short, it may require "'pagan realpolitik'" rather than Christian love to drive a nation to war. The kicker: "It would be interesting to hear the president"—a self-proclaimed evangelical Christian—"explain that at the next White House prayer breakfast."

According to the Bush administration script, the war in Iraq was a response to 9/11 and to global Muslim terrorism, but it was not to be taken as a crusade against Islam per se. According to the *Times,* 9/11's religion angles included the judgments made by various religious bodies about going to war and the president's "faith" in taking up the fight, considered critically, at least by Peter Steinfels. But it was necessary to consider the war from Muslim viewpoints, too.

Saddam Hussein himself became the subject of *Times* religious psychology. In order to understand Hussein's "grand obsession" with his image as "the natural leader of an Arab world yearning for past glories under the banner of Islam that fluttered atop the Arab armies that conquered much of the ancient world after the death of the prophet Muhammad in A.D. 632" (Burns 2002b), the *Times* examined his "empire of mosques," including the recently completed Mother of All Battles Mosque on the outskirts of Baghdad. In his "struggle for the hearts and minds" of Iraqi Kurds, Hussein issued "a religious fiat saying it was time to fight the Americans even as they prepare for war" (MacFarquhar 2002e).

Osama bin Laden, too, prepared for the American invasion by releasing an audiotape calling on Muslims worldwide to "repulse any United States attempt to invade Iraq, urging them to apply the lessons learned by al Qaeda, his terror network" (MacFarquhar 2003r). The *Times* printed excerpts from bin Laden's broadcast under the title, "Fight the 'Crusaders'" ("Bin Laden's Message" 2003).

In the United States, "in ways large and small, many Muslim Americans say, the backlash they have felt since the attacks of Sept. 11 has intensified since the United States attacked Iraq. Other Americans, they say, are making them feel scared, anxious and obligated to change their lifestyles and lower their profiles. Many say they have been made to feel like scapegoats, and the feelings are all too familiar" (Janofsky 2003b). The *Times* reported several attacks on Muslim Americans nationwide. In New York City, Mayor Michael R. Bloomberg "prayed and pleaded . . . with dozens of Muslim worshipers in Queens, urging them not to view the city's fight against terrorism and the nation's war with Iraq as anti-Islamic" (Christian 2003). On the national front, Muslims were "enraged" by the nomination of Daniel Pipes to a government-sponsored foreign-policy center, the United States Institute of Peace, during the Iraq offensive. Pipes was well known for his views that "mosques are breeding grounds for militants and that Muslims in government and military positions should be given special attention as security risks." The White House assured its critics that the president did not agree with Pipes and still regarded Islam as a "religion of peace" (Stevenson 2003).

American Muslims may have been reassured by officials' words; however, in much of the Muslim world and especially among Arabs, "driven by pride and religion," the "new jihad" was in Iraq. Said a Libyan in Syria on his way to answer the call from Iraq: "The Prophet Muhammad warned that there would be no judgment day until the Muslims fight with the Jews. . . . We see no difference between the Americans and the Jews and, God willing, we Arabs can settle all our accounts with the Americans and the British. Damn America." The Arab news media, in reporting on what they called the "massacres" and the "American Holocaust" of the Iraq War, conflated Iraqi and Palestinian scenarios, just as they equated the United States with Israel, Bush with Satan. This reportorial strategy, one Egyptian Muslim political scientist said, "is actually bringing everybody to the worst nightmare—the clash of civilizations" (MacFarquhar 2003e; see Sachs

2003b for the Arab media's take on war's "killing field"). In that potential context, Russia's fourteen million Muslims were "split . . . over whether to proclaim a jihad against the United States in response to the invasion of Iraq," and President Vladimir V. Putin acknowledged "concern for the nation's Islamic minority as a major factor in the government's decision to oppose military action in Iraq" (Wines 2003).

The American military had its own religious angles in fighting the war in Iraq. There were small but growing numbers of conscientious objectors among the ranks (Goodstein 2003i). The *Times* often depicted the prayers of American soldiers in the field (e.g., Ruth Fremson's photographs "Windows Shattered, but Faith Unbroken" [2003]); however, Laurie Goodstein (2003g) reported that an "Army Major General who commands Fort Bragg's training center for special operations forces has invited a group of predominantly Southern Baptist pastors to the base this month to participate in a military-themed motivational program for Christian evangelists." At least one Baptist invitee was offended by "the marriage of military and ministry." Reverend Barry Lynn, executive director of Americans United, said, "It's completely inappropriate to have the Army put on a revival meeting at a military base" in the course of a war with Muslim people. When Lieutenant General William G. Boykin's comments likening "the war against Islamic militants to a battle against 'Satan'" offended American Muslims and others, he apologized for his remarks (Jehl 2003c; see also "For Religious Bigotry" 2004, "General Said to Be Faulted over Speeches" 2004, and Jehl 2003a).

The connections between the military and religious fealty became even more personal with the deaths of American soldiers. "For One Pastor, the War Hits Home" (Blair 2003), read a headline about a black Baptist minister in Cleveland whose son was killed in Iraq. The *Times* article was an extended portrait of grief, with several photographs by Haraz Ghanbari. Ting-Li Wang's photographs of a Muslim family in Brooklyn illustrated Daniel J. Wakin's (2003d) article under the headline "Fear for a Navy Son, and the Fellow Muslims: Viewing Images of a War They Hate, a Brooklyn Family Is Proud and Sad." The AP article "Dissent: Antiwar Priest Removes Flag, but Not for Long" (2003), dateline San Antonio, Texas, told of a Catholic priest who took down an American flag in front of his church in protest to the Iraq War, but his archbishop ordered him to restore it to its place and not to force his political views on his parishioners. Doug Mills's (2003) front-page photograph "Burial at Arlington" showed Buddhist monks and

American marines delivering the flag-draped body of an American Buddhist soldier for military burial. In 2004, when US soldiers were killed and mutilated by a mob in Falluja, some of their families were pictured, "wrestling with outrage and grief, juxtaposed with a desire to forgive, based on their Catholic faith." "We can't hate," one mother said, "Hate is a sin" (Goodnough and Luo 2004). In Falluja, imams condemned the mutilations, and their fellow Muslims "expressed satisfaction and even pride in the deadly ambush but shame in its aftermath" (Gettleman 2004d).

In Iraq, the *Times* soon discovered the extent of the Christian minority composing less than 4 percent of the total Iraqi population. A feature on a 1,600-year-old Assyrian Christian monastery in the Kurdish-controlled region of northern Iraq raised the question of whether Christians had "benefited under Mr. Hussein's rule, or at least stood by as Kurds suffered," or whether Hussein had suppressed the Christians along with the Kurds and the Shiites (Rohde 2003c; see also Tavernise 2003b). The Christians expressed their desire for a godly peace in their land; an Agence France-Presse photograph of an Iraqi Christian lighting candles in Baghdad illustrated the wish. "Easter Arrives in an Unsettled City," read the headline (2003). On April 21, an AP photo by Brennan Linsley (2003) also emphasized Easter's theme, "A Day of Peace," displaying Chaldean Catholic altar boys during services. A photograph by James Hill (2003), "Footnotes to War," showed an Armenian Orthodox woman, framed by a cross in a cemetery, mourning for her husband and sons. Tariq Aziz's aunt, an Assyrian Christian like himself, expressed no charity toward her once-powerful relative. "Let them arrest him," she declared, posing for a picture beneath a cross on the wall of her home (Rohde 2003g).

The *Times* took interest in all manner of religious minorities in Iraq, including the Kurdish Yazidis, whose localized, syncretic traditions drew eclectically from Zoroastrianism, Christianity, and Islam. Despite a long history of persecution at the swords of the Ottoman Empire, the Yazidis practiced their faith, for "under the secularism of the Baath Party ruling Iraq, all religions [were] tolerated" (MacFarquhar 2003b). A photograph by Lynsey Addario/Corbis (2003) showed a baptism in the Tigris River in Baghdad, conducted by Mandeans—an ancient Gnostic "sect"—in preparation for their new year.

More significant, the news media had to learn quickly who the Shiite majority really was in Iraq: how to spell their names and titles, what were their organizations, leaders, and relations to one another (Mottahedeh 2003). The press focused its understanding of the Shiites on Ali (Muhammad's first cousin and husband of his eldest surviving child, Fatima), who was murdered in 661 and buried in Najaf (a religious center for Shiites). The Shiite imams were supposed to pass down Ali's infallibility as they were appointed, one to the next. The media also focused on Husayn (Ali's son and Muhammad's grandson through Fatima), who was murdered in 680 and was buried in Karbala, the second most important Shiite shrine city. Husayn's followers failed to help him, and to this day Shiites flagellate themselves on his death date during Ashura ceremonies to mark their everlasting shame. Writing in *Religion in the News,* Roy Parviz Mottahedeh (2003) claimed that newspapers skipped, more or less, from 680 to the present, missing much nuance about the Shiites' history and identity. Reports, including those in the *Times,* tended to focus on fatwas and on self-flagellation. Daniel Wakin (2003f) wrote about the latter—not in Iraq, but in Jamaica, Queens— which Mottahedeh (2003) described as "a characteristically interesting story" (27), but which he says also might have mentioned Opus Dei Catholics or Native American Christians in the Southwest, both of whom still flagellate themselves. In other words, Wakin might have used comparative religion to make some greater sense of Shiite ritual practice.

Whatever interest the *Times* took in Shiite religiosity, including that of Iranian Shiite pilgrims on their way to Karbala (Fisher 2003d), and whatever hopes its op-ed writers might have in Iraq's "golden age" as "the most secular of Arab states" at the "crossroads of culture" (Watson 2003), *Times* reporters were interested primarily in the political roles Shiites would play in the unfolding Iraqi drama. Neil MacFarquhar (2003o) predicted that the war's fate might rest on one of two figures whom the Shiites couldn't decide they hated more: "America or Saddam Hussein" (see also "A Religious Figure Speaks" 2003).

As Iraq fell to the Americans and chaos descended on the land, Shiites were at once relieved that they could now "pray without Saddam Hussein's forces listening in" (Santora 2003a). Nevertheless, the *Times* reported on April 11, 2003, that a "U.S.-backed Shiite cleric" was killed by a rival Shiite group at the mosque said to be at the tomb of Ali, the son-in-law of the Prophet Muhammad who was the cause of the Shiite sect's split from Islam's Sunni majority in the seventh century (C. Smith 2003k). A full page in the April 13 paper contained three articles on Iraqi Shiites, whose newfound freedom was turning—the reporters said—to internecine power struggles, vengeance, and the control of munitions (Feuer 2003; Miller 2003; C. Smith 2003i). *Times* photographs could capture the jubilation of Shiite pilgrims, "forbidden no more" from making their annual pilgrimage to the holy city of Najaf (Santora 2003b). At the same time, a Shiite "preacher" was said to "turn . . . up the heat on a stew of ethnic and religious rivalries" by declaring his command over one Iraq city (LeDuff 2003). The front page of the *Times* on April 19 spoke of "competing groups" in Baghdad—Sunnis and Shiites—"united in prayer" beneath the damaged tower of a mosque (see the photograph by AP's Hussein Malla) as they "put aside their differences to join in a demonstration calling for the expulsion of American troops in Iraq (Kifner and Smith 2003). American forces were barely establishing their checkpoints when the jump-page headline proclaimed: "Iraqi Muslims, Denouncing U.S. and Israel, Call for Creation of an Islamic State" (Kifner and Smith 2003).

In particular, Shiites were telling the "'infidels'" in an "anti-American sermon" to get out of Iraq and let an "'Islamic state'" take shape (C. Smith 2003f). On pilgrimage to "the holy city of Karbala for Ashura ceremonies, long banned under Saddam Hussein," a Shiite proclaimed, "We don't want Saddam, and we don't want Bush. . . . Islam, Islam!" (Kifner and Fisher 2003). "Elated Shiites, on Pilgrimage, Want U.S. Out" (C. Smith 2003b), declared the front-page headline on April 22. "Hotbed of Shiite Emotion: Clerics Jockey for Leadership," said another *Times* page-one headline (C. Smith 2003e)—beneath a photo by Ozier Muhammad of Muslim pilgrims in Karbala beating themselves bloody with whips and swords (see also Kifner 2003b on Shiite ritual "fervor"). A *Times* op-ed made clear the lack of uniformity among Iraqi Shiites, united in their desire for Americans to pack up and go (Hiro 2003).

In the wings, Iranian Shiite agents were said to be playing a role in the "fierce disputes among various Shiite leaders about the proper place of religion and politics in the Iraq of the future" (Jehl 2003b). As Iraqi Shiites were regaining their right to pray and process without government interference for the first time in several years (Smith 2003a), Iranian Shiites were urging them to "seize positions" in the Iraqi "power vacuum," leading to American consternation that "religious militancy may present a threat to the establishment of democracy" (Smith 2003h). Iraqi Shiites who had been exiled in Iran began a return to their homeland, but not all of them were enamored with the "hard-liners in Iran" (Fathi 2003b), and they were intent on creating in Iraq a religiopolitical balance appropriate to that country's populations and traditions. In an op-ed, a resident fellow at the American Enterprise Institute offered hope to the United States that the "age-old Shiite doctrine that clerics should keep their distance from politics" might lead to the "creation of a pluralistic, secular democracy under American guidance," something that Iraq's Grand Ayatollah Ali al-Sistani "might accept," although it was less likely that Iraq's "two most prominent revolutionary clerics," Muqtada al-Sadr and Muhammad Bakr al-Hakim, would embrace such a governmental solution (Gerecht 2003; cf. M. Rubin 2009).

Iraq's Sunnis were not to be ignored, and they, too, seemed intent on establishing a rule of law grounded in the "'way of life'" of Islam. Americans might hope for "moderate Islamic political parties," but "Islamist activity" was prevalent among Sunnis as well as Shiites. A Sunni in Mosul told the *Times* reporter, "Our democracy is not like your democracy. . . . We want the Koran to govern us." But the same man, an army veteran and craftsman, "criticized any religious parties that use violence and said Muslims can coexist with Christians, Jews and other religions. When asked about the Islamist party, he shook his head and said he feared that politicians might use religion for personal ends, as Mr. Hussein did. 'If you want to worship God in a pure way,' he said, 'you can't turn religion into a political issue'" (Rohde 2003d).

One can follow the numerous *Times* articles regarding Islam's cultural and political implications in Iraq through the second, third, fourth, and fifth anniversaries of 9/11. Analysis of them would make a study in its own right: the person, politics, and theology of "back-room theocrat" Muqtada al-Sadr (Maass 2003a); the efflorescence of "Islamic fundamentalism" (Kristof 2003b); ritual observance (MacFarquhar 2003k) and local Islamic jurisprudence after the disappearance of the Iraqi state (MacFarquhar 2003t); Iraqi women's fear that the rising "religious fervor may curtail their freedom" (Tavernise 2003a; see also Fathi 2003a); the reflection of Iraq's spiritual turmoil in its contemporary art (Lacey 2003a); the continuing Iranian influence over Iraq's Shiites (Burns and Worth 2004; Jehl and Fahti 2003; Rohde and Fathi 2003), including that of the US-friendly grandson of the late Ayatollah Ruhollah Khomeini, who warned against the creation of a Shiite theocracy (MacFarquhar 2003d); Ayatollah Muhammad Bakr al-Hakim's return from Iranian exile (Maass 2003a; Sachs 2003c, 2003g, 2003h); the tide of anti-American rhetoric and sentiment among Shiites and Sunnis, even as the United States recognized their importance to the future of Iraq's governmental formation

(Andrews and Tyler 2003; MacFarquhar 2003g, 2003m; Sachs 2003d; Tyler 2003); the rising number of foreign jihadists slipping into Iraq to fight on the "ultimate battleground" (MacFarquhar 2003h) against America and its Western allies; the spilling of the conflict into Saudi Arabia (MacFarquhar 2003c, 2003i, 2003j; "Victims of Saudi Attacks" 2003; Weisman 2003); Iraqi Shiism's evolving "power struggle pitting the older, established ayatollahs counseling patience with the occupation against a younger, more militant faction itching to found an Islamic state" (MacFarquhar 2003l); the American hope that "moderates" among the "Ayatollahs" would "save the day" for American electoral plans by voting in a Shiite majority (Tyler 2003), but also an American reminder of "a solution that has worked pretty well in the West: a secular constitution that favors no one religion at all" (Tepperman 2003); the death of the "moderate" cleric Ayatollah Bakr al-Hakim in a car bomb explosion outside the holy Shiite shrine in Najaf (MacFarquhar and Oppel 2003; see also MacFarquhar 2003s and Sachs 2003i), leading to greater Shiite determination—especially among Moktada al-Sadr and his followers—to gain control over Iraq's future (Fisher 2003c; MacFarquhar 2003f, 2003p) and to condemn the United States for the "'blood shed all over Iraq every day'" (MacFarquhar 2003a). And so on, virtually every day in the paper.

The religion angles on Iraq in the fall of 2003 through 2004 and beyond were directed mostly to politics, a continuing set of stories of factionalism, insurgency, and nation building without a predictable resolution in sight (see, e.g., Bannerjee 2004a; Burns 2004a, 2004b, 2004c, 2004e; Charney 2004; Eckholm 2004a; Filkins 2004b, 2004d, 2004e, 2004f, 2004g, 2004h; Filkins and Wong 2004; Fisher 2003b, 2004a; Gettleman 2004b, 2004c, 2004e; V. Nasr 2004; Oppel and Glanz 2004; Rieff 2004; J. Risen 2004; Sachs 2004a, 2004b; Al-Saeidy and Wong 2004; Sengupta 2004; "A Show of Strength in Baghdad" 2004; Wong 2004a, 2004b, 2004c, 2004d, 2004e, 2004f, 2004g; Wong and Filkins 2004). On many days, a reader had to ask if it was possible to separate religion from politics from culture in the warfare ignited by the US occupation of Iraq (Burns 2004d; Gettleman 2004a; Gettleman and Jehl 2004).

While concentrating on the "political nature of the war," *Times* correspondent Edward Wong (2007a) says that he tried to understand "Islam in Iraq and the Shiite–Sunni tensions" that escalated after the US invasion. He is grateful to the Iraqi reporters "who worked alongside us . . . in our newsroom," who were "extremely knowledgeable about various aspects of Islam and its history." Shiism was especially important to comprehend because "that branch of Islam has played a big role in shaping the history of pre-modern and modern Iraq," but so were all sects, Muslim and Christian, whose members composed the Iraqi populace.

In that context, American soldiers were hard pressed to avoid military action near mosques and other Iraqi holy places, including Christian churches, which were sometimes targets of Islamist fire (Fathi 2004c; "Firefights near Shiite Shrines" 2004; Fisher 2004c; Fisher and Wong 2004; Oppel 2004; Sengupta and Fisher 2004; "Worship and Unease in Baghdad" 2004; Worth 2004a). Many Iraqi Christians came under fire themselves because they were suspected of being American sympathizers and chose to flee their homeland or to lay low (Eckholm 2004b; Zoepf 2004).

When the tales were spread regarding American abuse of Muslim detainees at Abu Ghraib prison in Iraq and at the Guantánamo Bay facility, issues were raised in the press about the questionable morality of torture. That the recipients of the alleged mistreatment were Muslims and that their Muslim sensibilities were especially violated regarding sexuality, privacy, and the sacrality of the Koran raised particular interreligious concerns in the *Times* (Glassman 2004; "Q&A: Muslims Were Outraged" 2004). The *Times* was not blind to the atrocities committed by Muslim fighters in Iraq—for example, their "gruesome tactic" of beheadings (Wakin 2004c), which raised concerns about American hostages (Madigan and Sanford 2004). Seeking the big picture, Peter Steinfels (2004b) asked about civilian casualties in the Iraq War, wondering if many thousands of "innocents" had "become lost in the crossfire." He (2004a) also asked "ethical questions" about the torture of prisoners at Abu Ghraib and elsewhere.

In 2004 and 2005, the *Times* narratives regarding Iraq included not only continuing violence, but also the nation-building exercises of voting for a constitution and then for a government. In preparing *Times* readers for those momentous events, Ian Buruma (2004) presented a hopeful scenario for "an Islamic democracy" in Iraq, with Ali al-Sistani playing a pivotal role (see also Worth 2004b, 2004c). Edward Wong had attempted to highlight the "enigmatic cleric" (Wong 2004e) "who wielded vast influence over much of Iraq, and as a consequence also had a large impact on American policy in Iraq" (Wong 2007b). Unable to speak directly with Sistani—"the ayatollah rarely if ever meets with journalists"—Wong (2007b) tried to calculate the leader's place "in the devout Shiite heartland of the South." He acknowledges that "the article [Wong 2004e] is not a definitive profile of the ayatollah by any means—it only just scratched the surface. Even now, the ayatollah remains very much a mystery to us outsiders."

At the same time, the *Times* did not lose sight of Afghanistan, where Taliban assassins refused to acknowledge the American victory and killed their Afghan countrymen—including some senior Muslim clerics—who cooperated with the interim government of President Hamid Karzai and the electoral process that gave him a more permanent office (Gall 2003c). Even as a captured Taliban recruit "expressed disappointment with a movement he had idealized" (Rohde 2003f), the Taliban movement was far from destroyed, and Osama bin Laden continued to function as the head of Al Qaeda (Rohde 2003i; Van Natta 2004), even as Afghanistan created a constitution (Feldman 2003b), keeping in mind both Islamic and democratic principles, and elected a new government. Religious and political angles on the Taliban's continuing existence in Afghanistan endured through 2004 (S. Cohen 2004; Gall 2004) and well beyond, as the war dragged on.

With American wars on two fronts (Iraq and Afghanistan, both with Israel in mind), and with religious participants proliferating in the news, 9/11's religious angles had become fractals of the *Times'* conventional topoi in religion coverage. Religious traditions, worldviews, notions of the supernatural, ultimate and immediate concerns, rituals, ethics, and political loyalties all played roles in the combat and the contention, as the *Times* tried to aid its readers' comprehension.

PART IV | Meanings of 9/11

For decades, the *Times* had recognized the political dimensions of religious life around the world. Now two fronts of warfare made plain the inseparable, painful bonds between politics and religion in the wake of 9/11. On the pages of the paper and beyond it in books, *Times* authors tried to make sense of the maelstrom. These writers pondered modernity, moderation, tolerance, democracy, relativism, patriotism—all in relation to religious fervor and allegiance. In particular, essayists addressed the question whether 9/11 portended a "clash of civilizations" between the Judeo-Christian West and the Islamic world. Such a clash gave heightened meaning to the conventional notion of "culture wars."

Justifications and Significations

The official justification given for the US invasion of Iraq emphasized the task of building democratic institutions in the Muslim world as a bulwark against terrorism (Dao 2003). President Bush's "foreign policy was defined by Sept. 11," wrote a political scientist (Kengor 2004) who had authored a book about the president's faith. The author articulated the view in this *Times* op-ed that "Mr. Bush believes that God has implanted a desire for freedom in all human hearts. . . . Thus, he believes that Middle Eastern Muslims can be and should be free, because that is God's desire for them." Such a view was American to the core—"not that different from the systems of belief embraced by the founders—particularly the notion that all human beings are 'endowed by their Creator' with certain unalienable rights, one of which is liberty."

In Americans' minds, democracy entailed the value of religious freedom. Thus, the US State Department kept an eye on abuses of religious freedoms around the world, producing an annual report, which in 2001 found Taliban violations "'particularly severe'" (Marquis 2001), but which also found fault with crimps on religious rights in Saudi Arabia, Pakistan, and Israel. Post-9/11 America wished to represent itself as a bastion of religious liberty, especially while its soldiers waged war against Muslims in their own countries.

In the *Times,* many essayists—on the op-ed page and elsewhere—pondered the paradoxes and limits of freedom and tolerance as they framed the fault lines split asunder by the terrorist attacks of 9/11. Was the West at war with Islam or at least with a salient aspect of its tradition? Were Judaism and Christianity aligned against a common enemy? Was the basic conflict between secular civil society and spiritual fundamentalism? Were humanism and religiosity deeply at odds? And were tolerance and dogmatism situated in opposing camps, easily distinguished? Was the world embroiled in a struggle between modernity and the past—a past sometimes called tradition, at others medievalism?

These essays—attempts to understand the religious phenomena of 9/11 and its aftermath—by no means expressed the opinions of the *New York Times;* rather, they indicated the judgments of authors whom the *Times* editors chose to publish either because they were *Times* writers or because the outsiders' expertise was considered valuable enough for their submissions to be sought or accepted or both.

These particular essays suggested what 9/11 might *mean* by defining the conflict it symbolized and revealed. It was a conflict *about* crucial values, structures, institutions, and ways of life dearly important to the culture of the *Times,* including those who consume the paper as well as those who produce it: a conflict *about* religious freedom, secular humanism, the separation of church and state, tolerance, pluralism, democracy, relativism, patriotism, consensus, civilization, as well as *about* everything perceived as standing in opposition to these things.

In a speech, Osama bin Laden said that the events of September 11 "split the whole world into two camps: the camp of belief and the camp of disbelief." In rebuttal, Alan Wolfe (2001), a professor of political science and religion at Boston College, described how Americans had overcome their intolerant puritanical heritage, first by embracing Catholics, then Jews, and now Muslims and even those beyond the "'Abrahamic'" traditions. The American genius, he opined, was in its separation of church and state: "The war now going on between Americans and the forces of Osama bin Laden is not between belief and nonbelief. It is instead about two different ways of believing, only one of which allows for individual conscience and freedom. The refusal of the other to make that allowance is what makes terrorism against non-believers possible."

Wolfe's essay, published a month after 9/11, allowed that a "war" was taking place between Americans, who recognize "the God of a diverse people," and "the forces of Osama bin Laden," who wish to deny "individual conscience and freedom." Salman Rushdie (2001), the *Times'* favorite Muslim apostate for the preceding decade, weighed in with an op-ed about 9/11 entitled "Yes, This Is about Islam." Not just about bin Laden, but about *Islam.* But what *is* Islam, Rushdie asked, to most practicing Muslims? It is not so much theological; "after all, most religious belief isn't very theological." For most Muslims,

"Islam" stands, in a jumbled, half-examined way, not only for the fear of God—
the fear more than the love, one suspects—but also for a cluster of customs,
opinions and prejudices that include their dietary practices; the sequestration
or near-sequestration of "their" women; the sermons delivered by their mullahs of choice; a loathing of modern society in general, riddled as it is with
music, godlessness and sex; and a more particularized loathing (and fear) of
the prospect that their own immediate surroundings could be taken over—
"Westoxicated"—by the liberal Western style way of life.

There is also, Rushdie said, the "routine anti-Semitism" in popular and official
Muslim sentiment. No wonder, then, that millions of Muslims cheered the 9/11
attacks. But for Rushdie, this personal Islam, with its prejudices and faith, was
not the problem to be addressed. The problem was, rather, the dangerous politi-
cization of Islam. "The restoration of religion to the sphere of the personal, its
depoliticization, is the nettle that all Muslim societies must grasp in order to
become modern. The only aspect of modernity interesting to the terrorists is
technology, which they see as a weapon that can be turned on its makers. If terrorism is to be defeated, the world of Islam must take on board the secularist-
humanist principles on which the modern is based, and without which Muslim
countries' freedom will remain a distant dream."

The fault lines Rushdie delineated were not necessarily between Islam and
the West. He wrote that he did "not wholly" subscribe to "Samuel P. Huntington's
thesis about the clash of civilizations, for the simple reason that the Islamists'
project is turned not only against the West and 'the Jews,' but also against their
fellow Islamists. Whatever the public rhetoric, there's little love lost between the
Taliban and Iranian regimes. Dissensions between Muslim nations run at least
as deep if not deeper, than those nations' resentment of the West." But Rushdie
made clear a conflict between modernity based on "secularist-humanist principles" and Islamist (or did he imply *Islamic?*) refusal to allow religious freedom.

Wolfe and Rushdie seemed to define the 9/11 conflict similarly as a crux
between the principles of religious freedom grounded in secular government and
the dogmatic uniformity of religious rule. Jonathan Lear (2001), a member of the
Committee on Social Thought at the University of Chicago, reviewed *In the Name
of Identity: Violence and the Need to Belong* by Amin Maalouf (2001), a Christian,

Lebanese-born French journalist. The reviewer said that "in the aftermath of Sept. 11 we want to know more facts, . . . but we are also hungry for general reflection on what human beings are like." This book, he wrote, "argues that a politics of identity based on a sense of victimization—which reduces identity to a single affiliation—facilitates the creation of 'identities that kill.'" Lear continued, "The question that does concern Maalouf is why the Christian West, which has a tradition of intolerance, has founded societies that respect freedom of expression, while the Muslim world, which has a tradition of tolerance, is now a stronghold of fanaticism. Muslims attack the West, Maalouf thinks, not primarily because they are Muslim but because they feel downtrodden or derided. This sense of outrage is then taken up into a particular interpretation of Islam that offers redress and revenge." Maalouf, according to Lear, "'dreams' of a world in which there is religion and spirituality but in which those impulses are no longer attached to the need to belong to a group. . . . His hope is that by taking certain practical steps the world as a whole can accomplish what America has been struggling to accomplish: to embrace both diversity and unity."

Lear's review and Maalouf's book were not just reflections on innocence and victimhood: Israelis who hold to the victimhood of the Holocaust while crushing Palestinian self-determination; Palestinians who regard themselves as victims even as they perpetuate violence against Jews, whom they cannot think of as innocents; suicide bombers who consider themselves martyrs rather than terrorists (see Bennet 2003b; Burns 2003; Greenberg 2001; Van Natta 2003a; cf. Juergensmeyer 2003:72–75). More to the point, they framed the 9/11 encounter as a standoff between a society that allows for freedom of identity and one that does not. Maalouf (2001) wrote that "every individual should be able to identify, at least to some degree, both with the country he lives in and with our present-day world. . . . Each of us should be encouraged to accept his own diversity, to see his identity as the sum of all his various affiliations, instead of as only one of them raised to the status of the most important, made into an instrument of exclusion and sometimes into a weapon of war" (159). Nations that deny individuals the right to rise above identification with the state—doctrinaire patriotism, religio-nationalism—are excluding their citizens, Maalouf argued, "from the common civilisation that is coming into existence" (163). In like manner, Thomas L. Friedman's (2001b) column "Spiritual Missile Shield" stated that Americans' greatest defense for the future against Al Qaeda and its allies consisted not in military proliferation, but rather in the continuing will to "foster religious tolerance and pluralism." To Friedman, those principles were America's most abiding, most identifying, most powerful.

Tolerance became the subject of a *Times* article about a religion museum in Taiwan (Landler 2001) and of several *Times* essays during 2002, including one that asked, "The one true faith: Is it tolerance?" (Cahill 2002). This piece in the "Week in Review" traced the roots of modern American religious tolerance to the late eighteenth century, when Americans "officially refused to play the old game of whose religion was true, and took a generously agnostic view of religious truth: you may believe what you like and so may I, and neither can impose belief on the other." The author, an historian of Christianity's origins and accomplishments, asked significantly, "Is there an essentially different dynamic at work in Islamic countries that keeps them from arriving at the civic virtue of tolerance?" Was it also significant that the *Times* illustrated the essay with a painting of England's King Richard the Lionheart "setting off on a crusade" in the twelfth century? (See other images of religious wars in Jenkins 2001.) The author's hope was that Islam would be able to develop such ideals already functioning in the United States. Perhaps serving up an example, Jane Perlez (2002g) wrote about "an Islamic scholar's lifelong lesson: tolerance," focusing on Nurcholish Madjid, an Indonesian intellectual "known as the conscience of his nation." His eyes were always fixed on civil liberties, having "refined his taste for democratic values at the University of Chicago . . . , where he mixed his Islamic studies with courses in political science." He learned his American lessons and thus practiced as well as preached "the inclusive brand of Islam," welcoming a Jewish son-in-law to his family, thereby demonstrating the principle of religious pluralism.

Judith Shulevitz (2002) expounded on this theme in her column "The Close Reader: Other People's Religions" in the *New York Times Book Review.* "Americans don't like religious intolerance, and who can blame them?" she wrote in her lead. "When backed by state power, it can lead to murder and mayhem, which is why our founding fathers insisted on the separation of church and state. People who disparage other faiths no longer come off as commendably pious, as they did centuries ago; now they just seem boorish." After expressing what might be called the *Times*' "code" about religious tolerance, Shulevitz told the tale of Los Angeles school officials who took a Koran from a school library because it contained anti-Jewish comments. In Shulevitz's view, this act missed the point that intolerance is "an inevitable part of religion. Most world religions originally preached intolerance of other religions." The Koran regards Jews and Christians as failed religionists—especially Jews, who were seen "as sectarians who betrayed the universal nature of monotheistic truth." But let us remember, she said, that the Jewish Bible disparages the Canaanites, and the New Testament utters more than a few unkindnesses regarding the Jews. Shulevitz wanted youths in Los Angeles and elsewhere to "grasp [the idea] that systems of belief can be at once appealing and repugnant, and that the student's job is to discriminate between those qualities. That's what discrimination—the good kind—is for."

And that, seemingly, was what 9/11 was *about,* and essayists in the *Times* meant to help its readers "discriminate" between tolerant and intolerant traditions, as Shulevitz said. By way of an historical lesson for the post-9/11 world, María Rosa Menocal (2002a), author of *The Ornament of the World: How Muslims, Jews, and Christians Created a Culture of Tolerance in Medieval Spain* (2002b), wrote the op-ed "A Golden Reign of Tolerance," which summarized the title and content of her book about several hundred years of "cultural openness" in Andalusia (a thesis that Edward Rothstein [2003] questioned at length).

It was important for *Times* readers to realize that Americans did not invent religious tolerance and to see that Muslims were capable of practicing it as the hallmark of democratic, societal politics. Foreign-affairs columnist Thomas L. Friedman (2001a; see also Friedman 2002d) noted that 150 million Muslims live in India, making it the second-largest Muslim community in the world. India, he said, is a "multi-ethnic, pluralistic, free-market democracy" where Muslims participate and prosper.

The "fundamental question" facing *Times* readers was whether the modern practice of "democracy" was "compatible with Islam" or not. A *Times* reporter stated that "throughout most of the Muslim world the tension between Islam and modernity remains profound," with democracy being a signpost of modernity. He wondered if "it is the absence of a Reformation in the history of Islam that helps explain why universities in the Arab world that were once the most advanced centers of learning have often turned inward and backward" (Jehl 2001a). Despite his doubts, the *Times* provided a map of Muslim countries showing where democracy was taking observable, if "uneasy steps" in the "Islamic world." The map categorized that world into zones of "Democracy" (Turkey, Bangladesh, Senegal, Sierra Leone, and Suriname); "Emerging Democracy" (Indonesia, Albania, Gambia, Lebanon,

Niger); "Limited Democracy" (Egypt and sixteen other nations); "Authoritarian" (Iraq, Libya, Syria; cf. Dalrymple 2003 on "Syria's shades of gray"); "Monarchy" (Saudi Arabia and five other countries in the Middle East); "Monarchy/Limited Democracy" (Malaysia, Jordan, Kuwait, Morocco); "Theocracy" (Iran); "Transitional" (Pakistan, Nigeria, and several other African nations); and "No Functioning Central Government" (Afghanistan).

As if to demonstrate Islam's democratic "possibilities and perils," the *Times* "Week in Review" provided a full page analyzing "Turkey's secular experiment" (Sengupta 2001e) and Egypt's "effort to enforce lessons of tolerance" (Sachs 2001d). "Can Democracy Take Root in the Islamic World?" queried an op-ed page headline over three essays, all of which answered affirmatively. But whereas one urged the United States to "nudge" and "push" the "Arab autocrats—even those who woo the West with democratic language" (Gerges 2003)—another warned the United States against its own "arrogance of power" (Bin Talal 2003). The third cautioned American readers against regarding the notion of a "religious democracy" as an "oxymoron." Indeed, "the Jewish version of this ideal currently exists in Israel," so why should it not be workable in Iran and elsewhere in the Muslim world (Aslan 2003)?

If it was possible to perceive Islam's coexistence with—and even fostering of—democratic principles and processes, it was also necessary to recall how today's Muslims—and Americans, too—can fall short of the ideals of democratic tolerance. In his column "Bigotry in Islam—and Here," Nicholas D. Kristof (2002a) wrote:

> The Islamic world represses women, spawns terrorism, is prone to war, resists democracy and has contributed remarkably few great scientists or writers to modern civilization. So it's time to defend Islam. In speaking to Arab friends, I've reproached them for the virulent anti-Semitism in their societies. But it's a cheap shot for us to scold Arabs for acquiescing in religious hatred unless we try vigorously to uproot our own religious bigotry. Since 9/11, appalling hate speech about Islam has circulated in the U.S. on talk radio, on the Internet and in particular among conservative Christian pastors.

Quoting Teddy Roosevelt's idea that "the only good Indians are dead Indians," Kristof closed with the humbling thought that "history suggests that focusing on the moral deficiencies of other peoples simply underscores our own."

A review (Hilton 2003) of Jessica Stern's book *Terror in the Name of God* (2003) pointed to the same lesson in that book. In writing about religious militants, Stern said that "the bottom line . . . is that purifying the world through holy war is addictive. Holy war intensifies the boundaries between Us and Them, satisfying the inherently human longing for a clear identity and a definite purpose in life, creating a seductive state of bliss" (137). It is one thing to note Muslim terrorists' use of "spiritual dread"—their "most dangerous weapon" in that it "aims at destroying moral distinctions themselves" (296). But American policymakers must also ask themselves if they are falling into the same mindset: "We need to respond—not just with guns—but by seeking to create confusion, conflict, and competition among terrorists and between terrorists and their sponsors and sympathizers. We should encourage the condemnation of extremist interpretations of religion by peace-loving practitioners. . . . In the end, however, what counts is what we fight *for,* not what we oppose. We need to avoid giving into spiritual dread, and to hold fast to the best of our principles, by emphasizing tolerance, empathy, and courage" (296, italics in original).

In a sense, this idea has been the major 9/12 message of the *Times:* separating Muslims in general from militant Muslims, but, more important, defining liberal values as well as expressing and praising tolerance and empathy. The *Times* has been famously committed to tolerance, so much so that critics (e.g., Proctor 2000) have accused the newspaper of employing tolerance as its sacred, creedal truncheon by which it thumps everyone who disagrees with its editorial positions. Serge Schmemann's (2002d) "Us and Them: The Burden of Tolerance in a World of Division" provided a viewpoint sensitive to the limits of tolerance. Although recognizing that "from a passive, even reluctant accommodation, tolerance metamorphosed into a pillar of the American way, something to be taught, defended and promoted," Schmemann wrote that "the challenge is whether we must tolerate those who are murderously intolerant of us."

Schmemann (2007) tells how he came to write this essay. He was moderator at a post-9/11 interfaith panel—"one of those wishy-washy, 'we love each other' things," he recounts. The Christian and the Muslim representatives were expressing their mutual goodwill, but the rabbi was "hard-nosed" in defining difference among the Abrahamic faiths. "Religion is not always friendly," the rabbi uttered, eliciting a comment from the audience: "Do we all have to hold hands and be good? Are there not limits to tolerance?"

Schmemann acknowledges that 9/11 has been "a setback to ecumenism." Despite the initial "we are all together" sentiment in the United States, despite President Bush's immediate expressions of goodwill to Muslims, "polarization" and "mutual suspicion" have set in among the three traditions. Not only have neoconservatives, evangelical preachers, and people such as Bernard Lewis and Mel Gibson asked rude questions—"Is Islam inherently violent?"—but even moderate institutions such as the *Times* have expressed an "underlying hostility" to Islam. At the same time, Schmemann charges, "Islamic writers have been very weak" in responding to public criticism since 9/11, in part because they have not done enough to understand America and the West, in part because they have not been sufficiently self-critical, and in part because they will not admit in public to internal fractures and deficiencies within Islam. They have focused on their "perceived hurts" rather than on striving wholeheartedly toward needed reform.

As much as the *Times* essayists might emphasize religious tolerance and multicultural pluralism as aspects of American democratic principle and practice—the salient features of moderate modernity—the paper seemed far from committed to relativism in the period following 9/11. Indeed, eleven days after the attacks, Edward Rothstein (2001a) composed the essay "Attacks on U.S. Challenge the Perspectives of Postmodern True Believers" to criticize postmodern and postcolonial theorists' impulses. This is one of those times, Rothstein said, when right is right and wrong is wrong, and all this moral and cognitive relativism is twaddle. Rothstein quoted some of those who assigned US policies and injustices some fault in provoking the 9/11 attacks, but he found such views "ethically perverse. Rigidly applied, they require a form of guilty passivity in the face of ruthless and unyielding opposition."

Rothstein's position might have seemed akin to a *Fox News* executive's edict: "I don't believe that democracy and terrorism are relative things you can talk about, and I don't think there's any moral equivalence in those two positions." Yet the *Times* was willing to allow Stanley Fish (2001), dean of the College of Liberal Arts and Sciences at the University of Illinois at Chicago, to write a rebuttal to Rothstein's column. Fish stated that "postmodernism maintains only that there can be no independent standard for determining which of many rival interpretations of an event is the true one. The only thing postmodern thought argues against is the hope of justifying our response to the attacks in universal terms that would be persuasive to everyone, including our enemies." Postmodernism, he argued, does not allow us to reduce our enemies to irrational, evil madmen. They have their own brand of heroism that must be understood, their own reasons for attacking. He concluded, "If by relativism one means the practice of putting yourself in your adversary's shoes, not in order to wear them as your own but in order to have some understanding (far short of approval) of why someone else might want to wear them, then relativism will not and should not end, because it is simply another name for serious thought."

A year later *Times Book Review* columnist Judith Shulevitz (2002b) reflected on a year of American rhetoric about "'evil men'"—including President Bush's words. "But what exactly do we mean by evil?" she asked. Her reply was a conundrum, balanced on the slippery ground of human intent. "What if it could be proved that Osama bin Laden did in fact mean well?" she queried.

> Al Qaeda members and Palestinian suicide bombers are genuinely, sincerely convinced that they are doing the right thing. That doesn't make them less evil, but it does make them more terrifying, since they force us to face the chilly reality of a world in which sincerity and morality have nothing to do with each other. How strongly you believe in something is irrelevant; what matters is whether your beliefs are the correct ones, and we figure that out . . . by examining what your belief leads you to do. And that view demands humility, since it holds as true for us as it does for our enemies. If there is only a single standard of good behavior, then no matter how honestly we believe in our causes—in democracy, for instance, as opposed to tyranny or religious totalitarianism— we are never allowed to stop worrying about our own morality when we march forth to defend them.

In support of that inclination, an "Arts & Ideas" survey in the May 31, 2003, *Times* traced historians' notions of "an unholy alliance" between religion and nationalism (Stille 2003). According to one scholar, "The idea that religious intolerance is the 'original sin' of nationalism is getting more and more attention, . . . 'a healthy corrective to the modernist consensus. . . . Faced with the threat of Islamic fundamentalism, the West is more open to looking at the role of religion in the formation of nationalism.'" The "unholy alliance" may have arisen in reaction to the culture of tolerance among Muslims, Jews, and Christians in medieval Spain as Castille consolidated its power around its Christian base, and it has played a role in nation formation ever since, including in the United States. "Americans are in denial about their own nationalism," another scholar said. "They say, 'We don't do nationalism, we are a multiethnic country, we have patriotism.' But the U.S. still sees itself as the City on a Hill, fighting against 'the axis of evil.' Americans have a very theologically rooted sense of nation."

Relativism, Patriotism, and Their Perils

A newspaper such as the *New York Times* functions, perforce, as an agent of relativism—according to Stanley Fish's definition—because one of its major tasks is to make sensible to its readers (us) the worldview of other people(s) (them). The *Times* is a New York paper, telling (us) New Yorkers what is happening around our city. It is an American paper, telling (us) Americans about our country. But it also tells (us) Americans what the rest of the world is thinking and doing, especially when the world crashes into New York's metropolitan heart and we Americans need to understand why.

To learn about other people(s)—even about how their idea of heroism is our idea of terrorism—reporters must go out into the world. In order to persist in the world, reporters must accommodate their sources. They must, perforce, behave like relativists. The *Times Magazine* carried a piece by Peter Maass (2003b), "When Al Qaeda Calls," about Al Jazeera reporter Yosri Fouda, who got a scoop from Al Qaeda about its planning of the 9/11 assaults, and who failed to criticize the operatives publicly in order to maintain his relativistic, fence-sitting status with past and future sources. Maass called the process the "journalism of access." Smile and nod, he said, laugh at your sources' jokes, and do not cut off the flow of future information by offending them too much in your reports; that is what reporters must do to stay in business.

Maass was not content to rest his critique on reporters covering Al Qaeda and other foreigners. Indeed, the perils of the "journalism of access," he argued, are far greater in dealing with sources closer to home: "If you wish to remain popular in the mainstream media, you invite trouble by deviating too far from the views of your sources and audience. Harping on an unpopular truth is rarely a career-advancing or an audience-building move." The *Times* is not only a New York newspaper, but also an American institution, and it is expected, perforce, to present an American and even patriotic point of view.

Leftish critics of the American media have examined the language common to US opinion makers since 9/11, who are employed in aiding what can be called the national process of "manufacturing consent" (Collins and Glover 2002:3, using Noam Chomsky's expression). *Anthrax, blowback, civilization versus barbarism, cowardice, evil, freedom, fundamentalism, jihad, justice, targets, terrorism, unity, vital interests, "the war on . . .":* these are phrases the US government has used and the media have repeated since 9/11. Mainstream editors, publishers, and writers mostly took up America's official viewpoint in 9/11 coverage—and that meant the president's viewpoint—as canonical. There was a strong reluctance to dissent, to question, to probe, to look beyond patriotic bromides (Navasky 2002:xv–xviii), at least in the period immediately following 9/11.

In a book of essays about "journalism after September 11," a journalist complained that "there is a curtain of prescribed patriotism that has descended over the media, particularly television" (Carey 2002:88)—the cost, perhaps, of having news media owned by the entertainment industry. According to another critic, Robert McChesney (2002), in the same book, "The picture conveyed by the media was as follows: a benevolent, democratic, and peace-loving nation was brutally attacked by insane evil terrorists who hated the United States for its freedoms and affluent way of life" (93). Insofar as the United States was by the turn of the twenty-first century "the dominant economic and military power in the world, it has engaged in hundreds of wars and invasions and bombing missions across the planet" (92). But "establishment journalism" (98) or "media corporations" (99) in the United States were structurally incapable of telling the full truth about America. American news organizations covered 9/11 as Americans. They "became saturated with patriotic spirit after September 11" (Waisbord 2002:206). This saturation was perhaps the process and result of "commodifying" 9/11 for the purpose of "hegemony" (Christopher Campbell 2003)—for example, Dan Rather on the *David Letterman Show* announcing himself ready to follow his president's orders. In a steady state, says Sylvia Waisbord (2002), "Americanism is a bedrock value of US journalism" (206). That is part of the ideology of modernism practiced by most American news media, including the *Times*. In this crucial moment, however, the news media did more by covering 9/11 as a story of risk, threat, and patriotism concerning "'Fortress America,'" creating a "'culture of fear,'" according to Waisbord (202). For the most part, according to media commentators, "mainstream journalism was not willing to raise doubts about the merits of blatantly biased reporting such as Fox News' brand of journalism . . . : 'Be accurate, be fair, be American'" (208).

In this regard, the *Times* ran the article "Speech and Expression: In Patriotic Time, Dissent Is Muted" (Carter and Barringer 2001) about Americans who had fallen into post-9/11 patriotic step. Small-town journalists were fired, and sponsorship was withdrawn on television in revenge for the expressions of opinions at odds with the American consensus, thus giving real meaning to the notion of political correctness. "The surge of national pride that has swept the country after the terrorist attacks on Sept. 11 has sparked the beginnings of a new, more difficult debate over the balance among national security, free speech," and other competing American values. This article, it is said, "marked the end of overwhelming consensus in post-September 11 journalism" (Schedson 2002:36); however, the overwhelming coverage of 9/11 topics still fell in line with an American worldview. For all the rightist charges of a leftist media treasonous in its coverage, the opposite was true, and not just Fox was playing the role of one-sided jingoist.

The *Times* participated in American civil religion at 9/11. Most prominently, the series "A Nation Challenged" made it clear who the paper's readers were, what nation they belonged to, who was being attacked, and by whom, but its version of that religion included compassion, diversity, dissent, ecumenism, social activism—all covered in its stories. It even had the temerity to criticize *Fox News* on occasion. According to media critics on the left, the *Times* stood out from most mainstream media in its willingness to step back at times from the conformist flow, to be professional journalists again, covering conflict as well as consensus.

The *Times* has seen itself as a patriotic newspaper from its beginnings. It has replied to attacks on American properties—from the *Lusitania* to Pearl Harbor to the World Trade Center and the Pentagon—with patriotic indignation. However, since the late 1960s the paper has also on occasion been highly critical of American policies and has regarded its criticism as an act of patriotism. During the Vietnam War, some (e.g., Dinsmore 1969) charged the *Times* with appeasing Communists and undermining American national interests in its attempt to be neutral in reporting the news. In the minds of some, an American newspaper should be patriotic in its reportage and in its editorials, especially in a time of war.

If the attacks of 9/11 were acts of war, and if the United States was to respond by engaging in a prolonged military conflict with an identifiable enemy, where was the *Times* to stand in reporting and commenting on the crucial events to come? After 9/11, if the enemy was identifiable as Islamic, and if the United States and its Western allies were in the midst of what could be termed World War III, how well would the *Times* be able to remain neutrally descriptive in treating Islam? Was Islam to be treated as an evil threat to be fought or as a complex religious matrix—made up of those facets by which the *Times* had defined religion for decades—that needed to be understood? Would the *Times* act as priestly scribe in a civil religion, representing American interests as an American government might define them, or would the paper serve a more prophetic role, calling the nation to standards higher than patriotism? And what would those standards be, and from what source(s) would they derive? Would they be biblical or secular, humanistic or multicultural? And how would they define and regard "us" and "them"?

"Clash of Civilizations"

In the summer of 1993, as the Soviet bloc and the Cold War crumbled, distinguished professor of government and strategic studies Samuel P. Huntington published an article in *Foreign Affairs* in which he suggested that "the fundamental source of conflict in this new world will not be primarily ideological or primarily economic. The great divisions among humankind and the dominating source of conflict will be cultural" (22). In writing about "the fault lines between civilizations" and the "battle lines of the future," he discussed the "emergence of the modern international system with the Peace of Westphalia" (22) in the seventeenth century: the creation of nation-states and their ideologies. However, transcending state boundaries, he argued, were "civilizations, . . . the highest cultural grouping[s] of people and the broadest level of cultural identity people have short of that which distinguishes humans from other species," with "common objective elements, such as language, history, religion, customs, institutions, and by the subjective self-identification of people" (24). The most differentiating factor, he said, was "religion. The people of different civilizations have different views on the relations between God and man, the individual and the group, the citizen and the state, parents and children, husband and wife, as well as differing views of the relative importance of rights and responsibilities, liberty and authority, equality and hierarchy" (25).

Huntington argued that whereas Westphalia attempted to create secular states, in the late twentieth century the "'unsecularization of the world'" (26) has resulted in "'fundamentalist'" movements—"'Asianization,'" "'Hinduization,'" "'re-Islamization,'" and so on—that have attempted to redefine nationalism in religious terms. To some degree, these movements are matters of ethnicity, but Huntington emphasized their religious content and defined them as a trend toward "de-Westernization" (27). The upshot is that these fermenting religious nationalisms are defining themselves in opposition to Western civilization, a matter of "'us' versus 'them'" (29). The "fault lines between civilizations" (29) have long been apparent between eastern and western Europe, in essence between Western Christendom and Islam (and Orthodox Christianity). "The interaction between Islam and the West," he said, "is seen as a clash of civilization," and here is where "the West's 'next confrontation'" will come (32).

Although Huntington defined and surveyed the several "civilizations" of the world, he emphasized that "Islam has bloody borders" (35), with a heritage of jihad and martyrdom, and that Islam's primary nemesis is "the West." Citing intellectuals such as Bernard Lewis and V. S. Naipaul, Huntington distinguished between Western civilization and the rest: "Western concepts differ fundamentally from those prevalent in other civilizations. Western ideas of individualism, liberalism, constitutionalism, human rights, equality, liberty, the rule of law, democracy, free markets, the separation of church and state, often have little resonance in Islamic, Confucian, Japanese, Hindu, Buddhist or Orthodox cultures" (40). For whatever reasons, Huntington stressed a "Confucian–Islamic connection" (45) in opposition to the West in asking if "the next world war" (39) would constitute "the clash of civilizations" (22).

Huntington's article struck a responsive chord among some Western intellectuals despite widespread criticism of his ideas in academic circles (Abrahamian 2003). He expanded and calibrated his theory in a book, *The Clash of Civilizations and the Remaking of World Order* (1997), delineating the seven to nine civilizations in the world today; enumerating the core Western characterizations; defining the importance of Western "modernization" (68) since the eighteenth century; recognizing the end to "European colonialism" and "American hegemony" (91); portraying the varieties of "religious resurgence" worldwide (95); warning against Islam's "destabilizing force" (121) by means of burgeoning populations, resurgent religious vitality, and a "propensity toward violent conflict" (258); attending to Islam's critique of "Western secularism, irreligiosity, and hence immorality" (213); and exhorting Americans to resist the siren's call of multiculturalism in order to defend Western civilization. "The survival of the West depends," he said, "on Americans reaffirming their Western identity [as] unique not universal" (20–21). "Rejection of the [American] Creed and of Western civilization means the end of the United States of America as we have known it," he prophesied. "It also means effectively the end of Western civilization" (306–7).

For Huntington, the American "culture wars" are connected to the "clash of civilizations" because in order to win the latter, the former must be resolved in favor of a consensual "American Creed," which will defeat conflictual multiculturalists. His conclusion? "The clash between the multiculturalists and the defenders of Western civilization and the American Creed is . . . 'the *real* clash' within the American segment of Western civilization. Americans cannot avoid the issue: Are we a Western people or are we something else? The futures of the United States and the West depend upon Americans reaffirming their commitment to Western civilization" (307, italics in original).

Although Huntington's book was often coolly analytical—that is, until its diatribe against American multicultural turncoats, apostates, and schismatics—it was also stark in facing what Huntington felt was a "grim" (20) future. Between 1993 and 1997, he seems to have erased the question mark about a potential "clash of civilization." Rather, he stated that "the underlying problem for the West is not Islamic fundamentalism. It is Islam, a different civilization whose people are convinced of the superiority of their culture and are obsessed with the inferiority of their power. The problem for Islam is not the CIA or the U.S. Department of Defense. It is the West, a different civilization whose people are convinced of the universality of their culture and believe that their superior, if declining, power imposes on them the obligation to extend that culture throughout the world" (217–18). Huntington saw conflict between Islam and the West for two main reasons: (1) difference, "particularly the Muslim concept of Islam as a way of life transcending and uniting religion and politics versus the Western Christian concept of the separate realms of God and Caesar" (210); and (2) sameness, involving two religious systems of monotheistic intolerance and universalist expansion, in which jihad and crusade appear as symbolic mirrors of each other.

Why review Samuel Huntington's "controversial thesis" (Volkmer 2002:238) at length? Because its tenet regarding the "clash of civilizations" "routinely served in the media in both the U.S. and Europe as a justification of sorts for the otherwise inexplicable"—a constantly iterated dichotomy between "'us,' being the enlightened, modern, Christianized West," and "'them' being the anti-modern, anti-democratic Islam" (Volkmer 2002:238). Media critics (Llorente 2002), including the Dalai Lama (Goodstein 2003h), decried the media's adoption of Huntington's conflictual vocabulary, especially his notion of the "clash of civilizations," and they exhorted journalists to see the world in grays rather than in black and white and to be culturally self-critical rather than calling our nation's opponents "evil" (Rediehs 2002).

The media tended to see the post-9/11 world divided into the West and Islam; however, it was also newsworthy to learn how much the terrorists resembled "us"—using "our" Internet, watching "our" TV, going to "our" universities, enjoying "our" lifestyles. "Jihad" and "McWorld" seemed to be combined in a violent dialectic (Volkmer 2002:238–39). Indeed, one author, Mahmood Mamdani, accused the United States of having trained and funded the world's jihadists as a Cold War tactic: "The best-known C.I.A.-trained terrorist, he [Mamdani] notes dryly, is Osama bin Laden." Seen in this light, Al Qaeda's roots were in Western "politics, not [in] religion or culture" engendered solely by Islamic civilization (H. Eakin 2004).

In later works, Huntington (now deceased), most famous and most influential for his "clash of civilizations" thesis, seemed to regard values, globalization, diversity, and the human future in far less Manichaean ways and emphasized the congruence of Western and global cultures, but without denying the conflicts inhering to the interplay (see, e.g., Berger and Huntington 2002; Harrison and Huntington 2000). However, Huntington's book *Who Are We? The Challenges to America's National Identity* (2004) returned to the supposed dangers that "multiculturalism, diversity and bilingualism" pose to the "overarching national identity" of the United States (Kakutani 2004b). James Davison Hunter and Joshua Yates (2002)—Hunter best known for his work on the American "culture wars" (Hunter 1991)—wrote an appraisal of the many ways in which the world has adopted the technology of the West, a process that has had the ironic effect of alienating non-Westerners even further from the West.

The "culture wars" and the "clash of civilizations" were interconnected concepts in Huntington's writings and conjoined in the *New York Times* coverage of 9/11—both its matrix and its aftermath. These two popularized coinages pointed to religious dynamics, the former within American life and the latter primarily between American civilization (and that of its Western allies) and global Islam. The *Times* had reported on the "culture wars" for many years and had become embroiled in them, having been accused by critics on the religious right of being the leading advocate for secular humanism. When 9/11 came about as the narrative that marked the real shift from the twentieth to the twenty-first century and encoded viscerally the theory of the "clash of civilizations," it could be perceived as the event that tied the two stories together.

Scholars of recent religious nationalism have treated its parallels in America and around the world. Mark Juergensmeyer (1993) wrote of religious nationalism as a form of "antimodernism" (5). For him, the refusal to separate religion and politics—the rejection of the secular, social-contract notion of government that had established the modern nation-state beginning in the seventeenth century—made religious nationalism antimodern (5–7). Juergensmeyer saw the "rise of politically active right-wing preachers in the 1980's" (35) as America's version of religious nationalism—a challenge to modernity's "secular nationalism" (35). In its coverage of the "culture wars," the *Times* has taken a stance similar to Juergensmeyer's, and at times the paper seems to have written of the Islamic perpetrators of 9/11 as if they were ideological kin to American fundamentalists. For the *Times,* both the "culture wars" and the battle with militant Islam have been struggles between religious and secular nationalism.

When we look at the *Times* treatment of Islam after 9/11, it reads very much like the writings of scholars such as Bassam Tibi (2001), especially in the differentiation he makes between Islam, on the one hand, and political Islam, Islamic fundamentalism, and Islamism, on the other (1). Islam's mistrust of modernity but its embrace of contemporary science and technology (6), have been topics of concern for the *Times* in identifying contemporary Islam. The *Times* also shared Tibi's ambivalence toward religion in general—its supernaturalist, normative claims, its assertions of ultimacy—while acknowledging its importance as a cultural construct with a genealogy (28–29).

Hence, one can find the *Times* and scholars of religion on similar ground in their perspectives on issues raised by Huntington regarding Islam, Islamism, and the interplay between religion and nationalism. But, as exemplar of responsible journalism, the *Times* contained a range of views on these subjects after 9/11.

When in the weeks following 9/11 Italian premier Silvo Berlusconi called Western Christian civilization superior to Islamic civilization—in prosperity, human rights, and religious freedoms—the *Times* reported briefly on his views (Erlanger 2001a). *Times* correspondent Steven Erlanger (2007b), tipped off by an Italian journalist friend who heard Berlusconi's remarks, was "pretty shocked by his comments and also amused by them." To Erlanger, "it was simply a wonderful news story."

The paper devoted far more space, however, to humanizing Islam as part of its emphasis on cooperative religious diversity in the United States. But then over the weekend of October 6–8, 2001, as the United States attacked Afghanistan, the *Times'* coverage of Islam turned less hopeful and tolerant. Might there not be some truth to the idea that bin Laden represented a significant strand of Islam as well as of religious fundamentalism worldwide? And were not both—Islam and fundamentalism—at war with American democratic principles? The *Times* had been covering the "culture wars" in the United States—differences of opinion between conservative Christians and liberals regarding abortion, feminism, homosexuality, and so on—but now it was looking at a real culture war that might turn out to be a clash between civilizations.

Mark Lilla's (2001) op-ed "Extremism's Theological Roots" stated that American intellectuals—for example, Martin E. Marty—had not wanted to blame Islam for 9/11, but if we are going to hold Catholicism accountable for anti-Semitism during the Holocaust, Lilla argued, do we not have the obligation to hold Islam accountable for its militant fundamentalism? Judaism's settlers in Israel are motivated by a desire to bring on the Messiah; Islamic fundamentalists are motivated by something in their tradition (although he did not say what that might be). "In religion, as in nature," he concluded, "there is no such thing as spontaneous generation." Thus, religions that produce violence must hold the seeds of hatred within them.

Andrew Sullivan explored these themes to sensational effect in his October 2001 essay "This *Is* a Religious War" in the *Times Magazine*. "Perhaps the most admirable part of the response to the conflict that began on Sept. 11," he wrote, "has been a general reluctance to call it a religious war." But we must face reality, he said; we must not deny any longer the religious nature of this war. Sullivan argued, "It is a war of fundamentalism against faiths of all kinds that are at peace with freedom and modernity." He quoted the Koran in its espousal of war against unbelievers. He quoted the Taliban and bin Laden on their Islamic principles exhorting jihad. Not only did the article expose Islamic fundamentalism as a genuine expression of Islam, but Sullivan also took a hard look at Christian crusading mentality, which he called a monotheistic "terrorist temptation." Fundamentalism, he said, is comforting to the believer and damning to the nonbeliever.

The genius of the United States, in contrast, according to Sullivan, has been keeping its fundamentalists from gaining military-governmental power.

Separation of church and state is our great democratic virtue, he said. It is what we are fighting for now: "free religious faith" versus "intolerant, militaristic religion." He concluded: "We are fighting not for our country as such or for our flag. We are fighting for the universal principles of our Constitution—and the possibility of free religious faith it guarantees. We are fighting for religion against one of the deepest strains in religion there is. And not only our lives but our souls are at stake."

At the time of the publication of Sullivan's article, my students wondered aloud if the *Times* was using an analysis of Islamic fundamentalism to strike out at Christian fundamentalism in the United States. Would it be possible, they asked, to read every article about Islamic fundamentalism as a deflected criticism of American fundamentalism? Did *Times* editors commission Sullivan to scald monotheistic fundamentalism in its many forms?

When asked how he came to write this piece, Sullivan (2003) said that the *Times Magazine* editor called him up and asked him if he would write an article on the 9/11 aftermath with a religious angle. The editor did not tell him what religious angle to pursue, nor did the editor alter the article to tilt it in any direction. Having known the magazine editor for about ten years, Sullivan received complete freedom to write what he wanted, which he accomplished in two days. He had been thinking about these issues for a while, Sullivan said, so the thoughts came quickly.

Was it unfair for Sullivan to compare Islamic and Christian fundamentalism? Leah Renold (2002) looked at the use of the term *fundamentalism,* especially in the Sullivan article (see also an interview with V. S. Naipaul [Shatz 2001] in which Naipaul comments on this topic), which implied that Islam is fundamentalist at heart. Fundamentalism, Renold argued, is a specifically Christian movement with historical boundaries; the term should not be bandied about, she said.

Nonetheless, the *Times* already had a history of using the term as shorthand for types of religious movements beyond their American Christian counterparts. "Culture wars" coverage had already embedded the term in the *Times* vocabulary, and it meant a religious strain both antimodern and antimoderate; the term was not to be erased, especially when similarities could be found among Christian, Jewish, and Muslim fundamentalists.

In the *Times Magazine,* letters to the editor praised Sullivan's essay, but one commentator noted that "Sullivan pits fundamentalism, the 'subjugation of reason and judgment and even conscience to the dictates of dogma,' against modernity, which he defines as civil and political pluralism. This construction obscures a much more complicated cultural and intellectual reality" (Eugene MacCarraher in "This Is a Religious War" 2001). Yet the letter writer and others saw in 9/11 a cultural conflict within the United States as well as within Islam. At this moment of religiosecular "Armageddon," they wondered where the "silent . . . majority" stood.

In the period following 9/11, the *Times* reported and commented on church–state skirmishes in the "culture wars" of US domestic policy. Some might say (e.g., Marshall, Gilbert, and Ahmanson 2009) that the *Times* and other secular publications missed the point of religion's role in post-9/11 America; however, no one could accuse the *Times* of ignoring religion's prominence in 9/12 American public life. It covered:

- Vouchers for religious schools
- The place of religious displays and spiritual instruction in public schools
- The contest in public education between scientific evolution and creationism, now called "Intelligent Design"
- The debate over the moral standing of homosexuals in church, marriage, and public life—an issue in which the *Times* was far from neutral, although at least one writer in the *Times Magazine* recognized that the spark of homosexuality's legal rights was "how to reignite the culture wars" (Jeffrey Rosen 2003; indeed, the issue of same-sex marriages, beyond the scope of this study, was to play an important role in the "culture wars" affecting the presidential election of 2004)
- The judicial question of banning the phrase "under God" from the Pledge of Allegiance
- President Bush's "religion-based initiative"
- The very concept of the "separation of church and state"
- The continuing political clout of the Religious Right, especially as President Bush and his advisor Karl Rove worked to marshal their religious base for the 2004 presidential election

Throughout the prolonged drama concerning Justice Roy Moore's persistent, unconstitutional display of the Ten Commandments in the Alabama State Supreme Court building, the *Times* kept abreast of the public sparring between fundamentalist Christians and civil liberties groups. The "culture war" hackles raised by 9/11 made this clash all the more bitter.

Religious topics at a distance from 9/11 gained new-felt immediacy. So a review (Robert Wright 2003) of a book about the history of Mormon "fundamentalism" and "'faith-based violence'" in America led with a reference to 9/11's religious roots. The execution of Paul J. Hill, a former Presbyterian minister who assassinated a doctor performing abortions, raised the mighty issue of abortion's legality as a fixture in America's "culture wars," dating back to the early 1970s.

One might even say that the fracas concerning Mel Gibson's film *The Passion of the Christ* was both an internal American firefight and a cinematic outtake of America's sense of martyrdom at the hands of its evil enemies—a neat dovetailing of "culture wars" and "clash of civilizations" sentiment and imagery.

The presidential election year of 2004 heralded what Nicholas Kristof (2004a) called "a 'God gulf' of distrust, dividing churchgoing Republicans from relatively secular Democrats," and what a "Week in Review" headline called "The Culture Wars, Part II" (Toner 2004). Secularism found its proponents on the pages of the *Times* (e.g., in Michael Kazin's March 31, 2004, essay "Under God or Under Citizens: America's Long Culture War" regarding Susan Jacoby's *Freethinkers: A History of American Secularism* [2004]), but so did politically inclined Christian evangelicalism in authors such as Tim LaHaye and Jerry B. Jenkins, whose new "apocalyptic novel" *Glorious Appearing* (reviewed in Kirkpatrick 2004), foretold the Second Coming of a "warrior Jesus" who would destroy all his foes. According to the *Times'* reviewer, scholars of American religion found the novel especially significant: "The image of a fearsome Jesus who will turn the tables on the unbelieving earthly authorities corresponds to a widespread sense among many conservative Christians that their values are under assault in a culture war with the secular society around them." But the "culture war" had been ratcheted upward by the 9/11 attack, the war with Iraq, and President Bush's "discussions of a godly purpose behind American military actions in Afghanistan and Iraq." Mel Gibson's Jesus in *The Passion of the Christ* may have seemed like a submissive receptor of persecution—perhaps a symbol of America assaulted by its enemies on 9/11?—but according to one scholar quoted in Kirkpatrick's review, "the pendulum is swinging toward a darker, more martial, macho concept of the Messiah."

In the several months following 9/11, many, many articles in the *Times* seemed to be *about* "religion," defined one way or another. And for several years to come, it seemed as if most *Times* articles *about* "religion"—as tradition, institution, belief, supernaturalism, faith, ethics, ritual; as unifying and faction-alizing force in communities—possessed a 9/11 subtext. "Religion" was now largely politicized, and the politics were those of the "culture wars" in the United States and beyond.

Times reporters defined the divide between secularist and evangelist cultures in America; the paper's commentators provided the critique. Columnist and cultural correspondent Frank Rich (2002) was particularly opinionated on the left regarding conflicts about religion in American public life. Nicholas D. Kristof used his column now and again to douse the rhetorical flames of the "cultural wars"—but not always landing blows from the left. He wrote, for instance, "Evangelicals are usually regarded by snooty, college-educated bicoastal elitists (not that any read this newspaper) as dangerous Neanderthals. But while the old religious right was destructive when it launched the cultural wars, the new internationalists are saving lives in some of the most forgotten parts of the world. . . . I've lost my cynicism about evangelical groups party because I've seen them at work abroad" (Kristof 2002b; see also Kristof 2003e; cf. "Evangelicals and Their Critics" 2003). On the one hand, he praised evangelical missionaries in Africa (Kristof 2003d). On the other hand, he was glad to see the "'loving rebuke' by conservative Christians of their fire-breathing brethren" who called Islam a "vile faith," hence helping "move us back from the clash of civilizations that hard-liners in both Islam and Christianity are pushing us all toward" (Kristof 2003c). And he was concerned that "perhaps the most fundamental divide between America and the rest of the industrialized world" was "faith." How could it be, he wondered, that "Americans are three times as likely to believe in the Virgin Birth of Jesus (83 percent) as in evolution (28 percent)," and—having seen a similar move in Islam—he feared a drift in American Christianity "away from a rich intellectual tradition and toward the mystical. The heart is a wonderful organ, but so is the brain" (Kristof 2003a).

Paul Krugman (2002) accused the Bush administration of "removing long-standing barriers between church and state," not out of "interest in the substance of policy," but rather "to cater to a part of its base," meaning "fundamentalist" Christians. Bill Keller (2003a), the *Times'* new executive editor, penned a far less chilling word picture of George W. Bush's religiousness and the ways in which religion influenced his presidency. He depicted a man saved from his own demons by a faith-based twelve-step program, confident in his conversion, comfortable with other believers—including Muslims such as Turkey's Recep Tayyip Erdogan—and ready to "play the ecumenical healer by rebuking" foils such as Reverends Falwell and Robertson for "their attempt to turn the war on terror into a religious war." Keller also regarded the president and his "political genius" Karl Rove as masters of a plan to "make the religious right a captive of the Republican party." In 2004, columnist David Brooks added his voice to (the now late) William Safire's on the political right of the *Times* op-ed page, both weighing in on issues of national religious conflict and consensus (e.g., Brooks 2004c; Safire 2004b). On the international front, Brooks (2004a, 2004b) seemed sometimes fixated on "radical Islam." In short, *Times* columnists took a range of positions regarding post-9/11 "culture war" issues.

In Europe, considered far less pious than the United States (Ferguson 2003), a parallel set-to in the Western "culture wars" took place in the debate over whether to refer in the European Union Constitution to "'God as the source of truth'" as part of "Europe's 'spiritual heritage'" (Fuller 2003a; see also Fuller 2003b and Sciolino 2004l). Whereas the Roman Catholic Church lobbied heavily for God's inclusion (see "Pope Urges Europe to Avow Christianity" 2003), European minorities—Jews and Muslims—were concerned about an "'atavistic nostalgia of the Christian heritage'" in the economic confederation. *Newsweek* religion editor Kenneth L. Woodward (2003) wrote an impassioned *Times* op-ed about the "oxymoron" of "Europe without Christianity," when the "secularists" seemed victorious in erasing mention of Christianity's heritage in the Economic Union preamble (cf. "Europe, Christians, and History" 2003). The continent continued to "wring its hands over proclaiming its faith" (R. Bernstein 2003b) through 2003 and 2004 (see also Horowitz 2004).

If *Times* readers wished to witness a true "culture war," apart from squabbling over symbolic gestures, phrases in pledges and preambles, public policies, and the like, eastern Europe provided its share of examples—for instance, a "cycle of revenge" in Kosovo (Wood and Binder 2004), where Albanian Muslim and Serbian Orthodox Christian loyalists fought each other, sometimes to the death, and destroyed each other's houses of worship. Of course, a Huntingtonian might say that this ongoing battle constituted Exhibit A of the "clash of civilizations," right on the fault line between Muslim and Christian worlds. One might even argue that millions of Muslims had already crossed the fault line into Europe, creating a new "'Eurabia' that is hostile in equal measure to the United

States and Israel" (Ferguson 2004). Given the low fertility rates of Europeans, Muslim immigrants were filling in the void, taking jobs and spaces, and changing the ethos of a formerly Judeo-Christian civilization, portending perhaps "the death of the West." Deadly Muslim terrorist bombings in Madrid on March 11, 2003, gave solidity to such prophesying. If one could ignore for the moment that "most European Muslims are, of course, law-abiding citizens with little sympathy for terrorist attacks on European cities," the demographic changes could be perceived as ominous: "A youthful Muslim society to the south and east of the Mediterranean," stated Niall Ferguson (2004), "is poised to colonize—the term is not too strong—a senescent Europe." Considering the "decline of European Christianity"—a topic documented by the *Times* (e.g., Bruni 2003c)—"a creeping Islamicization of a decadent Christendom is one conceivable result." One might conjecture "a happy fusion between rapidly secularized second-generation Muslims and their post-Christian neighbors," but the evidence in 2004 suggested something less optimistic, at the least.

Did the *Times* adopt the idea that 9/11 was an offer to join the "clash of civilizations" that America could not refuse? In "21st-Century Jihad," a review of Peter L. Bergen's book *Holy War, Inc.: Inside the Secret World of Osama bin Laden* (2001), Ethan Bronner (2001) examined Bergen's argument against Huntington's thesis, which Bergen calls "seductive" (224) but simplistic and wrong. Bergen does not perceive bin Laden's hatred for the United States in cultural terms, but rather in political ones. Bin Laden did not condemn the United States for its constitution or for its drugs, alcohol, pornography, or entertainment industry. He left that for US fundamentalists such as Reverend Jerry Falwell. "What he condemns the United States for is simple," Bergen says of bin Laden: "its policies in the Middle East. Those are, to recap briefly: the continued U.S. military presence in Arabia; U.S. support for Israel, its continued bombing of Iraq; and its support for regimes such as Egypt and Saudi Arabia that bin Laden regards as apostates from Islam. Bin Laden is at war with the United States, but his is a *political* war, justified by his own understanding of Islam, directed at the symbols and institutions of American *political* power" (222, italics in original). If there is any cultural war going on, Bergen argues, it is within Islam rather than between Islam and the West. Bronner found Bergen's thesis "a cramped, literal parsing of bin Laden's few public statements, and in the end, simplistic and unsatisfying. You do not have to accept Huntington's argument entirely to see that this battle is over more than American foreign policy. Bin Laden is the product of a generation of Arab and Muslim failure to come to terms with much of the modern world," and that failure has produced a "clash" with the West—with modernity—that is "as much cultural as it is political."

Times essayists were not of one mind about the "clash of civilizations" thesis. Austrian scholar and ambassador Wolfgang Petritsch (2001) wrote in an op-ed from Sarajevo that "Islam is part of the West, too." His focus was on Bosnia-Herzegovina, which he represented at the time, but his more inclusive message was that Muslims are part of the European tradition. In rejecting the "us (the civilized, Western world) and them (the dangerous, suspect Muslims)" dichotomy, he concluded that "Bosnia is the place to render the notion of a clash of civilizations null and void and to prove that democracy, freedom and human rights are universal."

Mythographer and cultural historian Marina Warner (2001) warned implicitly against falling into the temptation of assigning Manichean oppositions in a complex world. In her "Week in Review" essay on "fantasy's power and peril," she wrote that "myths in which heroic figures are pitted in mortal combat against diabolical enemies have gained fresh energy in popular culture." The film versions of *Harry Potter* and *Lord of the Rings* made Americans feel comfortable with "the strength and familiarity of the good-vs.-evil tale." This theme in the West comes ultimately from the Middle East, she said, from the prophet Zoroaster, worshipped by the ancient Persians and by the prophet Mani in the third century A.D. in Persia. Manicheanism instructed both Christianity and Islam in dichotomizing the world into moral opposites. Her message was to see the other as oneself rather than as an inherent enemy. Her kicker? "These myths ultimately grant more power to their villains than they can ever take away." (For a different glance at Zoroastrianism, see Fathi 2001.)

Despite commentary criticizing the rhetoric of the "clash of civilizations," there was also a strong beating of Huntington's drum in the *Times*. Serge Schmemann's (2002a) "Analyzing the Cultural Collision That Gave Rise to Sept. 11," a review of Bernard Lewis's *What Went Wrong? Western Impact and Middle Eastern Response* (2002), noted that it was Lewis rather than Huntington who coined the phrase "clash of civilizations" in an article he wrote in 1990 for the *Atlantic Monthly*. It was Lewis's view, summarized by Schmemann, "that Muslims became accustomed in the early centuries of their history to perceiving themselves as the bearers of the final and true faith, and so never came to understand or accept the Christian civilization of Western Europe that he maintains has surpassed and humbled them." According to this view, "the shock of Western ascendancy has led, in our time to two responses: emulating the West and its secular culture or returning to the fundamentals of the faith—the path whose most extreme manifestation is Mr. bin Laden."

What Went Wrong? (2002) was surely a hard-edged look at Middle Eastern Islam. Despite the religion's storied past and its attempts to reform its lapses, in the twentieth century Muslims realized that, "compared with its millennial rival, Christendom, the world of Islam had become poor, weak, and ignorant . . . and therefore the dominance of the West was clear for all to see" (151). Rather than looking effectively at the question, "What have the Muslims done to Islam?" (156), Muslims blamed their failures on the Turks (for their secular nationalism), the Jews (for Israel), and the Americans (for imperialism). The outcome of this "'downward spiral of hate and spite, rage and self-pity, poverty and oppression'" (quoting Lewis) was revealed in 9/11, according to a second *Times* review of Lewis's book, as "the real culture wars," the "conflict between the West and Islam that has been centuries in the making" (P. Kennedy 2002). Both *Times* reviewers accepted Lewis's theses, more or less, regarding the "culture wars" and the "clash of civilizations." It is noteworthy, then, that Schmemann (2007) was "taken to task by conservatives" for not praising the book more roundly.

In his November 27, 2002, column "Defusing the Holy Bomb," Thomas L. Friedman (2002b) wrote what he wished George W. Bush would say to the "leaders of the Muslim world. . . . Let me be blunt: I am increasingly worried that we are heading toward a civilizational war." Friedman provided examples of this "civilizational war" that was taking shape. The Indonesian who masterminded the Bali explosion called his handiwork a "holy bomb." A US missionary nurse was killed in Lebanon because she was a Christian. "Do you know how much proselytizing Muslim groups do in America?" Friedman asked. He answered, "A lot. We have no problem with that. That's who we are. Who are you?" In Friedman's view, Palestinian suicide bombers think they are doing God's will. Muslims kill Americans in Kuwait and Jordan simply for being Americans. "You say all this is happening because we support Israel. I know we need to do more to bring peace, but I don't think that nurse was shot, or that Bali bomb was made 'holy,' because we support Israel." Friedman's conclusion? "The decent, but passive, Muslim center must go to war against this harsh fundamentalism. . . . Friends, unless you have a war within your civilization, there is going to be a war between our civilizations."

Friedman's was among the major conclusions one could draw from the *Times* for the several years following 9/11. Stories from around the world gave the impression of a "clash of civilizations" already taking place. Even with all the tolerant, multicultural articles about Muslims in the United States, the clash was a major motif in the newspaper. And *Times* essayists attempted to defuse an impending "clash of civilizations" by calling the Muslim world to a "culture war" within its own ranks, or, they warned, there would be war between Islam and the West.

Right next to Friedman's column was an op-ed by Salman Rushdie(2002), "No More Fanaticism as Usual," which reviewed recent events in the Islamic world: Nigeria sentenced a woman to beheading, and then riots broke out over a beauty contest; in Iran, a hero of the Iran–Iraq War was sentenced to death for speaking his mind; on Egyptian television there was anti-Semitic programming; a Muslim feminist had to flee the Netherlands because of death threats—all stories carried by the *Times*. Rushdie noted that at least in Iran the students were protesting. Everywhere else, he asked, where were the moderate Muslims? "As their ancient, deeply civilized culture of love, art and philosophical reflection is hijacked by paranoiacs, racists, liars, male supremacists, tyrants, fanatics and violence junkies, why are they not screaming? . . . As long as the majority remains silent, this will be a tough war to win."

Italian journalist Oriana Fallaci echoed Rushdie's sentiments in a *Times Magazine* interview, "Unquiet on the Western Front" (Aydintashas 2003). Fallaci had warned the West "about the threat from Islamic fundamentalism." In this interview, she told how much of a threat Islam was as a whole. The interviewer asked her, "Aren't you caricaturing the Muslim world . . . ?" She replied, "You want me to be optimistic. I am not. The day the Islamic world will start criticizing itself, the day it will give birth to some Luther or Calvin, then you call me and say, 'Fallaci, you were wrong.' I will then admit that the Western culture and Islamic culture can coexist." Until then, she saw unmitigated conflict. (See also "Italy: Oriana Fallaci Charged with Insulting Islam" [2005].)

With the war in Iraq in full battle dress and President Bush parading triumphantly but prematurely, Maureen Dowd (2003) devoted her column to "a tale of two Fridays." First, she looked upon Reverend Franklin Graham, preaching

"Christ" and "crusade" at the Pentagon over Muslim Pentagon employees' protests. Then she observed Shiites in Baghdad "shouting for America to 'leave our country.'" "Back here," she bemoaned, "the neo-cons and war planners were too busy gloating to worry about the ambient sound of civilizations clashing."

One could find the same message in an anonymously authored book (reviewed in Kakutani 2004a) that argued that Al Qaeda—the "'popular, worldwide, and increasingly powerful Islamic insurgency'"—was winning its war of terror against America. If the United States did not succeed in the short run, the book's author argued, that war "'has the potential to last beyond our children's lifetimes and to be fought mostly on U.S. soil.'"

As 2004 came to a close, however, the *Times* presented another story line, the one that Rushdie and Fallaci hoped for against hope. "Muslim Scholars Increasingly Debate Unholy War" (MacFarquhar 2004c), read the front-page headline, the article offering the news that "the long-simmering internal debate over political violence in Islamic cultures is swelling." Neil MacFarquhar wrote that "on one side" were "mostly secular intellectuals" and "ordinary Muslims dismayed by the ever more bloody image of Islam around the world." These "liberals" had "arrayed against them" the "powerful religious institutions," "prominent clerics," and "a whole different class of scholars" who might be called "extremists" but for their prestige among the "hard-core faithful." The reformers "provoked bedlam" when they questioned the validity and wisdom of violent messages traditionally attributed to Muhammad and when they criticized "'political Islam.'" They were called "'Zionists'" and "'infidels,'" but they held their ground. At least in the *Times* they got the last word: "This is the culture," they said, "and we have to change it."

The *Times* Beyond the *Times*

From September 12, 2001, through several years thereafter, the *Times* sought to understand "how a nightmare began and might continue" (Ramsey 2003). Reporters, columnists, photographers, editors, headline and caption writers, map makers and other illustrators, book reviewers, op-ed essayists, and other outsiders to the *Times* who wrote letters to the editors—all contributed to a complex narrative, certainly not a single-minded construction, in which the *Times* was a player in the larger story. The crucial quality of the 9/11 drama turned the overall *Times* coverage into a kind of epic, attaining the aspect of the mythic. The *Times* was not merely reporting and commenting on critical events with powerful, long-recognized religious dimensions, but also creating a chronicle of religious import, a saga of life-and-death importance to its multitudinous readership.

"Journalism, it's often said, is the first draft of history" (Wallace 2002). Mike Wallace, journalist and historian, said in his essay "Panorama and Pointillism on 9/11" that Richard Bernstein and the staff of the *New York Times* "provided us with a polished second draft" in their book *Out of the Blue: The Story of Sept. 11, 2001, from Jihad to Ground Zero* (2002). Leaving aside the question of the *Times'* practice of reviewing books published by the *Times* and written by *Times* employees, one may ask if *Out of the Blue* provides any insights about the *Times* coverage of 9/11? Its writers had time to frame the many stories into a single book, so does the singleness reveal *the story* that THE *Times* was trying to fashion? Or does its singleness differ from the many voices that expressed themselves on the many pages of the *Times* over time?

Out of the Blue is more vivid in its depiction (1–11) of people jumping from the World Trade Center than the *Times* was on September 12—even though Howell Raines mentions in the foreword (ix–xi) his editorial decision to print a photo of a man hurtling upside down to death. He thought the gatekeepers made the right decision. The photo was direct; it captured the extraordinary moment. This book does it more viscerally with words.

Chapter 2 reveals what was plain in hindsight about the *Times'* coverage of the causes of 9/11. The book's subtitle also points it out: *From Jihad to Ground Zero.* That is, the distant and immediate causes of 9/11 were in the "militant Islamic purism and the concept of jihad . . . born out of the Mongol invasion of the Middle East" (11) or even earlier in Islamic history. "As scholars have pointed out since the attacks on the World Trade Center in New York and the Pentagon in Washington, there has always been a powerful strain in Islam, one of the great monotheistic religions of the world, of a cult of death and sacrifice, a conviction that the highest calling, the quickest path to worldly prestige and heavenly reward, is through the slaughter of infidels and the enemies of Islam" (11).

Whereas this claim might be a single op-ed opinion, one among many, probably to be contradicted the next day on the same page, here is *the author* speaking. And even though he is quoting "scholars" and saying "perhaps," he is laying the blame squarely on Islam or at least on a "minority strand in a religion with many historical attributes, including tolerance and pluralism, pacific mysticism and gentleness" (11). The cause of the 9/11 story, Bernstein says, was a "story of a battle within Islam itself" (12). Did the *Times,* through its many authors and editors, come to the same clean conclusion?

Out of the Blue finds the more immediate intellectual cause of 9/11 in the Iranian Revolution, the "'holy warriors'" who fought the Soviet Union in Afghanistan, the "weird, perverse, radical utopianism in the air, fueled by the paranoid conviction that evil enemies, what they referred to as 'Jews and Crusaders' especially but Muslim heretics also, lurked everywhere" (25). Bernstein names Wahhabism and the Muslim Brotherhood as the "'hijackers' of Islam" (57).

That is Bernstein's take on the form of Islam that took hold of Mohamed Atta and his fellow terrorists. At Ground Zero, there were innocent US victims in their "openness" (46), "so guileless, almost innocent of the dark forces that destroyed them" (47). If the media played up the American people's innocence and their 9/11 "trauma" (Chermak, Bailey, and Brown 2003a:7), *Out of the Blue* certainly makes that image central to the 9/11 story. Bernstein mentions "journalistic neutrality" (110); however, his book is an interspersed contrast between the evil plotters and the good guys who walked into the trap, and it opines how the United States was "too soft" (132) on Osama bin Laden and Al Qaeda.

The drama was heightened by the instructions Atta gave to his fellow terrorists the night before 9/11. They were to read traditional war chapters in the Koran and reflect on their martyrdom and their reward: "'Remind your soul to listen and obey,' the instructions read, 'and remember that you will face a decisive situation that might prevent you from one hundred percent obedience, so tame your soul, purify it, convince it, make it understand, and incite it. God said, "Obey God and His messenger, and do not fight among yourselves or else you will fail. And be patient, for God is with the patient.

"'When the confrontation begins,' the instructions continued, 'strike like champions who do not want to go back to this world. Shout "Allah'u Akbar" [God is great] because this strikes fear in the hearts of the non-believers. God said: "Strike above the neck, and strike at all of their extremities." Know that the gardens of paradise are waiting for you in all their beauty, and the women of paradise are waiting, calling out, "Come hither, friend of God." They have dressed in their most beautiful clothing'" (173).

In the upper floors of the World Trade Center, there was a Jewish man, five days from a trip to Jerusalem to celebrate the Jewish New Year, who died reciting a Hebrew psalm: "The Lord is the earth and its fullness" (221). The victims cried out, "Oh, God!" The terrorists evoked Allah.

And there are the stories of heroism, generosity, consolation, and devotion to the dead, and there are even stories of revenge and the quest for justice (which is never equated with the first angle of motive, the jihad).

And finally, America's response is presented according to the angle of civil religion—the coming together of faiths in a single nation, including Muslims.

Four angles in *Out of the Blue*: the jihad motive; the drama between evil and innocence; selfless mourning; interfaith response. Were they the *Times'* religion angles, though? The newspaper was surely more complex, more expansive, in defining religion; however, maybe these angles were at the core of its 9/11 narrative, now codified in a single *Times* book.

Or perhaps they were the product of Richard Bernstein's perspective. Perhaps the book genre gave Bernstein an opportunity to express himself in ways he could not as a *Times* correspondent on the pages of the paper.

Bernstein was named Berlin bureau chief for the *Times* in January 2003 (he later left the paper). He was a former foreign correspondent and bureau chief in China and France as well as the *Times* United Nations bureau chief, then a cultural correspondent and book critic, covering the world of ideas. He was the author or coauthor of a handful of books before *Out of the Blue:* one on France (1990), two on China (1982; Bernstein and Munro 1997), one on multicultural-ism (1994), and a personal reflection on a medieval Buddhist monk (2001c).

Bernstein's works have an American feel to them. He expressed his respect for the "inscrutable" French, about to be eclipsed by the United States, not only politically but culturally, and they knew it (1990:3). He found the Chinese "lov-able" in their desire to rediscover their true character, having been thwarted by Communist rule (1982:243–54). His hope in the early 1980s was "that after all these decades of decline, of misdirection, of mediocrity, China might one day be great again" (1982:254). He was far less sanguine about China in the late 1990s, predicting that China and America "are bound to collide," not as a "clash of civilizations," as Samuel P. Huntington would have it, but rather "in the old-fashioned terms of political alliance and the balance of power" (Bernstein and Munro 1997:5, 12). Writing as an American nationalist, Bernstein has aimed to defend US interests in recognizing potential enemies and warning his country-men against them. On a moral scale, he and Munro wrote: "If China remains *aggressive* and the United States *naïve,* the looming conflict between the two countries could even lead to military hostilities" (3–4, emphases added).

In *Dictatorship of Virtue: Multiculturalism and the Battle for America's Future* (1994), Bernstein implied that multiculturalist virtue constituted a slide into a potential reign of terror—"fanaticism," "dogmatism," "narrow orthodoxy," and "petrified opinion" in his homeland (3–4). He compared multiculturalism to the Chinese Cultural Revolution: it was a "secularized religion" that was being forced on mainstream Americans. The book's inscription was from Maximilien de Robe-spierre: "Terror is naught but prompt, severe, inflexible justice; it is therefore an emanation of virtue." Bernstein's view was that multiculturalists—the remnants of 1960s countercultural leftists—created an ideology that criticized all things American and mistook the cultures of the world for their own "leftist . . . ideol-ogy" (7). For a civil rights liberal, as Bernstein identified himself, multiculturalism had skidded far from the ideals of that movement, becoming a "code word for an expanded concept of moral and cultural relativism" (9), which espoused a critique of the West and uncritical praise of everything exotic. Bernstein believed that Americans must instead uphold "the standards and modes of behavior that have always made for success in American life" (11)—traditional, conservative values.

What are the values that Bernstein has espoused? In his exposition of Hsuan Tsang (Bernstein 2001c), the seventh-century Buddhist who journeyed from China to India and back, "the greatest traveler in history" in search of "the law" of Buddhism, the author called himself "a secular non-Buddhist skeptic" (5). Trained in academia but having determined that "the academic life was not for me" (4), he found his home of meaning in Judaism. "In matters of the spirit I am a Jew" (31), he wrote, but regarding religious matters he was "essentially a nonbeliever," but "a strangely religious nonbeliever, a devout sort of atheist, attached to the forms of religious ritual, the music, the solemnity of it, the intonation of the word of God, but not to its literal content" (32). He led the family seder each year, but he was "simply not capable of belief in a Supreme Being" (32). "I am tied to Judaism by aesthetic sentiment, by respect for the *martyrdom* of others, and by a sense of history" (32, emphasis added).

Bernstein imported his nationalistic defenses—against aggressive outlanders and naive multiculturalists at home—to his book *Out of the Blue*. His sense of the nobility of martyrdom pervade the pages of this work. The attacks of September 11, 2001, provided him with an axial event through which he could express the concerns of his previous books with a clarity that was not so apparent in his *Times* essays and reports. Given the freedom of individual authorship—albeit with a staff of *Times* colleagues behind him—he composed a book that expresses his point of view as well as, perhaps, that of the *Times*.

Bernstein's point of view was not the *Times*' point of view, although in the main it corresponded to the central narrative motifs presented in the paper. Other *Times* authors who covered aspects of the 9/11 story had their own tales to tell. Chris Hedges was a foreign correspondent for the *Times*—reporting on wars in Central America, the Middle East, and the Balkans, and in subsequent years he covered global terrorism surrounding 9/11. He warns his readers in his book *War Is a Force That Gives Us Meaning* (2002e), that "war is a god, . . . and its worship demands human sacrifice" (10). Its altar is the nation-state. "Patriotism, often a thinly veiled form of collective self-worship," he writes, "celebrates our goodness, our ideals, our mercy and bemoans the perfidiousness of those who hate us" (10).

War Is a Force is a moral challenge to much of the consensual United States, including the *New York Times* order, to seek understanding that transcends the blinkers of wartime rhetoric. Hedges proclaims, "War makes the world understandable, a black and white tableau of them and us. It suspends thought, especially self-critical thought. All bow before the supreme effort. We are one" (10). He pulls no punches: "War is a crusade. President George W. Bush is not shy about warning other nations that they stand with the United States in the war on terrorism or will be counted with those that defy us. This too is a *jihad*" (4, italics in original). A reviewer in the *Times* remarked that Hedges's book could provide a "timely . . . instructive to President Bush and the members of his national security team, most of whom have not served in the military or witnessed the carnage of battle. They should heed Mr. Hedges not because it might actually dissuade them from war, but because it is a persuasive call for humility and realism in the pursuit of national goals by force of arms" (Mann 2002; for another review, see Verghese 2002).

Hedges was part of a tradition of concern about national war mentality and its corrosion in national life and specifically in journalism. "The first casualty when war comes is truth," said Senator Hiram Johnson in 1917 (quoted in Knightley 1975:frontispiece). Phillip Knightley wrote a whole book about war correspondents' struggles—against trying to make sense out of the chaos of war around them and against the concerted censorship by their own governments. From the Civil War to the Vietnam War, refusal to take a party line—all is well, the cause is just, and so on—has resulted in expulsion, jailing, blackballing, vilification, freezing out, Knightley asserted. As Secretary of State Dean Rusk once asked of the press corps in 1968, "Whose side are you on?" (quoted on 382). Knightly found that "some correspondents became part of the military propaganda machine, and 'got on side'" (382). Fortunately, he said, others told the truth "and caused Americans to make a serious reappraisal of the basic nature of their nation" (383).

When Garry Wills (1975) reviewed Knightley's book in the *Times Book Review,* he recounted the lessons he had learned: "*A nation at war lies on principle. . . . The populace gladly submits to these lies. . . . A liberal democracy submits to propaganda more readily than a totalitarian state. . . . America has been under virtual war discipline ever since 1941*" (italics in original). Those words were written as the United States retreated from Vietnam. They are still mighty lessons for covering news, including (perhaps especially) religion news in the post-9/11 era, and Hedges took them up.

In interviews, online discussions, and speeches, Hedges has warned not only about what he sees as the addictive insanity of war, but also about the press's role in fomenting wartime jingoism. He told Bill Moyers (2003), *Religion & Ethics Newsweekly* (Abernethy 2003), and *Poynteronline* (Hedges 2003a) that "in wartime, the press is always part of the problem," for providing war with a "mythic narrative that war, in fact, doesn't have." His May 2003 commencement speech at Rockford College (Hedges 2003b) spoke of "war and empire" in the heady days of America's invasion of Iraq. The speech, offering "harsh criticism" (Watters 2003) of US policy in Iraq and warning against blind patriotism, caused a reaction that Hedges called "heartbreaking" (quoted in Watters 2003). His microphone was pulled twice, members of the audience excoriated him, and his oration was trimmed to prevent further disturbance. *TimesWatch* ("Chris Hedges" 2003) called Hedges's speech "pompous pacifism" and devoted a topic index to Hedges, where he was termed "an Extreme Bush Hater" and "anti-war reporter," guilty of "condescending contempt" for his critics.

Like Bernstein, Hedges had a viewpoint about 9/11's causes and consequences that was more angular than the honed articles they wrote on the pages of the *Times*. The views Hedges expressed about the dehumanizing nature of war were also to be found in Peter Steinfels's nuanced essays on "just-war" theory and in other articles about religious war protesters during the Afghanistan and Iraq conflicts; however, Hedges's voice was like one crying in the wilderness when it is compared to the main currents of *Times* reportage and commentary. Indeed, Hedges found himself outside the mainstream of *Times* decorum. After his Rockford speech, his employer sent him a "letter of reprimand," saying that he had made "public remarks that could undermine public trust in the paper's impartiality" (quoted in Hedges 2005:100). He was called on the carpet, but he would not back down from his convictions. Rather, he left the *Times* for academic and think-tank engagements. When his book on the Ten Commandments was published, it received one paragraph of notice in the *Times Book Review* section, a dismissive reference to the book's "fevered condemnations" of America's moral condition, which were "no more persuasive than those shrilly emanating from the right," according to the reviewer (Heilbrunn 2005). Hedges was now a leftist, as seen from the moderatist newspaper that used to employ him.

Hedges continues to write—now about the threat of the "Christian right" (Hedges 2005b; see also Hedges 2006b) to America's pluralist, "open society" (Hedges 2006b). Having entered the fray of the "culture wars" rather than merely writing about them, he calls himself a "former reporter" not because he has ceased to gather and disseminate factual information about the world around him, but because he has chosen the freedom to write books from his point of view without editorial constraint. "That's why I left the *Times*," he says (2006b); "I didn't want my opinions muzzled. . . . I had a choice: I could have shut up, but that would have been a betrayal of my integrity." Hedges attests that he saw "from inside the newsroom" in the Jayson Blair and Judith Miller fiascos "how lost the *Times* is" and what an "identity crisis" the *Times* is undergoing. He is not against balance in "moderate middle media" coverage of religion and politics. He is against coverage that shies away from confronting the frequent "lies" of news sources, especially officials. Hedges states that the "contract between journalists and readers"—for reporters to "tell the truth"—"has been broken." Judith Miller, he claims, broke that contract by allowing that her reports on US justifications for invading Iraq could go only as far as her sources' claims even though she knew—as all reporters know—that almost all sources "lie." Finally, he speaks about the "awful paradox of tolerance" (Hedges 2007) in America at a time when the religious right—dominionists, who are absolutely intolerant and absolutely dangerous, in his view—are gearing up for something more totalizing than cultural warfare. Hedges states that the news media, universities, pulpits, the Democratic Party—those who should be speaking out against these "American Fascists" (see Hedges 2006a)—have failed America by insisting on total tolerance.

The *Times* of Thomas L. Friedman

Perhaps if Hedges had been a columnist, he might have been granted more freedom by the *Times* for his opinions. *Times* columnist Thomas L. Friedman had distinguished himself in books (1989, 1999) as well as in the newspaper for his observations on politics in the Middle East. For some time before 9/11, he had been warning his readers of a terrorist attack, and he was proven prescient on that fateful day (Waisbord 2002:202). In his book *Longitudes and Attitudes: The World in the Age of Terrorism* (2003a), he collects the columns he had written about 9/11 and then further explicates his point of view.

In *Longitudes* (2003a), Friedman writes that 9/11 turned his job from "fun" to "compelling." It was "the biggest news story in my life" (xi). In this axial moment, Friedman served as a prominent example of *Times* commentary on 9/11. He had points of view about Judaism, Islam, American civic religion, patriotism, tolerance, and so on before 9/11. To what degree did he change, and to what degree did he fall back on his previous paradigms?

Friedman declares in *Longitudes* his intellectual independence as a commentator. He had been foreign-affairs columnist for the *Times* since January 1995, and, he attests, in that time "I have never had a conversation with the Publisher of *The New York Times* about any opinion I've adopted—before or after any column I've written. . . . I have total freedom, and an almost unlimited budget, to explore" (xii). It could be said that he was chosen for this job because his employer perceived his opinion to coincide with that of *Times* corporate culture on most important issues. Thus, there was no need to second-guess or censor him because he was already their man. (On this topic, see Laurel Leff's [2005] argument that the *Times* publisher picks editors who agree with him or will know to agree with him on the issues that matter to him [189–191]. The culture of the place is created from the top, she states. See also Robert Darnton's [1990] argument that writers at the *Times* glance hierarchically upward to see what is expected of them in creating copy.) However much independence Friedman has, free of pressure from his bosses, it might be said that more than any other writer he represented *the* voice of the *Times* when addressing the volatile questions of religion in the heat and light of 9/11.

So much so that New York Times Television produced a video in 2003 summarizing the paper's take on the "roots of 9/11" (Friedman 2003b). Friedman was the reporter and writer for the video, which was coproduced by Discovery Channel; indeed, the film was as much about him as it was about 9/11. Calling himself "a tourist with an attitude," he avowed that his report constituted his own viewpoint only; nonetheless, it presented the main line of *Times* expression on 9/11's causes and ramifications—short of the American invasion of Iraq. He examined the feelings of deprivation and humiliation in the Muslim world, left behind by many aspects of modernity, and many Muslims' resentments directed at the United States and Israel. He made the distinction between normative Islamic spirituality—focused on the self—and the politicized system of Al Qaeda, which Friedman called a "cult" like those of Jim Jones and David Koresh. Friedman pointed to a "struggle for the soul of Islam" between the religion of Islam and cultish Islamism. Muslims might resent the stereotype of "Islamic terrorism" promulgated in the West; however, one could hardly deny the realities evidenced in 9/11. Finally, Friedman looked hopefully to a "conversation" taking place within Muslim societies about how to regard the violent movement "hijacking" their religion. "I don't want this to be a war of civilizations," Friedman said, "but unless there is a war within civilizations, between the good guys and the bad guys, there will be a war between civilizations." The video's story line followed very closely the interpretive angles in Friedman's column and his book.

It is necessary to note that Friedman is not a "religion" writer. His field is foreign affairs, and he therefore already had a lens on his topic before 9/11. In *Longitudes and Attitudes* (2003a), he writes about what he calls the "super-story," meaning the grand context for many, if not most foreign-affairs stories of our time, "the new international system . . . called globalization," its "integration," its "web," and its "global markets" (3, 4). In such a connected world, there are what he calls "super-empowered individuals" (5), such as Osama bin Laden, who are able to exert enormous influence over the globalized world through their ideals, their will, their skill in manipulating the world's integrative tools.

In that context and as collected in *Longitudes*, Friedman's columns about 9/11 expressed interest in two primary subjects. First, who were the suicide hijackers, "what motivated them to do what they did, and what motivated large parts of the Arab and Muslim worlds to give them passive support?" His second question was culturally introspective: "Who are we—America?" (xii).

On January 12, 2001, Friedman wrote in "Clinton's Last Memo": "What troubles me most about the mood on the Arab street today is the hostility I detect there to modernization, globalization, democratization, and the information revolution" (13). Yes, there were real concerns about Israel's control over "Muslim holy places in Jerusalem" (14), but Arabs should be more concerned about "what sort of education you offer your kids, what sort of economy you build, and what sort of rule of law you establish" (14). Friedman had already before 9/11 established several ideas in his columns: Muslims in the Arab world seemed opposed to modernity; the Palestinian concerns with Israel were real; education is one of the keys to a civilization.

Friedman was in Jerusalem on 9/11. He published his column "Walls," regarding Israel and the Palestinians, that day (29–30). His September 13 column, "World War III," asked, "Does my country really understand that this is World War III?" and stated that "there is a long, long war ahead" (33). Who were the combatants in this war? On the one side was "the world's only superpower and quintessential symbol of liberal, free-market Western values" (33), and on the other were "all the super-empowered angry men and women out there, . . . from failing states in the Muslim and third world. They do not share our values; they resent America's influence over their lives, politics, and children, not to mention our support for Israel; and they often blame America for the failure of their societies to master modernity" (33). "And unless we are ready to put our best minds to work combating them—the World War III Manhattan Project—in an equally daring, unconventional, and unremitting fashion, we're in trouble. Because while this may have been the first major battle of World War III, it may be the last one that involves only conventional nonnuclear weapons" (34). He closed the column with "Semper Fi" (35), shorthand Latin to indicate his fidelity—but to what or to whom? His book answered that question patriotically, without ambiguity.

Friedman said in his September 13 column that the United States must show its concern for the Palestinians and for Muslim economic grievances. At the same time, he asked, "Where are the Muslim leaders who will tell their sons to resist the Israelis—but not to kill themselves or innocent noncombatants? No matter how bad, your life is sacred. Surely Islam, a grand religion that never perpetrated the sort of Holocaust against the Jews in its midst that Europe did, is being distorted when it is treated as a guidebook for suicide bombing. How is it that not a single Muslim leader will say that?" (35).

Still writing from Jerusalem on September 14, 2001, Friedman cited Shimon Peres, Israel's foreign minister, who said of 9/11, "This is not a clash of civilizations—the Muslim world versus the Christian, Hindu, Buddhist, and Jewish worlds. The real clash today is actually not between civilizations, but within them—between those Muslims, Christians, Hindus, Buddhists, and Jews with a modern and progressive outlook and those with a medieval one. We make a great mistake if we simply write off the Muslim world and fail to understand how many Muslims feel themselves trapped in failing states and look to America as a model and inspiration" (quoted on 36). Friedman's worldview, like that of the *Times,* pitted the modern against the medieval. One finds this dichotomy throughout *Longitudes and Attitudes,* with the Protestant Reformation playing the crucial role in the shift from the medieval to the modern. Friedman's loyalty was to a vision of modernity that *Times* readers would comprehend from their experience with the paper's paradigms.

Friedman noted on September 14, 2001, that President Abraham Lincoln said of the South, "Remember, they pray to the same God" (quoted on 36). He then cited Middle East analyst Stephen P. Cohen: "The same is true of many, many Muslims. We must fight those among them who pray only to the God of Hate, but we do not want to go to war with Islam, with all the millions of Muslims who pray to the same God we do" (quoted on 36). Friedman continued: "These people [the Muslims who want war] . . . want to trigger the sort of massive U.S. retaliation that makes no distinction between them and other Muslims. That would be their ultimate victory—because they do see the world as a clash of civilizations, and they want every Muslim to see it that way as well and to join their jihad" (37). In a sense, there *was* a clash of civilizations from the viewpoint of the "terrorists . . . driven by pure hatred and nihilism" (37). But Friedman did not want to fight a war of civilizations, pressed by jihadists. Rather, he wrote, "Only their own religious communities and societies can really restrain and delegitimize them" (37). And so he encouraged "this civil war within Islam" (37) between the good Muslims who pray to the same God we do and those who pray to the "God of

Hate." What should the United States do? Friedman said, "To retaliate in a way that doesn't distinguish between those who pray to a God of Hate and those who pray to the same God we do is to invite an endless war between civilizations" (37).

It is said that the *New York Times* is a hypersecular newspaper. One would not know that by reading Friedman's theological premises about God, peoples, and prayers. Thus grounded, Friedman sought to lecture about Muslim traditions. In a fictional letter he composed on October 12, 2001, from George W. Bush to Osama bin Laden, he wrote:

> You really don't know much about Islamic history. The Muslim world reached the zenith of its influence in the Middle Ages—when it preserved the best of classical Greek and Roman teachings, and inspired breakthroughs in mathematics, science, medicine, and philosophy. That is also when Islam was at its most open to the world, when it enriched, and was enriched by, the Christian, Greek, and Jewish communities in its midst—whom you now disparage as infidels—and when it was actively trading with all corners of the world. Your closed, inward, hate-filled version of Islam—which treats women as cattle and all non-Muslims as enemies—corresponds with no period of greatness for Islam, and will bring none. (52)

One might call it chutzpah for Friedman to thus explicate Islamic history and in such legendary terms regarding past Islamic greatness—when it drew on its Christian, Jewish, and Greek neighbors—and about its decline and subsequent insularity. This vision was very much what the *Times* presented in its articles—where Islamic science, Islamic political prowess, and Islamic tolerance were depicted as things of the past.

Friedman recognized the struggles within national Muslim cultures. He noted on September 21, 2001, that Syria, Egypt, Algeria, and Tunisia had faced Islamist threats and "crushed them without mercy" (40). In some cases, these "fundamentalists" (40) escaped to weak states such as Afghanistan or to the freedom of America or Europe, where they became the world's problem. Some Arab states—most notably Saudi Arabia—"made a devil's pact with the fundamentalists" (40), allowing them to raise funds and recruit at home, so long as they left the regimes alone. These countries refrained from criticizing the Islamists in their midst, and the latter thereby gained followers. "The result: we must now fight a war against terrorists who are crazy and evil but who, it grieves me to say, reflect the mood in their home countries more than we might think" (41), Friedman wrote. To engage in this battle, Friedman called in a September 28, 2001, column for the United States to get the help of the "Russian mafia" to kill Osama bin Laden.

On October 2, 2001, Friedman took a turn at explicating his own country. He explained his American faith in education in a column about his daughter's school, "Eastern Middle School," in Silver Springs, Maryland. He said that what the terrorists do not understand is how important education is to our culture. "Their constant refrain is that America is a country with wealth and power but 'no values.' The Islamist terrorists think our wealth and power are unrelated to anything in the soul of this country—that we are basically a godless nation, indeed the enemies of God. And if you are an enemy of God, you deserve to die. These terrorists believe that wealth and power can be achieved only by giving up your values, because they look at places such as Saudi Arabia and see that many of the wealthy and powerful there lead lives disconnected from their faith." "Of course," he continued, "what this view of America completely misses is that American power and wealth flow directly from a deep spiritual source—a spirit of respect for the individual, a spirit of tolerance for differences of faith or politics, a respect for freedom of thought as the necessary foundation for all creativity, and a spirit of unity that encompasses all kinds of differences. Only a society with a deep spiritual energy, which welcomes immigrants and worships freedom, could constantly renew itself and its sources of power and wealth. . . . Lord know, ours is hardly a perfect country," he stated. However, "these terrorists so misread America. They think our strength lies only in the World Trade Center and the Pentagon—the twin pillars of our wealth and power. . . . Actually, our strength lies in the slightly dilapidated gym of Eastern Middle School on parent–teacher night, and in thousands of such schools across the land. That is where you'll find the spirit that built the Twin Towers and can build them over again anytime we please" (46, 47). In this column, Friedman used religious terms such as *spiritual* and expressions such as "Lord knows." He said that America "worships" freedom, commenting, perhaps in an enunciation of the Protestant work ethic, that it was this "spirit" that produced American power and wealth and was apparently consistent with the nation's values.

If Friedman's patriotism was apparent, what was his attitude toward Israel? Friedman wrote in his diary that he composed his October 5, 2001, column "Yes, but What?" in response to politically correct academics who were all too ready to see the terrorists' viewpoint. He wrote, "Yes, there is no question, America's support of Israel—even when Israel builds greedy, provocative settlements in the heart of the Gaza Strip—has produced understandable Muslim anger. But . . ." (48). Friedman could—and did—criticize Israel and US support for Israel's policies toward Palestinians. On October 16, 2001, he acknowledged that "no doubt there is deep Arab anger over U.S. support for Israel. I've gotten angry myself over the failure of successive U.S. governments to restrain Israel's voracious settlement-building program" (54). He recognized that the Israel–US alliance was a factor in triggering the 9/11 assault, but not the only factor and not one that would ever justify—or even explain—the 9/11 attacks.

As for America's other allies, he wrote on October 9, 2001, "The truth is, our real coalition partners can be counted on a few fingers: Britain, France, Canada, Germany, Australia, Japan" (50). He would observe later that American allies were reduced even further when the Iraq War began. Indeed, even on October 26, 2001, he proclaimed as an American writing for an American audience, "My fellow Americans, I hate to say this, but except for the good old Brits, we're all alone. And at the end of the day, it's U.S. and British troops who will have to go in, on the ground, and eliminate bin Laden" (61).

By this time, US military forces were engaged against the Taliban and Al Qaeda in Afghanistan, and Friedman discussed the ethics of battle. Arab Muslim allies were suggesting that the United States should stop fighting in Afghanistan during Ramadan in respect for the holy Muslim month of fasting. Friedman commented that Egypt and Syria launched the 1973 Middle East War during Ramadan. In fact, they called it "the Ramadan war" (60). He concluded, "I don't really care if that war coincides with Ramadan, Christmas, Hanukkah, or the Buddha's birthday—the most respectful and spiritual thing we can do now is fight until justice is done" (61). On November 2, 2001, he wrote: "A month into the war in Afghanistan, the hand-wringing has already begun over how long this might last. Let's all take a deep breath and repeat after me: Give war a chance" (64). He called bin Laden "a mass murderer" (64) who deserved the attack, and "ditto with Saddam. Whenever U.S. officials speak about Saddam, they should always say: 'Saddam Hussein, the man who has killed more Muslims in the twentieth century than any other human being'" (65) in his assaults on a million Iranians, Iraqis, Kurds, and Kuwaitis. Thus, Friedman found propriety in American battles in Afghanistan and Iraq as justified attacks on mass murderers.

During the Afghanistan War, Friedman sought to gain a better sense of the Islamic mood in South Asia. Writing from Peshawar, Pakistan, on November 13, 2001, Friedman told about the Osama bin Laden T-shirts, the posters calling for "Jihad Against America" (70), the wall graffiti calling for jihad against a putative Indian–Jewish alliance. In this context, he visited the biggest madrassa in Pakistan, with 2,800 students. (Mullah Muhammad Omar once attended it, did not graduate, but was given an honorary degree.) Friedman's portrait of this school contrasted to his depiction of his daughter's Eastern Middle School, symbol of American educational values. Here in the madrassa, all the students were "studying the Koran and the teachings of the Prophet Muhammad with the hope of becoming mullahs, or spiritual leaders" (70). Their learning was by "rote" (70). "Most will never be exposed to critical thinking or modern subjects" (71), Friedman stated. There were thirty-nine thousand such madrassas in Pakistan, a "disquieting" (71) thought, he said, because the curriculum was designed by the Mogul emperor in 1701, and the one shelf of science books dated largely from the 1920s. In a classroom donated by the Kingdom of Saudi Arabia, a boy chanted a Koranic verse: "The faithful shall enter Paradise and the unbelievers shall be condemned to eternal hellfire" (quoted on 71). Friedman asked one student about 9/11, and the boy replied that it was most likely caused by Americans, but he was glad to see Americans, like the rest of the world, face pain. And what did the students think of Americans? "They are unbelievers and do not like to befriend Muslims, and they want to dominate the world with their power" (71) was the response.

Friedman wrote on November 16, 2001, that despite the madrassas, bin Laden had unwittingly forced Muslims to confront "modernity" (72). As a Pakistani businessman wrote in the Pakistani daily *The Nation*, "We Muslims cannot keep blaming the West for all our ills. . . . Without a reformation in the practice of Islam that makes it move forward and not backward, there is no hope for us Muslims anywhere. We have reduced Islam to the organized hypocrisy of state-sponsored mullahism. For more than a thousand years Islam has stood still because the mullahs, who became de facto clergy instead of genuine scholars, closed the door on *itjihad* [reinterpreting Islam in light of modernity] and no one came forward with an evolving application of the message of the Holy Quran" (quoted on 73). Friedman added to this commentary that "the Protestant Reformation, melding Christianity with modernity, happened only when wealthy princes came along ready to finance and protect the breakaway reformers. But in the Muslim world today the wealthiest princes, like Saudi Arabia's, are funding antimodern schools" (73).

Friedman pondered the condition of Islam in Pakistan and contrasted it to the situation in its often adversarial neighbor, India. On November 20, 2001, he suggested that India had cauterized its nearly 150 million Muslims—the second-highest number of Muslims in the world—from the infection of terrorism through the flame of democracy (74–75). Friedman did not claim perfection in India's relations between Muslims and the majority Hindus; nonetheless, he felt that democracy made all the difference in regularizing social and political relationships and fostering healthy religious communities. He made this assertion several months before the outbreak of fatal violence between Indian Hindus and Muslims.

With these perspectives, on November 27, 2001, Friedman attempted to gather his thoughts about the conflict engendered by 9/11 in his column "The Real War." He began: "If 9/11 was indeed the onset of World War III, we have to understand what this war is about" (78). He explained: "We're fighting to defeat an ideology: religious totalitarianism. World War II and the cold war were fought to defeat secular totalitarianism—Nazism and Communism—and World War III is a battle against religious totalitarianism, a view of the world that says, My faith must reign supreme and can be affirmed and held passionately only if all others are negated. That's bin Ladenism" (78). This war is not to be fought by armies only. "It has to be fought in schools, mosques, churches, and synagogues, and can be defeated only with the help of imams, rabbis, and priests" (78).

He turned to Rabbi David Hartman from the Shalom Hartman Institute in Jerusalem, one of his column's main advisers, whose central idea is that "God speaks multiple languages and is not exhausted by just one faith" (78). Friedman asked Hartman how to combat religious totalitarianism. The rabbi replied, "All faiths that come out of the biblical tradition—Judaism, Christianity, and Islam—have the tendency to believe that they have the exclusive truth. When the Taliban wiped out the Buddhist statues, that's what they were saying. But others have said it too. The opposite of religious totalitarianism is an ideology of pluralism—an ideology that embraces religious diversity and the idea that my faith can be nurtured without claiming exclusive truth. America is the Mecca of that ideology, and that is what bin Laden hates, and that is why America has to be destroyed [according to Al Qaeda]" (78–79). Friedman concluded that Christianity and Judaism have struggled with these issues—modernity, pluralism, secularism, alternative faiths—and internally there are Christian and Jewish "fundamentalists" (79) as well as pluralists. The same must become true for Islam, "but a similar internal struggle within Islam to reexamine its texts and articulate a path for how one can accept pluralism and modernity—and still be a passionate, devout Muslim—has not surfaced in any serious way" (79). In short, the 9/11 clash was between a modern, pluralistic religious consciousness prevalent in Judeo-Christianity and a premodern, totalitarian religious consciousness holding sway in Islam.

As an example of religious modernity, Friedman referred on December 16, 2001, to a new synagogue he and his friends had founded, which was using a Presbyterian church for its Hanukkah party. There was nothing strange about that arrangement, Friedman said, unless you thought about it. "Whenever I encounter the reality of religious tolerance in America," Friedman commented, "it strikes me almost as a miracle. I know that religious intolerance is also alive and well in this country, but it is not the norm" (90). Expressing the value his newspaper has placed on religious tolerance, diversity, and ecumenism as crucial elements of America's way of life, he called this tradition of tolerance America's "spiritual missile shield" (90) in its battle with religious totalitarianism.

This attitude underlay Friedman's August 28, 2002, column "Cuckoo in Carolina," a comment on the to-do in North Carolina over Michael Sells's *Approaching the Qu'rán: The Early Revelations* (2001) being assigned as a required orientation reading at the University of North Carolina. He began: "The ruckus being raised by conservative Christians over the University of North Carolina's decision to ask incoming students to read a book about the Koran—to stimulate a campus debate—surely has to be one of the most embarrassing moments for America since September 11. Why? Because it exhibits such profound lack of understanding of what America is about, and it exhibits such a chilling mimicry of what the most repressive Arab Muslim states are about" (212). Friedman argued that in Saudi Arabia it is against the law to practice any religion other than Islam. It would be a good thing for Muslims (not just Saudis) to read the Bill of Rights, the US Constitution, the *Federalist Papers*. And, he said, it is a good thing for Americans to learn about Islam; indeed, he had studied Islam and Arabic at the University of Minnesota in 1971. His conclusion? Quoting the "religious philosopher David Hartman," he wrote, "'A monolithic framework does not create a critical mind'" (213).

Religious tolerance was an American domestic value Friedman prized; however, in foreign affairs he favored hard-nosed rhetorical judgments. On February 13, 2002, he allowed that he was "glad" that President Bush had used the expression "axis of evil" to describe potential nuclear-armed adversaries, Iraq, Iran, and North Korea, because it demonstrated America's intent to fight. Why was this so important? "Because the critics are missing the larger point, which is this: September 11 happened because America had lost its deterrent capability" (122), and Friedman, like his president, saw a need to regain it.

In 2002, Friedman's columns turned to implications of 9/11 in the proliferating tensions between Israelis and Palestinians as well as more generally in the Middle East. In London, an Arab editor asked Friedman, "Are Jews in the media behind the campaign to smear Saudi Arabia and Islam?" (120). Friedman replied in his February 10, 2002, column that Jewish reporters have covered Palestinians, Bosnian Muslims, Kosovars, and other Muslims in a fair and professional manner. "So, to begin with, maybe—just maybe—there is no Jewish conspiracy against Muslims or Saudi Arabia at work here" (120). In a May 5, 2002, column, Friedman found it risible that Muslim students in Indonesia harped on the supposed influence of American "Jewish" politicians such as Al Gore (164–65)! But he also expressed pride in Israel's achievements and a special sensitivity to questions of Jewish identity. On March 6, 2002, he opined that Muslims were envious of Israel because it has accomplished so much: "How could a tiny Jewish state amass so much military and economic power if the Islamic way of life—not Christianity or Judaism—is God's most ideal religious path?" he asked (134). He called this envy "the core of Muslim rage" (134), and he said that it was "educated, but frustrated, Muslim youth . . . who perpetrated 9/11 and who slit the throat of the *Wall Street Journal* reporter Danny Pearl—after reportedly forcing him to declare on film, 'I am a Jew and my mother is a Jew'" (135).

Whatever tensions there might be between Muslims and Jews, even in the Mideast, and despite his references to World War III, Freidman refused at first to adopt wholeheartedly as his own the Huntingtonian terminology of a "clash of civilizations." On March 10, 2002, Friedman noted that some in Israel and the

"American Jewish right" claimed that "a war of civilizations" (137) was already under way and that it must be fought totally. They called this attitude "'realism'" (137); however, Friedman said that if this view became dominant in Israel, that country was doomed because there were endless numbers of Palestinians who would wage war endlessly against Israel. On April 3, 2002, Friedman returned to this theme, but with a more hawkish angle: "A terrible disaster is in the making in the Middle East. What Osama bin Laden failed to achieve on September 11 is now being unleashed by the Israeli–Palestinian war in the West Bank: a clash of civilizations" (150). He concluded: "Either leaders of goodwill get together and acknowledge that Israel can't stay in the territories, but can't just pick up and leave without a U.S.–NATO force helping Palestinians oversee their state, or Osama wins—and the war of civilizations will be coming to a theater near you" (151). In post-9/11 perspective, Israel's security seemed a matter of crucial importance to America's defense.

As the first anniversary of 9/11 approached, Friedman took stock on September 3, 2002, of three lessons he had learned in the previous year.

First, who are the terrorists? They are "evil" "extremists" who chose to "lash out at the symbol of modernity" (216), the United States of America.

Second, who are we, especially in relation to them? "'We're good; they're evil, nothing is relative,'" Friedman claimed, quoting another writer. American goodness, however, was to be perceived as a matter of institutions and values, not as a matter of race or religious denomination. "We Americans are not better than any other people, but the Western democratic system we live by is the best system on earth. Unfortunately, in the Arab-Muslim world, there is no democracy, too few women's rights, and too little religious tolerance. It is the values and traditions of freedom embraced by Western civilization, and the absence of those values and traditions in the Arab-Muslim world, that explain the main difference between us" (216–27).

Finally, Friedman asked, "Why do so many foreigners reject the evil perpetrators of 9/11 but still dislike America?" His answer was imbued with patriotism: "It's because, while we have the best system of governance, we are not always at our best in how we act toward the world" (217).

Friedman chose September 11, 2002, to draw explicitly on his biblical heritage in his column "Noah and 9/11." The column was without a doubt a moral sermon deriving from Friedman's religious tradition, its discernment of God's will and human responsibility in personal behavior and public policy. One of Friedman's mentors, Rabbi Tzvi Marx, told him from the Netherlands, "We feel after 9/11 like we have experienced the flood of Noah—as if a flood has inundated our civilization and we are the survivors. What do we do the morning after?" Noah got drunk, making him "numb to the world"; however, said the rabbi, God laid down the "Noahite laws. His first rule was that life is precious, so man should not murder man" (quoted on 218). So, Friedman said, the analogy is clear: we can numb ourselves to the world, or we can insist ever more firmly on "rules and norms—both for ourselves and for others" (218). "Yes, we must kill the murderers of 9/11, but without becoming murderers and without simply indulging ourselves" (219).

Throughout 2002, Friedman returned repeatedly to the theme that America's enemies were not Muslims per se. Indeed, Islamist extremists had no abler foes than the progressives and reformists in their own societies. On June 2, 2002, he wrote that the West should hope for "a war within Islam over its spiritual message and identity, not a war with Islam" (181).

On June 19, 2002, he queried from Tehran: "What if a theocracy and a democracy had a baby? What would it look like? It would look like Iran" (188). He praised Iranian Muslims who were trying to create "a democratic, progressive Islamic alternative" (189). "Wish them well" (189), he said. And on December 4, 2002, Friedman wrote about Hashem Aghajari, an Iranian revolutionary who was now a college professor condemned to death by Iranian Islamic hardliners for giving a speech "on the need to rejuvenate Islam with an 'Islamic Protestantism'" (260). Just as Protestants wanted a religion in which individuals could escape the domination of clergy and speak with God directly, read the scriptures directly, thus Aghajari yearned for Islam: "We need a religion that respects the rights of all," he said, "a progressive religion, rather than a traditional religion that tramples the people" (261).

Friedman's hopes for a progressive Islam to counter the forces of Muslim extremism helped form his support for an American war in Iraq, which he saw from a post-9/11 perspective. On December 8, 2002, he stated, "We *are* at war. We are at war with a cruel, militant Islam, led by Al Qaeda, we are at war with a rising tide of global anti-Americanism, and we will probably soon be at war to disarm Iraq" (262, italics in original). Despite his "heretical thought" that Americans might be "overreacting to 9/11" (288); despite his "longing and nostalgia" for the post-9/11 "American solidarity" (294), which began to dissipate as the Iraq conflict commenced; despite his spiritual urge, derived from the kabbalah, toward "repairing the world" (297), Friedman's fidelities propelled him toward promoting in the pages of the *Times* a military conflict between "them" and "us."

Friedman's fidelities were clear enough in his columns; however, in his "diary" at the close of *Longitudes and Attitudes* (321–95), he revealed more about himself, and it is worth observing the several aspects of his identity that helped frame his "attitudes" in his commentary about 9/11, its causes, and its consequences. In a sense, one gains a glimpse into several dimensions of Friedman's faith, from which his attitudes derived.

Friedman's faith was an aspect of what he termed American "civic religion" (331). In loving detail, he described people who worked at the World Trade Center, kissing their spouses good-bye each morning, going to work, applying their energy toward something larger than themselves, a commonweal greater than their individual parts. "It was just like [my daughter's] school—one of a million such temples of America's civic religion, only the World Trade Center was home to ninety different nationalities instead of just forty" (331), Friedman wrote. He said that Americans learned from 9/11 to treat our firefighters, police officers, our institutions and regulations, with renewed respect. Why? "Because they protect and preserve the bedrock of our society—our workplaces and public schools. They are the guardians of the temples of our civic faith" (333). Friedman's "civic religion" was not just something that he described, but rather something he believed in: personal commitment, work in common, multiethnic colleagueship, a spirit of cooperation.

Friedman's fidelity to American civic religion led him to reject the Islamist critique of American culture: "For bin Laden, the Twin Towers were the symbol of a godless, corrupt, materialistic society—a society that got rich and powerful precisely because it had no values. Of course, what bin Laden never understood was that the truth was exactly the opposite: We are rich and powerful *because* of our values—freedom of thought, respect for the individual, the rule of law, entrepreneurship, women's equality, philanthropy, social mobility, self-criticism, experimentation, religious pluralism—not despite them" (332–33).

Friedman denied the applicability of bin Laden's denunciation of American culture. He also found himself at odds with the post-9/11 attitudes he encountered on college campuses. In the "Political Correctness 101" section of *Longitudes and*

Attitudes (333–38), he commented that he found his conversations in academia "depressing" because the American professors and students "just didn't seem to get it" (334). Get what? That America, despite its faults, "has done more to make this world a better, more livable place for more people than any other country in history. Some people don't like that. They detest the freedom, the pluralism, the religious toleration, the secularism, the gender equity, the democracy, the faith, the free markets, and the multiethnicity with which we have built our society, and which we urge others to emulate." Friedman continued, "There really are people who hate Christians, hate Jews, hate secularism, hate the equality of women. At some point you have to either kill those people or be killed by them. This is not a misunderstanding that can be cleared up by a few courses in multiculturalism" (334). According to Friedman, academics would do well to "teach Evil 101" (335) in order to understand our 9/11 foes.

One might ask what such a course might entail. Would it be a depiction of bin Laden's evil? Or would it examine the complexities and subtleties of defining evil, in America as well as in other lands and peoples? The *Times,* as we have seen, carried several thoughtful essays on this thorny topic. Friedman, however, had another message to deliver: that although many in the West did not see 9/11 and its aftermath as an aspect of war between civilizations, Osama bin Laden certainly did, and he was calling his fellow Muslims to total warfare against us. Even if we do not think that there is a war of civilizations taking place, there *is* because evil persons among the Muslim billions are bringing it to us. We must respond and with force.

On one campus, the professors said that bin Laden was responding to American policies, especially regarding Israel. Friedman argued that bin Laden had no such critique; his motive was hatred, his desire to destroy us. Later on, a campus security officer, an off-duty policeman or fireman, "a wonderfully earthy guy, the sort of cop or fireman America is built on," agreed with Friedman in private. It was this "political correctness," Friedman commented, "that prompted me to write the column 'Yes, but What?'" (337). It also led him to tell his daughters at dinner: "Girls, you can have any view you want—left, right, or center. You can come home with someone black, white, or purple. But you will never come in this house and not love your country and not thank God every day that you were born an American" (337).

Friedman's fidelity to American "civic religion" was thus made all the more fervent by the feeling of commitment toward the United States, which he termed "patriotism or love of country" (337). Friedman's patriotism, however, did not preclude cultural conflict at home. He cited Stephen P. Cohen, the Middle East analyst, who was "so right" when he stated: "'Either we have wars within civilization'—wars between those in each civilization who want to embrace modernity, integration, and coexistence with other cultures, faith, and peoples and those who oppose all that—'or we will end up with wars between civilizations'" (392–93). Taken seriously, this notion would suggest that the "culture wars" in the United States are a sign of our health. It is a good thing for there to be such open debate within our civilization about our basic values. Indeed, newspapers exist for the purpose of explicating and exemplifying that debate as a means of telling us who we are, what we care about, and how we contend with our civic compatriots. If only Islamic societies could struggle within their own circles, we might not find them at war with us.

"Them" and "us." Friedman's fidelity was decidedly with "us"—fractious, conflictual "us." One can follow Friedman's continuing commentary on the "war of ideas" (Friedman 2004b) in the 9/12 world. In that column and in *Longitudes,* Friedman's fidelities are apparent, and I would argue that they are the mainstream loyalties of the *Times,* for all its diversity of viewpoint and opinion.

The Battle of Lepanto Redux

Friedman's loyalties are with the United States. In its civil religion, his column has served as a kind of sermon calling Americans to the core values and behaviors of its better angels. He is clearly of America and with America, and America is at war. Call it "World War III" or a "clash of civilizations," it is a battle royal. It is intriguing, then, to ponder the scene of battle displayed on the cover of *Longitudes and Attitudes*.

The back jacket identifies the front as a detail from the mural *The Battle of Lepanto* painted by Giorgio Vasari (1511–74). The original is in the Sala Regia, Vatican Palace, Vatican State. In the narrow, horizontal band between Friedman's name and the book's title, one can discern men in water, swimming, drowning, clutching ships and longbows. Some wear helmets; some wear turbans. Their faces are grim.

The Gulf of Lepanto, by Oxia, is south of Corfu, on the western coast of Greece, in the sixteenth century at the fault line between the Ottoman-held Balkans and the Christian, western Mediterranean. It was the site of a military contest between Ottoman Istanbul, on the one hand, and a confederation of Venice, Spain, and the Papal States—that is, the Latin Mediterranean (and by extension, western Europe)—on the other.

Victor Davis Hanson's book *Carnage and Culture: Landmark Battles in the Rise of Western Power* (2001; reviewed twice in the *Times,* once before 9/11 [Parker 2001] and once after [E. Rothstein 2001b]) contains a chapter entitled "The Market—or Capitalism Kills: Lepanto, October 7, 1571" (233–75). There one can read about the Ottoman sea battle against newly invented Venetian galleasses, six "novel monstrosities" (233) that had more firepower than a dozen of Admiral Hassan Ali's galleys. Pope Pius V had convinced Philip II of Spain and the Venetian Senate to fight a "once and for all" battle (245) to save the western

Mediterranean from the Turks, led by Sultan Selim II, who were ravaging the coast and the islands, including Cyprus.

Philip made Don Juan of Austria the supreme commander of the allied fleets. Don Juan's *La Reale* flew the banner of the Crucifixion. Priests blessed the crews of the Holy League. Every ship had a crucifix on it. The Christians vowed to conquer or to die, "'as Heaven may determine'" (235) and as Don Juan commanded. Once the battle began, the Christians boarded the Turkish flagship *Sultana* and slaughtered the Ottomans. Ali's head was soon on a pike on the *Reale*'s quarterdeck. Then the "frenzied Christians . . . could systematically slaughter the Turkish peasants" who manned Ali's ships (236). The Holy League fighters freed 15,000 Christian galley slaves and "made it a point to butcher every dumbfounded and by now mostly defenseless Ottoman sailor and soldier" (237). The battle took but four hours, with combined dead estimated at 40,000 (of the 180,000 men present), one of the bloodiest one-day battles in history. The waters around Lepanto were said to be "a sea of blood" (241) as "murderous Christian gunners" (241) barraged the Turks hanging on to pieces of ships in the water. No prisoners were to be taken by the Christian armada, and as many as 10,000 Turkish seamen were killed at sea, their ships demolished. Christian pikemen harpooned the hapless Turks as they floundered in the roiling waters.

In the West, Lepanto immediately became a legendary victory, seen (in art, history, literature, and elsewhere) from Western eyes. "Don Juan's selflessness and his single-minded zeal in uniting the disparate nations of southern Europe" (245) were famed in his time, as was his generosity—sharing his prize money with the wounded in the fleet. There were Christian celebrations all over southern Europe, limned by many a Te Deum Laudamus, rosary, commemorative coin, woodcut, medal, sculpture, and painting (such as those by Veronese, Vicentino, Tintoretto, and Titian as well as, of course, the famous Vatican frescos by Vasari). Cervantes was a veteran of the battle and memorialized it in *Don Quixote*. The future king of England, James I, wrote eleven thousand lines of verse commemorating Lepanto. Paintings and songs "attributed the remarkable Christian victory to divine intervention" (253).

In 1572, Pope Pius V "summoned Vasari to Rome to celebrate the triumphal victory of the Christian League over the Turks in two grand frescoes" (Pietrangeli 1996:274) in the Sala Regia of the Vatican. Vasari painted *The Battle of Lepanto*,

April–May 1572, finishing so quickly that he remarked, "I thought as if I really had been present at the battle with the Turks" (274).

In the painting (Pietrangeli 1996:402–3, plate 378), the sea battle takes place in the center and lower right. The detail on Friedman's cover is from the very bottom of the scene. Christians and Turks fire at one another, Christians from the left, Turks from the right. At the top left, Jesus, St. Peter, other saints, and angels wield swords and thunderbolts from their celestial cloud. Devils and serpents flee, squirming off into darkness at the top right. At the center, the Angel Gabriel, surrounded by an aura, steadies the Christians onward to victory. At the lower left, the largest figure, a woman in white, presumably Mary or perhaps the Church, bears a large cross on her shoulder; in her left hand, she holds a chalice or ciborium bearing the heavenly host, the body of Christ. At her feet lie a handful of captive Muslims, and she sits on two of their backs. An angel lays a triumphal wreath on her head.

Pius V died in 1572, but Vasari continued his project under Pope Gregory XIII in 1573. He completed several scenes of the recent Saint Bartholomew's Eve (August 23–24, 1572) slaughter of Huguenots, interpreted in the Vatican as a defense of Catholicism against plotting French Protestants rather than as a massacre. To complete the triumphal theme, Vasari and his assistants painted the fresco *The Opposing Fleets of the Turks and the Holy League at Lepanto* in 1573 (Pietrangeli 1996:404, plate 380). In this scene, the ships face each other beneath their unfurled banners, ready for battle. Three females, representing the papacy, Spain, and Venice, embrace each other at lower left. A map of Lepanto sits at the center, bottom. To balance the three confident Christian women, receiving halos from angels, the lower right shows skeletal Death with his scythe. Angels empty a turban of serpents over several horrified, cringing Turks. It is said that Pope Gregory XIII was very pleased with the work as a representation of the crusading, triumphant spirit of Christendom against its Muslim enemies. Hanson (2001) remarks that in Giorgio Vasari's second "haunting canvas" of Lepanto, "the supernatural forces of good and evil watch as the six enormous galleasses lead out the Holy League's massive armada" (illustrations between 236 and 237).

Lepanto has long been considered "a watershed event in the history of East–West relations," Hanson writes—not just a "tactical victory" (267), but proof that the Westerners could defeat the Turks when they wished and willed to. Why did the Christians win? Because the battle was on a Sunday? Because of priestly blessings? Because of Turkish sacrileges on Corfu (Christian graves, churches, and priests defiled)?

Hanson puts aside these religious explanations; he attributes the victory to "capitalist economies" (254) capable of producing overwhelming firepower. The Western forces had more and superior cannon, better weaponry and protective devices, more experience with firearms. "At Lepanto," he writes, "heavier and more plentiful firearms, greater rates of fire, more reliable ammunition, and better-trained gunners added up to enormous European advantages" (248). The Turks had the manpower; the Christians had the firepower.

Europe was fragmented in the sixteenth century: Protestants versus Catholics, states versus states. France was an active ally of the Ottomans, using their help to take Corsica from Genoa in 1532, housing the Turkish admiral Barbarossa's fleet in the winter of 1543–44. No wonder the Ottomans expected to win at Lepanto: the Christians were, as Hassan Ali had said, "of different nations and held different religious rites" (255).

In addition, Europe had qualms about warfare—including just-war theories and even pacifism (something Islam has never developed—the idea that war is inherently evil); however, Christians seemed willing to fight this war. And because Islam had developed its concept of military jihad, there were two parties more than willing to fight. "Yet what gave the much smaller states of the Christian federation a fighting chance for victory was their remarkable ability—given their limited populations and territory—to create capital, and thereby to fabricate excellent vessels, mass-produce advanced firearms, and hire skilled crews" (258). The Turks copied their ship designs from the Italians; they had slave labor; but they lacked financial mobilization.

Venice, with a population of only two hundred thousand, possessed wherewithal unmatched by the Turks: "Its system of capitalism, consensual government, and devotion to disinterested research" (261–62). Muslims were not allowed to make a profit on their investments; *riba*—"over and above a thing"— was not allowed in investments, nor were loans, leading to a stagnant economy. With no banking system, the Ottomans had to hide their gold to protect it from tax collectors. Ali's huge personal fortune, consisting of 150,000 gold sequins, was on his ship when he died.

In short, according to Hanson, "true market economies never fully developed in the Muslim world because they were in jeopardy without freedom and antithetical to the Koran, which made no distinction between political, cultural, economic, and religious life, and therefore discouraged unfettered economic rationalism" (269). "Free capital is the key to war making on any large scale" (270), Hanson concludes. "Capital is the wellspring of technological innovation, which is inextricably tied to freedom, often the expression of individualism, and thus critical to military success throughout the ages" (270–71).

Hanson thus views the Battle of Lepanto as an unequal contest between two civilizations, one inspired and shackled by Islamic ideals, the other fueled by the interrelated values of free enterprise, rationalism, and invention.

In *The Unthought in Contemporary Islamic Thought* (2002), Mohammed Arkoun interprets the Battle of Lepanto—often called the Thirteenth Crusade—as a persistent expression of mutual hatred between Middle Eastern Islam and European Christendom. He says that "the Crusades have been and are still used in European and Muslim discourses, even in schools, as a theme of *mutual exclusion* and *contempt*" (275, italics in original). The battle has served, he claims, as a statement of the "collective *imaginaire* in the biased, nationalistic construction of the values, criteria, and regime of truth underlying the concept of *jihād* in Islam, Just War or Holy War in Christianity and secular Europe" (275, italics in original). In leading to, fighting, and reflecting on the Battle of Lepanto, "Islam and Christianity performed the same functions of masking reality, twisting the meaning of events and transcendentalizing profane behaviour, with the same later results of individual and collective alienation. This last, it will be claimed, is the price paid for the survival and temporal growth (*spiritual* growth, believers will insist) of each community" (289, italics in original).

It took centuries, says Arkoun, for European historians to "shift" their presentation of the Crusades from a one-sided, legitimating narration to a "modern, critical, open exploration of both sides, using archives and new interpretive approaches" (275). Arkoun's implication is that Islam has yet to attain this distance from which to assess the Crusades. His more challenging claim is that participants at Lepanto wished to see themselves as engaged religiously in the battle, but they were motivated more substantially by material forces.

Pius V called for a "thirteenth crusade against the Muslim infidel" (289); however, Arkoun sees the combatants as motivated by mercenary aims. "Religion counted for very little in the behaviour of the most visible protagonists" (291), he asserts, even though recruitment and other official language "employed all the stereotypes most likely to arouse eschatological visions and millenarian aspirations in the popular consciousness" (291). What was the battle about, in Arkoun's view? He suggests that we read Fernand Braudel's magisterial opus *The Mediterranean and the Mediterranean World in the Age of Philip II* (1972), which regards Lepanto as "an episode in the secular struggles between all the Mediterranean peoples" (Arkoun 2002:292). As Arkoun puts it, "In the minds of both sides, a religious motive was thus substituted for the real reasons[,] which were (and remain to this day) strategic and economic" (292).

We see in the documents surrounding Lepanto the religious language on both sides. Christians mocked Mohammed; they vanquished by Christ. (Muslims did not disparage Jesus, who is a prophet for them.) Each spoke of the other as infidels; each called upon God for grace, victory, providence. From 1571 to the present, Christians and Muslims have continued a process of "reciprocal exclusion," using religious "dogma" in the process (Arkoun 2002:297). Lepanto and the Crusades in general have provided the theological-historical language for Christians and Muslims to entrench the fault lines between them ever deeper. Hence, the concern over Hollywood's post-9/11 fascination with the "ferocious fight between Christians and Muslims over Jerusalem in the Crusade of the 12th century" in the film *Kingdom of Heaven* (Waxman 2004).

Given this heritage, why does Friedman use Lepanto to illustrate his book on "longitudes"—the fault lines themselves? His book cover speaks eloquently of Muslim–Christian conflict both in the age of Philip II and in our own day. It suggests that we are in the midst of "World War III," an epochal "clash of civilizations" akin to—and perhaps derived from—the Crusades, straddling the longitudes between Islam and the West. Is that Friedman's point? Is that a point suggested more subtly but persistently on the pages of the *Times?*

Fernand Braudel (1972) has much to say about the fault lines between the Ottoman Empire and the Christian principalities of the western Mediterranean. To the historical actors of the sixteenth century, the immediate clashes of the day could be read as episodes of religious warfare between two civilizations, Muslim and Christian. But Braudel places this old news in a more glacial context. One needs also, he states, to take a step back from immediate events to look at the contexts beyond the religious, the military, and the political to the deeper structures of social patterns, subsistence, environmental milieu in which Islam and Christianity vied. Today the context is global, as Friedman well knows. Is a patriotic American perspective the best or final word on the world's conflicts? How can it be?

To understand Lepanto, the battle, we must first understand its complex natural environment: the mountains, the plateaus, the plains, and peninsulas surrounding the Mediterranean, as well as the transhumance and nomadism of Mediterranean peoples; the sea itself, its coastlines and islands, its boundaries—Sahara to the south, Europe to the north, from the palms to the olives, the Atlantic, and the all-important fault line between eastern and western Mediterranean—directly in line with Lepanto.

Once we grasp the physical Mediterranean, we need to learn of the land and sea routes, the shipping, the urban markets, the populations, their appetites and economies—the spices, metals, cereals, and so on. Upon this knowledge, we come to know of the empires, Turkish and Spanish; the societies, from nobility to poverty and banditry; and the civilizations—Turkish, Christian, with Jews caught betwixt. Then piracy and the forms of war. Only with all these elements in mind can we come to understand the events, politics, and people leading up to Lepanto and its aftermath. This is the perspective we gain by reading the work of an historian such as Braudel, and it is for this reason that scholarship can have an advantage over journalism in providing depth to a field.

If we are to speak about a "clash of civilizations" today, as Friedman does and as do others in the *Times,* we might take heed from some remarks by Braudel (1972) about the Mediterranean civilizations of the sixteenth century. He writes, "The mark of a living civilization is that it is capable of exporting itself, of spreading its culture to distant places" (763). Its very dynamism threatens its neighbors. "There was once an Arab civilization: its importance and its decline are well known. . . . In the sixteenth century there was a Latin civilization (I have reservations about calling it Christian)" (763–64). They faced each other, borrowed from each other, and clashed with each other.

Living civilizations must all be able to "borrow wisely" (764), Braudel states. "But a great civilization can also be recognized by its refusal to borrow, by its resistance to certain alignments, by its resolute selection among the foreign influences offered to it and which would no doubt be forced upon it if they were not met by vigilance, or, more simply, by incompatibility of temper and appetite" (764). Mediterranean Latins, for example, resisted both Protestant Reformation and Islam in the sixteenth century and clashed with both. Most significant, the

Mediterranean was separated by geography and civilization not only north and south, but east and west, by "that immutable barrier" (771), the longitudinal fault line at Lepanto between the Latin and the Ottoman.

Can we apply these comments to today? Are we witnesses to two dynamic civilizations, each exporting itself, each resisting the other and asserting its own autonomy partially at the expense of the other? Can we also see ourselves today, in our reading of the news, as Braudel sees the past? "Events are the ephemera of history," he writes; "they pass across its stage like fireflies, hardly glimpsed before they settle back into darkness and as often as not into oblivion" (901). How soon will we be able to think about 9/11 in this way? Friedman (2003a) states that 9/11 is "one of those rare major historic events that will turn out to be even larger, even more important, than it first seemed. And we are not at the beginning of the end of understanding it or its implications" (387). Is he correct?

As Braudel (1972) points out, some say that "the fall of Constantinople in 1453 was a non-event and Lepanto, the great Christian victory of 1571, had no consequences at all, as Voltaire took great pleasure in pointing out. (These two opinions are both, let me hasten to say, open to debate)" (902). "Lepanto was the most spectacular military event in the Mediterranean during the entire sixteenth century," he states (1088). One might say that it did not settle anything right away. The Holy League lost battles and dispersed in the next few years. Turks still had victories to come. But "the spell of Turkish supremacy had been broken" (1088), and before long the Turks were greatly weakened vis-à-vis the Christians. The event was important, and it is remembered as such.

It is also remembered for its religious foundation, and rightly so, Arkoun to the contrary. Pope Pius V organized the Holy League, 1566–70, because of his "highly developed sense of the conflicts between Christendom and the Infidels and Heretics. His dream was to wage these mighty battles and to bring a speedy solution to the quarrels that divided Christendom against itself" (Braudel 1972:1029). Are we to follow Arkoun's interpretation, downplaying religion to a rhetorical role rather than a real cause? One might say that Lepanto was an articulation of environmental, economic, civilizational, cultural, and political forces greater than religion. Nonetheless, religion was surely a crucial factor, as it is in our day. "For this war of religion," Braudel concludes, "a war between hostile civilizations, spread spontaneously and rapidly over a land well-primed by hatred and poverty" (1061). It was a war of religion, whatever else it was.

Friedman meant to be "'provocative,'" I am told (Gelman 2006; cf. C. Vecsey 2006), in illustrating his 9/11 book with *The Battle of Lepanto*. Knowing what we do about the battle and the painting in the sanguinary history of Christian–Muslim relations, we might ask what Friedman wished to provoke. Surely his book repeatedly makes the point that American and Islamic cultures stand in sharp contrast to one another. Their institutions, beliefs, ethics, and rituals, their faith in the supernatural, and their sense of community—although historically related and comparable as modes of religiousness—are far removed from one another as cumulative traditions. For Friedman, as for the *Times* as a whole, to comprehend the conflictual milestone known as 9/11 is to fathom the groundwork of religion underlying it, along with its multilayered contexts.

(MORE)

One could have closed the story of 9/11's religious angles in 2004. By that time, many of the narratives had taken on the quality of evergreens—worth noting without offering anything substantial to a reader interested in religion in the 9/12 world.

By 2004, a *Times* reportorial scandal and shakeup beginning in the spring of 2003 had come and gone. Without much direct bearing on the 9/11 story, the unsavory case of Jayson Blair (see "*Times* Reporter Who Resigned" 2003) unveiled structural flaws in *Times* practices concerning hiring, reporting, and factual oversight. As a result, the paper appointed its first editor for standards at the level of assistant managing editor (Steinberg 2003) as well as a rotating position of public editor to question *Times* policies. Perhaps most shaking, Executive Editor Howell Raines lost his post and was replaced by Bill Keller.

By the end of 2004, the *Times* revolution had become the subject of book-length treatment. Timothy Noah (2004) reviewed Seth Mnookin's book *Hard News: The Scandals at "The New York Times" and Their Meaning for American Media* about Jayson Blair the "fabulist," Howell Raines the "bully," and their comeuppance. Noah made the point that Gay Talese had once amazed Americans by giving them an inside look at the very secretive organization of the *Times*. Today, however, "everyone's a media critic," and there are no *Times* secrets anymore. Even Raines wrote his own version of his rise and fall in the *Atlantic Monthly* in May 2004 (see Espin 2006). It was unclear what the meaning of these events was for American news media, except, perhaps, that they are being watched. December 2004 seemed a suitable moment of closure.

Nonetheless, the next year carried the religion angles on 9/11 still further. Stanley Fish wrote about religion in January 2005: "Nowadays, in the wake of September 11, there often seems to be nothing else in the news, as we continue to debate the questions that were being asked within hours of the attacks on the World Trade Center. Is this a religious war? If so, what exactly is our religion? If not, what kind of war is it? Do the terrorists represent Islam or only some perverted version of that faith? Who is to say?"

Religion surely filled the pages of the *Times,* and most articles were about something other than 9/11. The moral, political controversy over the life and death of Terri Schiavo made front-page news in the spring of 2005. On April 5, the death of Pope John Paul II created an avalanche of *Times* coverage, reviewing his papacy, focusing on his funeral, and documenting the ascension of his successor, Pope Benedict XVI.

Nonetheless, 9/11's shock waves continued to be felt in the press and reverberated in much consideration of religion in the news, in particular concerning Islam. Especially in regard to Iraq, but in regard to other places, too, the headlines often repeated stock phrases about Islam's threat to social order. References to "Islamic radicals" ("Britain: Radical Cleric" 2005), "militant clerics" (Eckholm 2005a), "Islamic terrorism" (McLean 2005a), "Islamic militants" (Perlez 2005), "Islamist revolution" (Griswold 2005), "militant imams" (Van Natta and Bergman 2005), "militant Muslims" (Simons 2005b), "Islamists" (C. Smith 2005c), and "jihad death threats" (Simons 2005a) were the order of the day. *Times* writers, such as David Rieff (2005b), continued to depict an American "conflict with jihadism" as "a contest between modernity and antimodernity."

Times correspondent John Tagliabue (2007a)—who wrote perceptively about post-9/11 developments in Islam and between Islam and other faiths, including Islamist "activist cells" in Europe—doubts that his reporting "contributed much to a reader's understanding of religion" beyond "a fanatic variation" of Islam. Although espousing an "idealistic" belief that "religious leaders can have an influence reinforcing the opposition of their faithful to radicalism and violence," he acknowledges that "all too often religious leaders stoke fanaticism"—witness Ian Paisley in Northern Ireland. Islamism struck many *Times* writers as a serious threat to world peace, and Tagliabue (2007b) muses that if "Muslim leaders were not fomenting fanaticism, I think there could be less violence among their followers."

In nations around the world—from Pakistan (Masood 2005b; "Pakistan Cabinet Split" 2005; "Pakistani Court" 2005; Sengupta 2005b; Sengupta and Masood 2005a; Sengupta and Rohde 2005), Afghanistan (Gall 2005a), India

(Sengupta 2005a, 2005c), Thailand and Malaysia (Cumming-Bruce 2005), Russia ("Islamic Group Says It Set Off Dagestan Blast" 2005), and Egypt (Slackman 2005) to France (C. Smith 2005d), Italy (Fisher 2005a), and England—especially England in July 2005, but France would have its own crisis of Muslim violence in November 2005 (Alvarez 2005a; Cowell 2005d; Lyall 2005b; "'Muhammad' Is Growing Popular in Britain" 2005)—Islam continued to be seen as a problematic, politicized, burgeoning faith, not always true to its earnest ideals (Bergen 2005a; Lacey 2005) and largely in turmoil. The *Times* seemed focused on what it considered "a tide of Islamic fury, and how it rose" (Kifner 2005b). Books continued to be reviewed about "globalized Islam" (e.g., Feldman 2005b), "the war for Muslim minds," "radical Islam," "terrorism," "jihadists," and "extremism," all as a "global warning" to *Times* readers about "political Islam" and the "willing recruits" (Kakutani 2005) it produced for hijacking on 9/11.

One book, Yaroslav Trofimov's *Faith at War: A Journey on the Frontlines of Islam* (2005) delivered the "bad news"—that is, "bad" to American readers—that "the United States is regarded, across large swaths of the Muslim world, with a mixture of suspicion and hatred that military action in Afghanistan and Iraq has fanned to a white hot intensity. Moderate Muslim voices are being drowned out by the screaming of fanatics." Trofimov found virulent anti-Semitism and "blood-thirsty ideas" among Middle East Muslims of "well-to-do and privileged" classes who had "some experience with the West" (Grimes 2005b; see also Caputo 2005). A *Times* op-ed added that more than half of "terrorists had either attended college or had received a college degree" (Bergen and Pandey 2005).

It was not clear whether it was good news to Western readers or not that "the jihad is a civil war" in which the West is "only a bystander" (Grimes 2005a). To see the contemporary contention within Islam as, in William Grimes's words, a "centuries-long struggle between traditionalists and rationalists," as Reza Aslan does in his book *No God but God* (2005), and not as "a monumental struggle between fundamentalist Islam and modern secular democracy," as Samuel P. Huntington did, seemed not to reduce the threat of conflagration beyond Islam's borders. "The war within Islam" (Rodenbeck 2005) was a matter of international concern. Thomas L. Friedman (2005e) saw for Islam a choice between "a culture of life or death," with significant ramifications for the West as well as for Muslim societies.

Amidst "factional unrest" (Eckholm 2005b, 2005d; Filkins 2005d), "suicide attacks" (Eckholm 2005c; cf. Pape 2005), as well as kidnappings and other forms of violence (Gettleman 2005) by a Muslim "insurgency" (Gettleman and Wong 2005), Iraqis voted on their constitution in February 2005. In a setting of evolving religiopolitics, the *Times* expressed hope and concern about the possibility for a "secular" (Filkins 2005b, 2005e) Iraqi government led by Shiites (Burns and Glanz 2005; Wong 2005e; Wong 2005f; Wong 2005k) and dreaded or merely tolerated by many Sunnis (Glanz 2005b; cf. Tavernise 2005d). The constitutional election— perhaps proof that "Allah and democracy can get along fine" (Hiro 2005; see also Feldman 2005a and Ibrahim 2005); perhaps a suggestion that there is "a world of ways to say 'Islamic Law'" (Rohde 2005b); perhaps a cause to give a Nobel Peace Prize to Grand Ayatollah Ali al-Sistani (Friedman 2005b); or perhaps a cause of concern to "secular Iraqis" (Filkins 2005c)—by no means closed the story of religion in conflict in Iraq (Burns 2005; Filkins 2005a; Filkins and Glanz 2005; Filkins and Worth 2005; C. Smith 2005a; L. Smith 2005; Tavernise 2005a, 2005b, 2005c; Tavernise and Oppel 2005; Wong 2005a, 2005c, 2005d, 2005h, 2005i, 2005j; Worth 2005a, 2005b, 2005c, 2005d, 2005e, 2005f, 2005h, 2005i, 2005j; and others).

Upon reflection, Erik Eckholm (2007b) says of the religious dimensions to the Iraq War: "I guess it was a given that religious sectarianism was involved in so much of the violence and politics but the true religious aspect, in my brief exposure, seemed pretty secondary to issues of politics, class and power." During "my two periods there in late 2004 and early 2005," he writes, "I was very struck by the support the Shiite lower classes had for Moktada al-Sadr and their resentment of more upper crust Shiite groups as well as Sunnis." Despite writing about "Sunni extremists" in Iraq and acknowledging the overall importance of Islam there, Eckholm (2007a) found religion to be less exclusively a motivating force in Iraq than in South Asia: "I didn't get the feeling of Islamic extremism the way one can see it in Pakistan," with its "violent fundamentalists."

Iraq's contention between Shiites and Sunnis had an impact on other Muslim lands, such as Saudi Arabia (MacFarquhar 2005c), which experienced a "push toward reform" (MacFarquhar 2005b) from writers, educators, and even theologians moved by post-9/11 realizations. In Jordan, religious leaders and curriculum planners aimed to "tone down the Islamic bombast in textbooks" (Fattah 2005c), but they encountered resistance. The Mideast sometimes witnessed reprisals against these reformers as well as faltering coalitions between Christians and Muslims, especially in Lebanon ("Anti-Syrian Christians in Lebanon" 2005; Kifner 2005a).

The *Times* seemed not to tire of memoirs (De Bellaigue 2005; Kakutani 2005b; Riding 2005b), news items (Glanz 2005a; MacFarquhar 2005a; Masood 2005a; Wong 2005b, 2005g; Worth 2005g), and op-eds (Rushdie 2005) concerning Muslim women thirsting to be free of religious restraint in their homelands. Canada's Irshad Manji continued to receive commendation for her "courageous book" *The Trouble with Islam Today* (2005a), which called for "a reformation of Islam" (Friedman 2005a). Ayaan Hirsi Ali's protection "from jihad death threats" in the Netherlands (Simons 2005a) still made international news concerning this "feminist," "legislator-apostate," and "daughter of the Enlightenment" (C. Caldwell 2005). Closer to home, Dr. Amina Wadud, a member of "a 'progressive Muslim' movement" in the United States (Elliott 2005e, 2005j) determined to lead public Islamic prayers in order to end the "second-class status" of women in Islam.

Islam's negative associations were exacerbated, to say the least, on July 7, 2005, when "jihadist militants" (Bergen 2005b) attacked the London underground—the British version of America's 9/11—leading Peter Bergen (2005b) to write in a *Times* op-ed of "a grim truth . . . : one of the greatest terrorist threats to the United States emanates not from domestic sleeper cells or, as is popularly imagined, from the graduates of Middle Eastern madrassas, but from some of the citizens of its closest ally, Britain." The deadly bombings raised yet again the specter of a "jihadist cancer" (Friedman 2005f) and "cult of death" (Friedman 2005d), now festering amidst Europe's democratic institutions.

A *Times* op-ed by French scholar Olivier Roy (2005) explicated the European Islamist phenomenon at hand, refusing to see it in purely religious terms or as a direct response to British policy in Iraq: "The Western-based Islamic terrorists are not the militant vanguard of the Muslim community; they are a lost generation, unmoored from traditional societies and cultures, frustrated by a Western society that does not meet their expectations. And their vision of a global ummah is both a mirror of and a form of revenge against the globalization that has made them what they are." Whatever the explanation, however, Roy's *Times* article highlighted the idea that "the terrorists' only true cause is global Islamic dominion." (See also David Brooks August 4, 2005, column for his reiteration of Olivier Roy's argument.)

While England's Muslim leaders tried to demonstrate their patriotic loyalty and deflect retaliatory acts against British Muslims (Cowell 2005a; Cowell and Van Natta 2005; Fattah 2005b, 2005f; C. Smith 2005e), investigators tried to tie together the threads and threats of Islamist terrorism in Britain and beyond (Alvarez 2005b; Sciolino and Van Natta 2005). "Revenge attacks and vandalism" (Alvarez 2005c) struck Muslim properties and persons in the bombing aftermath, and the "fringe of Britain's Muslims" (Fattah 2005a) burned with resentment and threat (Fattah 2005d; Mekhennet and Van Natta 2005; Waldman 2005)—some of which had already shaped the zealous bombers' motives on July 7 (Rohde and Khan 2005).

"Seeking moderate support" (Cowell 2005c), British prime minister Tony Blair tried to rally Muslim leaders to accept his plan to shut down mosques and organizations and deport imams and others who appeared to support Islamic violence in England (Lyall 2005a). Muslim groups, however, "condemned" the plan as "discriminatory" (Cowell 2005b; see also Van Natta and Mekhennet 2005), even as the Canadian Muslim Irshad Manji (2005b) wondered in a *Times* op-ed why the prime minister was required to "tolerate the hate" in his nation's midst. Several *Times* reporters (R. Bernstein et al. 2005) tried to parse a rhetorical path for England and other Western countries to distinguish between free speech and terrorism.

As the English reacted to homegrown Muslim terrorism and European Muslims rankled under "increased scrutiny" (Rosenthal 2005b) and "alienation . . . cultural, historical and above all religious, as much if not more than it is political" (Rieff 2005a), the Dutch were faced with the grisly details and theological justifications made palpable at the trial of Muhammad Bouyeri, Theo van Gogh's killer (Crouch 2005b), who vowed that "he would do it all over again if given the chance" (Crouch 2005a).

A poll of Muslims in Islamic lands suggested a shrinkage in support for "extremism" and violence" (R. Bernstein 2005a); an Australian Muslim organization urged its clerics to "preach moderation and speak out against terrorism and violence" (Bonner 2005); Dutch mosques "adopted a code of conduct to fight radicalism" (Tagliabue 2005b); and North American Muslim scholars produced a fatwa "to end extremism" in Muslim ranks (Goodstein 2005a). American Muslim leaders were now vocal about the need to "confront" the threat of religiously inspired violence "within Islam" and to "persuade American Muslims—especially the young—to beware of preachers peddling extremism and terrorism" (Goodstein 2005c). However, Muslims seemed solidly, perhaps increasingly, hostile to Western attempts to reform and "modernize" them (Dowd 2005a), especially when such attempts came in the guise of "public diplomacy" (Goodstein 2005b).

Not all images of Muslims focused on conflict. Pilgrimage to Mecca provided an opportunity to represent the "cosmopolitan" aspect of Islam (Fattah 2005e; "The Muslim World Gathers in Mecca" 2005). Id al-Adha exemplified the Muslim spirit of "sacrifice and celebration" ("Sacrifice" 2005). Sufis were sometimes held up as exemplars of Muslim "tolerance" and the "purely spiritual dimension of Islam" (Estrin 2005; Jefferson 2005; Martin 2005). In one *Times* feature from Iran, some Muslims were humanized amidst the "austerity of Islam" for their "yen for chic . . . clerical dress" (Fathi 2005). Another feature heralded a twenty-million-dollar "Islamic wing" to house art at the Louvre, funded by a Saudi prince (Tagliabue 2005). And yet another recalled an architectural "jewel of medieval Islam" in Spain (McLean 2005). A third raved about a "groundbreaking exhibition" in Barcelona—an explicit attempt to counteract "clash of civilization" rhetoric in the post-9/11 world—about Muslim "voyagers" (i.e., conquerors) in medieval Iberia (Riding 2005c).

Portraits of American Muslims still emphasized the "spiritual" aspects of a "far-flung culture" fitting into US societal patterns (Elliott 2005f). One television series, *Sleeper Cell,* featured a "practicing Muslim as a hero seeking to check the intentions of terrorists" (Steinberg 2005). (What about a series featuring "wacky terrorists" like the kooky Nazis of *Hogan's Heroes?* Not yet, the *Times* remarked [Halbfinger 2005]. Wait twenty years.)

But the view was more often of Christians and Muslims vying for converts and control around the world (Loewenberg 2005; Rohde 2005a) and of Jews and Muslims in mutual recriminations about Palestine, anti-Semitism, and the Holocaust (Arenson 2005; Eden 2005; Glaberson 2005b; "Palestinians Remove Hate Text" 2005; C. Smith 2005b). The Roman Catholic hierarchy under Benedict XVI puzzled over its relationship with Islam (Fisher 2005b; see also Rosenthal 2005) and made overtures to Muslim spiritual leaders (Fisher 2005c; "Pope Says Terror Mustn't Hurt Faiths' Ties" 2005), but it remained unclear whether Islam would be a "rival or [a] partner" with Christianity (Riding 2005)—shades of the Crusades? (See also Dargis 2005.)

Even in the United States, Muslims seemed sometimes at bitter odds with their non-Muslim neighbors, especially when they carried mutual resentments from the Old World. A murder of Coptic Christians in Jersey City set off rancorous accusations against Muslims of Egyptian heritage (Elliott 2005b, 2005h), who, it turned out, were innocent of the charges (McFadden and Holl 2005).

The *Times* continued to report on allegations, convictions, and intimations of innocence of Muslim Americans in a suspicious post-9/11 era of bias and discrimination against them (Abdrabboh 2005; N. Bernstein 2005; Broder 2005; Dao 2005; Dao and Lichtblau 2005; Glaberson 2005a, 2005c; Lichtblau 2005b; Lichtblau 2005c; C. Marshall 2005a, 2005b; Picker 2005; "Soldier Convicted in Deadly Attack" 2005; Worth 2005k). The paper increasingly paid attention to Muslim complaints and lawsuits regarding purportively abusive and discriminatory treatment by the Department of Homeland Security, the FBI, and other officials (Elliott 2005a, 2005c, 2005d, 2005i, 2005k; Elliott and Rashbaum 2005), above all at Guantánamo Bay (R. Bernstein 2005b) and Abu Ghraib prisons. One *Times* feature focused on a "strikingly bold" group of Muslim activists in Queens, the Islamic Thinkers Society, strongly opposed to American policies, both domestic and foreign (Elliott 2005g).

Although beyond the temporal scope of this study, Andrea Elliott's three-part series "An Imam in America" (Elliott 2006b, 2006c, 2006d; see also Elliott 2007) proved to be one of the *Times*' most searching looks into the post-9/11 lives of Muslims in America, and it won her paper the Pulitzer Prize for feature writing. *Times* reporter Joseph Berger (2007) remarks that

> 9/11 forced *The Times* to focus more energy, manpower and front-page space on the growing Muslim community in New York and the United States. That was the inspiration for Andrea Elliott's Pulitzer-winning series on the imam as well as other pieces by Laurie Goodstein and others. . . . By contrast, when I covered religion in the mid-1980s, I did only a handful of pieces on Muslim life in the city. . . . Until 9/11 we lamentably did too little on revealing and reporting on the lives of Muslims in our midst, and I'm sure broader pieces that may reflect on the wide variety of observance or non-observance among Muslims from many different nations here would be welcome as well.

He adds, "I'm sure the variety can more than match that of Jews and Christians."

In 2005, University of Colorado professor Ward Churchill's infamous essay—written immediately following the 9/11 attacks—created a furor ("Colorado: Professor Offers Explanation" 2005; Healy 2005b; Johnson 2005; York 2005b, 2005c) when the public realized that he had questioned the innocence of the World Trade Center victims. His published comments—comparing the World Trade Center "technocrats" to Nazi functionaries such as Adolph Eichmann—outraged many, causing his lecture at Hamilton College in upstate New York to be cancelled in February 2005 because of threats of violence there and calling his own tenure at Colorado into question. The Colorado House of Representatives composed a public document declaring the World Trade Center victims to be "'innocent in every sense of the word and should always be remembered as innocent'" (York 2005a).

Perhaps, a *Times* reporter suggested, "subjects like Sept. 11 have become 'sacred,' and cordoned off from impopular analysis" (Johnson 2005). Or perhaps the halo of innocence was an expression of the "beloved" status of those killed on 9/11 (Collins 2005). Whereas families of the victims tried to "put a human face" on the several thousands who died that day to shame terrorists around the world, Churchill refused to back down from his contention that "Sept. 11th was a natural and inevitable response to what the U.S. is doing in the world. . . . The United States," he said, "has no right to bomb innocent populations" (quoted in Collins 2005). Defining innocence seemed as important as defining terrorism in the post-9/11 *Times,* both terms serving as factors in a moral equation. Significantly, the Pentagon—also attacked on 9/11 as the symbol of American military might, corresponding to the World Trade Center's significance to economic power—seemed to be left out of the discussion of innocence. Daniel Okrent (2005c) defined "terrorism" as "an act of political violence committed against purely civilian targets . . . ; attacks on military targets are not."

If Americans were largely convinced about their own innocence before and in 9/11, they were gravely concerned about their morality in fighting the post-9/11 wars in Afghanistan and Iraq. The mistreatment of Muslim prisoners at Guantánamo and Abu Ghraib prisons, it was charged ("Ex-G.I. Writes about Interrogation Tactics" 2005), made especial effort to offend Islamic spirituality and sensibilities regarding sexual pollution, on the one hand, and Koranic sacrality, on the other. "Are we losing our soul?" Maureen Dowd (2005b) asked in her column regarding the "toxic combination of sex and religion" used "to break Muslim detainees."

If Americans were concerned about US military behavior, all the more were Muslims—in Afghanistan first, but then throughout the worldwide Islamic community—as they heard of reports (first carried in *Newsweek*) of offensive

treatment of the Koran by American troops (Gall 2005b). Riots led to deaths following the news—perhaps mistaken and later retracted, much to the detriment
of the news media's "credibility" (Healy 2005a)—that US soldiers engaged in pur-
posive "desecration" by flushing a Koran down a toilet (Bumiller 2005; Seelye
2005a, 2005b; Seelye and Lewis 2005). Thomas L. Friedman (2005c) reminded
readers—especially Muslims—that "jihadists" had engaged in "desecration" far
worse than the putative flushing of a Koran. Think "mass murders" and "dis-
memberment of real Muslims by other Muslims," he said.

Friedman did not excuse the United States for its alleged abuse of an Islamic
sacred symbol, though. Even if he had, the Muslim world was not about to forget
or forgive. The *Times* remarked that Guantánamo Bay had "come to symbolize
the view of the U.S. for many Muslims," noting the irony that a "champion of
rights" was "accused of torture" and now "desecrations" (Sengupta and Masood
2005b). It did not help US credibility when documents cited "abuse" of the Koran
in "repeated complaints" by Guantánamo prisoners (N. Lewis 2005), subsequently confirmed by an American military inquiry (Shanker 2005). Although
no "'credible evidence'" surfaced regarding the Koran's having been flushed
down a toilet, the overall "mishandling" of the Holy Book (Masood 2005c; see
also Schmitt 2005) ignited further Muslim protests worldwide and similar accusations within the United States (Lichtblau 2005a).

Americans and especially New Yorkers continued to grapple with increas-
ingly contentious questions about Ground Zero's future (see Kakutani 2005a; C.
Risen 2005). Plans for "a museum on sacred ground," an International Freedom
Center, described as "a temple of contemplation and conflict" at Ground Zero
(Ouroussoff 2005b), ran into trouble with critics on all sides of the political spectrum. Some suggested, according to Patrick Healy (2005c), that the center was "a
jingoistic propaganda tool," lacking "a sense of humility." Others, such as New
York's Governor George E. Pataki, refused to consider any future programming
at the Freedom Center, which "could offend 9/11 families and pilgrims to a proposed memorial nearby." In this story by Frank Rich (2005), Pataki was quoted
as saying, "I view that memorial site as sacred grounds," akin to the beaches of
Normandy or Pearl Harbor, "and we will not tolerate anything on that site that
denigrates America, denigrates New York or freedom, or denigrates the sacrifice or courage that the heroes showed on Sept. 11." The governor's "ultimatum
drew criticism from some arts groups and Democratic critics," who found his

preemptive "'censorship'" both "'inappropriate'" and "'anti-American.'" Pataki held firm, however, that there could not be complete "freedom of expression at the Freedom Center." In the struggle over Ground Zero's future—"pure unadulterated farce," according to Rich—the zone remained "a pit, a hole, a void."

A "small group of family members" of World Trade Center 9/11 victims ("Keeping Ground Zero Free" 2005), supported by municipal firefighters ("Manhattan: Firefighters Enter 9/11 Fray" 2005), tried to "preserve sacred ground" ("Fight Against Freedom Center" 2005) by lobbying against the Freedom Center. A *Times* editorial in favor of the center initiated a round of letters ("The Real Meaning of Ground Zero" 2005) and at least one personal feature pondering the "real meaning," the "underlying meaning," of Ground Zero (Finn 2005). Governor Pataki eventually barred the Freedom Center from the "sacred precinct" at Ground Zero (Dunlap 2005d), to the dismay of *Times* commentators (Dunlap 2005b; Pogrebin 2005).

Across the street from Ground Zero at St. Paul's Chapel, an artist installed his re-creation of a sycamore tree that fell in the churchyard under the blast of the World Trade Center's collapse. St. Paul's rector allowed the installation, regarding the sculpture as "a powerful cynosure, embodying religious sentiment without being an overtly religious symbol." Four years after 9/11, Trinity Church and St. Paul's were still receiving close to two million visitors a year, "many on pilgrimage to ground zero." They were determined to keep the memory of 9/11 alive (R. Kennedy 2005).

Religious symbols continued to weigh in the 9/11 memory. The *Times* ran a photo of the cruciform steel column that towered over the World Trade Center ruins ("At the Ruins Beneath Ground Zero" 2005). The oral history of New York's 9/11 still emphasized "faith" as well as "fear" (O'Donnell 2005b). Families still in grief over the loss of their loved ones in the World Trade Center sued New York City to preserve their remains in a "dignified burial site" (O'Donnell 2005a). One still encountered the language of spirituality—about "'sacred, hallowed ground'" at Ground Zero (Dunlap 2005c; see also Dunlap 2005e). And yet most of the *Times* articles about Ground Zero four years after the attacks lacked a religious dimension, leaning instead toward politics, architecture, psychology, and city planning (e.g., Dunlap 2005a, 2005d; Ouroussoff 2005a).

Four years after: 9/11 was still "a day no one can forget"; however, it seemed to have lost its encompassing emotional sacrality. "Immediately after the attacks," a *Times* reporter wrote, "politicians insisted that life should, wherever and whenever possible, return to normal. . . . But now," she continued, "it's hard to find any practical difference between bravely returning to normal and simply ignoring the day." The *Times* chided the Fox network for scheduling season premiers for football and cartoon comedies on 9/11. "'I didn't make any connection' to the terrorist attacks," said the Fox scheduler. 'People laugh, people cry, life goes on,' he said, speaking from Los Angeles." A Fox publicist, organizing a "premiere party near ground zero," seemed unconcerned about "offending anyone who might be observing Sept. 11. 'Literally no one's even brought that up, I'm not kidding you,' she said." So, the question in the *Times* seemed to be: "9/11: Light a candle or party on?" (Kantor 2005).

American representatives overseas were advised—by Bush administration undersecretary of state Karen P. Hughes, in charge of "'public diplomacy'"—to mark September 11, 2005, with a "'humble'" observance, perhaps by attending "interfaith services on that date. . . . 'This is not just about us,'" she observed (Weisman 2005).

And on the fourth anniversary, whose painted visage adorned the front cover of the *New York Times Magazine?* Osama bin Laden, his Christ-like, Semitic features framed by white turban and robe, his eyes fixed on the viewer, his lips pursed, as if to speak. "Seldom has an image so clearly marked the turning of the world," wrote Professor Mark Danner (2005), not about bin Laden's face, but rather about his handiwork, the "demise of the World Trade Center." That act—called by a contemporary composer "the greatest work of art in the history of the cosmos"—"was meant to serve, among other things, as a recruiting poster for jihad." Its agents were death-defying performance artists and also international, revolutionary propagandists who shifted history from the atomic age to an epoch of terrorism. This axial event, Danner wrote, had produced spiritual eruptions, expectations of apocalypse, expressions of moral clarity, claims of innocence, and mutual incriminations of evil. In the struggle that ensued, 9/11 occupied central space in American collective memory; policies were justified in its name, and meaning was measured by its scale. It seemed conceivable "four years on" that the ideological, faith-based war ignited by the events of 9/11 was proceeding as bin Laden hoped and planned.

And by the fifth anniversary? Amidst popular and documentary films, books, and memorials of a now historical 9/11, the *Times* continued to characterize "the plot against America" as "Islamic militancy" and "antimodernity" (Filkins 2006)—employing the tropes of moderatism and modernism to comprehend the religious motives that culminated in 9/11. The "modern Pietà" of Reverend Mychal Judge—the "Saint of 9/11"—was again recycled on film and in the *Times* as the icon of "religious devotion" in responding to the World Trade Center attacks (Holden 2006).

Indeed, places in New York City associated with Judge—in life and death— had already taken on the feel of reliquaries. According to David W. Dunlap (2004c), the Church of St. Francis of Assisi was now renowned as the "spiritual home to the Rev. Mychal F. Judge, . . . the fire Department chaplain who was officially the first casualty of the attack on September 11, 2001. The image of his ashen body being carried from the World Trade Center was one of the most powerful expressions of the human toll that day" (204). His corpse "was brought to St. Peter's [Church] by firefighters on September 11, 2001, and laid before the altar" (242), providing that church with a claim to spiritual fame.

Sacred spaces abounded, yet New York City was still waiting for action to formalize commemoration of that "'hole in the ground'" at Ground Zero, considered "'sacred'" by "people who assign theological significance to a devastation wrought by killers guided by religious motivations of their own" (Haberman 2006a). The steel cruciform icon still cast its shadow over the Ground Zero neighborhood (Konigsberg 2006), while dust of World Trade Center human remains lay in "'limbo'": in "climate-controlled, walk-in containers" under a tent on Manhattan's east side, next to an "altar-like fountain" and "a luminous, tranquil chapel where victims' relatives can gather privately to mourn" (Dunlap 2006b).

Under the title "Echoes of 9/11 Define Life 5 Years Later," the *Times* commemorated the 2001 attacks by reflecting on a Chicago Muslim woman who insisted on wearing a head scarf in the face of "religious bias," vowing, "I will never take it off again" (MacFarquhar 2006). Another Muslim woman, recently settled in Brooklyn from her native Pakistan, part of a growing emigration, took her scarf off five days after arriving. "I came to the United States because I want to improve myself," she said, describing her new way of thinking. "This is a second birth for me" (Elliott 2006a).

At the fifth anniversary, the *Times* reflected on "ways to avoid the next 9/11," including "an agenda of opportunity for the Islamic world," "giving Muslims hope" (Kean and Hamilton 2006). It may be impossible to "kill an ideology"

(Mahle 2006) epitomized by Al Qaeda; however, it is necessary to "keep American Muslims on our side" (Stern 2006).

On September 11, 2006, the *Times* focused on that momentous day more fully than it had since September 2001. Under the headline "Sept. 11, 2001–2006: Portraits of Grief," the paper revisited the lives of 9/11 mourners, some of whom emphasized the sustaining role of religion in their lives. One said, "If I didn't believe in God I wouldn't be here, I'd be in a mental home someplace." Another declared, "I remember Mohamed Atta in my prayers. Not because I condone what he has done. Not that I accept what he has done. But if I am to heal, I cannot let hate poison me" ("Revisiting the Families" 2006).

On September 11, 2006, as five years earlier, New York City's clergy "were being asked again to shoulder much of the burden for making sense of the tragedy and offering consolation" (Luo 2006)—although the arts, such as Mozart's Requiem, sung by thousands at Carnegie Hall, also provided "solace and catharsis" (Wakin 2006). On this "ritualistic, commemorative" occasion (Wakin 2007), perhaps not solely "religious" per se, but eliciting the human spirit at a singular moment, New Yorkers testified to their emotions. "I felt the need to experience community," said one participant. "Art heals. Sharing art has even a larger capacity to heal." Another added, "It is the Mass for the dead, and I feel it brings peace to our lives" (Wakin 2006).

Religion, seen in the *Times* as the root cause of 9/11, was also perceived as its most irenic, effective response. During the High Holy Days—the Days of Awe, as they are called—the *Times* recited the "redemptive" account of a Jewish couple who honored their son, killed in the north tower of the World Trade Center on 9/11, by establishing the Peter C. Alderman Foundation to help other victims of violence (Applebome 2006b). In his "Beliefs" column, Peter Steinfels (2006) quoted an Anglican divine, who in turn cited an Israeli rabbi who said he had learned from the Bible that "God tells Moses to take off his shoes in the divine presence," meaning that "we couldn't meet God if we were protected against the uneven and unyielding and perhaps stony or thorny ground." With this in mind, he said, "'Those who are responsible for violence of any kind, even when they think it is in a just cause, need to take off their shoes and recognize what it is like when flesh and blood are hurt. Terrorism,' he concluded, 'is the absolute negation of any such recognition,' and what will defeat terrorism in the end 'is "taking off our shoes," coming to terms with what we share as mortal beings who have immortal value.'"

Almost ten years have come and gone since 9/11 (cf. Kleinfeld 2007). Osama bin Laden's demise has not reduced his shadowy import for the past decade. Violence persists in Iraq, Afghanistan, and Pakistan, and still between Israelis and Palestinians. In the United States, cultural and political skirmishes erupt over the placement of mosques and the investigations of Muslim plots, real and imagined. The *Times* continues its coverage of these ongoing stories. To comprehend what we have learned about religion through the *Times* treatment of 9/11 and its aftermath is to be reduced, finally, to quoting headlines in a tale seemingly without end. Perhaps the story has become all too familiar, its angles all too articulated.

Readers might say the same of this book. Did you already know all that I have told you here? Why is that? It is probably because your worldview—not just your familiarity with the news, but your sense of contemporary reality—is shaped largely by the *New York Times*. I know that mine is.

It is time to close, knowing, however, that no matter when I finish, I might rightly end the book with the copywriter's notation to signal a continuing story: (MORE).

Epilogue

For five years, the events of 9/11 made religion front-page news almost on a daily basis. Even a decade after 9/11, the mass of religion reportage and commentary in the *Times'* 9/12 world looms large, and for good reason. Religion is now important—a motivating factor worldwide for good and ill—and the *Times* recognizes that fact.

One might assert that the *Times* was an artifact of the secularization movement of the mid–twentieth century (see Huntington 1997:95). One might even posit that the *Times* has been a causative agent of American secularism. True or not, one can ask, What has the paper's response been to the religious resurgence of the twenty-first century? The editors have already begun to take religion more seriously. Religion reporters have been hired, religion reports expanded. Has the *Times* found itself out of step with the changing times—ironic for an institution that regards itself as an engine of modernity, not only a carrier of news, but *news itself*—and is its management trying to catch up to change? If the current is toward religiosity, the *Times* must perforce keep up with the times and document what is happening and report what the public wants to observe. "Many voices at the *Times* are secular," says former *Times* religion editor Kenneth A. Briggs (2007), but now there are many voices that sound of appreciation for piety.

What does *Times* religion coverage look like in the decade following 9/11? On the day I copyread this epilogue for publication, April 12, 2011, the *Times* published nine substantial religion articles, from front page to editorial page, from foreign, national, and metropolitan sections to the pages of the "Science Times," with perspectives on Christianity, Judaism, Hinduism, Islam, civil religion in the United States, Europe, and Africa, theology, gender, meditation, ethics, ritual, personal life, politics, and the law—a full panoply of coverage and opinion.

According to Laurie Goodstein (2004b), the *Times* still tends to emphasize majority religions in the United States, such as Christianity, Roman Catholicism in particular. There are so many religious "miniworlds" even in the United States—Jews, Buddhists, Muslims, Mormons, and so on—and the paper has to look at each group's "numbers." The two largest religious groups are evangelicals, including the Southern Baptists, and Roman Catholics. Thus, they get the most coverage. Even though the paper does not consider "denominational" data—institutional structures, codes, hierarchies, and doctrines, the kind of stories that might appear in press releases from organizational bodies—to be newsworthy in and of themselves, the best-known churches still receive the bulk of coverage.

A graduate of the University of California at Berkeley and the Columbia Graduate School of Journalism, Goodstein was a repeat winner of both the Templeton Religion Reporter of the Year Award and the Supple Religion Writing Award before joining the *Times* staff. She (2004b) says that when she came to the *Times,* she was eager to focus on "grassroots" religion—"how people live their faith." She wanted to cover "folks" in the "living room" rather than officials in the church or the synagogue, personal religiosity—both "practices" and "doctrines"—rather than organizational arrangements. For instance, she enjoyed her report on young evangelical Christians in their redefinition of dating (Goodstein 2001l).

In general, however, she has been charged with covering more institutional matters rather than idiosyncratic spiritual "seekers." Denominations and religious agencies with political agendas have been vitally engaged with the sociocultural issues of the day (e.g., ethical concerns regarding sexuality, abortion, war, and peace), and these issues have been deemed more newsworthy than individual spirituality. The attacks of September 11, 2001, raised opportunities to investigate Islam in its many dimensions; however, the emphasis had to be placed on public religion and institutional responses to the 9/11 crisis. *Times* executive editor Howell Raines determined that his staff would cover 9/11 by flooding the paper with stories of public interest. For months, Goodstein had little or no time to pursue her "living room" angles, except insofar as they related to 9/11. Then the Catholic sexual abuse story in 2002—also covered by Raines's flooding technique—"forced" her to cover Roman Catholicism as an institution (Goodstein 2004b).

Goodstein had no question about the importance of the 9/11 and Catholic sex scandal stories. Her point is that a paper of the *Times'* size should have more reporters with a direct concern for religion—both breaking stories and the more "grassroots" phenomena. Peter Steinfels (2005b) remarks that the *Times,* "this *sui generis* institution," has so much more wherewithal than other papers—not just money, but smart, worldly editors, fact checkers, stringers, and so on, all of whom can be helpful in highlighting religion in the news. And, as he pointed out a decade earlier, "contrary to the assumption in some religious circles, there is very little hostility to religion and a good deal of respect for religion today, at least for the fact that Americans are overwhelmingly religious" (Steinfels 1993a:4). Steinfels and Goodstein think, however, that the *Times* can use far more religion coverage—meaning more personnel devoted primarily or exclusively to religious dimensions of contemporary life. It would take a staff of ten, Goodstein says (2004b), to report on all the major religious groups in the United States, not to mention in the world.

Goodstein does not recommend that the *Times* hire an expert on the world's religions. As it is, international coverage is by nation, not by topic. Thus, the Rome correspondent reports on everything in the region, including news from the Vatican. The New Delhi correspondent writes about religion as well as about politics, culture, and other aspects of life in India. Goodstein thinks that this is how it should be. She cannot picture someone reporting on Roman Catholic matters in the Vatican and then traveling to India to cover developments in Hinduism and then on to another country, another religion. In her mind, religions are best covered regionally in their national contexts.

In 2004, however, Goodstein was only one of two full-time religion writers at the *Times,* she on the national desk and Daniel J. Wakin on the metro. (Wakin subsequently moved to another beat, although he has received an occasional call to explicate Catholicism.) In 2004, Gustav Niebuhr, who left the *Times* at the end of 2001, had not been replaced, even though there were many reporters who wanted his job and some who had interviewed for it. No decision had been made about his successor still in 2004, so Goodstein was covering two jobs, supplemented by Peter Steinfels's (now Mark Oppenheimer's) "Beliefs" column and by occasional "Religion" items penned by various scribes, including Samuel J. Freedman.

When asked about the decision-making "intelligence" at the *Times,* which defines religious news and determines what stories get covered, Goodstein (2004b) replied that there is "no central" gatekeeping intelligence making these choices. The newsroom, she says, is filled with so many people who are "that smart," and each of them is working individually to develop stories for tomorrow, next week, next month. "Everyone is coming up with ideas." It is "more decentralized than you would think." She herself always has ten stories she wants to get out at any one time, pieces that she regards as "edgy."

Although Goodstein develops many of her own pieces, her editors on the national desk also assign her stories to pursue. She remarks that hundreds of reporters work for the national desk. Most of them are situated around the country, whereas she works out of New York City, so she has an advantage of face-to-face contact with her editors—albeit in a single, cacophonous room a city block long and half a block wide, with hundreds of people at their desks, headphones on, typing, talking on their telephones—giving her an opportunity to sell her religion angles to them. She has praise for her "bosses," who usually listen to her ideas, and she appreciates the Sulzberger family, which makes the *Times* work so well by providing ample funds to support the operation.

At the same time, she remarks, the *Times* is "very hierarchical," like the "military." During Howell Raines's regime, the operation was particularly "top down," which irked many people, including Gustav Niebuhr (2001t), who preferred to leave the paper rather than submit to its authoritarianism. As Goodstein (2004b) tells it, the main editors determine, in the end, what fills the paper's pages, and then there are "layers in between" the editors and the reporters: subeditors with varying degrees of authority.

Within this framework, however, there is a great degree of individual autonomy—not only among the "stars," such as Peter Steinfels or Thomas L. Friedman, who write "pretty much what they want," but also for a religion reporter such as Goodstein. When asked if she consults with other writers at the *Times* who cover religion in their own ways—for example, Steinfels or Friedman or art critic Holland Cotter—Goodstein reports that has never spoken or communicated in any way with either Friedman or Cotter. She has had only minimal contact with *Times* religion writers of the recent past, such as Ari L. Goldman or Edward B. Fiske, and she was unaware that a present-day sports columnist, George Vecsey, had once covered the religion beat. Every so often she has conversed with Steinfels, but for the most part her work is untethered to other projects in religion. She did not know, for instance, that Frank Rich was working on a major analysis of the film *The Passion of the Christ* when she was writing her own story about it. This is an example, she says, of how "the right hand doesn't know what the left is doing at the *Times*." The paper is so big that coordination takes place primarily at the level of management rather than between one writer and another. To that point, in interviews two *Times* writers with strong interest in religion and admiration for Goodstein's work in print mispronounced her name; they clearly did not know her personally.

Alan Finder (2007), who has covered higher education for the *Times,* describes this indirect interaction in the case of a front-page article he wrote in 2006 on Baptist colleges. His editors asked Goodstein to check his text for fact and tone, and she made several suggestions for changes. He found this critique "a useful exercise" and would be "not at all" offended if they were to ask her again in a similar situation. Nonetheless, he notes that each reporter is "quasi-independent" in framing stories, and he did not consult Goodstein in composing a recent piece on religious ferment on several college campuses. "Perhaps I should have," he muses.

Like any newspaper, the *Times* is intent on printing a story before its competitors do. Religion, like any other beat, has breaking news, and the *Times* editors want to get out in front. Goodstein (2004b) describes her job in such situations as "flying by the seat of our pants," trying to beat a deadline in a state of "panic." She tells, for example, how she learned about the possible election of Episcopal Gene Robinson to the bishopric in New Hampshire, and so went there to cover the election, knowing that he was openly gay. The vote on Robinson gave her only a half-hour to file her report so that it could be run the next day. So she wrote most of the story before the vote—the background material of the later paragraphs— and had to sit in the church, amidst the voters, and write the lead in a very brief period of time. The only other reporters there were Anglicans (from England and from Africa), so she was able to scoop all the other American papers and on the front page. (On this story, see Goodstein 2003c, 2003d, 2003e.)

Goodstein makes it clear that the *Times* is capable these days of regarding religion as front-page news of breaking significance. Although she wishes for more colleagues at the paper to take on the complexity and diversity of religious developments, she is satisfied with the level and focus of *Times* religion coverage—even if she is carrying a heavy portion of the burden, with help in the "Religion Journal" from Samuel G. Freedman, Marek Fuchs, Eric Goldscheider, Michael Luo, Kate Zernike, Katie Zezima, and their successors. Does Goodstein think that *Times* religion reporters should possess greater expertise about religion and religions? She retorts, "I am a journalist," not an "expert on religion." For all her interest in religion and her extensive experience covering it, her training is in journalism, not in religious studies scholarship. "My work is anecdotal," she says, "and that is appropriate to journalistic treatment of religion."

John W. Fountain (2005b), a black Pentecostal who for three years was Midwest correspondent for the *Times* at the beginning of the twenty-first century, thinks that "newspapers do not do a good job" of covering religion. Papers such as the *Times,* he says, cover the "seasonal stuff," the "scandals," but they still seem surprised by the power of people's faith. The story of conservative Christian voters of 2004 "seemed to sneak up on people" in the media because the media were not prepared to take the phenomenon seriously.

In his years at several prominent newspapers, Fountain usually found his editors open to religion angles he proposed; nevertheless, journalism and religion seemed a world apart. He is sometimes asked, "How do you deal with being a journalist and also being religious?" He replies, "As long as I don't speak in tongues in the newsroom, I'm OK." Like other reporters, he refuses to separate his identity—as a man, a black man, a Chicagoan, an American, a father, and, yes, a Christian—from his profession. "I've never read an objective story in my life," he testifies, understanding that journalists invest themselves in the work they produce. "We strive to be fair," he adds, and in writing the truth, he says, he is able to proclaim his faith. Like McCandlish Phillips, whom he met at a World Journalism Institute meeting, Fountain thinks that journalism can be a means of "living your faith," and the *Times* can support that calling. But it is difficult for him to tell if religion is a high priority at the newspaper.

Before 9/11, Mark Silk (1999) wrote that "institutionally the *Times* is more ambivalent about religion than just about any other newspaper I know. The result these days is that they are happy to have two good people doing religion as a national beat, and happy to have pieces on religion internationally, but very gingerly about religion in NYC. This doubtless relates to longstanding issues at the *Times* about local coverage, but ends up giving the world a distorted upper-westside [*sic*] view of New York."

Silk notwithstanding, the *Times* has developed considerable coverage of religion in the nation as a whole as well as in New York. Goodstein (2004b) rejects the notion that the *Times* has a parochial perspective on religious diversity or a jaundiced view of particular religions. When faced with the charge that *Times'* reports on religions in distant lands (e.g., India) are "stereotypical" or "hackneyed" to anyone knowledgeable about these foreign faiths, she replies that any insider—a ballplayer, an arbitrager—will invariably find newspaper coverage of their specialization superficial. At the same time, however, everyday readers of the paper need foundational knowledge and background information about religions to which they are outsiders. She thinks the *Times* strikes the right balance in its treatment of various faiths and in its religion coverage between insiders and outsiders as well as among New York, the nation, and the world.

"I've hung out more with evangelicals than with Jews," Goodstein says about her job at the *Times*. And although she recognizes that she herself is not an evangelical—"I am who I am, a mother, a Californian, a Jew"—and she does not subscribe to the "myth of objectivity" in journalism, she feels that evangelicals, Catholics, Jews, Buddhists, Hindus, and Muslims get a fair shake at her paper. "There are evangelical Christians in our newsrooms," she notes. "Not lots" of them, but they do exist. She would like to see more Muslims writing for the *Times,* adding their perspectives to reportage and commentary about Islam. At the same time, she warns against "conflicts of interests" when a member of a particular religious denomination reports on that group. The *Times* allows Catholics to write about Catholicism, Jews about Judaism, and so forth, but the paper will not countenance a Jewish or Catholic correspondent with a sectarian axe to grind, nor will it allow a Muslim or an evangelical in its employ to play that role.

Goodstein does not claim that the *Times* always gets it right in its religion coverage. Its reports, its captions, its headlines sometimes lack sufficient nuance. It is especially difficult, she says, for the "very talented" copy editors—who write all the headlines—to capture the essence of every story to the writers' or their subjects' satisfaction. She refers to an article of hers whose headline read, "Dalai Lama Says Terror May Need a Violent Reply" (Goodstein 2003h). The Dalai Lama's followers backtracked after the story ran, saying that he would never condone violence; however, Goodstein stood by her story, saying that on two occasions the Dalai Lama refused to criticize the US war against Iraq, and he decidedly left open the possibility of justified war. Hence, the headline writer did not really get it wrong, even though Goodstein's story was slightly more nuanced than the headline suggested.

Goodstein vouches for the accuracy of her religion reports, even though it occasionally happens that her subjects deny what they have said. It is possible that she can misinterpret or misunderstand what her sources say to her; however, she records her interviews with care, taping some conversations, transcribing rapidly typed notes over the phone, and taking handwritten notes in person. Of course, mistakes happen, she acknowledges, and thus the need for the corrections page in the *Times*.

In her view, *Times* religion coverage is comprehensive, taking in religious dimensions of contemporary life in almost every section of the paper. In addition, the *Times* has a virtual religion page, almost every Saturday, with a "Beliefs" column, a set of "Religion Journal" entries, and extended coverage of religious ideas that have played during the week. The word *religion* does not appear in bold on the Saturday masthead, but the paper pays close attention to religious developments week by week.

One of Goodstein's closest colleagues at the *Times* has been Daniel J. Wakin, who came to the paper in 2000 and took a religion assignment on the metro desk in October 2001. Wakin had studied classics at Harvard. The son of an esteemed scholar of Islamic law and a prolific journalist and professor of communications and sociology, Wakin worked as a summer clerk for the AP during college. "I really took to journalism," he recalls; "I loved it" (Wakin 2007). As a result, he took a job with AP, serving in the Newark, New Jersey, bureau and as an editor on the "Foreign" desk, during which time he studied Arabic. From 1992 until 1998, Wakin served in Rome, where the Vatican was part of his beat. After two years in southern Africa, he became attractive to the *Times*. He hired on, first on the "Continuous News" desk, at the time the department that supplied the Web site with real-time news. Like other reporters, he worked on the metro desk (beginning in May 2001), a standard base of "deployment" for other fields, he says. In 2004, he left the religion beat to cover classical music.

Why religion? Wakin's father had published many books about religion—especially Roman Catholicism. His mother had introduced him to knowledge of Muslim thought, language, and practice. Nonetheless, he states, it was "completely a coincidence" that he should focus his journalistic skills on religious topics. His father was interested in Wakin's religion coverage, especially Catholicism; however, he did not try to influence his son's career directly. Rather, he says, when he was offered a religion beat among several opportunities at the *Times,* his parents' background "made the job seem attractive" (Wakin 2010)—and especially appropriate, he muses, in "the largest Jewish city in the world" (Wakin 2007) and "one of the largest concentrations of Catholics in the country and a vast number of other faiths" (Wakin 2010). After 9/11, he agreed with *Times* editors that "we needed to increase our coverage of Islam" (Wakin 2007). In 2002, he took on the priestly sex scandals in the American Catholic community, and with his knowledge of Italian and Vatican contexts he helped the *Times* record the papal conclave following the death of Pope John Paul II.

Did Wakin see himself as part of "a tradition of religion writers" at the *Times?* No, he was not conscious of walking "in the shoes" (Wakin 2007) of those who went before, such as Kenneth A. Briggs, George Vecsey, and Gustav Niebuhr. Nor did he pore over the "old news" about religion in the "morgue." "I was basically 'lazy,'" he avers, tongue in cheek, and rarely "went back" to old clippings, except when updating particular topics. In those cases, however, he "read old clips with gusto if they were necessary to researching a story. In fact," he writes (Wakin 2010), "reporters read them constantly to absorb the proper background." For Wakin, news is about today, for today's audiences, not a repetition of old themes, even while taking stock of long-term trends. As a religion reporter, he tried to write something fresh in each article, to go beyond the past. In addition, his fear of plagiarism—his compulsion "not to use the words" (Wakin 2007) already appearing in the paper—made him keep his distance from his predecessors' work, except when necessary.

However, "as a reader" of the *Times,* Wakin (2007) could imagine his place in the tradition of religion journalism; and as a colleague, he admired certain writers—such as Holland Cotter on art and religion—and he "felt confident seeking advice" from Laurie Goodstein. "We trusted in each other," he states; we "traded tips"; we "bounced ideas off each other"; he "filled in" for her as stories arose and "sometimes collaborated"—for instance, during the papal conclave in 2005.

With his own extensive experience and with Goodstein's help, Wakin felt confident during his several years as a *Times* religion writer. "I like to think I wrote some good articles about Islam," he says (2007), and "I think I wrote well about the Catholic Church," its "hierarchy," the Holy See, and the relationship between American Catholics and the Vatican.

Goodstein and Wakin were colleagues in religion coverage in the years following 9/11. Peter Steinfels, the author of the *Times* "Beliefs" column (487 of them, until coming to a close in 2010), was more remote from their daily reportage. Hailing from Chicago, this Catholic intellectual (of partial Jewish heritage, with childhood heroes such as Albert Camus, G. K. Chesterton, and Dorothy Day) attended Loyola University, then received an M.A. and a Ph.D. in European history from Columbia University. As a lad, he already had an abiding interest in journalism. He and his brother even started "a national family newspaper" (Steinfels 2005b), and in the 1960s he began his work in "higher journalism" at the Catholic periodical *Commonweal* and became its executive editor in the 1980s. In 1979, he wrote a book about the emerging neoconservative movement in America (Steinfels 1979). He also coedited a journal dealing with ethical issues in medicine and science and a book on death and dying.

The *Times* hired Steinfels in 1988 as senior religion correspondent in order to continue the liberal Catholic tradition carried on so ably by John Cogley in the 1960s, especially during the Second Vatican Council. Both had been *Commonweal* editors before coming to the *Times*. Arthur Gelb and Abe Rosenthal wanted another Cogley on the *Times* staff, although Steinfels wondered if what they really wanted was another great story like Vatican II, which Cogley had illuminated with such grace. When offered this position at the *Times*, Steinfels demurred at first, discouraged in part by Rosenthal's reputed manner of bossing reporters. Further courted, however, Steinfels finally signed on.

Until 1997, Steinfels served as religion reporter; since then, he has written the "Beliefs" column while teaching at Georgetown, Notre Dame, and other Catholic universities. He and his accomplished wife, Margaret O'Brien Steinfels (also executive of *Commonweal* for a time), are now codirectors of the Fordham Center on Religion and Culture, and he is the author of *A People Adrift: The Crisis of the Roman Catholic Church in America* (2003g).

In his column as well as in his book, Steinfels has used a theologically trained, Catholic "language of intellectual refinement" (Schmalzbauer 2002:174), emphasizing nuance, ambiguity, fine-grained distinctions, rejecting the polarities of left and right, avoiding authoritarian Catholicism but also secular liberalism. Steinfels wants journalists to avoid oversimplifications in writing about religion: the winner/loser categories that work so easily for politics and sports. He also wants to avoid those tired plot lines that derive from the Enlightenment's struggle with religious faith: conservative/liberal, orthodox/dissenter. He wants religion journalism at the *Times* and elsewhere to perceive the spectrum rather than the dichotomy in diverse religiousness.

As a reporter, Steinfels (2007) shares Laurie Goodstein's "disappointment" "in not being able to do as many 'living room' stories" as he might have wished. "Of the major goals I set for myself, my biggest failure was in reporting the religious life of 'ordinary' people, people whose religion had significant consequences in their daily lives although they were not among those who had made some dramatic commitment to an exceptional religious life." His work as a columnist has offered him different opportunities.

Above all, he has wanted his "Beliefs" column to be a place—as with venues for arts, music, sports, and so on—where people knowledgeable about a subject, in this case religion, can engage sophisticated topics with a specialized frame of reference. He thinks of "Beliefs" readers as people who already know what the Apostles' Creed is (alas, he is sometimes disappointed, and his copy editors urge him to define many religious references). Steinfels draws upon his religious background and training, although he cautions that "being religious is no protection against bias." Indeed, it brings potential biases of its own to reporting and commentary.

His column has been, for him, an arena for serious investigation of religion. He cites current scholarship about religion, presenting authors' ideas and crediting their books. He writes his essays not only with religious readers in mind, but also with a "secular" audience, such as the "editors on the editorial pages of the *Times*" (Steinfels 2005a), hoping to challenge their presuppositions, to provoke and inform them. Asked about the thesis that the *Times* constitutes a self-perpetuating news loop, with writers producing work to fulfill their editors' expectations, Steinfels disagrees. He says that even as a reporter he tended to produce copy that countered editors' proclivities, and rarely have his stories or columns been "spiked" by offended management gatekeepers.

It is a leitmotif voiced by *Times* spokespersons that the paper has long been vigilant in "maintaining the clear line of separation that exists between the News and Editorial departments" (Talese 1970:171; see also Garst 1945). Goodstein (2004b) replies to the right-wing assertion that liberal editorial policy dictates liberal news slants by stating that the *Times* maintains a "church–state separation" between editorials and news. "Honestly," she attests, "we reporters have nothing to do with the editorial writers." Steinfels (2005a) refers to the separation as a "Chinese wall," noting, "In all my years at the *Times* I never experienced any pressure from the editorial pages." *Times* public editor Daniel Okrent (2005a) has gone even further, in writing of the twelve hundred newsroom employees at the *Times*, "In 16 months, I haven't found a soul here who has ever experienced any pressure, or even endured a suggestion, to conform to the opinions expressed on the editorial page."

Okrent has avowed the truth of this universal assertion, telling cynics, "If you don't want to believe this, feel free to be wrong." At the same time, he has noted that the "line between news and opinion" was frequently crossed with personal license by columnists such as Peter Steinfels, Clyde Haberman, Edward Rothstein, and others—especially on the sports pages—whose task was "to report *and* explain" (italics in original). Their "freedom to mouth off" was often "distinguished by the typesetting convention of what's called ragged-right formatting," alerting readers to the "commentary" therein. But—to repeat—the *Times* continues to insist that reporters and commentators, including those who cover religion, are free of both editorial and management impingement. Their commitment is to reporting the truth, insofar as it can be reported.

"Journalism is obviously not a religion, and newsrooms are hardly cathedrals," writes Clyde Haberman (2006b) in a column about Abraham Rosenthal, who "fired" Haberman as City College campus correspondent for fabricating a minor detail. "But the concept of sin exists nonetheless. If there is a mortal sin, it is the willful publishing of an untruth. Sure, we get things wrong, but it is generally as the result of human fallibility, not deliberate transgression."

Mark Silk (2001b) opined that religion writers who have come to the *Times* from elsewhere—for example, Gustav Niebuhr from the *Atlanta Constitution* and the *Wall Street Journal* and Laurie Goodstein from the *Washington Post*—wrote better stuff at their earlier locations. He wondered if the *Times* has not provided a milieu conducive to the best in religion reporting. When Niebuhr left the *Times* in fall 2001, he was discouraged by a lack of management receptivity to innovations in religion reporting (Niebuhr 2001h). Niebuhr's religion colleagues observed that he seemed unable to "sell" (Steinfels 2005a) his religion stories to editors. Ignoring his overtures, the editors gave him the assignments they favored, perhaps missing his insights regarding religion news. Niebuhr ironically might have had more opportunity to develop his talents at the *Wall Street Journal,* a paper that, Steinfels (2007) comments, "felt much less obligation to give ongoing coverage to religion." There, Niebuhr "could spend weeks on what would be a page-one story," whereas at the *Times* he had daily duties to fulfill.

But does all this mean that the *Times* possesses an antireligion mindset? Some evangelical Christians think so, or at least they claim that *Times* opinion writers express a bias against their religion. "In such a media mindset," claims William David Sloan (2000), "it therefore does not surprise one to read a religion columnist for the *New York Times* declaring that Baptists, the largest Protestant group in the nation, are 'small-minded' and 'obstreperous'" (viii, source of quotations unverifiable; see also Sloan 2006). John McCandlish Phillips (2005)—for two decades a leading metro writer for the *Times,* until he quit in 1973—recently accused *Times* and *Washington Post* columnists of lavishing "fear and loathing" upon "my brethren, fellow evangelicals along with traditional Catholics," presenting them as theocrats on a "'jihad'" in "a ghastly arcade mirror" of reality. Phillips holds up Maureen Dowd, Frank Rich, and Paul Krugman as examples of bigotry against religion, but he implies that the newspaper at large—reporters and editors, as well as op-ed page writers—has animus toward Christian believers.

Phillips might have turned to other *Times* columnists, such as David Brooks and others, who share his concern about the opinions expressed on their own op-ed page. In doing so, however, Phillips might discover a greater diversity and balance in *Times* commentary than he claims exists. Nicholas D. Kristof (2003e), for instance, stated in his column "God, Satan, and the Media" that "there may be an element of messianic vision in the plan to invade Iraq and 'remake' the Middle East." However, he wrote, in the news business many people are "out of touch" with evangelical Christian messianic ideas, which are common in the United States. "Liberal critiques" of such ideas often take a "sneering tone about conservative Christianity itself," Kristof observed, concluding, "Such mockery of religious faith is inexcusable."

Can it be said accurately that the *Times*—in news articles as well as in commentary—takes a "sneering tone" about evangelical Protestantism, Catholicism, Orthodox Judaism, and Islam or about religion in general? I can say no more than that the jury is out about *Times* examination of these and other religious groups. Do I see evidence of a "sneering tone" in *Times* religion coverage? The occasional piece does have such a tone, particularly in regard to the politicized controversy over "intelligent design" creationism and especially outside of straight news coverage, but I have not detected the presence of this tone in general regarding religious dimensions of 9/11. Does the *New York Times* have a particular view or set of views about religion, part of its corporate perspective on the world? William E. Paden (1994) reminds us that all interpretations of "worlds"—including religious "worlds"—are also the product of "worlds" (58). So, one might argue, the *Times* analysis of religion comes from somewhere. It is shaped by a culture, and it inhabits and creates its own "world."

Like most mainstream journalism, the *Times* worldview is modernist and materialist in its appreciation of skeptical, rationalist, empirical, and scientific investigation. In treating supernaturalist claims, the *Times* is apt to quote visionaries about their experiences, balancing their testimonies with cautionary responses by others, without taking a side in the matter. But for assertions of supernatural powers—the magical, the exorcistic, the paranormal, the divinational, the miraculous, especially when scientific and medicinal prerogatives are impinged or usurped, *Times* writers frequently display a skepticism colored by contempt. The paper seems at times to share the methodological agnosticism of social sciences such as sociology. But is the *Times* hostile to religion as a whole? No, it is perhaps hostile only to certain claims of gnostic insight and power to manipulate supernatural efficacy in the material world.

The *Times* worldview assumes its readers to be rationalists like its own skeptical editors and reporters, who are amazed that there are people out there who believe in magic and miracle. Unlike the *Sun,* the *Examiner,* the *National Enquirer,* the *Weekly World News,* and other supermarket tabloids, the *Times* is not in the habit of headlines such as "Quick Test Tells If You're Going to Heaven or Hell!" or "Baby Born with Angel Wings" (quoted in Steinfels 1992).

And yet the *Times* sometimes expresses sympathy for "wonderment": belief in Santa Claus and Christmas, belief in journalism, belief in belief. In a skeptical age, in a skeptical city, in a skeptical newspaper, there is sometimes need to recall the "importance and difficulty of faith, hope and belief" (Applebome 2006a)—as the *New York Sun* did in 1897 with its oft-reprinted editorial "Is There a Santa Claus?"

Most *Times* staffers may think that "supernaturalism" is "just going too far" (Briggs 2007). It is beyond their pale of intellectual respectability. We are "a rational crowd," they think. But are they drawn in print to atheism? Largely not. They may be "patronizing" to claims of supernatural realities, yet they have "their ears to the ground," says Kenneth A. Briggs. They know that a large majority of Americans are supernaturalists to some degree. *Times* journalists also believe, according to Briggs, that this religiousness is "part of the glue that holds this democracy together," it is part of our cultural and civic heritage, and thus it must be reported. Furthermore, "people like that stuff." They like to read about it. For these reasons, the "news judgment" at the *Times* is that supernaturalism is worth its ink.

The issue here is not whether the *Times* is friendly or hostile to religion's supernaturalism, nor is it necessary to mount a defense or an accusation regarding putative liberalism at the *Times*. My aim, rather, much like a reporter's, has been to examine—copiously citing the *Times* itself with a minimum of theoretical interpretations on my part—how the *Times* has defined religion and its many dimensions in contemporary life in the shadow of 9/11.

We speak of "the *Times*" as an institution, a culture, a world, an individual. It must be said, however, that the *Times* does not have a single viewpoint, nor does it have a single standard or method. Who writes all the religion pieces for the *Times*? It has several religion writers with a variety of religious and professional backgrounds. Then there are many other reporters who cover religion stories on other beats: metropolitan, regional, national, political, international, science, food, family, arts, sports, and so on. How do they inform themselves and their audience without religious studies on their résumé? They sometimes turn to the experts for quotations and angles: academics, firsthand players in religious developments, denominational officials, and the like. Finally, the experts and interested parties themselves are called upon or volunteer to write op-ed pieces and features of all sorts.

One might say that the *Times* management cares not a whit about defining religion or studying it. Its editors and writers and photographers' concern is to understand contemporary life, and insofar as religion—however defined—is an important causative agent, it is worthy of documentation and commentary. Steven Erlanger (2007a), *Times* Jerusalem bureau chief, writes, "i don't know why anyone would want to read the ny times to study religion. we don't write religious articles; we cover religion, well or badly. my job isn't to contribute to a better understanding of religion, but of the world i cover, and religion plays a role in that world" (lowercase in original). Daniel J. Wakin (2007), who reported on religion for the *Times* metro desk after 9/11, questions the very premise of this book: "Is a newspaper a place to gain an education about something," such as religion? He thinks not. "I . . . look at it as a chronicle of current events, themes and ideas percolating in society at the moment."

That being said, the *Times* pays heed to the academic study of religion. On the pages of the *Times*—for example, in obituaries and book reviews, on the pages of the magazine—we occasionally meet the leaders, past and present, of religious studies as a discipline. The paper not only hires reporters with interest and some expertise in religious topics for the religion beat but also commissions scholars whose professional training it is to analyze religious phenomena. Op-eds, obits, and book reviews hire on theologians, historians, sociologists, anthropologists, and other skilled observers of religion who do care about characterizing religion, its pluralism, its vocabulary, its symbols, its mystery, its faith, its wisdom, its spirituality, its quest for meaning, its connection to human needs and divine calling, its temptations, and its transcendence. It would appear, then, that the *Times* brings as much expertise to its pages as most academic authors do in writing a book. From report to commentary to essay to editorial, there are different ways to treat the variety of religious subjects.

Nonetheless, *Times* employees avow that different parts of the paper, such as the *Times Book Review* or the *Times Magazine,* have a different feel for their religious topics, especially in recent years with the growth of special magazine-type sections on various topics. Daniel Okrent (2004), *Times* public editor in 2004, has commented on the "antipathy directed toward *The Times Magazine* by many of the daily paper's writers and editors," an animosity that is "decades old." The reporters claim that the magazine writers play loose and fast with the facts. "Magazine people say most newspaper stories aren't written well enough, or dramatically enough, to engage the reader; newspaper people say magazine writers excel not at storytelling but at embroidery," he commented.

Kenneth A. Briggs (2007) expresses skepticism regarding the notion of "the *Times* as an actor" who speaks "in a voice." Rather, he says, the paper is a "locality"— a "bulletin board"—for "many voices" to be posted. Of course, there is "approval at certain levels" of the perspectives printed in the *Times,* and those views are "filtered" through the editorial process; however, one cannot say what "the *Times* believes" or "wishes," only what "gets reported." Indeed, news reporters might find the opinions expressed in book reviews to be "off the wall." Sports columnist George Vecsey (2007) says that it would be "misleading" to assume that there is "one central position at the *NYT* ordering up articles and essays." In the "new age of accessibility via e-mail," he (2010) often has readers accuse him of "following the *NYT* line on one thing or another." He says, "The *NYT* is a complicated democracy where writers and particularly columnists are not told what to write or think." He says, with assurance gained through experience, that "readers would be surprised to learn how hard it is to pin down a unified *Times* worldview, if indeed one exists."

When we read books, let's say of history, that try to characterize a national temper or the weltenschauung of the era, we can often discern the countervailing tendencies in the evidence; however, authors try to smooth over these tendencies for the sake of analytical continuity, even while allowing for complexity in analysis. In newspapers, the various articles are not expected to add up to a single conclusion; they are allowed to contradict each other. A newspaper is not a single-minded tract. It is the creation, says Gustav Niebuhr (2006), of many individual "entrepreneurs," all with their own angles, working both separately and together in the "chaos" of the newsroom. One might say that it is "amazing that the paper gets produced" in this way. At the same time, it can be said that through this process we get a textured picture of our age in its contradictory details. This is why I have been interested in an exhaustive examination of *Times* religion coverage rather than in picking out a few articles on a common theme with a common viewpoint. I have been interested in what we would learn about post-9/11 religion, politics, and journalism by reading the *Times* in an encyclopedic manner, over time, with all the complexity included.

How much depth does the *Times* give a story? Does the *Times* cover the same stories year after year, Christmas after Christmas, Passover after Passover, and now Ramadan after Ramadan? Does each story start from scratch and never go beyond etching the surface? Does the paper merely report, or does it analyze and provide context? Does it cite historical precedents or theoretical models? Should it aim for these kinds of profundity? I think it does. I also wonder if there is not strength to straight reportage without all the overlay and background. Is there not cumulative effect to the *Times* reiterative coverage of themes? Does a reader not develop deeper knowledge through memory over time by following the *Times* in its religion coverage?

I think that there is wisdom in the myriad journalistic details. One cannot feel so cocksure about an opinion when faced with thousands of quotations—a panorama of people's perspectives, all saying what they think and feel and what they stand for. Being a professor of the humanities, I celebrate the complexity, the diversity, the expressiveness of the details without neglecting or reducing them. There is richness in the coverage. You can swim in it; you can drown in it. With its immensity, it can take your breath away and your voice. It can also educate you. I do not say that you can learn everything you need to know about religion in these times by reading the newspaper—even if that paper is the *New York Times*. But it is an edifying place to start.

Perhaps *Times* reportage and commentary might constitute not only a "first draft of history," but also a more accurate version of that history—because it includes many perspectives under the same canopy—than subsequent, single-authored works on the same period. The *Times* offers a multiperspectival, even a "cubist" (Reinitz 1969), set of visions, which might be more true to the complex realities of the world than any single interpretive reduction. Far from a constraining corporate culture with a single-minded gospel, the *Times* is an institution that allows—encourages!—multiple knowledges, multiple disciplines, multiple ideologies, multiple conventions to find expression on its pages.

Within reason, of course. In the long run, the *Times* favors—privileges?—certain views over others. More liberal than not? More secular than not? Perhaps, but always with an eye toward the moderate center. There is a core and periphery to *Times* coverage, both built with respect to a perceived mainstream center. Moderatism is the paper's code, if not exactly its gospel.

I have found the *Times*' post-9/11 religion coverage to be responsible, estimable journalism—not just in any single article in which the reporter tries to define the issue and find viewpoints on its many sides, but also in the totality of reportage. One op-ed contradicts another; one report adds a dimension that a previous report left out. There is a constant reaching toward other perspectives. Balance comes from this range of views; however, it is balance built on its own and its readership's conventional worldview as locally, regionally, and nationally defined. The *New York Times* is not published in Kabul or Baghdad. If it were, its center of gravity would be significantly different in these places.

Good journalism, Ari L. Goldman writes (1991), is like good Talmud. Each issue begins with a summary statement, fair and inclusive, followed by argument—one voice, another voice, expressing valid opinions, each "worth listening to and recording." Each may be right, even though they diverge and disagree. Neither Talmud nor good journalism is willing to "settle for only one opinion." For Goldman, Talmud "is the ultimate newspaper of Judaism," striving toward "equality and justice" with "logic and perseverance" (138–39). In my view, the *Times* seems committed to the same goals. For that reason, among others, there seems no better place to learn about religion, politics, and journalism reported in these times, in this epoch of ours following 9/11.

References

Index

References

"2 Gatherings Reflect U.S. Muslims' Divide" (AP). 2003. *New York Times,* Aug. 30.

"13 Nigerians Die in Christian–Muslim Fighting" (AP). 2001. *New York Times,* Oct. 15.

"14 Killed in Ritual at Annual Muslim Pilgrimage in Saudi Arabia" (Reuters). 2003. *New York Times,* Feb. 12.

"244 Die in Saudi Stampede during Muslim Pilgrimage" (Reuters). 2004. *New York Times,* Feb. 2.

Abdallah, Aslam. 2005. "Post-9/11 Media and Muslim Identity in American Media." In *Quoting God: How Media Shape Ideas about Religion and Culture,* edited by Claire Hoertz Badaracco, 123–28. Waco, TX: Baylor Univ. Press.

Abdrabboh, Fatina. 2005. "Veiled Praise." *New York Times,* June 23.

Abernethy, Bob. 2003. "Interview: Chris Hedges." *Religion & Ethics Newsweekly,* Jan. 31. Available at http://www.pbs.org/wnet/religionandethics/week622/hedges.html# right.

Abou El Fadl, Khaled. 2002. "Moderate Muslims under Siege." *New York Times,* July 1.

———. 2003. "9/11 and the Muslim Transformation." In *September 11 in History: A Watershed Moment?* edited by Mary L. Dudziak, 70–135. Durham, NC: Duke Univ. Press.

Abrahamian, Ervand. 2003. "The US Media, Huntington, and September 11." *Third World Quarterly* 24, no. 3: 529–44.

"Action Alert: Whose Human Rights Matter? NYT on Hezbollah and Israeli Attacks on Civilians." 2007. *FAIR (Fairness & Accuracy in Reporting),* Sept. 11. Available at http://www.fair.org/index.php?page=3176.

Adams, Marilyn McCord. 1999. *Horrendous Evils and the Goodness of God.* Ithaca, NY: Cornell Univ. Press.

Addario, Lynsey. 2001. "Jihad's Women" (photo essay). *New York Times Magazine,* Oct. 21.

———. 2003. "An Old Faith, a New Year" (photo). *New York Times,* July 22.

"Afghanistan Closes a Christian Relief Office" (AP). 2001. *New York Times,* Aug. 6.

"Afghans to Keep 24 Christian Aid Workers in Jail during Inquiry" (AP). 2001. *New York Times*, Aug. 7.

"After the Attacks: A Day of Prayer" (photos). 2001. *New York Times*, Sept. 15.

Ajami, Fouad. 1995. "Surrounded by Zealots." Review of *Allah O Akbar: A Journey Through Militant Islam*, by Abbas. *New York Times Book Review*, Jan. 15.

———. 2001a. "Nowhere Man." *New York Times Magazine*, Oct. 7.

———. 2001b. "What the Muslim World Is Watching." *New York Times Magazine*, Nov. 18.

"Alabama Court Refuses Plaque for Dr. King." 2001. *New York Times*, Aug. 29.

Albanese, Catherine. 1999. *America: Religions and Religion*. Belmont, CA: Wadsworth.

Alvarez, Lizette. 2003a. "Helping Retrieve Muslim Children, Including Her Own." *New York Times*, June 16.

———. 2003b. "Iranian Lawyer, Staunch Fighter for Human Rights, Wins Nobel." *New York Times*, Oct. 11.

———. 2004. "Britain Charges Muslim Cleric Sought by U.S." *New York Times*, Oct. 20.

———. 2005a. "Britain's Mainstream Muslims Find Voice." *New York Times*, Mar. 6.

———. 2005b. "The Fourth Bomber: New Muslim at 15, Terror Suspect at 19." *New York Times*, July 18.

———. 2005c. "Violent Aftermath: Revenge Attacks and Vandalism Unnerve Muslims in Britain." *New York Times*, July 12.

"American Muslims: Community Lends Its Support after Vandals Strike Mosque" (AP). 2002. *New York Times*, Jan. 3.

Amiri, Rina. 2001. "Muslim Women as Symbols—and Pawns." *New York Times*, Nov. 27.

———. 2002. "The Fear Beneath the Burka." *New York Times*, Mar. 20.

"Andrea Haberman: Planning for Two." 2001. *New York Times*, Dec. 31.

Andrews, Edmund L. 2002. "Frankfurt: In Rich Detail, Algerian Describes Plot to Blow up French Synagogue." *New York Times*, Apr. 24.

Andrews, Edmund L., and Patrick E. Tyler. 2003. "As Iraqis' Dissatisfaction Grows, U.S. Offers Them a Greater Political Role." *New York Times*, June 7.

"Annual Pilgrimage to Mecca Nears Culmination" (photograph). 2003. *New York Times*, Feb. 11.

"Anti-Semitic Book Distributed at Rally for Malaysian Leader" (Reuters). 2003. *New York Times*, June 22.

"Anti-Syrian Christians in Lebanon Split from Their Muslim Allies" (AP). 2005. *New York Times*, May 25.

Applebome, Peter. 2004. "Our Towns: A Lasting Gift, from a Terrific Club Nobody Wanted to Join." *New York Times*, Sept. 5.

———. 2006a. "Our Towns: Tell Virginia the Skeptics Are Still Wrong." *New York Times,* Dec. 13.

———. 2006b. "Our Towns: To Honor a Son Lost on 9/11, Parents Help Others Torn by Violence." *New York Times,* Sept. 24.

Archibold, Randal C. 2001. "St. Patrick's: City Celebrates Its Heroes, and Grieves over Their Loss." *New York Times,* Sept. 18.

Arenson, Karen W. 2002a. "Education: Student Project: Redesign Church Hit Sept. 11." *New York Times,* Jan. 23.

———. 2002b. "Harvard President Sees Rise in Anti-Semitism on Campus." *New York Times,* Sept. 21.

———. 2005. "Columbia Panel Clears Professors of Anti-Semitism." *New York Times,* Mar. 31.

Arkoun, Mohammed. 2002. *The Unthought in Contemporary Islamic Thought.* London: Saqi Books.

Armstrong, Karen. 2001. "Breaking the Sacred." *New York Times,* Mar. 11.

"Army Rebukes Muslim Chaplain over Adultery and Pornography" (Reuters). 2004. *New York Times,* Mar. 23.

Aronson, Deb. 2003. "A Telling Effect." *Illinois Alumni Magazine* (Mar.–Apr.). Available at http://www.uiaa.org/urbana/illinoisalumni/utxt0302e.html.

"Arson Suspected at Dutch Mosque" (Reuters). 2004. *New York Times,* Nov. 14.

Asayesh, Gelareh. 1999. *Saffron Sky: A Life Between Iran and America.* Boston: Beacon Press.

———. 2001. "Lives: Shrouded in Contradiction." *New York Times Magazine,* Nov. 25.

Ashton, John, and Tom Whyte. 2001. *The Quest for Paradise: Visions of Heaven and Eternity in the World's Myths and Religions.* New York: HarperCollins.

Aslan, Reza. 2003. "Why Religion Must Play a Role in Islam." *New York Times,* July 18.

———. 2005. *No God but God: The Origins, Evolution, and Future of Islam.* New York: Random House.

"At the Ruins Beneath Ground Zero, Ghosts of the Past and Stirrings of the Future" (photo). 2005. *New York Times,* July 25.

Atran, Scott. 2003. "Who Wants to Be a Martyr?" *New York Times,* May 5.

Auletta, Ken. 1997. "The Man Who Disappeared." *The New Yorker* (Jan. 6). Available at http://www.kenauletta.com/themanwhodisappeared.html.

Aydintashas, Asia. 2003. "Questions for Oriana Fallaci: Unquiet on the Western Front." *New York Times Magazine,* Feb. 2.

Ayoob, Mohammed. 2001. "How to Define a Muslim American Agenda." *New York Times,* Dec. 29.

Ayres, B. Drummond, Jr. 2001. "Robertson Resigns from Christian Coalition." *New York Times,* Dec. 6.

"Backer of Wife-Beating to Return to France" (AP). 2004. *New York Times,* Apr. 24.

Bahrampour, Tara. 2001. "Where Islam Meets 'Brave New World.'" *New York Times Education Life,* Nov. 11.

Baker, Al. 2004. "Arrest of Mosque Leaders Surprises Neighbors, Who Describe Both as Peaceful Men." *New York Times,* Aug. 6.

"Bangladeshi Court Acts to Protect Hindus" (Agence France-Presse). 2001. *New York Times,* Nov. 27.

Bannerjee, Neela. 2004a. "Cleansing Iraqi Bomb Victims Takes Its Own Toll." *New York Times,* Mar. 4.

———. 2004b. "Equal Rights: Iraqi Women's Window of Opportunity for Political Gains Is Closing." *New York Times,* Feb. 26.

"Baptist Head Urges Prayers for Muslim Conversion" (AP). 2001. *New York Times,* Nov. 27.

Barrett, Amy. 2002. "Questions for Aukai Collins: Holy Warrior." *New York Times Magazine,* Aug. 4.

Barringer, Felicity, and Erik Eckholm. 2002. "Missing American Journalist Wasn't Spy, Friends Say." *New York Times,* Jan. 29.

Barron, James. 2001. "The Fallen: Cardinal Egan Leads Prayers for Victims, and Applause for Rescuers." *New York Times,* Sept. 17.

———. 2006. "Bringing Relief to 9/11 Families, and a Man's Flaws to Light." *New York Times,* Apr. 3.

Barry, Dan. 2001a. "In Coffin Making, an Abbey Finds Fiscal Rebirth." *New York Times,* Sept. 6.

———. 2001b. "The Survivor: In Pulpits, a Grateful Christian Testifies to Deliverance." *New York Times,* Nov. 6.

———. 2001c. "The Vigils: Surrounded by Grief, People Around the World Pause and Turn to Prayer." *New York Times,* Sept. 15.

———. 2003a. "For One 9/11 Family, Five Waves of Grief." *New York Times,* Sept. 10.

———. 2003b. "Preaching the Gospel of Sept. 11 to Visitors." *New York Times,* Mar. 21.

———. 2004. *Pull Me Up: A Memoir.* New York: W. W. Norton.

Bawer, Bruce. 2004. "Perspective / Security vs. Freedom: Tolerant Dutch Wrestle with Tolerating Intolerance." *New York Times,* Nov. 14.

Bearak, Barry. 2001a. "2 Americans Allowed to See Their Jailed Daughters in Kabul." *New York Times,* Aug. 28.

———. 2001b. "Accused Aid Workers Face Islamic Judges in Afghanistan." *New York Times,* Sept. 9.

———. 2001c. "Afghan Says Destruction of Buddhas Is Complete." *New York Times,* Mar. 12.

———. 2001d. "Afghans Present Aid Team's Sins, Complete with Theology Lesson." *New York Times,* Sept. 7.

———. 2001e. "Afghans Shut Offices of 2 More Christian Relief Groups." *New York Times,* Sept. 1.

———. 2001f. "The Afghans: Taliban Plead for Mercy to the Miserable in a Land of Nothing." *New York Times,* Sept. 13.

———. 2001g. "Another Strange Kabul Problem: Finding a Lawyer." *New York Times,* Sept. 10.

———. 2001h. "Death to Blasphemers: Islam's Grip on Pakistan." *New York Times,* May 12.

———. 2001i. "Kabul Retraces Steps to Life before Taliban." *New York Times,* Dec. 2.

———. 2001j. "Kandahar Journal: This Job Is Truly Scary: The Taliban Are Watching." *New York Times,* June 1.

———. 2001k. "Over Protests, Taliban Say That They Are Destroying Buddhas." *New York Times,* Mar. 4.

———. 2001l. "The Purists: Taliban: From Vigilantes to Strict Rulers." *New York Times,* Sept. 19.

———. 2001m. "Red Cross Makes First Visit to 8 Jailed Aid Workers in Kabul." *New York Times,* Aug. 27.

———. 2001n. "Religious Arrests Cast a Pall over Afghanistan Aid Efforts." *New York Times,* Aug. 23.

———. 2001o. "Taliban Propose an Identity Label for the 'Protection' of Hindus." *New York Times,* May 23.

———. 2001p. "Taliban Will Allow Access to Jailed Christian Aid Workers." *New York Times,* Aug. 26.

———. 2003. "Commencement Address." Univ. of Illinois at Urbana-Champlain, May 18. Available at http://www.uiuc.edu/commencement/bearak.html.

Becker, Elizabeth. 2001. "The Protest: Marchers Oppose Waging War Against Terrorists." *New York Times,* Oct. 1.

Bellah, Robert N. 1967. "Civil Religion in America." *Daedalus* 96, no. 1: 1–21.

Belluck, Pam. 2001. "American Muslims: Caught in the Middle, with Disdain for bin Laden and Criticism for the U.S." *New York Times,* Oct. 13.

Bennet, James. 2001. "Christmas Eve in Bethlehem: Santas, Songs but No Arafat." *New York Times*, Dec. 25.

———. 2003a. "Crossing Jordan: The Exit That Isn't on Bush's 'Road Map.'" *New York Times*, May 18.

———. 2003b. "How 2 Took the Path of Suicide Bombers." *New York Times*, May 30.

———. 2003c. "Israeli Gadfly Hopes to Separate Religion and State." *New York Times*, Jan. 17.

———. 2003d. "Jerusalem Holy Site a Tense Crossroad Again." *New York Times*, Aug. 29.

Bennett, William J. 2002. *Why We Fight: Moral Clarity and the War on Terrorism*. New York: Doubleday.

Benowitz, June Melby, ed. 1998. *Encyclopedia of American Women and Religion*. Santa Barbara, CA: ABC-CLIO.

Benzel, Jan. 2001. "Centers of Solace for the Self." *New York Times*, Oct. 28.

Bergen, Peter L. 2001. *Holy War, Inc.: Inside the Secret World of Osama bin Laden*. New York: Free Press.

———. 2005a. "Brothers in Alms." *New York Times*, Jan. 8.

———. 2005b. "Our Ally, Our Problem." *New York Times*, July 8.

Bergen, Peter [L.], and Swati Pandey. 2005. "The Madrassa Myth." *New York Times*, June 14.

Berger, Joseph. 2004a. "Israel Sees a Surge in Immigration by French Jews, but Why?" *New York Times*, July 4.

———. 2004b. "A Muslim Santa's Gift to an Interfaith Group: Free Rent." *New York Times*, Dec. 24.

———. 2004c. "Prayer amid the Office Machines." *New York Times*, Jan. 19.

———. 2007. E-mail correspondence with the author. Aug. 20.

Berger, Peter L., and Samuel P. Huntington, eds. 2002. *Many Globalizations: Cultural Diversity in the Contemporary World*. Oxford, UK: Oxford Univ. Press.

Berkow, Ira. 2001. "Sports of the Times: Calm Needed during Time of Anger." *New York Times*, Sept. 19.

Berman, Paul. 2003a. "Listening to Terrorists." Review of *Just War Against Terror: The Burden of American Power in a Violent World* by Jean Bethke Elshtain and *The Great Terror War* by Richard Falk. *New York Times Book Review*, Apr. 27.

———. 2003b. "The Philosopher of Islamic Terror." *New York Times Magazine*, Mar. 23.

———. 2003c. *Terror and Liberalism*. New York: W. W. Norton.

Bernstein, Nina. 2004. "From Immigrants, Stories of Scrutiny, and Struggle." *New York Times*, July 20.

———. 2005. "Girl Called Would-Be Bomber Was Drawn to Islam." *New York Times*, Apr. 8.

Bernstein, Richard. 1982. *From the Center of the Earth: The Search for the Truth about China*. Boston: Little, Brown.

———. 1990. *Fragile Glory: A Portrait of France and the French*. New York: Knopf.

———. 1993. "A Growing Islamic Presence: Balancing Sacred and Secular." *New York Times*, May 2.

———. 1994. *Dictatorship of Virtue: Multiculturalism and the Battle for America's Future*. New York: Knopf.

———. 2001a. "Books of the Times: Challenging the Vatican on Role in Anti-Semitism." Review of *The Popes Against the Jews: The Vatican's Role in the Rise of Modern Anti-Semitism* by David I. Kertzer. *New York Times*, Sept. 19.

———. 2001b. "Experts on Islam Pointing Fingers at One Another." *New York Times*, Nov. 3.

———. 2001c. *Ultimate Journey: Retracing the Path of an Ancient Buddhist Monk Who Crossed Asia in Search of Enlightenment*. New York: Knopf.

———. 2002. "Books of the Times: The Saudis' Brand of Islam and Its Place in History." Review of *The Two Faces of Islam: The House of Sa'ud from Tradition to Terror* by Stephen Schwartz. *New York Times*, Nov. 6.

———. 2003a. "A Conference in Austria Denounces Anti-Semitism." *New York Times*, June 21.

———. 2003b. "Letters from Europe: Continent Wrings Its Hands over Proclaiming Its Faith." *New York Times*, Nov. 12.

———. 2004a. "European Security Group Takes Aim at Anti-Semitism." *New York Times*, Apr. 29.

———. 2004b. "European Union Mends Rift with Jewish Groups." *New York Times*, Jan. 9.

———. 2004c. "German Police Raid Mosque Said to Show Jihad Videos." *New York Times*, July 13.

———. 2004d. "Germany Struggles to Assess True Aims of Islamic Group." *New York Times*, Sept. 26.

———. 2004e. "Letters from Europe: Lessons of Islam in German Classrooms." *New York Times*, June 30.

———. 2004f. "The Saturday Profile: The Fear Born of a Much Too Personal Look at Jihad." *New York Times*, Nov. 27.

———. 2005a. "Muslim Approval of Terror Drops, Poll Finds." *New York Times*, July 15.

———. 2005b. "One Muslim's Odyssey to Guantánamo." *New York Times*, June 5.

Bernstein, Richard, and Ross H. Munro. 1997. *The Coming Conflict with China*. New York: Knopf.

Bernstein, Richard, and the staff of the *New York Times*. 2002. *Out of the Blue: The Story of September 11, from Jihad to Ground Zero*. New York: Henry Holt and Times Books.

Bernstein, Richard, et al. 2005. "What Is Free Speech, and What Is Terrorism?" *New York Times*, Aug. 14.

"Bias Incidents Against Muslims Are Soaring, Islamic Council Says." 2002. *New York Times*, May 1.

"Bin Laden's Message: Fight the 'Crusaders'" (Reuters). 2003. *New York Times*, Feb. 15.

"Bin Laden's Statement: 'The Sword Fell.'" 2001. *New York Times*, Oct. 8.

"Bin Laden's Words: 'God Willing, America's End Is Near.'" 2001. *New York Times*, Dec. 28.

Bin Talal, Hassan. 2003. "Seeing Iraq's Future by Looking at Its Past." *New York Times*, July 18.

Blair, Jayson. 2003. "For One Pastor, the War Hits Home." *New York Times*, Apr. 7.

Blank, Dennis. 2001. "Florida Religious Theme Park Fights for Property Tax Exemption." *New York Times*, Nov. 23.

Bohlen, Celestine. 2001a. "Facing the Limits of a Just War." *New York Times*, Sept. 22.

———. 2001b. "Museum Helps Jewish Family Regain Relic Nazis Stole." *New York Times*, August 29.

Bonner, Raymond. 2002. "2 Americans Killed in Attack on Pakistan Church." *New York Times*, Mar. 18.

———. 2003a. "The Asian Arena: Radical Cleric Is Charged with Treason in Indonesia." *New York Times*, Apr. 15.

———. 2003b. "Islamic Cleric Gets Mixed Verdict in Indonesian Trial for Terrorism." *New York Times*, Sept. 3.

———. 2005. "Australia: Muslims Urged to Preach Against Terror." *New York Times*, July 26.

Boof, Kola. 2001. *Long Train to the Redeeming Sin*. Fullerton, CA: North African Book Exchange.

Bragg, Rick. 2001a. "Florida Minister Defies Drug Dealers, Despite Threat on Life." *New York Times*, Aug. 28.

———. 2001b. "Protesters: A Pro-Taliban Rally Draws Angry Thousands in Pakistan, Then Melts Away." *New York Times*, Oct. 6.

———. 2001c. "Seeking Miracles from Cruelty and Beauty." *New York Times*, Oct. 28.

———. 2001d. "Shaping Young Islamic Hearts and Hatreds." *New York Times*, Oct. 14.

Bragg, Rick, and Ruth Fremson. 2001. "Prayers Sustain Pakistani Church in Hard Times." *New York Times*, Nov. 4.

Braudel, Fernand. 1972. *The Mediterranean and the Mediterranean World in the Age of Philip II*. 2 vols. Translated by Siân Reynolds. New York: Harper and Row.

Breithaupt, Fritz. 2003. "Rituals of Trauma: How the Media Fabricated September 11." In *Media Representations of September 11*, edited by Steven Chermak, Frankie Y. Bailey, and Michelle Brown, 67–81. Westport, CT: Praeger.

Briggs, Kenneth A. 2007. Telephone interview by the author. Feb. 26.

Brill, Steven. 2003. *After: How America Confronted the September 12 Era*. New York: Simon & Schuster.

Brinkley, Joel. 2002. "Bethlehem: Vowing to Stay at a Holy Site as Troops and Impasse Linger." *New York Times*, Apr. 7.

"Britain: Radical Cleric Faces July Trial" (AP). 2005. *New York Times*, Jan. 5.

Broder, John M. 2004. "American Being Sought by the F.B.I. Found His Place in Islam, Relatives Say." *New York Times*, May 28.

———. 2005. "Judge Orders Islamic Fund-Raiser Deported." *New York Times*, Feb. 9.

Bronner, Ethan. 2001. "21st-Century Jihad." Review of *Holy War, Inc.: Inside the Secret World of Osama bin Laden* by Peter L. Bergen. *New York Times Book Review*, Nov. 18.

———. 2002. "Suspect Thy Neighbor." Review of *American Jihad: The Terrorists Living among Us* by Steven Emerson. *New York Times Book Review*, Mar. 17.

Brooke, James. 2002. "Muslims in the Philippines, Echoes of an Era: Pershing Was Here." *New York Times*, Jan. 27.

Brooks, David. 2004a. "The Hookie Awards." *New York Times*, Dec. 25.

———. 2004b. "The Hookie Awards, Part 2." *New York Times*, Dec. 28.

———. 2004c. "One Nation, Enriched by Biblical Wisdom." *New York Times*, March 23.

———. 2005. "Trading Cricket for Jihad." *New York Times*, Aug. 4.

Brown, Jen. 2004. "Denied Time Off for Ramadan, Brooklyn Students Start Petition." *New York Times*, Oct. 14.

Brown, Patricia Leigh. 2003. "At Muslim Prom, It's a Girls-Only Night Out." *New York Times*, June 9.

Bruni, Frank. 2002. "Nearly 40 Jewish Graves Are Desecrated in a Rome Cemetery." *New York Times*, July 19.

———. 2003a. "Athens Journal: Muslims' Unanswered Prayer: A Place to Worship." *New York Times*, Apr. 22.

———. 2003b. "Baghdad's Diplomacy: Iraqi Minister, Visiting Pope, Warns Europe That a War Would Be Seen as Anti-Muslim." *New York Times*, Feb. 15.

———. 2003c. "Faith Fades Where It Once Burned Strong." *New York Times*, Oct. 13.

———. 2003d. "Iraq's Campaign: At Assisi, Iraqi Envoy Traces Saint's Footsteps and Publicly Prays for Peace." *New York Times*, Feb. 16.

———. 2003e. "The Vatican: Pope Is Sending Envoy to Baghdad in Effort to Avert a War." *New York Times*, Feb. 10.

———. 2003f. "The Vatican: Pope Voices Opposition, His Strongest, to Iraq War." *New York Times*, Jan. 14.

———. 2003g. "Vatican: Threat of Iraq War Draws World Leaders, with Different Views, to the Pope's Door." *New York Times*, Feb. 22.

Bumiller, Elisabeth. 2001. "Bin Laden, on Tape, Boasts of Trade Center Attacks; U.S. Says It Proves His Guilt." *New York Times*, Dec. 14.

———. 2003. "White House Letter: Religious Leaders Ask If Antiwar Call Is Heard." *New York Times*, Mar. 10.

———. 2005. "White House Presses *Newsweek* in Wake of Koran Report." *New York Times*, May 18.

Burns, John F. 2001a. "Afghans Suggest Bin Laden Leave." *New York Times*, Sept. 21.

———. 2001b. "Bin Laden Taunts U.S. and Praises Hijackers." *New York Times*, Oct. 8.

———. 2001c. "Gunmen Kill 16 Christians in Church in Pakistan." *New York Times*, Oct. 29.

———. 2001d. "International Memo: America Inspires Both Longing and Loathing in Arab World." *New York Times*, Sept. 16.

———. 2001e. "Islamabad: Pakistani Officials Say They Have No Firm Suspects in Massacre at Christian Church." *New York Times*, Nov. 4.

———. 2001f. "Kashmir's Islamic Guerrillas See Little to Fear from U.S." *New York Times*, Dec. 24.

———. 2001g. "Taliban Link Fate of Aid Workers to U.S. Action." *New York Times*, Oct. 7.

———. 2001h. "U.S. Rescues 8 Aid Workers South of Kabul." *New York Times*, Nov. 15.

———. 2002a. "Bin Laden Stirs Struggle on Meaning of Jihad." *New York Times*, Jan. 27.

———. 2002b. "Hussein's Obsession: An Empire of Mosques." *New York Times*, Dec. 15.

———. 2002c. "Relishing Beautiful New Freedoms in Kabul." *New York Times*, Sept. 15.

———. 2003. "The Attacker: Bomber Left Her Family with a Smile and a Lie." *New York Times*, Oct. 7.

———. 2004a. "At Least 143 Die in Attacks at Two Sacred Sites in Iraq." *New York Times*, Mar. 3.

———. 2004b. "Cleric May Warn Iraqis to Reject New Government." *New York Times*, Mar. 28.

———. 2004c. "Insurgents: Cleric, Surrounded by U.S., Hints at Easing His Resistance." *New York Times*, Apr. 14.

———. 2004d. "Ordeal: Anxious Moments in Grip of an Outlaw Iraqi Militia." *New York Times*, Apr. 7.

————. 2004e. "U.S. Soldiers Die in Iraq as a Shiite Militia Rises Up." *New York Times,* Apr. 5.

————. 2005. "Iraq Government Calls for an End to Mosque Raids." *New York Times,* May 17.

Burns, John F., and James Glanz. 2005. "Iraqi Shiites Win, but Margin Is Less Than Projection." *New York Times,* Feb. 14.

Burns, John F., and Robert F. Worth. 2004. "Iraqi Campaign Raises Question of Iran's Sway." *New York Times,* Dec. 15.

Buruma, Ian. 2004. "Essay: An Islamic Democracy for Iraq?" *New York Times Magazine,* Dec. 5.

Buruma, Ian, and Avishai Margalit. 2004. *Occidentalism: The West in the Eyes of Its Enemies.* New York: Penguin.

Bush, George W. 2001. "President's Proclamation." *New York Times,* Nov. 20.

Butler, Desmond. 2002. "Germany Plans to Raise Status of Nation's Jews." *New York Times,* Nov. 15.

Byrnes, Timothy A. 1991. *Catholic Bishops in American Politics.* Princeton, NJ: Princeton Univ. Press.

————. 2001. *Transnational Catholicism in Postcommunist Europe.* Lanham, MD: Rowman and Littlefield.

Byrnes, Timothy A., and Peter J. Katzenstein, eds. 2006. *Religion in an Expanding Europe.* Cambridge, UK: Cambridge Univ. Press.

Byrnes, Timothy A., and Mary C. Segers, eds. 1992. *The Catholic Church and the Politics of Abortion: A View from the States.* Boulder, CO: Westview Press.

Cahill, Thomas. 2002. "The One True Faith: Is It Tolerance?" *New York Times,* Feb. 3.

Caldwell, Christopher. 2005. "Daughter of the Enlightenment." *New York Times Magazine,* Apr. 3.

Caldwell, Deborah. 2003. "Should Christian Missionaries Heed the Call in Iraq?" *New York Times,* Apr. 6.

"California: Jewish Radical Is Dead." 2002. *New York Times,* Nov. 15.

Campbell, Christopher P. 2003. "Commodifying September 11: Advertising, Myth, and Hegemony." In *Media Representations of September 11,* edited by Steven Chermak, Frankie Y. Bailey, and Michelle Brown, 47–65. Westport, CT: Praeger.

Campbell, Colin. 1984. "Moslem Students in U.S. Rediscovering Islam." *New York Times,* May 13.

Canedy, Dana. 2002. "Lifting Veil for Photo ID Goes Too Far, Driver Says." *New York Times,* June 27.

"Captain Yee's Ordeal" (editorial). 2003. *New York Times,* Dec. 14.

Caputo, Philip. 2005. "Why They Hate Us." Review of *Faith at War: A Journey on the Frontlines of Islam, from Baghdad to Timbuktu* by Yaroslav Trofimov. *New York Times Book Review,* July 17.

Capuzzo, Jill P. 2004. "Coasters, Islam, and a Case of Nerves." *New York Times,* Sept. 18.

Cardwell, Diane. 2003a. "The Immigrants: Muslims Face Deportation, but Say U.S. Is Their Home." *New York Times,* June 13.

———. 2003b. "Memorial: Families Pay Respects to Victims of '93 Attack." *New York Times,* Feb. 27.

Carey, James W. 2002. "American Journalism on, before, and after September 11." in *Journalism after September 11,* edited by Barbie Zelizer and Stuart Allan, 71–90. London: Routledge.

Carroll, James. 2002. "Articles of Faith." Review of *The Heart of Islam: Enduring Values for Humanity* by Seyyed Hossein Nasr. *New York Times Book Review,* Sept. 8.

Carter, Bill, and Felicity Barringer. 2001. "Speech and Expression: In Patriotic Time, Dissent Is Muted." *New York Times,* Sept. 28.

Carter, Stephen L., et al. 2002. "Reflections on an America Transformed." *New York Times,* Sept. 8.

Castelnuovo, Rina. 2001. "Ramadan Begins, Outside the Walls." *New York Times,* Nov. 17.

"Ceremonies of Healing, Old and New" (photo essay). 2002. *New York Times,* Sept. 9.

Charfi, Mohamed. 2002. "Reaching the Next Muslim Generation." *New York Times,* Mar. 12.

Charney, Marc D. 2004. "Q&A / Amatzia Baram." *New York Times,* Aug. 22.

Chen, David W. 2002. "In Year of Attacks, Passover Preparations Are Somber." *New York Times,* Mar. 27.

Chermak, Steven, Frankie Y. Bailey, and Michelle Brown. 2003a. "Introduction." In *Media Representations of September 11,* edited by Steven Chermak, Frankie Y. Bailey, and Michelle Brown, 1–13. Westport, CT: Praeger.

———, eds. 2003b. *Media Representations of September 11.* Westport, CT: Praeger.

"Chirac Condemns Attacks on Muslim Sites" (Reuters). 2004. *New York Times,* Mar. 7.

Chivers, C. J. 2004. "Mourning and Anger at School Caught Up in Terrorism." *New York Times,* Oct. 13.

"Choice of Words: To Avoid Offending Muslims, Mission's Name Will Probably Change." 2001. *New York Times,* Sept. 21.

"Chris Hedges." 2003. *TimesWatch,* May 21. Available at http://www.mrc.org/timeswatch/articles/2003/0521.asp.

Christian, Nichole M. 2001. "Worshipers Hail the Miraculous at Cathedral." *New York Times,* Dec. 26.

———. 2003. "Bloomberg Tries to Reassure Muslim Worshipers." *New York Times*, Mar. 29.

Church, Kenneth. 2002. "Jihad." In *Collateral Language: A User's Guide to America's New War*, edited by John Collins and Ross Glover, 109–24. New York: New York Univ. Press.

"Church, State, and Joe Lieberman" (editorial). 2001. *New York Times*, Sept. 1.

"Claim in Killing of Christian Family in India" (Agence France-Presse). 2002. *New York Times*, Feb. 5.

Clark, Andrew. 2001. "Arts Abroad: Comics, Muslim and Jewish: Sharing a Toronto Stage." *New York Times*, Nov. 6.

"Cleansing before the Fasting." 2004. *New York Times*, Oct. 15.

Clemetson, Lynette. 2003. "'Just Shoot Me.'" *New York Times*, Apr. 20.

Cohen, Roger. 2002. "Barry Bearak." *Times Talk* (Apr.).

———. 2004. "The War on Terror: An Obsession the World Doesn't Share." *New York Times*, Dec. 5.

Cohen, Stephen P. 2004. "Television Review: Going Home to Discover the Face of Islam." *New York Times*, Feb. 9.

Collins, Glenn. 2001. "Public Lives: A Cross, a Shield, and a Prayer for Firefighters." *New York Times*, Nov. 27.

———. 2005. "Global Word to Terrorists: You Killed My Beloved." *New York Times*, Mar. 20.

Collins, John, and Ross Glover. 2002. "Introduction" In *Collateral Language: A User's Guide to America's New War*, edited by John Collins and Ross Glover, 1–13. New York: New York Univ. Press.

"Colorado: Professor Offers Explanation" (AP). 2005. *New York Times*, Feb. 9.

Conde, Carlos H. 2003. "Blasts at Philippine Mosques Follow Bombing at Terminal." *New York Times*, Apr. 4.

Conover, Ted. 2003. "Essay: Ministering to the Enemy." *New York Times Magazine*, Oct. 12.

"Convictions Dropped for Muslim Chaplain at Guantánamo Bay" (Reuters). 2004. *New York Times*, Apr. 15.

Cooper, Ann. 2002. "Daniel Pearl's Essential Work." *New York Times*, Feb. 23.

Coq, Guy. 2004. "Scarves and Symbols." *New York Times*, Jan. 30.

Cornell, George. 1990. "The Evolution of the Religion Beat." In *Reporting Religion: Facts & Faith*, edited by Benjamin J. Hubbard, 20–35. Sonoma, CA: Poleridge Press.

"Correction: Hadhrat Mirza Tahir Ahmad, Muslim Spiritual Leader, 74." 2003. *New York Times*, May 17.

Cotter, Holland. 2001a. "Art Review: Kicking Up a Storm to Keep Chaos and Evil at Bay." *New York Times*, Sept. 21.

———. 2001b. "Beauty in the Shadow of Violence." *New York Times*, Oct. 7.

———. 2001c. "Buddhas of Bamiyan: Keys to Asian History." *New York Times*, Mar. 3.

———. 2001d. "Cosmopolitan Trove on the Road to China." *New York Times*, Nov. 16.

———. 2001e. "Lowly Everyday Objects as High Art." *New York Times*, Oct. 7.

———. 2001f. "Shelf Life: The Story of Islam's Gift of Paper to the West." *New York Times*, Dec. 29.

———. 2002. "Art Review: Modernism Gets a Revolutionary Makeover in Iran." *New York Times*, Sept. 27.

———. 2003a. "Art Review: In 16th-Century Iran, a Dynasty Hunts a Signature Style." *New York Times*, Oct. 17.

———. 2003b. "An Often Misunderstood and Marginalized Category of Art." *New York Times*, May 27.

———. 2003c. "Renovation Project Will Close Islamic Galleries at the Met." *New York Times*, May 27.

———. 2004. "Art Review: Polyphony for the Eye." *New York Times*, July 16.

"Court Upholds Stoning for Nigerian Mother" (AP). 2002. *New York Times*, Aug. 20.

Cowan, Alison Leigh. 2001. "Doing Good Deeds, and Windows." *New York Times*, Dec. 4.

Cowell, Alan. 2001a. "A Cycle of Hatred Is Visited on a New Generation in Northern Ireland." *New York Times*, Sept. 8.

———. 2001b. "Tug of Faith Unsettles British Muslims." *New York Times*, Oct. 24.

———. 2002. "Religious Violence in Nigeria Drives Out Miss World Event." *New York Times*, Nov. 23.

———. 2004. "British Arrest Radical Cleric U.S. Seeks." *New York Times*, May 28.

———. 2005a. "Arrests: Show of Resolve as Religious Leaders Try to Cool Tensions." *New York Times*, July 11.

———. 2005b. "Blair Is Seeking to Curb Radicals Who Preach Hate." *New York Times*, Aug. 6.

———. 2005c. "Seeking Moderate Support, Blair Meets Muslim Leaders." *New York Times*, July 20.

———. 2005d. "War Is Muted as Issue in Britain, but Not for Its Muslims." *New York Times*, Apr. 22.

Cowell, Alan, and Joel Greenberg. 2002. "In Church of Nativity, the Refuse of a Siege." *New York Times*, May 11.

Cowell, Alan, and Don Van Natta Jr. 2005. "Top Muslims in Britain Reject Call to Violence." *New York Times*, Sept. 3.

Cox, Cher Patric. 2003. "The Philosopher of Islamic Terror" (letter to the editor). *New York Times Magazine,* Apr. 6.

"Critics Say Draft of Head Scarf Ban in French Schools Is Too Vague" (AP). 2004. *New York Times,* Apr. 22.

Crossette, Barbara. 2001a. "In Montreal: A Sense of Foreboding in Canada's Diverse Muslim Haven." *New York Times,* Sept. 16.

———. 2001b. "(Mid) East Meets (Far) East: A Challenge to Asia's Own Style of Islam." *New York Times,* Dec. 30.

———. 2001c. "Militancy: Living in a World Without Women." *New York Times,* Nov. 4.

———. 2001d. "Taliban Explains Buddha Demolition." *New York Times,* Mar. 19.

———. 2002. "A Tough Time to Talk of Peace." *New York Times,* Feb. 12.

Crouch, Gregory. 2005a. "Man on Trial in Dutch Killing Says He'd Do 'Same Again.'" *New York Times,* July 13.

———. 2005b. "Suspect in Killing of Dutch Filmmaker Maintains His Silence." *New York Times,* July 12.

Crowley, Stephen. 2003."A Chorus of Grief at Ground Zero" (photo). *New York Times,* Sept. 9.

"Cult Statue Destroyed." 2001. *New York Times,* Sept. 7.

Cumming-Bruce, Nick. 2005. "Ethnic and Religious Tension on the Thailand–Malaysia Border." *New York Times,* Sept. 3.

Daley, Suzanne. 2001. "Europe Wary of Wider Doors for Immigrants." *New York Times,* Oct. 20.

———. 2002a. "Gang Attacks Jews on Sports Field in France." *New York Times,* Apr. 13.

———. 2002b. "Surge in Anti-Semitic Crime Worries French Jews." *New York Times,* Feb. 26.

Dalrymple, William. 2003. "Syria's Shades of Gray." *New York Times,* June 7.

"Dan Barry." 2003. Feature on the Web site of the Russell J. Jandoli School of Journalism Mass Communication, St. Bonaventure Univ. Available at http://www.sbu.edu/jmc/events/barry03commday.html.

Danner, Mark. 2005. "Taking Stock of the Forever War." *New York Times Magazine,* Sept. 11.

Dao, James. 2003. "Vatican: War on Iraq Was Just, Powell Says to Pope." *New York Times,* June 5.

———. 2004a. "3 American Muslims Convicted of Helping Wage Jihad." *New York Times,* Mar. 5.

———. 2004b. "Mystery Cloaks Firing of Iranian Couple." *New York Times,* Dec. 12.

———. 2005. "Muslim Cleric Found Guilty in the 'Virginia Jihad' Case." *New York Times,* Apr. 27.

Dao, James, and Eric Lichtblau. 2005. "Case Adds to Outrage for Muslims in Northern Virginia." *New York Times,* Feb. 27.

Dargis, Manohla. 2005. "Film Review: An Epic Bloodletting Empowered by Faith." *New York Times,* May 6.

Darnton, Robert. 1990. *The Kiss of LaMourette: Reflections in Cultural History.* New York: W. W. Norton.

"David Hunter, 90, Pioneer in Interfaith Ties." 2001. *New York Times,* Aug. 31.

Davidson, Adam. 2003. "Encounter: Loves Microsoft, Hates America." *New York Times Magazine,* Mar. 9.

Day, Sherri. 2001. "Dwindling Numbers, Constant Faith." *New York Times,* Oct. 13.

"Deadly Violence Erupts Again in India's Hindu–Muslim Conflict." 2002. *New York Times,* May 9.

De Bellaigue, Christopher. 2005. "Sleeping with the Enemy." Review of *Husband of a Fanatic: A Personal Journey Through India, Pakistan, Love, and Hate* by Amitava Kumar. *New York Times Book Review,* Mar. 20.

"Defending France's Jews" (editorial). 2003. *New York Times,* Jan. 16.

Dillon, Sam. 2003a. "Research: Islamic World Less Welcoming to American Scholars." *New York Times,* Apr. 18.

———. 2003b. "Suddenly, a Seller's Market for Arabic Studies." *New York Times,* Mar. 19.

———. 2004. "Columbia to Check Reports of Anti-Jewish Harassment." *New York Times,* Oct. 29.

Dinsmore, Herman H. 1969. *All the News That Fits: A Critical Analysis of the News and Editorial Contents of "The New York Times."* New Rochelle, NY: Arlington House.

"Dissent: Antiwar Priest Removes Flag, but Not for Long" (AP). 2003. *New York Times,* Apr. 12.

"Doctor Is Charged in Plot" (AP). 2002. *New York Times,* Aug. 24.

"Does the Koran Belong in Class?" (letters to the editor by Michael Dobkowski and others). 2002. *New York Times,* Sept. 3.

Donovan, Aaron. 2002. "Here, Islamic Law Guides How the Food Is Killed." *New York Times,* Mar. 26.

Dowd, Maureen. 2001. "Bush's Women's Rights Promotion Rings Hollow." *New York Times,* Nov. 20.

———. 2002a. "Rapture and Rupture." *New York Times,* Oct. 6.

———. 2002b. "Sacred Cruelties." *New York Times,* Apr. 7.

———. 2002c. "Under the Ramadan Moon." *New York Times,* Nov. 6.

———. 2003. "A Tale of Two Fridays." *New York Times,* Apr. 20.

———. 2005a. "Reformer Without Results." *New York Times,* Aug. 13.

————. 2005b. "Torture Chicks Gone Wild." *New York Times,* Jan. 30.

Dowden, Richard. 2002. "This Woman Has Been Sentenced to Death by Stoning." *New York Times Magazine,* Jan. 27.

Dowd-Timonen, Patricia. 2003. "Daniel Pearl" (letter to the editor). *New York Times Magazine,* Jan. 12.

D'Souza, Dinesh. 2002. *What's So Great about America.* Washington, DC: Regnery.

Dubner, Stephen J. 2001. "Looking for Heroes—and Finding Them." *New York Times,* Oct. 6.

Dugan, George, Caspar H. Nannes, and R. Marshall Stross. 1979. *RPRC: A 50-Year Reflection.* New York: Religious Public Relations Council.

Dugger, Celia W. 2002a. "Court Bars Hindus' Rite Where They Razed Mosque." *New York Times,* Mar. 14.

————. 2002b. "Discord over Killing of India Muslims Deepens." *New York Times,* Apr. 29.

————. 2002c. "Fire Started on Train Carrying Activists Kills 57." *New York Times,* Feb. 28.

————. 2002d. "Hindu Justifies Mass Killings of Muslims in Reprisal Riots." *New York Times,* Mar. 5.

————. 2002e. "Hindu Rioters Kill 60 Muslims in India." *New York Times,* Mar. 1.

————. 2002f. "Indian Town's Seed Grew into the Taliban's Code." *New York Times,* Feb. 23.

————. 2002g. "More Than 200 Die in 3 Days of Riots in Western India." *New York Times,* Mar. 2.

————. 2002h. "Religious Riots Loom over Indian Politics." *New York Times,* July 27.

Dugger, Celia W., et al. 2001. "Islam: Thousands Hear Call of Prayer and Politics at World's Mosques." *New York Times,* Oct. 13.

Dunlap, David W. 2001a. "From the Rubble, Icons of Disaster and Faith." *New York Times,* Dec. 25.

————. 2001b. "Trinity Church: Amid the Rubble, a Steeple Stands." *New York Times,* Sept. 17.

————. 2002. "Blocks: Messages in Concrete: The Aesthetics of Safety." *New York Times,* Aug. 15.

————. 2003a. "At Ground Zero Oasis, a Path Is Restored." *New York Times,* Nov. 7.

————. 2003b. "Blocks: Looking for God in the Details at Ground Zero." *New York Times,* Jan. 9.

————. 2003c. "Blocks: Seeking the Sublime in the Simple to Mark 9/11." *New York Times,* Nov. 27.

———. 2004a. "Blocks: A Reflective View at Ground Zero, with Images from Your Sponsors." *New York Times,* Aug. 19.

———. 2004b. Email correspondence with the author, Aug. 26.

———. 2004c. *From Abyssinian to Zion: A Guide to Manhattan's Houses of Worship.* New York: Columbia Univ. Press.

———. 2004d. "Historic Chapel Embraces Role as Monument to Sept. 11." *New York Times,* Apr. 28.

———. 2004e. "Solace on the Site of Disaster." *New York Times,* May 14.

———. 2005a. "At Ground Zero, a Place to Recall a Lost Era." *New York Times,* Aug. 29.

———. 2005b. "Blocks: Pataki Solution on Museum Flies in Face of Planning." *New York Times,* Sept. 29.

———. 2005c. "Blocks: Varying Boundaries of Hallowed Ground." *New York Times,* Sept. 8.

———. 2005d. "Governor Bars Freedom Center at Ground Zero." *New York Times,* Sept. 29.

———. 2005e. "Seeking Trees, and Healing, for Ground Zero." *New York Times,* Sept. 8.

———. 2006a. "Plan to Move Ground Zero 'Cross' Upsets Priest." *New York Times,* Apr. 12.

———. 2006b. "Renovating 'Sacred Space,' Where the Remains of 9/11 Wait." *New York Times,* Aug. 29.

Dunlap, David W., and Joseph J. Vecchione. 2001. *Glory in Gotham: Manhattan's Houses of Worship: A Guide to Their History, Architecture, and Legacy.* New York: A City & Company Guide.

"Dutch Filmmaker Critical of Islam Is Shot and Killed." 2004. *New York Times,* Nov. 3.

Dwyer, Jim, and Susan Sachs. 2001. "The Reaction: A Tough City Is Swept by Anger, Despair, and Helplessness." *New York Times,* Sept. 12.

Eakin, Emily. 2001a. "New Accusations of a Vatican Role in Anti-Semitism." *New York Times,* Sept. 1.

———. 2001b. "Suddenly, It's Nostradamus, the Best Seller." *New York Times,* Sept. 18.

Eakin, Hugh. 2004. "When U.S. Aided Insurgents, Did It Breed Future Terrorists?" *New York Times,* Apr. 10.

"Easter Arrives in an Unsettled City." 2003. *New York Times,* Apr. 20.

Eberstadt, Fernanda. 2004. "A Frenchman or a Jew?" *New York Times Magazine,* Feb. 29.

Eck, Diana L. 2001. *A New Religious America: How a "Christian Country" Has Now Become the World's Most Religiously Diverse Nation.* New York: HarperSanFrancisco.

Eckholm, Erik. 2001a. "China Seeks World Support in Fight with Its Muslim Separatists." *New York Times,* Oct. 12.

———. 2001b. "In Kandahar, a Top School Reopens, and Girls Are Welcome." *New York Times,* Dec. 23.

———. 2002. "Struggle to Control What Islamic Schools Teach." *New York Times,* Jan. 15.

———. 2004a. "Attacks on Iraqi Shiite Leaders Raise Fears of Civil Strife." *New York Times,* Dec. 28.

———. 2004b. "Religion: A Day before Christmas, Fear Keeps Pews Empty in Baghdad." *New York Times,* Dec. 25.

———. 2005a. "Campaigning: Ally of Militant Cleric Is on the Stump in Sadr City." *New York Times,* Jan. 5.

———. 2005b. "Insurgents: Sunni Group Says It Killed Cleric's Aide in Bombing." *New York Times,* Jan. 15.

———. 2005c. "Iraq at the Brink: Is Shiite Good Will a Good Bet?" *New York Times,* Jan. 16.

———. 2005d. "Politics: Factional Unrest Is Dividing the Shiites of Southern Iraq." *New York Times,* Jan. 15.

———. 2007a. Email correspondence with the author, Aug. 17.

———. 2007b. Email correspondence with the author, Aug. 21.

Eden, Ami. 2005. "Playing the Holocaust Card." *New York Times,* Jan. 29.

Egan, Timothy. 2001. "Tough but Hopeful Weeks for the Muslims of Laramie." *New York Times,* Oct. 18.

———. 2002. "Muslim Held after Bags Failed Check Is Denied Bail." *New York Times,* Sept. 11.

"Egyptians Mourn an Islamic 'Guide.'" 2004. *New York Times,* Jan. 10.

Eichenwald, Kurt. 2001a. "The Financial Web: U.S. Help Sought to Monitor Aid Groups." *New York Times,* Dec. 15.

———. 2001b. "U.S. Jews Split on Washington's Shift on Palestinian Status." *New York Times,* Oct. 5.

Elliott, Andrea. 2003. "In Brooklyn, 9/11 Damage Continues." *New York Times,* June 7.

———. 2004a. "Muhammad at the Movies: Venerated, and Animated." *New York Times,* Nov. 15.

———. 2004b. "Study Finds City's Muslims Growing Closer since 9/11." *New York Times,* Oct. 5.

———. 2005a. "5 Muslims to Sue Homeland Security in Border Detentions." *New York Times,* Apr. 20.

———. 2005b. "A Bloody Crime in New Jersey Divides Egyptians Once Again." *New York Times,* Jan. 21.

———. 2005c. "Immigrants Fear Filing Suits, Advocates Say." *New York Times*, Apr. 30.

———. 2005d. "In a Suspicious U.S., Muslim Converts Find Discrimination." *New York Times*, Apr. 30.

———. 2005e. "Muslim Group Is Urging Women to Lead Prayers." *New York Times*, Mar. 18.

———. 2005f. "Nourishing a Far-Flung Culture." *New York Times*, Mar. 9.

———. 2005g. "Queens Muslim Group Says It Opposes Violence, and America." *New York Times*, June 22.

———. 2005h. "Rage Explodes at Egyptian Family's Funeral." *New York Times*, Jan. 18.

———. 2005i. "Study by Muslim Group Says Bias Crimes Up 50% in 2004." *New York Times*, May 12.

———. 2005j. "With Women at the Forefront, a Muslim Service Challenges Tradition." *New York Times*, Mar. 19.

———. 2005k. "You Can't Talk to an F.B.I. Agent That Way, or Can You?" *New York Times*, June 4.

———. 2006a. "More Muslims Are Coming to U.S. after a Decline in Wake of 9/11." *New York Times*, Sept. 10.

———. 2006b. "A Muslim Leader in Brooklyn, Reconciling 2 Worlds." *New York Times*, Mar. 5.

———. 2006c. "Tending to Muslim Hearts and Islam's Future." *New York Times*, Mar. 7.

———. 2006d. "To Lead the Faithful in a Faith under Fire." *New York Times*, Mar. 6.

———. 2007. "A Cleric's Journey Leads to a Suburban Frontier." *New York Times*, Jan. 28.

Elliott, Andrea, and William K. Rashbaum. 2005. "Anti-Muslim Bias Seen in Charges Against Man Linked to Al Qaeda." *New York Times*, June 1.

Elshtain, Jean Bethke. 2003. *Just War Against Terror: The Burden of American Power in a Violent World*. New York: Basic Books.

Eltahawy, Mona. 2002. "Keeping Faith with Islam in a New World." *New York Times*, Sept. 3.

Emerson, Steven. 2002. *American Jihad: The Terrorists Living among Us*. New York: Free Press.

Erlanger, Steven. 2001a. "Italy's Premier Calls Western Civilization Superior to Islamic World." *New York Times*, Sept. 27.

———. 2001b. "A Memory-Strewn Celebration of Germany's Jews." *New York Times*, Sept. 10.

———. 2002a. "Jab at a Jew Is Rattling Book World in Germany." *New York Times*, June 6.

———. 2002b. "The Jewish Question: Europe Knows Who's to Blame in the Middle East." *New York Times*, Apr. 7.

———. 2002c. "Specter of High-Level Anti-Semitism Taints German Campaign." *New York Times*, May 29.

———. 2007a. Email correspondence with the author, Aug. 20.

———. 2007b. Email correspondence with the author, Aug. 26.

Espen, Hal. 2006. "I'd Rather Be. . . ." Review of *The One That Got Away: A Memoir* by Howell Raines. *New York Times Book Review*, June 11.

Estrin, James. 2001. "In Memoriam" (photo). *New York Times*, Dec. 7.

———. 2005. "Lens: Observance." *New York Times*, Aug. 3.

"Europe, Christians, and History" (letters to the editor by Elain R. Samet and others). *New York Times*, June 17.

"Evangelicals and Their Critics" (letters to the editor by Michael O'Reilly and others). 2003. *New York Times*, Mar. 5.

"Ex-G.I. Writes about Interrogation Tactics" (AP). 2005. *New York Times*, Jan. 28.

"The Explosion in the Moslem World: A Roundtable on Islam." 1979. *New York Times*, Dec. 11.

Falk, Richard. 2003a. "Books of the Times: Waging a War of Words on the Very Idea of War." Review of *The Unconquerable World: Power, Nonviolence, and the Will of the People* by Jonathan Schell. *New York Times*, May 24.

———. 2003b. *The Great Terror War*. New York: Olive Branch Press.

"Falwell Calls Muhammad a Terrorist" (AP). 2002. *New York Times*, Oct. 4.

"Farrakhan Wants Evidence Released in Terrorist Attacks" (AP). 2001. Oct. 18.

Farzami, Farouz. 2004. "Iran's Lonely Crowd." *New York Times*, Nov. 27.

Fathi, Nazila. 2001. "Iranians Welcome Winter with a Ritual from Ancient Persia." *New York Times*, Dec. 23.

———. 2002a. "3rd Day of Protests in Tehran over Scholar's Death Sentence." *New York Times*, Nov. 12.

———. 2002b. "Iranian Refuses to Challenge His Death Sentence for Apostasy." *New York Times*, Nov. 14.

———. 2002c. "Iran Legislators Vote to Give Women Equality in Divorce." *New York Times*, Aug. 27.

———. 2002d. "Iran Sentences Reformist to Death for Insult to Prophet Muhammad." *New York Times*, Nov. 8.

———. 2002e. "Iran's President Trying to Limit Power of Clergy." *New York Times*, Aug. 29.

———. 2002f. "Protests Grow in Iran over Death Sentence for Professor." *New York Times*, Nov. 13.

———. 2003a. "The Clergy: Iraqi Career Women Ponder a Future under Shiite Rule." *New York Times*, May 25.

———. 2003b. "Exiles: As Iraqi Clerics Go Home, Talk of Schism with Shiite Hard-Liners in Iran." *New York Times,* Apr. 28.

———. 2003c. "Political Fervor of Iranian Clerics Begins to Ebb." *New York Times,* Jan. 17.

———. 2003d. "Protests in Iran Spread, and an Imam Urges Severe Punishment." *New York Times,* June 21.

———. 2004a. "As Repression Eases, More Iranians Change Their Sex." *New York Times,* Aug. 2.

———. 2004b. "Film Has Everyone but Clerics Giggling in Iran." *New York Times,* May 5.

———. 2004c. "International Reaction: Shiite Muslims Condemn U.S. for Attacks on Holy City." *New York Times,* Aug. 13.

———. 2004d. "Iran Drops Death Penalty for Professor Guilty of Blasphemy." *New York Times,* June 29.

———. 2004e. "President Khatami Warns Clerics Ruling Iran Against Extremism." *New York Times,* Feb. 12.

———. 2005. "Qum Journal: Where the Austerity of Islam Yields to a Yen for Chic." *New York Times,* June 7.

Fattah, Hassan M. 2005a. "Anger Burns on the Fringe of Britain's Muslims." *New York Times,* July 16.

———. 2005b. "Britain's Muslims Take Tough Line on Militants." *New York Times,* Aug. 11.

———. 2005c. "Jordan Is Preparing to Tone Down the Islamic Bombast in Textbooks." *New York Times,* June 12.

———. 2005d. "Leeds: New Incidents Heighten Tensions among British Muslims." *New York Times,* July 23.

———. 2005e. "Mecca Journal: Islamic Pilgrims Bring Cosmopolitan Air to Unlikely City." *New York Times,* Jan. 20.

———. 2005f. "Neighbors: Longtime Haven for Arabs Now Must Ask: Why Us?" *New York Times,* July 10.

Feldman, Noah. 2003a. *After Jihad: America and the Struggle for Islamic Democracy.* New York: Farrar, Straus and Giroux.

———. 2003b. "A New Democracy, Enshrined in Faith." *New York Times,* Nov. 13.

———. 2005a. "Agreeing to Disagree in Iraq." *New York Times,* Aug. 30.

———. 2005b. "Chronicle Political Islam: Global Warning." Review of *Globalized Islam: The Search for a New Ummah* by Olivier Roy. *New York Times Book Review,* Feb. 6.

Ferguson, Niall. 2003. "Why America Outpaces Europe (Clue: The God Factor)." *New York Times,* June 7.

————. 2004. "The Way We Live Now: Eurabia?" *New York Times Magazine,* Apr. 4.

"A Festive Time for Muslims." 2004. *New York Times,* Feb. 3.

Feuer, Alan. 2003. "Muslims: Vengeful Chaos Clouds Long-Suffering Shiites' New Freedom." *New York Times,* Apr. 13.

"Fight Against Freedom Center Plan Continues." 2005. *New York Times,* July 11.

"Fight the 'Crusaders.'" 2003. *New York Times,* Feb. 15.

Files, John. 2004. "Man Sets Himself Aflame near White House." *New York Times,* Nov. 16.

Filkins, Dexter. 2001. "Afghans at Queens Mosque Are Divided over bin Laden." *New York Times,* Sept. 19.

————. 2002a. "Kenya's Muslims: Resentments Both Local and International." *New York Times,* Dec. 1.

————. 2002b. "Now Playing in Turkey: Can Islamists Run a Democracy?" *New York Times,* Nov. 24.

————. 2002c. "Turkey Turns to Moderate in Islamic Party as New Premier." *New York Times,* Nov. 17.

————. 2004a. "The Constitution: Iraqi Women 1, Islamists 0." *New York Times,* Feb. 28.

————. 2004b. "Insurgents Quit Mosque in Najaf after Peace Deal." *New York Times,* Aug. 28.

————. 2004c. "Iraq Tape Shows the Decapitation of an American." *New York Times,* May 12.

————. 2004d. "Militant Cleric Is Testing Entry in Iraqi Politics." *New York Times,* Oct. 3.

————. 2004e. "Repatriation: Iraqi Council Weighs Return of Jews, Rejecting It So Far." *New York Times,* Feb. 28.

————. 2004f. "Sunni Clerics Call for an End to Killing, of Iraqis, That Is." *New York Times,* Mar. 1.

————. 2004g. "Top Shiite Cleric Is Said to Fear Voting in Iraq May Be Delayed." *New York Times,* Sept. 23.

————. 2004h. "Top Shiites Drop Their Resistance to Iraqi Charter." *New York Times,* Mar. 8.

————. 2005a. "On Bus, Bicycle, and Foot, Suicide Aim at a Shiite Holy Day." *New York Times,* Feb. 20.

————. 2005b. "Politics: A Top Shiite Candidate for Premier's Post Offers a Secular Vision for Iraq." *New York Times,* Feb. 10.

————. 2005c. "Secular Iraqis Say New Charter May Curb Rights." *New York Times,* Aug. 24.

————. 2005d. "Shiite Faction Ready to Shun Election in Iraq." *New York Times,* Jan. 29.

———. 2005e. "Shiites in Iraq Say Government Will Be Secular." *New York Times,* Jan. 24.

———. 2006. "The Plot Against America." Review of *The Looming Tower: Al-Qaeda and the Road to 9/11* by Lawrence Wright. *New York Times Book Review,* Aug. 6.

Filkins, Dexter, and James Glanz. 2005. "Shiites and Kurds Halt Charter Talks with Sunnis." *New York Times,* Aug. 27.

Filkins, Dexter, and Edward Wong. 2004. "Attempt to Kill Iraqi Ayatollah Reported." *New York Times,* Feb. 6.

Filkins, Dexter, and Robert F. Worth. 2005. "Leaders in Iraq Sending Charter to Referendum." *New York Times,* Aug. 29.

Finder, Alan. 2006. "Education: Essay Stirs Debate about Influence of a Jewish Lobby." *New York Times,* Apr. 12.

———. 2007. Telephone interview by the author, Mar. 19.

Finley, Bill. 2002. "Robertson Selling His Horses in Response to Protests from His Followers." *New York Times,* May 9.

Finn, Robin. 2001. "Public Lives: A Daughter of Islam, and an Enemy of Terror." *New York Times,* Oct. 25.

———. 2005. "Public Lives: Fighting for the Underlying Meaning of Ground Zero." *New York Times,* Aug. 12.

"Firefights near Shiite Shrines." 2004. *New York Times,* May 15.

Firestone, David. 2001a. "After a Long, Slow Climb to Respectability, a Muslim Charity Experiences a Rapid Fall." *New York Times,* Dec. 10.

———. 2001b. "Religion: For Some Jewish Leaders, Partnership with Muslims Is a Casualty of Sept. 11 Attacks." *New York Times,* Oct. 22.

———. 2002a. "60's Firebrand, Now Imam, Is Going on Trial in Killing." *New York Times,* Jan. 6.

———. 2002b. "Billy Graham Responds to Lingering Anger over 1972 Remarks on Jews." *New York Times,* Mar. 17.

———. 2002c. "The Charity: Muslim Group Can Be Sued, Judges Decide." *New York Times,* June 6.

———. 2002d. "Evangelical Christians and Jews Unite for Israel." *New York Times,* June 9.

———. 2003. "Divisive Words: Lawmaker under Fire Quits Leadership Post." *New York Times,* Mar. 15.

"First School of Astrology Is Accredited" (AP). 2001. *New York Times,* Aug. 28.

Fish, Stanley. 2001. "Condemnation Without Absolutes." *New York Times,* Oct. 15.

———. 2005. "One University under God?" *Chronicle of Higher Education,* Chronicle Careers, Jan. 7. Available at http://chronicle.com/jobs/2005/01/2005010701c.htm.

Fisher, Ian. 2001. "Europe's Muslims Seek a Path amid Competing Cultures." *New York Times*, Dec. 8.

———. 2002a. "Account of Punjab Rape Tells of a Brutal Society." *New York Times*, July 17.

———. 2002b. "How an Atheist Helps Protect Islamists in Turkey." *New York Times*, Nov. 26.

———. 2002c. "Pakistani Clerics Fight School Plans." *New York Times*, Aug. 4.

———. 2002d. "Turkey Waits and Wonders: How Closely Bound to Islam Is Election Victor?" *New York Times*, Nov. 7.

———. 2002e. "Voters in Turkey Expel Leadership." *New York Times*, Nov. 4.

———. 2003a. "Defining Hamas: Roots in Charity and Branches of Violence." *New York Times*, June 16.

———. 2003b. "Iraqi Shiite Anger Raises New Fears for U.S. Soldiers." *New York Times*, Oct. 11.

———. 2003c. "The Resistance: An Anti-American Iraqi Cleric Declares His Own Government, but Few Rally to Support Him." *New York Times*, Oct. 12.

———. 2003d. "Resolute Iranian Pilgrims Meet Awed G.I.'s." *New York Times*, Oct. 7.

———. 2003e. "Victims: Nine Bullets That Ended Baptists' Work in Yemen." *New York Times*, Jan. 16.

———. 2004a. "The Clerics: Iraqi Liquor Store Owners Fear Fundamentalists' Rise." *New York Times*, July 16.

———. 2004b. "Italian Woman's Veil Stirs More Than Fashion Feud." *New York Times*, Oct. 15.

———. 2004c. "Leading Muslim Clerics in Iraq Condemn Bombing of Churches." *New York Times*, Aug. 3.

———. 2005a. "Flow of Muslim Immigrants Strains the Reputation for Tolerance of a Small Italian Town." *New York Times*, Aug. 27.

———. 2005b. "Issue for Cardinals: Islam as Rival or Partner in Talks." *New York Times*, Apr. 12.

———. 2005c. "Pope Urges Muslims to Confront Terrorism." *New York Times*, Aug. 21.

Fisher, Ian, and Edward Wong. 2004. "The Military: Shrine in Najaf Damaged Again as Clashes Continue." *New York Times*, May 26.

Fiske, Edward B. 1974a. "He Converted to Islam and Took a Wife." *New York Times*, Sept. 13.

———. 1974b. "Islam Today: India's Moslems, Once-Powerful Minority, Are Slow to Play a Role in Secular Society." *New York Times*, Sept. 17.

———. 1974c. "Islam Today: Islam Growing Fastest in a Malaysian State; Charges of Pressure to Convert Are Heard." *New York Times*, Sept. 18.

———. 1974d. "Islam Today: The Koran as a Constitution." *New York Times*, Sept. 16.

———. 1974e. "Islam Today: Moslem Faith Strong in a Secular Era." *New York Times*, Sept. 15.

———. 1974f. "Modernist Stirrings Felt, but Islam Strongly Resists Change." *New York Times*, Sept. 18.

"Footnotes: Brigitte Bardot." 2003. *New York Times*, May 15.

"Footnotes to War." 2003. *New York Times*, Apr. 19.

"For Religious Bigotry" (editorial). 2004. *New York Times*, Aug. 26.

Fountain, John W. 2001a. "African-American Muslims: Sadness and Fear as a Group Feels Doubly at Risk." *New York Times*, Oct. 5.

———. 2001b. "The Muslims: Blending Day of Feasting into Month of Fasting." *New York Times*, Nov. 23.

———. 2001c. "Prayer Warriors Fight Church–State Division." *New York Times*, Nov. 18.

———. 2001d. "Public Lives: An Island of Peace in the Midst of an Abortion Debate." *New York Times*, Sept. 8.

———. 2002a. "Death Abroad Fails to Dim Bible Students' Resolve." *New York Times*, Nov. 23.

———. 2002b. "A Phone Call Brings Sad News but Fails to Dent Faith." *New York Times*, June 6.

———. 2003a. *True Vine: A Young Black Man's Journey of Faith, Hope, and Clarity*. New York: Public Affairs.

———. 2003b. "Waiting: In Prayers, Kansas Town Shows Unity." *New York Times*, Mar. 25.

———. 2005a. "The God Who Embraced Me." On "This I Believe," *All Things Considered*, National Public Radio, Nov. 28. Available at http://www.npr.org/templates/story/story.php?storyId=5016108.

———. 2005b. Telephone interview by the author, Dec. 29.

———. n.d. Web site at http://www.johnwfountain.com/.

Fouquet, Hélène. 2004. "Switzerland: Barred Islamic Scholar Gives Up U.S. Teaching Post." *New York Times*, Dec. 15.

"France Scolds Sharon for Calling Jews to Israel" (Reuters). 2004. *New York Times*, July 19.

"France: Students to Protest Anti-Semitism" (Reuters). 2004. *New York Times*, Oct. 23.

Frankel, Max. 2001. "Turning Away from the Holocaust." *New York Times*, Nov. 14.

Frantz, Douglas. 2001a. "American Parents Afraid for Two Held by Afghans." *New York Times*, Sept. 21.

———. 2001b. "The Captives: U.S. Relief Workers Tell of Fear and Faith." *New York Times*, Nov. 17.

———. 2001c. "Minutes from Cries of Jihad, Town Dreams of U.S." *New York Times,* Oct. 24.

———. 2001d. "Pakistan: Islamist Who Rallies Followers Against U.S." *New York Times,* Oct. 8.

———. 2001e. "Quetta Journal: Giving Proper Burial to Holy Books." *New York Times,* Sept. 29.

———. 2002. "Turkey, Well along Road to Secularism, Fears Detour to Islamism." *New York Times,* Jan. 8.

Frantz, Douglas, and Desmond Butler. 2002. "Imam at German Mosque Preached Hate to 9/11 Pilots." *New York Times,* July 16.

Frantz, Douglas, and David Rohde. 2001. "How bin Laden and Taliban Forged Jihad Ties." *New York Times,* Nov. 22.

Freedman, Samuel G. 2002. "Looking at Arab-American Lives with Care, and One Eye Closed." *New York Times,* Sept. 1.

Fremson, Ruth. 2001a. "Allure Must Be Covered: Individuality Peeks Through." *New York Times,* Nov. 4.

———. 2001b. "A Day for Meditation" (photo). *New York Times,* Sept. 19.

———. 2003. "Windows Shattered, but Faith Unbroken" (photos). *New York Times,* Apr. 21.

French, Howard W. 2002. "Video of Death of Journalist Is Seen in Court in Pakistan." *New York Times,* May 15.

Fried, Joseph P. 2001. "Following Up: A Son's Murder, a Mother's Nightmare." *New York Times,* Sept. 9.

———. 2003. "Following Up: Rehashing the Verdicts in a Synagogue Incident." *New York Times,* May 18.

Friedman, Thomas L. 1989. *From Beirut to Jerusalem.* New York: Farrar, Straus, Giroux.

———. 1999. *The Lexus and the Olive Tree.* New York: Farrar, Straus, Giroux.

———. 2001a. "Foreign Affairs: Today's News Quiz." *New York Times,* Nov. 20.

———. 2001b. "Spiritual Missile Shield." *New York Times,* Dec. 16.

———. 2002a. "Cuckoo in Carolina." *New York Times,* Aug. 28.

———. 2002b. "Defusing the Holy Bomb." *New York Times,* Nov. 27.

———. 2002c. "An Islamic Reformation." *New York Times,* Dec. 4.

———. 2002d. "Where Freedom Reigns." *New York Times,* Aug. 14.

———. 2003a. *Longitudes and Attitudes: The World in the Age of Terrorism.* New York: Random House and Anchor Books.

———. 2003b. *Searching for the Roots of 9/11* (documentary film). Silver Springs, MD: Discovery Communications and New York Times Television Video.

———. 2004a. "War of Ideas, Part 2." *New York Times,* Jan. 11.

———. 2004b. "War of Ideas, Part 6." *New York Times,* Jan. 25.

———. 2005a. "Brave, Young, and Muslim." *New York Times,* Mar. 3.

———. 2005b. "A Nobel for Sistani." *New York Times,* Mar. 20.

———. 2005c. "Outrage and Silence." *New York Times,* May 18.

———. 2005d. "A Poverty of Dignity and a Wealth of Rage." *New York Times,* July 15.

———. 2005e. "Reaping What It Sowed." *New York Times,* May 4.

———. 2005f. "Rooting Out the Jihadist Cancer." *New York Times,* July 8.

Friese, Kai. 2002. "Hijacking India's History." *New York Times,* Dec. 30.

Fuchs, Dale. 2004. "Spain Weighs Muslim Rights and Concerns about Safety." *New York Times,* May 23.

Fuchs, Marek. 2002. "Religion Journal: After 9/11, Inmates Search for True Nature of Islam." *New York Times,* Sept. 21.

Fuller, Thomas. 2003a. "Europe Debates Whether to Admit God to Union." *New York Times,* Feb. 5.

———. 2003b. "In Europe, One Continent under God. Or Not." *New York Times,* Feb. 9.

Gall, Carlotta. 2003a. "Islamic Militants: In Pakistan Border Towns, Taliban Has a Resurgence." *New York Times,* May 6.

———. 2003b. "Tackling a Tall Order: The Bamiyan Buddha." *New York Times,* Apr. 23.

———. 2003c. "Taliban Are Killing Clerics Who Dispute Holy War Call." *New York Times,* Aug. 4.

———. 2004. "Rescued and Patched, Afghan Art Back on View." *New York Times,* Dec. 28.

———. 2005a. "Gunmen Kill Afghan Cleric Who Condemned Taliban Leaders." *New York Times,* May 30.

———. 2005b. "Muslims' Anti-American Protests Spread from Afghanistan." *New York Times,* May 14.

Garbarine, Rachelle. 2001. "Residential Real Estate: Church Rents Out a Redone Building." *New York Times,* Sept. 7.

Garst, Robert E., ed. 1945. *The Newspaper: Its Making and Its Meaning. By Members of the Staff of the "New York Times."* New York: Charles Scribner's Sons.

Gelman, David. 2006. Communication with the author, Nov. 9.

"General Said to Be Faulted over Speeches" (AP). 2004. *New York Times,* Aug. 20.

Genzlinger, Neil. 2001. "A Few among the Thousands Who Offered Time and Expertise: Their Donation: An Oasis Amid Chaos." *New York Times,* Nov. 12.

Gerecht, Reuel Marc. 2003. "How to Mix Politics with Religion." *New York Times,* Apr. 29.

Gerges, Fawaz A. 2001. "A Time of Reckoning." *New York Times,* Oct. 8.

————. 2003. "Empty Promises of Freedom." *New York Times*, July 18.

"German Cause Célèbre: A Teacher's Head Scarf." 2003. *New York Times*, June 30.

Gettleman, Jeffrey. 2003. "Court Case: Deployment of Suspect Was Opposed." *New York Times*, June 19.

————. 2004a. "At Word of U.S. Foray, a Baghdad Militia Erupts." *New York Times*, Apr. 7.

————. 2004b. "Ex-Rivals Uniting: Signs That Shiites and Sunnis Are Joining to Fight Americans." *New York Times*, Apr. 9.

————. 2004c. "Holy Day: A Ritual of Self-Punishment, Long Suppressed, Is Shattered by Mortar Attack." *New York Times*, Mar. 3.

————. 2004d. "Mob Attack: Falluja's Religious Leaders Condemn Mutilation, but Not Killing, of Americans." *New York Times*, Apr. 3.

————. 2004e. "A Young Radical's Anti-U.S. Wrath Is Unleashed." *New York Times*, Apr. 5.

————. 2005. "Insurgents: Gunmen Kidnap the Catholic Archbishop of Mosul as Pre-Election Violence Flares in Iraq." *New York Times*, Jan. 18.

————. 2006. "Africa: A Kenyan Town's Offer of Aid Pays Dividends for Its Youth." *New York Times*, Sept. 11.

Gettleman, Jeffrey, and Douglas Jehl. 2004. "Up to 12 Marines Die in Raid on Their Base as Fierce Fighting Spreads to 6 Iraqi Cities." *New York Times*, Apr. 7.

Gettleman, Jeffrey, and Edward Wong. 2005. "Insurgency: Archbishop Freed in Iraq." *New York Times*, Jan. 19.

Giuliani, Rudolph W. 2003. "How Europe Can Stop the Hate." *New York Times*, June 18.

Glaberson, William. 2001. "Interpreting Islamic Law for American Muslims." *New York Times*, Oct. 21.

————. 2004. "Man Burned at White House Is Called Central to Terror Case." *New York Times*, Nov. 17.

————. 2005a. "Defense Calls F.B.I. Informer in Terror Case Against Sheik." *New York Times*, Feb. 12.

————. 2005b. "Sheik Prayed for Jews' Death, Says Prosecutor." *New York Times*, Jan. 29.

————. 2005c. "Video, Previously Excluded, Is Shown at Sheik's Terror-Financing Trial." *New York Times*, Feb. 24.

Glanz, James. 2005a. "Some Fear Iraq's Charter Will Erode Women's Rights." *New York Times*, Aug. 8.

————. 2005b. "Too Angry or Fearful to Vote, Sunni Iraqis Are Marginalized." *New York Times*, Feb. 12.

Glassie, John. 2003. "In Good Faith: Questions for Irshad Manji." *New York Times Magazine*, Dec. 21.

Glassman, Mark. 2004. "Broadcast: U.S. Religious Figures Offer Abuse Apology on Arab TV." *New York Times*, June 11.

Goldberg, J. J. 1996. *Jewish Power: Inside the American Jewish Establishment*. Reading, MA: Addison-Wesley.

Goldberger, Paul. 1996. "God's Stronghold at Mammon's Door." *New York Times*, May 14.

Golden, Tim. 2004. "How Dubious Evidence Spurred Relentless Guantánamo Spy Hunt." *New York Times*, Dec. 19.

Goldman, Ari L. 1991. *The Search for God at Harvard*. New York: Random House and Times Books.

———. 1993. "Thriving amid Harmony, a Mosque Is Transformed." *New York Times*, May 4.

———. 2001. "'Avoid Israel so We Can Be Safe and Sound in New York?'" *Jerusalem Post*, Sept. 14.

Goldscheider, Eric. 2002. "Religion Journal: Colleges Are Scrambling for Muslim Chaplains." *New York Times*, Feb. 26.

Goldsmith, Jeanette. 2001. "The Uncomfortable Question of Anti-Semitism" (letter to the editor). *New York Times Magazine*, Dec. 9.

Goode, Erica. 2001. "Letting Bygones Be Bygones Is Often a Challenge." *New York Times*, Dec. 11.

Goodnough, Abby, and Michael Luo. 2004. "The Victims: Families of Men Slain by Mob Focus on Their Lives, Not How They Died." *New York Times*, Apr. 3.

Goodstein, Laurie. 2001a. "Abortion Advertising Campaign." *New York Times*, Aug. 30.

———. 2001b. "As Attacks' Impact Recedes, a Return to Religion as Usual." *New York Times*, Nov. 26.

———. 2001c. "Child Sex Case Brings Battle on Admission to Clerics." *New York Times*, Aug. 31.

———. 2001d. "Civil Rights: American Sikhs Contend They Have Become a Focus of Profiling at Airports." *New York Times*, Nov. 10.

———. 2001e. "The Cleric: Muslim Leader Who Was Once Labeled an Alarmist Is Suddenly a Sage." *New York Times*, Oct. 28.

———. 2001f. "Finding Fault: Falwell's Finger-Pointing Inappropriate, Bush Says." *New York Times*, Sept. 15.

———. 2001g. "Influential American Muslims Temper Their Tone." *New York Times*, Oct. 19.

———. 2001h. "The Legal Opinion: Muslim Scholars Back Fight Against Terrorists." *New York Times*, Oct. 12.

———. 2001i. "Military Clerics Balance Arms and Allah." *New York Times,* Oct. 7.

———. 2001j. "Muslim-Americans: Some Muslims Say Tape Removes Previous Doubt." *New York Times,* Dec. 15.

———. 2001k. "Muslims Nurture Sense of Self on Campus." *New York Times,* Nov. 3.

———. 2001l. "New Christian Take on the Old Dating Ritual." *New York Times,* Sept. 9.

———. 2001m. "Ramadan: Muslims See Acceptance and Scrutiny as Holy Month Nears." *New York Times,* Nov. 16.

———. 2001n. "Relations: In U.S., Echoes of Rift of Muslims and Jews." *New York Times,* Sept. 12.

———. 2001o. "The Role of Religion: Scholars Call Attacks a Distortion of Islam." *New York Times,* Sept. 30.

———. 2001p. "Stereotyping Rankles Silent, Secular Majority of American Muslims." *New York Times,* Dec. 23.

———. 2001q. "U.S. Muslims Push Stamp as Symbol of Acceptance." *New York Times,* Nov. 20.

———. 2002a. "Bishops Turn to Writing Antiwar Policy." *New York Times,* Nov. 13.

———. 2002b. "Civil Liberties: Jewish Groups Endorse Tough Security Laws." *New York Times,* Jan. 3.

———. 2002c. "O Ye of Much Faith! A Triple Dose of Trouble." *New York Times,* June 2.

———. 2002d. "The Religious Leaders: Evangelical Figures Oppose Religious Leaders' Broad Antiwar Sentiment." *New York Times,* Oct. 5.

———. 2002e. "War on Iraq Not Yet Justified, Bishops Say." *New York Times,* Nov. 14.

———. 2003a. "American Jews: Divide among Jews Leads to Silence on Iraq War." *New York Times,* Mar. 15.

———. 2003b. "American Muslims: Resentful of Treatment, Muslims Still Work with Authorities." *New York Times,* Mar. 21.

———. 2003c. "Anglican Leaders Work to Avoid a Split over Gay U.S. Bishop." *New York Times,* Oct. 16.

———. 2003d. "Anglicans in Angry Split over Homosexuality Issue." *New York Times,* Oct. 12.

———. 2003e. "Anglicans Warn of a Split If Gay Man Is Consecrated." *New York Times,* Oct. 17.

———. 2003f. "Catholics: Conservative Catholics' Wrenching Debate over Whether to Back President or Pope." *New York Times,* Mar. 6.

———. 2003g. "Church Event Set for Base Stirs Concern." *New York Times,* Apr. 6.

———. 2003h. "Dalai Lama Says Terror May Need a Violent Reply." *New York Times,* Sept. 18.

———. 2003i. "Dissent: Conscientious Objector Numbers Are Small but Growing." *New York Times*, Apr. 1.

———. 2003j. "Muslims Hesitating on Gifts as U.S. Scrutinizes Charities." *New York Times*, Apr. 17.

———. 2003k. "Pentagon Says It Will Review Chaplain Policy." *New York Times*, Sept. 28.

———. 2003l. "Religions' View: Diverse Denominations Oppose the Call to Arms." *New York Times*, Mar. 6.

———. 2003m. "Seeing Islam as 'Evil' Faith, Evangelicals Seek Converts." *New York Times*, May 27.

———. 2003n. "Top Evangelicals Critical of Colleagues over Islam." *New York Times*, May 8.

———. 2004a. "American Muslims Back Kerry." *New York Times*, Oct. 22.

———. 2004b. Interviewed by the author, Hamilton, NY, Mar. 23.

———. 2004c. "Muslim Women Seeking a Place in the Mosque." *New York Times*, July 22.

———. 2004d. "Since 9/11, Muslims Look Closer to Home." *New York Times*, Nov. 15.

———. 2004e. "Woman's Mosque Protest Brings Furor in the U.S." *New York Times*, July 22.

———. 2005a. "From Muslims in America, a New Fatwa on Terrorism." *New York Times*, July 28.

———. 2005b. "From State Dept., Advice for Muslim Convention." *New York Times*, Sept. 3.

———. 2005c. "Muslim Leaders Confront Terror Threat within Islam." *New York Times*, Sept. 2.

Goodstein, Laurie, and Tamar Lewin. 2001. "Victims of Mistaken Identity, Sikhs Pay a Price for Turbans." *New York Times*, Sept. 19.

Goodstein, Laurie, and Gustav Niebuhr. 2001. "Attacks and Harassment of Middle-Eastern Americans Rising." *New York Times*, Sept. 14.

"G.O.P. Web Site Apologizes for Anti-Islam Link." 2002. *New York Times*, Dec. 28.

Gordis, Daniel. 2002. "Needing Israel." *New York Times*, Apr. 13.

"Graham Modifies Comments" (AP). 2001. *New York Times*, Dec. 5.

"Graham's Son Defends Him" (AP). 2002. *New York Times*, Apr. 4.

Gramling, Oliver. 1940. *AP: The Story of News*. New York: Farrar and Rinehart.

Green, John C., James L. Guth, Corwin E. Smidt, and Lyman Kellstedt. 1996. *Religion and the Culture Wars: Dispatches from the Front*. Lanham, MD: Rowman and Littlefield.

Green, Peter S. 2001. "Arts Abroad: Polanski Film about Holocaust and Suffering in Poland." *New York Times*, Sept. 6.

Greenberg, Joel. 2001. "The Suicide Bomber: A Family Is Left 'Sad and Happy' by a Violent Death." *New York Times,* Dec. 7.

———. 2002a. "The Church: Hymns, Not Gunfire, Fill Bethlehem." *New York Times,* May 13.

———. 2002b. "Mosque near Christian Shrine Is Blocked by Israeli Officials." *New York Times,* Jan. 10.

Greenfield, Lauren, and Amy M. Spindler. 2001. "Beauty: Beheld." *New York Times Magazine,* Sept. 9.

Grimes, William. 2005a. "Books of the Times: The Jihad Is a Civil War, the West Only a Bystander." Review of *No God but God: The Origins, Evolution, and Future of Islam* by Reza Aslan. *New York Times,* May 4.

———. 2005b. "Books of the Times: Where the Evil Empire Is Us and the Veil Liberation." Review of *Faith at War: A Journey on the Frontlines of Islam, from Baghdad to Timbuktu* by Yaroslav Trofimov. *New York Times,* June 3.

Griswold, Eliza. 2005. "The New Islamist Revolution?" *New York Times Magazine,* Jan. 23.

Gross, Jane. 2001a. "Jewish Ritual Is Adapted for Dead of Sept. 11." *New York Times,* Nov. 6.

———. 2001b. "A School Finds Strength in a Network of Grief." *New York Times,* Dec. 18.

———. 2002. "A Year of Study Abroad, a Year of Great Danger." *New York Times,* July 3.

"Groups Lose Sole Authority on Chaplains for Muslims" (AP). 2003. *New York Times,* Oct. 15.

Gussow, Mel. 2003. "A New Play Encounters Muslims' Ire in Cincinnati." *New York Times,* Feb. 3.

Haberman, Clyde. 2001a. "NYC: When the Unimaginable Happens, and It's Right Outside Your Window." *New York Times,* Sept. 12.

———. 2001b. "A Perilous Road in Israel Becomes a Death Trap Again." *New York Times,* Aug. 27.

———. 2002. "NYC: Among Jews, Urge to Panic Is Premature." *New York Times,* June 18.

———. 2003a. "NYC: Rational Talk by 2 Faiths across Divide." *New York Times,* Mar. 14.

———. 2003b. "NYC: The Sacred and the Tacky, Inseparable." *New York Times,* May 6.

———. 2004a. "NYC: A Little Late, but a Stand Against Hate." *New York Times,* Nov. 16.

———. 2004b. "NYC: A Spot to Rest, and to Honor Love and Loss." *New York Times,* July 16.

———. 2006a. "NYC: Call It a Hole in the Ground. We Can Take It." *New York Times,* Aug. 29.

———. 2006b. "NYC: The Guy Who Fired Me Was Right." *New York Times,* May 12.

Habila, Helon. 2003. "Justice, Nigeria's Way." *New York Times,* Oct. 4.

Halbfinger, David M. 2002. "After the Veil, a Makeover Rush." *New York Times,* Sept. 1.

———. 2003. "The Prisoners: Amid Easter Finery, a Celebrated Return to U.S. Soil for Former P.O.W.'s." *New York Times,* Apr. 21.

———. 2005. "The Pitch: A Series about Wacky Terrorists." *New York Times,* Sept. 1.

Hamill, Pete. 2004. "Who Can Reach the Dead?" Review of *Up from Zero: Politics, Architecture, and the Rebuilding of New York* by Paul Goldberger. *New York Times Book Review,* Sept. 12.

Hanley, Robert. 2001. "Archbishop Is Installed for the Newark Diocese." *New York Times,* Oct. 10.

Hanson, Victor Davis. 2001. *Carnage and Culture: Landmark Battles in the Rise of Western Power.* New York: Doubleday.

Harden, Blaine. 2001a. "Saudis Seek to Add U.S. Muslims to Their Sect." *New York Times,* Oct. 20.

———. 2001b. "U.S. Patriots from Mideast Want to Pursue bin Laden." *New York Times,* Oct. 12.

———. 2002. "The Role of Religion: Once Calmed by Faith, Suspect Turned Furious." *New York Times,* Oct. 27.

Harden, Blaine, and Kevin Sack. 2001. "One for His Country, and One Against It." *New York Times,* Dec. 11.

Harris, Mark. 1974. "The Last Article." *New York Times Magazine,* Oct. 6.

Harrison, Lawrence E., and Samuel P. Huntington, eds. 2000. *Culture Matters: How Values Shape Human Progress.* New York: Basic Books.

Hart, Steve. 2001. "Muslim Prayers" (photo). *New York Times,* Nov. 18.

Hartocollis, Anemona, and Charlie LeDuff. 2001. "Relations: Parents Fear Their Children Will Be the Targets of Bigotry." *New York Times,* Sept. 15.

Hasan, Asma Gull. 2000. *American Muslims: The New Generation.* New York: Continuum.

———. 2002. "Learning a Lesson for Ramadan." *New York Times,* Nov. 6.

———. 2004. *Why I Am a Muslim: An American Odyssey.* London: Element.

Hasan, Nader R. 2002. "Jihad and Veritas." *New York Times,* June 5.

"Hate Crimes Up Against Muslims" (AP). 2002. *New York Times,* Nov. 26.

Hauser, Christine. 2004. "Getting Out the Muslim Vote." *New York Times,* Mar. 1.

Hays, Matthew. 2004. "Act of Faith: A Film on Gays and Islam." *New York Times,* Nov. 2.

Healy, Patrick D. 2003. "A Drive to Register Muslims as Voters in New York State." *New York Times,* June 16.

———. 2005a. "Believe It: The Media's Credibility Headache Gets Worse." *New York Times,* May 22.

————. 2005b. "College Cancels Speech over 9/11 Remarks." *New York Times,* Feb. 2.

————. 2005c. "Pataki Warns Cultural Groups for Museum at Ground Zero." *New York Times,* June 25.

Hedges, Chris. 2001a. "Best Address in Jerusalem." Review of *The Rock: A Tale of Seventh-Century Jerusalem* by Kanan Makiya. *New York Times Book Review,* Nov. 25.

————. 2001b. "La Courneuve Journal: In Suburban Squalor near Paris, Echoes of Jihad." *New York Times,* Oct. 16.

————. 2002a. "Muslims Return from Mecca with Joy, Yet Concern." *New York Times,* Mar. 8.

————. 2002b. "Public Lives: A Minister's Star-Struck Path to Ground Zero." *New York Times,* Sept. 18.

————. 2002c. "Public Lives: Separating Spiritual and Political, He Pays a Price." *New York Times,* June 13.

————. 2002d. "Tunisia: Explosion at Synagogue Tied to Jihad; Arrest Made." *New York Times,* Apr. 24.

————. 2002e. *War Is a Force That Gives Us Meaning.* New York: Public Affairs.

————. 2003a. "Chris Hedges on War and the Press." *Poynteronline,* Mar. 25. Available at http://www.poynter.org/content/content/_view.asp?id=25766.

————. 2003b. "War and Empire: Text of the Rockford College Graduation Speech [May 17]." *Rockford Register Star,* May 21. Available at http://www.rrstar.com/localnews/your_community/rockford/20030521-4971.shtml.

————. 2004a. "Public Lives: An Actor's Craft and His Faith Intersect." *New York Times,* Sept. 7.

————. 2004b. "Public Lives: A Muslim in the Middle Hopes Against Hope." *New York Times,* June 23.

————. 2005a. *Losing Moses on the Freeway: The 10 Commandments in America.* New York: Free Press.

————. 2005b. "Soldiers of Christ II: Feeling the Hate with the National Religious Broadcasters." *Harper's Magazine,* May 30. Available at http://www.harpers.org/FeelingTheHate.html.

————. 2006a. *American Fascists: The Christian Right and the War on America.* New York: Free Press.

————. 2006b. "The Christian Right and the Open Society." Colloquium given at Colgate Univ., Hamilton, NY, Feb. 7.

————. 2007. "American Fascists: The Christian Right and the War on America." Public lecture given at Colgate Univ., Hamilton, NY, Feb. 12.

Heilbrunn, Jacob. 2005. "Nonfiction Chronicle." Review of *Losing Moses on the Freeway: The Ten Commandments in America* by Chris Hedges. *New York Times Book Review*, Aug. 21.

Henneberger, Melinda. 2001a. "Archbishop Bids Brotherly Goodbye to Wife, and Returns to Fold." *New York Times*, Aug. 30.

———. 2001b. "Delicately, Pope Deplores 1915 Killings of Armenians." *New York Times*, Sept. 27.

———. 2001c. "Harsh Words at Christian–Muslim Meeting." *New York Times*, Oct. 5.

———. 2001d. "Jews on Panel Examining Wartime Pope Say Vatican Singled Them Out for Blame." *New York Times*, Sept. 12.

———. 2001e. "The Papal Trip: Pope, in Central Asia, Speaks Out Against Any Overzealous Military Response by the U.S." *New York Times*, Sept. 24.

———. 2001f. "Politics and Piety: The Vatican on Just Wars." *New York Times*, Sept. 30.

———. 2001g. "Pope Condemns Extremism behind Terror." *New York Times*, Sept. 25.

———. 2001h. "The Pope, in Central Asia, Urges Peace." *New York Times*, Sept. 23.

———. 2001i. "Pope to Leave for Kazakhstan and Armenia This Weekend." *New York Times*, Sept. 21.

———. 2001j. "Rome Journal: So Many to Mourn: An Envoy's Sad Baptism." *New York Times*, Sept. 18.

———. 2001k. "Reading Italy's Signs of the Cross." *New York Times*, Nov. 11.

———. 2001l. "Social Justice and Terror Offer Bishops Tough Issue." *New York Times*, Oct. 28.

———. 2001m. "La Spezia Journal: Are There Crosses in Schools? Is Italy Catholic?" *New York Times*, Nov. 10.

———. 2001n. "Vatican Journal: Between a Melodrama's Lines: Interfaith Battle." *New York Times*, Aug. 29.

———. 2001o. "The Vatican: Pope, Not Mentioning U.S., Urges Military 'Restraint.'" *New York Times*, Dec. 12.

———. 2002a. "Pope Sees 'Intolerable' Violence." *New York Times*, Apr. 9.

———. 2002b. "Vatican to Hold Secret Trials of Priests in Pedophilia Cases." *New York Times*, Jan. 9.

Henriques, Diana B. 2002. "Charity Overwhelmed in Bid to Meet Attack Victims' Bills." *New York Times*, Jan. 5.

Herszenhorn, David M. 2001a. "An Afternoon of Prayer in a Wounded City." *New York Times*, Aug. 27.

———. 2001b. "McGreevey Sidesteps Politics in Ramadan Speech at Mosque." *New York Times*, Nov. 24.

————. 2004. "Time Off Is Given for Ramadan for Students at Brooklyn School." *New York Times,* Oct. 15.

Higgins, Chester, Jr. 2001. Untitled photo. *New York Times,* Sept. 19.

Hill, James. 2003. "Footnotes to War" (photo). *New York Times,* Apr. 19.

Hilton, Isabel. 2003. "Everybody Hates Somebody Somewhere." Review of *Terror in the Name of God: Why Religious Militants Kill* by Jessica Stern. *New York Times Book Review,* Nov. 16.

"Hindu Temple Plan in India Stokes Tensions" (Reuters). 2003. *New York Times,* July 20.

Hiro, Dilip. 2003. "Why the Mullahs Love a Revolution." *New York Times,* Apr. 23.

————. 2005. "Allah and Democracy Can Get Along Fine." *New York Times,* Mar. 1.

Hoge, Warren. 2001. "The Convert: Shoe-Bomb Suspect Fell in with Extremists in London." *New York Times,* Dec. 27.

————. 2003. "London: Britain Moves to Deport Muslim Cleric as a Radical." *New York Times,* Apr. 6.

Holden, Stephen. 2006. "Film Review: The Gentle Life of a Priest, Made Famous in Death." *New York Times,* Sept. 6.

"Holy Month Comes to End in Kashmir." 2004. *New York Times,* Nov. 15.

"Holy Places: A Church and a Site Revered by 3 Faiths" (Agence France-Presse). 2002. *New York Times,* Apr. 4.

"Holy Sites, Bitter Passions." 2002. *New York Times,* Apr. 7.

Hoover, Dennis R. 2002a. "Choosing Up Sides in the Middle East." *Religion in the News* 5, no. 3 (Fall 2002): 8–10, 20–21.

————. 2002b. "Missionaries or Not?" *Religion in the News* 5, no. 1 (Spring): 16–18, 31.

Hoover, Stewart M., Barbara M. Handley, and Martin Radelfinger. 1989. *The RNS-Lilly Study of Religion Reporting and Readership in the Daily Press.* Philadelphia: School of Communications and Theater, Temple Univ.

"Hoping to Give Buddha Back to Afghanistan" (photo). 2002. *New York Times,* Apr. 12.

Horowitz, Jason. 2004. "Europe, Seeking Political Unity, Stumbles over Issue of Religion." *New York Times,* Nov. 7.

Hubbard, Benjamin J. 1990. "The Importance of the Religion Angle in Reporting on Current Events." In *Reporting Religion: Facts & Faith,* edited by Benjamin J. Hubbard, 3–19. Sonoma, CA: Poleridge Press.

Hunter, James Davison. 1991. *Culture Wars: The Struggle to Define America.* New York: Basic Books.

Hunter, James Davison, and Joshua Yates. 2002. "In the Vanguard of Globalization: The World of American Globalizers." In *Many Globalizations: Cultural Diversity in the*

Contemporary World, edited by Peter L. Berger and Samuel P. Huntington, 323–57. Oxford, UK: Oxford Univ. Press.

Huntington, Samuel P. 1993. "The Clash of Civilizations?" *Foreign Affairs* 72, no. 3 (Summer): 22–49.

————. 1997. *The Clash of Civilizations and the Remaking of World Order.* New York: Simon & Schuster and Touchstone Books.

————. 2004. *Who Are We? The Challenges to America's National Identity.* New York: Simon & Schuster.

Husain, Muhammad Ishrat, and Bernard Haykel. 2001. "Think Tank: Two Views: Can the Koran Condone Terror?" *New York Times,* Oct. 13.

Ibrahim, Saad Eddin. 2005. "Islam Can Vote, If We Let It." *New York Times,* May 21.

Ignatieff, Michael. 2001. "Exhibit A: Blood Sisters." *New York Times Magazine,* Sept. 9.

"In a Kabul Mosque, There Is New Vigor among Dervishes." 2001. *New York Times,* Dec. 1.

Inderfurth, Karl F. 2001. "Teaching the Taliban about Human Rights." *New York Times,* Aug. 29.

"Iran Pardons Cleric Who Was Jailed for Insulting Islam." 2002. *New York Times,* Nov. 6.

"Islamic Anti-Semitism" (editorial). 2003. *New York Times,* Oct. 18.

"Islamic Group Says It Set Off Dagestan Blast." 2005. *New York Times,* July 3.

"Italy: Oriana Fallaci Charged with Insulting Islam" (Reuters). 2005. *New York Times,* May 26.

Jackson, Sherman A. 2003. "Islam(s) East and West: Pluralism Between No-Frills and Designer Fundamentalism." In *September 11 in History: A Watershed Moment?* edited by Mary L. Dudziak, 112–35. Durham, NC: Duke Univ. Press.

Jacobs, Andrew. 2001. "Faith: Delivering the Gospel to Ground Zero Streets." *New York Times,* Oct. 18.

Jacoby, Susan. 2004. *Freethinkers: A History of American Secularism.* New York: Holt.

James, Caryn. 2001. "The Media: Islam and Its Adherents Ride the Publicity Wave." *New York Times,* Oct. 6.

James, Edwin L. 1945. "The Organization of a Newspaper." In *The Newspaper: Its Making and Its Meaning. By Members of the Staff of the "New York Times,"* edited by Robert E. Garst, 3–21. New York: Scribner's.

James, George. 2002. "After Sept. 11 Losses, Then a Fire, a New Jersey Church Worships On." *New York Times,* Jan. 14.

Janofsky, Michael. 2003a. "The Missing: Vigil for Soldier Brings Common Ground for 2 Tribes That Are Usually at Odds." *New York Times,* Mar. 28.

————. 2003b. "Muslim Americans: War Brings New Surge of Anxiety for Followers of Islam." *New York Times,* Mar. 29.

———. 2004. "Soldier Is Facing Charges of Trying to Aid Al Qaeda." *New York Times,* Feb. 13.

Jefferson, Margo. 2005. "Theater Review: Timeless Lessons on Tolerance Imparted by a Sufi Sage from Colonial Africa." *New York Times,* Apr. 7.

Jehl, Douglas. 2001a. "Democracy's Uneasy Steps in Islamic World." *New York Times,* Nov. 23.

———. 2001b. "For Saudi Cleric, Battle Shapes Up as Infidel vs. Islam." *New York Times,* Dec. 5.

———. 2001c. "Guardians of the Faith: Speaking in the Name of Islam." *New York Times,* Dec. 2.

———. 2001d. "Moderate Muslims Fear Their Message Is Being Ignored." *New York Times,* Oct. 21.

———. 2001e. "The Muslims: More Extremists Find Basis for Rebellion in Islam." *New York Times,* Sept. 22.

———. 2003a. "Bush Says He Disagrees with General's Remarks on Religion." *New York Times,* Oct. 23.

———. 2003b. "Iran Said to Send Agents into Iraq." *New York Times,* Apr. 23.

———. 2003c. "Pentagon: U.S. General Apologizes for Remarks about Islam." *New York Times,* Oct. 18.

Jehl, Douglas, and Nazila Fathi. 2003. "The Shiites: Gingerly, Pro-Iranian Iraqi Muslim Group Lobbies for Washington Favor." *New York Times,* May 7.

Jenkins, Ron. 2001. "Refighting Old Religious Wars in a Miniature Arena." *New York Times,* Dec. 9.

"Jewish Defense League Leader Is Declared Dead in a Suicide" (AP). 2002. *New York Times,* Nov. 5.

"Jewish Group Plans Armed Patrols in Brooklyn." 2002. *New York Times,* June 10.

"Jewish Groups Want a Teenager's Novel Withdrawn in France." 2002. *New York Times,* Dec. 12.

"Jews Discuss Attacks at Brussels Meeting" (Reuters). 2002. *New York Times,* Apr. 23.

"Jihad's Women" (letters to the editor by Paul Chernis and others). 2001. *New York Times Magazine,* Nov. 18.

Johnson, Kirk. 2005. "Incendiary in Academia May Now Find Himself Burned." *New York Times,* Feb. 11.

Jones, Richard Lezin. 2002. "New Jersey: Arab Paper Is Assailed for Inflaming Anti-Semitism." *New York Times,* Nov. 8.

Jordan, Lewis, ed. 1976. *The "New York Times" Manual of Style and Usage.* New York: New York Times Company.

Judah, Tim. 2002. "The Sullen Majority." *New York Times Magazine,* Sept. 1.

Juergensmeyer, Mark. 1993. *The New Cold War? Religious Nationalism Confronts the Secular State.* Berkeley and Los Angeles: Univ. of California Press.

———. 2003. *Terror in the Mind of God: The Global Rise of Religious Violence.* Berkeley and Los Angeles: Univ. of California Press.

Kahn, Joseph. 2001. "A Business Plan for Islam Inc." *New York Times,* Dec. 30.

———. 2002. "American Muslims: Raids, Detentions, and Lists Lead Muslims to Cry Persecution." *New York Times,* Mar. 27.

Kakutani, Michiko. 2001. "Critic's Notebook: Rituals for Grieving Extend Past Tradition into Public Displays." *New York Times,* Sept. 18.

———. 2003. "Books of the Times: Book Study as Insubordination under the Mullahs." Review of *Reading Lolita in Tehran: A Memoir in Books* by Azar Nafisi. *New York Times,* Apr. 15.

———. 2004a. "Books of the Times: A Dark View of U.S. Strategy." Review of *Imperial Hubris: Why the West Is Losing the War on Terror* by anonymous. *New York Times,* July 9.

———. 2004b. "Books of the Times: An Identity Crisis for Norman Rockwell America." Review of *Who Are We? The Challenge to America's National Identity* by Samuel P. Huntington. *New York Times,* May 26.

———. 2005a. "Books of the Times: After a Day of Terror, a Long Architectural Tug of War." Review of *Sixteen Acres: Architecture and the Outrageous Struggle for the Future of Ground Zero* by Philip Nobel. *New York Times,* Jan. 18.

———. 2005b. "Books of the Times: As if the Mullahs Were All Young at Heart." Review of *Lipstick Jihad: A Memoir of Growing up Iranian in America and American in Iran* by Azadeh Moaveni. *New York Times,* Feb. 25.

———. 2005c. "Books of the Times: Ordinary but for the Evil They Wrought." Review of *Perfect Soldiers: The Hijackers, Who They Were, Why They Did It* by Terry McDermott. *New York Times,* May 20.

Kandall, Jonathan. 1978. "Religious Revival Is Sweeping across the World of Islam." *New York Times,* Nov. 23.

Kantor, Jodi. 2005. "9/11: Light a Candle or Party On?" *New York Times,* Aug. 18.

Kaplan, Robert D. 2002. *Warrior Politics: Why Leadership Demands a Pagan Ethos.* New York: Random House.

Karim, Karim H. 2002. "Making Sense of the 'Islamic Peril': Journalism as Cultural Practice." In *Journalism after September 11,* edited by Barbie Zelizer and Stuart Allan, 101–16. London: Routledge.

———. 2003. *Islamic Peril: Media and Global Violence.* Montreal: Black Rose Books.

Kaufman, Leslie, and Constance L. Hays. 2001. "Red, White, and Blue Christmas." *New York Times,* Sept. 27.

Kazin, Michael. 2004. "Books of the Times: Under God or under Citizens: America's Long Culture War." Review of *Freethinkers: A History of American Secularism* by Susan Jacoby. *New York Times,* Mar. 31.

Kean, Thomas H., and Lee H. Hamilton. 2006. "Giving Muslims Hope." *New York Times,* Sept. 10.

Kearney, John. 2004. "My God Is Your God." *New York Times,* Jan. 26.

Keddie, Nikki R. 2001. "Divine Inspiration." *New York Times,* Dec. 16.

"Keeping Ground Zero Free" (editorial). 2005. *New York Times,* July 12.

Keller, Bill. 2003a. "God and George W. Bush." *New York Times,* May 17.

———. 2003b. "Here's a Model for How to Shape a Muslim State." *New York Times,* May 4.

Kelley, Tina. 2002. "In Chapel's Closing, a Ground Zero Sanctuary Is Lost." *New York Times,* Mar. 24.

Kengor, Paul. 2004. "What Bush Believes." *New York Times,* Oct. 18.

Kennedy, Paul. 2002. "The Real Culture Wars." Review of *What Went Wrong? Western Impact and Middle Eastern Response* by Bernard Lewis. *New York Times Book Review,* Jan. 27.

Kennedy, Randy. 2001. "Tunnel Vision: In a Simple Memo, F.Y.I., a Tense Tale of Survival." *New York Times,* Nov. 6.

———. 2005. "Uprooted in the Attacks, Now Planted in Bronze." *New York Times,* July 6.

Kepel, Gilles. 2002. *Jihad: The Trail of Political Islam.* Translated by Anthony F. Roberts. Cambridge, MA: Belknap Press of Harvard Univ. Press.

Kershaw, Sarah. 2001a. "Army Chaplain in Detention Sought to Teach about Islam." *New York Times,* Sept. 25.

———. 2001b. "New Bishop Is Installed for Long Island Diocese." *New York Times,* Sept. 6.

———. 2001c. "A Prayer before Flying." *New York Times,* Oct. 6.

———. 2002. "Mourning and Prayers near 16 Empty Acres." *New York Times,* June 3.

———. 2003. "Guantánamo Chaplain and His Wife Speak Out." *New York Times,* Dec. 5.

———. 2004. "Washington Guardsman Charged with Trying to Spy for Al Qaeda." *New York Times,* Feb. 19.

Kertzer, David I. 2003. "The Modern Use of Ancient Lies." *New York Times,* May 9.

Khan, Muqtedar. 2003. "Putting the American in 'American Muslim.'" *New York Times,* Sept. 7.

Khouri, Norma. 2003. *Honor Lost: Love and Death in Modern-Day Jordan.* New York: Atria Books.

Kifner, John. 1980. "Marx and Mosque Are Less Compatible Than Ever." *New York Times,* Sept. 14.

———. 2001. "Public Lives: On the Front Line, Pursuing the God of Peace." *New York Times,* Oct. 4.

———. 2003a. "Islamic Traditionalists Sweep Liberals in Kuwaiti Election." *New York Times,* July 7.

———. 2003b. "Karbala: Iraqi Shiites Show Their Fervor in City They Hold Holy." *New York Times,* Apr. 23.

———. 2004. "Massacre Draws Self-Criticism in Muslim Press." *New York Times,* Sept. 9.

———. 2005a. "A Fine Line Between Civil War and Politics." *New York Times,* June 26.

———. 2005b. "A Tide of Islamic Fury, and How It Rose." *New York Times,* Jan. 30.

Kifner, John, and Ian Fisher. 2003. "Marines End Role in Iraq's Capital as Army Moves In." *New York Times,* Apr. 21.

Kifner, John, and Craig S. Smith. 2003. "Competing Groups Display Influence in Iraq's Capital." *New York Times,* Apr. 19.

Kilborn, Peter T. 2001. "Christmas 2001: Santa, Snowmen, and Old Glory." *New York Times,* Dec. 25.

Kilgannon, Corey. 2001. "New York Harbor Journal: Cruise Has Time to Repent and Time to Party." *New York Times,* Sept. 10.

———. 2003a. "All-American? U.S. Says No." *New York Times,* Apr. 21.

———. 2003b. "Miracle? Dream? Prank? Fish Talks, Town Buzzes." *New York Times,* Mar. 15.

———. 2003c. "Pakistani, 18, Wins Fight Against Order to Leave U.S." *New York Times,* Apr. 30.

———. 2004a. "Afghan Mosque's Founders Say Imam Who Ejected Them Must Go." *New York Times,* July 3.

———. 2004b. "Mosque Remains Divided, Despite Ruling from Court." *New York Times,* Aug. 7.

———. 2004c. "New Church at St. John's Awaits Dedication." *New York Times,* Nov. 20.

———. 2004d. "They're Not Heavy: They're His People." *New York Times,* July 1.

———. 2007. Telephone interview by the author. Sept. 12.

Kimmelman, Michael. 2002. "Many Heavens, Many Ways to Get There." *New York Times,* Jan. 5.

Kinzer, Stephen. 2002. "A Clash of Symbols: Defining Holy Sites on Faith." *New York Times,* Apr. 28.

———. 2003. "Annemarie Schimmel, Influential Scholar of Islam, Dies at 80." *New York Times,* Feb. 2.

————. 2004. "The Teacher: Muslim Scholar Loses U.S. Visa as Query Is Raised." *New York Times,* Aug. 26.

Kirk, Don. 2001a. "Filipinos Fear More Violence as 5 Muslim Provinces Vote." *New York Times,* Nov. 26.

————. 2001b. "U.S. Couple Held in Philippines Describe Their Ordeal on Tape." *New York Times,* Nov. 27.

Kirkpatrick, David D. 2004. "Wrath and Mercy: The Return of the Warrior Jesus." *New York Times,* Apr. 4.

Kirn, Walter. 2004. "9.12.04: The Way We Live Now: Forget It?" *New York Times Magazine,* Sept. 12.

Kleinfeld, N. R. 2007. "As 9/11 Nears, a Debate Rises: How Much Tribute Is Enough?" *New York Times,* Sept. 2.

Knightley, Phillip. 1975. *The First Casualty: From Crimea to Vietnam: The War Correspondent as Hero, Propagandist, and Myth Maker.* New York: Harcourt Brace Jovanovich.

Konigsberg, Eric. 2006. "Brief Journey for an Icon of the Attack on New York." *New York Times,* Oct. 6.

Kramer, Martin S. 2001. *Ivory Towers on Sand: The Failure of Middle Eastern Studies in America.* Washington, DC: Washington Institute for Near East Policy.

Krauss, Clifford. 2002. "Montreal Journal: A Sikh Boy's Little Dagger Sets Off a Mighty Din." *New York Times,* June 3.

————. 2003. "The Saturday Profile: An Unlikely Promoter of an Islamic Reformation." *New York Times,* Oct. 4.

————. 2004a. "Letter from the Americas: When the Koran Speaks, Will Canadian Law Bend?" *New York Times,* Aug. 4.

————. 2004b. "Police Investigate 2 Canadian Muslims over Comments about Jews." *New York Times,* Oct. 31.

Kristof, Nicholas D. 2002a. "Bigotry in Islam—and Here." *New York Times,* July 9.

————. 2002b. "Following God Abroad." *New York Times,* May 21.

————. 2002c. "A Life of Balances." *New York Times,* Feb. 22.

————. 2002d. "Saudis in Bikinis." *New York Times,* Oct. 25.

————. 2002e. "Stoning and Scripture." *New York Times,* Apr. 30.

————. 2002f. "Watch What You Say." *New York Times,* June 21.

————. 2003a. "Believe It, or Not." *New York Times,* Aug. 15.

————. 2003b. "Cover Your Hair." *New York Times,* June 24.

————. 2003c. "Giving God a Break." *New York Times,* June 10.

————. 2003d. "God on Their Side." *New York Times,* Sept. 27.

————. 2003e. "God, Satan, and the Media." *New York Times,* Mar. 4.

———. 2004a. "The God Gulf." *New York Times,* Jan. 1.

———. 2004b. "Martyrs, Virgins, and Grapes." *New York Times,* Aug. 4.

———. 2004c. "Overdosing on Islam." *New York Times,* May 12.

Krugman, Paul. 2002. "Gotta Have Faith." *New York Times,* Dec. 17.

Kuczynski, Alex. 2001. "Spiritual Balm, at Only $23.95." *New York Times,* Oct. 21.

Lacey, Marc. 2001. "Traditional Spirits Block a $500 Million Dam Plan in Uganda." *New York Times,* Sept. 13.

———. 2002a. "Fiery Zealotry Leaves Nigeria in Ashes Again." *New York Times,* Nov. 29.

———. 2002b. "Where 9/11 News Is Late, but Aid Is Swift." *New York Times,* June 3.

———. 2002c. "Zanzibar Journal: Tourists and Islam Mingle, Not Always Cozily." *New York Times,* Mar. 6.

———. 2003a. "Basra: Mixed Emotions Emerge in Iraqi Art." *New York Times,* May 25.

———. 2003b. "In Remotest Kenya, a Supermodel Is Hard to Find." *New York Times,* Apr. 22.

———. 2004. "In Sudan, Hunter and Hunted Alike Invoke the Prophet." *New York Times,* Aug. 22.

———. 2005. "Abu Sroug Journal: Nobody Danced. No Drums. Just Fear. Some Holiday!" *New York Times,* Apr. 22.

Laderman, Gary. 2002. "9/11 on Our Mind." *Religion in the News* 5, no. 3 (Fall): 2–3, 22.

Landler, Mark. 2001. "Yonghe Journal: Religion Museum in Taiwan Promotes Tolerance." *New York Times,* Dec. 3.

———. 2002a. "Afghan Artist Erases Layers of Repression." *New York Times,* Jan. 13.

———. 2002b. "Kabul Journal: 2 Jews Outlast Taliban. Maybe Not Each Other." *New York Times,* Jan. 18.

———. 2003. "A German Court Accepts Teacher's Head Scarf." *New York Times,* Sept. 25.

Lavery, Brian. 2001. "Target of Attack in Belfast: Little Girls Going to School." *New York Times,* Sept. 6.

Lear, Jonathan. 2001. "The Enemy of My Enemy." Review of *In the Name of Identity: Violence and the Need to Belong* by Amin Maalouf. *New York Times Book Review,* Nov. 25.

Lears, Jackson. 2003. "How a War Became a Crusade." *New York Times,* Mar. 11.

LeDuff, Charlie. 2002. "Jail Incident Is Not Fatal to Chairman of the J.D.L." *New York Times,* Nov. 6.

———. 2003. "A Cleric Assumes a Bully Pulpit." *New York Times,* Apr. 19.

Lee, Felicia R. 2002. "Seeking Campus Dialogue, Not Diatribe." *New York Times,* Oct. 5.

———. 2004. "An Islamic Scholar with the Dual Role of Activist." *New York Times,* Jan. 17.

Leff, Laurel. 2005. *Buried by the "Times": The Holocaust and America's Most Important Newspaper.* New York: Cambridge Univ. Press.

Leland, John. 2004. "Tension in a Michigan City over Muslims' Call to Prayer." *New York Times,* May 5.

Lelyveld, Joseph. 2001. "All Suicide Bombers Are Not Alike." *New York Times Magazine,* Oct. 28.

"Letter on Filmmaker's Body Threatened Official" (Agence France-Presse). *New York Times,* Nov. 5.

Levin, Andrea. 1997. "Schmemann Leads the Herd." CAMERA (Committee for Accuracy in Middle East Reporting in America), Apr. 27. Available at http://www.camera.org/index.asp?x_context=6&x_article=128.

Lévy, Bernard-Henri. 2004. "A Tale of Love and Death in Afghanistan." *New York Times,* Apr. 17.

Lewin, Tamar. 2001. "Sikh Owner of Gas Station Is Fatally Shot in Rampage." *New York Times,* Sept. 17.

———. 2002. "Web Site Fuels Debate on Campus Anti-Semitism." *New York Times,* Sept. 27.

Lewin, Tamar, and Gustav Niebuhr. 2001. "Violence: Attacks and Harassment Continue on Middle Eastern People and Mosques." *New York Times,* Sept. 18.

Lewis, Bernard. 2002. *What Went Wrong? Western Impact and Middle Eastern Response.* Oxford, UK: Oxford Univ. Press.

———. 2003. *The Crisis of Islam: Holy War and Unholy Terror.* New York: Modern Library.

Lewis, Flora. 1979a. "Basis of the New Moslem Fervor Seen as Rejection of Alien Values." *New York Times,* Dec. 28.

———. 1979b. "Language a Key to the Spirit of an Islamic Revival." *New York Times,* Dec. 30.

———. 1979c. "Students and the Young Leading Moslem Fundamentalist Revival." *New York Times,* Dec. 29.

Lewis, James R., ed. 1998. *The Encyclopedia of Cults, Sects, and New Religions.* Amherst, NY: Prometheus Books.

Lewis, Neil A. 2001. "Legal Issues: Could Seized American Face Treason Count?" *New York Times,* Dec. 4.

———. 2002. "Leader of Islamic Charity Is Accused of Lying to Court." *New York Times,* May 1.

———. 2003a. "Case Against Ex-Chaplain Opens Focusing on Affair." *New York Times,* Dec. 9.

———. 2003b. "Lawyer Upset by Treatment of Ex-Chaplain for Detainees." *New York Times,* Oct. 25.

———. 2003c. "Prosecutors Say It's Unclear Papers Chaplain Carried Were Classified." *New York Times,* Dec. 10.

———. 2004. "Charges Dropped Against Chaplain." *New York Times,* Mar. 20.

———. 2005. "Documents Say Detainees Cited Abuse of Koran." *New York Times,* May 26.

———. 2007a. Email correspondence with the author, Aug. 18.

———. 2007b. Email correspondence with the author, Aug. 27.

Lewis, Neil A., and Thom Shankar. 2004. "Missteps and Confusion Seen in Muslim Chaplain's Spy Case." *New York Times,* Jan. 4.

Lewis, Paul. 2003. "Hadhrat Mirza Tahir Ahmad, 74, Leader of Muslim Sect, Who Claimed to Be Prophet." *New York Times,* May 7.

Lichtblau, Eric. 2003a. "American Muslims: F.B.I. Tells Offices to Count Local Muslims and Mosques." *New York Times,* Jan. 28.

———. 2003b. "Group of Muslims Charged with Plotting Against India." *New York Times,* June 28.

———. 2004. "Islamic Charity Says F.B.I. Falsified Evidence Against It." *New York Times,* July 27.

———. 2005a. "Detainee at Brig in Charleston Accuses His Jailers of Abuse." *New York Times,* Aug. 9.

———. 2005b. "From Advocacy to Terrorism, a Line Blurs." *New York Times,* June 5.

———. 2005c. "Scholar Is Given Life Sentence in 'Virginia Jihad' Case." *New York Times,* July 14.

Lichtblau, Eric, and William Glaberson. 2003. "Millions Raised for Qaeda in Brooklyn, U.S. Says." *New York Times,* Mar. 5.

Liddle, R. William, and Saiful Mujani. 2003. "The Real Face of Indonesian Islam." *New York Times,* Oct. 11.

Lilla, Mark. 2001. "Extremism's Theological Roots." *New York Times,* Oct. 7.

Lincoln, Bruce. 2003. *Holy Terrors: Thinking about Religion after September 11.* Chicago: Univ. of Chicago Press.

Lind, Michael. 2002. "Their Country 'Tis of Them." Review of *30 Reasons for Loving Our Country* by Roger Rosenblatt; *Why We Fight: Moral Clarity and the War on Terrorism* by William J. Bennett; and *What's So Great about America* by Dinesh D'Souza. *New York Times Book Review,* July 7.

Linsley, Brennan. 2003. "A Day of Peace" (photo). *New York Times,* Apr. 21.

Lippy, Charles H., and Peter W. Williams, eds. 1988. *Encyclopedia of the American Religious Experience: Studies of Traditions and Movements.* 3 vols. New York: Charles Scribner's Sons.

Lipton, Eric. 2003. "Surplus History from Ground Zero." *New York Times,* Dec. 19.

———. 2004. "Islamic Scholar from Virginia Is Charged in Holy War Plot." *New York Times,* Sept. 24.

Llorente, Marina. 2002. "Civilization versus Barbarism." In *Collateral Language: A User's Guide to America's New War,* edited by John Collins and Ross Glover, 39–51. New York: New York Univ. Press.

Loconte, Joseph. 2003. "The Prince of Peace Was a Warrior, Too." *New York Times,* Jan. 1.

Loewenberg, Samuel. 2005. "Christian Rock for Muslims." *New York Times,* May 10.

Lohr, Steve. 2001. "Internet Access Providers Curb Both Terrorist Postings and an Anti-Islamic Backlash." *New York Times,* Sept. 17.

Lopate, Phillip. 2004. "U.F.O. Tour." Review of *Pull Me Up: A Memoir* by Dan Barry. *New York Times Book Review,* May 16.

Lubet, Steven. 2002. "A Muslim Lawyer for Moussaoui." *New York Times,* Apr. 25.

Lueck, Thomas J. 2001. "Group Grew Out of Militancy." *New York Times,* Dec. 13.

———. 2004. "L.I. Man Charged in Bias Assault of Sikh Leader." *New York Times,* July 13.

Lule, Jack. 2002. "Myth and Terror on the Editorial Page: The *New York Times* Responds to September 11." *Journalism and Mass Communication Quarterly* 79, no. 2 (Summer): 275–93.

Luo, Michael. 2004. "M.T.A. Is Sued over Its Policy on Muslim Head Coverings." *New York Times,* Oct. 1.

———. 2006. "Religion: Clergy Again Shoulders Burdens of Consoling and Explaining." *New York Times,* Sept. 11.

"Lutheran Panel Reinstates Pastor after Post-9/11 Interfaith Service." 2003. *New York Times,* May 13.

Lyall, Sarah. 2003. "What Drove 2 Britons to Bomb a Club in Tel Aviv?" *New York Times,* May 12.

———. 2005a. "Britain Says It Will Bar Return of Firebrand Muslim Cleric." *New York Times,* Aug. 13.

———. 2005b. "British Court Says Banning Muslim Gown Violates Student's Rights." *New York Times,* Mar. 3.

———. 2007. Email correspondence with the author, Aug. 18.

Maalouf, Amin. 2001. *In the Name of Identity: Violence and the Need to Belong.* Translated by Barbara Bray. New York: Arcade.

Maass, Peter. 2001a. "The Volunteer." *New York Times Magazine,* Oct. 7.

———. 2001b. "The Zealot." *New York Times Magazine,* Sept. 30.

———. 2003a. "Back-Room Theocrat." *New York Times Magazine,* May 11.

———. 2003b. "When Al Qaeda Calls." *New York Times Magazine,* Feb. 2.

MacFarquhar, Neil. 2001a. "Anti-Western and Extremist Views Pervade Saudi Schools." *New York Times,* Oct. 19.

———. 2001b. "Bin Laden's Wildfire Threatens Might of Saudi Rulers." *New York Times,* Nov. 6.

———. 2001c. "Memoirs: Fighters Uplifted Muslims, bin Laden Aide Says in Book." *New York Times,* Dec. 5.

———. 2001d. "Mixed Views of bin Laden in Homeland." *New York Times,* Oct. 5.

———. 2001e. "Teachings: Bin Laden and His Followers Adhere to an Austere, Stringent Form of Islam." *New York Times,* Oct. 7.

———. 2001f. "The Video: Bin Laden, in a Taped Speech, Says Attacks in Afghanistan Are a War Against Islam." *New York Times,* Nov. 4.

———. 2002a. "3 U.S. Citizens Slain in Yemen in Rifle Attack." *New York Times,* Dec. 31.

———. 2002b. "Egyptian Group Patiently Pursues Dream of Islamic State." *New York Times,* Jan. 20.

———. 2002c. "A Few Saudis Defy a Rigid Islam to Debate Their Own Intolerance." *New York Times,* July 12.

———. 2002d. "Killing Underscores Enmity of Evangelists and Muslims." *New York Times,* Nov. 25.

———. 2002e. "The Kurdish Region: Iraq Courts Its Kurds with an Anti-U.S. Islamic Edict." *New York Times,* Dec. 24.

———. 2002f. "Many Arabs Say Bush Misreads Their History and Goals." *New York Times,* Jan. 31.

———. 2003a. "Ayatollah's Funeral: Thousands at Burial of Slain Cleric." *New York Times,* Sept. 3.

———. 2003b. "Bashiqa Journal: A Sect Shuns Lettuce and Gives the Devil His Due." *New York Times,* Jan. 3.

———. 2003c. "A Bombing Shatters the Saudi Art of Denial." *New York Times,* May 18.

———. 2003d. "Clerics: A Khomeini Breaks with His Lineage to Back U.S." *New York Times,* Aug. 6.

———. 2003e. "For Arabs, New Jihad Is in Iraq." *New York Times,* Apr. 2.

———. 2003f. "Iraqi Shiites Flex Muscle Even as They Mourn." *New York Times,* Sept. 1.

———. 2003g. "Iraqi Unrest: In Shiite Holy City of Najaf, a Sudden Anti-U.S. Storm." *New York Times,* July 21.

———. 2003h. "Rising Tide of Islamic Militants See Iraq as Ultimate Battlefield." *New York Times*, Aug. 13.

———. 2003i. "Riyadh: A Saudi Editor Who Offended Clerics Is Ousted from His Post." *New York Times*, May 28.

———. 2003j. "Saudis Re-Examine an Islamic Doctrine Cited by Militants to Condone Jihad." *New York Times*, May 25.

———. 2003k. "A Shiite Burial Ground Awaits Foreign Faithful." *New York Times*, Aug. 18.

———. 2003l. "Shiite Clerics Clashing over How to Reshape Iraq." *New York Times*, Aug. 26.

———. 2003m. "Shiite Group Plans Militia to Protect Holy Sites From G.I.'s." *New York Times*, Aug. 16.

———. 2003n. "Shiites in Southern Iraq Loom as a Serious Threat to Hussein." *New York Times*, Jan. 14.

———. 2003o. "The South: Shiites, Resenting Both Sides, Are Swing Group." *New York Times*, Apr. 8.

———. 2003p. "A Stilled Voice: After Cleric's Assassination, Fears for the Future." *New York Times*, Sept. 2.

———. 2003q. "Students Roil Iranian Capital in 3rd Night of Protests." *New York Times*, June 13.

———. 2003r. "The Terrorists: Tape Ascribed to bin Laden Urges Muslims to Stand with Iraq." *New York Times*, Feb. 12.

———. 2003s. "Thousands Mourn Iraqi Ayatollah Killed in Bombing." *New York Times*, Aug. 31.

———. 2003t. "With Iraqi Courts Gone, Young Clerics Judge." *New York Times*, Aug. 4.

———. 2003u. "Young Iranians Are Chafing under Aging Clerics' Edicts." *New York Times*, June 16.

———. 2004a. "Cairo Journal: God Has 4,000 Loudspeakers; the State Holds Its Ears." *New York Times*, Oct. 12.

———. 2004b. "A Kiss Is Not Just a Kiss to an Angry Arab TV Audience." *New York Times*, Mar. 5.

———. 2004c. "Muslim Scholars Increasingly Debate Holy War." *New York Times*, Dec. 10.

———. 2004d. "New Violence, Old Problem: The Saudies Fight Terror, but Not Those Who Wage It." *New York Times*, June 6.

———. 2004e. "Saudis Support a Jihad in Iraq, Not Back Home." *New York Times*, Apr. 23.

———. 2005a. "Iranian Women's Dress Code Is Modest but Golf Friendly." *New York Times,* July 5.

———. 2005b. "Saudi Reformers: Seeking Rights, Paying a Price." *New York Times,* June 9.

———. 2005c. "Saudi Shiites, Long Kept Down, Look to Iraq and Assert Rights." *New York Times,* Mar. 2.

———. 2006. "Religious Bias: A Simple Scarf, but Meaning Much More Than Faith." *New York Times,* Sept. 8.

MacFarquhar, Neil, and Richard A. Oppel Jr. 2003. "Car Bomb in Iraq Kills 95 at Shiite Mosque." *New York Times,* Aug. 30.

Machacek, David W. 2003. "The Case of Chaplain Yee." *Religion in the News* 6, no. 3 (Fall): 7–8, 22.

Madigan, Nick, and Melissa Sanford. 2004. "In Utah, Two Faiths and One Prayer." *New York Times,* July 1.

Mahle, Melissa Boyle. 2006. "We Can't Kill an Ideology." *New York Times,* Sept. 10.

Makiya, Kanan. 2001. *The Rock: A Tale of Seventh-Century Jerusalem.* New York: Pantheon Books.

"Manhattan: Firefighters Enter 9/11 Fray" (AP). 2005. *New York Times,* Aug. 17.

Manji, Irshad. 2004. "Under the Cover of Islam." *New York Times,* Nov. 18.

———. 2005a. *The Trouble with Islam Today.* New York: St. Martin's.

———. 2005b. "Why Tolerate the Hate?" *New York Times,* Aug. 9.

Mann, Robert. 2002. "A Reporter Scrutinizes War and Its Myths." Review of *War Is a Force That Gives Us Meaning* by Chris Hedges. *New York Times,* Oct. 22.

Al-Marayati, Salam. 2002. "Indict Individuals, Not Charities." *New York Times,* Oct. 11.

Mark, Mary Ellen, and Samantha M. Shapiro. 2001. "Faith: Keeper of the Flame." *New York Times Magazine,* Sept. 9.

Marquis, Christopher. 2001. "The State Department: An American Report Finds the Taliban's Violation of Religious Rights 'Particularly Severe.'" *New York Times,* Oct. 27.

———. 2003. "Religious Services: Muslims Object to Graham." *New York Times,* Apr. 18.

Marshall, Carolyn. 2005a. "Deportation Set for Imam in F.B.I. Case." *New York Times,* Aug. 16.

———. 2005b. "Pakistani Imam Is Accused of Planning Terror Training." *New York Times,* Aug. 10.

Marshall, Paul. 2009. "Religion and Terrorism: Misreading al Qaeda." In *Blind Spot: When Journalists Don't Get Religion,* edited by Paul Marshall, Lela Gilbert, and Roberta Green Ahmanson, 31–46. New York: Oxford Univ. Press.

Marshall, Paul, Lela Gilbert, and Roberta Green Ahmanson, eds. 2009. *Blind Spot: When Journalists Don't Get Religion.* New York: Oxford Univ. Press.

Martin, Douglas. 2001. "Robert M. Brown, a Champion of Ecumenism, Is Dead at 81." *New York Times,* Sept. 7.

———. 2005. "Martin Lings, a Sufi Writer on Islamic Ideas, Dies at 96." *New York Times,* May 29.

Marty, Martin E. 2002. "The Sensitive Crown of the Human Heart." Public lecture given at Colgate Univ., Hamilton, NY, Sept. 11.

———. 2005. "Making Headlines." *Sightings,* Apr. 4. Available at http://listhost.uchicago.edu/pipermail/sightings.

Mason, Debra L. 1995. "God in the News Ghetto: A Study of Religion News from 1944 to 1989." Ph.D. diss., Ohio Univ.

Masood, Salman. 2004a. "Bombing: At Least 40 in Pakistan Die in Attack on Holy Day." *New York Times,* Mar. 3.

———. 2004b. "Gunmen Kill a Leading Pro-Taliban Sunni Cleric in Pakistan." *New York Times,* May 31.

———. 2004c. "Pakistan Bans Public Meetings after 40 Die in a Car Bombing." *New York Times,* Oct. 8.

———. 2004d. "Possible Suicide Bombing Kills 23 at a Mosque in Pakistan." *New York Times,* Oct. 2.

———. 2004e. "Suicide Bomber Kills 3 Others at a Shiite Mosque in Pakistan." *New York Times,* Oct. 11.

———. 2005a. "Islamic Court for Pakistan Rejects Ruling in Rape Case." *New York Times,* Mar. 12.

———. 2005b. "Kiss a Hindu? Just Imagine. Islamists Did, with Outrage." *New York Times,* Mar. 27.

———. 2005c. "Reports of Mishandling Koran Bring Protest Worldwide." *New York Times,* May 28.

Mattingly, Terry. 2000. "The Man Who Didn't Disappear." *On Religion,* Sept. 20. Available at http://matt.gospelcom.net/column/2000/09/20/.

McCalman, Iain. 2004. "The Empty Chador." *New York Times,* Aug. 4.

McChesney, Robert W. 2002. "September 11 and the Structural Limitations of U.S. Journalism." In *Journalism after September 11,* edited by Barbie Zelizer and Stuart Allan, 91–100. London: Routledge.

McDowell, Edwin. 2003. "Residential Real Estate: Financing Is Arranged for Observant Muslims." *New York Times,* Feb. 14.

McFadden, Robert D. 2001a. "In Profile: Bin Laden's Journey from Rich, Pious Lad to the Mask of Evil." *New York Times,* Sept. 30.

———. 2001b. "The Service: In a Stadium of Heroes, Prayers for the Fallen and Solace for Those Left Behind." *New York Times,* Sept. 24.

———. 2002a. "The Dead: Victims Shared Affection for Yemenis, Families Say." *New York Times,* Dec. 31.

———. 2002b. "Heads Turn and Eggs Roll, but Perilous Times Darken Easter." *New York Times,* Apr. 1.

McFadden, Robert D., and John Holl. 2005. "2 Robbers Killed Jersey City Family of 4, Prosecutors Say." *New York Times,* Mar. 5.

McGivena, Leo, et al. 1969. *The News: The First Fifty Years of New York's Picture Newspaper.* New York: News Syndicate.

McLean, Renwick. 2004a. "Spain Arrested More Than 130 Suspects in Islamic Terrorism in '04." *New York Times,* Jan. 6.

———. 2004b. "Spain Considers Financing for Major Religions." *New York Times,* Aug. 3.

———. 2004c. "Spanish Prisons Provide Pool of Recruits for Radical Islam." *New York Times,* Oct. 31.

———. 2005. "Medina Azahara Journal: Growth in Spain Threatens a Jewel of Medieval Islam." *New York Times,* Aug. 16.

McMorris, Christine. 2002. "Bush and the Burqa." *Religion in the News* 5, no. 1 (Spring): 14–15, 29.

McNeil, Donald G., Jr. 2001. "More and More, Other Countries See the War as Solely America's." *New York Times,* Nov. 4.

———. 2002a. "France Vows Harsh Action after More Synagogues Burn." *New York Times,* Apr. 2.

———. 2002b. "Tunisian Jews at Blast Site: A Stalwart Remnant." *New York Times,* Apr. 15.

———. 2002c. "Tunisian Synagogue Blast Called Accident." *New York Times,* Apr. 13.

Meeker, Richard H. 1983. *Newspaperman: S. I. Newhouse and the Business of News.* New Haven, CT: Ticknor & Fields.

Mehio, Saad. 2001. "How Islam and Politics Mixed." *New York Times,* Dec. 2.

Mekhennet, Souad, and Don Van Natta Jr. 2005. "Outspoken Cleric: Militant London Sheik Had Predicted More Terror Attacks." *New York Times,* July 12.

Menocal, María Rosa. 2002a. "A Golden Reign of Tolerance." *New York Times,* Mar. 28.

———. 2002b. *The Ornament of the World: How Muslims, Jews, and Christians Created a Culture of Tolerance in Medieval Spain.* Boston: Little, Brown.

"Milk and Dates at Sunset." 2004. *New York Times,* Oct. 16.

Miller, Judith. 1983. "Moslem World Is Unsettled by Surge in Fundamentalism." *New York Times,* Dec. 18.

———. 2001a. "A Glimpse, Guard Down." *New York Times,* Dec. 14.

———. 2001b. "The Suspect: Bin Laden: Child of Privilege Who Champions Holy War." *New York Times,* Sept. 14.

———. 2002. "Naming the Evildoers." Review of *Militant Islam Reaches America* by Daniel Pipes. *New York Times Book Review,* Sept. 29.

———. 2003. "Weapons: Shiite Clerics Seek Control of Munitions at 2 Factories." *New York Times,* Apr. 13.

Milloy, Ross E. 2001a. "Frozen Assets: In Texas, Donors to Muslim Charity Seethe at Raids by Government." *New York Times,* Dec. 6.

———. 2001b. "Relief after Release: Hometown Is Jubilant Aid Workers Are Free." *New York Times,* Nov. 16.

Mills, Doug. 2003. "Burial at Arlington" (photo). *New York Times,* Apr. 29.

Mishra, Pankaj. 2002. "Hinduism's Political Resurgence." *New York Times,* Feb. 25.

———. 2003a. "India's Muslim Time Bomb." *New York Times,* Sept. 15.

———. 2003b. "The Other Face of Fanaticism." *New York Times Magazine,* Feb. 2.

Mitgang, Herbert. 1993. "Books of the Times: Of Islam, Fundamentalism, and Western Values." Review of *The New Cold War? Religious Nationalism Confronts the Secular State* by Mark Juergensmeyer and *Islam and the West* by Bernard Lewis. *New York Times,* Aug. 11.

"The Money Trail: Accused Helper of Al Qaeda Pleads Guilty." 2003. *New York Times,* Apr. 15.

Morris, Bob. 2001. "Looking for Solace in a Spirit World." *New York Times,* Dec. 16.

Moss, Michael, and Jenny Nordberg. 2003. "Muslims: Imams Urged to Be Alert for Suspicious Visitors." *New York Times,* Apr. 6.

Mottahedeh, Roy Parviz. 2001. "Islam and the Opposition to Terrorism." *New York Times,* Sept. 30.

———. 2003. "Keeping the Shi'ites Straight." *Religion in the News* 6, no. 2 (Summer 2003): 4–6, 27.

Moyers, Bill. 2003. "Transcript: Bill Moyers [*sic*] Talk with Chris Hedges." *NOW,* Mar. 7. Available at http://www.pbs.org/now/transcript/transcript_hedges.html.

Muhammad, Ozier. 2003. "A Day to Honor Their Faith." *New York Times,* Sept. 29.

"'Muhammad' Is Growing Popular in Britain" (Reuters). 2005. *New York Times,* Jan. 7.

Murphy, Dean E. 2001. "Christmas Mass Beneath a Cross of Fallen Steel." *New York Times,* Dec. 26.

————. 2002. "As Public Yearns to See Ground Zero, Survivors Call a Viewing Stand Ghoulish." *New York Times*, Jan. 13.

"Muslim-Americans: Florida License Trial Opens in Lawsuit by Veiled Woman" (AP). 2003. *New York Times*, May 28.

"Muslim Leader among Blacks Resigns Post" (AP). 2003. *New York Times*, Sept. 1.

"Muslim Mobs, Seeking Vengence [*sic*], Attack Christians in Nigeria" (AP). 2004. *New York Times*, May 13.

"Muslim Rebels in Philippines Make a Deal and Free 89" (AP). 2001. *New York Times*, Nov. 29.

"Muslims in European Schools" (editorial). 2003. *New York Times*, Oct. 8.

"The Muslim World Gathers in Mecca." 2005. *New York Times*, Jan. 20.

"Mychal Judge, 68, Chaplain for Fire Dept." 2001. *New York Times*, Sept. 13.

"Mychal Judge: Where He Was Needed." 2001. *New York Times*, Dec. 31.

Mydans, Seth. 2001a. "Bush Meeting Jakarta Leader; Islamic Militancy Is Likely Topic." *New York Times*, Sept. 19.

————. 2001b. "In Indonesia, Once Tolerant Islam Grows Rigid." *New York Times*, Dec. 29.

————. 2001c. "Lau Journal: An Outpatient Exorcism (It Was Only a Crab)." *New York Times*, Aug. 27.

————. 2001d. "Militant Islam Unsettles Indonesia and Its Region." *New York Times*, Sept. 21.

————. 2001e. "The Pacific: Indonesia Radicals Issue Threats of Holy War." *New York Times*, Sept. 29.

————. 2002a. "Bomb in Pakistan Mosque Kills 12 and Hurts Dozens." *New York Times*, Apr. 27.

————. 2002b. "By Barring Religious Garb, Singapore School Dress Code Alienates Muslims." *New York Times*, Mar. 2.

————. 2002c. "In Pakistan, Rape Victims Are the 'Criminals.'" *New York Times*, May 17.

————. 2002d. "Jihad Seethes, and Grows, on Indonesian Island." *New York Times*, Jan. 10.

————. 2002e. "Pakistan: Bomb Attack Chills Churchgoers in Islamabad." *New York Times*, Apr. 1.

————. 2002f. "Sentenced to Death, Rape Victim Is Freed by Pakistani Court." *New York Times*, June 6.

————. 2003a. "Asian Front: Trials to Begin in Bombing on Bali That Shocked Indonesia." *New York Times*, May 12.

————. 2003b. "The Saturday Profile: A Friendship Sundered by Muslim Code of Honor." *New York Times*, Feb. 1.

———. 2003c. "Southeast Asia: In Far East of Many Muslims, Press Is Anti-U.S. but Hardly Pro-Jihad." *New York Times*, Apr. 11.

———. 2004a. "Reaction: Moscow's Gloom Deepens As Fear Becomes Routine." *New York Times*, Sept. 6.

———. 2004b. "Thai Troops Kill 107 in Repelling Muslim Attackers." *New York Times*, Apr. 29.

Myers, Steven Lee. 2001. "At U.S. Base: Marines Build Firepower in the South, Bolstering Their Patrols and Readiness." *New York Times*, Dec. 3.

Myre, Greg. 2003a. "27 Israeli Reserve Pilots Say They Refuse to Bomb Civilians." *New York Times*, Sept. 25.

———. 2003b. "In a Christian–Muslim Dispute, Israel Blocks a New Mosque." *New York Times*, July 2.

Naby, Eden, and Richard N. Frye. 2003. "The Martyr Complex." *New York Times*, Sept. 14.

Nafisi, Azar. 2003. *Reading Lolita in Tehran: A Memoir in Books.* New York: Random House.

Nair, Meera. 2002. "Lives: A Show of Faith." *New York Times Magazine*, Apr. 28.

Naparstek, Michael. 2001. "Falwell and Robertson Stumble." *Religion in the News* 4, no. 5 (Fall): 5, 27.

Napoli, James J. 2002. "Covering Islam in Egypt." *Religion in the News* 5, no. 1 (Spring): 20–22, 31.

Nasr, Seyyed Hossein. 2002. *The Heart of Islam: Enduring Values for Humanity.* San Francisco: HarperSanFrancisco.

Nasr, Vali. 2004. "Iraq's Real Holy War." *New York Times*, Mar. 6.

Nathan, Joan. 2001. "A Challah of Prayers and Memories." *New York Times*, Sept. 19.

———. 2004. "Breaking Ramadan's Fast with a Family Meal." *New York Times*, Oct. 20.

Navarro, Mireya. 2001. "Sacramento's Shaken Ukrainian Residents Hold Funeral for 6 Slain Relatives." *New York Times*, Aug. 27.

Navasky, Victor. 2002. "Foreword." In *Journalism after September 11*, edited by Barbie Zelizer and Stuart Allan, xiii–xviii. London: Routledge.

Newman, Andy. 2001. "In Temple, Seeking Meaning and Promise in a New Year." *New York Times*, Sept. 19.

———. 2002a. "Good Friday Ritual Is Cast with the Backdrop of 9/11." *New York Times*, Mar. 30.

———. 2002b. "Patrols in Jewish Neighborhoods Face Arrest, Commissioner Says." *New York Times*, June 11.

———. 2002c. "Rabbi Halts Plan to Bring Armed Patrol to Brooklyn." *New York Times*, June 17.

————. 2002d. "Remembering Sept. 11 in a Personal Way, or Maybe Ignoring It." *New York Times*, Aug. 8.

————. 2003. "The Mosque: Brooklyn Muslims, Disputing Any Ties to Terror." *New York Times*, Mar. 5.

————. 2004. "On Brooklyn's Avenue of Babel, Cultures Entwine." *New York Times*, Mar. 26.

————. 2005a. "Admirers of Fallen 9/11 Hero Disdain the Vatican's Likely Plan to Bar Gays as Priests." *New York Times*, Sept. 25.

————. 2005b. "Fire Dept. Chaplain Resigns after Remarks about 9/11." *New York Times*, Oct. 1.

————. 2005c. "Group to Visit Gaza Strip to Oppose Israeli Pullout." *New York Times*, June 5.

————. 2007. Telephone interview by the author. Aug. 21.

Newman, Andy, and Daryl Khan. 2003. "Brooklyn Mosque Becomes Terror Icon, but Federal Case Is Unclear." *New York Times*, Mar. 9.

Newman, Maria. 2003. "Region: Calling Fire an Accident, Leaders of Mosque Say They Will Rebuild." *New York Times*, July 15.

New York Times. 2002. *A Nation Challenged: A Visual History of 9/11 and Its Aftermath.* New York: Callaway.

Niebuhr, Gustav. 2001a. "The Catholic Church: Bishops Draft Principles to Guide Response to Terrorism." *New York Times*, Nov. 13.

————. 2001b. "Christian Arabs, Too, Are Harassed." *New York Times*, Oct. 15.

————. 2001c. "The Churches: At Houses of Worship, Feelings Are Shared and Comfort Is Sought in Greater Numbers." *New York Times*, Sept. 17.

————. 2001d. "The Evangelist: Muslim Group Seeks to Meet Billy Graham's Son." *New York Times*, Nov. 20.

————. 2001e. "Excerpts from Sermons across the Nation." *New York Times*, Sept. 17.

————. 2001f. "A Faith-Based Effort to Save Ailing Marriages." *New York Times*, Sept. 1.

————. 2001g. "Finding Fault: U.S. 'Secular' Groups Set Tone for Terror Attacks, Falwell Says." *New York Times*, Sept. 14.

————. 2001h. Interviewed by the author. Hamilton, NY, Nov. 30.

————. 2001i. "Mormons Paying $3 Million to Settle Sex Abuse Case." *New York Times*, Sept. 5.

————. 2001j. "Muslims and the Military: Ties Between a Mosque and Fort Bragg Stay Strong and Neighborly." *New York Times*, Oct. 6.

————. 2001k. "Peace Activists: Groups Plan Vigils and Rallies to Urge Alternatives to War." *New York Times*, Oct. 5.

———. 2001l. "Placing Blame: Falwell Apologizes for Saying an Angry God Allowed Attacks." *New York Times*, Sept. 18.

———. 2001m. "Religion Journal: American Islamic Media: Assorted and Aspiring." *New York Times*, Nov. 24.

———. 2001n. "Religion Journal: Clergy of Many Faiths Answer Tragedy's Call." *New York Times*, Sept. 15.

———. 2001o. "Religion Journal: How to Link Two Media, and Two Faiths as Well." *New York Times*, Sept. 1.

———. 2001p. "Religion Journal: In Devastation's Shadow, a Landmark's Renewal." *New York Times*, Nov. 3.

———. 2001q. "Religion Journal: Iran's President Speaks on Faith and Civilization." *New York Times*, Nov. 17.

———. 2001r. "Religion Journal: Shrines Serve the Need for Healing in Public Spaces." *New York Times*, Oct. 6.

———. 2001s. "Religions Ponder the Stem Cell Issue." *New York Times*, Aug. 27.

———. 2001t. "Reporting on Religion, before September 11th and After." Public lecture given at Colgate Univ., Hamilton, NY, Nov. 30.

———. 2001u. "Studies Suggest Lower Count for Number of U.S. Muslims." *New York Times*, Oct. 25.

———. 2001v. "Support from Churches: Bishops Write Bush to Back U.S. Efforts." *New York Times*, Sept. 21.

———. 2002. "Q&A: Acknowledging That God Is Not Limited to Christians." *New York Times*, Jan. 12.

———. 2006. "The Innovative Impulse in American Religion." Public lecture given at Oneida Community, Sherrill, NY, Sept. 26.

Nieves, Evelyn. 2001a. "A New Minority Makes Itself Known: Hispanic Muslims." *New York Times*, Dec. 17.

———. 2001b. "A U.S. Convert's Path from Suburbia to a Gory Jail for Taliban." *New York Times*, Dec. 4.

———. 2002. "The American Prisoner: A Cousin, Also a Convert to Islam, Calls Lindh a 'True Hero' and Says He Is Innocent." *New York Times*, Mar. 18.

"Nigerian State Government Urges Muslims to Kill Fashion Writer" (Agence France-Presse). 2002. *New York Times*, Nov. 27.

"Nigerian Woman Cleared in Stoning Case." 2003. *New York Times*, Sept. 26.

"Nigerian Woman Condemned to Death by Stoning Is Acquitted." 2003. *New York Times*, Mar. 26.

Noah, Timothy. 2004. "Troubled Times." Review of *Hard News: The Scandals at "The New York Times" and Their Meaning for American Media* by Seth Mnookin. *New York Times Book Review*, Dec. 26.

Al-Nogaidan, Mansour. 2003. "Telling the Truth, Facing the Whip." *New York Times*, Nov. 28.

Nomani, Asra Q. 2004. "Hate at the Local Mosque." *New York Times*, May 6.

Nordin, Kenneth Dayton. 1975. "Consensus Religion: National Newspaper Coverage of Religious Life in America, 1849–1960." Ph.D. diss., Univ. of Michigan.

Nunberg, Geoffrey. 2004. "Lexical Lessons: What the Good Book Says: Anti-Semitism, Loosely Defined." *New York Times*, Apr. 11.

O'Donnell, Michelle. 2005a. "9/11 Families to Sue City over Remains." *New York Times*, Aug. 17.

———. 2005b. "9/11 Rescuer Recalls Fear and Faith." *New York Times*, Aug. 14.

Okrent, Daniel. 2004. "The Public Editor: What Do You Know, and How Do You Know It?" *New York Times*, Feb. 29.

———. 2005a. "The Public Editor: A Few Points along the Line Between News and Opinion." *New York Times*, Mar. 27.

———. 2005b. "The Public Editor: The Hottest Button: How the *Times* Covers Israel and Palestine." *New York Times*, Apr. 24.

———. 2005c. "The Public Editor: The War of the Words: A Dispatch from the Front Lines." *New York Times*, Mar. 6.

Onishi, Norimitsu. 2001a. "Long Ordeal Ends Happily in Pakistan." *New York Times*, Nov. 16.

———. 2001b. "Rising Muslim Power in Africa Causes Unrest in Nigeria and Elsewhere." *New York Times*, Nov. 1.

———. 2001c. "A Tale of the Mullah and Muhammad's Amazing Cloak." *New York Times*, Dec. 19.

———. 2002a. "Industrious Senegal Muslims Run a 'Vatican.'" *New York Times*, May 2.

———. 2002b. "Mother's Sentence Unsettles a Nigerian Village." *New York Times*, Sept. 7.

———. 2004. "Korean Missionaries Carrying Word to Hard-to-Sway Places." *New York Times*, Nov. 1.

Oppel, Richard A., Jr. 2004. "Insurgents: 5 Churches Are Attacked; Bombs Kill 4 Servicemen." *New York Times*, Oct. 17.

Oppel, Richard A., Jr., and James Glanz. 2004. "More Iraqi Army Dead Found in Mosul; Cleric Is Slain." *New York Times*, Nov. 23.

Ouroussoff, Nicolai. 2005a. "Critic's Notebook: A Deepening Gloom about Ground Zero's Future." *New York Times*, Sept. 10.

————. 2005b. "A Museum on Sacred Ground: Architecture Review: A Temple of Contemplation and Conflict." *New York Times,* May 20.

Overbye, Dennis. 2001. "How Islam Won, and Lost, the Lead in Science." *New York Times,* Oct. 30.

Oz, Amos. 2001. "Struggling Against Fanaticism." *New York Times,* Sept. 14.

Ozel, Soli. 2002. "Islam Takes a Democratic Turn." *New York Times,* Nov. 5.

Pace, Eric. 2001. "Herbert Haag, 86, Priest Who Challenged Vatican." *New York Times,* Aug. 30.

Paden, William E. 1994. *Religious Worlds: The Comparative Study of Religion.* Boston: Beacon Press.

"Pakistan Cabinet Splits on Religion and Passports" (Reuters). 2005. *New York Times,* Jan. 7.

"Pakistan Holds 19 Suspects in Mosque Raid" (Reuters). 2003. *New York Times,* July 7.

"Pakistani Court Rules Against Islamic Bill." 2005. *New York Times,* Aug. 5.

"Pakistan's Cruel Blasphemy Law" (editorial). 2001. *New York Times,* Aug. 30.

Pala, Christopher. 2003. "Kazakhstan Faith Talks Seek to Subdue Religious Clashes." *New York Times,* Sept. 25.

"Palestinians Remove Hate Text from Web Site" (Reuters). 2005. *New York Times,* May 19.

Palmer, Allen W., and Abdullahi A. Gallab. 2001. "Islam and Western Culture: Navigating Terra Incognita." In *Religion and Popular Culture: Studies on the Interaction of Worldviews,* edited by Daniel M. Stout and Judith M. Buddenbaum, 109–23. Ames: Iowa State Univ. Press.

Pape, Robert A. 2003. "Dying to Kill Us." *New York Times,* Sept. 22.

————. 2005. "Blowing Up an Assumption." *New York Times,* May 18.

Pareles, Jon. 2003. "Television Review: A Rock Star's Struggle Where Militant Islam Rules." *New York Times,* July 17.

————. 2004. "Critic's Choice/New CD's: From a Senegalese Master, a Tolerant Side of Islam." *New York Times,* July 5.

Parker, Geoffrey. 2001. "The Way of the West." Review of *Carnage and Culture: Landmark Battles in the Rise of Western Power* by Victor Davis Hanson. *New York Times Book Review,* Aug. 12.

Pearl, Judea. 2002. "Death Images Hide the Truth of Danny Pearl." *New York Times,* June 18.

Perlez, Jane. 2002a. "Asian Arena: Hopes for Easter Release of Missionary Couple Held in Philippine Jungle Prove Unfounded." *New York Times,* Apr. 1.

————. 2002b. "Asian Militants: School in Indonesia Urges 'Personal Jihad' in Steps of bin Laden." *New York Times,* Feb. 3.

————. 2002c. "Jakarta Journal: A TV Preacher to Satisfy the Taste for Islam Lite." *New York Times,* Aug. 23.

————. 2002d. "Jakarta Rejects Muslim Law and Alters Presidential Voting." *New York Times,* Aug. 12.

————. 2002e. "Muslim-as-Apple-Pie Videos Are Greeted with Skepticism." *New York Times,* Oct. 30.

————. 2002f. "Muslims' U.S. Hostage Is Killed in Gun Battle in the Philippines." *New York Times,* June 8.

————. 2002g. "The Saturday Profile: An Islamic Scholar's Lifelong Lesson: Tolerance." *New York Times,* Mar. 16.

————. 2002h. "U.S. Tries to Win Over Angry Indonesian Muslims." *New York Times,* June 22.

————. 2002i. "With Indonesia Politics up for Grabs, Islam's Role Grows." *New York Times,* Apr. 30.

————. 2003a. "Islam Lite in Indonesia Is Looking More Scary." *New York Times,* Sept. 3.

————. 2003b. "Maumere Journal: On an Indonesian Island, a Reverence for Tolerance." *New York Times,* Mar. 11.

————. 2003c. "Saudis Quietly Promote Strict Islam in Indonesia." *New York Times,* July 5.

————. 2003d. "U.S. Asks Muslims Why It Is Unloved: Indonesians Reply." *New York Times,* Sept. 27.

————. 2004. "Cracks in Thailand's Peace." *New York Times,* Mar. 8.

————. 2005. "Recovery Effort: Islamic Militants Volunteer to Aid Muslims in Indonesia." *New York Times,* Jan. 10.

Peterson, Iver. 2001. "City: In Troubled Times, Episcopal Diocese Welcomes Its 15th Bishop." *New York Times,* Sept. 30.

Petit, Robert B. 1986. "Religion Through the *Times:* An Examination of the Secularization Thesis Through Content Analysis of *The New York Times,* 1855–1975." Ph.D. diss., Columbia Univ.

Petritsch, Wolfgang. 2001. "Islam Is Part of the West, Too." *New York Times,* Nov. 20.

Phelps, Robert H. 2009. *God and the Editor: My Search for Meaning at "The New York Times."* Syracuse, NY: Syracuse Univ. Press.

Phillips, John McCandlish. 2001. *Faith in the Daily News Chase.* Asheville, NC: World Journalism Institute, Aug. 17.

————. 2005. "When Columnists Cry 'Jihad.'" *Washington Post,* May 4.

Picker, David. 2005. "Olajuwon Says He Gave in Good Faith." *New York Times,* Feb. 16.

Pietrangeli, Carlo. 1996. *Paintings in the Vatican.* Boston: Little, Brown.

"Pilgrims near End of Hajj." 2004. *New York Times,* Feb. 1.

Pipes, Daniel. 2002a. "Harvard Loves Jihad." *New York Post,* June 11.

———. 2002b. *Militant Islam Reaches America.* New York: W. W. Norton.

Pogrebin, Robin. 2005. "News Analysis: Is Culture Gone at Ground Zero?" *New York Times,* Sept. 30.

"Police Say Man Accused in Plot Had Explosives" (AP). 2002. *New York Times,* Aug. 25.

Pollack, Kenneth M. 2002. *The Threatening Storm: The Case for Invading Iraq.* New York: Random House.

———. 2003. "Faith and Terrorism in the Muslim World." Review of *The Crisis of Islam: Holy War and Unholy Terror* by Bernard Lewis. *New York Times Book Review,* Apr. 6.

"Pope Makes Plea for Mideast Peace during New Year's Mass" (AP). 2003. *New York Times,* Jan. 2.

"Pope Says Terror Mustn't Hurt Faiths' Ties" (Reuters). 2005. *New York Times,* July 21.

"Pope Urges Europe to Avow Christianity" (AP). 2003. *New York Times,* Feb. 17.

"Pope Urges World to 'Save the Children' Affected by Conflicts" (AP). 2001. *New York Times,* Dec. 26.

Portraits: 9/11/01: The Collected "Portraits of Grief" from "The New York Times." 2003. New York: Henry Holt and Times Books.

"Prayers for the Youngest Survivors of the School Siege in Russia." 2004. *New York Times,* Sept. 8.

"Pre-Islam Idols Being Broken under Decree by Afghans" (Agence France-Presse). 2001. *New York Times,* Mar. 2.

Press, Eyal. 2001. "It's a Volatile, Complex World. . . ." *New York Times Education World,* Nov. 11.

Preston, Julia. 2004. "Man Who Led a Mosque Is Convicted of Visa Fraud." *New York Times,* Sept. 24.

Pristin, Terry. 2002. "Civil Liberties: Behind the Legal and Private Worlds of the Veil." *New York Times,* Aug. 11.

Proctor, William. 2000. *The Gospel According to "The New York Times."* Nashville, TN: Broadman & Holman.

Purdy, Matthew, and Lowell Bergman. 2003. "Unclear Danger: Inside the Lackawanna Terror Case." *New York Times,* Oct. 12.

Purnick, Joyce. 2001. "Metro Matters: Our Daily Tribute to Differences Provokes Dislike among Many." *New York Times,* Sept. 20.

Pyne, Robert. 2003. "The True Good Samaritans." *New York Times,* Apr. 19.

"Q&A: Muslims Were Outraged; So Were Christians." 2004. *New York Times,* May 9.

Quealy, Gerit. 2004. "Vows: Rachel Uchitel and Steven Ehrenkranz." *New York Times,* Dec. 12.

Queen, Edward L., II, Stephen R. Prothero, and Gardiner H. Shattuck Jr., eds. 1996. *The Encyclopedia of American Religious History.* 2 vols. New York: Facts on File.

"Raid on Church: Grenade Attack in Pakistani Village Kills 3 at Christmas Service" (AP). 2002. *New York Times,* Dec. 26.

Raines, Howell. 2002a. "Foreword." In *Out of the Blue: The Story of September 11, from Jihad to Ground Zero,* by Richard Bernstein and the staff of the *New York Times,* ix–xi. New York: Henry Holt and Times Books.

———. 2002b. "Introduction." In *A National Challenged: A Visual History of 9/11 and Its Aftermath,* by the New York Times. 8–9. New York: Callaway.

———. 2003. "Foreword." In *Portraits: 9/11/01: The Collected "Portraits of Grief" from the "New York Times,"* vii–viii. New York: Henry Holt and Times Books.

———. 2004. "My Times." *Atlantic Monthly* (May). Available at http://www.theatlantic .com/doc/200405/raines.

Ramadan, Tariq. 2004. "Too Scary for the Classroom?" *New York Times,* Sept. 1.

"Ramadan Begins, Outside the Walls" (photo). 2001. *New York Times,* Nov. 17.

Ramirez, Anthony. 2004. "Tempest in a Translation? Jewish Leader Denies Insult." *New York Times,* July 28.

Ramsey, Nancy. 2003. "Television Review: How a Nightmare Began and Might Continue." *New York Times,* Mar. 25.

Rao, Ramesh. 2002. "Media Coverage of the Events in Gujarat." Mar. 13. Available at http://www.hinduunity.org/antihinddugger.htm.

Raver, Anne. 2001. "Human Nature: A Place of Solace in a Time of Grief." *New York Times,* Sept. 13.

"The Real Meaning of Ground Zero" (letters to the editor by John Ferrari and others). 2005. *New York Times,* July 14.

Rediehs, Laura J. 2002. "Evil." In *Collateral Language: A User's Guide to America's New War,* edited by John Collins and Ross Glover, 65–78. New York: New York Univ. Press.

Reinitz, Richard. 1969. "Cubism and the Writing of History." *University of Denver Quarterly* 4, no. 1 (Spring): 7–16.

"Religion Journal: Abhorring Terror at an Ohio Mosque." 2001. *New York Times,* Sept. 22.

"Religion Journal: Christianity and Islam Seek Way to Go Forward." 2001. *New York Times,* Dec. 8.

"Religious and Ethnic Clashes in Nigeria Spread, Killing at Least 165" (Reuters). 2001. *New York Times,* Sept. 12.

"A Religious Figure Speaks." 2003. *New York Times,* Apr. 4.

"The Religious Right: Islam Is Violent in Nature, Pat Robertson Says" (AP). 2003. *New York Times,* Feb. 23.

"Religious Strife in Nigeria Leaves Bodies in the Streets" (AP). 2001. *New York Times,* Sept. 10.

Renold, Leah. 2002. "Fundamentalism." In *Collateral Language: A User's Guide to America's New War,* edited by John Collins and Ross Glover, 94–107. New York: New York Univ. Press.

"Repeated Vandalism of Mosque Is to Be Investigated as Bias Crime" (AP). 2004. *New York Times,* Apr. 24.

"Revisiting the Families: Getting Past the Pain of 9/11, in Steps Both Big and Small." 2006. *New York Times,* Sept. 11.

"Rev. James Ford, 70, Chaplain of U.S. House of Representatives" (AP). 2001. *New York Times,* Sept. 5.

Rich, Frank. 2002. "Religion for Dummies." *New York Times,* Apr. 27.

———. 2003. "They Both Reached for the Gun." *New York Times,* Mar. 23.

———. 2005. "Ground Zero Is so Over." *New York Times,* May 29.

Richardson, Lynda. 2004. "Public Lives: He Lost a Brother on 9/11, and Gained a Calling." *New York Times,* Dec. 24.

Riding, Alan. 2002a. "The Church: Vatican Aims Sharp Rebuke at 'Reprisals' by Israelis." *New York Times,* Apr. 4.

———. 2002b. "French Author Acquitted of Charges for Anti-Islam Comment." *New York Times,* Oct. 23.

———. 2003. "Philosopher on the Trail of Daniel Pearl's Killer." *New York Times,* Aug. 30.

———. 2004. "Islamic Art as a Mediator for Cultures in Confrontation." *New York Times,* Apr. 6.

———. 2005a. "The Crusades as a Lesson in Harmony?" *New York Times,* Apr. 24.

———. 2005b. "A Muslim Woman, a Story of Sex." *New York Times,* June 20.

———. 2005c. "Muslim Voyagers in a Distant Land (the West)." *New York Times,* Sept. 3.

———. 2007. Email correspondence with the author, Aug. 15.

Rieff, David. 2004. "The Shiite Surge." *New York Times Magazine,* Feb. 1.

———. 2005a. "An Islamic Alienation." *New York Times Magazine,* Aug. 14.

———. 2005b. "Their Hearts and Minds?" *New York Times Magazine,* Sept. 4.

"Rightists Protest in Milan, Seeking Curbs on Muslims in Italy" (Reuters). 2001. *New York Times,* Oct. 20.

Rimer, Sara. 2001. "On Sept. 11, Even Monks Watched Television." *New York Times,* Oct. 21.

Risen, Clay. 2005. "Rebuilding Ground Zero." Review of *Sixteen Acres: Architecture and the Outrageous Struggle for the Future of Ground Zero* by Philip Nobel. *New York Times Book Review*, Jan. 30.

Risen, James. 2004. "Account of Broad Shiite Revolt Contradicts White House Stand." *New York Times*, Apr. 8.

Rives, Bob. 2001. "A Ramadan That Is Now Different" (photo). *New York Times*, Nov. 16.

Robertson, Nan. 1992. *The Girls in the Balcony: Women, Men, and "The New York Times."* New York: Random House.

Rockwell, John. 2003. "Is 'Klinghoffer' Anti-Semitic?" *New York Times*, May 4.

Rodenbeck, Max. 2005. "The War within Islam." Review of *No God but God: The Origins, Evolution, and Future of Islam* by Reza Aslan. *New York Times Book Review*, May 29.

Rohde, David. 2002a. "9 Hindus Die in Attack on Pilgrims in Kashmir." *New York Times*, Aug. 7.

———. 2002b. "Bethlehem: Church of Nativity Damaged and a Monastery Is Scorched." *New York Times*, Apr. 9.

———. 2002c. "Bethlehem: Clerics Tell of Ritual and Danger under Siege." *New York Times*, Apr. 12.

———. 2002d. "Braving Nature and Militants, Hindus Trek for a Peek at a God's Icy Symbol." *New York Times*, Aug. 5.

———. 2002e. "Gunmen Kill 6 at a Christian School in Pakistan." *New York Times*, Aug. 6.

———. 2002f. "Gunmen Kill 7 Workers for Christian Charity in Pakistan." *New York Times*, Sept. 26.

———. 2002g. "Raids in Pakistan Raise New Fears." *New York Times*, Aug. 10.

———. 2002h. "Turning Away from U.S., Pakistan's Elite Gravitate toward Islamic Religious Parties." *New York Times*, Oct. 13.

———. 2003a. "48 Pakistanis Die in Attack on Shiite Rites." *New York Times*, July 5.

———. 2003b. "Excavation's Finding at Mosque Site in India Could Fuel Dispute. *New York Times*, Aug. 27.

———. 2003c. "In the Field / Christian Sanctuary: View from Ancient Monastery as Yet Another War Intrudes." *New York Times*, Apr. 10.

———. 2003d. "Mosul: Free of Hussein's Rule, Sunnis in North Flaunt a Long-Hidden Piety." *New York Times*, Apr. 23.

———. 2003e. "Muslims Recant, and Hindus Are Acquitted in Riot Trial." *New York Times*, July 1.

———. 2003f. "A Prisoner's Journey from the Classroom to the Taliban." *New York Times*, Sept. 1.

———. 2003g. "Relatives: 'Let Them Arrest Him,' Tariq Aziz's Aunt Says." *New York Times,* Apr. 21.

———. 2003h. "Survivors Tell of Massacre at Mosque in Pakistan." *New York Times,* July 6.

———. 2003i. "Why America Still Can't Find Osama bin Laden." *New York Times,* Sept. 14.

———. 2005a. "Mix of Quake Aid and Preaching Stirs Concern." *New York Times,* Jan. 22.

———. 2005b. "A World of Ways to Say 'Islamic Law.'" *New York Times,* Mar. 13.

———. 2007. Email correspondence with the author, Aug. 17.

Rohde, David, and Nazila Fathi. 2003. "Islam: Power Moves May Be Uniting Hard-Liners in Iraq and Iran." *New York Times,* June 24.

Rohde, David, and Mohammed Khan. 2005. "Ex-Londoner's Diary of Jihad: A Portrait Sprinkled with Koran Verses and Epithets." *New York Times,* Aug. 8.

Rohrlich, Marianne. 2001. "Personal Shopper: Reshaping the Festival of Lights." *New York Times,* Dec. 6.

Roof, Wade Clark, ed. 2000. *Contemporary American Religion.* 2 vols. New York: Macmillan Reference USA.

Rosen, Gary. 2003. "What Would Woodrow Wilson Do?" Review of *Terror and Liberalism* by Paul Berman. *New York Times Book Review,* Apr. 13.

———. 2004. "Books of the Times: Terrorists' Hatred of the West the West's Own Bastard Child?" Review of *Occidentalism: The West in the Eyes of Its Enemies* by Ian Buruma and Avishai Margalit. *New York Times,* Mar. 27.

Rosen, Jeffrey. 2003. "How to Reignite the Culture Wars." *New York Times Magazine,* Sept. 7.

Rosen, Jonathan. 2001. "The Uncomfortable Question of Anti-Semitism." *New York Times Magazine,* Nov. 4.

———. 2004. "Books of the Times: Arguing That Israel Should Return Land and Apologize." Review of *How Israel Lost the Four Questions* by Richard Ben Cramer. *New York Times,* July 2.

Rosenthal, Elisabeth. 2002. "Asian Terror: Beijing Says Chinese Muslims Were Trained as Terrorists with Money from bin Laden." *New York Times,* Jan. 22.

———. 2005a. "Pope Benedict Reaches Out to Muslims." *New York Times,* Apr. 26.

———. 2005b. "Surveillance: Muslims in Italy Unsettled over Increased Scrutiny." *New York Times,* Aug. 1.

Rothstein, Adam. 2003. "Jihad for Journalists." *Religion in the News* 6, no. 2 (Summer): 9–10.

Rothstein, Edward. 2001a. "Connections: Attacks on U.S. Challenge the Perspectives of Postmodern True Believers." *New York Times,* Sept. 22.

———. 2001b. "Shelf Life: Why Western Soldiers Have Always Been Such Fierce Fighters." Review of *Carnage and Culture: Landmark Battles in the Rise of Western Power* by Victor Davis Hanson. *New York Times,* Dec. 1.

———. 2002a. "Connections: Anti-Semitism as Fear of Too-Rapid Change." *New York Times,* Apr. 13.

———. 2002b. "Connections: Hateful Name-Calling vs. Calling for Hateful Action." *New York Times,* Nov. 23.

———. 2003a. "Connections: Islam and the Unveiled Photograph." *New York Times,* June 14.

———. 2003b. "Connections: Mutating Virus: Hatred of Jews." *New York Times,* May 17.

———. 2003c. "Shelf Life: Looking for Roots of War and Terror." Review of *Terror and Liberalism* by Paul Berman. *New York Times,* Apr. 5.

———. 2003d. "Was the Islam of Old Spain Truly Tolerant?" *New York Times,* Sept. 27.

———. 2004. "Connections: Those Who Were Inspired to Hate the Modern World." *New York Times,* July 10.

Roy, Olivier. 2005. "Why Do They Hate Us? Not Because of Iraq." *New York Times,* July 22.

Rubin, Elizabeth. 2004. "The Jihadi Who Kept Asking Why." *New York Times Magazine,* Mar. 7.

Rubin, Michael. 2009. "Three Decades of Misreporting Iran and Iraq." In *Blind Spot: When Journalists Don't Get Religion,* edited by Paul Marshall, Lela Gilbert, and Roberta Green Ahmanson, 47–64. New York: Oxford Univ. Press.

Ruda, Richard. 2001. "Weekend Excursion: An Oasis of Peace and Contemplation." *New York Times,* Oct. 19.

Rudoren, Jodi. 2007. Email correspondence with the author, Aug. 18.

Ruethling, Gretchen. 2004. "Judge Awards $156 Million in Terror Death." *New York Times,* Dec. 9.

Rushdie, Salman. 2001. "Yes, This Is about Islam." *New York Times,* Nov. 2.

———. 2002. "No More Fanaticism as Usual." *New York Times,* Nov. 27.

———. 2005. "India and Pakistan's Code of Dishonor." *New York Times,* July 10.

Rutenberg, Jim. 2001. "Fox Portrays a War of Good and Evil, and Many Applaud." *New York Times,* Dec. 3.

Sachs, Susan. 2001a. "The 2 Worlds of Muslim-American Teenagers." *New York Times,* Oct. 7.

———. 2001b. "Cairo Journal: Muslim Televangelist Delivers a Winning Message." *New York Times,* Dec. 24.

———. 2001c. "Cairo Journal: A Tree Drooping with Its Ancient Burden of Faith." *New York Times,* Dec. 26.

———. 2001d. "In One Muslim Land, an Effort to Enforce Lessons of Tolerance." Dec. 16.

———. 2001e. "Where Muslim Traditions Meet Modernity." *New York Times,* Dec. 17.

———. 2002a. "Anti-Semitism Is Deepening among Muslims." *New York Times,* Apr. 27.

———. 2002b. "Baptist Pastor Attacks Islam, Inciting Cries of Intolerance." *New York Times,* June 15.

———. 2002c. "Relations: For Many American Muslims, Complaints of Quiet but Persistent Bias." *New York Times,* Apr. 25.

———. 2003a. "American Muslims: Pilgrims Find Changes on Both Ends of Journey." *New York Times,* Feb. 16.

———. 2003b. "Arab Media Portray War as Killing Field." *New York Times,* Apr. 4.

———. 2003c. "Back in Iraq, a Cleric Urges Islamic Rules." *New York Times,* May 11.

———. 2003d. "Baghdad: Shiite Clerics' Ambitions Collide in an Iraqi Slum." *New York Times,* May 25.

———. 2003e. "In Harlem's Fabric, Bright Threads of Senegal." *New York Times,* July 28.

———. 2003f. "A Muslim Missionary Group Draws New Scrutiny in U.S." *New York Times,* July 14.

———. 2003g. "Postwar Politics: Iraqis More Bemused Than Enthused by Cleric." *New York Times,* May 12.

———. 2003h. "Shiites: One Faith, One Political Goal, and Set to Collide." *New York Times,* May 13.

———. 2003i. "A Victim: An Iraqi Shiite Who Moved Between Religion, Revolt, and Politics." *New York Times,* Aug. 30.

———. 2004a. "Iraq Navigates Between Islam and Democracy." *New York Times,* Mar. 7.

———. 2004b. "Power Broker: Theocracy and Democracy: The Cleric Spoiling U.S. Plans." *New York Times,* Jan. 18.

Sack, Kevin. 2001. "Apocalyptic Theology Revitalized by Attacks." *New York Times,* Nov. 23.

Sack, Kevin, and Gustav Niebuhr. 2001. "After Stem-Cell Rift, Groups Unite for Anti-Abortion Push." *New York Times,* Sept. 4.

"Sacrifice and Celebration." 2005. *New York Times,* Jan. 21.

Al-Saeidy, Abdul Razzaq, and Edward Wong. 2004. "Najaf: Radical Cleric Isn't Wanted by His Neighbors." *New York Times,* Apr. 24.

Safi, Omid. 2001–2004. "Study of Islam Section." Available at http://groups.colgate.edu/aarislam/default.htm.

Safire, William. 2004a. "Arab and Jewish Votes." *New York Times,* Oct. 25.

———. 2004b. "Of God and the Flag." *New York Times,* Mar. 24.

Said, Edward W. 1981. *Covering Islam: How the Media and the Experts Determine How We See the Rest of the World.* New York: Pantheon Books.

Saint Louis, Catherine, and Andres Serrano. 2001. "The Looks They Get." *New York Times Magazine,* Sept. 23.

Salamon, Julie. 2002a. "Fatwa Victim or a Fraud?" *New York Times,* Dec. 11.

———. 2002b. "Television Review: Instant Islam: Trying to Find a Global Faith in the Details." *New York Times,* May 9.

Sanneh, Lamin. 2001. "Faith and the Secular State." *New York Times,* Sept. 23.

Santora, Marc. 2003a. "In the Field / Basra's Shiites: No More Fear That Prayer Falls on the Wrong Ears." *New York Times,* Apr. 12.

———. 2003b. "Once Dangerous Pilgrimage Is Forbidden No More." *New York Times,* Apr. 19.

Saulny, Susan. 2002. "The Reaction: In New York, Arabs and Jews Share Many Concerns." *New York Times,* Mar. 31.

———. 2003. "Muslim Workers Claim Bias at the Plaza." *New York Times,* Oct. 1.

"Saved from Stoning" (editorial). 2003. *New York Times,* Sept. 27.

"Scenes of Rejoicing and Words of Strategy from bin Laden and His Allies." 2001. *New York Times,* Dec. 14.

Schedson, Michael. 2002. "What's Unusual about Covering Politics as Usual." In *Journalism after September 11,* edited by Barbie Zelizer and Stuart Allan, 36–47. London: Routledge.

Schell, Jonathan. 2003. *The Unconquerable World: Power, Nonviolence, and the Will of the People.* New York: Henry Holt and Metropolitan Books.

Schemo, Diana Jean. 2001a. "A Drive Against Gossip." *New York Times,* Sept. 6.

———. 2001b. "Revival of School Prayer Has Limited Success." *New York Times,* Oct. 23.

———. 2002. "Mideast Strife Loudly Echoed in Academia." *New York Times,* July 11.

———. 2003. "Terrorism: American Dies in a Land Whose Faith Called Him." *New York Times,* May 16.

Schillinger, Liesl. 2004. "The New 'Arab' Playwrights. They're Female, They're Organized, and They're . . . Not All Arab." *New York Times,* Apr. 4.

Schmalzbauer, John. 2002. "Between Objectivity and Moral Vision: Catholics and Evangelicals in American Journalism." In *Practicing Religion in the Age of the Media: Explorations in Media, Religion, and Culture,* 165–87. New York: Columbia Univ. Press.

Schmemann, Serge. 2001a. "Taliban Lose Grip on Wider Regions; Aid Workers Free." *New York Times,* Nov. 15.

———. 2001b. "U.S. Attacked: President Vows to Exact Punishment for 'Evil.'" *New York Times,* Sept. 12.

———. 2002a. "Books of the Times: Analyzing the Cultural Collision That Gave Rise to Sept. 11." Review of *What Went Wrong? Western Impact and Middle Eastern Response* by Bernard Lewis. *New York Times,* Jan. 23.

———. 2002b. "House of Worship: In Shift, Israel Bars Building of a Mosque near a Church." *New York Times,* Mar. 4.

———. 2002c. "Jerusalem Journal: Atop Church, Another, Less Deadly Holy War." *New York Times,* Aug. 26.

———. 2002d. "Us and Them: The Burden of Tolerance in a World of Division." *New York Times,* Dec. 29.

———. 2007. Telephone interview by the author, Aug. 28.

Schmitt, Eric. 2003. "Ex-Chaplain with Detainees Is Charged." *New York Times,* Oct. 11.

———. 2005. "Military Details Koran Incidents at Base in Cuba." *New York Times,* June 4.

Schmitt, Eric, and Frank Bruni. 2004. "Cheney Sees Pope, Who Makes Plea for Peace." *New York Times,* Jan. 28.

Schoenbaum, David. 2002. "Books of the Times: Opening Western Eyes to a View of Islam." Review of *Militant Islam Reaches America* by Daniel Pipes. *New York Times,* Aug. 28.

Schultz, Jeffrey D., John G. West Jr., and Iain MacLean, eds. 1999. *Encyclopedia of Religion in American Politics.* Phoenix: Onyx Press.

Schwartz, Stephen. 2002. *The Two Faces of Islam: The House of Sa'ud from Tradition to Terror.* New York: Doubleday.

Sciolino, Elaine. 2001. "Hair as a Battlefield for the Soul." *New York Times,* Nov. 18.

———. 2002a. "For Outsiders in Saudi Arabia, Worship Comes with a Risk." *New York Times,* Feb. 12.

———. 2002b. "Jidda Journal: Where the Prophet Trod, He Begs, Tread Lightly." *New York Times,* Feb. 15.

———. 2002c. "Muslims Feel Sept. 11 Chill as Mecca Plays It Cautious." *New York Times,* Feb. 5.

———. 2002d. "Putin Unleashes His Fury Against Chechen Guerillas." *New York Times,* Nov. 12.

———. 2002e. "Servicemen Win, Doffing Their Veils in Saudi Arabia." *New York Times,* Jan. 25.

———. 2002f. "Word for Word / Temper, Temper: From bin Laden's Native Land, a Voice to Calm the Angry American." *New York Times*, Mar. 17.

———. 2003a. "Ahwaz Journal: In Iran's Hair Salons, the Rebels Wield Scissors." *New York Times*, Feb. 7.

———. 2003b. "Daughter of Iran Revolution Struggles Against the Veil." *New York Times*, Apr. 2.

———. 2003c. "Freed Ayatollah Again Makes Voice Heard." *New York Times*, Feb. 1.

———. 2003d. "French Islam Wins Officially Recognized Voice." *New York Times*, Apr. 14.

———. 2003e. "French Minister Threatens to Expel Extremist Muslims." *New York Times*, Sept. 20.

———. 2003f. "French Officials and Muslims Celebrate New Islamic Council." *New York Times*, Jan. 15.

———. 2003g. "Iran to Lift Dissident Cleric's House Arrest after 5 Years." *New York Times*, Jan. 28.

———. 2003h. "Letters from Europe: France Envisions a Citizenry of Model Muslims." *New York Times*, May 7.

———. 2003i. "A Maze of Identities for the Muslims of France." *New York Times*, Apr. 9.

———. 2003j. "A Muslim in the Middle in France." *New York Times*, Apr. 21.

———. 2003k. "Muslim Lycée Opens in Secular France, Raising Eyebrows." *New York Times*, Sept. 9.

———. 2004a. "1789 to 2004: France Has a State Religion: Secularism." *New York Times*, Feb. 8.

———. 2004b. "2 Muslim Sites Attacked in France, and Reaction Rankles." *New York Times*, Mar. 6.

———. 2004c. "Bobigny Journal: French Sikhs Defend Their Turbans and Find Their Voice." *New York Times*, Jan. 12.

———. 2004d. "Car of Acclaimed Muslim Appointee Is Bombed in France." *New York Times*, Jan. 19.

———. 2004e. "Debate Begins in France on Religion in the Schools." *New York Times*, Feb. 4.

———. 2004f. "Europeans and Americans Seek Answer to Anti-Semitism." *New York Times*, Feb. 20.

———. 2004g. "Europe Struggling to Train New Breed of Muslim Clerics." *New York Times*, Oct. 18.

———. 2004h. "France Seems to Try Acting Affirmatively on Muslims." *New York Times*, Jan. 15.

———. 2004i. "France Turns to Tough Policy on Students' Religious Garb." *New York Times,* Oct. 22.

———. 2004j. "French Assembly Votes to Ban Religious Symbols in Schools." *New York Times,* Feb. 11.

———. 2004k. "French Muslims Protest Rule Against Scarves." *New York Times,* Jan. 18.

———. 2004l. "God's Place in Charter Is Dividing Europeans." *New York Times,* May 26.

———. 2004m. "Here's News for Cowboys: Bandana Can Be Religious." *New York Times,* Jan. 21.

———. 2004n. "Hostages: France Won't Meet Demand to Stop Ban on Head Scarves." *New York Times,* Aug. 30.

———. 2004o. "A New French Headache: When Is Hate on TV Illegal?" *New York Times,* Dec. 9.

———. 2004p. "Religious Symbols: Ban on Head Scarves Takes Effect in a United France." *New York Times,* Sept. 3.

———. 2004q. "Terrorism: Hostages Urge France to Repeal Its Scarf Ban." *New York Times,* Aug. 31.

Sciolino, Elaine, and Don Van Natta Jr. 2005. "For a Decade, London Thrived as a Busy Crossroad of Terror." *New York Times,* July 10.

Scott, A. O. 2004. "Film Review: In a Land of Female Repression, a Girl Survives as a Boy." *New York Times,* Feb. 6.

Scott, Janny. 2001. "The Portraits: Closing a Scrapbook Full of Life and Sorrow." *New York Times,* Dec. 31.

———. 2003. "Introduction." In *Portraits: 9/11/01: The Collected "Portraits of Grief" from the "New York Times,"* ix–x. New York: Henry Holt and Times Books.

Scott, Paul. 2001. "Questions for Martin E. Marty: Sacred Battles." *New York Times Magazine,* Sept. 30.

Seelye, Katharine Q. 2005a. "*Newsweek* Apologizes for Report of Koran Insult." *New York Times,* May 16.

———. 2005b. "Red Cross Reported Koran Abuses." *New York Times,* May 20.

———. 2007. Email correspondence with the author, Aug. 16.

Seelye, Katherine Q., and Neil A. Lewis. 2005. "*Newsweek* Says It Is Retracting Koran Report." *New York Times,* May 17.

Segers, Mary C., and Timothy A. Byrnes, eds. 1995. *Abortion Politics in American States.* Armonk, NY: M. E. Sharpe.

Sella, Marshall. 2001. "How a Grief Ritual Is Born." *New York Times Magazine,* Oct. 7.

———. 2003. "Did You Hear the One about the Suicide Bomber?" *New York Times Magazine,* June 15.

Sells, Michael. 2001. *Approaching the Qur'án: The Early Revelations.* Ashland, OR: White Cloud Press.

Sengupta, Somini. 2001a. "Endorsements: A Rabbi Who Serves Satmars Is Backing Vallone for Mayor." *New York Times,* Sept. 6.

———. 2001b. "Joining Hindu and Muslim Icons in Art." *New York Times,* Dec. 26.

———. 2001c. "Muslim-Americans: Torn Between Silence and Open Discussion." *New York Times,* Sept. 19.

———. 2001d. "Relations: Arabs and Muslims Steer Through an Unsettling Scrutiny." *New York Times,* Sept. 13.

———. 2001e. "Turkey's Secular Experiment." *New York Times,* Dec. 16.

———. 2002a. "After Riots, Some Muslims Fear for Their Future in India." *New York Times,* Mar. 21.

———. 2002b. "Again, Indian Holy City Braces for a Hindu Mob." *New York Times,* Mar. 15.

———. 2002c. "Fear and Flight in Deadly Kashmir: Islamic Militants Brutalize Hindus, Dramatizing a Land's Divisions." *New York Times,* Jan. 16.

———. 2002d. "Hindu Right Goes to School to Build a Nation." *New York Times,* May 13.

———. 2002e. "In Religious Tinderbox, India Snuffs Spark." *New York Times,* Mar. 16.

———. 2002f. "Riots Shake Friendships and Faiths in India." *New York Times,* Mar. 24.

———. 2003a. "As Stoning Case Proceeds, Nigeria Stands Trial." *New York Times,* Jan. 26.

———. 2003b. "Facing Death for Adultery, Nigerian Woman Is Acquitted." *New York Times,* Sept. 26.

———. 2003c. "Kaduna Journal: Piety and Politics Sunder a Riot-Torn Nigerian City." *New York Times,* Feb. 21.

———. 2003d. "When Do-Gooders Don't Know What They're Doing." *New York Times,* May 11.

———. 2004. "In the Ancient Streets of Najaf, Pledges of Martyrdom for Cleric." *New York Times,* July 10.

———. 2005a. "Attack at Temple in India Leaves 6 Dead; Sectarian Strife Is Feared." *New York Times,* July 6.

———. 2005b. "Letter from Asia: Staunch Islam and Its Many Foes (Including Apathy)." *New York Times,* Aug. 3.

———. 2005c. "Thousands Are Arrested in India in Unrest over Temple Site." *New York Times,* July 7.

Sengupta, Somini, and Ian Fisher. 2004. "Bombs Explode Near Churches in 2 Iraqi Cities." *New York Times,* Aug. 2.

Sengupta, Somini, and Salman Masood. 2005a. "Blast Kills 19 at Pakistani Shrine during Muslim Festival." *New York Times,* May 28.

———. 2005b. "Guantánamo Comes to Define U.S. to Muslims." *New York Times,* May 21.

Sengupta, Somini, and David Rohde. 2005. "To Many, Talk of a Crackdown in Pakistan Seems Hollow." *New York Times,* July 20.

Severson, Kim. 2004. "Turkey Is Basic, but Immigrants Add Their Homeland Touches." *New York Times,* Nov. 25.

Shanker, Thom. 2004. "U.S. Fails to Explain Policies to Muslim World, Panel Says." *New York Times,* Nov. 24.

———. 2005. "Inquiry by U.S. Reveals 5 Cases of Koran Harm." *New York Times,* May 27.

Shatz, Adam. 2001. "Questions for V. S. Naipaul: Literary Criticism." *New York Times Magazine,* Oct. 28.

Sheets, Hilarie M. 2001. "Stitch by Stitch, a Daughter of Islam Takes on Taboos." *New York Times,* Nov. 25.

Shenon, Philip. 2001. "The Money Trail: F.B.I. Raids 2 of the Biggest Muslim Charities; Assets of One Are Seized." *New York Times,* Dec. 15.

———. 2004. "Senate Committee Requests Tax and Fund-Raising Records for 27 Muslim Charities." *New York Times,* Jan. 15.

Shenon, Philip, and David Johnston. 2001. "The Investigation: Will Suggests Suspect Had Long Planned to Die for Beliefs." *New York Times,* Oct. 4.

"Shooting in France in Wave of Anti-Jewish Attacks" (AP). 2002. *New York Times,* Apr. 1.

"A Show of Strength in Baghdad." 2004. *New York Times,* Apr. 4.

Shulevitz, Judith. 2001. "The Close Reader: At War with the World." *New York Times Book Review,* Oct. 21.

———. 2002a. "The Close Reader: Other People's Religions." *New York Times Book Review,* Mar. 24.

———. 2002b. "The Close Reader: There's Something Wrong with Evil." *New York Times Book Review,* Oct. 6.

Sifton, John. 2001. "Essay: Beyond the Khyber Pass." Review of *Reaping the Whirlwind: The Taliban Movement in Afghanistan* by Michael Griffin; *Taliban: Militant Islam, Oil, and Fundamentalism in Central Asia* by Ahmed Rashid; *Afghanistan's Endless War: State Failure, Regional Politics, and the Rise of the Taliban* by Larry P. Goodson; *Afghanistan* by Chris Steele-Perkins; and *The Search for Peace in Afghanistan* by Barnett R. Rubin. *New York Times Book Review,* Nov. 18.

Silk, Mark. 1998. *Unsecular Media: Making News of Religion in America.* Urbana: Univ. of Illinois Press.

———. 1999. Communication with the author, Oct. 27.

———. 2000. "Wars of Religion." *Religion in the News* 3, no. 1 (Spring): 3.

———. 2001a. "The Civil Religion Goes to War." *Religion in the News* 4, no. 5 (Fall): 1.

———. 2001b. Interviewed by the author, Hamilton, NY, Nov. 15–16.

———. 2001c. "Islam and the Media since September 11th." Public lecture given at Colgate Univ., Hamilton, NY, Nov. 16.

———. 2001d. "Islam Is Everywhere." *Religion in the News* 4, no. 5 (Fall): 6–8, 28.

———. 2002. "Our Muslim Neighbors." *Religion in the News* 5, no. 3 (Fall): 1, 22.

Simons, Marlise. 2002a. "The Mideast in Marseille: Violence Shakes a City." *New York Times,* Apr. 8.

———. 2002b. "The Saturday Profile: Behind the Veil: A Muslim Woman Speaks Out." *New York Times,* Nov. 9.

———. 2004a. "Amsterdam Journal: Graphic Film of Protest, and Cries of Blasphemy." *New York Times,* Sept. 27.

———. 2004b. "Dutch Filmmaker, an Islam Critic, Is Killed." *New York Times,* Nov. 3.

———. 2004c. "Police Arrest 8 Tied to Suspect in Killing of Dutch Filmmaker." *New York Times,* Nov. 4.

———. 2004d. "Spain Is Seeking to Integrate Growing Muslim Population." *New York Times,* Oct. 24.

———. 2005a. "The Hague Journal: 2 Dutch Deputies on the Run, from Jihad Death Threats." *New York Times,* Mar. 4.

———. 2005b. "Militant Muslims Act to Suppress Dutch Film and Art Show." *New York Times,* Jan. 31.

Slackman, Michael. 2005. "With No Status as a Party, Egyptian Group Wields Power." *New York Times,* Aug. 16.

Sloan, William David. 2000. "Introduction: Media History and Religion." In *Media and Religion in American History,* edited by William David Sloan, vii–x. Northport, AL: Vision Press.

———. 2006. Email correspondence with the author, Jan. 12, Feb. 22.

Smaby, Jonathan E. 2001. "American Ramadan." *New York Times,* Nov. 18.

Smith, Craig S. 2001a. "China, in Harsh Crackdown, Executes Muslim Separatists." *New York Times,* Dec. 16.

———. 2001b. "Fearing Unrest, China Presses Muslim Group." *New York Times,* Oct. 5.

———. 2002a. "Arabs and America: Saved by U.S., Kuwait Now Shows Mixed Feelings." *New York Times,* Oct. 12.

———. 2002b. "Jidda Journal: Underneath, Saudi Women Keep Their Secrets." *New York Times,* Dec. 3.

———. 2002c. "A Movement in Saudi Arabia Pushes toward an Islamic Ideal, and Frowns on the U.S." *New York Times,* Dec. 9.

———. 2003a. "Cleric in Iran Says Shiites Must Act." *New York Times,* Apr. 26.

———. 2003b. "Elated Shiites, on Pilgrimage, Want U.S. Out." *New York Times,* Apr. 22.

———. 2003c. "French Jews Tell of a New and Threatening Wave of Anti-Semitism." *New York Times,* Mar. 22.

———. 2003d. "Granada Journal: Where the Moors Held Sway, Allah Is Praised Again." *New York Times,* Oct. 21.

———. 2003e. "In Hotbed of Shiite Emotion, Clerics Jockey for Leadership." *New York Times,* Apr. 23.

———. 2003f. "Iraqi Shiites Jockeying for Power, Preach an Anti-American Sermon." *New York Times,* Apr. 20.

———. 2003g. "Letters from Europe: Minarets and Steeples: Can France Balance Them?" *New York Times,* Oct. 1.

———. 2003h. "Muslims: On a Friday in Baghdad, Shiites Gather for Prayer for First Time in Four Years." *New York Times,* Apr. 26.

———. 2003i. "Najaf: A Long-Simmering Power Struggle Preceded Killings at an Iraqi Holy Shrine." *New York Times,* Apr. 13.

———. 2003j. "Skien Journal: Where East Meets West Warily, She Makes Them Laugh." *New York Times,* Nov. 14.

———. 2003k. "U.S.-Backed Shiite Cleric Killed at Shrine in Najaf." *New York Times,* Apr. 11.

———. 2004a. "Chirac Condemns Desecration of Jewish Graves, Latest in a Wave." *New York Times,* Aug. 11.

———. 2004b. "Dutch Charge 7 Muslim Men in Killing of a Critic of Islam." *New York Times,* Nov. 6.

———. 2004c. "Dutch Look for Qaeda Link after Killing of Filmmaker." *New York Times,* Nov. 8.

———. 2004d. "Dutch Muslim School Bombed; Link to Killing Suspected." *New York Times,* Nov. 9.

———. 2004e. "Dutch Try to Thwart Terror Without Being Overzealous." *New York Times,* Nov. 25.

———. 2004f. "Europe Fears Islamic Converts May Give Cover for Extremism." *New York Times,* July 19.

———. 2004g. "France Is Struggling to Suppress Extremist Muslim Clerics." *New York Times,* Apr. 30.

————. 2004h. "French Politician Stirs Debate over Limits of Secular Society." *New York Times*, Oct. 27.

————. 2004i. "'Ideology of Contestation': Europe's Muslims May Be Headed Where the Marxists Went Before." *New York Times*, Dec. 26.

————. 2004j. "In Mourning Slain Filmmaker, Dutch Confront Limitations of Their Tolerance." *New York Times*, Nov. 10.

————. 2004k. "Islam in Jail: Europe's Neglect Breeds Angry Radicals." *New York Times*, Dec. 8.

————. 2004l. "Letter from North Africa: Islam and Democracy: Algerians Try to Blaze a Trail." *New York Times*, Apr. 14.

————. 2004m. "Militant Mullah Meets Match in Comic at Norway Nightclub." *New York Times*, Apr. 30.

————. 2004n. "Neo-Nazis in Paris Vandalize and Burn a Jewish Community Center." *New York Times*, Aug. 23.

————. 2004o. "Third Bomb Attack Directed at France's First Muslim Prefect." *New York Times*, Jan. 30.

————. 2004p. "Thwarted in Germany, Neo-Nazis Take Fascism to France." *New York Times*, Aug. 13.

————. 2004q. "Turkey Offers Reassurance on Adultery Issue in Bid to Join Europe." *New York Times*, Sept. 24.

————. 2005a. "Correspondence / Return of a Renegade: The Man Who Would Set Shiite Against Shiite." *New York Times*, Sept. 11.

————. 2005b. "Europe's Jews Seek Solace on the Right." *New York Times*, Feb. 20.

————. 2005c. "Fear of Islamists Drives Growth of Far Right in Belgium." *New York Times*, Feb. 12.

————. 2005d. "Muslim Group in France Is Fertile Soil for Militancy." *New York Times*, Apr. 28.

————. 2005e. "Muslims: At Mosque That Recruited Radicals, New Imam Calls for Help in Catching Bombers." *New York Times*, July 9.

Smith, Craig S., and Don Van Natta Jr. 2004. "Officials Fear Iraq's Lure for Muslims in Europe." *New York Times*, Oct. 23.

Smith, Lee. 2005. "The World Turns: Bush, the Great Shiite Liberator." *New York Times*, May 1.

Smith, Roberta. 2001. "Art Review: Displaying Hindu Ritual with Reverence and Graciousness." *New York Times*, Sept. 7.

Smyth, Frank. 2002. "Iraq's Forgotten Majority." *New York Times*, Oct. 3.

"Soldier Convicted in Deadly Attack on His Camp" (AP). 2005. *New York Times*, Apr. 22.

Sontag, Deborah. 2003. "The Erdogan Experiment." *New York Times Magazine,* May 11.

———. 2004a. "Mystery of the Islamic Scholar Who Was Barred by the U.S." *New York Times,* Oct. 6.

———. 2004b. "Terror Suspect's Path from Streets to Brig." *New York Times,* Apr. 25.

Spiegel, Shondell. 2002. "The Pearl Murder" (letter to the editor). *New York Times,* Feb. 27.

Sreberny, Annabelle. 2002. "Trauma Talk: Reconfiguring the Inside and Outside." In *Journalism after September 11,* edited by Barbie Zelizer and Stuart Allan, 220–34. London: Routledge.

Stanley, Alessandra. 2002a. "Frail Pope Takes His Message of Peace to the Azerbaijanis." *New York Times,* May 23.

———. 2002b. "The TV Watch: A Portrait of the Prophet behind Islam." *New York Times,* Dec. 18.

Steinberg, Jacques. 2003. "*Times* Names First Editor for Standards." *New York Times,* Sept. 10.

———. 2005. "On a New Showtime Series, America's Protector Is a Muslim." *New York Times,* July 4.

Steinfels, Peter. 1979. *The Neoconservatives: The Men Who Are Changing America's Politics.* New York: Simon & Schuster.

———. 1992. "Beliefs: If Only You Read *The Weekly World News,* You'd Know God Is a Green-Eyed 9-Footer." *New York Times,* July 18.

———. 1993a. "Constraints of the Religion Reporter." *Nieman Reports* 47, no. 2 (Summer): 3–5, 55.

———. 1993b. "Despite Role on World Stage, Muslims Turn to the Personal." *New York Times,* May 7.

———. 2001a. "Beliefs: In the Venture into Stem Cell Research, Just Where Are the Ethical Limits? And Will They Prove Lasting?" *New York Times,* Sept. 8.

———. 2001b. "Beliefs: A Military Campaign, the Calls for Caution and Some Complex Roots in Christian Thought." *New York Times,* Nov. 10.

———. 2001c. "Beliefs: A Philosopher-Priest's New Look at the Old Question: God in a World of so Much Evil." *New York Times,* Oct. 13.

———. 2001d. "Beliefs: Violence Can Breed Justice as Well as Injustice: When History and Common Sense Make the Case." *New York Times,* Oct. 27.

———. 2002a. "Beliefs: Churches and Ethicists Loudly Oppose the Proposed War on Iraq, but Deaf Ears Are Many." *New York Times,* Sept. 28.

———. 2002b. "Beliefs: In the Heat of War, Confronting a Moral Principle of Keeping Civilians Immune from Direct Attack." *New York Times,* Apr. 6.

———. 2002c. "Beliefs: Where Was God? It Is a Question That Might Be Asked Every Day—or Perhaps Not at All." *New York Times,* Aug. 31.

———. 2002d. "Beliefs: With More Than a Year Gone By, American Muslims Debate Islam, Intolerance, Terrorism, and the Significance of Sept. 11." *New York Times,* Dec. 7.

———. 2003a. "Beliefs: History's Pagans Might Have Approved of President Bush's Iraq Policy, an Author Suggests." *New York Times,* Apr. 5.

———. 2003b. "Beliefs: In a Poll, Few Say That Religion Shaped Their Views of Iraq. The Truth May Be More Complex." *New York Times,* Mar. 22.

———. 2003c. "Beliefs: In the Aftermath of War, What Is There to Be Said about the Pope's Opposition to It?" *New York Times,* May 24.

———. 2003d. "Beliefs: The Just-War Tradition, Its Last-Resort Criterion, and the Debate on an Invasion of Iraq." *New York Times,* Mar. 1.

———. 2003e. "Beliefs: A New Poll Gauges the Evolving Attitudes about Islam and about Gay Marriage." *New York Times,* Aug. 2.

———. 2003f. "Beliefs: 'Pacem in Terris,' and Debate on It, Echo Anew." *New York Times,* Feb. 1.

———. 2003g. *A People Adrift: The Crisis of the Roman Catholic Church in America.* New York: Simon & Schuster.

———. 2004a. "Beliefs: The Ethical Questions Involving Torture of Prisoners Are Lost in the Debate over the War in Iraq." *New York Times,* Dec. 4.

———. 2004b. "Beliefs: In the Brutality of War, the Innocents Have Become Lost in the Crossfire." *New York Times,* Nov. 20.

———. 2004c. "Beliefs: A Leading Scholar on Just-War Theory Turns His Thoughts Elsewhere: To Just Aftermaths." *New York Times,* Sept. 4.

———. 2005a. Interviewed by the author, Hamilton, NY, Nov. 1.

———. 2005b. "The Short, Happy Life of a Religion Reporter." Public lecture given at Colgate Univ., Hamilton, NY, Nov. 1.

———. 2006. "Beliefs: An Archbishop Suggests a Pause to Breathe Deeply and to Let Some of Our Demons Walk Away." *New York Times,* Sept. 16.

———. 2007. Email correspondence with the author, Feb. 23.

Steinglass, Matt. 2002. "Why Is Nigerian Islam so Radical?" *New York Times,* Dec. 1.

Steinhauer, Jennifer. 2001. "The Site: A Symbol of Faith Marks a City's Hallowed Ground." *New York Times,* Oct. 5.

———. 2004. "A Mission, and a Trail of Crumbs." *New York Times,* Dec. 13.

Stern, Jessica. 2003. *Terror in the Name of God: Why Religious Militants Kill.* New York: HarperCollins.

————. 2006. "Keep American Muslims on Our Side." *New York Times,* Sept. 10.

Stevens, Dana. 2004. "Film Review: Animated Retelling of the Birth of Islam." *New York Times,* Nov. 13.

Stevenson, Richard W. 2002. "The White House: As Ramadan Draws to a Close, Bush Praises Muslims for 'Spirit of Tolerance.'" *New York Times,* Dec. 6.

————. 2003. "Washington Memo: For Muslims, a Mixture of White House Signals." *New York Times,* Apr. 28.

————. 2004. "Bush Meets Pope, Who Voices His Displeasure over Iraq." *New York Times,* June 5.

Stille, Alexander. 2001. "Islam Experts Off on a Wild Ride, Willing or Not." *New York Times,* Nov. 10.

————. 2002. "Scholars Are Quietly Offering New Theories of the Koran." *New York Times,* Mar. 2.

————. 2003. "Historians Trace an Unholy Alliance." *New York Times,* May 31.

Stone, Robert. 2003. "The Survivors." Review of *After: How America Confronted the September 12 Era* by Steven Brill. *New York Times Book Review,* Apr. 20.

Stout, David. 2001. "The First Lady: Mrs. Bush Cites Abuse of Women and Children by the Taliban." *New York Times,* Nov. 18.

Strawson, John. 2003. "Holy War in the Media: Images of Jihad." In *Media Representations of September 11,* edited by Steven Chermak, Frankie Y. Bailey, and Michelle Brown, 17–28. Westport, CT: Praeger.

Strom, Stephanie. 2004. "Arab's Gift to Be Returned by Harvard." *New York Times,* July 28.

Sullivan, Andrew. 2001. "This *Is* a Religious War." *New York Times Magazine,* Oct. 7.

————. 2003. Interviewed by the author, Hamilton, NY, Dec. 2.

————. 2004. "Decent Exposure." Review of *The Trouble with Islam: A Muslim's Call for Reform in Her Faith* by Irshad Manji. *New York Times Book Review,* Jan. 25.

Swarns, Rachel L. 2003a. "More Than 13,000 May Face Deportation." *New York Times,* June 7.

————. 2003b. "Muslims Protest Monthlong Detention Without a Charge." *New York Times,* Apr. 20.

Swarns, Rachel L., and Christopher Drew. 2003. "Fearful, Angry or Confused, Muslim Immigrants Register." *New York Times,* Apr. 25.

Tagliabue, John. 2002a. "Pope, at Ecumenical Meeting, Denounces Violence in Religion's Name." *New York Times,* Jan. 25.

————. 2002b. "Pope Says Talks, Not Fighting, Can End Mideast Violence." *New York Times,* Apr. 1.

———. 2002c. "Synagogue in Paris Firebombed; Raids Go On." *New York Times*, Apr. 5.

———. 2005a. "Louvre Gets $20 Million for New Islamic Wing." *New York Times*, July 28.

———. 2005b. "The Netherlands: Mosques Fight Militancy." *New York Times*, Sept. 6.

———. 2007a. Email correspondence with the author, Aug. 17.

———. 2007b. Email correspondence with the author, Aug. 23.

Talese, Gay. 1970. *The Kingdom and the Power*. New York: Bantam Books.

"Taliban Decree Orders Statues Destroyed" (Agence France-Presse). 2001. *New York Times*, Feb. 27.

"Taliban Suspect Christian Plot among Western Aid Workers" (AP). 2001. *New York Times*, Aug. 13.

Talwalkar, Sumit A. 2002. "Celia Dugger's Anti-Hindu Article." Aug. 9. Available at http://www.media-watch.org/responses/0802/1.html.

Tavernise, Sabrina. 2002. "Bomb Attack Shows That Russia Hasn't Rooted Out Anti-Semitism." *New York Times*, June 1.

———. 2003a. "Iraqi Women Wary of New Upheavals." *New York Times*, May 5.

———. 2003b. "Minorities: In a Muslim City in Iraq, a Christian Group Enjoys Its Lively Quarter." *New York Times*, May 23.

———. 2005a. "Cycle of Bloodshed: Many See Sectarian Roots in Wave of Killings in Iraq." *New York Times*, May 27.

———. 2005b. "Religious Battles: Quiet Killings Split Neighborhood Where Sunnis and Shiites Once Lived Side by Side." *New York Times*, July 4.

———. 2005c. "Sunni Accuses a Shiite Militia of Killing Clerics." *New York Times*, May 19.

———. 2005d. "Sunnis to Accept Offer of a Role in Constitution." *New York Times*, June 17.

Tavernise, Sabrina, and Richard A. Oppel Jr. 2005. "Sunnis in Iraq Unite to Compete with Shiites in Elections." *New York Times*, May 22.

Taylor, Craig. 2003. "What They Were Thinking." *New York Times*, Mar. 2.

"Tehran's Well Veiled Denounce Laxity in Women's Attire." 2004. *New York Times*, Sept. 4.

Tepperman, Jonathan D. 2003. "A Delicate Balance." Review of *After Jihad: America and the Struggle for Islamic Democracy* by Noah Feldman. *New York Times Book Review*, July 6.

Testa, Andrew. 2001. "In a Kabul Mosque, There Is New Vigor among Dervishes" (photos). *New York Times*, Dec. 1.

"This Is a Religious War" (letters to the editor by Eugene McCarraher and others). 2001. *New York Times Magazine*, Oct. 28.

Thomas, Jo, and Ralph Blumenthal. 2002. "Rural Muslims Draw New, Unwanted Attention." *New York Times,* Jan. 3.

"Threats Close Thai Schools in Muslim Area" (Reuters). 2004. *New York Times,* Feb. 19.

"Thumbs Up to Clyde Haberman." 2001. CAMERA (Committee for Accuracy in Middle East Reporting in America), Sept. 12. Available at http://www.camera.org/index .asp?x_context=6&x_article=332.

Tibi, Bassam. 2001. *Islam Between Culture and Politics.* New York: Palgrave.

Tierney, John. 2002. "The Big City: Downtown, a Necropolis Is Rising." *New York Times,* Jan. 25.

"*Times* Reporter Who Resigned Leaves Long Trail of Deception." 2003. *New York Times,* May 11.

Toner, Robin. 2004. "To the Barricades: The Culture Wars, Part II." *New York Times,* Feb. 29.

Toumani, Meline. 2003. "Ambassador for a Silenced Music." *New York Times,* May 25.

Trofimov, Yaroslav. 2005. *Faith at War: A Journey on the Frontlines of Islam.* New York: Henry Holt.

"Two Dozen Cars Vandalized." 2003. *New York Times,* Jan. 17.

"Two Years Later: Acts Large and Small." 2003. *New York Times,* Sept. 12.

Tyler, Patrick E. 2003. "Fledgling Shiite Moderates: In Iraq's Disorder, the Ayatollahs May Save the Day." *New York Times,* July 6.

———. 2004a. "British Cultural Official Tied to Slurs Against Muslims." *New York Times,* Aug. 7.

———. 2004b. "British Singer Calls His Deportation a Mistake." *New York Times,* Sept. 24.

Tyler, Patrick E., and Don Van Natta Jr. 2004. "Militants in Europe Openly Call for Jihad and the Rule of Islam." *New York Times,* Apr. 26.

"The Uncomfortable Question of Anti-Semitism" (letters to the editor by Roy Lawrence and others). 2001. *New York Times Magazine,* Nov. 25.

"U.N. Pleads with Taliban Not to Destroy Buddha Statues" (AP). 2001. *New York Times,* Mar. 3.

"U.S. Charges Islamic Leader Who Met Bush." 2003. *New York Times,* Sept. 30.

"Using the News to Teach Religion." 2004. *Religion & Ethics NewsWeekly,* Thirteen/ WNET (PBS). Available at http://www.religionethics.com/teach/.

"Vandals' Motive Wasn't Anti-Semitism" (AP). 2002. *New York Times,* July 31.

Van Natta, Don, Jr. 2003a. "Big Bang Theory: The Terror Industry Fields Its Ultimate Weapon." *New York Times,* Aug. 24.

———. 2003b. "Radical Islam: London Imam Is Removed as Leader of Mosque." *New York Times,* Feb. 5.

————. 2004. "Sizing Up the New Toned-Down bin Laden." *New York Times,* Dec. 19.

Van Natta, Don, Jr., and Lowell Bergman. 2005. "Insurgency: Militant Imams under Scrutiny across Europe." *New York Times,* Jan. 25.

Van Natta, Don, Jr., and Souad Mekhennet. 2005. "Islamic Groups Condemn Blair's Anti-terror Proposals." *New York Times,* Aug. 7.

Vecsey, Christopher. 2004. Email communication to David W. Dunlap, Aug. 13.

————. 2006. Email communication to Thomas L. Friedman, Nov. 10.

————. 2009. "Religion, Reported in *The New York Times:* Articles, 1970–2001." Available at http://www.colgate.edu/portaldata///imagegallery/faculty/18913/imagegallery/faculty/Religion_NYT_1970-2001.pdf.

Vecsey, George. 2002. Interviewed by the author. Port Washington, NY, July 20.

————. 2005. Email correspondence with the author, Aug. 4.

————. 2007. Correspondence with the author, Jan. 2.

————. 2010. Email correspondence with the author, July 30.

Verghese, Abraham. 2002. "Wars Are Made, Not Born." Review of *War Is a Force That Gives Us Meaning* by Chris Hedges. *New York Times Book Review,* Nov. 17.

"Victims of Saudi Attacks Are Mourned." 2003. *New York Times,* May 17.

"Visiting the Shiite Ancestors." 2004. *New York Times,* Feb. 2.

Volkmer, Ingrid. 2002. "Journalism and Political Crises in the Global Network Society." In *Journalism after September 11,* edited by Barbie Zelizer and Stuart Allan, 235–46. London: Routledge.

Von Zielbauer, Paul. 2003. "Ceremony: Vial of Blood Is Laid to Rest as Fire Dept. Salutes Its Last." *New York Times,* Sept. 9.

Wadler, Joyce. 2001. "At Historical Temple, a Joyous Revival" (photos). *New York Times,* Sept. 10.

Waisbord, Silvio. 2002. "Journalism, Risk, and Patriotism." In *Journalism after September 11,* edited by Barbie Zelizer and Stuart Allan, 201–19. London: Routledge.

Wakin, Daniel J. 2001a. "At Edge of Ground Zero, Gospel and Giving." *New York Times,* Dec. 1.

————. 2001b. "The Imam: New Head of Main Mosque on Spot." *New York Times,* Nov. 2.

————. 2001c. "Memorial Service: A Tribute of Tibetan Horns and Aged Chants for the Trade Center Victims." *New York Times,* Oct. 30.

————. 2001d. "Muslims in America: Moderates Start Speaking Out Against Islamic Extremism." *New York Times,* Oct. 28.

————. 2001e. "No Day Too Holy: War Rarely Pauses." *New York Times,* Oct. 28.

————. 2001f. "Public Lives: St. Patrick's Ceremony All in a Morning's Work." *New York Times,* Dec. 25.

———. 2001g. "Safekeeping Faith and Tradition." *New York Times,* Nov. 16.

———. 2001h. "Terror Attacks Could Change Paths of Faith." *New York Times,* Sept. 30.

———. 2001i. "Thanksgiving in a Time of Fasting: In Brooklyn, Healing Rhythms of Ramadan." *New York Times,* Nov. 21.

———. 2002a. "Anti-Semitic 'Elders of Zion' Gets New Life on Egypt TV." *New York Times,* Oct. 26.

———. 2002b. "Chapel and Refuge Struggles to Define Role." *New York Times,* Nov. 28.

———. 2002c. "Clerics' Daunting Task: Forming 9/11 Sermons." *New York Times,* Sept. 8.

———. 2002d. "For Muslims, an Uneasy Anniversary." *New York Times,* Aug. 19.

———. 2002e. "Killed on 9/11, Fire Chaplain Becomes Larger Than Life." *New York Times,* Sept. 27.

———. 2002f. "Online in Cairo, with News, Views, and 'Fatwa Corner.'" *New York Times,* Oct. 29.

———. 2002g. "Preparing to Take on His Church." *New York Times,* July 10.

———. 2002h. "Ranks of Latinos Turning to Islam Are Increasing." *New York Times,* Jan. 2.

———. 2002i. "Seeing Heresy in a Service for Sept. 11." *New York Times,* Feb. 8.

———. 2003a. "Beirut: Video Game Created by Militant Group Mounts Simulated Attacks Against Israeli Targets." *New York Times,* May 18.

———. 2003b. "Christian Charity to Help a Mosque." *New York Times,* Feb. 4.

———. 2003c. "Dissent: A Prominent Rabbi Reconsiders His Recent Antiwar Remarks." *New York Times,* Mar. 28.

———. 2003d. "Fear for a Navy Son, and for Fellow Muslims: Viewing Images of a War They Hate, a Brooklyn Family Is Proud and Sad." *New York Times,* Apr. 11.

———. 2003e. "Religious Violence: Missionaries' Friend Killed in Lebanon Bombing." *New York Times,* May 8.

———. 2003f. "Scenes of Ritual Flagellation Resonate at Mosque." *New York Times,* Apr. 25.

———. 2003g. "Sermons of 1776, with a Spirit of 2003." *New York Times,* Mar. 16.

———. 2004a. "In New Jersey, Shia Finds Its Voice." *New York Times,* Apr. 10.

———. 2004b. "Keeping the Faith as the Meter Runs." *New York Times,* May 28.

———. 2004c. "Reaction: Assessing a Gruesome Toll after a Rash of Beheadings." *New York Times,* June 24.

———. 2006. "Ceremony: Gathering at Carnegie Hall to Find Solace and Catharsis in the Music of Mozart." *New York Times,* Sept. 12.

———. 2007. Telephone interview by the author. Oct. 8.

———. 2010. Email correspondence with the author, July 26.

Waldman, Amy. 2001a. "Changed Lives: Religious Leader Takes His Calling to Ground Zero." *New York Times,* Sept. 20.

———. 2001b. "Holiday: Fast Ends in Kabul, but a Hunger Grows for a New, Better Life." *New York Times,* Dec. 17.

———. 2001c. "Iran Shiites Celebrate and Mourn a Martyr." *New York Times,* Dec. 15.

———. 2001d. "No TV, No Chess, No Kites: Taliban's Code, from A to Z." *New York Times,* Nov. 22.

———. 2001e. "Public Lives: American Imam Refutes Attacks and Defends Islam." *New York Times,* Oct. 9.

———. 2001f. "Rosh Hashana: Rabbis Revise Sermons to Soften a Stark Prayer." *New York Times,* Sept. 18.

———. 2001g. "Shackles Off, Russia's Muslims Are Still Chafing." *New York Times,* Nov. 9.

———. 2001h. "Word for Word / Taboo Heaven: More No-Nos Than You Can Shake a Stick At. (Hey, No Stick-Shaking.)" *New York Times,* Dec. 2.

———. 2002a. "10 Killed in Attack on Temple in Kashmir." *New York Times,* Nov. 25.

———. 2002b. "At Least 25 Are Killed in Raid on Hindu Temple in India." *New York Times,* Sept. 25.

———. 2002c. "Hindu Nationalists Win Landslide Vote in Indian State." *New York Times,* Dec. 16.

———. 2002d. "How in a Little English Town Jihad Found Young Converts." *New York Times,* Apr. 24.

———. 2002e. "In Massacre of Hindus, a Grim Omen for All India." *New York Times,* Sept. 26.

———. 2002f. "Life in Kabul: Keeping Their Faiths under Taliban Rule Drew Sikhs and Hindus Together." *New York Times,* Jan. 20.

———. 2002g. "A Secular India, or Not? At Strife Scene, Vote Is Test." *New York Times,* Dec. 12.

———. 2003a. "The 15 Women Awaiting Justice in Kabul Prison." *New York Times,* Mar. 16.

———. 2003b. "Anxiety Rises in a Muslim Enclave near Bombay." *New York Times,* Sept. 1.

———. 2003c. "Ramdevra Journal: Shoes, and Religious Ire, Fall Away at a Saint's Feet." *New York Times,* Sept. 8.

———. 2004a. "Free of Taliban's Yoke, 2 Afghan Women Rise Again." *New York Times,* Oct. 17.

———. 2004b. "Indian Muslims' Hope Is One Good Policewoman." *New York Times*, Oct. 17.

———. 2004c. "Religious Leader's Arrest in Killing Incites Holy Men and Hindu Nationalists." *New York Times*, Dec. 5.

———. 2004d. "Violence in Kashmir Invades a Most Sacred Space." *New York Times*, June 16.

———. 2005. "Seething Unease Shaped British Bombers' Newfound Zeal." *New York Times*, July 31.

Wallace, Mike. 2002. "Books of the Times: Panomara and Pointillism on 9/11." Review of *Out of the Blue: The Story of Sept. 11, from Jihad to Ground Zero* by Richard Bernstein and the staff of the *New York Times*. *New York Times*, Aug. 29.

Walsh, Andrew. 2001. "Good for What Ails Us." *Religion in the News* 4, no. 5 (Fall): 2–5, 26.

———. 2002. "Returning to Normalcy." *Religion in the News* 5, no. 1 (Spring): 26–28.

———. 2003. "The Trouble with Missionaries." *Religion in the News* 6, no. 2 (Summer): 7–8, 27.

Warner, Marina. 2001. "Fantasy's Power and Peril." *New York Times*, Dec. 16.

"Washington: Army Chaplain Quits" (AP). 2004. *New York Times*, Aug. 3.

Watson, Peter. 2003. "Crossroads of Culture." *New York Times*, Apr. 21.

Watters, Carrie. 2003. "Democracy, Civility Debated at College." *Rockford Register Star*, May 21. Available at http://www.rrstar.com/localnews/your_community/rockford/20030521-4971.shtml.

Waxman, Sharon. 2004. "Film on Crusades Could Become Hollywood's Next Battleground." *New York Times*, Aug. 12.

Wayne, Leslie. 2004. "Sikh Group Finds Calling in Homeland Security." *New York Times*, Sept. 28.

Weber, Bruce. 2002a. "Critic's Notebook: A Spectacle, Moving Yet Mysterious." *New York Times*, July 19.

———. 2002b. "Musical Drama on a Story Sacred to Shiite Muslims." *New York Times*, July 15.

Weiner, Tim. 2001. "Man in the News: Seizing the Prophet's Mantle: Muhammad Omar." *New York Times*, Dec. 7.

Weinraub, Bernard. 2003. "With Battle Ahead, Sober Time for Troops." *New York Times*, Mar. 20.

Weiser, Benjamin. 2001. "The Jihad: Captured Terrorist Manual Suggests Hijackers Did a Lot by the Book." *New York Times*, Oct. 28.

Weisman, Steven R. 2003. "Islam: Suicide Bombings Are Condemned in Saudi Mosques." *New York Times*, May 17.

———. 2005. "Bush Aide Urges 'Humble' 9/11 Observance by Overseas Envoys." *New York Times*, Sept. 1.

"When Faith Guides a President" (letters to the editor by Claude M. Gruener and others). 2003. *New York Times*, Mar. 14.

Wicker, Tom. 1978. *On Press*. New York: Viking.

Wilgoren, Jodi. 2001a. "American Muslims: Islam Attracts Converts by the Thousand, Drawn before and after Attacks." *New York Times*, Oct. 22.

———. 2001b. "Captured Missionaries' Family Prays and Waits." *New York Times*, Nov. 30.

———. 2001c. "The Pakistani-Americans: Isolated Family Finds Support and Reasons to Worry in Illinois." *New York Times*, Oct. 1.

———. 2001d. "Struggling to Be Both Arab and American." *New York Times*, Nov. 4.

———. 2002a. "Arab and Muslim Comics Turn Fear into Funny." *New York Times*, Sept. 1.

———. 2002b. "Going by 'Joe,' Not 'Yussef,' but Still Feeling Like an Outcast." *New York Times*, Sept. 11.

Wills, Garry. 1975. Review of *The First Casualty: From the Crimea to Vietnam: The War Correspondent as Hero, Propagandist, and Myth Maker* by Phillip Knightley. *New York Times Book Review*, Sept. 14.

———. 2001. "Before the Holocaust." Review of *The Popes Against the Jews: The Vatican's Role in the Rise of Modern Anti-Semitism* by David I. Kertzer. *New York Times Book Review*, Sept. 23.

———. 2003. "With God on His Side." *New York Times Magazine*, Mar. 30.

Wilson, Michael. 2002a. "Evangelist Says Muslims Haven't Adequately Apologized for Sept. 11 Attacks." *New York Times*, August 15.

———. 2002b. "How to Say 'Enough,' Gracefully." *New York Times*, Oct. 11.

———. 2002c. "St. Paul's Chapel near Ground Zero Slowly Dismantles 9/11 Memorial." *New York Times*, Nov. 8.

Winerip, Michael. 2001a. "Our Towns: After Too Many Funerals, a Priest Could Use a Blessing." *New York Times*, Oct. 28.

———. 2001b. "Our Towns: The High Cost of Looking Like an All-American Guy." *New York Times*, Oct. 21.

Wines, Michael. 2003. "Islamic Minority: 2 Leaders of Russia's Muslims Split over Jihad Against U.S." *New York Times*, Apr. 4.

Winter, Greg. 2001a. "2 Held in Plot to Attack Mosque and Congressman." *New York Times*, Dec. 13.

———. 2001b. "Court Blocks Evangelist's Effort to Reopen a Refinery." *New York Times*, Nov. 9.

———. 2001c. "In a Shift, Muslim Groups Cast Themselves as Loyal Critics." *New York Times,* Oct. 25.

———. 2001d. "Jewish Militant's Road to Jail Was Filled with Arrests." *New York Times,* Dec. 15.

———. 2002. "Grand Plan Haunts Pat Robertson." *New York Times,* Feb. 3.

Wolfe, Alan. 2001. "The God of a Diverse People." *New York Times,* Oct. 14.

Wong, Edward. 2004a. "The Ayatollah: U.S. Calls Report of Bid to Kill Sistani False." *New York Times,* Feb. 7.

———. 2004b. "Factions: Cleric's Militia Upends Shiite Power Balance." *New York Times,* Apr. 21.

———. 2004c. "The Government: Iraq Secular Leaders Seek to Thwart Islamist Power." *New York Times,* Feb. 22.

———. 2004d. "Iraqi Factions: Once-Ruling Sunnis Unite to Regain a Piece of the Pie." *New York Times,* Jan. 12.

———. 2004e. "Iraq's Path Hinges on Words of Enigmatic Cleric." *New York Times,* Jan. 25.

———. 2004f. "Sermons: Clerics Urge End to Clashes Between U.S. and Rebels." *New York Times,* May 22.

———. 2004g. "Transition Politics: Uprising Has Increased the Influence of Sunni Clerics." *New York Times,* May 31.

———. 2005a. "Can the Sunnis Count?" *New York Times,* July 17.

———. 2005b. "Draft for New Iraqi Constitution Includes Curbs to Women's Rights." *New York Times,* July 20.

———. 2005c. "Iraq Holy City Suffers Lack of Utilities and Pilgrims." *New York Times,* Feb. 16.

———. 2005d. "Iraqi Politics: Clerics' Group Says It Won't Urge Sunnis to Boycott Votes." *New York Times,* July 24.

———. 2005e. "Najaf: Shiite Leader Inspires Many to Cast Ballots." *New York Times,* Jan. 31.

———. 2005f. "Politics: Najaf's Clerics Praise Iraqi Voters and Appear Confident That Shiites Will Gain Power." *New York Times,* Feb. 1.

———. 2005g. "Radio: On the Air, on Their Own: Iraqi Women Find a Forum." *New York Times,* Sept. 4.

———. 2005h. "Religion: As Sunni Divisions Widen, Iraq's Sufis Are under Attack." *New York Times,* Aug. 21.

———. 2005i. "Shiite Morality Takes Hold in Iraq's 2nd-Largest City." *New York Times,* July 7.

———. 2005j. "Suicide Bomber Kills 10 at Iraq Gathering of Sufi Muslims on Day of Dozens of Deaths." *New York Times,* June 4.

———. 2005k. "Top Iraq Shiites Exert Influence on Constitution." *New York Times,* Feb. 6.

———. 2007a. Email correspondence with the author, Aug. 19.

———. 2007b. Email correspondence with the author, Sept. 8.

Wong, Edward, and Dexter Filkins. 2004. "U.S. Strikes Mosque Held by Iraqi Cleric's Militia." *New York Times,* May 12.

Wood, Nicholas, and David Binder. 2004. "Treasured Churches in a Cycle of Revenge." *New York Times,* Apr. 3.

Woodward, Kenneth L. 2003. "An Oxymoron: Europe Without Christianity." *New York Times,* June 14.

"Worship and Unease in Baghdad." 2004. *New York Times,* Oct. 9.

Worth, Robert F. 2001. "The Deep Intellectual Roots of Islamic Terror." *New York Times,* Oct. 13.

———. 2002. "Duality of Gay Muslims Is Tougher after Sept. 11." *New York Times,* Jan. 13.

———. 2004a. "Insurgents Bomb 2 Churches in Northern Iraq City." *New York Times,* Dec. 8.

———. 2004b. "Politics: Rift among Shiite Factions May Hurt Them in Election." *New York Times,* Dec. 7.

———. 2004c. "Politics: Shiite Groups Agree to Unite for the Election, and Sunnis Register for It." *New York Times,* Dec. 9.

———. 2005a. "950 Die in Pilgrims' Stampede on a Baghdad Bridge." *New York Times,* Sept. 1.

———. 2005b. "Bombs Kill 5 in Iraq Cities at Holy Time for the Shiites." *New York Times,* Apr. 1.

———. 2005c. "For Some in Iraq's Sunni Minority, a Growing Sense of Alienation." *New York Times,* May 8.

———. 2005d. "Gunmen Open Fire on Sunni Worshipers in Southern Iraq, Killing One." *New York Times,* Sept. 3.

———. 2005e. "A Haircut in Iraq Can Be the Death of the Barber." *New York Times,* Mar. 18.

———. 2005f. "In Iraq, a Tug of War over the Truth." *New York Times,* Apr. 24.

———. 2005g. "In Jeans or Veils, Iraqi Women Are Split on New Political Power." *New York Times,* Apr. 13.

———. 2005h. "On a Bridge to Unity, or Perhaps to War." *New York Times,* Sept. 4.

———. 2005i. "Sunni Arabs Rally to Protest Proposed Iraqi Constitution." *New York Times,* Aug. 27.

———. 2005j. "Sunni Leader Vows Support for Insurgents." *New York Times,* Mar. 29.

———. 2005k. "Yemeni Cleric, Convicted in Terror Case, Is Sentenced to the Maximum, 75 Years." *New York Times,* July 29.

Wren, Christopher S. 1978. "The Moslem World Rekindles Its Militancy." *New York Times,* June 18.

Wright, Robert. 2003. "Thou Shalt Kill." Review of *Under the Banner of Heaven: A Story of Violent Faith* by Jon Krakauer. *New York Times Book Review,* Aug. 3.

Wright, Robin. 1985. *Sacred Rage: The Crusade of Modern Islam.* New York: Simon & Schuster and Linden Press.

———. 2001. *Sacred Rage: The Wrath of Militant Islam.* New York: Simon & Schuster and Touchstone Books.

———. 2002. "Mosque and State." Review of *Jihad: The Trail of Political Islam* by Gilles Kepel. *New York Times Book Review,* May 26.

Wuthnow, Robert. 1998. *After Heaven: Spirituality in America since the 1950s.* Berkeley and Los Angeles: Univ. of California Press.

Wyatt, Edward. 2001a. "Board Votes to Require Recitation of Pledge at Public Schools." *New York Times,* Oct. 18.

———. 2001b. "Teachers Don't Need Note for a Religious Day." *New York Times,* Sept. 11.

Yardley, Jim. 2001a. "Differences Portray Microcosm of Islamic World." *New York Times,* Dec. 15.

———. 2001b. "The Mastermind: A Portrait of the Terrorist: From Shy Child to Single-Minded Killer." *New York Times,* Oct. 10.

York, Michelle. 2005a. "Professor Is Assailed by Legislature and Vandals." *New York Times,* Feb. 3.

———. 2005b. "Professor Quits a Post over a 9/11 Remark." *New York Times,* Feb. 1.

———. 2005c. "Remark on 9/11 Sparks Storm at College." *New York Times,* Jan. 31.

Zanganeh, Lila Azam. 2004. "When Timbuktu Was the Paris of Islamic Intellectuals in Africa." *New York Times,* Apr. 24.

Zelizer, Barbie. 2002. "Photography, Journalism, and Trauma." In *Journalism after September 11,* edited by Barbie Zelizer and Stuart Allan, 48–68. London: Routledge.

Zelizer, Barbie, and Stuart Allan. 2002a. "Introduction: When Trauma Shapes the News." In *Journalism after September 11,* edited by Barbie Zelizer and Stuart Allan, 1–24. London: Routledge.

———, eds. 2002b. *Journalism after September 11.* London: Routledge.

Zernike, Kate. 2002a. "Assigned Reading on Koran in Chapel Hill Raises Hackles." *New York Times,* Aug. 20.

———. 2002b. "Harvard Student Drops 'Jihad' from Speech Title." *New York Times,* June 1.

Zezima, Katie. 2004. "The Muslim Patient Will See You Now, Doctor." *New York Times,* Sept. 1.

Zhao, Yilu. 2001. "Notebook: Police Officer Visits to Reassure a Queens Mosque." *New York Times,* Sept. 22.

———. 2002a. "Campus Evangelists Seek Out Foreign Students." *New York Times,* Jan. 9.

———. 2002b. "Steering Clear of Politics at Islamic Day Schools." *New York Times,* Mar. 11.

Ziad, Waleed. 2004. "How the Holy Warriors Learned to Hate." *New York Times,* June 18.

Zinser, Lynn. 2004. "Free at Last, Islamic Women Compete with Abandon." *New York Times,* Aug. 21.

Zoepf, Katherine. 2004. "Exodus: Many Christians Flee Iraq, with Syria the Haven of Choice." *New York Times,* Aug. 5.

Zonis, Marvin. 1994. "An Islamic Identity Crisis." Review of *A History of the Modern Middle East* by William L. Cleveland. *New York Times Book Review,* Jan. 30.

Index